Real-Time Systems Development

Rob Williams

ELSEVIER

AMSTERDAM • BOSTON • HEIDELBERG • LONDON
NEW DELHI • NEW YORK • OXFORD • PARIS • SAN DIEGO
SAN FRANCISCO • SINGAPORE • SYDNEY • TOKYO
Butterworth-Heinemann is an imprint of Elsevier

B H

Real-Time Systems Development
Williams

Butterworth Heinemann
An Imprint of Elsevier
Linacre House, Jordan Hill, Oxford OX2 8DP
200 Wheeler Road, Burlington, MA 01803

Original ISBN : 978-0-7506-6471-4

First Printed in India 2008
Reprinted 2009, 2013

Indian Reprint ISBN : 978-81-312-1520-3

Published by Elsevier, a division of Reed Elsevier India Private Limited.

Registered Office: 305, Rohit House, 3 Tolstoy Marg, New Delhi-110 001.
Corporate Office: 14th Floor, Building No. 10B, DLF Cyber City, Phase-II, Gurgaon-122 002, Haryana, India.

Printed and bound at Saurabh Printers Pvt. Ltd.
A-16, Sector IV, Noida-201 301.

Contents

Real-Time Systems Development

Preface

As more and more of our daily technology depends on embedded microprocessors, the demand for good real-time software has grown enormously. So it is unfortunate that computer science students frequently only develop and run programs on standard desktop Windows platforms. This leaves them somewhat unprepared for the extra problems encountered should they end up producing code for a new DVD player, a mobile handset or an Internet packet router. This text reveals some of the particular difficulties encountered when designing for real-time systems, and the alternative routes available for software realization. It is perhaps a shame that so few programmers have the opportunity to study the science and art of real-time systems before being confronted by their first real-time project. As a large proportion of new domestic and leisure equipment relies on microprocessors for basic operations, the world might be a safer and less frustrating experience for all of us if this situation could be rectified.

My own commercial experience in the field of microprocessor applications influenced my academic direction when I returned to university life. It had struck me that the normal computer science courses did not cover enough basic material in low-level programming and electronics which was necessary to support a career in real-time, embedded development. There had also been a continuing trend to separate the study of hardware from software, reducing students' ability to understand the operational totality of microprocessor-based systems. When debugging faulty equipment, computing graduates suffered from a serious disadvantage. Should they require some more graphical evidence from their limping software, they dared not turn on an oscilloscope. On the other side of the fence, electronic engineers scratched away at assembler spaghetti code, or naively marvelled at the irredeemable wonders of Basic.

What was needed was a synthesis of the two disciplines, a harmonization of software and electronic engineering. With this in mind we proposed and validated the BSc Computing for Real-time Systems. This text came from the experience of teaching on that four-year honours programme. It represents the content of a two-semester, senior year module called 'Real-time Systems

Design' which we have presented to our undergraduates, in a variety of evolving versions, for 20 years. It has also been delivered in a modified, accelerated form as a masters-level module within our MSc Software Engineering. On the whole, students enjoy the module, and manage to gain considerable benefit from the down-to-earth approach and practical challenges.

Recommended lab sessions

It is anticipated that the majority of the readers of this text will be advanced undergraduates or masters-level students pursuing a course called Computer Science, Computing, Software Engineering, or some similar title. They will probably have chosen to take an option in Real-time Systems Design, or Development. Such modules normally include weekly lectures and practical work in laboratories. So, the material covered in the following chapters represents only one component of their learning experience. The following list of extended practical exercises is not a recommended schedule for a single semester's laboratory activity because each individual student will bring different experience and skills to the course. They have different ambitions and expectations, so what they actually decide to do during the practical sessions will vary. A variety and choice of laboratory work is always a popular factor with students.

1. Introduction to I/O programming with Linux
2. Real-time motor control
3. Finite state methodology
4. SA/SD, real-time Yourdon, case study
5. OOD, case study
6. Configuring gcc cross-compilers
7. Cross-development methods
8. Synchronization and communications
9. Petri net methods
10. Point Of Sale (POS) network case study

An alternative and very effective strategy is to organize an extended case study project, which involves design, implementation and test activities. This develops and extends the students' understanding throughout the semester, and can be subdivided into component parts for each member of the team. In this way, a wide range of technical skills and interests, from embedded microcontrollers to Oracle database servers, can be integrated into a single project, and assessed partly individually and partly as a team. Such activity offers the extra benefit of enabling groups to work together on a much larger assignment, certainly an important experience for undergraduate students. A suitable idea which we have used recently is the development of a POS network, with POS terminals, data concentrator and central database server. This supplies a broad scope for design variation and allows for regular enhancement to keep the technology up to date.

Acknowledgements and thanks

There are many individuals, colleagues, students and graduates from our BSc Computing for Real-time Systems degree, who have contributed to this text, directly or indirectly. In particular I would like to thank a colleague Bob Lang who generously provided detailed, technical reviews of all the chapters, based partly on his own commercial experience working with real-time systems. Also, Craig Duffy tolerating the repeated requests to read drafts and responded with a sustained counterstream of cross-development news from his Linux porting activities. In addition, I have enjoyed useful discussions on many real-time topics with Richard Barry, Adam Budd, Andy Clymer, Mark Cridge, Tony Gibbs, Will Skinner, and Rob Voisey. They may recognize their influence in some parts of the book.

The duckshoot game, among many other ideas, was lucidly explained to me many years ago by Jonathan Bromley, and it has survived to provide an intriguing programming exercise. I must also warmly thank my colleagues Jeff Graham, Nigel Gunton, Ian Johnson, Peter Martin, Laurence O'Brien and Chris Wallace for engaging so generously in technical discussions and accepting the regular outbreaks of author's obsession.

There are too many students to mention individually, but throughout the past 20 years, they have trusted us with their careers by enrolling onto our BSc Computing for Real-time Systems degree. Fundamentally, it is their good humour and continuing curiosity which provided the spur for this text. The best reward for any teacher is to see students progress and develop their technical confidence, leading to successful graduation and rewarding careers.

I must also once again give praise to Brian Kernighan for his wonderfully small pic language, which I used to construct all the line diagrams throughout the book. The original text was edited with emacs and the formatting was all carried out using groff from Richard Stallman's GNU suite. It was here that I discovered the fun of using pic to code diagrams. I would also like to thank Richard Stallman for the guidance he generously offered concerning the General Public License which is discussed in Section 9.13.

The book would not have been possible without the energy and persistence of the editors, initially David Hatter, and latterly Alfred Waller at Elsevier. Many thanks to them both for their patient encouragement throughout, and also to Deborah Puleston for her flawless and patient editing.

Finally credit and thanks to the my wife Val, who several times struggled through the draft text, in a heroic effort to eliminate my worst grammatical errors. Apologies to our cat Cassie who has not yet forgiven my purchase of a flat panel screen, removing her favourite warm perch on top of the CRT. I witnessed her discouraging encounter with modern technology as she teetered on the top edge of the new LCD panel, and then slowly, silently toppled backwards onto my keyboard.

Dr Rob Williams
UWE
Bristol
rob.williams@uwe.ac.uk

Chapter 1

Introduction to real-time systems

1.1 Chapter overview

The role of real-time software grows larger and larger, and in a competitive marketplace any marginal improvement in usability or performance, provided by more effective software, will give a significant sales advantage. This introductory chapter tries to outline the source of some of the problems which programmers and engineers are likely to encounter and provides a set of guidelines for identifying potential real-time systems by looking at a number of their characteristics. It also introduces associated key ideas through example applications which, at this early stage, may be more helpful than offering abstract principles.

1.2 Real-time systems development

Real-time processing normally requires both parallel activities and fast response. In fact, the term 'real-time' is often used synonymously with 'multi-tasking' or 'multi-threading', although this is not strictly correct: small real-time systems, as used in dedicated equipment controllers, can perform perfectly adequately with just a simple looping program. Indeed, the period I spent developing commercial embedded systems taught me that such simplicity of design has much merit, and with the massive increase in processor speeds, it is now possible to use such crude software schemes for a much wider range of applications. As long as the response is *good enough*, no further complexities need be introduced. But, if a large number of different inputs are being monitored by a single processor, or the input data streams are complex and structured, the simple polling loop approach will prove inflexible and slow, and a multi-tasking solution will be required. Whatever style of implementation is chosen as appropriate, the need remains to deal with several concurrent activities over a period of time.

Real-time systems often seem like juggling

1.3 System complexity

A lot of the problems encountered with any software development involve 'complexity management'. Good practice, prior experience and team work are essential factors in achieving a successful outcome. Problems often appear impossible until they are subdivided, then each component part becomes much more manageable. Real-time software suffers from the same set of problems as traditional DP (Data Processing) applications, but adds the extra dimension of time to confuse the developer. To help in the preliminary analysis and design work, a rigorous method, which can be understood by all the team members, should be adopted. This will provide discipline and guidance. The main reason for undertaking design activity is to arrive at some well-structured code. Design without a subsequent implementation is mostly a futile activity. If you follow a good design technique, appropriate questions will emerge at the right moment, disciplining your thought processes.

A design method should provide intellectual guidance for system partitioning as well as documentation standards to ensure you record your decisions and supporting rationale. Without an effective method, you could end up with the complexity of a bramble patch, as illustrated opposite.

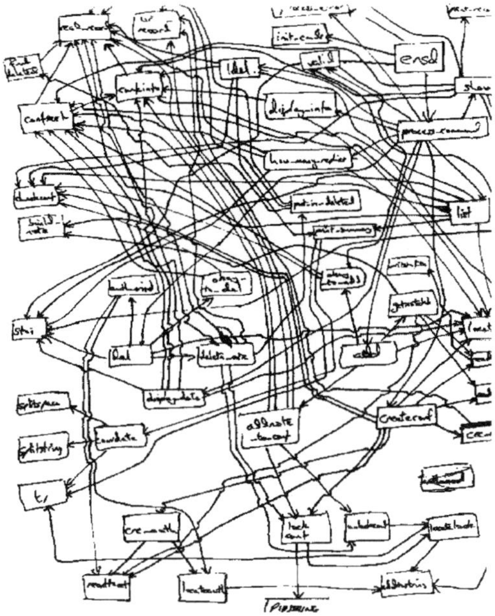

A *very* preliminary design schema illustrating complexity (thanks to Les Carleton)

Perhaps surprisingly, suitable alternatives for real-time systems design are not very numerous. In this text we have selected: Structured Analysis/ Structured Design (SA/SD), Concurrent Design Approach for Real-time Systems (CODARTS), Finite State Methods (FSM), and Object-Oriented Design (OOD) for study. The actual tools used to solve problems clearly constrain the set of solutions available, and so the choice of design method is vital.

1.4 Microprocessors and real-time applications

We are all familiar with real-time applications, they surround us in our everyday lives. Vending machines, mobile phones, alarm systems, washing machines, motor car engine controllers, heart monitors, microwave ovens, point-of-sale terminals, all operate courtesy of an embedded microcontroller running dedicated software. Before microprocessors appeared in the late 1970s, such functionality, in as far as it was possible, was conferred by electronic circuits often built using 7400 series TTL logic packs. Each application required a completely different circuit to be designed and manufactured. This was not an attractive prospect for equipment suppliers who were struggling to control their expanding warehouse stock levels, inflated by the gush of new silicon products. The arrival of embedded software, which allowed many different applications to share the same hardware, was most welcome. The term

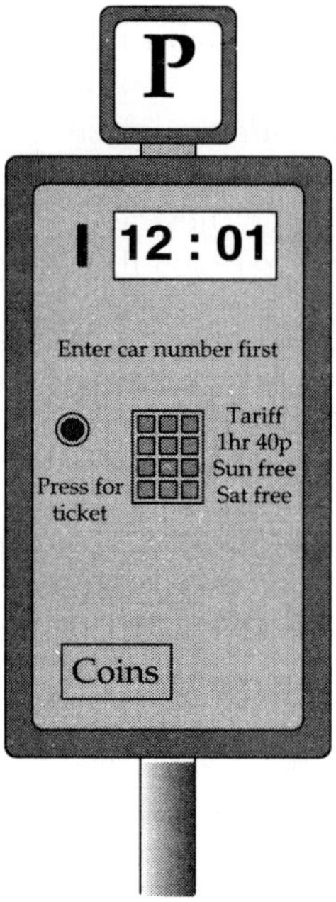

A familiar real-time application

'real-time' is also used in the USA to describe on-line terminal services such as ATMs (Automatic Teller Machines, or cash dispensers), database enquiry, and on-line reservation and payment systems. Recently the term 'responsive system' has been introduced to further distinguish such computer-based applications. The list expands as technology elaborates. In practice, all computer systems have some aspects which are relevant to real-time programming and so the specific skills presented in this text are in great demand.

1.5 Definition of a real-time system

Although there is no clear dividing line between real-time and non-real-time systems, there are a set of distinguishing features (listed below) which can assist with an outline classification schema to identify real-time applications.

- *Timing* The most common definition of a real-time system involves a statement similar to 'Real-time systems are required to compute and deliver correct results within a specified period of time.' Does this mean that a *non-real-time* system such as a payroll program, could print salary cheques two years late, and be forgiven because it was *not* a real-time system? Hardly so! Obviously there are time constraints on non-real-time systems too. There are even circumstances in which the

- Specified limit on system response latency
- Event-driven scheduling
- Low-level programming
- Software tightly coupled to special hardware
- Dedicated specialized function
- The computer may be inside a control loop
- Volatile variables
- Multi-tasking implementation
- Run-time scheduling
- Unpredictable environment
- System intended to run continuously
- Life-critical applications

Outline real-time categorization scheme

early delivery of a result could generate more problems than lateness of delivery. A premature newspaper obituary could sometimes create as much havoc as an early green on a traffic light controller.

Response time sensitivity

- *Interrupt driven* After the requirement for maximum response delay times, the next characteristic of real-time systems is their involvement with events. These often manifest themselves in terms of interrupt signals arising from the arrival of data at an input port, or the ticking

Event-driven pre-emption

of a hardware clock, or an error status alarm. Because real-time systems are often closely coupled with special equipment (a situation that is termed 'embedded') the programmer has also to gain a reasonable understanding of the hardware if the project is to be a thorough success. Once again, however, the demarcation between traditional data processing and real-time systems is not easy to draw because *event-driven* GUI interfaces are so widely used within all desktop applications.

- *Low-level programming* The C language is still favourite for writing device drivers for new hardware. But because high-level languages, including C, do not generally have the necessary instructions to handle interrupt processing, it has been common for programmers to drop down to assembler level to carry out this type of coding. Because ASM and C are classified as low-level languages by many programmers, who may be more familiar with database systems and windowing interfaces, it has been suggested as a distinguishing characteristic of real-time programmers that they prefer to use low-level languages. This can be seen as somewhat misleading, when the real-time high-level languages Modula-2 and ADA are taken into consideration.
- *Specialized hardware* Most real-time systems work within, or at least close beside, specialized electronic and mechanical devices. Unfortunately, to make matters more difficult, during development these are often only prototype models, with some doubt surrounding their functionality and reliability. This is especially true for small embedded microcontrollers which may even be required to perform as critical component parts within a feedback control loop. The oven power controller illustrated below could employ an integrated microcontroller to monitor the oven temperature and adjust the electrical power accordingly. Such applications place a heavy responsibility on the programmer to fully understand the functional role of the software and its contribution to the feedback delay which governs the system response. Code may have to run synchronously with the hardware or other software systems, such as when telephone transmissions are sequenced 8000 times a second to maintain acceptable voice quality. Very often this leads the programmer

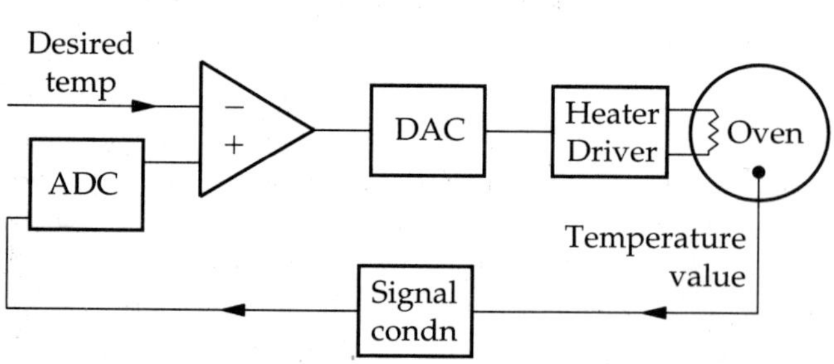

Feedback control loop for specialized hardware

into other disciplines: electrical theory, mechanics, acoustics, physiology or optics. Real-time programmers rarely have a routine day.

- *Volatile data I/O* Another special issue for real-time software concerns 'volatile data'. These are variables which change their value from moment to moment, due to the action of external devices or agents, through interrupts or DMA. This is distinguished from the situation where input data is obtained from a disk file, or from the keyboard under program control. The most common example encountered by real-time programmers involves input channels which operate autonomously to bring in new values for memory variables when data arrives at an input port. The software must then be structured to check for changes at the correct rate, so as not to miss a data update.

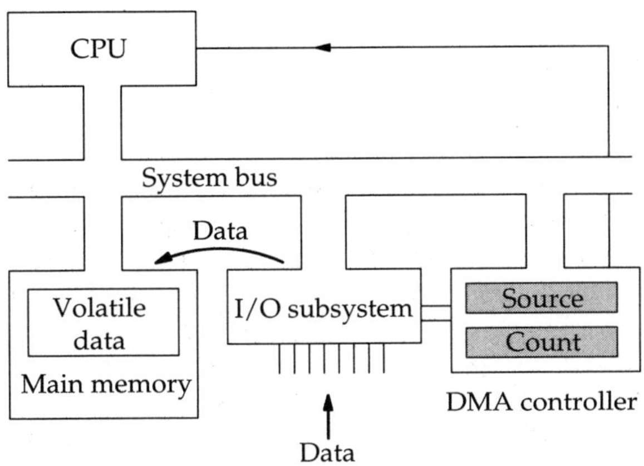

Volatile variables with a DMA controller

- *Multi-tasking* Real-time systems are often expected to involve multitasking. In this situation, several processes or tasks cooperate to carry out the overall job. When considering this arrangement, there should be a clear distinction drawn between the static aggregation of groups of instructions into functions for compilation, and the dynamic sequencing of tasks which takes place at run-time. It has already been suggested that full multi-tasking is not always necessary, but it can be positively advantageous to programmers in simplifying their work. It is also widely accepted that many computer systems have become so complex that it has become necessary to decompose them into components to help people to understand and build them. In the traditional data processing field, for example, the production of invoices from monthly accounts requires several distinct operations to be carried out. These can be sequenced, one after the other, in separate phases of processing. With real-time systems this is rarely possible; the only way to partition the work is to run components in parallel, or concurrently. Multi-tasking provides one technique which can assist programmers to partition their systems into manageable components which have delegated responsibility to carry out some part of the complete activity. Thus, multi-tasking, although generally seen as an implementation strategy, can also offer an intellectual tool to aid the designer.

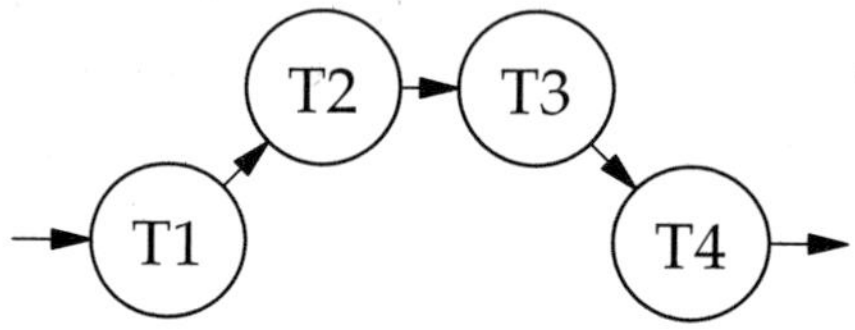

Component sequencing

- *Run-time scheduling* The separation of an activity into several distinct, semi-autonomous tasks leads to the question of task sequencing. In traditional DP applications the sequence planning is largely done by the programmer. Functions are called in the correct order and the activity is completed. But for real-time systems this is only half the story. The major part of sequencing takes place at run-time, and is accomplished by the operating system through the action of the scheduler. It is as if the sequencing decisions have been deferred, it is a kind of 'late sequencing', to draw a parallel with the established term 'late binding', used with regard to code linking. This is perhaps the most interesting feature of real-time systems. The manner in which the various activities are evoked in the correct order is quite different from that of a traditional DP system which normally relies on the arrival of data records from an input file to sequence the functions, and so it is predetermined and fixed.
- *Unpredictability* Being event driven, real-time systems are at the mercy of unpredictable changes in their environments. It is just not feasible to anticipate with 100 per cent certainty all the permutations of situations which may arise. In my experience, the worst offenders are actually the human users, who seem totally unable, or unwilling, to understand what the designer intended. Any choice offered by a menu or sequence of YES/NO alternatives will soon reveal unexpected outcomes during field trials. The exact ordering or sequencing of all the functions which deal with these interactions has to be decided at run-time by the scheduler, giving much more flexibility in response. Considerable effort is now put into extensive simulation testing in order to trap as many of these bugs as possible, even before the designs are released.

Unpredictability

- *Life-critical code* Although not always the case, real-time systems can involve serious risk. A failure to run correctly may result in death or at least injury to the user and others. Such applications are becoming more and more common, with the aircraft and automobile industries converting their products to 'fly by wire' processor technology. This removes from the driver/pilot all direct, muscular control over the physical mechanism, relying entirely on digital control systems to carry out their commands. The burden of developing real-time, life-critical software, with all the extra checking, documentation and acceptance trials

Life risking applications

required, may raise the cost beyond normal commercial projects, of similar code complexity, by an astonishing factor of 30. Most real-time applications are intended to run continuously, or at least until the user turns off the power. Telephone exchanges, for example, contain millions of lines of real-time code, and are expected to run non-stop for 20 years. The increasing use of embedded microprocessors within medical monitoring and life-support equipment, such as radiological scanners and drug infusion pumps, makes consideration of software reliability and systems integrity even more urgent. Some research effort has been expended in devising a method to formally prove correct a computer program, much in the same way that mathematicians deal with algebraic proofs. So far, the products resulting from this work have not generated much commercial interest.

1.6 Programming structures

It is now well accepted that computer programs can all be broken down into three fundamental structures:

- Linear sequences of instructions
- Iterative loops of instructions
- Branches guarded by selection statements

But as indicated above, the *sequencing* of real-time code is not straightforward. In addition, multi-tasking code requires two more structures:

- Parallel or concurrent instructions
- Critical groups of exclusive instructions

SEQ
IT
SEL
PAR
CRIT

More structures in real-time programs

While all DP systems may benefit from utilizing parallel or concurrent coding, it is rarely *essential*, as it frequently is in the case of real-time systems. This formally indicates the increased complexity that arises when working in the real-time field.

1.7 Response latency

There is also an interesting contradiction in citing 'minimum response delay' (latency) as the key factor when characterizing real-time systems. For example, when using more sophisticated real-time executives (RTE), the full response to a Receiver Ready or Transmitter Ready (RxRdy or TxRdy) interrupt is often deferred in order to balance the processing load. Thus the executive attempts to impose its own processing schedule on all the activities, which can actually result in a delayed response. This could be seen as transforming unpredictable, asynchronous demands into scheduled, synchronous processing.

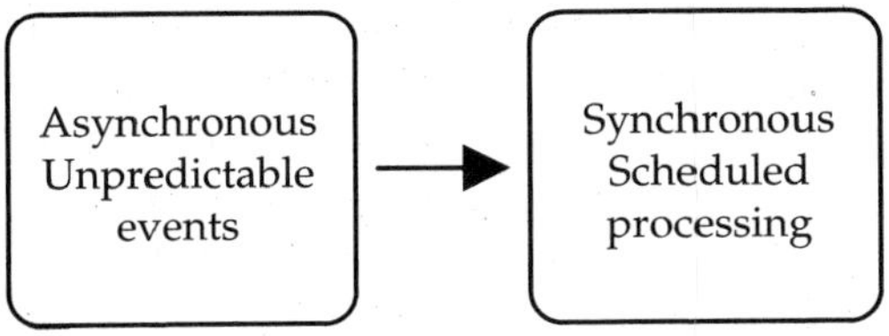

Rapid response compromised for processing efficiency

1.8 Relative speeds

1.8.1 Polling an input too fast

An important factor that needs to be clearly understood by newcomers to real-time programming is the vast disparity in speed between the modern, electronic computer and the human, physical world. Whereas even a slow microcontroller will zip through instructions at a rate of 10 million per second, humans can rarely handle a keyboard at two key strokes per second. The problem is due more to the *relative* speeds than their absolute values. Such an enormous disparity in speed leaves programmers in quite a quandary, since the voracious processing capacity of a modern CPU demands to be fed at all times!

Consider the oscilloscope trace below, which shows how the output voltage changes when a microswitch is closed. The contact bounces for a period of up to one millisecond (1 ms, one thousandth of a second) before finally settling down. Humans are not aware of this high speed dithering, but a computer, sampling an input port one million times a second, can wrongly record that the switch has been turned on and off several times when it has only been pressed once.

Such errors often show up in 'monitoring and counting' systems and may lead to the use of more expensive optical or magnetic switch units which do not suffer from contact bounce.

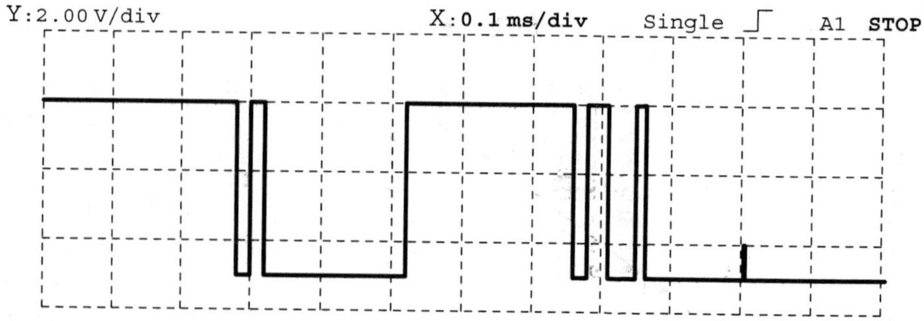

Voltage from a key switch showing a contact bounce of nearly 1 ms

Alternatively, extra logic gates can be included to eliminate the effects of contact bounce as shown below. But perhaps the best solution is to deploy some debouncing software. This can subject the incoming, raw signals to low-pass filtering, at no extra expense. We will return to this issue in Chapter 4 with an example system.

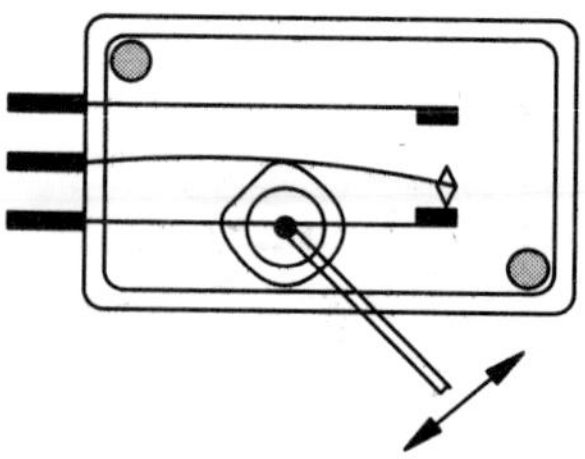

Mechanical switch

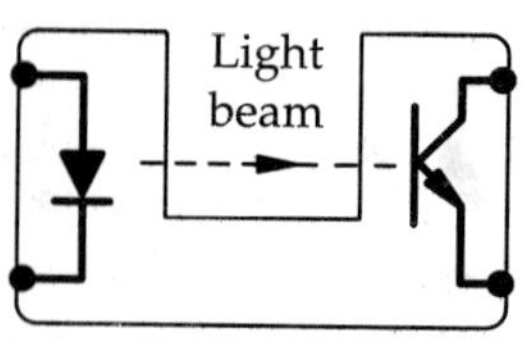

Optical switch

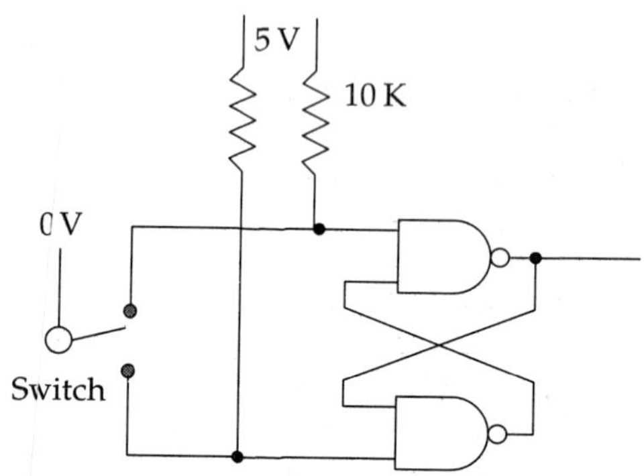

Debouncing logic

1.8.2 Polling an input too slowly

It scarcely needs to be said that if a computer checks an input too infrequently it runs the risk of missing an occasional event, such as a counting pulse. To avoid this happening, it is common to require the sampling rate to be at least twice as fast as the mean pulse frequency. If the system has to detect a pulse occurring no more often than every 10 ms, the port should be checked at least every 5 ms (200 times a second). Sometimes the input events are recorded on a hardware latch in an attempt to reduce the required sampling rate.

However, this still runs the risk of losing an event when a following event overruns the previous one before the software reads and clears the earlier event from the latch.

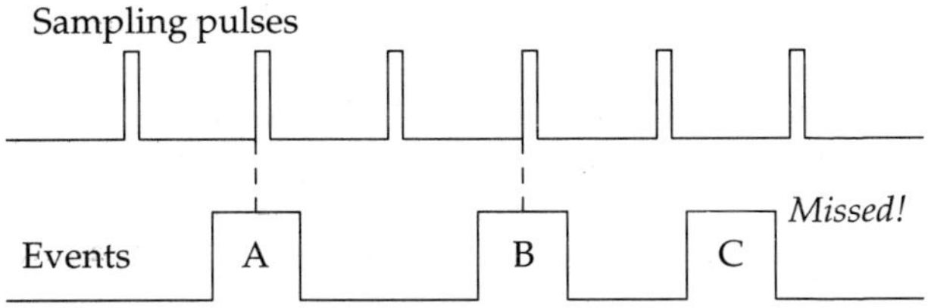

Sampling too infrequently

The term 'aliasing' is used to describe a similar situation which occurs when an analogue signal is sampled too slowly. If the input signal contains frequencies above *half* the sampling rate, the sampled version of the signal will appear to contain frequencies not in the original signal. Look closely at the figure below. The original signal ('A') is printed with a thick line and shows 12 cycles (∩∪). The sampling points are shown as dashed lines, with the captured values as thick vertical bars. Notice that there are fewer than the minimum two samples per signal cycle. There are only 20 samples in 12 cycles, whereas there should be at least 24. Now reconstruct the signal using only the sample values. The resulting synthesized wave ('B') is drawn with a thin line. 'A' and 'B' are not the same. This artifact is called aliasing and is avoided by filtering all the high frequency components from the original signal before sampling occurs. The maximum frequency threshold of half the sampling rate is referred to as the Nyquist limit. You may be familiar with old Hollywood films, where stagecoach wheels appear to turn backwards because the movie cameras ran too slowly.

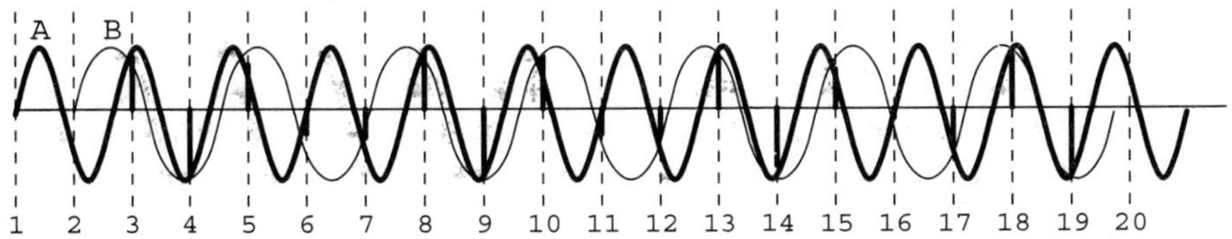

Aliasing error through sampling too slowly: only 20 sample points in 12 cycles

1.8.3 Light sensing

Another example problem, illustrating the relative timing issue, involves the use of light sensors. Normal office lighting relies on fluorescent tubes. These actually flicker very strongly at 100 Hz. The human eye is normally insensitive to flicker rates above 40 Hz, but a surface inspection computer could easily be confused by large variation in illumination. If the program is periodically reading a value given by a photodiode, the exact moments when the samples are taken would have more influence on the result than the darkness of the surface being scanned. If the polling is carried out fast enough, say 5 kHz, the 100 Hz brightness modulation would get averaged out. Once again, the timing of computer activity is critical to obtaining a correct result.

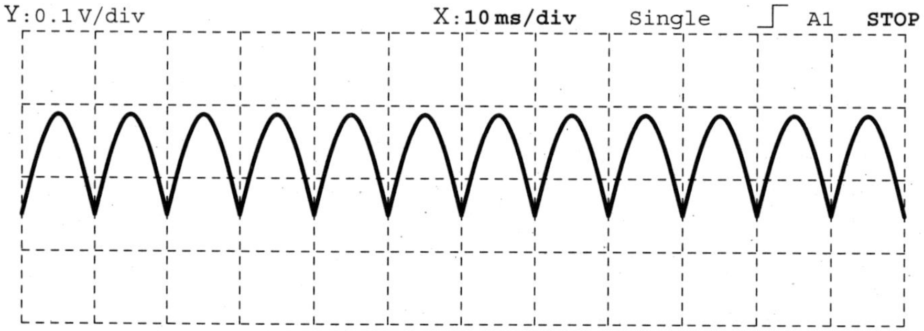

Voltage from a light sensor showing 100 Hz mains flicker

The application areas described above, switch scanning, pulse detection and light sensing, show that calling input routines too *frequently* or too *infrequently* can both generate artifacts which can blossom into serious errors.

1.9 Software timing

Another problem for programmers involved with real-time systems is the need to understand more exactly what the compiler is creating. With desktop systems it is now commonplace to write and run, with little attention being

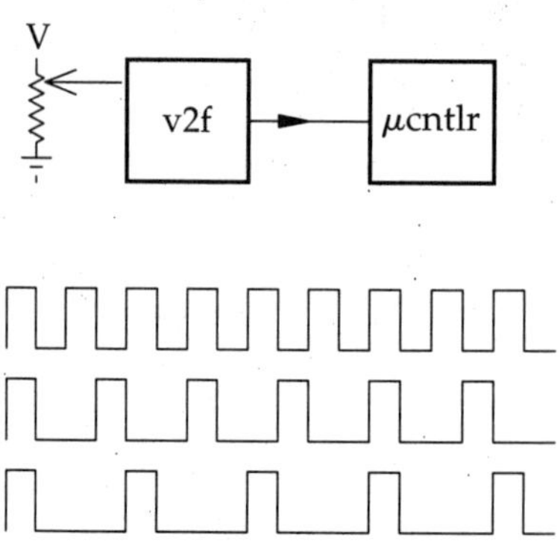

Voltage-to-frequency converter

paid to the final executable code. There are circumstances where this optimistic disregard may lead to difficulties. A commonly used environmental monitoring arrangement involves a transducer being interfaced to a voltage-to-frequency converter (thanks to Laurence O'Brien for sharing this lop-sided bug with me). The cost advantage of not using an ADC interfaced to a serial transmission link is the prime motivation. With a V2F unit, the transducer analogue voltage is converted to a pulse frequency code: the larger the voltage, the higher the frequency; the lower the voltage, the lower the frequency. The computer only has to dedicate a single bit input port to accept the information in serial mode. However, there remains the problem of converting this pulse frequency code into normal integer format. For an HLL programmer the following code might appear attractive. It runs and offers the beguiling appearance of success, but it entails an interesting bug related to the code generated by the compiler. Unfortunately, the time spent in the two opposing arms of the `IF/ELSE` structure is not matched. So with an actual 50/50 situation, the results would not come out as 50/50, because of the dwell time bias. This can be checked by reversing the code and running both versions back to back. Inspecting assembler code listings from the compiler will also reveal the discrepancy.

```
loop for 100 msec {                          loop for 100 msec {
   if (input_bit) <-----------------------------> if (!input_bit)
        hcount++;                                       hcount++;
   else                                            else
        lcount++;                                       lcount++;
}                                               }
temp1 = tempX*hcount/                           temp2 = tempX*hcount/
       (lcount+hcount)                                  (lcount+hcount)
```

1.10 High speed timing

Perhaps an example would now be useful of the opposite situation, when processors simply cannot run fast enough. Consider a laser range-finder, intended for use in civil surveying, or more ominously for battlefield targeting. It works by preparing a pulse laser for firing, emitting a pulse of light, waiting for the reflected echo to return, and, by timing the duration of the flight, calculating the distance travelled.

The speed of light is 3×10^8 m/sec.

For a target 20 km away, the pulse of light will travel 40 km (4×10^4 m).

$$\text{So } \textit{time taken} = \frac{\textit{distance}}{\textit{speed}} = \frac{4 \times 10^4}{3 \times 10^8} = 1.3 \times 10^{-4}\,\text{s} = 130\,\mu\text{s}$$

If the item being surveyed is only 50 m distant, the time of flight will be reduced to 325 ns.

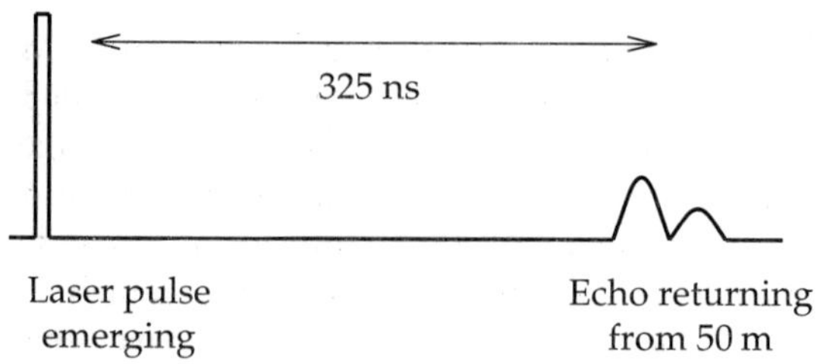

Light travels very fast!

Thus the timing mechanism must be able to cope with the range 0.3–150 μs. Instructions executed on a 500 MHz, dedicated processor could maximally complete instructions every 2 ns, with the code running from LI cache. However, any disturbance to the instruction fetch/execute pipeline sequence, such as cache elimination, task swapping, interrupts, or even conditional branches in the code, would reduce the instruction rate considerably. Therefore, the only reliable timing method for this application is to employ a high speed hardware counter which is cleared down and restarted when the light pulse leaves the laser, and stopped when the echo returns. The number captured is a measure of the distance travelled by the laser pulse, there and back. Only a close interplay of software and hardware can provide the solution to this problem.

1.11 Output timing overload

There is a similar set of timing problems facing the programmer when dealing with periodic, or cyclic, output data. A typical example involves the control of motors. These may be used in continuous mode, to turn wheels at a desired speed, or to position a unit and hold it against a varying resistant pressure.

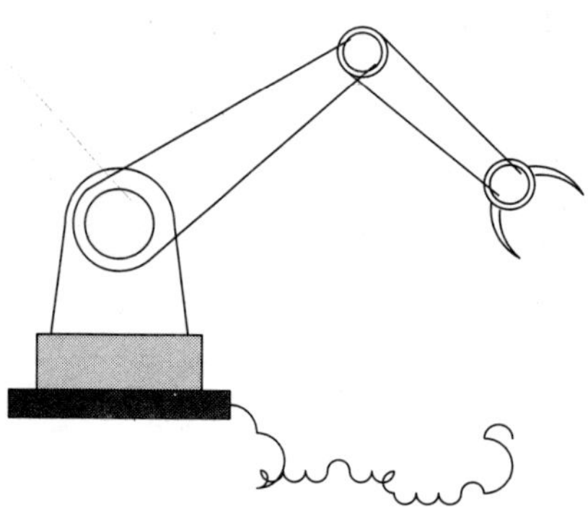

Motor drive problems

Both situations may involve responding to sensors providing feedback information. There are several different types of motor available, each with its own special area of application: stepper, DC servo, universal AC, induction AC, and synchronous AC. DC servo and stepper motors are most commonly controlled with microprocessors; the latter we will meet again in Chapter 2. Both DC servo and steppers can provide rotation and dynamic positioning. Stepper motors in particular require accurately timed sequences of pulses to control their speed and direction.

Microprocessor-based controllers can handle such a problem by holding pulse pattern tables in memory and accessing the entries in sequence at the correct rate. Another interesting type of positioning servo motor is supplied by Futaba for model makers. It also uses a digital pulse input to specify the required angular position of the motor shaft. Commonly, a 2 ms pulse will indicate a central, neutral position, a 1.5 ms pulse sets the shaft to $-45°$ and a 2.5 ms pulse sends the shaft to $+45°$. Unfortunately, unlike the stepper motor, the positioning pulses need to be repeated every 20 ms, to refresh the controller. This is quite a problem for a processor when several positioning units have to be serviced simultaneously, as is the case with a robot arm. Arranging for five timing pulses to be dispatched every 20 ms, with an accuracy of 50 μs, really does benefit from some special hardware support.

1.12 Debugging real-time systems

When debugging real-time code extra difficulties emerge, such as the impossibility of usefully single stepping through doubtful code, or reproducing elusive, time critical input situations. Inserting a neanderthal `printf( )` statement in an attempt to isolate the bug will completely change the execution timing (my aged PC/200 takes nearly 1 ms to complete a call to printf). Confusion often arises when dealing with prototype hardware. Errors can be blamed on the software, when in fact the problem is due to the new electronics. Such uncertainty makes debugging more difficult and challenging. Extra equipment may need to be acquired, by purchase, hire or loan, to generate complex test signals, and capture the results using sophisticated logic analysers, In Circuit Emulators (ICE) or digital storage oscilloscopes. Initially, a very useful trick is to insert a couple of output instructions within your code, which will emit a short indicator pulse from a spare output port. This can be picked up by the oscilloscope and viewed. It is an enormous advantage to be able to see the relative timings of ongoing processing activity, set against traces obtained from external events. When dealing with systems which are processing fast streams of data interleaved with intermittent, much slower events, capturing the correct sequences for analysis can be tricky. In this situation, you may be able to get your software to trigger the viewing trace, and so synchronize the oscilloscope display to the events under investigation.

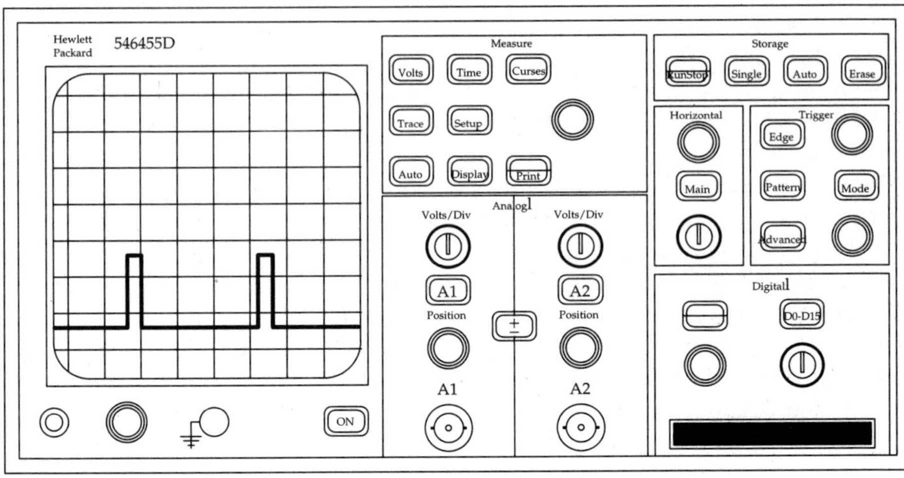

Oscilloscopes can display timing information from software, too

1.13 Access to hardware

Because real-time computer systems are often working in tight integration with the surrounding equipment, they need to have efficient access to hardware. This means that the normal hardware/software separation, imposed by an operating system for security purposes, has to be broached. The application software must be able to directly read input ports and write to output ports. With Unix and Windows, these operations are forbidden to all but supervisor-level code. To run all the application tasks with supervisor permission would incur unnecessary risk, so special device driver routines are needed to provide the I/O facilities that real-time programs require. Operating systems can get in the way.

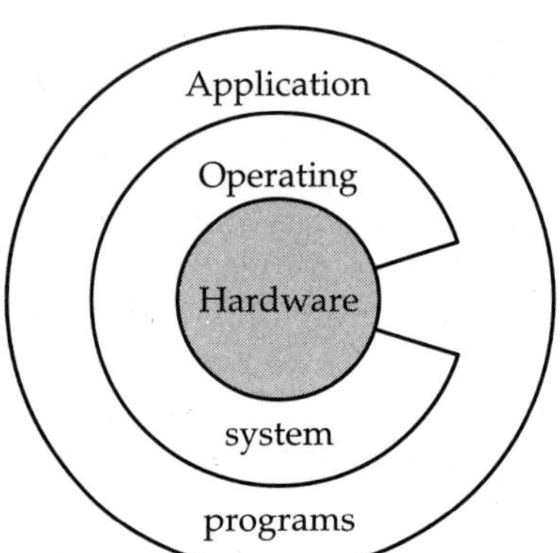

Direct access to hardware

1.14 Machine I/O

All machine instruction sets must include some mechanism allowing the programmer to transfer data into and out of the computer. To that end, Intel provides its CPUs with special `IN` and `OUT` instructions which operate solely on ports located within a designated I/O address space. In a more unified, von Neumann approach Motorola chose to avoid separate I/O instructions and address spaces, and so enabled programmers to use the normal group of data transfer instructions with I/O ports.

This is possible because all the ports are located within memory address space, alongside the RAM or ROM chips. From the CPU's perspective, ports, ROM and RAM can look much the same for access purposes. Only when data caching facilities are included does this homogeneity break down.

- Dedicated and periodic **polling**
- **Interrupt** driven
- Direct Memory Access (**DMA**)

Different I/O techniques

From the software point of view there are three principal techniques used to initiate and control the transfer of data through a computer I/O port. Direct Memory Access (DMA) is distinct in that it depends substantially on autonomous hardware which is required to generate the bus cycle control sequences in order to carry out data transfers independently of the main CPU. We will discuss each I/O method in greater detail later in this chapter. All require software driver routines to work closely with associated hardware units. These routines are normally part of the operating system and not infrequently written in assembly language. In the PC marketplace, extension card suppliers provide such driver routines on CD or floppy disk, along with the hardware, so that they may be installed by the user. It is also increasingly

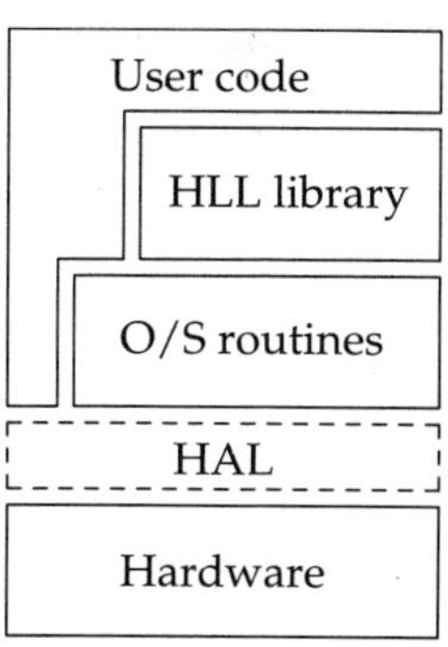

Software access to hardware

common to have access to driver routine libraries via the Internet. Following the pioneering example of Unix, modern operating systems are written as far as possible in HLL, probably C. In this way, porting the operating system to a new processor is faster and more reliable, once a good C compiler has been obtained. Windows NT has defined a specific hardware interface layer of software, HAL, which acts as a virtual machine layer to aid porting to new processors. The traditional view of software is a hierarchy of intercommunicating layers as presented above. Each layer has a specific data processing role and exchanges messages with adjoining layers.

HAL hides much of the specific hardware differences between Pentium, ALPHA and MIPS processors, from the main part of the operating system code, making it easier to port and maintain the system code. Although Windows 98 allows direct access to the I/O hardware, with Unix and Windows NT/XP it is strictly denied for security reasons. Such a limitation does not concern most application programmers who only ever access I/O facilities by calling library procedures provided with the HLL compiler, such as `getc( )` and `putc( )`. These library procedures may then call underlying operating system functions to gain access to the actual hardware.

The introduction of a 'virtual machine' software layer has also been used in the development of a version of Linux, RTAI, for real-time applications. We will discuss this more in Chapter 19.

1.15 Programmed I/O

The fundamental method of reading data from an input port involves the simple execution of either a MOVE or IN instruction, depending on whether the port is memory mapped or I/O mapped. An example of input by programmed polling from an I/O mapped port is presented in C and Pentium assembler code below. This would only work on a system running DOS or Windows 98 because Linux expressly denies direct access to hardware in this fashion for security reasons. Access to all port addresses is limited to processes running with root permissions, so if you have the supervisor password, and are prepared to risk a complete system rebuild should you inadvertently blunder into an unexpected port, you are free to try your hand! The Linux 'suid'

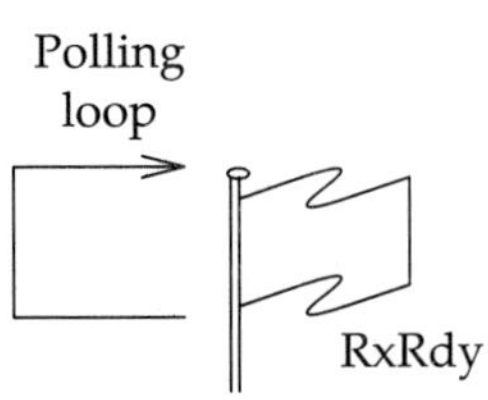

Spin polling

permissions, explained in Chapter 10, offer a middle path through the security quagmire. Operating system code handles all the I/O operations, so all the assembler-level IN and OUT instructions are hidden inside device driver routines. The receive ready flag (RxRdy) in the status register (STATUS) is repeatedly checked in a tight polling loop until it has been set to 1 by the port hardware, indicating that a new item of data has arrived in the data receive register (RxData). The loop then drops through and the newly arrived data byte is read from the data receive register. In this example, it is then checked for zero because this would indicate the end of the current data transfer. If it is non-zero, the item is saved into the data array using a pointer, and the loop continues.

```
do  {
    while (!(INP(STATUS) & RXRDY)) { };       /* wait for data */
}   while (*pch++ = INP(RXDATA));             /* check data for a NULL */
```

The ASM equivalent of the above code uses the Pentium `IN` input instruction and might look something like this. Again, the status port register is checked before reading the data port itself.

```
        MOV EDI,PCH             ;init pointer to start of data buffer
TLOOP:  IN AL,STATUS            ;read status port
        AND AL,RXRDY            ;test device status bit
        JZ TLOOP                ;blocking: if no data go round again

DATAIN: IN AL,RXDATA            ;data from Rx port & clear RXRDY flag
        OR AL,AL                ;test for EOS marker
        JZ COMPLETE             ;jmp out if finished
        MOV [EDI],AL            ;save character in data buffer
        INC EDI                 ;bump buffer pointer to next location
        JMP TLOOP               ;back for more input
COMPLETE: ....                  ;character string input complete
```

Example input polling loop in C and ASM code

It is also very important to understand that I/O port hardware detects the action of data being read from the data register, RxData, and clears down the RxRdy flag. This prepares the hardware for the arrival of the next item of data. The complementary version which *outputs* data is nearly identical, except the TxData flag in the status register is polled until it changes to 1, indicating that the data transmit register is empty and available. The next data item is then moved from memory into TxData, the data transmit register. At this point the polling loop starts all over again.

1.16 Hardware/software cost tradeoff

To an increasing extent, product functionality has been invested in the embedded software rather than special purpose hardware. It was immediately appreciated, with the introduction of microprocessors in the 1970s, that the cost of duplicating and distributing software was trivial compared to manufacturing and transporting hardware units. Although this may still be true, it is apparent that hardware *production* costs are falling, and software *development* costs dramatically increasing. In addition, the lifetime maintenance cost of software has often been neglected because it was not really understood how software could deteriorate over time in a similar way to corroding metal parts. The need to fund continual software maintenance can in part be attributed not to an ageing process within the system, but rather to an evolving environment which no longer fits the software. Maybe this is paralleled in the theatre, where Shakespeare is continually reinterpreted, generation after generation, seeking to match the evolving expectation of audiences. Since 1606, the accumulated maintenance cost of *King Lear* has certainly far outstripped the original commissioning fee. In fact, software suppliers may still not fully understand the problems associated with the management and maintenance of their products; hardware revisions remain more visible and controllable. But perhaps the most problematic issue for all software products is the ease with which changes can be made, and the future need for documentation forgotten.

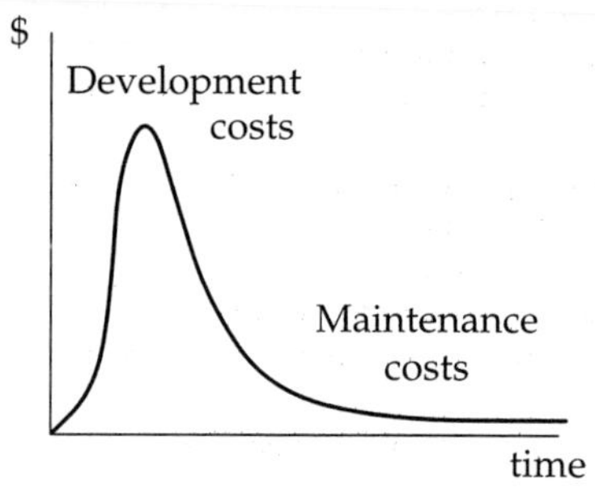

Software lifetime costs

1.17 Hard, soft and firm

Often the distinction is drawn between 'hard' and 'soft' real-time systems. Hard systems impose tight limits on response times, so that a delayed result is a wrong result. The examples of a jet fuel controller and a camera shutter unit illustrate the need to get a correct value computed and available at the right time. Soft real-time systems need only meet a time-average performance target. As long as most of the results are available before the deadline, the system will run successfully, with acceptably recognizable output. Audio and video transmission and processing equipment are examples of real-time systems which must achieve an average throughput performance. A single lost speech sample or image frame can normally be covered up by repeating the previous item. Only when responses are delayed repeatedly will a seriously unacceptable error occur. The category of 'firm' is also being mooted as a crossover between the other two, because real-world systems do not always fall into either category for response deadlines.

A somewhat clearer distinction is visible between 'large' and 'small' real-time systems development. Design techniques, management methods, implementation languages and many other critical aspects are dealt with differently by groups operating at the two extremes of this application spectrum. Typical projects on the small side would be coffee or ticket vending machines, entertainment equipment, or protocol converter units. Large systems could be production plant monitoring equipment, air traffic control and telecommunication networks. Real-time systems, large and small, are becoming a routine part of our everyday life.

1.18 Software Quality Assurance (SQA)

The production and maintenance of high quality software has been the special concern of software engineers since the 1970s, when the term 'Software Engineering' was first coined in an attempt to express the frustration of programmers with the repeated failures of large software projects. By studying the separate activities involved in designing and realizing programs, it was hoped to improve the industry's performance. The complete lifecycle of a software product spans several distinct but overlapping phases which can, to some extent, be discussed in isolation. The software engineering approach to real-time systems emphasizes the importance of the early requirements acquisition phase and later product testing activity. As software continues to grow in size and sophistication, the need to coordinate large teams of analysts and programmers, all working on the same project, becomes more problematic. Some parallels can be drawn with traditional engineering methods, and benefits can be derived from their long experience, but this can also be misleading. The techniques which have evolved to successfully support large civil engineering projects or automobile production plants may not necessarily be appropriate for computer programmers. Remember that bridges still collapse and cars fail due to design faults, so the admiration and emulation should be cautious. Undoubtedly the complexity of software will increase still further and automated methods will have to be developed to assist the development process. In particular, real-time systems have suffered from some disasterously public failures, such as the loss of the Ariane 5 rocket during its initial

> 'Hardware degrades despite maintenance, software degrades because of it.'

A depressing aphorism

launch and the recall of engine management units for bug fixes, which have contributed to a general scepticism about all computer-based projects.

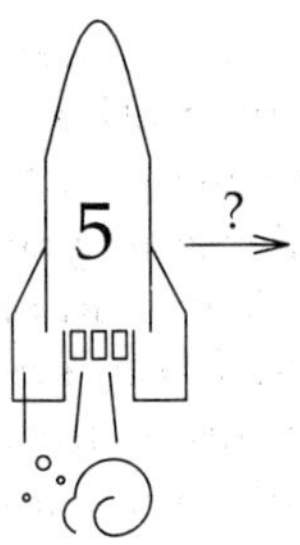

Costly software failures

1.19 Experience and history

Unfortunately, in computing, the lessons learned during earlier eras are often overlooked. Pioneering mainframe programmers despised the small DEC PDP-8 minicomputers when they first arrived, and the Intel 8080 microprocessors were initially ignored by everyone except hobby-mag readers and hardware engineers. In my own department, an experienced CS colleague expressed the now ludicrous view that he could see no reason to include details of the recently introduced Z80 microprocessor and CP/M operating system into university curricula. Each generation seems determined to recapitulate earlier discoveries and waste vast effort in the process. With the introduction of the PC, Microsoft and IBM spurned many well-designed, field proven operating systems in favour of DOS. This now seems an incredible leap backwards in developmental terms.

When re-reading the RTL/2 reference book written by John Barnes in 1976, I am struck by the freshness of its focus, the continuing relevance of the ideas and the apparent lack of progress achieved in dealing with the same set of software problems during the intervening three decades. The perceived need to adopt the latest jargon and intellectual style seems to have created a fashion-conscious industry which refuses to sift out and carry forward the best ideas.

Part of the problem could be that the modern computer science textbook rarely contains much technical information about past achievements in hardware and software. If there is a history section, it occurs along with the introduction, and concentrates on industry 'heroes' and archive photographs of shiny sales-room cabinets. Comments on their tiny 16 Kbit core memories do not draw out our admiration for the efficiency of the code, but rather laughter at the ludicrous idea of programs running in such confined space. Indeed, the subtle ideas and algorithms contained within them are not often discussed or explained. History is bunk, but if we ignore it, we are condemned to repeat its mistakes and continually suffer the same frustrations.

1.20 Futures?

For real-time developers, a very relevant revolution, which may parallel that triggered by the arrival of 8 bit microprocessors, could be in progress at this very moment with the introduction of large Field Programmable Gate Arrays (FPGAs). These are configured for a particular application by writing a specification program in a language such as VHDL or Verilog. With the size and gate density achievable at present, it is possible to install several fast RISC processors on the same FPGA, and still leave space for peripheral devices. So the opportunity for 'roll your own' microcontrollers is available now, with the possibility of powerful bespoke clustering not far off. Such a development is not so revolutionary, but if the expressive potential of VHDL is pushed a bit further, it may be capable of capturing the complete application, with all its algorithms, in digital hardware without recourse to processors and software. The advantage of parallel, synchronous circuits implementing all the functionality is yet to be thoroughly investigated. Such an approach draws back together the divergent skills and traditions developed by software and hardware engineers. Those involved in real-time systems design and implementation should keep their eyes open for evolving developments from this direction.

1.21 Chapter summary

This chapter introduces the key issues which make the development of real-time software more challenging than desktop, or traditional DP applications. A set of characteristics is offered which can be used to identify those applications which may require special real-time expertise. But a clear distinction is not really valid because most modern programs have some measure of real-time features. The key significance of designing systems to handle many discrete, concurrent activities has been emphasized because of the extra complexity that this introduces. The sequencing of code at run-time in response to changing environmental circumstances is possibly the principal defining characteristic. Handling I/O activity with unusual devices can be a particular problem for real-time programmers which demands extra hardware knowledge. Hard real-time systems need to meet strict response deadlines, while soft real-time systems only have to achieve a satisfactory average performance. It is now recognized that large real-time systems require special expertise, tools and techniques for their successful development. The current revolution in the field of embedded systems centres on the application of FPGA chips as a replacement for programmable microcontrollers.

Considerations of timing must be appreciated by the system designer and programmer.

1 ms, a millisecond, one thousandth of a second	10^{-3}
1 μs, a microsecond, one millionth of a second	10^{-6}
1 ns, a nanosecond, one thousandth of a millionth of a second	10^{-9}
1 ps, a picosecond, one millionth of a millionth of a second	10^{-12}
1 fs, a femtosecond, one thousandth of a millionth of a millionth of a second	10^{-15}

1 year	32 nHz	year number rollover
6 months	64 nHz	GMT<->BST changeover
8 hr	30 μHz	AGA coal stove cycle time
10 s	0.1 Hz	photocopier page printing
1 s	1 Hz	time-of-day rate
300 ms	3 Hz	typing speed
300 ms		human reaction time
150 ms	7 Hz	mechanical switch bounce time
15 ms	70 Hz	motor car engine speed
	260 Hz	middle C
	440 Hz	concert pitch A
1 ms	1 kHz	serial line data rate
125 μs	8 kHz	digitized speech, telephone quality
64 μs	15.6 kHz	TV line rate
50 μs		Mc68000 interrupt latency
0.5 μs	2 MHz	Mc68000 instruction rate
0.074 μs	13.5 MHz	video data rate
0.050 μs		semiconductor RAM access time
0.01 μs	100 MHz	Ethernet data rate
10 ns	100 MHz	memory cycle, PC motherboard
2.5 ns	400 MHz	logic gate delay
555 ps	1.8 GHz	cellular telephone transmissions
500 ps	2 GHz	single instruction issue, Pentium IV
0.3 ps	3 THz	infrared radiation
16 fs	600 THz	visible light

$2^{10} \approx 10^3$	1000, known as 1 kilo
$2^{20} \approx 10^6$	1000_000, known as 1 mega
$2^{30} \approx 10^9$	1000_000_000, known as 1 giga
$2^{40} \approx 10^{12}$	1000_000_000_000, known as 1 tera
$2^{50} \approx 10^{15}$	1000_000_000_000_000, known as 1 peta
$2^{60} \approx 10^{18}$	1000_000_000_000_000_000, known as 1 exa

Timing parameters, from slow to fast

1.22 Problems and issues for discussion

1. What should be the intellectual basis of computer science, the CPU fetch–execute cycle or the use of abstract languages to specify functionality?

   Will the use of VHDL or Verilog to configure large FPGA chips become as significant for programmers as the traditional HLLs: C/C++ and Java?
2. With the increase in CPU speeds from 20 to 2000 MHz in 20 years (1980 to 2000), have many of the original reasons for using complex multi-tasking software been rendered irrelevant by enhanced hardware performance?
3. What aspects of code sequencing can be set at compile time, and what aspects still have to be determined at run-time? (This concerns the 'granularity' of concurrency.)
4. If every process had its own private CPU, what facilities, currently offered by operating systems, would no longer be required?
5. Look up the circumstances of the Ariane 5 launch catastrophe (4/6/96), and see whether too little or too much software engineering was principally to blame. Would the rocket have crashed if the programming had been carried out in C rather than Ada, or if the 'trusted and proven' Ariane 4 software had not been reused?
6. Compare the technical specifications for several microprocessors:

	Clock speed	*MIPS*	*Max memory*	*MMU*	*External interrupts*	*H/W timer*	*FPU*
PIC 12C508							
Intel 8051							
Motorola MCF5282							
ARM-7							
Intel Pentium-4							
Itanium 2							

1.23 Suggestions for reading

Allworth, S. & Zobel, R. (1987). *Introduction to Real-time Software Design.* Macmillan.

Barnes, J. (1976). *RTL/2, Design and Philosophy.* Hayden & Sons.

Bruyninckx, H. (2002). Real-time and Embedded Guide. From: herman.bruyninckx@mech.kuleuven.ac.be

Burns, A. & Welling, A. (2001). *Real-time Systems and Programming Languages.* Addison Wesley.

Cooling, J. E. (2003). *Software Engineering, Real-time Systems.* Addison Wesley.

Gomaa, H. (1993). *Software Design Methods for Concurrent and Real-time Systems.* Addison Wesley.

Lawrence, P. & Mauch, K. (1985). *Real-time Microcomputer Systems Design: An Introduction.* McGraw Hill.

Shaw, A. C. (2001). *Real-time Systems and Software.* Wiley.

Şimon, D. (1999). *An Embedded Software Primer.* Addison Wesley.

Chapter 2

Implementing simple real-time systems

2.1 Chapter overview

This chapter describes the use of serial tasking loops to demonstrate how simple real-time systems can be implemented using round robin, cooperative scheduling. This simple approach serves to eliminate the task swapping overhead associated with pre-emptive multi-tasking. By introducing the extra facility of interrupt service routines, a quite reasonable real-time embedded system can be achieved. The problem of resource sharing, or critical data, is also discussed within the context of cooperative scheduling. The chapter concludes with some practical examples using the standard printer port of a Linux-based PC for initial device control experiments.

2.2 Multi-tasking

When working with a single CPU, it is common to share this pivotal resource by rapidly switching between all the active tasks. Operating systems, such as Unix and Windows, select one task to run on the CPU for a 10 ms time slice, then select another. Multi-tasking or multi-threading programs are readily implemented using modern High-Level Languages (HLL), such as Java or C++, through the low-level facilities provided by the operating system. My Linux workstation is currently handling 66 tasks, of which only a dozen are directly attributable to my endeavours; the remainder are carrying out background jobs, such as handling the LAN connection, managing my desktop and various X sessions. In this way a multi-tasking operating system gives the impression of having multiple CPUs, when in fact it does not. The term *concurrent* processing is normally used to express how multi-tasking can be achieved by serially sharing a single CPU. If multiple CPUs can be used simultaneously for the different tasks, this is referred to as *parallel* processing. Concurrent processing is only viable because the speed and processing capability of a modern CPU, in most cases, far outstrips the demands of a single task. Deciding when and how the tasks are swapped and what strategy is used to choose the next active task to run on the CPU are responsibilities of the system scheduler.

```
rob>  ps -A|wc -l
      66
rob>
```

Linux multi-tasking: 66 tasks

Initially, the habit of sharing a CPU among competing tasks started in the days of large, expensive mainframes. The cost of running programs would have been prohibitive if multi-tasking had not been developed to rapidly share the resources and running costs among many users. But when the first cheap microprocessors emerged onto the market, it seemed a good opportunity to ditch the growing burden of operating systems code, and allocate each process to a separate microprocessor. For some reason this simple vision has not been adopted, instead, as the microprocessors grew in power and sophistication, so did their operating software. So today, each desktop, or laptop, PC is running the equivalent of a 1975 super-minicomputer operating system. It does seem rather strange.

2.3 Task loops

As already stated in Chapter 1, small real-time systems may simply employ a continuous loop of functions to carry out all the necessary activities. This avoids the 'expensive' overhead of pre-emptive task swapping by simply coding the change from one function to the next as a cooperative hand-over. However, such a loop of function/tasks, which can regularly scan for significant changes at the input ports, or update output ports, does not really provide an event-driven real-time system; moreover, much of the processor time is spent in fruitless status-flag testing, sometimes termed 'skip-polling'. The average response time to an active device is half the loop period, with a worst case latency which is the sum of all the other functions, on their longest paths. A more significant problem arises because the simple cyclic looping of procedures cannot deliver dependable timing when required to periodically schedule activities. The immediate solution to undependable response times is to tie each response-critical task directly to a device-driven interrupt. This uses the interrupt hardware to prioritize and pre-emptively schedule tasks. Such hardware-based scheduling can work well for very small applications, but it is rather inflexible, not integrated with the wider task priority settings, and will always lead eventually to intractable difficulties. In general, there are never enough interrupt levels, the application is tied to specific hardware, varying the relative priority among Interrupt Service Routines (ISR)

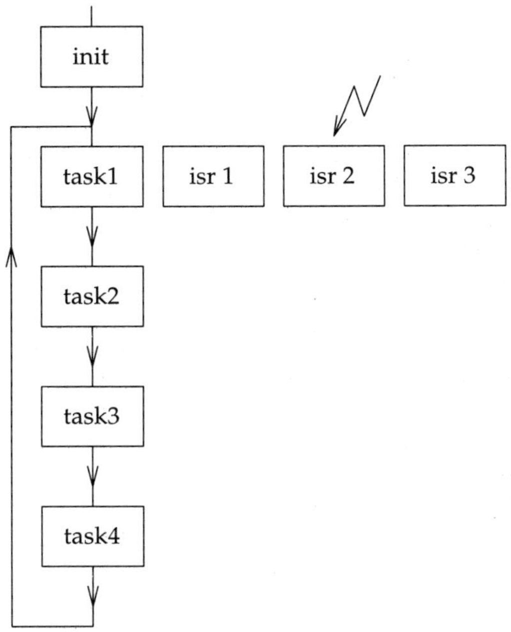

Simple task loop with interrupt routines

is nearly impossible, and debugging the full application becomes more and more difficult. These issues will be explored further in Chapter 4, when the simple task loop structure is expanded into a cyclic executive.

2.4 Code timing problems

As already stated, the simple cyclic looping of tasks does not always provide sufficient timing accuracy. This is referred to as the 'jitter' problem, whereby all code suffers some indeterminacy in its run-time. We can use an oscilloscope to watch the time taken for a section of code to execute, all that you need to add to your code is an output instruction at the start and another

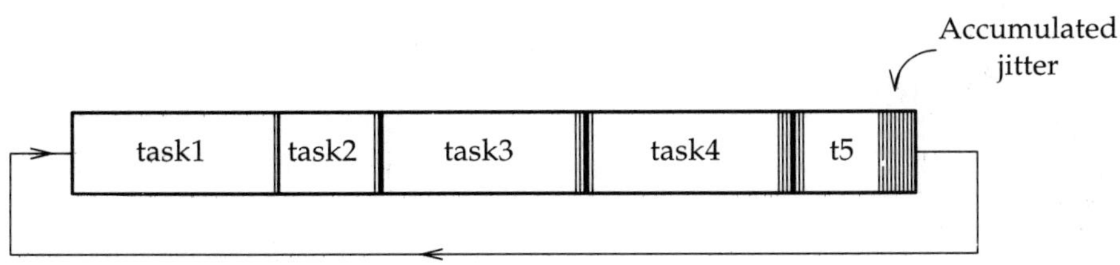

Jitter: code run-time uncertainty

at the end, to raise and lower the voltage on a single bit of an output port. The run-time variation will show up as a horizontal shudder or jitter on the back edge of the pulse. This is due to intervening interrupts and unavoidable uncertainty in the execution of the IF/ELSE selections within the code. Some specialist application areas deal with this run-time uncertainty by carefully padding out the code to match up each arm of all the IF/ELSE statements. Alternatively, the hardware can be used to drive a group of interrupt service routines, one for each task, but this will never be satisfactory in the long run because it is intrinsically inflexible, beyond the programmer's control. Also, doubt has been expressed on the safety of systems which rely too heavily on interrupts. Testing all the combinations and situations in which interrupts can occur is impossible, leaving the nagging issue of reliability.

The task loop also imposes a minimum response latency on I/O activity. Taking the average, a device will have to wait one half of a loop period before its associated task comes round to deal with the request. This constraint may impose too fast a loop frequency, reducing the amount of useful processing that a task can complete each cycle. The quick fix of splitting loop tasks into several phases, each to be executed on subsequent passes through the loop, is not to be pursued. A further caution regarding this implementation plan involves the risk of tasks blocking or crashing; however unlikely the external events and circumstances, however well tested your code, this *will* occur (trust me). Unfortunately, a loop task crashing leads to a catastrophic failure of the whole system, even if the problem, trivially, only involved a single input channel.

2.5 Interrupt-driven tasks

A fuller description of the details of interrupt handling will be presented in Chapter 3. So this paragraph simply introduces the topic as it relates to elementary tasking techniques. Most CPUs are provided with one or more interrupt request lines which play an important part in keeping the computer system on its toes and providing a timely service to all its attached devices. Using the interrupt facilities, it is possible to arrange for specially written subroutines to be evoked by externally triggered interrupt signals. So the interrupt signal arriving at the CPU forces it to stop executing the current

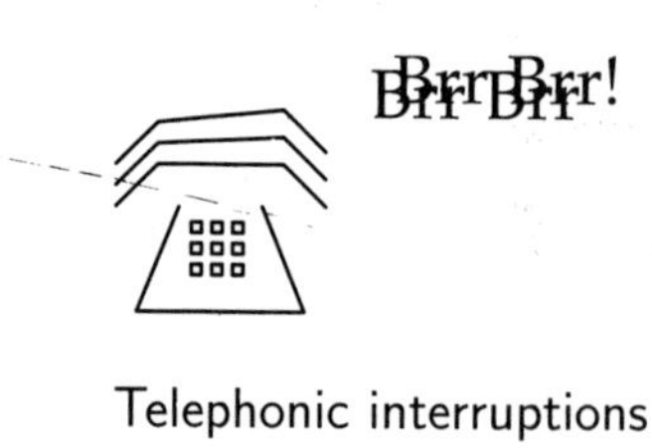

Telephonic interruptions

program and change to another routine, known as the Interrupt Service Routine (ISR). When the ISR is complete, the CPU *resumes* the interrupted program. In some circumstances, ISRs may be considered to be hardware scheduled tasks. The way an interrupt works is quite simple, though the startup initialization that needs to be carried out can be more complex.

2.6 Task swapping: How? When? Which?

- **How?**
- **When?**
- **Which?**

Scheduling issues

It should be noted that the 'scheduling' of tasks within a straightforward looping scheme is actually fully planned by the programmer, and is referred to as 'cooperative scheduling'. Each task has to *yield* to the next one in the sequence, exiting gracefully. Whereas in a more sophisticated operating environment, tasks are switched in and out transparently by a run-time scheduling process whose action may be difficult to predict in every circumstance. This need to multiplex access to the CPU poses several questions. How does a task swap occur? When is it time to carry out a task swap? Which task will be selected for the next turn? In general, task interleaving and code re-entry can be handled in a number of ways with different levels of 'visibility' to the application programmer.

2.7 Task re-entry

Re-entry capsule with precious cargo

Multi-tasking systems have a more sophisticated software structure than traditional programs. Switching between tasks is more complex than calling and returning from functions because the function entry/exit conditions are established and maintained by the compiler. Re-entry after a function call is a simple affair involving a limited number of local variables and parameters usually stored in an orderly fashion on the stack. The equivalent situation of *task swapping* in a multi-tasking system demands a total volatile environment save/restore operation. This requires all the CPU registers to be saved on the stack, as well as those within the Memory Management Unit (MMU), if it is being used, and may even encompass peripheral units should their status change from task to task. Carrying out such operations on the CPU registers and system stack requires the use of assembler code because HLLs do not offer efficient means to PUSH and POP registers. So specialist, systems programmers, with skills beyond straightforward HLLs, are required.

2.8 Causes of task swapping

In simple terms it is either data or time that determines the order of task execution. When data arrives at an *input* port it will either generate an external interrupt signal to the CPU or be spotted by an intermittent polling operation, often itself triggered by a timer interrupt. In both situations the arrival of data changes the balance of priorities among the tasks. If the input data is not quickly read from the port register, into a larger memory buffer, there is a risk of it getting overwritten by subsequent items of data. Thus, the tasks dedicated to dealing with incoming data suddenly assume a much greater urgency when the items appear. In a similar vein, when data is *output*, transmission should be as fast as possible. But given the bandwidth limitations of even high speed output channels, the CPU will outpace the port, requiring pauses between the transfer of items of data from memory to the output port. A common technique is again to employ an interrupt signal, this time to alert the system to the availability of a free channel, a 'transmit ready' interrupt in place of the 'receive ready' interrupt we have previously described. Thus, tasks require scheduling according to a dynamic balance of changing priorities directly affected by data movements or elapsed times. The moment-to-moment sequence of activities undertaken by tasks should always be governed by the demands of data or time. No other motivation

- Explicit coding, cooperative scheduling
- R-t HLL, co-routining support
- RTE, pre-emptive and cooperative scheduling
- O/S, priority-based tasking through system calls

Multi-tasking implementation options

exists. When real-time systems are characterized as 'event driven', what is really intended is 'data driven', but with the data arrival pattern being somewhat unpredictable and often inconvenient.

2.9 Resource sharing

An important problem is introduced when resources are shared through multi-tasking or, on a more limited scale, through the use of interrupt service routines. With pre-emptive multi-tasking, the risk occurs that a task gets swapped out while it is writing to a shared, global data area. Should a subsequent task then need to access the same data, it will unfortunately be in an unusable, corrupted state. How to ensure exclusive access to shared data resources, also termed 'critical data', introduces the programmer to the subject of mutual exclusion and semaphore facilities. A simple illustrative example comes from displaying the time of day (TOD). Should a time update happen right in the middle of a procedure to refresh the front panel display, some bizarre time values can be seen. Other examples can be found involving intercomputer communications and data transmission. There are several solutions to the problem of protecting critical data, referred to as 'mutual exclusion'.

- Disable task switching during a critical access
- Serialize all critical data accesses
- Use semaphore process queues to control access to critical data

Techniques for protecting critical data

Disabling all interrupts for the period of the access is frowned on by many programmers because it halts task scheduling and most of the I/O activity, even that unrelated to the contentious access. Interestingly, the second technique, serializing accesses, is exactly the regime which the cyclic scheduler imposes, thus removing the need for semaphores. Programmers recognize that one of the principal contributions that operating systems and real-time executives make is the provision of semaphore queues to deal with this situation in an orderly fashion. However, as we will see later, using semaphores can introduce a new set of problems and dangers for the unwary.

2.10 Using the printer port for digital I/O

This section changes focus from the theoretical consideration of critical resource protection to the very practical area of I/O interfacing. It describes how a simple experimental setup can be arranged to carry out some basic I/O programming exercises with a PC running Linux. For many students, the excitement of practical I/O programming starts with controlling a device hooked up to a parallel port. Luckily, most PCs are still provided with such a port known as LP1, or /dev/lp. But because direct access to hardware registers is restricted by Linux for security reasons, a special device driver has to be used to give ordinary application programmers the power to read and write to the printer port. Rather than side-tracking to describe the full intricacies of developing and installing a Linux device driver (this is left to Chapter 19) here we are using the Parapin C library package from Jeremy Elson. By using a library (libparapin.a) and the associated header file (parapin.h), it is possible to write programs which monitor 4 input lines and control 8 output lines on the PC parallel port. The output byte uses the regular 8 pins which normally carry data to the printer, while the input nibble is carried on lines intended for flow control and printer error status signals: ACK, BUSY, OUT-OF-PAPER, SELECT.

All that is needed is a small circuit board equipped with four switches and eight LEDs with a parallel cable and 25 pin D-type plug which can then be connected to the parallel port for experimental demonstrations. No external power supply is required, as the printer output lines can handle the 2.5 mA taken to illuminate a low-current LED. Pin 25 is the common signal earth provided by the PC printer port. This should *not* be connected to another earth point. It is indicated explicitly in figure below only to indicate where to attach an oscilloscope probe earth lead, and for no other reason. The printer port input lines are pulled up internally, meaning that the switches only have to short down to earth, or remain open, in order to signal 1 or 0.

The code fragment listed below illustrates the use of programmed I/O with access directly to the PC hardware. Normally such code is hidden within the operating system. In this case, Linux requires the task to be run under root privilege, which is done by using `su` before launching the program. In addition, the level of I/O privilege has to be adjusted within the task to get access to the printer port registers. Working directly on bare hardware is now only found when dealing with microcontroller developments, where the size of the application does not justify the provision of full operating system functionality, such as a disk filing system, or multi-user password management.

The primary PC printer port has three byte-wide registers: the control register at 0x37A, the status register at 0x379, and the data output register at 0x378. The data register is normally used to output ASCII character codes to the printer, while the status register relays back into the computer status and error conditions from the printer. It is easy to use these for experimental purposes. The circuit for this is given below. Direct port access in this manner requires the security controls to be set aside, so it is not recommended in normal circumstances.

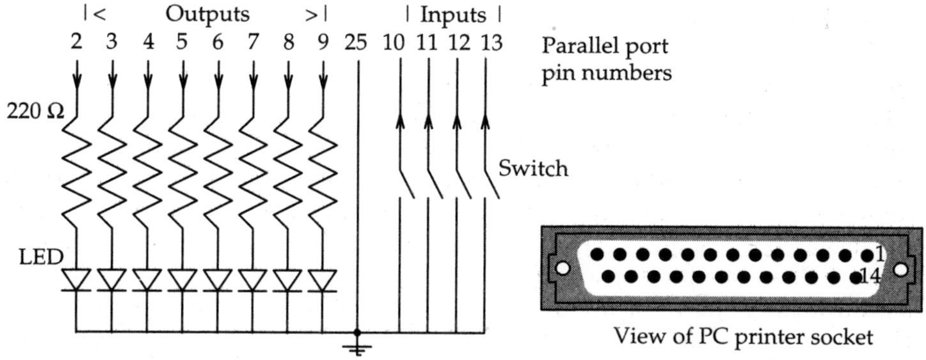

Using the PC parallel port for I/O programming

```
/* Outputs slow binary count to printer port (Centronics lines 2-9),
   while waiting for printer status bit 0x40 (Centronics line 10) to be
   set. Must be run as root
*/
#include <asm/io.h>
#include <time.h>

#define SLOW 500000000
#define CONTROL_REG    0x37A
#define STATUS_REG     0x379
#define DATA_REG       0x378
#define SWITCH1        0x40


main ()
   {
   int i;
   unsigned char c;
   struct timespec tr, tt={ 0, SLOW };

   iopl(3);

   while ((inb(STATUS_REG) & SWITCH1)) { // check an input switch for a quit
          i++;
          outb(0xff&i, DATA_REG);        // output pattern to LEDS
          nanosleep( &tt, &tr);
   }
}
```

Basic programmed I/O under Linux

2.11 Electric motors

Real-time systems quite frequently involve the control of electric motors. There is a wide, even somewhat confusing, choice of different types of motor, each suited for a particular application area. While it is possible for programmers to handle correctly such devices with only a very superficial knowledge of their internal mechanism, it always helps to have a more detailed understanding. The fundamental principle of all electric motors is the same, namely the production of a rotating magnetic field, which drags round a central magnetic armature. How this rotating field is produced distinguishes the various types of motor. AC induction motors use the three-phase mains power supply to circulate the magnetic field round and round. DC motors require a commutator switch on one end of the armature which directs electric current into the correct electromagnet coils. Stepper motors use external circuitry to rapidly switch current between coils in order to rotate the magnetic field. Of the range of motors listed below, the stepper motor is suitable for microcontroller products, so they are of particular interest to real-time programmers. These small motors have become the popular choice for low power, small mechanisms such as vending machines, printer plotters, clocks and robots. Besides being relatively cheap and easy to interface, they offer the extra ability to stop and hold at a particular position. So, stepper motors can be used to manoeuvre component parts within equipment, and maintain their position indefinitely, or as long as the loading does not exceed the maximum holding torque. They can readily be acquired with a positioning accuracy of a few degrees of arc.

- Stepper
- DC with brushed commutator
- AC brushless induction (squirrel cage)
- DC brushless
- Servo
- Universal with commutator

Types of electric motor

2.12 Operational details of stepper motors

Although programmers can, and do, reproduce cookbook code to drive stepper motors, it is more satisfying to appreciate how the hardware actually responds to your carefully timed pulses. The figure below shows a sequence of three 30° steps of a three pole stepper motor. This indicates how the stator magnetic field is switched from coil to coil, dragging the central armature round. The top row illustrates the situation at one end of the motor, with the bottom row representing the opposite end. Perhaps the best way to visualize the stepping sequence is to copy the figure onto a separate sheet of paper, and fold it in half across the middle. Then the two motor ends will be correctly sitting back to back. Notice how the central armature has one less pole than the surrounding stator, and so can only exactly align one of its three magnetic 'teeth' or 'cogs' at any time. In the diagram, one tooth is marked with a dot to make it easier for you to track its progress from step to step.

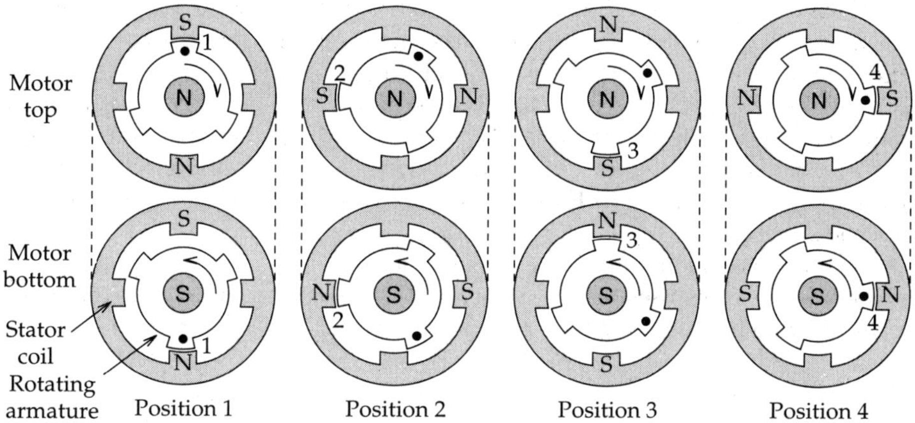

Three steps in the operation of a stepper motor (based on Lawrence and Mauch, 1987)

The central rotating armature is constructed with a single permanent magnet along its axis. One end is always north, the other always south. This polarity affects the cog teeth, so all the teeth at one end of the armature are magnetized north, while the others are magnetized south. Note that the magnetic cog teeth at the north and south ends of the central armature are not in alignment. The stator body is equipped with four electromagnet coils,

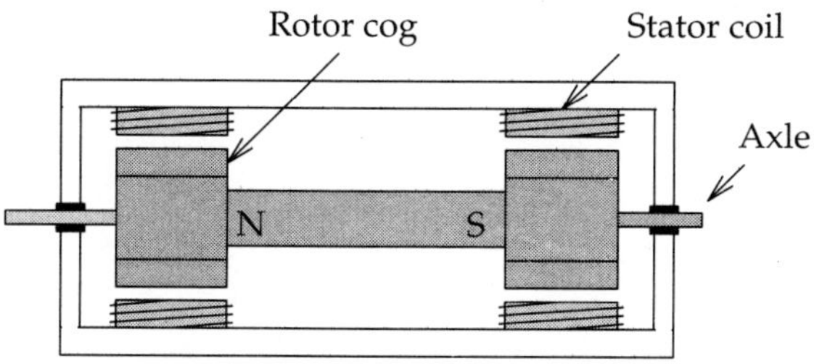

Cross-section of stepper motor

numbered 1, 2, 3 and 4. With a three cog, four pole configuration, the fundamental step equals a quarter of the intercog angle. So for this motor, it takes 12 steps for a complete rotation. The four coils in the surrounding armature (at north, south, east and west) are wound with fine copper wire to permit strong magnetic fields to be induced. To effect a rotation step, the magnetic fields from the two energized stator coils attract the nearest cogs of opposite polarity. The new rotor position will be maintained until the armature currents are changed, which can be very useful in many applications where occasional, accurate displacements are required.

Each coil has to produce magnetic fields in both orientations, N–S and S–N, which can be done by reversing the direction of current flow. To reduce the complexity of the transistor drive circuitry needed to achieve this, it is common to wind the coils with a centre tap, a scheme known as a bifilar winding. The centre tap is normally connected to the positive power supply voltage, with the two end taps feeding down to earth through NPN power transistors, or N channel FETs. These can then be switched on and off by a microcontroller.

A more common axial construction found in small stepper motors is shown below. This uses multiple stator pole fingers arranged as interlocking 'crowns' which, when excited, produce a ring of N–S–N–S poles all around

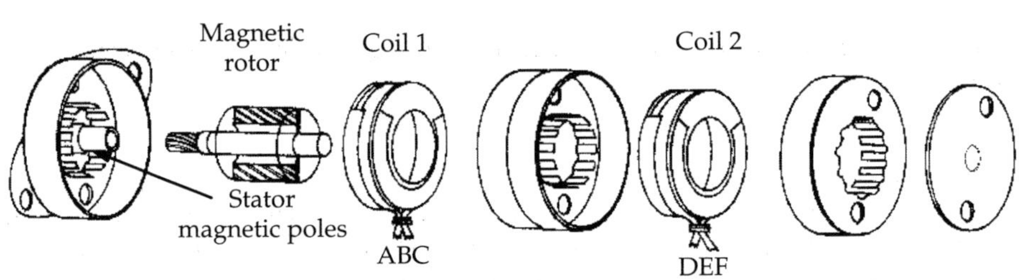

Exploded view of a small stepper motor

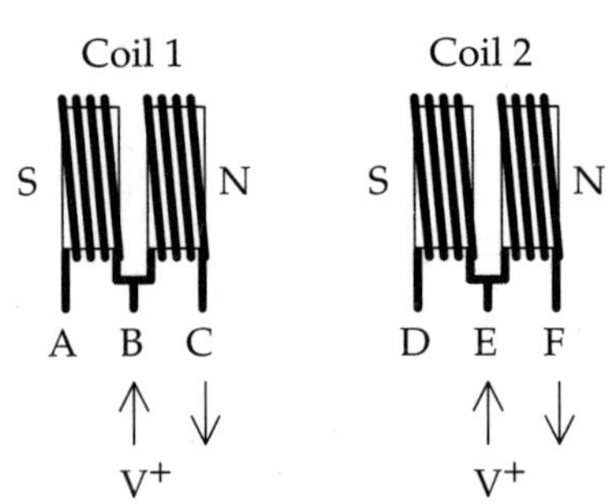

Activation of bifilar stator coils

the rotor. As the direction of the magnetic field reverses when the coil current is reversed, the resulting N–S–N–S poles appear to rotate around the inside of the stator body. The rotor has been manufactured with a ribbed pattern of permanent magnetic poles which react to the rotating magnetic field created by the stator coils, by physically turning in the reverse direction to the magnetic field. The magnetic stator fields can be set by a microprocessor switching currents between the coils. Although the split coil, *bifilar* wiring scheme does suffer from the disadvantage of only employing half the coil windings to generate magnetic fields, it does need only half the number of power transistors of the non-bifilar arrangement. A straightforward single phase excitation stator drive pattern is tabulated below. But there are more complex drive patterns possible with the same hardware, reducing the stepping angle, giving better precision and smoother running. This excitation sequence for half stepping involves driving two stator coils simultaneously. Alternative stepping patterns are provided in the example program at the end of this chapter.

Stator coil excitation sequence					
	A	C	D	F	B & E
Full stepping mode, single excitation					
Position 1	On	Off	Off	Off	V+
Position 2	Off	Off	On	Off	V+
Position 3	Off	On	Off	Off	V+
Position 4	Off	Off	Off	On	V+
Full stepping mode, double excitation					
Position 1	On	Off	Off	On	V+
Position 2	On	Off	On	Off	V+
Position 3	Off	On	On	Off	V+
Position 4	Off	On	Off	On	V+
Half stepping mode, double excitation					
Position 1	On	Off	Off	Off	V+
Position 1.5	On	Off	On	Off	V+
Position 2	Off	Off	On	Off	V+
Position 2.5	Off	On	On	Off	V+
Position 3	Off	On	Off	Off	V+
Position 3.5	Off	On	Off	On	V+
Position 4	Off	Off	Off	On	V+
Position 4.5	On	Off	Off	On	V+

Driving a stepper motor

2.13 Lifecycle of a professional programmer

There is quite a common professional pattern to the way practising programmers deal with real-time systems. Their first project starts as a simple sequential loop of procedures with extra interrupt routines and ad hoc global status flags introduced as the development progresses. Unfortunately, the initial laboratory prototype often works reliably. But further modifications or improvements to the production model induce a nightmare of unforeseen side-effects. This is usually termed the **Bodge** method of system development, bottom-up from beginning to end. The second project can be a disastrous attempt to apply a more theoretical ideal to the practical lessons learnt from the first experience. Second projects rarely get completed because the goal of thorough perfection can never be attained within 3.5 person-months. The code grows and grows, the design gets reworked many times, and the test schedule never gets finished. Perhaps we can call this phase the **Bloat** phase. After this, the only sane decision left for the third project is to reuse well-proven software. **Buy** as much as possible! So beware the 'Second System Syndrome'.

- **Bodge**
- **Bloat**
- **Buy**

Psychology of a systems programmer

2.14 Chapter summary

A simple program loop of tasks, running periodically at a fixed rate, with help from some interrupt service routines, can satisfy many straightforward embedded applications. However, the problem of inadvertently corrupting shared data must be carefully considered. Using the printer port on a PC demands running processes with root privilege, but with the Unix `setuid` facility, a process using direct I/O code can be launched with only normal user rights. Until a programmer has had to interface with real-world devices, the timing discrepancy between the computer and its surrounding physical world will never be fully appreciated. The control of different kinds of electric motors is a common requirement for real-time programmers.

```
/* Example driver routine for a dual, two phase stepper motor
*
*/
#include <stdio.h>
```

```
#include <string.h>
#include <unistd.h>
#include <fcntl.h>
#include "../PIO.h"          //gcc keypad.c -L. -lfab -o keypad
#include <sys/time.h>
#include <ctype.h>

typedef unsigned char BYTE;
typedef unsigned int DWORD;

// alternative driving patterns for a dual, two phase stepper
// motor

const BYTE
  steptab1[]={8, 4, 2, 1, 8, 4, 2, 1, 8, 4, 2, 1, 8, 4, 2, 1};
const BYTE
  steptab2[]={9,12, 6, 3, 9,12, 6, 3, 9,12, 6, 3, 9,12, 6, 3};
const BYTE
  steptab3[]={8,12, 4, 6, 2, 3, 1, 9, 8,12, 4, 6, 2, 3, 1, 9};
int control, portA, portB, portC;
int portCstatus = 0; // motor attached to C0-C3 of 8255 PIO

void inithw(void) {
   int x=0x90;
   initFAB(&control, &portA, &portB, &portC);
   write(control, &x, 1); // 8255 mode 0
}
void stepit(void) {
   static int step;
   int s;
   step = (step++)&0x0F;
   s = steptab2[step];
   portCstatus = (s & 9) | ((s&2)<<1) | ((s&4)>>1);
   write(portC, &portCstatus, 1);
}
int main () {
   struct timeval tim;
   BYTE key;
   DWORD then, now, rround;

   initFAB(&control, &portA, &portB, &portC);
   gettimeofday(&tim, 0);
   now = tim.tv_sec*1000000 + tim.tv_usec;

   while (1) {
           rround =0;
           then = now+4000;
           if (now > then) rround = 1; // roll round flag

        while (rround ? (now > then):(then > now)) {
```

```
            gettimeofday(&tim, 0);
            now = tim.tv_sec*1000000 + tim.tv_usec;
          //printf("%d pc=%x \r", then, portCstatus);

      }
          stepit();
  } // while

  closeFAB(&control, &portA, &portB, &portC);
    return 0;
}
```

2.15 Problems and issues for discussion

1. What do you see as the principal purpose of operating a multi-tasking environment within the modern computer? Why does the PC contain only one main processor? (Note that the keyboard, graphics card, Ethernet interface and other ancillary units may use small, dedicated microcontrollers.)
2. What are the advantages and disadvantages of using a simple polling loop to cyclically schedule tasks? Does this offer a reliable basis for accurate timing?
3. What is a 'critical resource', and why can it be a major problem for real-time programmers? How could you enforce exclusive access to an identified critical resource?
4. What role can interrupts serve in an embedded computer? What is the difference between a CPU which can nest interrupt calls, and one which cannot? Why is the suggestion that mutual exclusion may be provided by momentarily inhibiting all interrupt requests, often rejected by programmers?
5. What are the major differences between using multiple tasks and calling several subroutines within a single task?
6. What determines the relative priorities of interrupts? How are the normal task priorities related to those of interrupt service routines?
7. Draw a 4×4 matrix keypad and mark two switches on the same horizontal scan row as closed. Explain how a 'phantom closure' could now appear.
8. Draw a timing diagram which describes the sequence of signals required to drive a stepper motor clockwise one full rotation, then anticlockwise one full rotation.
9. Look up the excitation sequence, using simultaneous twin coil activation, to advance the stepper motor by half steps.
10. Using five of the eight LEDs connected to the printer port, as in Section 2.10, directly program the I/O to implement an electronic dice display.

2.16 Suggestions for reading

Elson, J. PARAPIN: a parallel port pin programming library for Linux. USC. From: http://www.circlemud.org/jelson/software/parapin

Heidenstrom, K. (1999). PC parallel port mini-FAQ. From: http://www.programmersheaven.com

Lawrence, P. & Mauch, K. (1987). *Real-time Microcomputer System Design*. McGraw Hill.

Li, Q. & Yao, C. (2003). *Real-time Concepts for Embedded Systems*. CMP Books.

Saikkonen, R. Linux IO port programming mini-HOWTO.

Chapter 3

Basic input and output

3.1 Chapter overview

Dealing with input/output (I/O) activity can be the central challenge for many real-time programmers because routine desktop computing successfully hides its complexity, structure and dynamics. This chapter suggests that real-time programmers often need a good understanding of the underlying hardware, in terms of port address mapping and register functionality. Interrupt processing introduces further complexity for the programmer, including critical data protection and relative timing issues.

3.2 Memory-mapped ports

For the programmer, accessing hardware usually means reading or writing to ports or registers belonging to a peripheral device. The instructions used for such activity depend on the addressing scheme adopted by the system

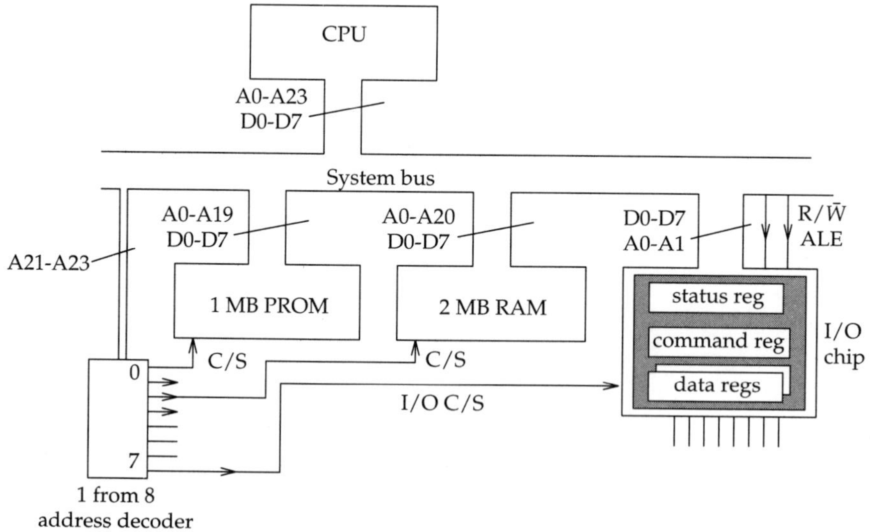

Memory-mapped I/O, showing the address decoding for a 24 bit CPU

designer. With memory-mapped ports, the I/O registers behave like memory locations, responding to the same main bus control signals as RAM and ROM chips. Thus, programmers can access memory-mapped ports using standard variable access instructions, such as `indata = *portpointer;`. The compiler translates this code using machine instructions such as `MOVE`, which are also used to access memory. The peripheral devices are allocated addresses within some part of the memory map. Generally all the ports are clustered together so as not to fragment the physical memory, rendering it less usable for contiguous blocks of RAM or ROM.

The I/O chip in the figure opposite is memory-mapped and positioned within a 16 Mbyte address space. It contains four registers (Status, Command, Data-in and Data-out) and so only requires two address lines for internal addressing. To distinguish it from other devices connected to the system bus it has been allocated one chip select line (C/S line 7) emerging from the memory map, address decoder logic. It is also connected to the Address Latch Enable (ALE) and Read/NOTWrite (R/$\overline{\text{W}}$) memory control lines. ALE is used by the CPU to tell the memory chips when the address bus holds a good value. The CPU uses the line to ask for a read/fetch or write operation. Decoding an instruction, if a memory access is requested, will trigger the correct sequence of control bus pulses.

Device	Size	Address pins	24 bit address bus	Address range
PROM1	1 MB	20	000x ++++ ++++ ++++ ++++ ++++	00 0000–0F FFFF
RAM1	2 MB	21	001+ ++++ ++++ ++++ ++++ ++++	20 0000–3F FFFF
RAM2	2 MB	21	010+ ++++ ++++ ++++ ++++ ++++	40 0000–5F FFFF
RAM3	2 MB	21	011+ ++++ ++++ ++++ ++++ ++++	60 0000–7F FFFF
I/O	4 B	2	111x xxxx xxxx xxxx xxxx xx++	E0 0000–E0 0003
				E0 0004–E0 0007
			Aliases	E0 0008–E0 000B
				E0 000C–E0 000F
				. . .

\+ – used internally by device
x – unused, don't care
1 – needs to be a 1 for memory decoding
0 – needs to be a 0 for memory decoding

Memory map table for the computer system opposite

Any devices attached to a common bus, and so sharing the same address space, require selection, or having their base addresses distinguished, by using their chip select pins. The *within device* address is then carried by the group of lower address lines, marked with a '+' in the memory map table.

In this case the registers are located at the following addresses: E00000H – command register, E00001H – status register, E00002H – receive and transmit data.

When you study the memory decoding circuit, you can see that the total address space of 16 Mbytes is split by the most significant three address bits into eight 2 Mbyte pages. The top memory page is reserved for the I/O devices, while the lower seven are available for RAM or ROM. A formal memory map table can be used to define all the address allocations. Note that because we have not applied full decoding, the I/O chip would act promiscuously and respond enthusiastically to each block of four addresses in the upper page, giving 524, 288 equivalent addresses for the same chip. This unwelcome aliasing effect would make it impossible to install any other devices in the top 2 Mbyte page without modifying the whole memory decoding circuit. Such an adjustment would require all the remaining 19 address lines to be incorporated into the decoding logic.

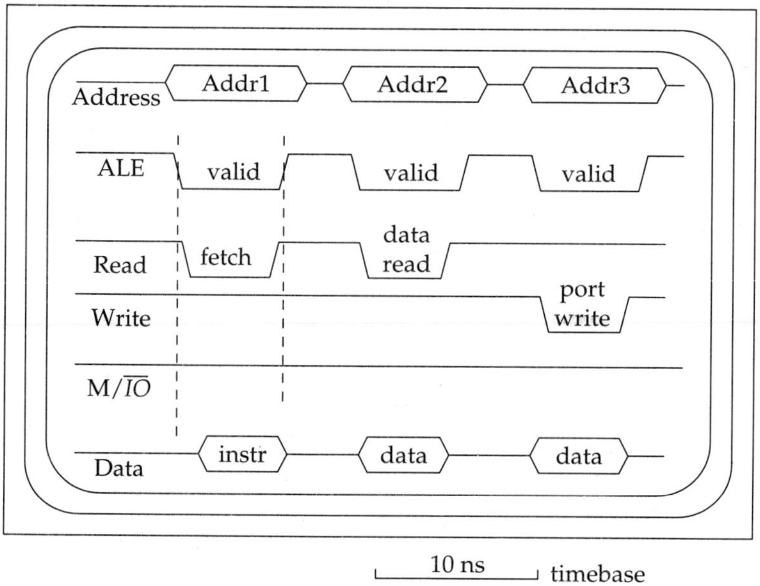

Bus activity while accessing memory-mapped ports

Bus signal timing is schematically displayed in the above figure. The relative moment when bus signal lines change value, and pulse edges occur, is very significant for the electronic interfaces. The ALE pulse indicates valid signals on the address bus, at any other time the bus will carry meaningless noise. The READ and WRITE bus lines can be separate, as in this diagram, or combined into a single Read/NOTWrite (R/$\overline{\text{W}}$) control line. Where separate an I/O address space is supported by the CPU, another control line (M/$\overline{\text{IO}}$) is required to indicate which of the two spaces the current address is referencing.

3.3 I/O mapped ports

An alternative to mapping ports into memory space is offered by some CPUs, including the Intel range of processors. In this case, through the provision of more bus control lines and extra instructions, a completely independent addressing space for I/O ports is provided. The PC utilizes this 64 Kbyte port address space supported by the Pentium, which also offers the IN and OUT machine instructions. The advantage of a clear memory space unbroken by the occasional I/O device is easy to appreciate, especially when extra RAM modules need to be inserted in a contiguous block. When the address space decoding logic is being planned, the limited size of I/O space is actually much welcomed by systems engineers, who rarely find the need to integrate anywhere near 65 536 ports onto a single computer bus. In addition, there is considerable advantage gained in the security realm by explicitly separating I/O from memory. Should the CPU have a data cache to speed up its operations, it is very important to ensure that all I/O activity reads data directly from the ports, and not a previously cached value. With I/O mapping it is easy to cancel all caching activity, while leaving the parallel memory activity open to caching. Finally, it is not uncommon for I/O devices to lag somewhat in performance, requiring much longer access times than DRAM or Flash chips. It is very frustrating to discover that your overall bus clock speed cannot be increased simply due to the unavailability of a faster version of an otherwise insignificant I/O chip.

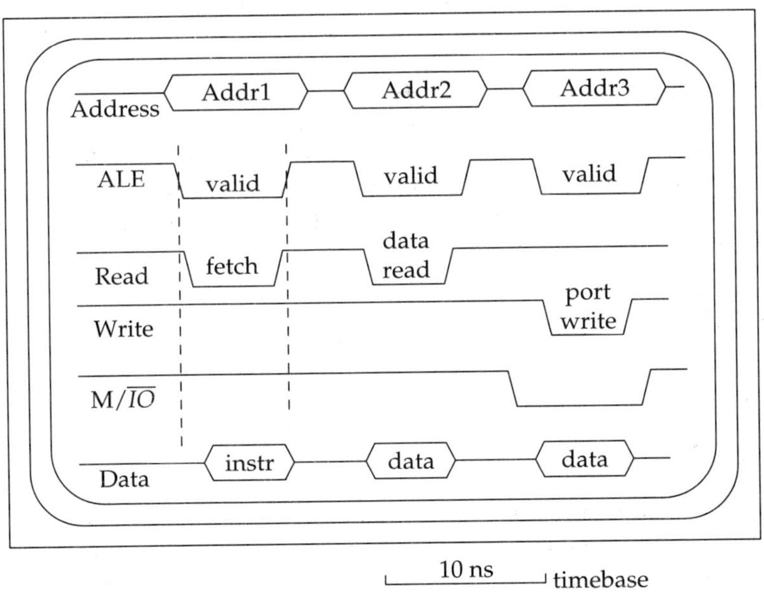

Bus activity while accessing I/O-mapped ports

The C language has been extended for relevant compilers to cover the IN and OUT machine instructions with the `inb()` and `outb()` functions, as already demonstrated in the example program in Section 2.10. In some compilers these are termed `inp()` and `outp()`. Other processors, which do not have this distinct I/O address space, require the I/O ports to be mapped into the memory address space alongside the RAMs and ROMs. In this situation, when working with a CPU which is endowed with a Memory Management Unit (MMU), it is possible to map the physical port addresses into several different virtual address values for programmers to access. This can be thought of as an interesting novelty.

3.4 Port registers – the programmers' view

If you need to address the I/O ports directly, assuming the operating system security controls will allow this, you will have to know the base address of the I/O chip in the memory map and the layout and function of its internal registers.

In this situation, a copy of the technical data sheet from the I/O chip manufacturer with some helpful application notes are invaluable, if not essential. When confronted with such literature, programmers, not being electronic engineers, have to quickly learn the art of selective reading, paying attention only to those aspects of relevance to programming. (See figure opposite for an example page from such a data sheet.) Programmers would certainly need the information to ascertain the port addresses of the internal registers and be clear about their function. Reading the hardware users' guide for a peripheral interface chip, despite the initial appearance of complexity, is no more difficult than reading a text on programming. The majority of I/O chips only contain three types of register as listed below. There may be none or several of each type. I/O registers may be accessed as bytes rather than words, and sometimes each bit corresponds to a separate feature or facility. When reading technical data sheets about I/O chips it is advisable to start by identifying these three register types.

- Command Registers
- Status Registers
- Data Registers

Types of port register

The purpose of command registers is to allow the programmer to specify more exactly the action of the I/O chip. There may be a wide range of options provided, such as transmission speeds, buffer sizes and error handling techniques, all to cater for different circumstances and a variety of applications. This allows the chip manufacturer to supply a single product which can be set up, using the command register, to fit in with a variety of applications. The particular choice is made during system initialization by writing the appropriate bit pattern to a command register. Sometimes the hardware makes command registers appear as write-only, which creates further programming difficulties if some bits in the register need to be updated by different tasks at different times.

On the other hand, **status registers** are provided so that the software can keep a watch on the I/O chip by reading and testing the contained status flags. These registers may be read-only, which is not too surprising.

The **data registers** are the 'letter boxes' through which the data actually passes during its journey into or out of the computer. Generally, you expect to write to an output port, and read from an input port, but sometimes the opposite, too, is allowed.

Functional Description

Data Bus Buffer

This three-state bi-directional 8-bit buffer is used to interface the 82C55A to the system data bus. Data is transmitted or received by the buffer upon execution of input or output instructions by the CPU. Control words and status information are also transferred through the data bus buffer.

Read/Write and Control Logic

The function of this block is to manage all of the internal and external transfers of both Data and Control or Status words. It accepts inputs from the CPU Address and Control busses and in turn, issues commands to both of the Control Groups.

(CS) Chip Select. A "low" on this input pin enables the communication between the 82C55A and the CPU.

(RD) Read. A "low" on this input pin enables 82C55A to send the data or status information to then CPU on the data bus. In essence, it allows the CPU to "read from" the 82C55A.

(WR) Write. A "low" on this input pin enables the CPU to write data or control words into the 82C55A.

(A0 and A1) Port Select 0 and Port Select 1. These input signals, in conjunction with the RD and WR inputs, control the selection of one of the three ports or the control word register. They are normally connected to the least significant bits of the address bus (A0 and A1).

82C55A BASIC OPERATION

A1	A0	RD	WR	CS	INPUT OPERATION (READ)
0	0	0	1	0	Port A → Data Bus
0	1	0	1	0	Port B → Data Bus
1	0	0	1	0	Port C → Data Bus
1	1	0	1	0	Control Word → Data Bus
					OUTPUT OPERATION (WRITE)
0	0	1	0	0	Data Bus → Port A
0	1	1	0	0	Data Bus → Port B
1	0	1	0	0	Data Bus → Port C
1	1	1	0	0	Data Bus → Control
					DISABLE FUNCTION
X	X	X	X	1	Data Bus → Three-State
X	X	1	1	0	Data Bus → Three-State

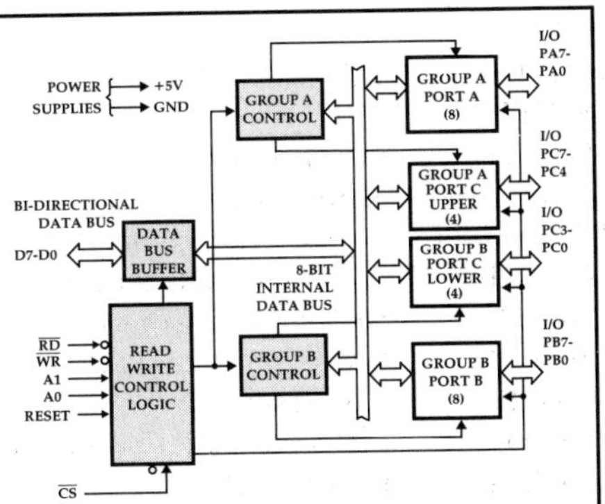

FIGURE 1. 82C55A BLOCK DIAGRAM. DATA BUS BUFFER, READ/WRITE, GROUP A & B CONTROL LOGIC FUNCTIONS

(RESET) Reset. A "high" on this input initializes the control register to 9Bh and all ports (A, B, C) are set to the input mode. "Bus hold" devices internal to the 82C55A will hold the I/O port inputs to a logic "1" state with a maximum hold current of 400 μA.

Group A and Group B Controls

The functional configuration of each port is programmed by the systems software. In essence, the CPU "outputs" a control word to the 82C55A. The control word contains information such as "mode", "bit set", "bit reset", etc., that initializes the functional configuration of the 82C55A.

Each of the Control blocks (Group A and Group B) accepts "commands" from the Read/Write Control logic, receives "control words" from the internal data bus and issues the proper commands to its associated ports.

Control Group A - Port A and Port C upper (C7 - C4)

Control Group B - Port B and Port C lower (C3 - C0)

The control word register can be both written and read as shown in the "Basic Operation" table. Figure 4 shows the control word format for both Read and Write operations. When the control word is read, bit D7 will always be a logic "1", as this implies control word mode information.

Data sheet (p. 3) for an Intersil 82C55A, parallel port I/O chip. (The full version of the 8255 data sheet can be found on the web at: http://www.intersil.com.docs/data/fn/fn2/fn2969/index.htm. If this fails, try a search at: http://www.netcomponents.com for '8255A'.)

Port address	Function
3F8-3FFH	COM1
3F0-3F7H	FDC
3C0-3DFH	Graphics card
3B0-3BFH	Graphics card
3A0-3AFH	
380-38CH	SDLC controller
378-37FH	LPT1
300-31FH	
2F8-2FFH	COM2
278-27FH	LPT2
210-217H	Expansion unit
200-20FH	Games port
1F0-1F8H	Primary IDE controller
170-178H	Secondary IDE controller
0E0-0FFH	8087 coprocessor slot
0C0-0DFH	DMA controller (4 channels)
0A0-0BFH	NNI reset
080-09FH	DMA controller (4 channels)
060-07FH	Digital I/O
040-05FH	Counter/timer
020-02FH	PIC
000-01FH	DMA

A listing of PC I/O-mapped port addresses with standard function

The Programmable Peripheral Interface (8255) was originally produced by Intel as a member of the family of I/O support chips intended for the i8080 microprocessor. Despite its ancient origins back in the 1970s, it is still found on PC I/O cards offering three byte-wide parallel ports for interconnecting equipment to the computer. The data sheet shows three bi-directional ports which are referred to as A, B and C. Port C has various alternative functions and can be split into two 4 bit sections under certain conditions. From the addressing table on p. 51, the two address lines, A_0 and A_1, can be seen to select one of the ports, while the READ and WRITE control lines determine whether the current access is an input or output activity. The advantage of using a 'programmable' I/O device comes from the flexibility that it offers. For example, the program initializes major aspects of the functionality, including whether it is acting as an input or an output port. The

Mode 0 – basic byte-wide input and output ports
Mode 1 – bytes passed by strobed (asynchronous) handshake
Mode 2 – tri-state bus action

Modes of activity for an i8255 PIO

control, or command, register must be set up correctly before any data can be transferred. There are three modes of action as listed on p. 52.

The three byte-wide ports, A, B and C, can operate simultaneously under differing modes of activity. The figure below presents the function of the individual bits within the control register, and offers a fragment of code to initialize the 8255 for routine I/O operation.

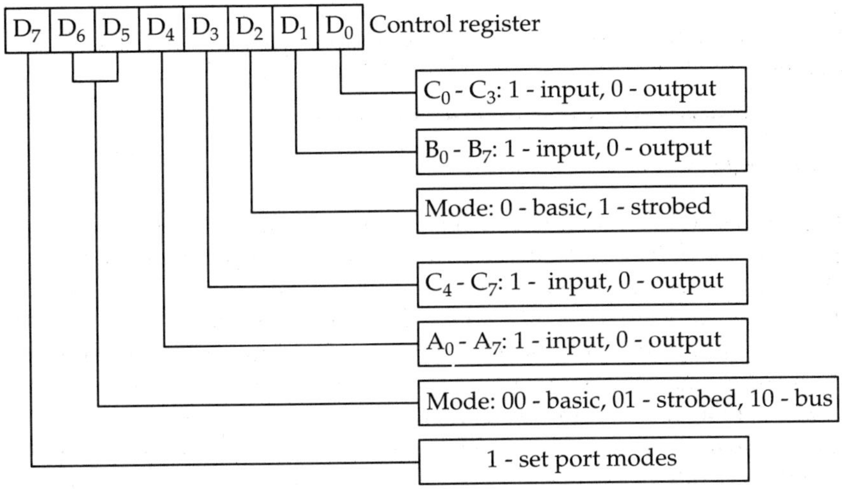

Control register functions for the 8255 PPI

```
// Win-98. Initializes 8255 at 0x1f3: Port A IN; B OUT; C OUT
   outp((short)0x1F3, 0x90);    // Initialize 8255 Command
                                // Register
```

In summary, the command registers contain writeable bit flags. These allow the programmer to control the activity of the chip, which is usually done by writing to the register during the initialization phase, whereas the status registers contain readable bit flags which indicate chip activities and errors. The data registers, usually designated as input or output, are the windows through which data items pass to and from the external device.

3.5 Port polling

Spin polling has already been introduced in Section 1.15 with a code example which accessed a serial UART. The technique of 'spin testing' a status bit, waiting for a TRUE condition to occur before continuing with the main processing, is employed in a much wider way than for just I/O. There are many circumstances when a status flag can be used to communicate between two tasks. Because the CPU operates so much faster than peripheral devices, and their human attendants, if a computer depended solely on this method to communicate with peripheral devices it would spend most of its time in *wasteful* polling loops, testing each device in turn to see if it is ready and requires service.

System buses operate at	500 Mbytes/sec
Blocks of characters can be moved at	100 Mbytes/sec
Ethernet transfers data at	10 Mbytes/sec
Telephone call needs	8Kbytes/sec
Serial lines frequently run at	1Kbytes/sec
Epson printers operate at	100 bytes/sec
Keyboards send at	4bytes/sec

Data transfer rates

Polling is like a telephone with a broken bell: *making* a call is perfectly all right, but the only way to *receive* a call would be to regularly pick up the handset and check by listening to determine if anyone is on the line. The likely frequency of occurrence of events, and the seriousness of any penalty which befalls should any be missed, need to be determined before choosing which I/O technique to employ. The disparate data transfer rates demanded by different I/O activities indicate the need for a range of methods.

Some improvement can be gained when devices are only polled at regular, timed intervals, which is referred to as 'intermittent polling'. This is found in many embedded systems around the home, in environmental monitoring equipment and in traffic counting systems. The polling interval is chosen to suit the needs of the application. It could be once a second (1 Hz) or every 10 microseconds (100 kHz). Sometimes a quite ancillary requirement determines the cycle timing, such as the need to reduce front panel display flicker to a minimum. By only polling the device intermittently, the

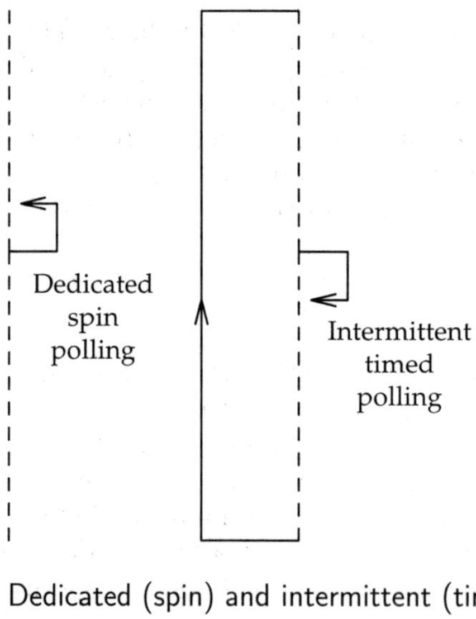

Dedicated (spin) and intermittent (timed) polling

time lost in spin polling is avoided. Such a method works well and avoids the complexity of interrupt processing. This suggestion is slightly disingenuous because to achieve a 25 ms, intermittent polling rate would require the assistance of an interrupt-driven clock tick, so we have simply swapped one interrupt requirement for another. However, it is useful to clearly distinguish between *dedicated* (spin) and *intermittent* (timed) polling when discussing the advantages and disadvantages of the technique.

Although dedicated polling wastes much CPU time, when peripherals run so slowly, the alternatives of interrupt-driven I/O and autonomous DMA are more demanding in terms of hardware and software support. Some equipment, such as radar echo processing systems, require such a fast reaction to incoming data that even an interrupt response is too slow. In these circumstances only a fast dedicated polling loop might suffice. Also, in many developmental projects, polling is considered as a first option because it is readily implemented and straightforward to debug and test. In fact, it is often employed as a first step towards the full, interrupt-driven implementation.

3.6 I/O access permissions

Policing interprocess security, through login privilege and file access permissions, is an important consideration for operating systems. In fact, it is far more complex than immediately apparent. Consider the problem of accessing a sensitive file, such as /etc/passwd, or allowing the utilities chat, kill, and ps. The basic problem is that Unix does not permit one task to see or affect any other task's private information, nor, understandably, is it possible to interfere with kernel data.

There are two situations to deal with. The first is where a utility, such as kill or ps, needs to access data belonging to another task. To allow this, the source and target can both be running under the control of the same effective user, or the source must have root privilege. The second situation occurs when kernel information is required, such as a lock list, or the list of active processes. In that case, the task must be running with effective root privileges.

To avoid the need to have all tasks running under root, or even the same UID, which would defeat all of the security safeguards, there has to be a means of temporarily obtaining higher privileges, but in a way that limits its abuse. The Unix setuid mechanism offers this facility by providing a special directory bit for executable commands, which then causes the running task to assume the privileges of the owner/creator of the command, rather than the invoker's privileges. For example, the ps utility employs this technique to allow any user to execute ps and temporarily acquire root privileges so as to read the kernel process table.

A task normally runs with the invoker's privileges. So the EUID (effective user id) is set to be the same as the user's login id, termed the RUID (real user id). However, if the executable file's setuid bit has been set (`chmod +s doitall`) the task gets a copy of the original *file owner*'s privileges, not the current user's. If, then, an executable file is owned by root, and is given world executable rights (`chmod 777 doitall`), as well as the setuid bit, any user may evoke it to run under root permissions. A potentially dodgy arrangement, from the security viewpoint.

The `setuid()` command gives a running task a limited power for changing its effective ID (EUID). Predictably, a user task cannot jump up to root privilege, but a task which has been started under root setuid permissions may shrug off that responsibility, after completing the initialization phase, and revert to being a normal user-level task with EUID set to RUID. This demonstrates how to overcome the problem of directly accessing ports within a program, when the user does not have root privileges.

```
rob> su
Password: ******
root> ls -al duckshoot
root> -rwxr-xr-x 1 rob rob 14336 Apr 17 11:26 duckshoot
root> chown root:root duckshoot
root> ls -al duckshoot
root> -rwxr-xr-x 1 root root 14336 Apr 17 11:26 duckshoot
root> chmod +s duckshoot
root> ls -al duckshoot
root> -rwsr-sr-x 1 root root 14336 Apr 17 11:27 duckshoot
root> exit
rob> ./duckshoot
```

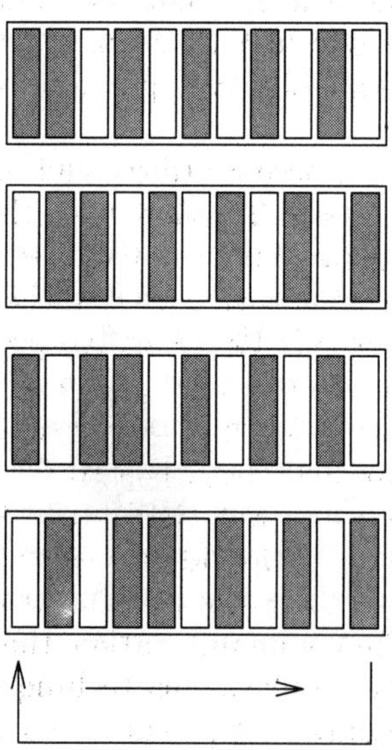

Duckshoot output sequence

The duckshoot program runs a small game which can be implemented with only eight or ten LEDs and a couple of switches. An initial illuminated pattern, or 'flock', is made to pass across the LED array, rotating from one end to the other. The speed of passing is a parameter of the game: faster makes it more difficult to play. The aim is to 'shoot all the ducks' by extinguishing each of the LEDs. One of the switches is designated as a trigger, and only single shot operation is allowed, no machine gunning. If the flock is flying to the left, the left position is taken as the target. If the flock is flying towards the right, the target is the rightmost position. Should the trigger be operated when the target LED is illuminated, a kill has occurred, and the LED is extinguished, removing a duck from the flock. However, if the shot is taken when the target LED is off, effecting a miss, a penalty occurs. This results in the insertion of an extra duck back into the flock. So a game is won when all LEDs (ducks) are extinguished, and the game is lost when all LEDs are on simultaneously, indicating a sky full of ducks. Besides the trigger switch, speed and direction can be controlled by other switches. The timing of the flock display, and the polling rate of the trigger switch, are critical to the success of the program.

```
/* duckshoot.c,
 * demo of parallel port facilities for I/O
 * Trigger button has to be relaxed between shots
 */
#include <stdio.h>
#include <stdlib.h>
#include <unistd.h>
#include <parapin.h>                 // gcc -O duckshoot.c -lparapin
                                     // -o duckshoot

#define OUTPUT_PINS 0x00FF
#define INPUT_PINS 0xF000            // obtained from parapins.h

void right_rot(unsigned char * f) {
  unsigned char t = *f;
    *f = (*f>>1) | ((t & 1) ? 0x80 : 0);
}

void left_rot(unsigned char * f) {
  unsigned char t = *f;
    *f = (*f<<1) | ((t & 0x80) ? 1 : 0);
}

void put_byte(unsigned char b) {
  unsigned int i, mask=1;

  for (i=0; i<8; i++)
     if (b & mask<<i)
         set_pin(LP_PIN[i+2]);
     else
         clear_pin(LP_PIN[i+2]);
}
```

```
int main() {
  unsigned char flock = 0x0f;          // initial flock of 4
                                       // ducks
  int i, snore, trigger, direction;

  if (pin_init_user(LPT1) < 0) exit(0);

  pin_output_mode(OUTPUT_PINS);        // 8 LEDs to display
                                          current state of flock
  pin_input_mode(INPUT_PINS);          // direction, speed, and
                                          trigger

  while (flock && flock<0xFF) {        // continue until flock
                                          empty or full

    put_byte(flock);                   // update LED display
    printf(" %2x \n", flock);

    if (pin_is_set(LP_PIN12) )
       snore=250000;
    else
       snore=50000;

    trigger = pin_is_set(LP_PIN10);    // get state of trigger

    direction = pin_is_set(LP_PIN13);  // get direction of
                                          flight

    usleep(snore);

    if(trigger && !pin_is_set(LP_PIN10))
         flock ^= direction ? 0x01 : 0x80;

    if (direction)                     // rotate flock
          right_rot(&flock);
     else
        left_rot(&flock);
  };
  if (flock==0)                        // end of game!
        printf("You won!\n\n");
  else
        printf("You lost!\n\n");

  for (i=0; i<10; i++) {
    set_pin(OUTPUT_PINS);    usleep(100000);
    clear_pin(OUTPUT_PINS);  usleep(100000);
  }
    clear_pin(OUTPUT_PINS);
  return 0;
}
```

3.7 To block or not to block

When attempting to read in data from a device, it is important to decide from the start whether you intend to *block* on the read or not. This refers to the situation where you commit the thread of execution to wait until some data is available. In an HLL program it may involve a call such as `scanf( )` which will not return until it has satisfied the complete parameter list. The host operating system handles the complex details of I/O within a multitasking environment, but it does still appear like a dedicated polling loop to the programmer. Such single-minded perseverance may not be to your liking when your program has many other things to do. A simple solution is to make sure that there is always some data waiting to be read before going into a blocking read. In the Windows environment, it is still possible to use the old DOS function `kbhit()` which returns TRUE or FALSE depending on whether a new keyboard character is ready and waiting to be read. But with Linux a different and more generally applicable approach is used. The *blocking time* for a device can be set to a very low value which makes it appear as if there is no delay when data is unavailable. When returning from a `read()` or other input function, either the data itself or the number of items received must be checked to ascertain if data has been successfully read.

```
 /* Example showing use of Linux tcsetattr() function to disable
    keyboard blocking & buffering, allowing single char entry
*/
#include <stdio.h>
#include <sys/termios.h>
#include <ctype.h>

void setterm(void) {
  struct termios kbd;

  tcgetattr(0, &kbd);              // file descriptor 0 = stdin
    kbd.c_lflag &= ~(ICANON);
    kbd.c_cc[VTIME] = 0;
    kbd.c_cc[VMIN] = 0;
  tcsetattr(0, TCSANOW, &kbd);     // console device
}

main ( ) {
  int letter = 'a';
    setterm( );
    while (letter != 'q') {
      letter = getchar( );
      putchar('.');
    }
}
```

Reconfiguring keyboard input on Linux

It is often necessary to avoid both *blocking* and *buffering* when reading console keyboard input. The code on p. 59 achieves this. But for other devices, such as serial ports, the code can also be adjusted using the file descriptor for that device, as in the figure below. Note that setting the device to NOBLOCK does not cancel input buffering, a CR/ENTER will still be required to flush the characters out of the buffer and make them accessible by an application read.

```
int fd;
struct termios tty;

fd = open("/dev/ttyS0", O_RDWR | O_NOCTTY | O_NONBLOCK);
if (fd <0) {perror("failed to open /dev/ttyS0"); exit(-1); {

tcgetattr(fd, &tty);
    tty.c_lflag &= ~(ICANON);
    tty.c_cc[VTIME] = 0;
    tty.c_cc[VMIN]  = 0;
tcsetattr(fd, TCSANOW, &tty);
```

Setting the COM port with `tcgetattr()`

A similar problem exists when using an output function such as `putc()`. If the output device is not ready to dispatch data, perhaps because it is still busy transmitting the previous item, it will block the next write request and not return from the call until it is free to service it. To avoid the situation of a program blocking on every output function, operating systems are capable of carrying out an availability check using status checking functions, such as or `GetOutputState()` in Windows. Unfortunately, these are not part of the standard set of C library calls. Each operating system has its own approach to the 'blocking' problem. Linux offers the powerful `ioctl()` facilities for reconfiguring channels, but to set non-blocking, there is also the `fcntl()` function illustrated opposite code fragment. This function is also useful when initializing signals. We will return to it later.

It is important, however, to note that task blocking is an essential part of fair scheduling within most multi-tasking systems. If the higher priority tasks do not yield, or block, it would be impossible for the lower priority tasks ever to gain access to the CPU. Indeed, on many computers, should a task not yield or block, even equal priority sister tasks will fail to run if time-slicing has not been enabled. They would suffer from what is termed *starvation.*

When *multi-threading* is supported, as it is with Java, a common approach for dealing with several blocking activities is to spawn off a thread for each. Thus, with three inputs, two outputs and a bi-directional network socket all to be watched, the program can spawn six threads. Each thread blocks on one channel until data is available, then the thread is rescheduled so

```
#include <unistd.h>
#include <fcntl.h>

main() {
int fd;

fd = open("/dev/lp0", O_RDWR);
if (fd <0) {perror("failed to open /dev/lp0"); exit(-1); }

fcntl(fd, F_SETFL, O_NONBLOCK);
  ....
}
```

Setting non-blocking devices using `fcntl()`

as to process the item. Communications between the threads can conveniently be carried out using shared variables or methods in the parent object. A similar, but non-threaded, approach to handle intermittent, asynchronous activity is provided by the `select()` function, which acts as a 'lookout' for file descriptor requests. The program blocks on the call to `select()`, until one of the registered file descriptors indicates that it is active. When this happens, the execution continues beyond `select()`, and the file descriptors can then be polled using the macro `FD_ISSET(fd1,&fdset)`. This is a common approach when handling multiple sockets.

3.8 Exception and interrupt processing – service on demand

If a device requires only occasional attention then the interrupt method works better than polling. The peripheral just demands CPU help when it needs it. Using interrupts does require special hardware to be available, but that is not usually a serious drawback. Interrupts offer the ability for external devices to signal to the CPU that they need immediate attention. This can be a great advantage when developing demand-driven, real-time systems because it provides fast, hardware mediated, task switching. Such a facility can eliminate, or at least reduce, the need for continual programmed polling to look out for I/O activity. The CPU must, however, be equipped with the means to handle interrupt signals, and respond to them in the correct fashion. Since the introduction of microprocessors in the 1970s, the provision of interrupt capability has been routine, and the basic manner of dealing with externally generated interrupts has been fairly standardized. The CPU is constructed so that once every fetch cycle the incoming interrupt line is checked, and if an active request is present the current processing sequence is paused and a selected service routine is executed, after saving the instruction pointer. At the end of the service routine, the instruction pointer is restored and processing continues from where it was paused. The response time to an interrupt may be very short, of the order of 10 μs.

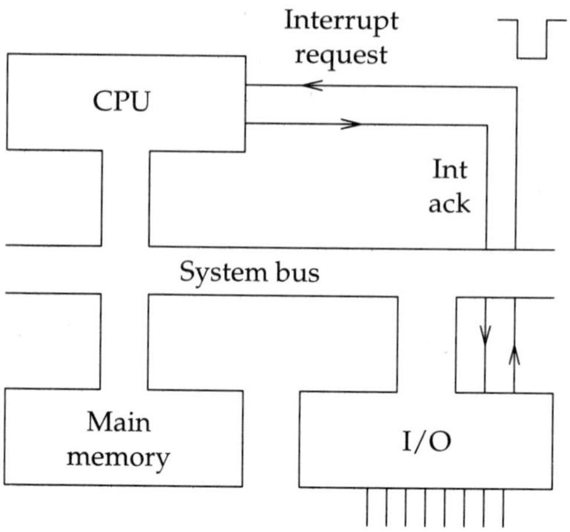

Using the CPU interrupt request and acknowledge lines

Computer systems also exploit an extension of the interrupt technique, known as exception processing. In this case the source of the interrupt signal is internally generated, from a CPU error condition or a memory access violation. Such an event may require immediate action half way through an instruction, giving a serious headache to the CPU hardware engineers. In addition, a special form of subroutine call, known as a `TRAP` instruction, can be provided which also utilizes the interrupt mechanism to achieve fast and secure action.

It is convenient to deal with such events through exception handler routines which are installed and accessed in the same manner as interrupt service routines. Indeed, the term 'exception' is often used as a generic category which includes device-driven interrupts, error exceptions and software `TRAP` instructions.

- External interrupts
- System errors
- TRAP instructions

Exception types

3.9 Multiple interrupt sources

CPUs are generally equipped with very few, sometimes only a single, interrupt signal line. Yet systems normally have to respond to multiple sources of interrupt, which raises the difficulty, when an interrupt occurs, of determining which device has requested the interrupt. Every interrupting device is provided with its own service routine, stored in memory, which must be

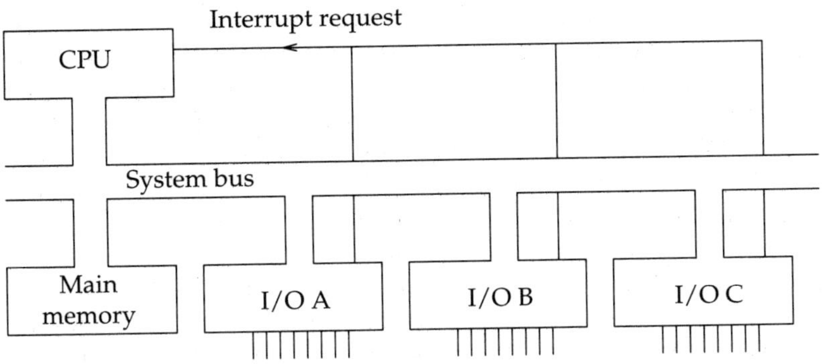

Connection of many interrupting devices to the CPU

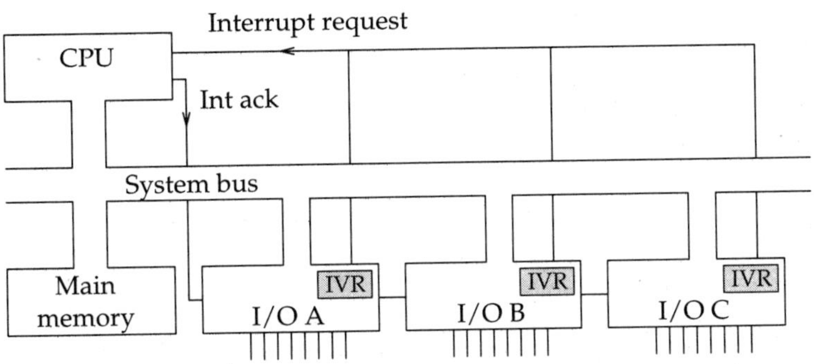

Vectored interrupts using a daisy-chain prioritization line

run as rapidly as possible after the interrupt occurs. There is also the associated difficulty of devices firing interrupt requests simultaneously. Then a *prioritization* decision has to be taken as to which to service immediately and which to defer to later.

There are generally three methods of discovering the active, interrupting device and then selecting the correct service routine. The first and simplest method only requires a single interrupt request line and relies on the main interrupt service routine undertaking a polling activity, to check all the possible culprits, by reading a status flag available within each device. The correct service code can then be chosen. This serial testing and jumping activity can introduce some unacceptably long delays into the interrupt response time, but does not require any extra hardware. If there are only a few external devices using interrupts, it is perfectly adequate to use simple polling. It can also be used when the CPU offers several interrupt request lines because more than one device is attached to each line, each line being set at a different priority level.

The second is a better method, but demands special peripheral devices equipped with Interrupt Vector Registers (IVR). It is used by the Motorola Mc68000 family. Each peripheral chip holds its own self-identifying interrupt vector number within an 8-bit register. Now, after the interrupt request has been detected, the CPU broadcasts an interrupt acknowledge signal which asks any device of that priority level to own up if it has an active interrupt request pending. The response from the device is the interrupt vector held in the IVR. The 8 bit vector number is arranged to be an offset into the Interrupt Vector Table (IVT). Here will be found the address of the device's Interrupt Service Routine (ISR). Storing interrupt vectors inside the peripheral chip does mean that they have to include a vector register in order to participate in the game of vectored interrupts. Not all I/O chips do so.

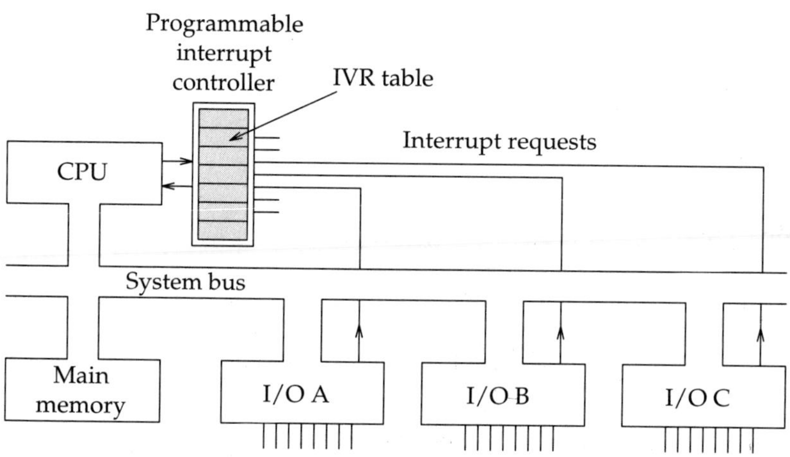

Vectored interrupts using PIC hardware

The third method uses a Programmable Interrupt Controller (PIC), as implemented in the PC. The PIC acts as a centralized, prioritizing encoder, and takes the responsibility away from the device for replying to the CPU's interrupt acknowledge cycle with an identifying vector number.

- Device polling
- Device returns vector
- Interrupt controller (PIC)

Device identification

When an interrupt takes control, the CPU first saves the current value of the program counter and CPU status register onto the system stack for later. Then the entry address of the appropriate ISR is obtained from the IVT and written into the PC. In this way it starts executing the ISR, whose first job is

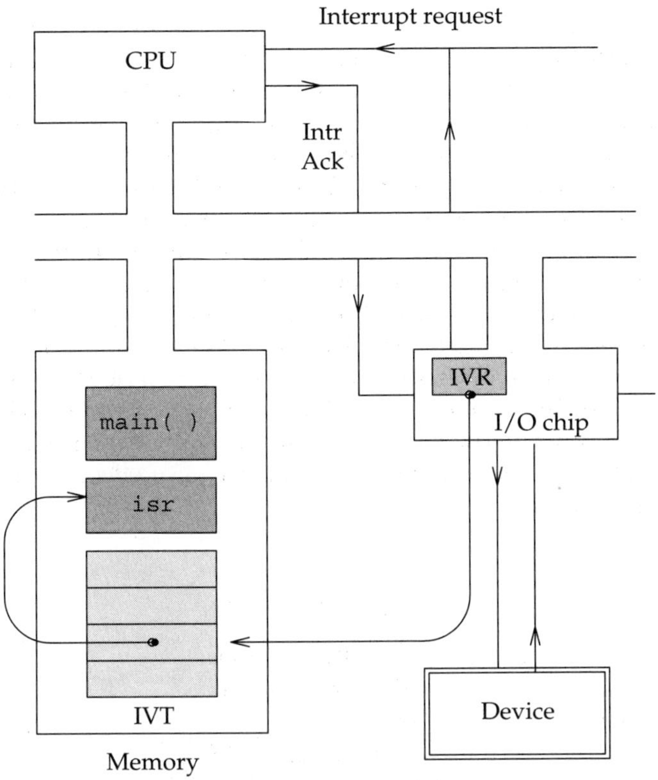

Locating interrupt service routines with IVR vectoring facilities

to protect all the other CPU registers used in the ISR from getting *corrupted.* This simply involves PUSHing the register contents onto the stack, from where they will be restored at the completion of interrupt processing. Then the source of the interrupt has to be verified, perhaps by testing a peripheral device flag bit, and the cause of the interrupt removed. Until this is done, there is the danger of suffering a repeated interrupt from the same source, even though all the processing has been completed. It may then be necessary to *reinitialize* the peripheral device to ready it for another interrupt request, although sometimes this is not required. The end of the ISR is marked by POPping the saved registers from the stack and the execution of a special 'return from interrupt' (`RTE`) instruction to restore the Instruction Pointer (IP) and status register values.

3.10 Powerfail detection

The ability to detect and warn of imminent power loss is a common requirement for many embedded systems. By monitoring the AC power line, as in the figure below, it is possible to detect the onset of the emergency 100 ms before the DC supply to the microcontroller starts to dip below the minimum level. The simple circuit involves two opto-couplers run back to back, supplying a retriggable monostable with a 100 Hz stream of trigger pulses derived from the mains power line. A monostable, such as the well-known 555, is an analogue timer circuit, using a capacitor and resistor to produce a fixed width output pulse. In this case, the pulse is set for 15 ms, 50 per cent longer than a single European mains power half cycle. So, as long as the 100 Hz trigger stream keeps retriggering the timer, its output will remain high. However, should the AC line fail, the monostable would receive no more trigger pulses, and within a maximum of 15 ms, a high priority power fail interrupt signal would be sent to the microcontroller. Using the same circuit, a 50 Hz pulse stream can be generated to be directed into a lower priority interrupt pin. This can be used for synchronizing the control of power triacs with particular phases of the mains cycle in order to reduce radio interference effects when switching large inductive loads.

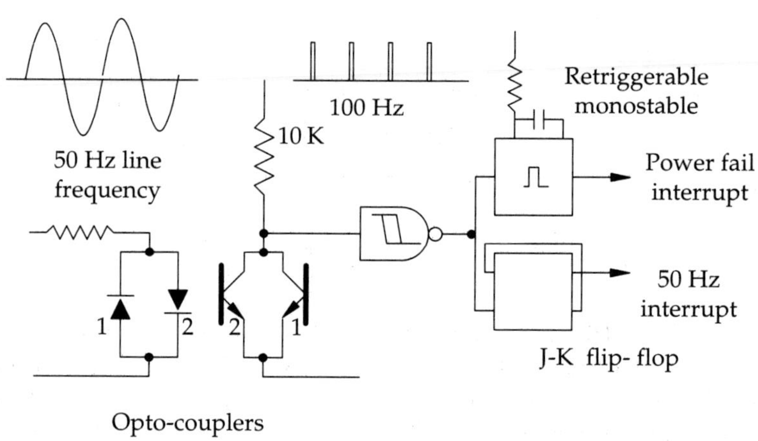

Sources of power line interrupt signals

A power fail interrupt service routine is somewhat different from the normal example because the system is expected to close down during the `delay` routine, so there is no return from interrupt instruction (RETI or RTE) at the end. The required activities are: stop all user services, turn off 'heavy' devices to conserve power, switch to power-down mode, save internal audits to back up RAM, clear front panel display and positively kill the processor.

When power returns, a possible problem occurs if a second powerfail then occurs immediately, right in the middle of the power-up code sequence. In this example, there was a particular difficulty due to the length of time the clock readjustment routine could take. So the powerfail had to detect if the failure was clean, or right in the middle of a critical routine.

```
/* Example power fail interrupt routine for an i8051 vending
   machine.
*  Stop users, motor and printer off, power-down mode, save RAM
   audits
*  clear front display, kill CPU.
*/
POWRFL:    MOV A,#037H        ;
           OUTL P1, A         ;coin slot blocked, reset CPU
           ORL P2, #0FFH      ;printer port select
           ANL P2, #0EFH      ;
           CLR A
           CPL A
           MOVD P4, A         ;clear lower nibble
           SWAP A             ;
           MOVD P5, A         ;clear upper nib and motor
           ORL P2, #0FFH      ;port deselect

           CPL F1             ; 0 - power-up fail
           JF1 RAMSAV         ; 1 - normal power fail

PUPF:      MOV R0, #034H      ;countback values to internal RAM
                               for backup
           MOV A, T           ;save TF in R34
           MOV @R0, A         ;
           MOV A, #001H       ;aux register for countback
           MOV T, A
           MOV R0, #3AH
           MOV @R0, #38H      ;minutes
           DEC R0
           MOV @R0, #01H      ;hours
           DEC R0
           MOV @R0, #06H      ;days
           DEC R0
           MOV @R0, #00H      ;weeks

RAMSAV:    MOV A, #0DFH
           OUTL P2, A         ;select backup RAM (nibble wide)
           MOV R0, #00H       ;external pointer
           MOV R1, #03FH      ;internal pointer

RMS1:      MOV A, @R1
           MOVX @R0, A        ;save upper nib
           SWAP A
           INC R0             ;bump external pointer
           MOVX @R0, A        ;save lower nib
           INC R0             ;bump external pointer
           DJNZ R1, RMS1
```

```
            MOV A, T              ; normal operation if T=1
            MOVX @R0, A
            INC R0
            SWAP A
            MOVX @R0, A
            ORL P2, #0FFH         ;deselect backup RAM

CLEAR:      MOV R7, #0FFH         ;
            MOV R6, #0DEH         ;clear display
            CALL DISPR
            MOV R6, #07BH         ;
            CALL DISPR

            JF1 PF2
            ORL P1, #040H         ;kill processor thro reset line
PF2:        MOV R5, #00FH         ;if INTEMPT low reset X counter
            CALL SWTEST
            MOV A, #00H
            CALL DELAY
            JMP RESET             ;jump to reset if KILL fails
```

3.11 Interrupt structure on the PC

Extra hardware can be employed to prioritize the incoming interrupt signals, as with the Intel **PIC** (Programmable Interrupt Controller) chip which allows through a single **IRQ** from the most urgent device. Even then, the CPU may still not accept the request because it has disabled all interrupt processing. The Pentium has a CPU status flag which indicates whether it is prepared to respond to interrupts or not. To control this, there is a pair of instructions to set and clear the interrupt flag: **STI** and **CLI**. However, these instructions are only available to privileged users.

Once an interrupt is accepted by the CPU there remains the problem of identifying the source of the request and then locating the correct ISR in memory. The PIC identifies which IRQ was responsible for the interrupt. However, when asked by the CPU for the identification it does not return the IRQ number, but an 8 bit number, known as the vector. This is used by the CPU to access the correct entry in the **IVT** (Interrupt Vector Table) held in memory. The IVT data table holds the addresses of the entry points for all possible ISRs. Every source of interrupt has a unique entry in this address table or IVT (Interrupt Vector Table).

The relatively small number of interrupt lines available on the PC would seem to be a major disadvantage when trying to add further devices. But so far people have got by, often by disabling existing devices or even unplugging boards in order to share an IRQ. Suffering an IRQ conflict was a common problem when installing new ISA cards. PCI cards share the primary IRQ levels allocated to the bus.

Int Number	Function	Source
77	Hard Disk2	IRQ15
76	Hard Disk1	IRQ14
75	8087	IRQ13
74	PS/2 mouse	IRQ12
73	Soundcard	IRQ11
72	Network	IRQ10
71	Redirected	IRQ2
70	RTC	IRQ8
. . . .		
18	BIOS/TOD	INT
17	BIOS/softboot	INT
16	BIOS/print	INT
15	BIOS/KBD	INT
14	BIOS/comms	INT
13	BIOS/disk	INT
12	BIOS/msize	INT
11	BIOS/check	INT
10	BIOS/video	INT
0F	LPT1:	IRQ7
0E	FDC	IRQ6
0D	SoundCard	IRQ5
0C	COM1:	IRQ4
0B	COM2:	IRQ3
0A	----	IRQ2
09	KBD:	IRQ1
08	System timer	IRQ0
07		
06		
05	Screen dump to printer	
04	Numeric overflow	
03	Breakpoint	
02	NMI, power fail	
01	Single step trace	
00	Integer divide error	

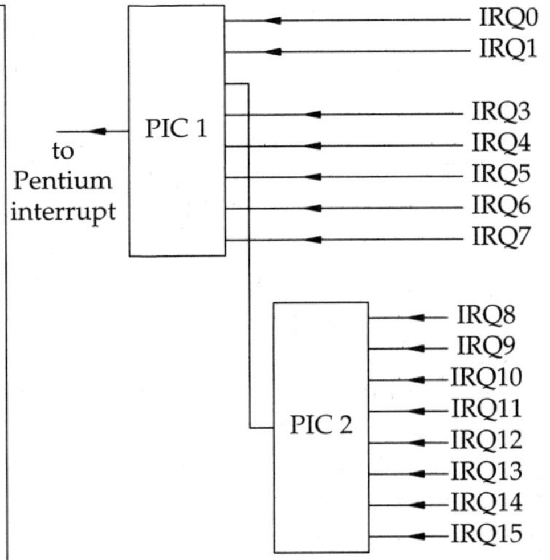

IRQ7	IRQ6	IRQ5	IRQ4	IRQ3	IRQ2	IRQ1	IRQ0

PIC Interrupt Mask Register (21H)
1 – disable
0 – enable

	EOI		0	0	I_2	I_1	I_0

PIC Interrupt Control Register (20H)
EOI – write 1, re-enable interrupts
$I_0 - I_2$ – read, current interrupt number

Part of the PC interrupt vector table and related PIC connections

The highest priority is IRQ0, with IRQ15 the lowest and not all the IRQ lines are mapped through to the ISA and PCI expansion buses.

IRQ0 – committed for the principal system timer. This generates the ticks which enable the operating system (Unix, Windows) to regain control from any process at the end of its allocated time slot.

IRQ1 – committed to the keyboard controller.

IRQ2 – committed to the cascaded, second PIC which offers IRQ8–IRQ15. IRQ9 takes on the role of IRQ2 inputs, but is not commonly used, to avoid the possibility of conflict.

IRQ3 – designated as COM2 serial port, but widely used for modems internal as well as external, which leads to frequent conflicts. This may be avoided by relocating the modem to an unused IRQ, or disabling the COM2 activity in the BIOS setup parameters. Sometimes a sound card may try to take on this IRQ, which adds to the confusion. An extra problem is that unfortunately COM4 is designated to this interrupt as well.

IRQ4 – committed to COM1/mouse, an RS232 port which is often dedicated to serial mouse activity. Like the COM1/COM3 situation, this interrupt is shared with COM3, which is unfortunate because modems are often preconfigured to COM3, thus guaranteeing a conflict with the serial mouse. A simple solution is the PS/2 mouse!

IRQ5 – designated as LPT2, a second parallel port initially for another printer, but now more commonly used for the SoundBlaster card. Not many PCs have a requirement for two printers, but the parallel port can also be interfaced to other plug-in devices, so conflicts may still occur.

IRQ6 – committed to the Floppy Disk Controller (FDC).

IRQ7 – committed to LPT1, parallel printer port.

IRQ8 – committed to a hardware timer for real-time programmers.

IRQ9 – often used for network cards and other PCI-based devices.

IRQ10 – available and often used for network cards, SoundBlaster or SCSI adapters. Available for the PCI bus.

IRQ11 – available as for IRQ10.

IRQ12 – committed to PS/2 mouse if it is provided, otherwise much the same as IRQ10 and IRQ11.

IRQ13 – committed to the maths coprocessor unit (8087).

IRQ14 – committed to the first IDE disk controller.

IRQ15 - committed to the second IDE controller.

The situation for the Pentium, PIC, IVT and peripheral device is illustrated on p. 69. The ritual of asking for a vector number, indexing into an address table and jumping to an address, appears somewhat laborious. Why could not the PIC simply return the full 32-bit address of the ISR to the CPU? There is some history entailed in the answer. Back in the 1970s, the PIC was built to respond to an interrupt acknowledge signal by jamming a full CALL instruction, complete with ISR address, onto the bus. This forced the i8080 CPU into the appropriate ISR. This method, involving a 3 byte 'interrupt fetch' by the CPU from the PIC rather than main memory, was abandoned as too inflexible. The current PC interrupt scheme is still generally judged as very restricting.

Both the Mc68000 and i8086 CPUs required their Interrupt Vector Tables (IVT) to start at memory address 0000. Happily, the facility to relocate the IVT anywhere in main memory was made available with the introduction of the Mc68010 and i80386 processors. This was possible through the provision of another CPU register which could be loaded with the current start address of the IVT. Motorola referred to it as the Vector Base Register (VBR) and Intel called it the Interrupt Descriptor Table Register (IDTR). To move the IVT you simply copy the contents, with any needed revisions, into the new memory position and point the VBR/IDTR to the base of the new table. This is extremely useful because it is common to position boot PROMs in

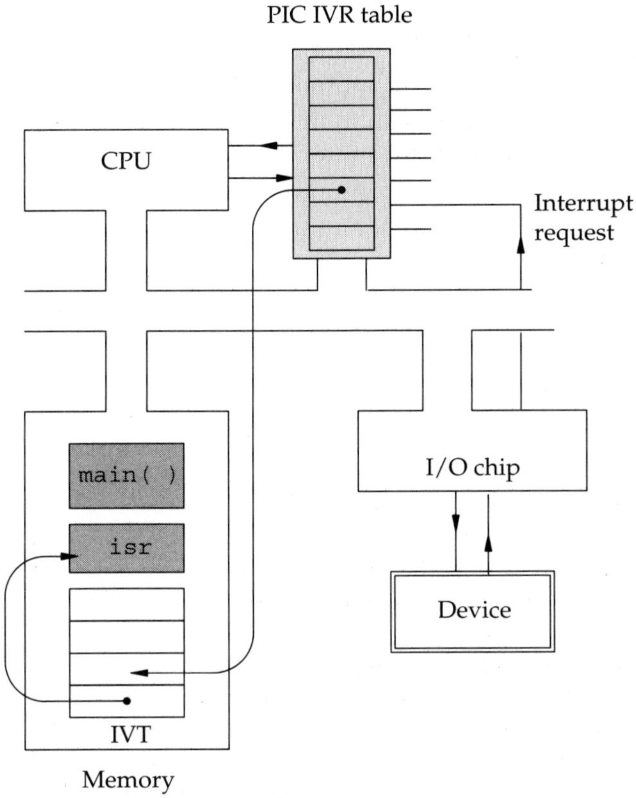

Locating interrupt service routines

the lowest memory page, thus locking the IVT for writing, not very useful during development.

Some small microcontrollers do not allow interrupt processing itself to be interrupted. The ability to accept and honour higher priority interrupts at any time is known as interrupt nesting. In this situation, a high priority device, such as a hard disk, could break into a low priority service routine without delay. The CPU finishes the high priority ISR, returns to the interrupted low priority ISR, and then finally returns to the main processing which was originally interrupted.

3.12 Deferred interrupt processing

Extensive use of interrupt routines delivers a problem to the programmer because the prioritization mechanism, necessary to handle simultaneous interrupts, is implemented in hardware circuitry, beyond the control of software. Thus, the relative priorities of event-driven tasks are fixed by the soldering iron. If dynamic priority reassignment is needed, a scheme used

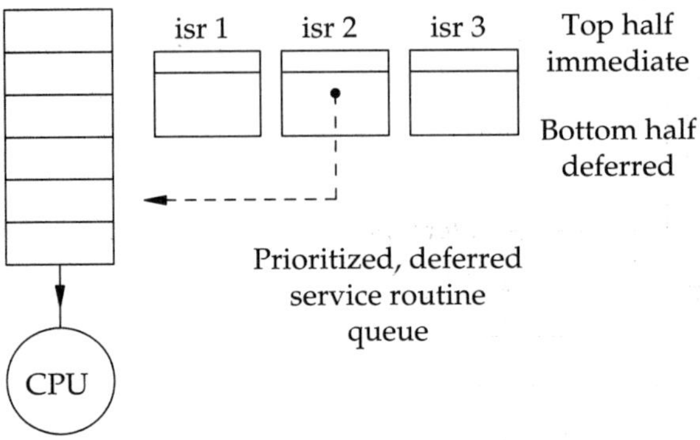

Deferred interrupt processing

by some early microprocessor coders, and taken up by Windows/NT, called 'deferred interrupt processing', may be the only solution. Here, the interrupt service routines are split into two parts, the immediate service code and the larger, deferred portion. While the short immediate code behaves the same as any interrupt service routine, it has the extra responsibility of entering the deferred section onto a queue for later processing. This gives the scheduler an opportunity to take into account relative priorities and reorder the deferred parts of the interrupt service routines. An additional advantage which comes from splitting interrupt routines occurs if an interrupt routine takes rather long to execute. As interrupt routines have higher priority than normal tasks, they effectively hold up all mainline processing until they complete. This need not be the case for deferred procedures.

3.13 Use of exceptions and interrupts

For most systems, the interrupt facilities are used for a wide variety of purposes as listed below. It seems that the external interrupt, fired by an attached device, is no longer so important.

- I/O data transfer request
- Software TRAP (SVC)
- Machine failure
- Real-time tick
- Run-time software error
- Single-step facility
- System reset or watchdog

Possible sources of interrupts

A very significant use of modern interrupt facilities has been introduced by the requirement for access control. By allocating CPU facilities and memory segments either 'User' or 'Privileged' status, the system can protect its core functions from ordinary users, reserving for 'root', or super-user, the more risky capabilities. This is often illustrated with the privilege levels represented as concentric spheres. Such access control is essential for modern multi-user operating systems and depends on all interrupts switching the CPU into privileged mode.

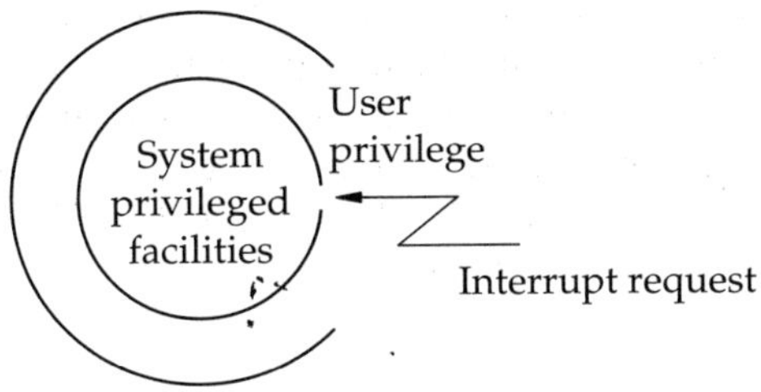

How interrupts assist operating system security

Thus, interrupts provide a small entry window to the system facilities that can be policed by ISR code, which is now included as part of the operating system. This could be seen as the most significant use of the software interrupt, or TRAP instruction.

3.14 Interrupt unpredictability

There is an extra problem when trying to debug systems running interrupt routines. With ordinary subroutines, the programmer should be able to tell exactly when each subroutine will run, taking into account the variation from moment to moment of IF-THEN-ELSE statements which may test changeable environmental conditions. In fact, some subroutines may never run at all because it happens to be a leap year, or Sweden doesn't recognize Euro-travel passes, or whatever. But the role of Interrupt Service Routines (ISR) is to run when the CPU interrupt signal gets activated by circumstances which are rarely under the direct control of the programmer. Thus we say that subroutines are predictable and synchronous, while interrupt service routines are asynchronous and unpredictable. This makes debugging software systems, where several interrupts are likely to fire at any time, much more demanding, especially when the debugger software confuses the situation by using the trace interrupt for its own ends. Because of this unpredictability, using interrupts on digital computers has been criticized as dangerous and programmers building embedded computer systems for life-critical applications often try to avoid them. But when working in less risky areas, hardware interrupts can offer an efficient technique to introduce some measure of responsive multi-tasking to the system.

3.15 Critical data protection – how to communicate with interrupts

There is a particular problem with passing data back from an ISR. Communication between an ISR and the main loop code is carried out through global variables, sufficient in itself to condemn this scheme in many programmers' eyes. Nevertheless, an early generation of 8 bit embedded applications, using the i8080 and Mc6800 microprocessors, often relied heavily on the CPU interrupt facilities to provide event-driven, pre-emptive task scheduling. Motorola extended the hardware support for interrupts offered by the 32 bit 68000 CPU to remove some of the limitations, but problems remained.

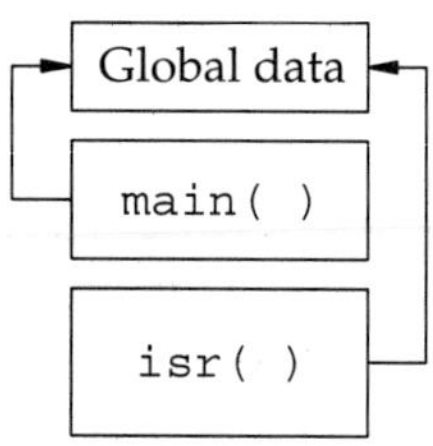

Interrupts using global data for communication

Consider the situation shown in the two component Time-of-Day (TOD) program on p. 75. There is a Real-time Clock (RTC) ISR being triggered every 10 ms to increment the seconds, minutes and hours values, and there is a display routine to refresh a set of front panel digits showing the TOD. The msec, sec, min and hours data is held in memory. The routine which refreshes the display runs regularly, about twice a second as a low priority task, perhaps in the main processing loop. It takes the current secs value, converts it to 7-segment format and writes it to the display. Then it does the same for mins and then for hrs.

The RTC ISR is more urgent and will break into any main process so that it can update the clock data in main memory. Now, what happens if the display is being refreshed when a RTC interrupt occurs? Consider the situation 01:59:59, with the display refresh having just written new values for secs and mins, and being poised to read the hrs from memory – and just then the RTC ISR occurs. It will rollover increment msecs to 00, then secs to 00, then mins to 00, then hrs to program. This happens to be right on the point of refreshing the hrs display. Which it does, leaving the incorrect value 02:59:59 for all to see. The false value will remain visible until the next display refresh occurs to correct it. In this example, the clock values in memory have not been corrupted so no lasting damage is done, unless you missed your train. If the display update routine also served a network connection, there would be scope for a larger disaster.

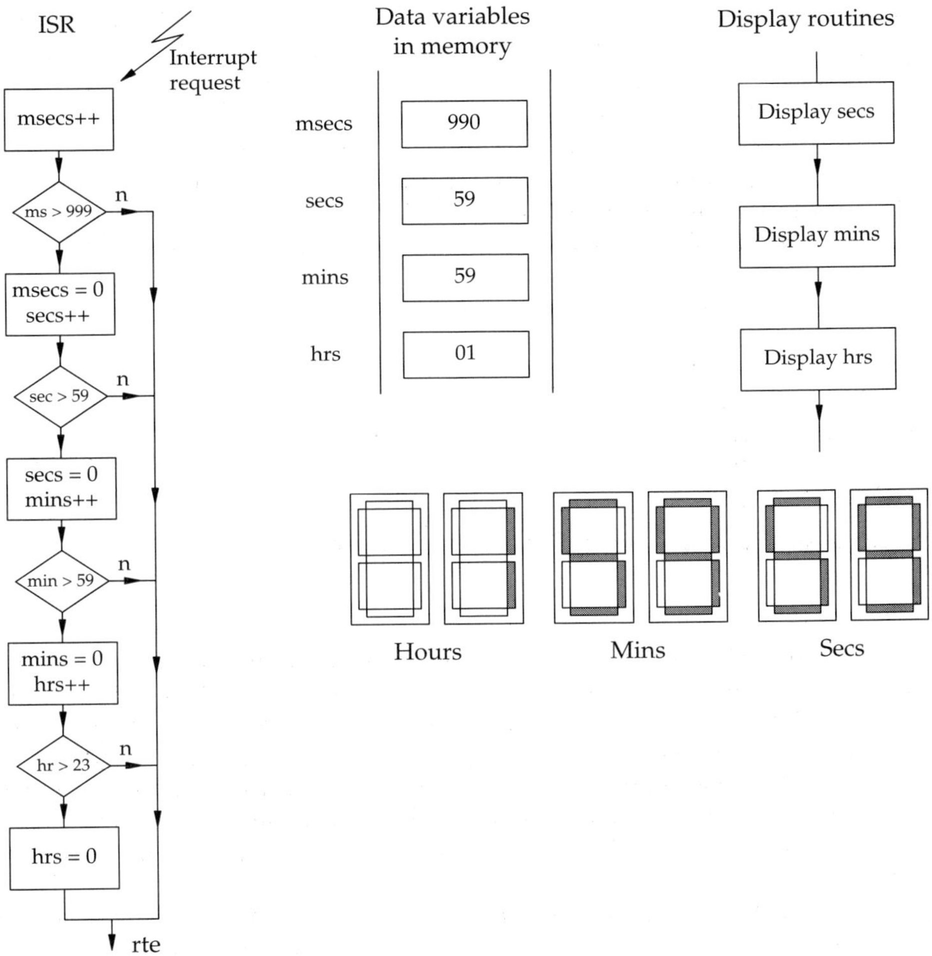

Real-time clock and time-of-day display sharing critical data

The problem described arises from the complexity of the data being processed and the need for simultaneous, unsynchronized access by two or more processes. In a more general form you may encounter the same problem when programming a multi-tasking application for Unix or NT. It is known as the critical resource problem. In this case, it is worth noting that if time was simply stored as a 32 bit integer, perhaps as seconds after boot-up, there would be no problem because the value would always be valid: interleaved update and display operations could not result in corrupted data, unless the computer had multiple processors capable of pre-empting access to the bus. There are several solutions which can be tried to clear up this difficulty. If the interrupts were disabled to block the RTC interrupt request on entry to the display update routines, and then re-enabled at the completion of the display refresh, the display would remain coherent but would progressively go wrong. When the system receives an RTC interrupt its response would be delayed if the interrupts are disabled, so there is a risk that the TOD would become out of true. This is a more significant issue when the ticks occurred more rapidly than 100 Hz. In fact, turning off all of the interrupts is far too drastic, because it would interfere with other interrupt-driven activity, such as I/O transfers. This solution is only acceptable for small microcontroller systems, where interrupt deferment would not be too disruptive.

- Disable interrupts
- Serialize the access
- Use a semaphore

Alternative solutions to protecting a critical resource

A better solution in this clock example is to serialize access to the critical data region as presented below. This means moving all the code across from the RTC ISR to the main program flow, just before the display refresh routines. This makes it impossible to read partly updated data. But now the RTC ISR must indicate to the main program through a flag or simple integer that a tick has occurred since the last display update. A check on the value of the RTC flag will determine whether a clock increment needs to take place.

It should be recognized that the tick flag is now a critical, shared resource in itself, which could also be in danger of corruption. This exposes a general problem with using access and status control flags. When three discrete machine instructions are used for the read, check and clear operation, a write operation, by interrupt in this example, can occur between reading and clearing, which could lead to a data corruption, a loss of time in this example. To assist with this the Pentium has a special non-interruptible mode for a small group of instructions, including BTS, BTR, and BTC (Bit-Test-and-Set, Bit-Test-and-Reset, Bit-Test-and-Complement). These are useful for testing and resetting single bit flags and, when preceded by the LOCK instruction, are guaranteed to run to completion even if an interrupt or DMA request is received half way through execution.

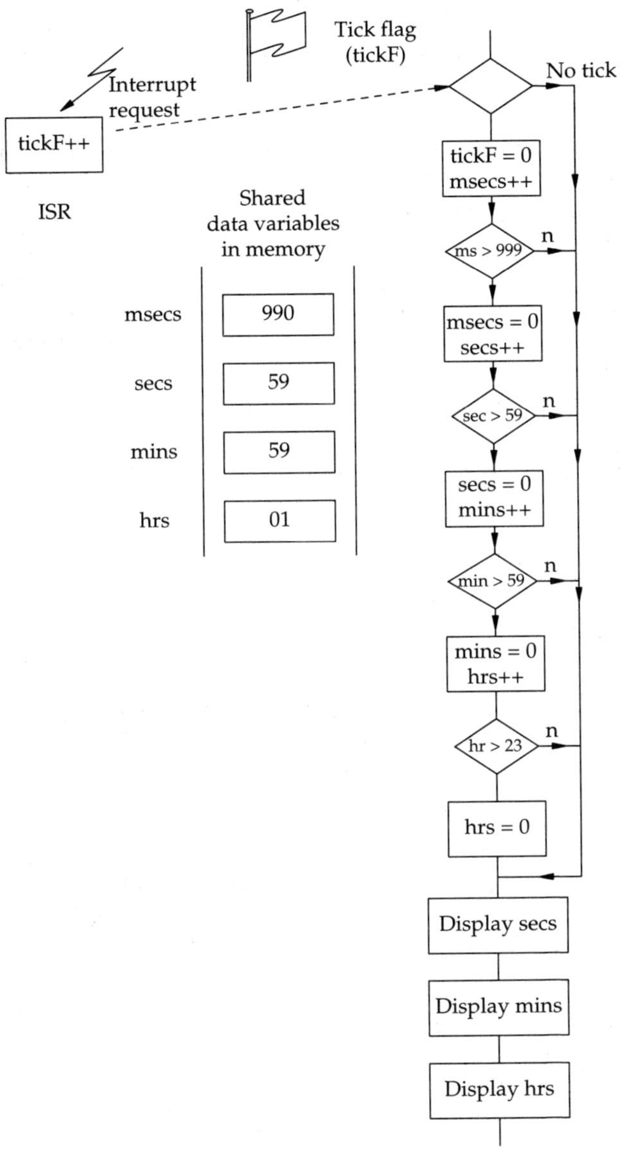

Serializing access to shared data

3.16 Buffered I/O – interrupt device drivers

When computers are furnished with sophisticated, multi-tasking operating systems, neither simple hardware polled I/O nor interrupt routines are directly accessible to the application programmer. The former due to dire inefficiency, the latter because of the risks involved in allowing ordinary users control over the interrupt system. All the data transfers into and out of the computer have to be handled by the trusted operating system routines known as device drivers. In both Unix and Windows these routines run in privileged mode and are responsible for the direct hardware interface. This includes flow control and error trapping when necessary. Frequently they also include software data buffers to smooth out any hiccoughs in the flow of data. Later, in Chapter 19, we will find out how the I/O interrupts, and the device driver service routines, are essential components in the wider process scheduling scheme. Application programmers gain access to the device driver routines either through HLL library functions such as printf() or putc() or through specially provided library functions which need to be explicitly linked into the code. In the figure below, the outline structure and action of interrupt device drivers is presented. You can see that the device driver code is split into two parts: the front end and the interrupt service routine. Between them is the data buffer where data is temporarily stored before moving onward.

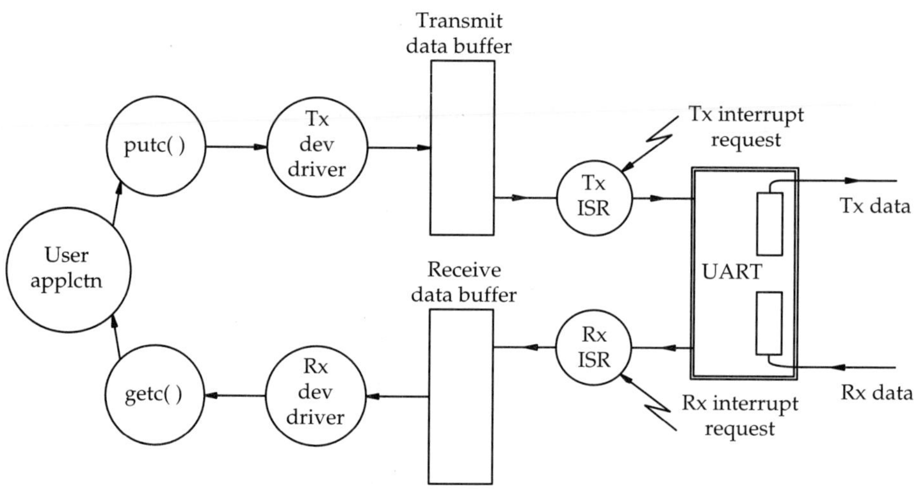

Using buffered, interrupt-driven I/O

Consider a data output operation illustrated above. The application program calls an output function with the data item as a parameter (`putc()`). Control then passes to a library routine which in turn calls an operating system routine. This checks to see if there is space in the transmit buffer associated with the specified device. If there is space, the item is entered at the back of the queue, the queue pointers are updated and control returns to the original program. If there happens to be no space in the buffer, perhaps due to a failure of the link, an error status code is returned, or the program will block until space becomes available. The data will hang about in the transmit buffer for a moment before it gets transferred to the output port by the transmit ISR. This is triggered by the port hardware when it is ready to receive more data. So an application program may appear to have satisfactorily written some data out to a device, when it actually got no further than the transmit buffer.

The sequence of operations is similar for the receive channel. Data arrives at the receive port and triggers an interrupt which evokes the receive ISR. This moves the data into the receive buffer, from where it may be read by an application program.

3.17 Chapter summary

When dealing with I/O intensive programs, several new problems emerge for the real-time programmer. Access to ports may be easier when working on bare hardware, but then all the useful operating system facilities disappear. Interrupt processing will always demand careful implementation and testing because of its unpredictability. Real-time programmers require a greater understanding of the underlying hardware, such as port address mapping and register bit flags. Operating systems hide the gory detail of I/O processing within their device driver modules, which are only accessible with root privilege, making it more difficult for students to practise the necessary skills.

3.18 Problems and issues for discussion

1. Using a search engine (such as Google), find and download a data sheet for a peripheral chip, such as a timer/counter, UART, parallel port. Read through the sheet, highlighting all references to internal registers. Ensure you have their access address and functions clearly distinguished. Plan an initialization routine written in C.
2. Allocate the following I/O activities to deal with through polling, interrupt or DMA, giving your justifications: roadside vehicle sensor, car engine speed transducer, audio microphone, burglar/intrusion detector, photodetector input for a laser range-finder, computer system power fail signal, high resolution X-ray scanner, ECG electrode signal monitor.
3. Why does the use of interrupt routines introduce the problem of critical data? How can a real-time system deal with this danger?
4. Investigate the interrupt facilities offered by commercial microcontrollers, such as 8051, 68307, ATM91 or LPC2124. How do these compare to those offered by the Pentium?
5. How can HLL programmers gain access to interrupt facilities?
6. Estimate the minimum polling rate for the following applications: car accelerator pedal position and inlet manifold pressure sensor, vending machine coin channel, LAN/Ethernet card, credit card swipe device, printer drum position, PC mouse, computer keyboard.

7. List in general terms the operations that are required within an ISR.
8. In high reliability systems, where failures may endanger life, the use of interrupts are viewed with some suspicion. Why is this?

3.19 Suggestions for reading

Buchanan, W. (1999). *PC Interfacing, Communications and Windows Programming.* Addison Wesley.

Lawrence, P. & Mauch, K. (1987). *Real-time Microcomputer System Design.* McGraw Hill.

Messmer, H-P. (2002). *The Indispensible PC Hardware Book.* Addison Wesley.

Williams, R. (2001). *Computer Systems Architecture: A Networking Approach.* Addison Wesley.

Chapter 4

Cyclic executives for bare hardware

4.1 Chapter overview

Small cyclic systems are based on the test-and-skip looping scheme described in the last chapter but include interrupt and 'burn' routines to maintain accurate loop timing. This chapter shows how they can be implemented using a function pointer table, with an associated dispatcher routine. The function names are all held in an array, and evoked in round-robin sequence by the dispatcher code. This simple scheme enables subsequent modifications to be readily undertaken. In conclusion, an example keypad application is described.

4.2 The basic system

The activity of a basic cyclic scheduler is illustrated below. Several functions are called in a prearranged sequence. In academic terms, the loop tasks are submitting themselves to a regime of 'cooperative scheduling', meaning that

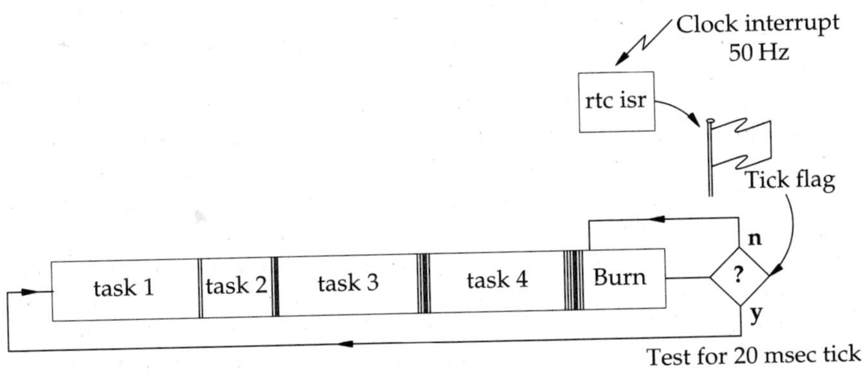

Timed cyclic loop with burn task

the programmer decides when a task will hand on to the next, with little scope for dynamic, run-time priority modification. At the end of the list, a special idle or burn function spins round in a tight loop testing a tick flag status bit. This flag is set once every 20 ms by an interrupt service routine. As soon as the burn task sees that the flag has been set, it stops spinning and returns to the start of the main loop, clearing the tick flag in readiness for the next burn. In this simple way, it is possible to be sure that each of the tasks runs at a rate of 50 Hz, once every 20 ms.

Small cyclic executives do offer the advantage of efficiency and testability. Because their structure is so simple, testing is straightforward. For life-critical applications, where simplicity is a great advantage, cyclic schedulers have sometimes been adopted instead of the more complex r-t executives.

4.3 System tick

The tick is an essential requirement for any r-t software system. Besides allowing the program to maintain the Time-of-Day (TOD), hours/minutes/seconds values, it enables task rescheduling as well as periodic scanning. It is the heartbeat of the scheduler. All r-t systems need timer-counter hardware to generate this regular tick by supplying an interrupt request every 5–25 msec.

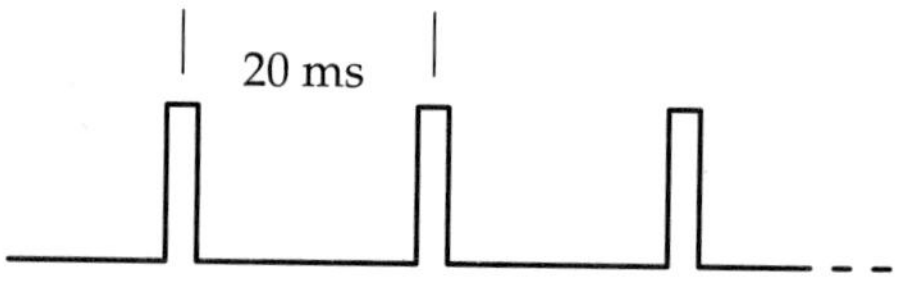

The 50 Hz r-t clock, or tick

The actual counter device may be found within the CPU or a specific Counter Timer Chip (CTC), but the programmer must be able to initialize it to the correct frequency of interrupt. If the application is hosted by an operating system, such as Linux or Windows, it is still possible to read a hardware clock using an API function call. On small embedded systems the exact cycle rate is sometimes determined by the unlikely issue of human visual flicker-fusion sensitivity! If the refresh rate of front panel LEDs is too slow (<25 Hz, every 40 msec) the display will generate a worrying flicker for observers. There is an extra advantage to using the main scheduling tick to scan the front panel display, which becomes apparent during debugging. When the display scanning stalls on one digit, it indicates that basic task scheduling has failed. Don't be afraid to hook an oscilloscope to the interrupt line to check the RTC interrupt rate. An error of ×100 in the frequency can be hard to diagnose using only a VDU and printer, but is immediately obvious with an oscilloscope.

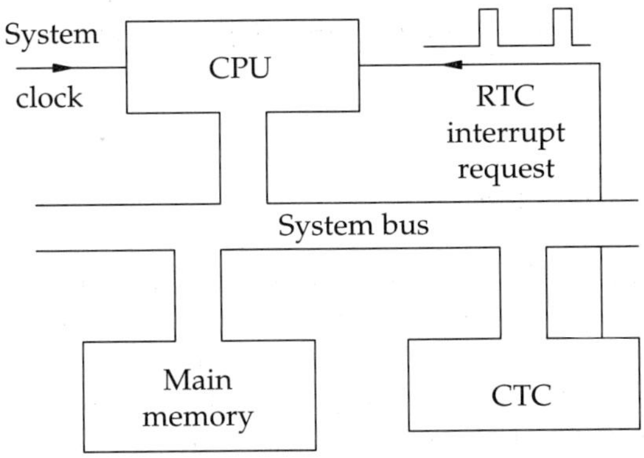

Generating the r-t tick

In fixed priority cyclic schemes, tasks can usually be allocated to one of the three priority levels according to their scheduling need: interrupt, clock and base.

Interrupt	– event-driven pre-emption, rapid response but little processing
Clock	– periodic scanning with fixed run-time
Base	– no strict requirements, background activity

Task priority levels for a cyclic executive

4.4 Extended tasks

The situation with large tasks has to be dealt with carefully. If a single task should overrun its clock slot, the whole timing sequence could be thrown out. So large tasks may need to be cut up into a number of parts, to be run in separate phases. This then maintains the correct looping period but effectively merges application code with scheduler code. Intermingling application code with scheduling code makes the programmer's job much more difficult. But it does highlight one of the main problems for multi-tasking: code re-entry.

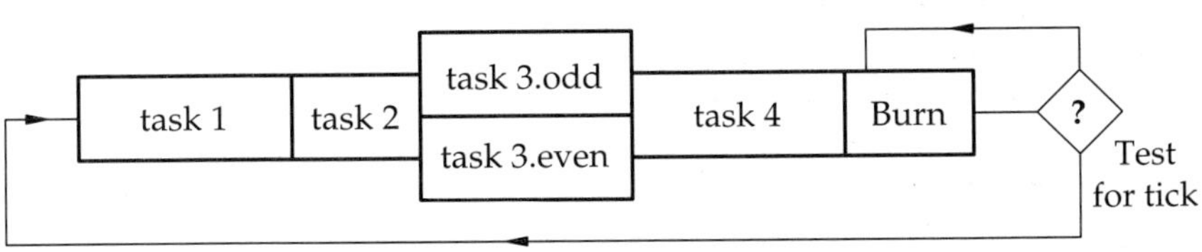

Cyclic loop with a split clock task

This is the requirement to break off from a task and restart it later on with no negative impact on the task's data.

4.5 Implementation of a cyclic executive

Each task appears as a function, much the way *threads* are implemented in larger operating systems. Thus, all the tasks can see the same global data, and use global variables as a convenient, if rather risky, way of communicating. A fairly simple cyclic executive, based on the three priority levels, can be implemented in C. One of the interrupt tasks must deal with the tick signal in order to support the clock level scheduling. Clock tasks are entered into slot lists arranged within a scheduling frame. Each slot will hold several tasks which will be scheduled at a fixed rate, imposed by the tick. If the processing of tasks in a slot completes before the next tick occurs, the base, or burn task, is taken up. This will continue until the next tick breaks in to start the next clock slot. Should clock slot overrun occur, time synchronization may be recovered before the end of the frame. Only a clock frame overrun is seen as serious, leading to slippage in polled values and time-of-day integrity. The relative priority of clock tasks can roughly be handled by entering higher priority tasks in several slots, so that they run more often.

External event interrupt routines return to clock-level tasks to allow them to run to completion, but pre-empt base-level tasks to allow rescheduling to take place. This is a hybrid arrangement, partly cooperative and partly demand pre-emption. A description of such a small executive, FreeRTOS, which uses a similar mix of task scheduling techniques, is to be found in Barry (2001). FreeRTOS has been proved on a number of different microcontrollers, and is perfectly adequate to host embedded applications which are not too ambitious in scope. The Cyclic Mosaic Scheduler can readily support the requirements of a periodic clock task, where regular actions are required at fixed intervals. If the need is for variable delays or irregular intervals the scheme is less attractive and an alternative Task Queue Scheduler could be

2 ms allocated per slot

0	1	2	3	4	5	6	7
t1	t1	t1	t1	t1	t1	t1	t1
t2	t3	t2	t3	t2	t3	t2	t3
t4	t4	t4	t4	t4	t4	t4	t4
t5	burn	burn	burn	burn	burn	burn	burn
t6							
t7							
burn							

A 16 ms time frame with eight execution slots

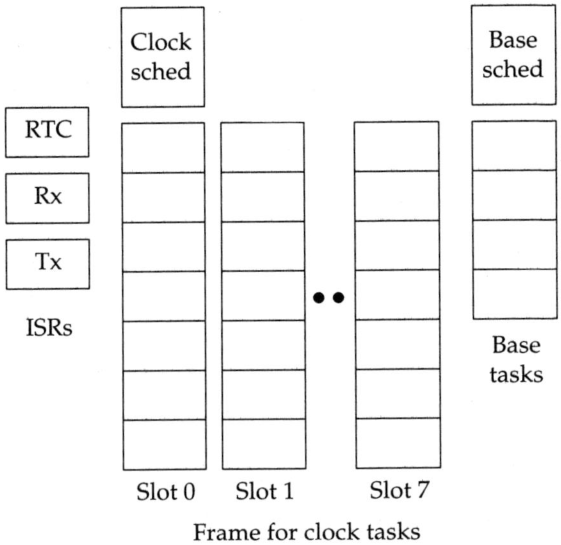

Cyclic executive task scheme

included. A FIFO queue of 'ready to run' tasks is checked and dispatched as part of the base-level activity. This is also a cooperative method because the tasks themselves have to include rescheduling or `sleep()` calls to enter themselves onto the task queue and return control to the dispatcher. This design of r-t system can also be developed, with some coding effort, into the full multitasking executive which is provided with queues for other resources besides the CPU. A major disadvantage of cyclic executives, which we will return to in future chapters, is the need to compile and link all tasks and scheduling code together. This is partly due to the close working of the application code with the clock and base schedulers, referred to as 'cooperative scheduling', and partly the lack of dynamic task loading.

4.6 Cyclic executive execution pattern

The execution sequence of tasks within a cyclic executive will not vary in the same unpredictable manner as tasks within a fully featured operating system or pre-emptive r-t executive, such as Unix, Windows, or VXWorks.

The clock-level tasks are dispatched one after the other, from the current slot, by the clock scheduler. The clock tasks quickly run to completion, handing back to the clock scheduler. When that slot's tasks are completed, the base scheduler runs 'burn' tasks until the next clock tick indicates that it is time to start on the next clock slot. The loop of base tasks provides a better way of benefiting from the excess slot time than the single burn task put at the end of each slot.

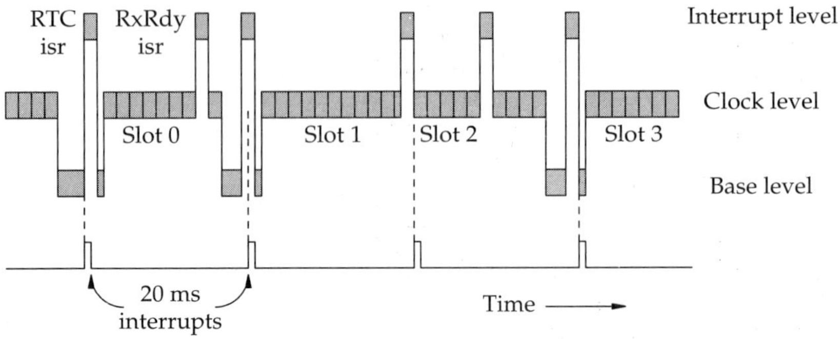

Execution pattern with interrupt, clock and base tasks

4.7 Demonstation cyclic executive code

A table-based cyclic dispatcher, as described in Section 4.5, can be implemented in C to run on Linux. The following example code uses the 10 ms tick supplied by Linux, but everything is massively slowed down for this demonstration. Each task prints a message and then sleeps for 1 sec. The slots are set for a 5 sec period, with the burn task telling us how long it has been waiting for the next 5 sec tick to arrive.

```
/* Demo table-based cyclic task dispatcher for Linux with
   multiple task slots */
#include <stdio.h>
#include <ctype.h>
#include <unistd.h>
#include <sys/times.h>                       // gcc cyclicx.c -o cyclicx
#define SLOTX 4
#define CYCLEX 5
#define SLOT_T 5000                          // 5 sec slot time

    int tps, cycle=0, slot=0;
    clock_t  now, then;
    struct tms  n;

    void one() {                             // task code
      printf("task 1 running\n");
      sleep(1);
    }
    void two() {
      printf("task 2 running\n");
      sleep(2);
    }
    void three() {
      printf("task 3 running\n");
      sleep(3);
    }
```

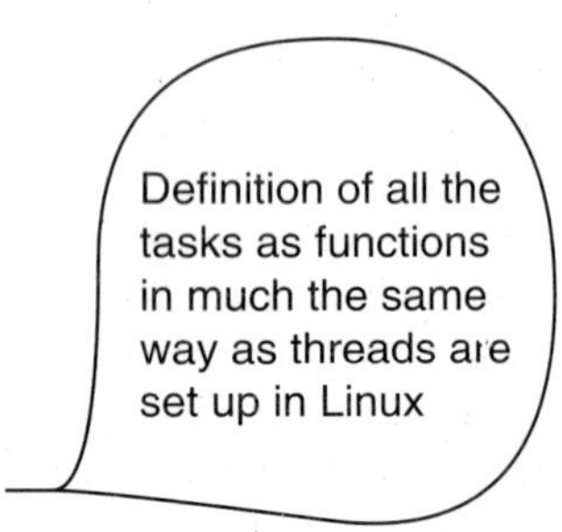

```
    void four() {
      printf("task 4 running\n");
      sleep(4);
    }
    void five() {
      printf("task 5 running\n");
      sleep(5);
    }
    void burn() {
      clock_t bstart = times(&n);

      while ( ((now=times(&n))-then) < SLOT_T*tps/1000 ) {
                    /* burn time here */
      }
      printf("burn time = %2.2dms\n\n", (times(&n)-bstart)*
          1000/tps);
      then = now;
      cycle = CYCLEX;
    }

    void (*ttable[SLOTX][CYCLEX])() = {
      {one,  two,   burn,  burn,  burn},
      {one,  three, burn,  burn,  burn},
      {one,  four,  burn,  burn,  burn},
      {burn, burn,  burn,  burn,  burn}
  };
  main () {
     tps = sysconf(_SC_CLK_TCK);
     printf("clock ticks/sec = %d\n\n", tps);
     while  (1)  {
      for(slot=0; slot<SLOTX; slot++)
        for(cycle=0; cycle<CYCLEX; cycle++)
           (*ttable[slot][cycle])(); // dispatch next task
                                     // from table
     }
  }
```

Task table holds tasks in rows each executed on a round-robin basis every 5 sec tick

4.8 Keypad application

A common example of a simple r-t application is the keypad/display scanner which is still regularly used as a cheap front panel or engineer's console on processor controlled equipment. This requires three parallel ports, two for output, and one for input. In the example below, there is a 16 button keypad, structured as a 4×4 matrix. The lines of the C output port are strobed low, one at a time, in rotating sequence under the control of the scanning software. The A port is then read, any lines which are low indicate a closed switch in the strobed column. All the rows are pulled high by the $10\,\text{k}\Omega$ resistors.

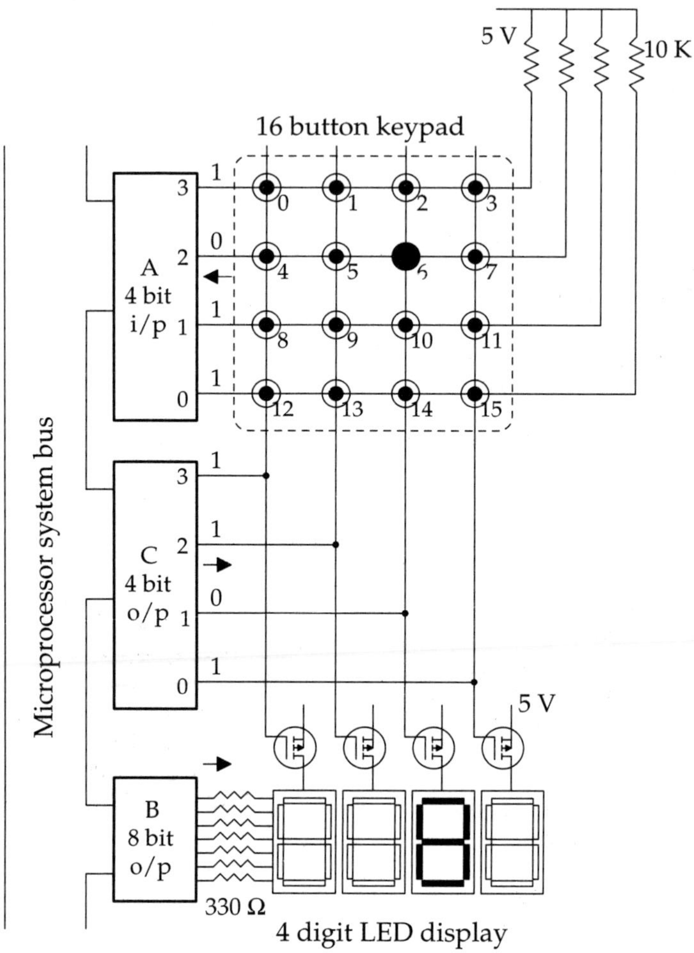

Engineer's console: keypad and display

Because manual keypads often suffer from contact bounce (see Section 1.8), several readings are taken and compared before a change in switch status is recorded. The regular pulse pattern from C can also be used to cyclically select a digit from the display. LEDs only emit light when they are actually pulsed, so most of the time, at least 75 per cent in this case, they are off. The eight LED segments are controlled by the byte-wide output port B, but because the segments from the four digits are wired in parallel, the column strobe pulse from port C is used to select the *active* digit. So, by rapidly cycling around the display, at a rate above the human flicker threshold, to the human eye it will appear as if all the digits are illuminated simultaneously. In normal lighting conditions, you cannot detect on–off flicker above 60 Hz. After the low pulse has been started on the current output line of port C, port A is read and any input line at 0 is assumed to have been shorted to the currently strobed output line through an active switch contact. All unconnected lines remain at 5 V because of the 10 k pull-up resistors.

The keypad push buttons may be replaced by optical switches or opto-couplers. These offer the extra advantage of only passing current in one direction, which eliminates the 'phantom closure' effect that occurs when three or more crosspoints are closed at the same time. Imagine switches 4, 6 and 0 held closed. This allows a zero strobe pulse from port C_1 to affect the port A_3 line as well as the port A_2. Unfortunately the scanner software incorrectly interprets this as if switch 2 is closed. A simple solution involves inserting diodes in line with all the switches to prevent the backflow of signals. The output transistor in the optical units already has this incorporated in the emitter junction.

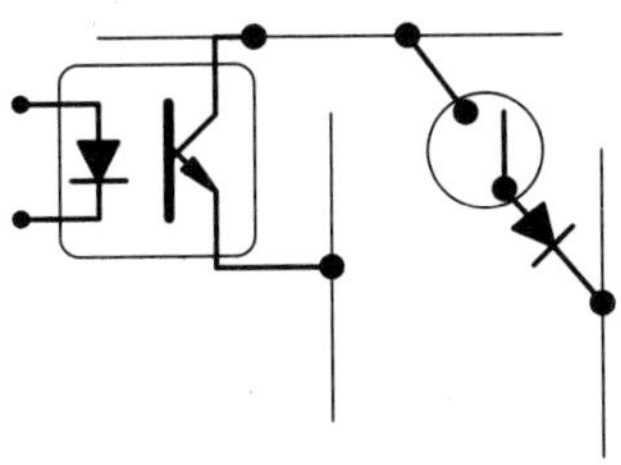

Optical or manual crosspoint switch

As described above, port B has to output each digit pattern in turn, as the port C strobe pulse runs round and round selecting each digit in turn. The frequency of the strobe is usually about 50 Hz, to reduce annoying visual flicker, but a faster rate may be employed to avoid missing any status changes on the input lines. Remember that if mechanical switches are being polled, the old problem of contact bounce will need to be dealt with by filtering the input samples. This can be handled very conveniently by a clock-level task in a small cyclic executive system.

```
/* Keypad.c (16 switches) scanner and 7-seg digit LED refresh
 *   tasks needs to be run at least every 20ms (50Hz minimum)
 *   Linux version, 28-2-04
 */
#include <stdio.h>
#include <string.h>
#include <unistd.h>
#include <fcntl.h>
#include "../PIO.h"              // gcc keypad.c -L. -lfab -O keypad
#include <sys/termios.h>
#include <ctype.h>

#define COLSX 4
#define ROWSX 4
```

```
typedef unsigned char BYTE;
typedef unsigned int DWORD;

DWORD keyflags;
BYTE colsel=0;
BYTE kpd0[COLSX];
BYTE kpd1[COLSX];
BYTE kpd2[COLSX];
BYTE ktrue[COLSX];          //current true keypad status
BYTE kedge[COLSX];
BYTE kchange[COLSX];        //1 - key status changed
BYTE digits[COLSX] = {3,2,1,0};
const BYTE segtab[] = {0xC0,0xF9,0xA4,0xB0,0x99,0x92,0x82,
     0xF8,0x80,0x90,0x88,0x83,0xA7,0xA1,0x86,0x8E,0xFF};
const BYTE keytab[] = {1,2,3, 15,4,5,6,14,7,8,9,13,10,0,11,12};

int control, portA, portB, portC;
int portAstatus = 0;
int portBstatus = 0;
int portCstatus = 0;

void initFAB(int *control, int *porta, int *portb, int *portc);
void closeFAB (int *control, int *porta, int *portb, int *portc);

void inithw(void) {
  int x;
  setterm();
  initFAB(&control, &portA, &portB, &portC);
  x = 0x90;
  write(control, &x, 1);        // mode 0
}

BYTE colscan(void) {
  int i;
  BYTE know;

  colsel = (++colsel) % COLSX;

  portCstatus = (BYTE) (01 << colsel);
  portBstatus = segtab[digits[colsel]];

  write(portB, &portBstatus, 1);
  write(portC, &portCstatus, 1);
  for(i=0;i<1000;i++);

  read(portA, &portAstatus, 1);
  kpd2[colsel] = kpd1[colsel];
```

```
  kpd1[colsel] = kpd0[colsel];
  kpd0[colsel] = (BYTE)portAstatus;

  kchange[colsel] = (kpd0[colsel] ^ kpd1[colsel]) |
      (kpd1[colsel]^ kpd2[colsel]);
  know = (kpd2[colsel] & ~kchange[colsel]) |
          (ktrue[colsel] & kchange[colsel]);
  kedge[colsel] = (know ^ ktrue[colsel]) & know;
  ktrue[colsel] = know;
  keyflags = 0;
  keyflags |=  ktrue[0] & 0x0F;
  keyflags |= (ktrue[1] & 0x0F) << 4;
  keyflags |= (ktrue[2] & 0x0F) << 8;
  keyflags |= (ktrue[3] & 0x0F) << 12;
  keyflags &= 0x0000ffff;
  for (i=0; keyflags&1; keyflags>>=1) i++;
   return i;
}

int main() {
  struct tms *tim;
  BYTE key;
  DWORD then;
  inithw();

  while (1) {
            key = colscan();
            if (key <16) {
                              digits[0]= keytab[key];
                              digits[1]= 16;
                              digits[2]= key % 10;
                              digits[3]= key / 10;
            } else {
                              digits[0]= 16;
                              digits[1]= 16;
                              digits[2]= 16;
                              digits[3]= 16;
            }

            printf("  key = %x \n", key);
            then = (DWORD)times(&tim)+1;
             while (then > (DWORD)times(&tim))  { };

   }
   closeFAB(&control, &portA, &portB, &portC);
     return 0;
 }
```

4.9 Chapter summary

The structure and function of small cyclic executives, implemented on bare hardware, has been described with example applications. Only three fixed levels of priority are readily supported: interrupt, clock and base. This can be judged as too inflexible for many of the more complex r-t applications. But this scheme does offer the developer good testability and low cost which may be significant for high distribution products. There is a close relation between the operation of cyclic executives and finite state machines which are described in the next two chapters.

4.10 Problems and issues for discussion

1. Explain the advantages of using a cyclic executive to dispatch a sequence of tasks rather than a simple round-robin loop of functions. How do you distinguish different levels of task priority?
2. The clock tick rate, given by a hardware timer, determines when the dispatcher moves onto the next task slot. What happens if the tasks run too long, and don't finish before the tick occurs? What steps could be taken to prevent this occurring in the future?
3. Why is the problem of critical data not so significant with cyclic executives?
4. If a task is taking too long to execute, causing clock slot overrun, what steps can be taken to eliminate or reduce the undesirable effects?
5. Get the cyclic executive example (page 86) running on a Linux system. Alter the task run-times by changing the `sleep( )` parameters. You are allowed integers up to 5. Beyond five seconds you will necessarily encounter clock slot overrun because the slot processing time is set for 5 secs, set by SLOT_T. Edit the task table.
6. Choose an example r-t system, such as a vending machine, engine control unit or burglar alarm. Identify the principal input, processing and output activities (tasks) and classify them as interrupt, clock (periodic) or base, according to the requirements of a cyclic executive.
7. Draw up a truth table, or Karnaugh map, to express a debouncing protocol which requires the recorded status of a switch (TruStat) to be changed only when two successive values of the reading (KeyStat,

PrevStat) are the same. You could start by filling in the following truth table and identifying the valid changes:

KeyStat	*PrevStat*	$TruStat_n$	$TruStat_{n+1}$
0	0	0	0
0	0	1	0
0	1	0	0
0	1	1	1
:	:	:	:

Now write a Boolean expression for updating TruStat, given the values of KeyStat, PrevStat and current TruStat.

8. Draw up a flowchart for the operation of software for keypad matrix scanning. Now include the 7-segment LED digits for display and contact debouncing.

4.11 Suggestions for reading

Allworth, S. & Zobel, R. (1996). *Introduction to Real-time Software Design.* MacMillan.

Alam, J. & Birtles, B. (2004). Porting FreeRTOS to the Coldfire Platform, UTS (University of Technology, Sydney) report.

Barry, R. (2001). FreeRTOS, http://www.freertos.org.

Bennett, S. (1994). *Real-time Computer Control: An Introduction.* Prentice Hall.

Shaw, A. (2001). *Real-time Systems and Software.* Wiley.

Chapter 5

Finite state machines – design tool

5.1 Chapter overview

The use of Finite State Machines (FSM) is at the base of several software design methods, and they can provide strong support during both design and implementation phases of software development. This chapter focuses on the use of Finite State Diagrams (FSD) for specifying the dynamic operation of software. Before planning an FSD, it is usual to draw up a context diagram to define the system perimeter. The transformation of FSDs into runnable code is deferred until the following chapter.

5.2 Defining the perimeter

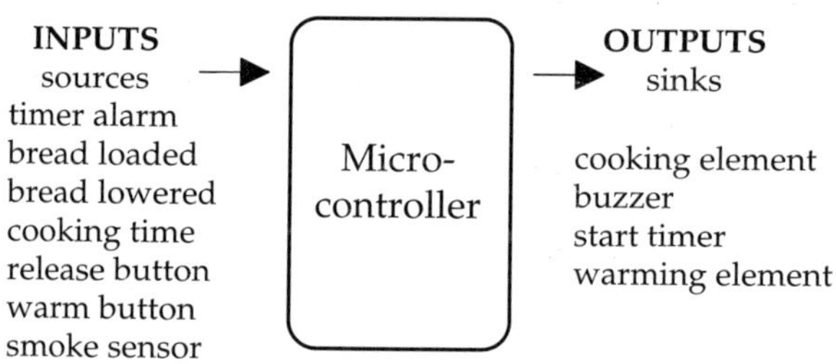

Context diagram for a toaster

Before any design activity can take place some clear and exact decisions have to be taken about the system perimeter. This is often referred to as establishing the system context and may not be entirely straightforward. For example, when confronted by an obvious, free-standing piece of equipment, such as a microwave oven or digital camera, it is often misleading to assume that the system perimeter should be the cabinet casing as most of the equipment controlled by the software is located inside the cabinet. The designer needs to establish what is in the system, and what is outside, from a *functional* point of view. In addition, it is convenient to treat countdown timers as if they are external devices with both input and output channels. So the first step is to isolate the central system controller, and then analyse its input and output data. This leads to an understanding of what data streams the system will have to deal with, and what the new system is expected to generate by way of actions and data. While drawing up the context diagram it is a convenient time to investigate the characteristics of the data streams, such as: data types, average data rate and typical arrival patterns. With this information the system designer can start to make basic decisions concerning hardware provision and software architecture. Drawing up a simple context diagram in this manner will suffice for most embedded microcontroller systems; however, with larger and more elaborate applications it is often necessary to carry out an extensive requirements investigation with a team of analysts before drafting the context definition. This predesign activity has often been identified as seriously deficient in some less than successful real-time projects. If the original requirements are wrong, or inexactly defined, no matter how good the design and code, the customer will not be satisfied.

Input	Type	Rate Hz
timer alarm	bool	0.2
bread loaded	bool	0.01
bread lowered	bool	0.01
cooking time	BYTE	–
release button	bool	?
warm button	bool	?
smoke sensor	bool	?
Output		
cooking element	bit	0.01
buzzer	bit	0.2
start timer	bit	0.2
warming element	bit	0.01

Fully specifying I/O

5.3 Channel bandwidths

Whatever the complexity and size of the system involved, designers have to define the interface between the system and its contextual environment. This is sometimes referred to as establishing the bit rate or bandwidth of the I/O channels. It includes identifying all the input and output streams which cross this boundary, and establishing the type and rate of data transfers. It is also useful to think about the likely *penalties* if new values of data are missed for a period, or a cyclical deadline is overshot. When the system is connected to other equipment, there will be protocols to investigate, and interfaces to comply with. Such information is crucial to get a picture of the likely scheduling patterns that may emerge within the running system and is often as important as understanding the core system functionality.

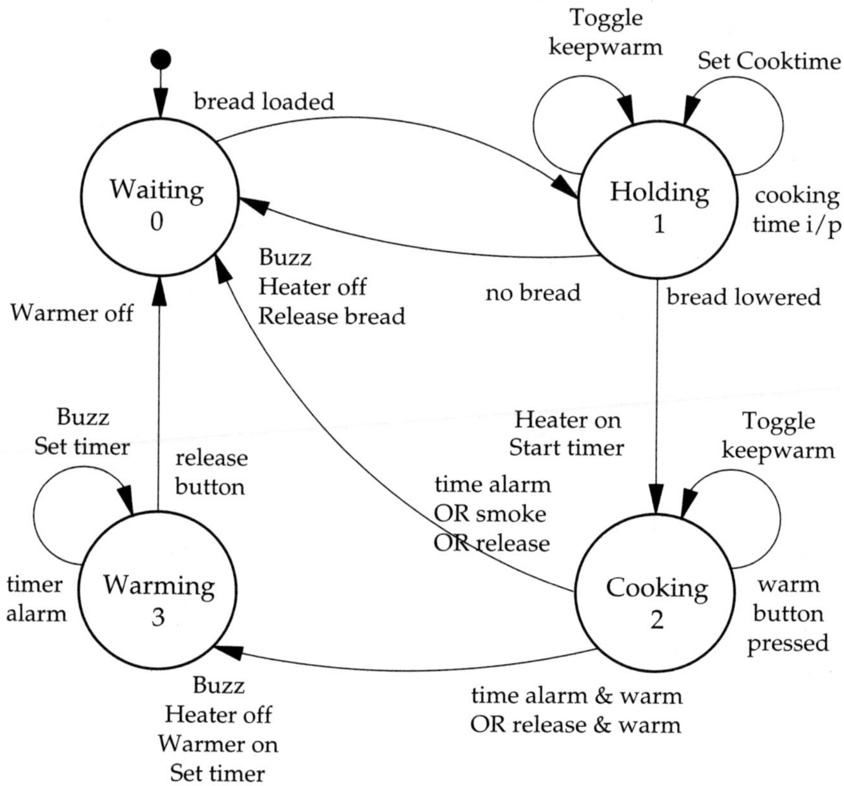

Example FSD: the toaster

Indeed, in many circumstances, this preliminary analysis phase can determine the long-term success or failure of a project because it is here that potential future expansion opportunities can inadvertently be excluded. This happens because the designer has to take a simplified view of the world in order to achieve project completion within a finite timescale. The implicit world model may allow a clever algorithm to be used in order to limit memory use, or reduce processing time. However, when the satisfied customer reappears with a shopping list of extra requirements for their next model, the constraints imposed by the 'clever' algorithm may no longer look so irrelevant. Designing for easy maintenance and future expansion is a skill that often only comes from long commercial experience.

5.4 Finite State Diagrams (FSD)

FSDs or State Transition Diagrams (STD) are very widely used to describe and analyse event-driven, cyclical systems. Both hardware and software can be dealt with using this simple technique. Indeed, both structured analysis/design and object-oriented design/programming methodologies employ finite state descriptions to capture and specify system dynamics. System behaviour is represented on an FSD as a group of discrete, mutually exclusive states, only one of which is occupied at any time. A transition between two of the system states is triggered by an event which commonly arises from a change in the status of an input port, perhaps generating an interrupt. All states and valid transitions must be clearly and completely specified. This can appear as a daunting prospect to new users of the finite state methodology, but can usually be accomplished by starting with an operational 'walkthrough'. The designer pretends to be a user observing the system as it passes through the various phases of a normal operational sequence. In this way, an FSD, with states and interstate transitions, can be seen as carrying a model of the 'world' with which the system is intended to interact.

In all cases, finite state models involve a very reduced version of the world as humans see it, limited to the immediate embedded context of the computer. States can be seen as representing periods when the system is stable, with unchanging output conditions, waiting for one of a number of valid trigger events. Transitions between states, triggered by particular events, can also have associated activities. So, every transition must have a trigger event, and may also have the capacity to evoke an activity to carry out some processing and possibly change the status of output ports. The length of dwell time at

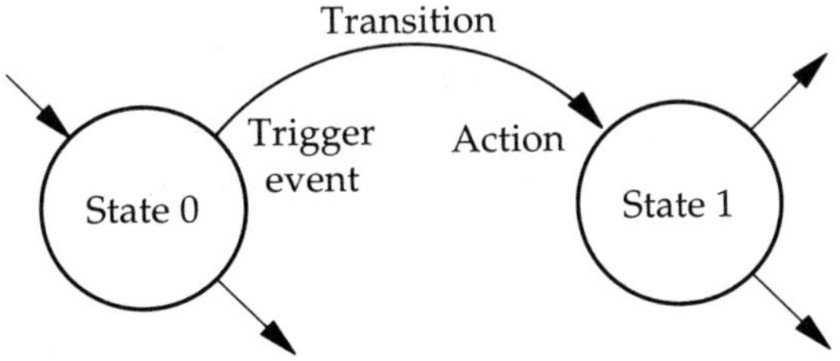

state:	unchanging, waiting condition
transition:	valid routes between states, triggered by events
event:	triggers transition between states, often an input signal
action:	activity/procedure undertaken on entry to a new state

States, transitions trigger events and actions. Component parts of finite state diagrams each state may vary from 5 nsec to 5 years, so this should not be used by the designer as the sole criterion for identifying system states. The transitions between states are considered as instantaneous. But it is during these state switches that all the real actions taken by the system are started. Often it is possible to change an output in order to start an activity, such as motor_on or ADC_start, and then wait in the following state for an acknowledgement input event before proceeding further.

Some descriptions of the FSM design method distinguish between transition 'trigger events' and 'guard conditions'. In other words, a transition will occur *when* the event happens, but only if the associated guard conditions are favourable. In the next chapter we will describe an alternative approach to handling events which need to be identified from both enduring status and instantaneous happenings.

In summary, the transition between system states is triggered by input events which must be clearly and completely specified. During the transitions, output actions are initiated which provide the overt functionality of the system. So in finite state designs there are states and transitions. States are identified as periods when the system is stable, with unchanging output conditions, and waiting for one of a number of valid trigger events to occur. Transitions between states, often triggered by input changes, can cause a change in the system output status through the associated activities.

The precise moment when the activities are carried out by subroutines, provides a choice. For a Mealy state machine, the activities can be evoked on entry to a state, while for a Moore machine, they occur on leaving a state, or within the state itself. Programmers see little significance in the two alternatives. I choose to use a mix of the two in my software implementation, associating actions with transitions, but clearly clocking the outputs to change only at fixed periods. The Moore type of FSM provides outputs which are determined solely by the current state, while for the Mealy type, both state and transition event are needed to determine the current output (activity). The distinction is quite significant for hardware engineers concerned with clock pulse rising edges and the like, but software provides a more flexible implementation medium. The operational sequence of a washing machine using an FSD is shown below.

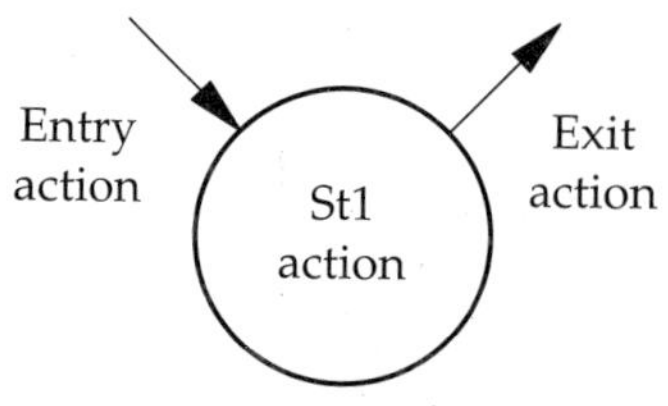

Entry, state and exit actions

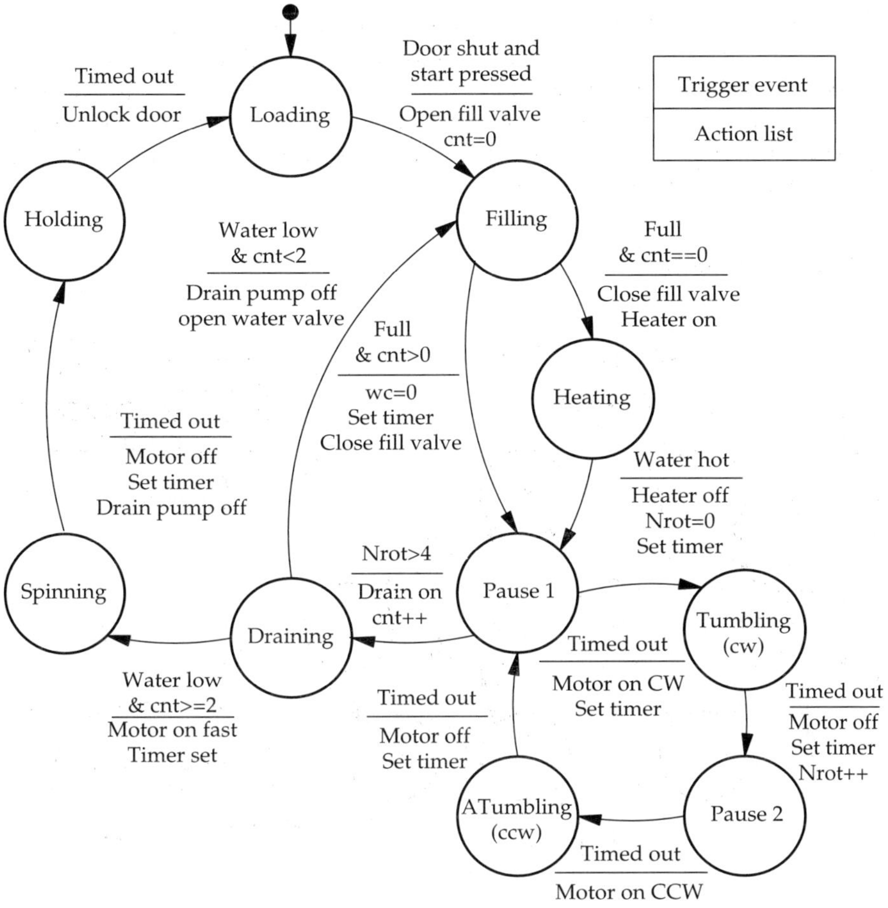

FSD for a basic washing machine

5.5 Auxiliary variables

An important characteristic of a pure finite state methodology is the complete representation of system history by the current state. So if there are several possible routes into a state, tracking different episodes and events, these differences are forgotten once the paths merge onto a single state. There should be no trace left of the different experiences which led to the current state. In our washing machine FSD, however, you can see references in the event fields to counters and timers. These are auxiliary variables introduced to reduce the size and complexity of the initial FSD, but their existence invalidates the principle of 'single state history'. When considering the filling state, it is really a dual state, the first that fills ready for heating and washing, and the second that fills for rinsing. Using the `cnt` variable reduces the size of the FSD, without introducing too much complexity. Without the cycle counter it would have been necessary repeatedly to draw in the tumble cycle 10 times, and expand the diagram to separately describe the rinse phase. It is clear that the auxiliary variables have simplified the diagram, without losing any exactness. Be warned though, excessive use of auxiliary variables undermines the whole philosophy of the finite state method, and leads to a very muddled theoretical situation.

5.6 Vehicle detection

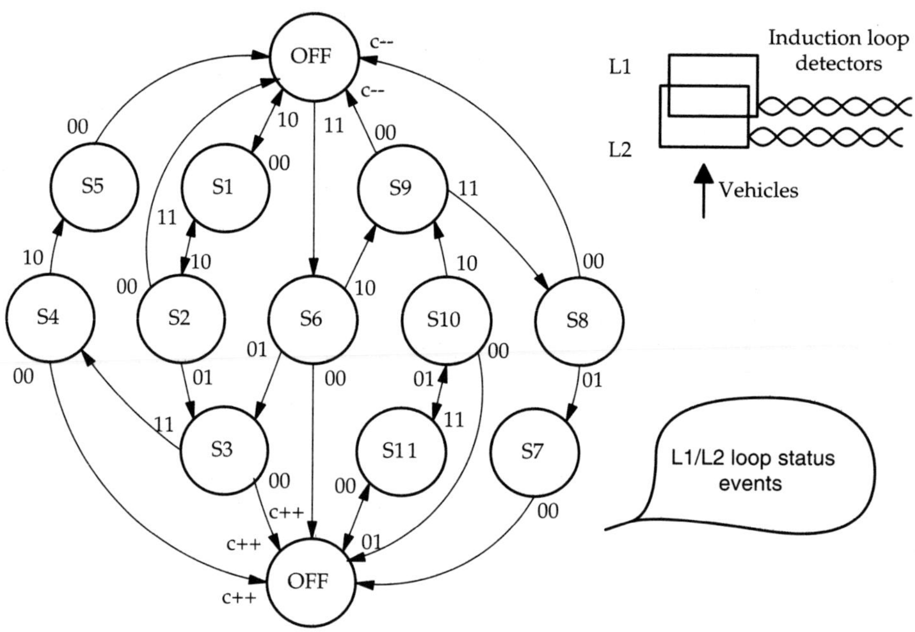

FSD for a vehicle induction loop detector unit

Vehicles are commonly detected, entering car parks or approaching traffic lights, using induction loops embedded in the road surface tarmac. These loops act as tuned aerials, oscillating at a particular radio frequency and so, when a steel axle or sump passes overhead, the resonance frequency changes which the oscillator circuit then registers as an event. To detect the direction of travel, it is common to use a pair of loops so that the order of the detection events gives the direction of travel. For the FSD presented above, the normal vehicle progression is from state OFF to S1 to S2 to S3 and back to OFF. The dual representation of the OFF state simplifies the diagram. There is really only one OFF state. The variable c is incremented and decremented as vehicles pass forwards or backwards across the pair of loops. The transitions actually model possible vehicle behaviour as seen by the detectors. They do not represent a complete description of all possible vehicle transit patterns, only the most common.

Data	Conditions	Exiting from state	Go to state
Start pressed and door shut		Waiting	Filling
Water full	& cnt==0	Filling	Heating
Water hot		Heating	Pause1
	Time out	Pause1	TumbleCCW
	Time out	TumbleCCW	Pause2
	Time out	Pause2	TumbleCW
	Time out	TumbleCW	Pause1
	Nrot>4	Pause1	Draining
Water low	& cnt<2	Draining	Filling
Water low	& cnt>=2	Draining	Spinning
	Time out	Spinning	Holding
	Time out	Holding	Waiting

An event table, showing the required data values and conditions

5.7 Simplification techniques

There are a couple of other techniques besides the use of auxiliary variables, which can help to simplify a state diagram. Sometimes you may find that the problem contains implicit symmetry or reversibility which can be exploited by using reverse direction transitions. When you review an FSD, look for states with only single exit transitions. It is often possible to eliminate them completely, moving the input transitions forward to the next downstream state. But do not pursue state reduction too enthusiastically. If the eventual outcome is a single, all-encompassing state you probably have gone too far in search of a simple diagram. It will not help you structure your program! If an FSD becomes too large to manage, it can readily be split into parts. These parts may even then be promoted to autonomous, separate FSDs, each with its own state index. Communication and synchronization between sister FSMs can be achieved using an activity from one FSD to send an event to its neighbour. Such an interaction could be 'loose' (asynchronous) or 'tightly coupled' (synchronous).

The intention of the finite state method is that each state should represent a uniquely defined moment in the system history. Using auxiliary condition variables, such as flags and counters, clouds this simplicity. 'Pure' finite state methodologists look askance at the use of timers, counters and pass flags. All these undermine the mathematical basis of finite state automata and their provability. But nevertheless, in limited quantities, they are very helpful to the practical programmer.

5.8 Input data and trigger events

Trigger events should not be viewed simply as input data. Rather, a trigger event may result from a logical combination of input data values, the current time and the existence of some internal status condition. This mapping from raw data to event numbers can be problematic for systems designers, and so it may be useful to draw up a table to enumerate the values. This also assists in simplifying the implementation because it identifies the unconditional time out event as common to six states.

At any moment, several potential events could exist, some of which are relevant to the current state, so a prioritization of events may be necessary. One example of this situation occurs when an overriding EXIT or CANCEL button is provided to the system user. Clearly this event should take precedence over the routine events. A question exists as to how long valid events are stored before being recognized or cancelled. Sometimes this issue is dismissed as incompatible with the basic principles of finite state machines. Alternatively, an approach is adopted which samples and prioritizes the events through a software encoder. In practice, incoming data, or even interrupt signals, may get latched by hardware and so stored for a moment until dealt with. As it is often convenient and cheaper, in microcontroller systems, to replace such peripheral hardware facilities with software, it results in the system effectively storing a potential event. How, then, to handle this situation when a pure FSM deals with all events afresh on each scan and dispatch cycle? Note that the Windows event-driven interface does queue events over periods of time, for consideration several times over. We return to this in the next chapter in the discussion of FSM implementation.

5.9 Teas-made

Another simple state-based example is the bedside teamaker, which can wake you up with an audible alarm, turn on the radio and brew a fresh pot of tea. The original equipment manufactured by Goblin relied on electric motors and cam operated switches, but this new high-tech design employs a microcontroller.

Devices: Kettle weight sensor
Teapot weight sensor
Water heater control relay
Radio power control relay
Alert buzzer
Reading light relay
User control panel
with selection buttons

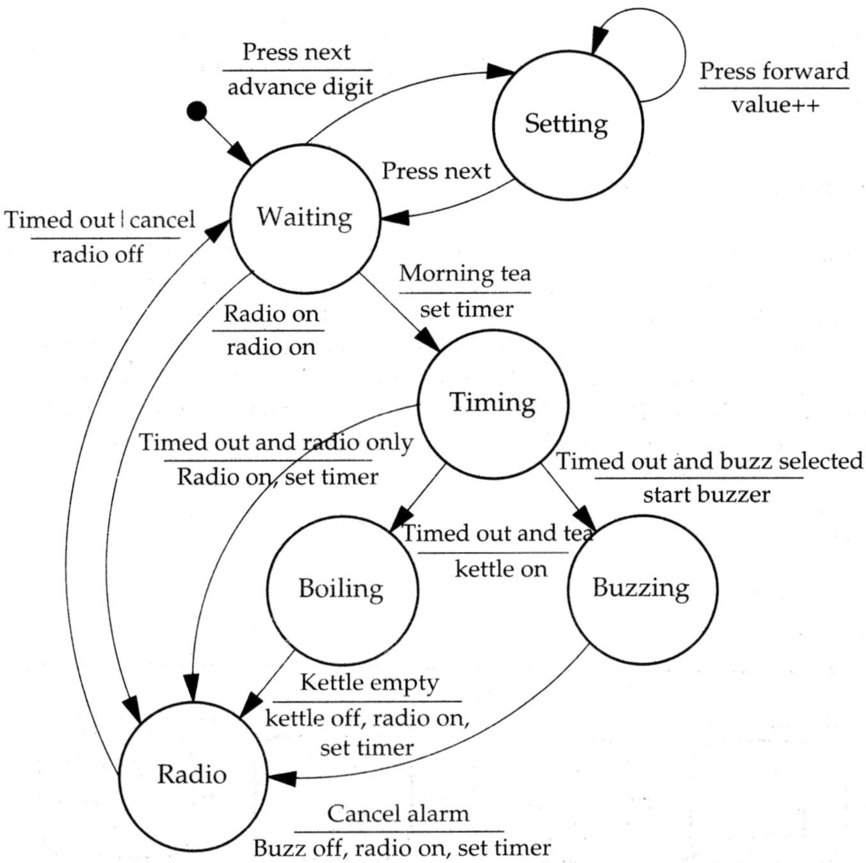

FSD for a Teas-made bedside alarm

The users can arrange to be woken up by either a buzzer, or the radio, with a pot of piping hot, aromatic beverage. The tea is made by forcing boiling water out of the sealed kettle under steam pressure, through a spout into the teapot where tea bags will need to be waiting. After the water has been expelled from the kettle, it is imperative to close off the heating current, or the system will self-destruct. For this safety reason, both the kettle and teapot are position and weight sensed. If no teapot is in position the operation should be cancelled. No heating current is passed if the kettle is empty. The user panel buttons are: TIME SET, ALARM SET, TEA NOW, ALARM ON, SELECT RADIO/BUZZER for ALARM, RADIO ON/OFF, ALARM OFF.

The radio is available at any time. The user may set the alarm time by advancing the alarm display. The alarm can be by buzzer or radio. If the kettle and teapot are prepared and in position, tea will be made when the timer has tripped and the alarm will then sound. If the buzzer is activated it will need to be cancelled manually. The radio will need to be timed out after 30 mins. At some time in the future, an Internet connection may also be demanded.

5.10 Hierarchical state charts

Criticism of FSM as a design tool is often focused on its lack of expressive power when dealing with complex problems. It provides no immediate facilities to handle large systems which would generally be viewed hierarchically, to assist with their progressive decomposition into parts. This enables people to cope with all the low-level details separately. With the introduction of statecharts, David Harel (1987) introduced the concept of nested FSMs, where every state is capable of sequestering another 'internal' FSM.

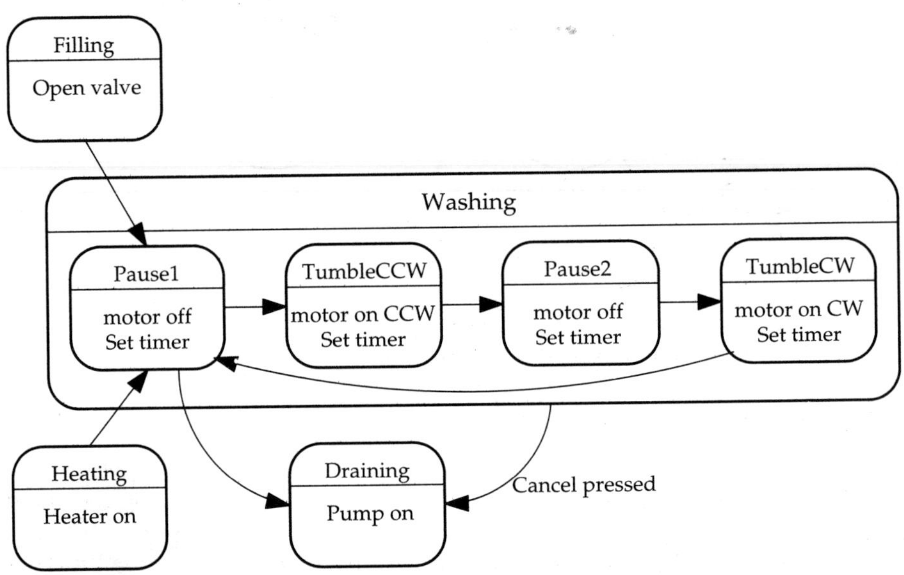

Washing machine as a hierarchical FSD

Now, following the above figure, if the client wants a manual override button to drain the water immediately, whichever of the four washing substates it is in, all that is needed is a single transition arrow coming from the washing superstate. This is then interpreted as originating from all the contained substates, which saves confusing the diagram with repetitive, extra transitions. In the case of a transition onto a superstate, one component substate may be designated as the default start or entry state. In such a situation, where a sub-FSM is hidden inside a superstate, all inward transitions are routed on to the 'initial' substate, and it is not necessary to save the substate index number when leaving the superstate. However, there is also the option of directing incoming transitions back to the same substate from which a superstate exit was last achieved. This is referred to as 'entry with history', and requires the superstate to store its own state index number.

Another example of the application of statecharts is presented below. This involves the sequence of button presses used to set up a digital watch. The NEXT button selects the time or date display, and also moves through the digits when initializing time or alarm values. So a button pressing sequence of NEXT, SET, NEXT, INCR, END would set the display to time, enter

Digital watch buttons

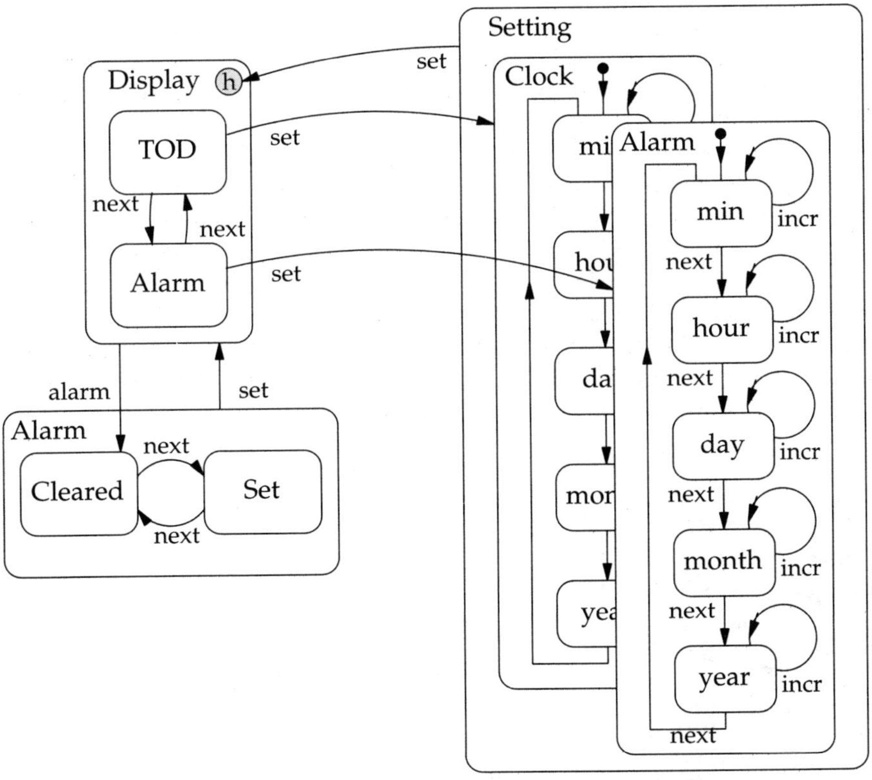

Hierarchical statechart for the digital watch

change time mode, move to the hours digit, advance one hour, for the winter to summer change, and return to the normal mode and time display. An INCR, NEXT, EXIT will toggle the status of the alarm pinger.

The implementation of hierarchical finite state machines is also promoted by Merak Spiv (2002) by using the class inheritance facilities provided by C++ and the constructor/destructor methods to carry out activities which are common to a group of substates held inside a superstate. This does require a non-static treatment of the FSM, using dynamically creating state objects, viewed by some as a more risky style of implementation. Although this might offer a solution in some applications, it does not address the real limitation that finite state diagrams are perfect for expressing detailed cyclic sequences, but much less suitable for expressing broad relationships between system level entities. We will return in Chapter 12 to a discussion of the use of statecharts by UML.

5.11 Concurrent FSMs

As mentioned earlier in Section 5.10, it is quite practicable to model larger systems using several FSMs running in parallel. These mostly act autonomously, accepting their own events and tıansitioning independently of each other. They can also run synchronously, as in a discrete simulation, where all transitions are carried out only when the master clock tick occurs. When implemented on a single CPU computer, parallel FSMs can be run concurrently as independent threads, sharing common dispatch code. Any interaction between the FSMs can be mediated by a shared event, global variables, or by one FSM executing an *action* which causes an *event* in another. Data can also easily be transferred asynchronously by passing it between *data out* and *data in* buffers. The accepted manner of drawing parallel statechart FSMs is shown below. Here there are two FSMs represented on either side of the dashed dividing line. The example below demonstrates the statechart notation for two parallel FSMs.

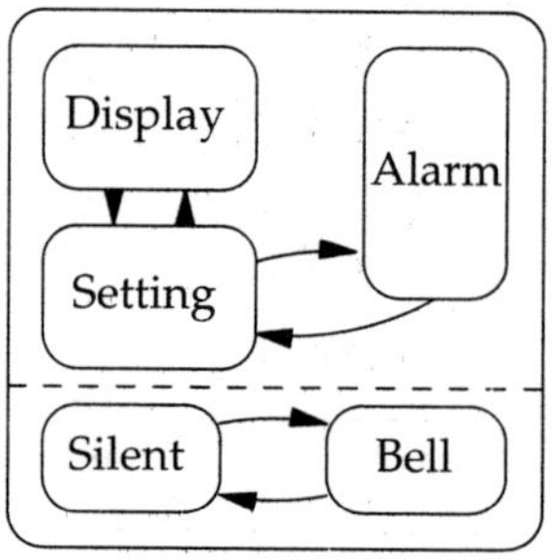

Parallel statecharts

5.12 OO design patterns and state machines

Object-oriented design has always included the use of state transition diagrams as an important technique to specify the full range of dynamic sequences that a system is permitted to follow during run-time. The UML object collaboration diagram, the event diagram, and the sequence diagram also express similar but slightly different views of the system's dynamic activity, and these will be described in more detail in Chapter 14. At a more abstract level, there has been a lot of recent work to identify and reveal the more common software design structures used by programmers. Perhaps unsurprisingly, this has proposed that the event-driven state machine is one of the basic paradigms or *patterns* which can be drawn on for assistance when carrying out an OO design for a real-time application. In the figure below, the state design pattern is expressed using UML, which is described later in Chapter 13. The diagram represents an application class, AppClass, evoking an abstract superclass, aState, which spawns a set of subclasses, one for each system state. This could be seen as a startling departure from the previously presented FSM schemes, especially when it comes to the implementation phase, because the idea of the 'state-as-an-object' could imply a more active responsibility for the individual state within the overall state sequencing process.

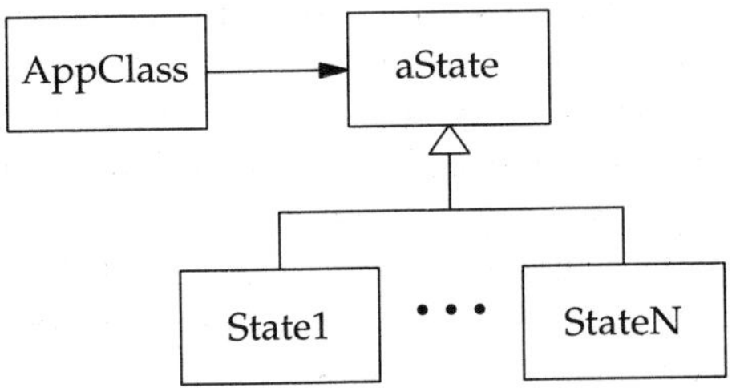

OO state design pattern

5.13 Chapter summary

The Finite State Diagram (FSD) provides a very useful design tool, which offers strong support for system analysis and documentation. After a systems context diagram has been drawn up, FSDs only require system states, transitions and events to be identified by the designer. The focus is on system dynamics rather than data structures. Harel statecharts extend the basic FSD format by supporting a hierarchical capability which enables the finite state method to be applied to much larger systems. Subsequent transformation of FSDs into runnable code is explained in the next chapter.

5.14 Problems and issues for discussion

1. Draw a state diagram for a set of traffic lights controlling a two-way intersection. Start with a simple time dependent system, completely blind to the traffic flows. Deal with the timer as if it were an external device, even though it may eventually be implemented in software. Next, include trigger events from vehicle sensors. Finally, impose time delays to prevent one direction hogging the intersection.

2a. Draw up a context diagram for a ticket issuing, pay-and-display parking machine. List input and output devices, taking care to identify the system perimeter with respect to the central microcontroller rather than the metal cabinet.

2b. Progress the pay-and-display design to a full finite state diagram. Start by imagining a motorist walking up to a machine to buy a ticket. List the actions required, in the correct order, and propose the states which the machine has to go through in order to complete the transaction. Assume the coins are validated by a autonomous device which relays the value of current cash accepted back to the main microcontroller.

3. Draw up a context diagram and FSD for a familiar piece of domestic equipment, such as a microwave oven, a minidisc player, a VCR or a breadmaking machine.
4. The vehicle detector discussed earlier in this chapter, and illustrated on p. 100, can be equipped with extra facilities to make it operationally more robust. For example, one induction loop may occasionally stop working. Normally you would expect an identical number of detection events from loop A and loop B. By keeping a count of the detection events, loop A incrementing and loop B decrementing, it is possible to use this count to set a discrepancy threshold, say ± 5, and then fail over to a backup mode of operating with only events from the active loop incrementing the count c. Insert the new Actions (inc/dec/reset ev_count) onto the FSD.
5. Draw up a full context diagram for the Teas-made equipment, defining all the input sensors and output actuators. Modify the FSD to include the facility to delay the tea until the alarm has gone off and 2 minutes have passed. A manual 'tea now' button might be useful, so insert this facility, too.
6. Translate the Teas-made FSM into Harel statecharts, using the facilities of hierarchical decomposition and expression.
7. Install the FSKC case tool on Linux for generating table-based FSMs in C code. Use the tool to build the washing machine simulator (p. 99).
8. Consider this FSD for a burglar alarm system and describe its operation to a friend after amending the system so that the alarm will time out after 15 minutes.

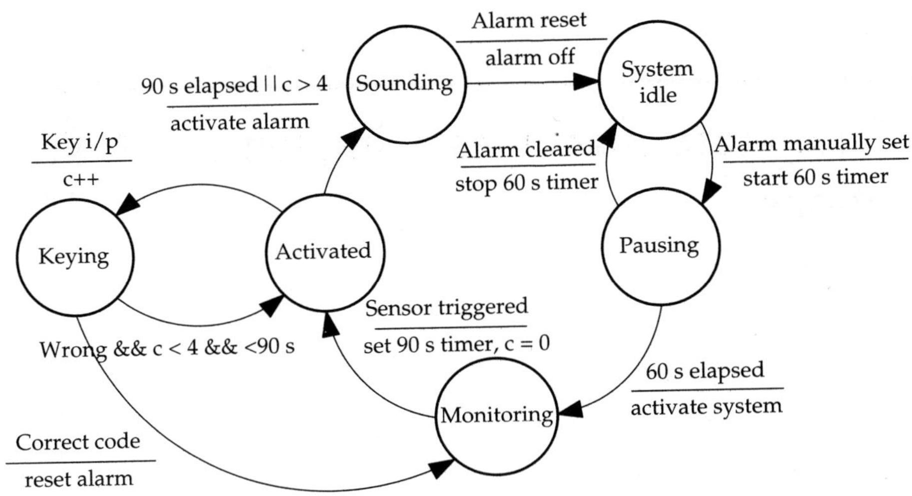

5.15 Suggestions for reading

Cureington, J. (2001). Finite State Kernel Creator (FSKC). From: tonyc@acm.org

Douglass, B. (2004). *Real Time UML*. Addison Wesley.

Harel, D. (1987). Statecharts: a visual formalism for complex systems. *Sci. Comp. Prog.*, 8, 231–274.

Harel, D. & Naamas, A. (1996). The STATEMATE semantics of statecharts. *ACM Trans. on SWEng. & Method.*, 5/4, Oct 1996, 293–333.

Shaw, A. (2001). *Real-time Systems and Software*. Wiley.

Chapter 6

Finite state machines – implementation options

6.1 Chapter overview

In the previous chapter, the use of Finite State Diagrams (FSD) for designing computer systems was presented. Here, a variety of alternative transformation techniques for obtaining runnable code from an FSD will be described. An example application for the recommended Finite State Table (FST) implementation technique is presented in greater detail.

6.2 Implementing an FSD

The FSM design method is readily understood and quite easily transformed into software for implementation. The five principal approaches for carrying out this transformation are listed below. These will now be presented in code form using the simulation of an electric toaster as an exemplar case study.

- Sequential code
- Multiple SWITCH-CASE
- GOTOand labels
- FST: Finite State Table method
- Object-oriented design pattern with dynamic states

Implementation techniques for FSDs

A crucial distinction depends on the way that input data and events are monitored and recorded. The first two techniques often employ simple blocking reads, holding the thread of execution while waiting for the expected input or status change. Such an approach may not always be compatible with the demands of system enhancement and maintenance.

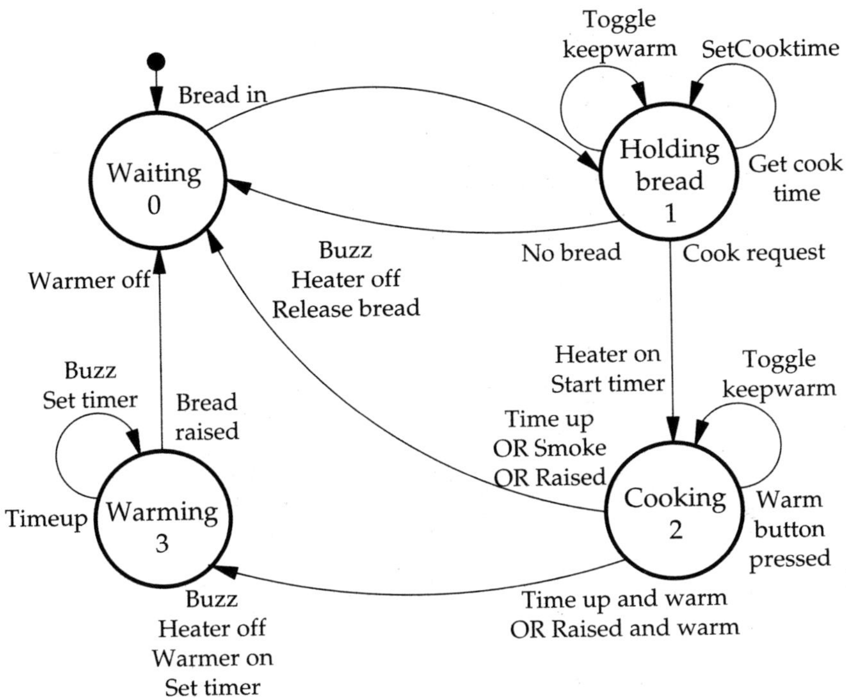

Finite state diagram for the toaster

During implementation, one of the biggest dangers to be avoided is becoming blocked within a transition action due to unsuccessful I/O or an overlong algorithm. This would lead to the system stalling, deadlocked until the action completes. During such intervals some polled input data could be missed, and certainly a user would detect a general drop in system responsiveness. A highly unwelcome circumstance where several input channels need to be scanned for events.

6.3 Implementation by direct sequential coding

The first FSD implementation method requires the program to follow closely the FSD topology. Initially this might appear reasonably straightforward, but by simply following the network of transitions the code can get quite intricate. This is especially true when relying on the IF-ELSE and WHILE statements from a block structured language. You may even feel the need to deploy an occasional GOTO, or resort to code replication to solve the coding challenge. Deriving C code directly from an FSD can be tricky. Similarly, when coding with block structured high-level languages, structure charts are much easier to follow that flowcharts. But whereas structure charts may readily be transformed into finite state diagrams, the reverse is not always

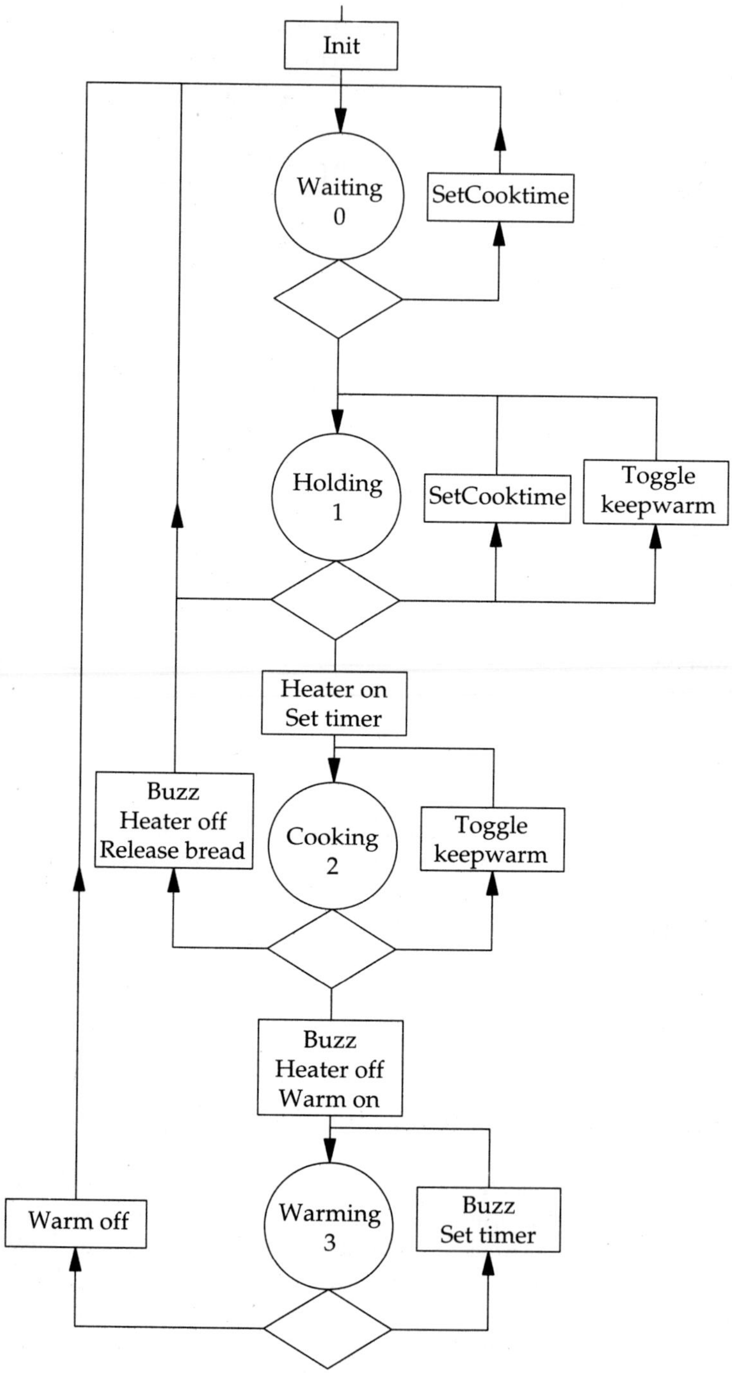

Algorithmic state machine for a toaster

so easy. Structure charts can be seen as one dimensional, whereas finite state diagrams offer more of a two-dimensional capability. This is implemented by using a tree diagram to express the structure chart as opposed to an arc/node network for the finite state diagram. To assist with the translation, you might find it helpful to convert your original FSD into a pseudo-flowchart, called an Algorithmic State Machine (ASM) as shown opposite.

Implementing the toaster directly in C, if you are able to manage it, could look as follows:

```
/* toaster1.c, direct sequential coding of FSD for Linux
   implementation*/

#include <stdio.h>
#include <ctype.h>
#include <ncurses.h>
#include <sys/times.h>
#include <unistd.h>
```

Link to libncurses.so library:
gcc toaster1.c -incurses -otoaster1

```
#define PrintWAITING printf("WAITING 0, Cook time=%2d secs \r",
#cooktime)
#define PrintHOLDING printf("HOLDING 1, Cook time=%2d secs,
#Warming %s, \r", \ cooktime,(warm)?"ON":"OFF")
#define PrintCOOKING printf("COOKING 2, Warming %s, time=%3.1d
#\r", (warm)?" ON": "OFF", \ (delay-times(&n))/tps)
#define PrintWARMING printf("WARMING 3 \r")
#define BREADIN 'B'
#define BREADUP 'N'
#define RELEASE 'R'
#define WARMTOGGLE 'T'
#define COOKRQ 'C'
#define BUZZTIME 5

main() {
clock_t delay, cooktime=1;
struct tms n;
int key = '0';
unsigned int warm = 0;
unsigned int tps;

initscr();
cbreak();
nodelay(stdscr, TRUE);
tps = sysconf(_SC_CLK_TCK);                    // ticks per second
```

Initialize screen and
keyboard handling
to prevent blocking
on read using Unix
curses library

```
while (1) {
      do {
            do {
              putchar('\n');
```

```
                do {
                        if (isdigit(key)) cooktime = (key - '0');
                        PrintWAITING;                         //State 0
                        key = getch();
                  } while (toupper(key) != BREADIN);

                putchar('\n');
                do {
                        if (isdigit(key)) cooktime = (key - '0');
                        if (key==WARMTOGGLE) warm=!warm;
                        PrintHOLDING;
                        key = toupper(getch());               //State 1
                } while (key!=COOKRQ && key!=BREADUP);
        } while (key != COOKRQ);
        printf("\nheater turned on\n");
        delay = times(&n) + cooktime*tps;
        do {
                if (key == WARMTOGGLE) warm = !warm;
                PrintCOOKING;
                key = toupper(getch());
        } while ((delay > times(&n)) && (key!=RELEASE));
                                                              //State 2
    } while (!warm);
    putchar('\n');
    do {
        putchar('\007');
        delay = times(&n) + BUZZTIME*tps;
        do {
                PrintWARMING;
        } while (delay > times(&n));                          //State 3
    } while (toupper(getch())!=RELEASE);
  }
}
```

6.4 THE **SWITCH-CASE** IMPLEMENTATION MODEL

Another very common method for implementing FSMs depends heavily on the SWITCH-CASE statement to deal with state selection by using the state number as a switch index. It is popular with programmers and also used by automatic code generators, including the case of hardware specification languages, such as VHDL. In this way, the execution thread is steered into whichever `case` arm has code for that particular state. Here it may wait, either in a tight spin polling loop, or by sleeping, for a relevant event which is checked and then serves to select the correct transition activity and the next state index value. In the toaster example which follows, the main `while(FOREVER)` loop runs continuously, checking for keyboard input and delay timeouts. These events are then used in the `if-elseif` chains to select the next state value and call action functions when required. Although popular, this method does suffer from the disadvantage of requiring a complete rework for each application, not much code can be transferred across to a new project. The equivalent structure chart can also be viewed, as a curiosity, on p. 118.

```
/* toaster2.c, a keyboard/screen simulation using Linux timing &
   I/O Implemented using switch/case with centralised input
   scanning
*/
#include <stdio.h>
#include <ctype.h>
#include <ncurses.h>  // compile with: gcc toaster2.c -lncurses
                      // -otoaster2
#include <sys/times.h>
#include <unistd.h>

#define FOREVER 1
#define COOKRQ 'C'
#define BREADIN 'B'
#define BREADUP 'N'
#define RELEASE 'R'
#define WARMTOGGLE 'T'
#define BUZZTIME 5
```

The FSM events are simulated by simple keyboard input

```
#define WAITING 0
#define HOLDING 1
#define COOKING 2
#define WARMING 3

unsigned int events, state, state_events;
clock_t cooktime, targettick;
struct tms n;
int keep_warm;
unsigned int ccount, tps;
int key;

void wait() {
      printf("Waiting\n\r");
}
void hold() {
      printf("Holding bread\n\r");
}
void cook() {
      printf("Heater on full, set delay for cooking time\n\r");
```

The FSM activities are generally reduced to basic printf output in this simulation

```
      printf("Cooking toast for %d secs\n\r", cooktime);
      targettick = times(&n) + cooktime*tps; // setting cooking
                                              // period
}
void warm() {
      printf("\07 \07 \07 Buzz, Heater on half, set delay for
        buzz\n\r");
      targettick = times(&n) + BUZZTIME*tps; // 5sec interval on
                                              // buzzer
      printf("Toast ready and warming\n\r");
}

void off() {
      printf("\007 \007 \007 Buzz, Timer off, Heater Off\n\r");
      printf("Toast ready\n\r");
}
void buzz() {
      printf("\007 \007 \007 BUZZ, BUZZ, Warming, set delay for
        next buzz\n\r");
      targettick = times(&n) + BUZZTIME*tps; // 5sec interval
                                              // on buzzer
}
void setcooktime() }
      cooktime = key - '0';
      printf("\ncooking time set to %d secs\n\r", cooktime);
}
void toggle() {
      keep_warm = !keep_warm;
      printf("\ntoggle warming status to %s\n\r", (keep_warm ?
        "ON":"OFF"));
}
main() {
      state = 0;
      printf("\n\n");
      initscr();
      cbreak();
      nodelay(stdscr, TRUE);
      tps = sysconf(_SC_CLK_TCK);
while (FOREVER) {
      key = 0;
      key = toupper(getch());
      printf("State = %2d \r",state);
switch (state) {
  case WAITING:
      if (key == BREADIN) {
            state = HOLDING;
      }
```

Continual looping

I/O carried out above the FSM switch-case

```
      else if (isdigit(key) ){
            setcooktime();
      }
      else if (key == WARMTOGGLE) {
            toggle();
      }
  break;
  case HOLDING:
      if (key == BREADUP) {
            state = WAITING;
      }
      else if (isdigit(key) ){
            setcooktime();
      }
      else if (key == WARMTOGGLE) {
            toggle();
      }
      else if (key == COOKRQ) {
            cook();
            state = COOKING;
      }
  break;
  case COOKING:
      if (key == WARMTOGGLE) {
            toggle();
            break;
      }
      if ( targettick < times(&n) || key == BREADUP) {
            off();
            if (keep_warm) {
                  warm();
                  state = WARMING;
            } else {
                  state = WAITING;
            }
      }
  break;
  case WARMING:
      if ( targettick < times(&n) ){
            buzz();
      }
      if(key == RELEASE) {
            off();
            state = WAITING;
      }
  break;
} } }
```

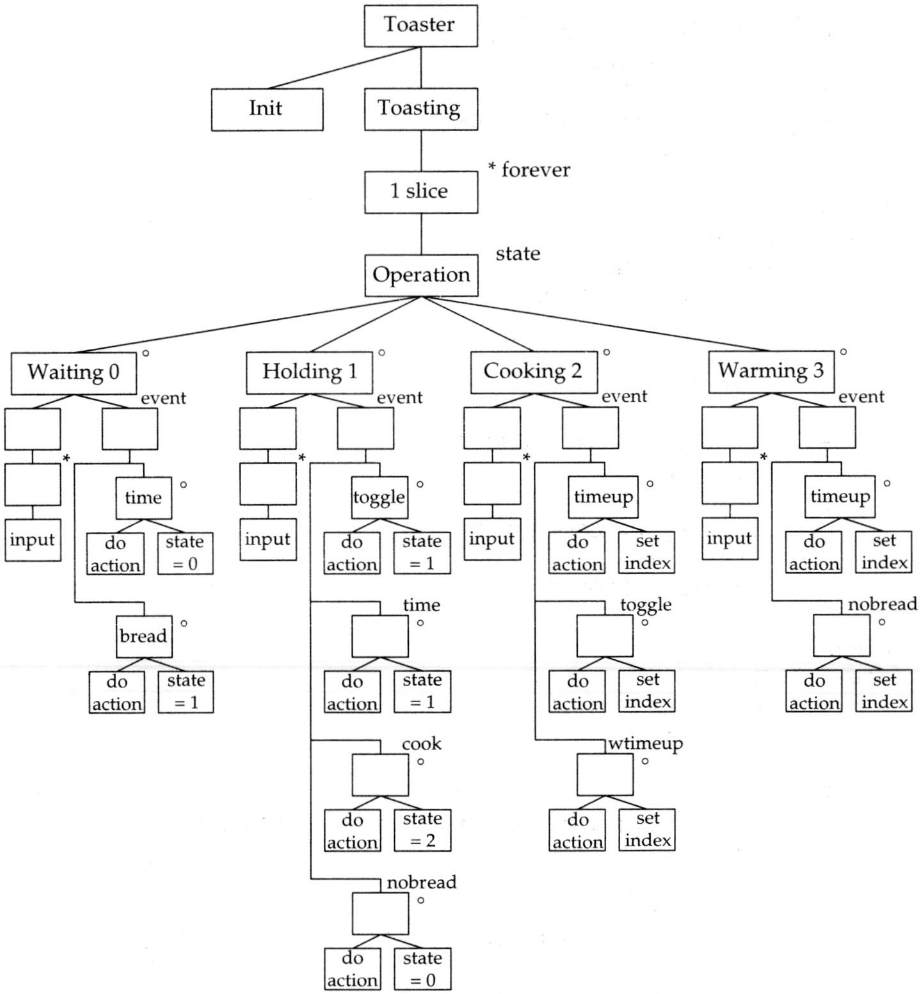

Structure chart equivalent for the toaster FSD

6.5 The **GOTO/LABEL** implementation model

Many HLL purists would deride this suggestion unmercifully because of its dependence on the dreaded `GOTO` instruction. But it is actually quite neat and easy to carry out, whatever the complexity of the FSM.

```
/* toaster3.c, a keyboard/screen simulation for Linux timing &
 * i/o. Implemented using goto/label jump structure
*/
#include <stdio.h>
```

```
#include <ncurses.h>        //link to libcurses.so: gcc toaster3.c
                            //-lncurses -otoastie
#include <sys/times.h>
#include <unistd.h>


#define COOKRQ 'C'
#define BREADIN 'B'
#define BREADUP 'N'
#define RELEASE 'R'
#define WARMTOGGLE 'T'
#define BUZZTIME 5


clock_t targettick, cooktime;
struct tms n;
int keep_warm = ~0;
int key, tps;

void wait() {
printf("Waiting \n\r");
}
void hold() {
  printf("Holding bread \n\r");
}
void cook() {
  printf("Heater on full, set delay for cooking time\n\r");
  printf("Cooking toast for %d secs\r\n", cooktime);
  targettick = times(&n) + cooktime*tps;  // setting cooking
                                          // period
}
void warm() {
  printf("Buzz, Heater on half, set delay for buzz\n\r");
  printf("Toast ready and warming\n\r");
  targettick = times(&n) + BUZZTIME*tps;  // 5sec interval on
                                          // buzzer
}
void off() {
  printf("Buzz, Timer off, Heater Off\n\r");
  printf("Toast ready and cooling\n\r");
}
void buzz() {
  targettick = times(&n) + BUZZTIME*tps;  // 5sec interval on
                                          // buzzer
  putchar('\007');
}
void setcooktime() {
  cooktime = key - '0';
  targettick = times(&n) + cooktime*tps;
  printf("\ncooking time set to %d secs\n\r", cooktime);
}
```

```
void toggle() {
  keep_warm = !keep_warm;
  printf("\ntoggle warming status to %s\n\r", (keep_warm ? "ON":
  "OFF"));
}
main() {
struct tms n;


      initscr();
      cbreak();
      nodelay(stdscr, TRUE);
      noecho();
      tps = sysconf(_SC_CLK_TCK);
```

I/O carried out within the application code – leads to difficulties

```
Waiting:
printf("WAITING 0   \r");
      key = toupper(getch());
      if (key == BREADIN) {
            hold();
            goto Holding;
      }
      if (isdigit(key)) {
            setcooktime();
      }
      goto Waiting;

Holding:
printf("HOLDING 1, Warming is %s \r", (keep_warm) ? "ON":"OFF");
      key = toupper(getch());
      if (key == BREADUP) {
            wait();
            goto Waiting;
      }
      if (key == COOKRQ) {
            cook();
            goto Cooking;
      }
      if (key == WARMTOGGLE) keep_warm = ~keep_warm;
      if (isdigit(key)) setcooktime();
      goto Holding;
Cooking:
printf("COOKING 2     \r");
      key = toupper(getch());
      if ( (targettick < times(&n)) || (key == RELEASE)) {
            if (keep_warm) {
                  warm();
                  goto Warming;
            } else {
                  off();
```

```
                    goto Waiting;
              }
        }
        if (key == WARMTOGGLE) {
            toggle();
        }
        goto Cooking;
Warming:
printf("WARMING 3    \r");
        if (targettick > times(&n)) {
          key = getch();
          if (toupper(key) == RELEASE) {
              off();
              goto Waiting;
           }
         } else {
           buzz();
         }
        goto Warming;
}
```

6.6 FST implementation model

The most interesting implementation method, offering most flexibility and good maintainability, uses a state transition table or Finite State Table (FST). The core of this technique is a two-dimensional table, with states and events indexing the columns and rows. The FST cells indicate whether an event may trigger a transition from the associated state. Not all events are recognized by all states, and not all interstate transitions are valid. State tables are usually sparsely populated. The active cells hold the destination state number for the transition, and the associated activity, if any. This leads to a criticism that a large part of most state tables is functionally irrelevant, only indicating *illegal* transitions. But these unused transition cells do enable future revisions to be easily inserted, and anyway, where memory is tight, the FSTs can be stored in ROM which generally is less precious than RAM. Another interesting aspect of finite state systems is the manner in which they

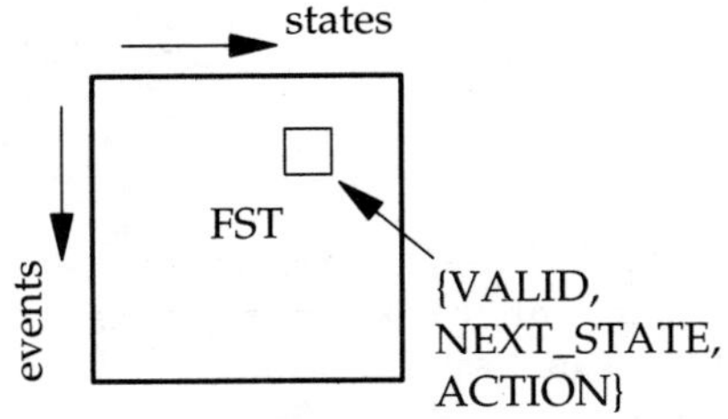

Finite state table layout

maintain a model of the real world. Conventional computer programs step through a sequence of instructions, shadowing, or simulating, changes in the world, moment by moment. The current position of the model is held by the CPU program counter and the program code itself simulates the world. With finite state systems, it can be very different. If the implementation involves a state transition table, the code is no more than a dispatcher, concerned with routine operations. The state model is held in a data structure not in a sequence of code. The running position of the model is held in the state index variable, not the CPU program counter. This arrangement means that the basic code structure can be used again and again within different applications. The toaster example implemented in C using the FST method is presented next.

Before the FST coding can start each state and each trigger event must be assigned unique identifier *numbers.* These will act as index values into the finite state table, and so for C they must run from 0. When an input takes place, it enables the associated trigger event value, and in this way, the coding of the state dispatcher becomes quite straightforward. The FST method normally implements input polling in non-blocking format to allow for several concurrent activities to be sustained.

```
/* toaster4.c, a keyboard/screen simulation using Linux timing
   Implemented using FST with table dispatcher.
*/
#include <stdio.h>
#include <ctype.h>
#include <ncurses.h>              //compile: gcc -lncurses toaster4.c
#include <sys/times.h>
#include <unistd.h>
#define STATESX 4                 // number of states
#define EVENTSX 9                 // number of distinct events
#define BUZZTIME 150
                                  // definition of event flags
#define BREADIN 0x01              //event 0
#define NOBREAD 0x02              //event 1
#define COOKREQUEST 0x04          //event 2
#define TIMEUP 0x08               //event 3
#define SMOKE 0x10                //event 4
#define TIMEUPWARM 0x20           //event 5
#define RELEASE 0x40              //event 6
#define COOKTIME 0x80             //event 7
#define PRINTdebug \r")
      printf("current_tick=%d cook_time=%d keep_warm=%d state=%d
             events=%x event=%d\r",\ current_tick, cook_time,
             keep_warm, state, events, last_event);
unsigned int events, state, state_events;
clock_t cook_time, current_tick, next_tick;
struct tms n;
```

```
unsigned int tps, target_count = 0;
unsigned int keep_warm, key, fcount, scount;

void wait() {
  printf("Waiting for bread\n\r");
}

void hold() {
  printf("Bread ready in slot\n\r");
}

void cook() {
  printf("Heater on full, set delay for cooking time\n\r");
  printf("Cooking toast for %d secs\n\r", cook_time);
  target_count = scount + cook_time*50;//setting cooking period
}

void warm() {
  printf("\07 \07 \07 Buzz, Heater on half, set delay for
    buzz\n\r");
  target_count = scount + BUZZTIME;     // 5sec interval on
                                           buzzer
  printf("Toast cooked and warming\n\r");
}

void off() {
  printf("\07 \07 \07 Buzz, Timer off, Heater Off\n\r");
  target_count = 0;
  printf("Toast ready and cooling\n\r");
}

void buzz() {
  printf("\07 \07 \07 BUZZ, BUZZ, and set delay for next
    buzz\n\r");
  target_count = scount + BUZZTIME;     // 5sec interval on
                                           buzzer
}

void sct() {
  cook_time = key - '0';
  printf("\ncooking time set to %d secs\n\r", cook_time);
}

void togg() {
  keep_warm = !keep_warm;
  printf("\ntoggle warming status to %s\n\r", (keep_warm ? "ON":"OFF"));
}
```

```
void null() { }
typedef void (*TPT)();

struct state_table {
unsigned int active;
unsigned int next_state;
TPT action;
} state_table[EVENTSX][STATESX] = {

// Waiting      Holding       Cooking       Warming       // Events
{ {1,1,null}, {0,1,null}, {0,2,null}, {0,3,null} },//0 Bread
{ {0,0,null}, {1,0,null}, {0,2,null}, {0,3,null} },//1 Removed
{ {0,0,null}, {1,2,cook}, {0,2,null}, {0,3,null} },//2 Cook
{ {0,0,null}, {0,1,null}, {1,0,off }, {1,3,buzz} },//3 Timeup
{ {0,0,null}, {0,1,null}, {1,0,off }, {0,3,null} },//4 Smoke
{ {0,0,null}, {0,1,null}, {1,3,warm}, {1,3,buzz} },//5 TimeWar
{ {0,0,null}, {0,1,null}, {0,2,null}, {1,0,off } },//6 Release
{ {1,0,sct }, {1,1,sct }, {0,2,null}, {0,3,null} },//7 CookTim
{ {0,0,null}, {1,1,togg}, {1,2,togg}, {0,3,null} },//8 Togglewarm
};

/* getmask, builds an event bit mask for a state from the FST
*  enabling the dispatcher to eliminate irrelevant events
*/
unsigned int getmask(unsigned int staten) {
   unsigned int mask=0;
   int i;
   for(i = EVENTSX-1; i >= 0; i--) {
      mask <<=1;
      mask |= state_table[i][staten].active;
   }
return mask;
}

/* geteventn, using the current state's event mask to select
 * only relevant events it then identifies the active event
 * with the highest priority, returning its number
*/
unsigned int geteventn() {
 unsigned int i, bitmask = 1;
 state_events = events & getmask(state);
 for(i=0; i < EVENTSX; i++) {
     if (state_events & bitmask) {     //mask out irrelevant
                                       //events
        events &= ~bitmask;            //cancel selected event
                                       //flag
        return i;
     }
```

```
      bitmask <<= 1;
 }
return ~0;
}

main() {
unsigned int last_state, event, last_event=0;
                                             // Initialization
                                             // code

scount = 0;
fcount = 0;
initscr();
cbreak();
nodelay(stdscr, TRUE);
tps = sysconf(_SC_CLK_TCK);

do {
     next_tick = times(&n) + tps/100;
     scount++;                              // cycle count, 50 Hz,
                                            // every 20ms

                                            // slow cyclic scanner
                                            // section
key = 0;
if ((key = getch()) != -1) {
                                            // slow laundry
                                            // Set event flags from
                                            // data etc
    key = toupper(key);
    if (key == 'W') keep_warm = ~keep_warm;
    if ( (key >= '0') && (key <= '9') ) events | = COOKTIME;
    if (key == 'B')  events | = BREADIN;
    if (key == 'N') {events | = NOBREAD; events &= ~BREADIN;}
    if (key == 'C')  events | = COOKREQUEST;
    if (key == 'S')  events | =, SMOKE;
    if (key == 'R')  events | = RELEASE;
}
if (target_count) {
        if (target_count < scount) {
               if (keep_warm ) events |= TIMEUPWARM;
               else            events |= TIMEUP;
        }
}
                                            // slow debug output
                                            // section

                                            // fast scanner section
do {
    fcount++;
```

```
                                            // fast laundry
                                            // Set event flags from
                                            // fast data
/* if (somethingfast) events |= fasteventflag; */

   PRINTdebug;                              // fast debug output
                                            // section

   current_tick = times(&n);
} while ( next_tick > current_tick);
                                            // periodic dispatcher
if ( (event = geteventn()) != ~0 ) {
    last_event = event;
    last_state = state;
    (*(state_table[event][state].action))();      // transition
                                                  // ACTION
    state = state_table[event][state].next_state;// Get next
                                                    state
    if(state != last_state) events = 0;           // Clear event
                                                  // flags
    }                                             // if change
                                                  // of state
  } while (key != 'Q');
endwin();
} //main
```

It is important to recognize that within each state, the events are implicitly given relative priorities so that when two events occur simultaneously, the outcome is predictable. The functions `getmask()` and `geteventn()` are responsible for building the current state event mask and using it to select an active event to trigger the next transition. With the structure of the FST presented in the toaster4.c example, the higher priority events are positioned at the top of the table, and the lower priority events towards the bottom, because `geteventn()` always scans from top to bottom. Each state can have its events ordered correctly, within the constraint of the needs of other states which may be using the same events, such as 'timeout'. If a clash of relative priorities does occur, the solution is to duplicate the event, relabel the new version, and extend the table to include the new row.

Dealing with a variety of input data and status changes from a variety of sources can be tricky for the programmer. The simplest solution is to collect all the afferent data, check and identify them and then enter the FSM dispatcher with the current state number and a single event number as indices for the FST. The transformation from a confusing mishmash of input data, interrupt event flags and timer/counter values, into an array of event flags, is represented as the Event Laundry.

The event laundry is situated in the main loop just after the input polling code. It assembles all the relevant information and updates the event flag

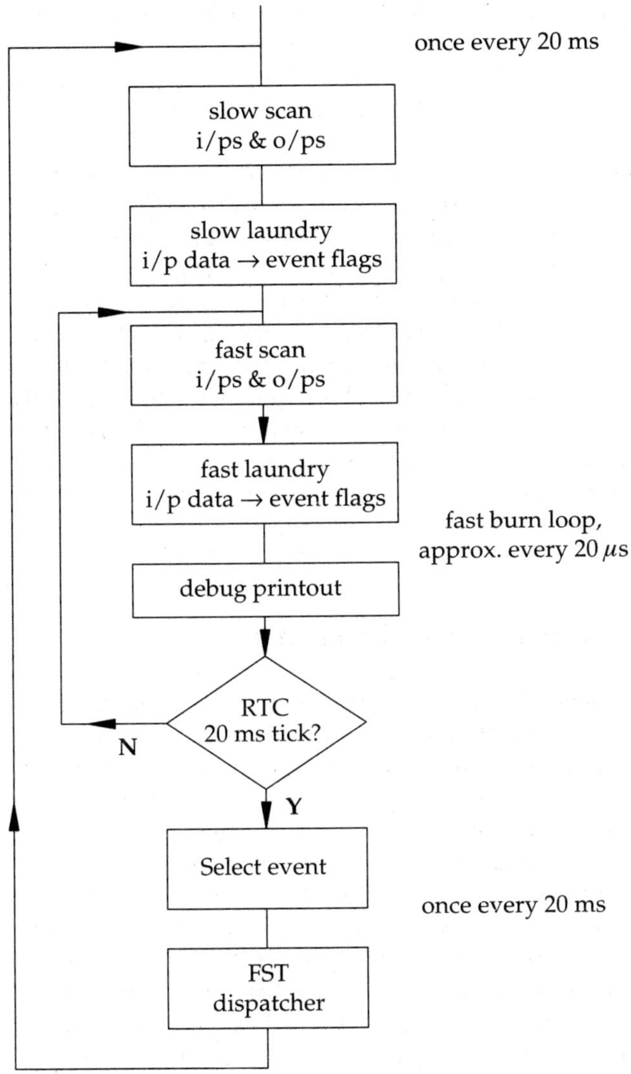

Functional arrangement for the FST implementation

array to indicate clearly which events are active. Then a current state bit mask is built to select only those events which are relevant to the current state. After which, the highest priority event is found and its number registered.

It is also preferable to enter the state dispatcher section at fixed time intervals. This will give the appearance of a steady performance even when extra actions or trigger events are added to the scheme. The rate can be selected to fit in with the application under development: 10 Hz for keypad operation, 1000 Hz for serial line, 0.1 Hz for a washing machine. A burn loop should be employed. with periodic checks on a hardware tick.

Debugging code can also usefully be inserted in the burn loop to wait for a single-stepping key, or just print out the current state, input values and event numbers.

Because the FSM analysis is limited to a single process, while implementations frequently involve many processes, several independent FSMs can be interlinked and all exercised by the same Finite State Engine (FSE). This is pursued further in Section 6.10. Dispatcher code can readily be evoked with different {table, state, event} tuples. Two different approaches can be adopted for handling multiple FSM designs: flat or hierarchical. The former exposes all the FSMs side by side, intercommunicating through an activity on FSM_1 triggering an event on FSM_2. The FSM are quasi-independent, only interacting through the loose coupling of an occasional event exchange. The latter scheme of hierarchically embedding FSMs within states, as advocated by David Harel and exploited in the StateMate system, is more complex, perhaps too complex for normal usage.

6.7 An object-oriented approach to implementation

The last of the five implementation methods will now be presented. When following an OO approach to FSM design and implementation, there is the option of taking a traditional route which means encapsulating all the details of each FSM within a single class, and using a `switch-case` or state table to implement the sequencing using a local method. This is a *static* approach. But alternatively there is a much more interesting *dynamic* approach to handling an FSM. In this case, each state is represented by a distinct class, supplied with the necessary activity methods and transition data. The UML state design pattern, p. 107, suggests that each state should be represented by sister substates derived from a single abstract superstate in order to achieve the maximum separation and encapsulation. Although this pattern is acknowledged as elegant and efficient to run, it is a bit of a mess to implement, and is not capable of supporting hierarchical expression. State methods cannot access the attributes belonging to the application context using the implicit `this` pointer, which reduces the effectiveness of data encapsulation. The addition of new states requires a change to the subclassing and the addition of new events requires adding new methods to the common interface. An implementation of the toaster in object-oriented C++ is presented next.

```
/* toaster5.cc, a keyboard/screen simulation using Linux timing
   Implemented in C++ using FSM patterns
*/
// Purpose. State design pattern versus table-driven approach
//
```

```
// Intent. Allow an object to alter its behavior when its
// internal state changes. The object will appear to change
// its class.
//
//
#include <errno.h>
#include <stdio.h>          //needed for non-blocking kbd input
#include <sys/ioctl.h>
#include <sys/termios.h>
#include <unistd.h>
#include <string.h>
#include <sys/times.h>

#include <unistd.h>
#include <ctype.h>
#include <iostream>
#define BUZZTIME 5
#define TIMEOUT -1
using namespace std;
unsigned int targettick, cooktime, tps;
int sindex;

class FSM;
// State base class. Implements default behavior for all its
   methods.
class FSMstate {  // Could be: empty implementation, or error
  message.
public:
  virtual void breadin  { cout << "ano state change\r" << endl;}
    (FSM*)
  virtual void breadup  { cout << "bno state change\r" << endl;}
    (FSM*)
  virtual void release  { cout << "cno state change\r" << endl;}
    (FSM*)
  virtual void          { cout << "dno state change\r" << endl;}
    warmtoggle (FSM*)
  virtual void cookrq   { cout << "eno state change\r" << endl;}
    (FSM*)
  virtual void settime  { cout << "fno state change\r" << endl;}
    (FSM*, int)
  virtual void timeup   { cout << "gno state change\r" << endl;}
    (FSM*)
  virtual void timeupW  { cout << "eno state change\r" << endl;}
    (FSM*)
protected:
  void changeState( FSM*, FSMstate* );
  void changeWarmState(FSM*);
  void changeTimeState(FSM*, int);
  void setTimer(FSM*);
  void clearTimer(FSM*);
```

```
  int getcookTime(FSM*);
  int getwarmState(FSM*);
};

// State machine. Reproduces the State interface, and delegates all
// behavior to the State derived class private data member.
class FSM {
public:
   FSM();
   void breadin()       { _state->breadin(this); }
   void release()       { _state->release(this); }
   void warmtoggle()    { _state->warmtoggle(this); }
   void cookrq()        { _state->cookrq(this); }
   void settime(int t)  { _state->settime(this, t); }
   void timeup()        { _state->timeup(this); }
   void timeupW()       { _state->timeupW(this);}
   int getTarget()      { return targettime; }
   int getcookTime()    { return cooktime; }
   int getwarmState()   { return WARMstate; }
private:
   friend class FSMstate;
   FSMstate* _state;
   int WARMstate ;
   int cooktime ;
   int targettime;
   void setTimer() {
      struct tms n;
      targettime = times(&n) + cooktime*tps;
    }
   void clearTimer() {
      targettime = -1;
    }
   void changeState( FSMstate* s ) {
      _state = s;
  }
  void changeWarmState() {
     WARMstate = ~WARMstate;
     cout<< (WARMstate&01)<<" ";
  }
  void changeTimeState(int t){
     cooktime = t;
     cout << "cooktime= " << cooktime << endl;
  }
};
void FSMstate::changeState( FSM* fsm, FSMstate* s ) {
   fsm->changeState( s );
}
void FSMstate::changeTimeState( FSM* fsm, int t) {
   fsm->changeTimeState(t);
}
```

```
void FSMstate::changeWarmState( FSM* fsm) {
   fsm->changeWarmState();
}
int FSMstate::getwarmState( FSM* fsm) {
   fsm->getwarmState();
}
void FSMstate::setTimer( FSM* fsm) }
   fsm->setTimer();
}
void FSMstate::clearTimer( FSM* fsm) }
   fsm->clearTimer();
}
int FSMstate::getcookTime( FSM* fsm) {
   fsm->getcookTime();
}
// State derived class. Each state overrides only the messages
// it responds to.
class Waiting : public FSMstate {
public:
   static FSMstate* instance() {
      if ( ! _instance ) _instance = new Waiting;
      return _instance;
   };
   virtual void settime( FSM*, int t);
   virtual void breadin( FSM* );
   virtual void warmtoggle( FSM* );
private:
   static FSMstate* _instance;
};
FSMstate* Waiting::_instance = 0;

class Holding: public FSMstate {
public:
   static FSMstate* instance() {
      if ( ! _instance ) _instance = new Holding;
      return _instance;
   };
   virtual void settime( FSM*, int );
   virtual void warmtoggle( FSM* );
   virtual void release( FSM* );
   virtual void cookrq( FSM* );
private:
   static FSMstate* _instance;
};
FSMstate* Holding::_instance = 0;

class Cooking : public FSMstate {
public:
   static FSMstate* instance() {
      if ( ! _instance ) _instance = new Cooking;
```

```
      return _instance;
   };
   virtual void release( FSM* );
   virtual void timeup( FSM* );
   virtual void timeupW( FSM* );
   virtual void warmtoggle( FSM* );
   virtual void settime( FSM*, int);
private:
   static FSMstate* _instance;
};
FSMstate* Cooking::_instance = 0;

class Warming: public FSMstate {
public:
   static FSMstate* instance() {
      if ( ! _instance ) _instance = new Warming;
      return _instance;
   };
   virtual void release( FSM* );
   virtual void timeupW( FSM* );
private:
   static FSMstate* _instance;
};
FSMstate* Warming::_instance = 0;

void Waiting::breadin(FSM* fsm) {
    cout << "Holding bread\r" << endl;
    sindex = 1;
    changeState(fsm, Holding::instance());
}
void Waiting::warmtoggle(FSM* fsm) {
    cout << "toggle warm hold\r" << endl;
    changeWarmState(fsm);
}
void Waiting::settime(FSM* fsm, int t) {
    cout << "Setting time\r" << endl;
    changeTimeState(fsm, t);
}
void Holding::cookrq(FSM* fsm) {
struct tms n;
   cout << "Heater on full, set delay for cooking time\r"
     << endl;
   cout << "Cooking toast for "<< getcookTime(fsm)<<" secs\r"
     << endl;
   setTimer(fsm);
   sindex = 2;
   changeState(fsm, Cooking::instance());
}
void Holding::release(FSM* fsm) {
```

```
    cout << "Release bread\r" << endl;
    sindex = 0;
    changeState(fsm, Waiting::instance());
}
void Holding::warmtoggle(FSM* fsm) {
    cout << "toggle warm hold\r" << endl;
    changeWarmState(fsm);
}
void Holding::settime(FSM* fsm, int t) {
    cout << "Setting time\r" << endl;
    changeTimeState(fsm, t);
}

void Cooking::release(FSM* fsm) {
    cout << "Release bread\r" << endl;
    cout << "Heater off\r" << endl;
    sindex = 0;
    clearTimer(fsm);
    changeState(fsm, Waiting::instance());
}
void Cooking::timeup(FSM* fsm) {
    cout << "Release bread\r" << endl;
    cout << "Heater off\r" << endl;
    sindex = 0;
    clearTimer(fsm);
    changeState(fsm, Waiting::instance());
}
void Cooking::warmtoggle(FSM* fsm) {
    cout << "toggle warm hold\r" << endl;
    changeWarmState(fsm);
}
void Cooking::settime(FSM* fsm, int t) {
    cout << "Setting time\r" << endl;
    changeTimeState(fsm, t);
}
void Cooking::timeupW(FSM* fsm) {
    cout << "Buzz Buzz\r" << endl;
    cout << "Heat reduced\r" << endl;
    sindex = 4;
    setTimer(fsm);
    changeState(fsm, Warming::instance());
}

void Warming::release(FSM* fsm) {
    cout << "Release bread\r" << endl;
    cout << "Heater off\r" << endl;
    sindex = 0;
    clearTimer(fsm);
    changeState(fsm, Waiting::instance());
}
```

```
void Warming::timeupW(FSM* fsm) {
   struct tms n;
   cout << "Buzz Buzz\r" << endl;
   setTimer(fsm);
}

// Start state is Cmd
FSM::FSM() {
   cout << "Waiting\r" << endl;
   changeState( Waiting::instance() );
}

void setterm(void) {
   struct termios tty;
   int status;
   status = ioctl(0, TCGETS, &tty);
   tty.c_lflag &= ~ICANON;
   tty.c_cc[VTIME] = 0;
   tty.c_cc[VMIN] = 0;
   status = ioctl(0, TCSETS, &tty);
   if (status == -1) {
            printf("ioctl error\n");
            exit(1);
   }
}

main() {
clock_t cook_time, current_tick, next_tick;
struct tms n;
unsigned int target_count = 0;
unsigned int t, keep_warm, key, fcount, scount=0;
FSM   toaster;
char  input[20];

    setterm();
    sindex = 0;
    tps = sysconf(_SC_CLK_TCK);
   while (1) {
        next_tick = times(&n) + 100;
            scount++; //cycle count, 50 Hz, every 20ms

        while (next_tick > times(&n)) { cout << sindex
          << " " << times (&n) << "\r";}
        t = toaster.getTarget();
        if ((t >0 ) && (t < times(&n))) {
                if (toaster.getwarmState())
                 toaster.timeupW();
                else toaster.timeup();
        } else if ((key = toupper(getchar())) != -1) {
                   if (isdigit(key)) {
```

```
                toaster.settime(key - '0');
              } else {
            switch (key) {
                case 'B': toaster.breadin();
                     break;
                case 'R': toaster.release();
                     break;
                case 'T': toaster.warmtoggle();
                     break;
                case 'C': toaster.cookrq();
                     break;
            }
        }
      }
   }
}
```

6.8 FSM scheduling issues

While carrying out debugging operations on the practical examples, a fundamental question concerning the timing of transitions may have been raised. When exactly do the interstate transitions occur? In fact, this is sometimes left entirely to the natural occurrence of input-driven events. So, the faster the events come, the more frequently the states change. This is reminiscent of a Mealy machine in which the output is affected immediately by input changes. However, such an uncontrollable situation has several disadvantages which can lead to significant problems. A better scheme is where the events are handled at a preset rate, synchronously locked to a suitable system clock. So the state and outputs only change periodically, in the manner of a Moore machine. It is worth noting that finite state machine events can arise from a variety of sources: external interrupts, timer interrupts, internal data changes or a polled status value. With a clocked FSM, each change is registered and stored until an RTC tick indicates that it is time for the next state transition to take place. At this moment the current event list is used

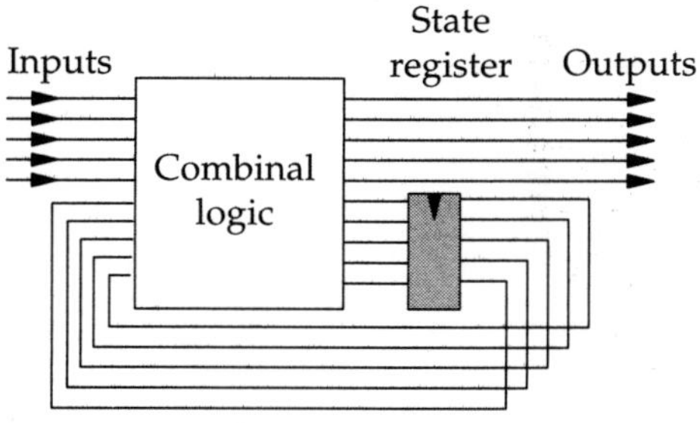

Mealy FSM in hardware

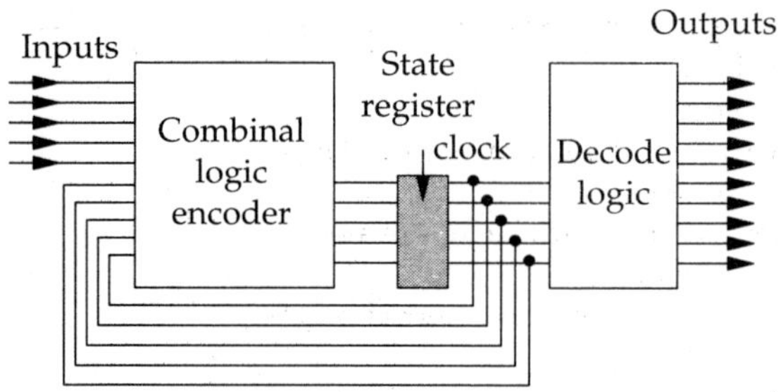

Moore FSM in hardware

to select the new state and initiate actions. A usual action would involve updating an output port, but many other examples have to be catered for. Actions may complete immediately, taking the form of an initialization or data transfer. In such circumstances the action may be implemented as a function call; however, should the action require an extended period of processing there may be the necessity of evoking a separate *task* to sustain the action concurrently with the FSM.

The optimum timing for the tick depends on the maximum interval allowed between input data reads. Usually the scan rate is set as slow as possible without running the risk of missing a rapid change of input status. Common values would be in the range 200 Hz (every 5 ms)–10 Hz (every 100 ms). For a 1 GHz CPU, this would allow the execution of 5–100 million instructions between each tick.

The two previous figures show the difference between hardware implementations of Moore and Mealy FSMs. It may be useful to present a similar schematic for our software implementation. Note that the events are latched, rather like a sample-and-hold circuit, in order to maintain the output signals constant between update points. The event masking logic is hidden within the final decoder, alongside the state index generation logic. New state index values and output signals are only generated when the two latches (shaded

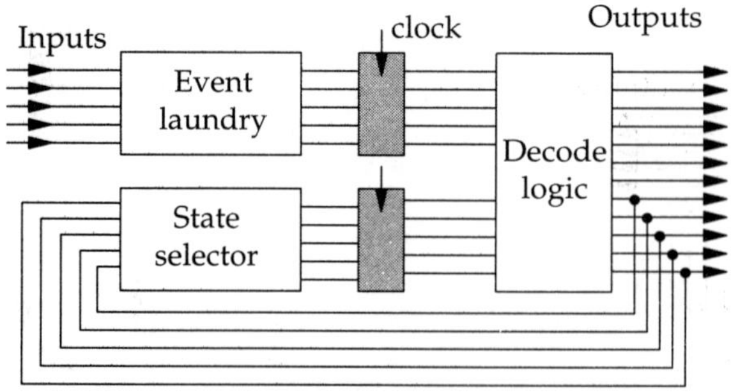

Schematic for an FST implementation in software

boxes) are clocked. In most of the examples in this chapter this would happen once every 10 or 20 ms. The choice of the dispatch rate is one of the principal implementation decisions which depends on a variety of characteristics specific to the application. An alternative approach which routinely blocks, waiting for the next event to appear, may work well if there is an underlying operating system to take benefit from the waiting time by running other tasks. But it does lead to more complicated I/O coding, critical data issues and full multi-tasking.

6.9 More FST

A more complex FST implementation is now presented which emulates a washing machine using an educational application board which is connected to an auxiliary parallel interface card. Many different parallel interface cards are on sale for both the ISA and PCI buses. When working with Linux, such a card will need a special device driver to be installed. This could be provided by the card manufacturer, or downloaded from an open source website, or specially written for the application. Access to the hardware is then made available, after initialization, through the standard `read()` and `write()` functions.

The FAB (Flite Applications Board) board, or any similar microprocessor applications board, offers a good range of hardware interface devices for the novice real-time programmer to experiment with. The FAB board is equipped with a small 9 V DC motor, a heater, temperature sensing thermister, digital to analogue converter (DAC), input switches and output LEDs: just perfect to play at being a washing machine. No involvement with real water though!

```
// Washing machine simulation using FAB board, follows FSM from
   page 99
// Author: Rob Williams 28/2/03
// Converted to Linux - Jan 2004
#include <stdio.h>
#include <string.h>
#include <unistd.h>
#include <fcntl.h>
#include "../PIO.h"      // compile with gcc washingmachine.c
                                  -lpio
#include <sys/termios.h>
#include <ctype.h>

#define PRINTdebug \
            printf("state = %d event = %d tcount=%d scount=%d
              switches=%x ctick=%d \r",\
            state, last_event, target_count, slowcount,
              portAshadow, current_tick);
```

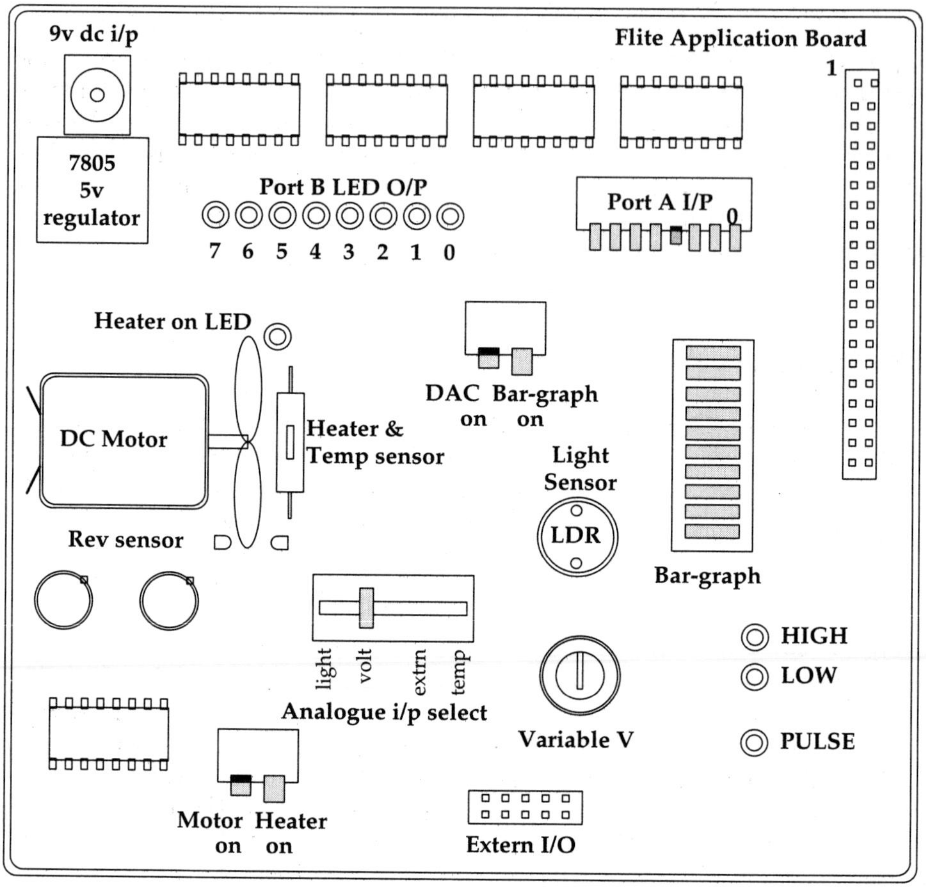

Educational applications board suited to real-time experiments (this application trial board was obtained from Flite Electronics International Ltd and has served well for many years, through several changes in processor: Z80 to 68000 to 68030 to Pentium and to Strong Arm (http://www.flite.co.uk))

```
// STATES
#define STATESX          10
#define LOADING           0
#define FILLING           1
#define HEATING           2
#define PAUSE1            3
#define TUMBLE            4
#define PAUSE2            5
#define ATUMBLE           6
#define DRAINING          7
#define SPINNING          8
#define HOLDING           9
```

```
// EVENTS
#define EVENTSX          10
#define DOORCLOSED     0x01
#define FULL           0x02
#define EMPTY          0x04
#define WASHEND        0x08
#define WATERHOT       0x10
#define TCOUNT         0x20
#define TIMEOUT        0x40
#define WCOUNT         0x80
#define DOOROPEN      0x100
#define SPINONLY      0x200

// INPUT SWITCHES PORT A
#define DOOR_SWITCH     0x01
#define WATER_HIGH      0x02
#define WATER_LOW       0x04
#define COMPAR          0x08 // reserved
#define FANSPEED        0x10 // reserved
#define SPIN_SPEED      0x20
#define TEMP_SELECT     0x40
#define SPIN_ONLY       0x80

// OUTPUT LEDS PORT B
#define INLETVALVE      0x01
#define DRAINPUMP       0x02

// MOTOR & HEATER CONTROL PORT C
#define MOTOR1          0x40
#define MOTOR2          0x80
#define HEATER          0x20

#define PAUSE_TIME         3
#define WASH_TIME          6
#define SPIN_TIME         10
#define TUMBLECYCLES       3
#define HITEMP            60
#define LOTEMP            45

#define DWORD unsigned int
#define BYTE unsigned char

DWORD events, cw = 0;
DWORD state, state_events, last_state;
DWORD water_heat, current_tick, next_tick;
DWORD target_count=0, slowcount=0, wcount=0, tcount=0,
  fastcount=0;
```

```
DWORD speed = 0;
BYTE watertemp;

int control, port_a, port_b, port_c;
int portAshadow=0, portBshadow=0, portCshadow=0;
int key, direction=0;

// FAB library routines for the ISA parallel port card
void initFAB(int *control, int *port_a, int *port_b, int
  *port_c);
void closeFAB (int *control, int *port_a, int
  *port_b, int *port_c);

// set console keyboard for nob-blocking and no buffering
void setterm(void) {
  struct termios tty;
          tcgetattr(0, &tty);
          tty.c_lflag &= ~(ICANON);
          tty.c_cc[VTIME] = 1;
          tty.c_cc[VMIN] = 0;
          tcsetattr(0, TCSANOW, &tty);
}

// initialize the ISA parallel card, an i8255 PIO with 3 byte-wide
   ports
void inithw(void) {
  int x;
          setterm();
          initFAB(&control, &port_a, &port_b, &port_c);
          x = 0x90;
          write(control, &x, 1);       // 8255 mode 0
}
void load() {
          printf( "\nLoading \n");
          wcount=0;
          tcount=0;
}
void fillh() {
          portBshadow |= INLETVALVE;
          printf("\nDoor closed, open water valve\n");
          write(port_b, &portBshadow, 1);
          tcount=0;
          wcount = 0;
}
void fillc() {
          portBshadow &= ~DRAINPUMP;
          portBshadow |= INLETVALVE;
          printf("\nOpen water valve, pump off\n");
          write(port_b, &portBshadow, 1);
```

```
            tcount=0;
            wcount++;
}
void heat() {
            portBshadow &= ~INLETVALVE;
            printf("\nClose valve\n");
            write(port_b, &portBshadow, 1);


            portCshadow | = HEATER;
            printf("\nHeater on\n");
            write(port_c, &portCshadow, 1);
}
void paus() {
            portBshadow &= ~INLETVALVE;
            write(port_b, &portBshadow, 1);
            portCshadow &= ~HEATER;
            printf("\nMotor & Heater off\n");
            write(port_c, &portCshadow, 1);
            speed = 0;
            target_count = slowcount + PAUSE_TIME*10;
            tcount++;
}
void tumble() {
            speed = 100;
            direction = 0;
            printf("\nClockwise Tumbling\n");
            target_count = slowcount + WASH_TIME*10 ;
}
void atumble() {
            speed = 100;
            direction = 1;
            printf("\nAnticlockwise Tumbling\n");
            target_count = slowcount + WASH_TIME*10 ;
}
void drain() {
            portBshadow | = DRAINPUMP;
            write(port_b, &portBshadow, 1);
            printf ("\nPump on\n");
            watertemp = 0;
            target_count = 0;
}
void spin() {
            speed = 255;
            portBshadow |= DRAINPUMP;
            write(port_b, &portBshadow, 1);
            printf("\nPump and spin motor on");
            target_count = slowcount + SPIN_TIME*10;
}
```

```
void hold() {
            speed = 0;
            portBshadow &= ~DRAINPUMP;
            write(port_b, &portBshadow, 1);
            printf("\n Pump and motor off, Please take your
              clothes\n");
}

// speed control by voltage chopping, fastcount: 0-speed, ON;
   speed-255, OFF
void motor_control() {
    BYTE motbits=0;
            portCshadow &= ~(MOTOR1 | MOTOR2);      //clear motor
                                                    //bits
            if(speed) {
                if(direction) motbits = MOTOR1;    // clockwise
                else          motbits = MOTOR2;    // counter
                                                   // clockwise
                if((fastcount&0xFF) < (speed&0xFF)) portCshadow |
                  = motbits;
            }
            write(port_c, &portCshadow, 1);
}

// ADC successive approximation routine, uses an 8 bit DAC chip
BYTE succapprox() {
            BYTE step, guess = 128;
            int switches;
            for(step = 64; step > 0; step >>= 1) {
                write(port_b, &guess, 1);
                read(port_a, &switches, 1);
                guess += (switches & COMPAR)? +step : -step;
            }
            return guess;
}

void null () {

}

typedef void (*TPT) ();

// defines a STATE TABLE entry
struct st {
  DWORD active ;
  DWORD next_state;
  TPT action ;
};
```

Table split for page display

```
// STATE TABLE
struct st state_table[EVENTSX][STATESX] = {

//states
//    0                 1                2               3               4
// LOADING          FILLING          HEATING         PAUSE1          TUMBLING
{{ 1,1,fillh}, { 0,1,null }, { 0,2,null}, { 0,3,null }, { 0,4,null },
{{ 0,0,null }, { 1,2,heat }, { 0,2,null}, { 0,3,null }, { 0,4,null },
{{ 0,0,null }, { 0,1,null }, { 0,2,null}, { 0,3,null }, { 0,4,null },
{{ 0,0,null }, { 0,1,null }, { 0,2,null}, { 0,3,null }, { 0,4,null },
{{ 0,0,null }, { 0,1,null }, { 1,3,paus}, { 0,3,null }, { 0,4,null },
{{ 0,0,null }, { 0,1,null }, { 0,2,null}, { 1,7,drain}, { 0,4,null },
{{ 0,0,null }, { 0,1,null }, { 0,2,null}, { 1,4,tumble},{ 1,5,paus },
{{ 0,0,null }, { 1,3,paus }, { 0,2,null}, { 0,3,null }, { 0,4,null },
{{ 0,0,null }, { 0,1,null }, { 0,2,null}, { 0,3,null }, { 0,4,null },
{{ 1,8,spin }, { 0,1,null }, { 0,2,null}, { 0,3,null }, { 0,4,null },
                    5               6              7             8
                 PAUSE2        ATUMBLING       DRAINING      SPINNING
               { 0,5,null }, { 0,6,null}, { 0,7,null },{ 0,8,null},
               { 0,5,null }, { 0,6,null}, { 0,7,null },{ 0,8,null},
               { 0,5,null }, { 0,6,null}, { 1,1,fillc},{ 0,8,null},
               { 0,5,null }, { 0,6,null}, { 1,8,spin },{ 0,8,null},
               { 0,5,null }, { 0,6,null}, { 0,7,null },{ 0,8,null},
               { 0,5,null }, { 0,6,null}, { 0,7,null },{ 0,8,null},
               {1,6,atumble}, {1,3,paus}, { 0,7,null },{ 1,9,hold},
               { 0,5,null }, { 0,6,null}, { 0,7,null },{ 0,8,null},
               { 0,5,null }, { 0,6,null}, { 0,7,null },{ 0,8,null},
               { 0,5,null }, { 0,6,null}, { 0,7,null },{ 0,8,null},
                                 9
                              HOLDING        //events
                          { 0,9,null }},     //DOORCLOSED
                          { 0,9,null }},     //FULL
                          { 0,9,null }},     //EMPTY
                          { 0,9,null }},     //WASHEND
                          { 0,9,null }},     //WATERHOT
                          { 0,9,null }},     //TCOUNT
                          { 0,9,null }},     //TIMEOUT
                          { 0,9,null }},     //WCOUNT
                          { 1,0,load }},     //DOOROPEN
                          { 0,9,null }},     //SPINONLY
 };

/* Build event mask for current state, using STATE TABLE
 * returns: 32 bit event mask
 */
DWORD getmask(DWORD staten) {
  DWORD mask=0;
  int i;

  for ( i= EVENTSX-1; i>=0; i--) {
      mask <<= 1;
      mask |= state_table[i][staten].active ;
  }
```

```
  return mask ;
 }

/* Use current state event mask to get the highest priority active
   event number
 * returns: current event number
 */
DWORD geteventn() {
  DWORD i, bitmask = 1;

  state_events = events & getmask(state);
  for ( i=0; i< EVENTSX; i++ ) {
    if ( state_events & bitmask ) {
        events &= ~bitmask;
        return i;
    }
    bitmask <<= 1;
 }
 return ~0;
}

/***********************************************************/
main() {
  struct tms *tim;
  int zero = 0;
 DWORD event, last_event=0;
 slowcount = 0;
 fastcount = 0;

   inithw(); //Initialize hardware, B_8255

while (1)
{
  next_tick = (DWORD)times(&tim) + 10; // advance tick clock

  slowcount++;

  read(port_a, &portAshadow, 1);      // read in panel switches
```

```
// Data Laundry, collects events
if (~portAshadow & DOOR_SWITCH)
   if (portAshadow & SPIN_ONLY)          events |= DOORCLOSED;
   else                                  events |= SPINONLY;
if ((~portAshadow & WATER_HIGH)          events |= FULL;
        && (wcount == 0))
if ((~portAshadow & WATER_HIGH)          events |= WCOUNT;
        && (wcount > 0 ))
```

```
if ( watertemp > ((portAshadow                    events|= WATERHOT;
      & TEMP_SELECT)?HITEMP:LOTEMP))
if((target_count )&&(target_count                 events |= TIMEOUT;
      < slowcount))
if (tcount > TUMBLECYCLES)                        events |= TCOUNT;

if ((~portAshadow & WATER_LOW)                    events |= EMPTY;
      && (wcount == 0) )
if ((~portAshadow & WATER_LOW)                    events |= WASHEND;
      && (wcount > 0) )

if (portAshadow & DOOR_SWITCH)                    events |= DOOROPEN;
do {
            fastcount++;
            motor_control();
           if ( state == HEATING) watertemp = succapprox();
           PRINTdebug;
           current_tick = (DWORD)times(&tim);
} while (next_tick > current_tick );

if ( (event = geteventn() ) != ~0 )
{
            last_event = event ;
            last_state = state;

            ( * ( state_table [event][state].action ) ) () ;
            state = state_table [event][state].next_state ;
            if (state != last_state ) events = 0 ;
}

}// while
  zero =0 ;
  write(port_b, &zero, 1);
  closeFAB(&control, &port_a,
   &port_b, &port_c);
} //main
```

Debug info printout

State dispatch code

6.10 Run-time environment

The five examples of toaster code used different styles of FSM implementation but are all hosted on the operating system Linux. However, such a full and rich run-time environment is not necessary. In fact, FSM code can be configured without too much trouble to run with a simple cyclic executive, or even directly on bare hardware with no separate run-time support. The choice really depends on considerations of cost and convenience. Simple systems are often destined to run on a cheap microcontroller, loading directly onto bare hardware, and executing without extra run-time support. In this case, all the hardware interfacing has to be carried out by the application itself, and little in the way of task scheduling is possible, beyond pre-emptive interrupt routines. Before anything else can happen, all the hardware has to be initialized to carry out the essential functions. This will certainly include writing initial values to the CPU stack pointer, I/O port command registers and a tick timer to produce the real-time interrupts.

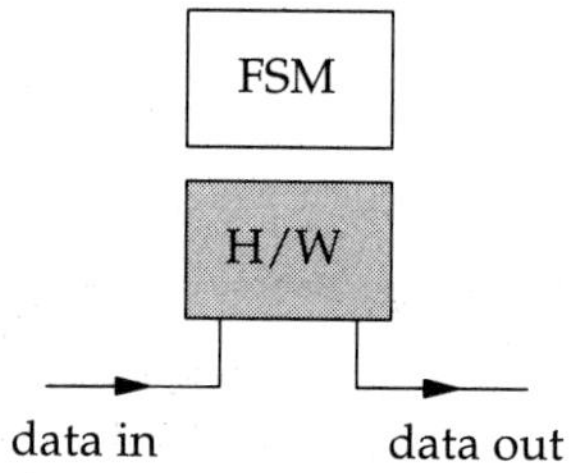

Single FSM directly on hardware

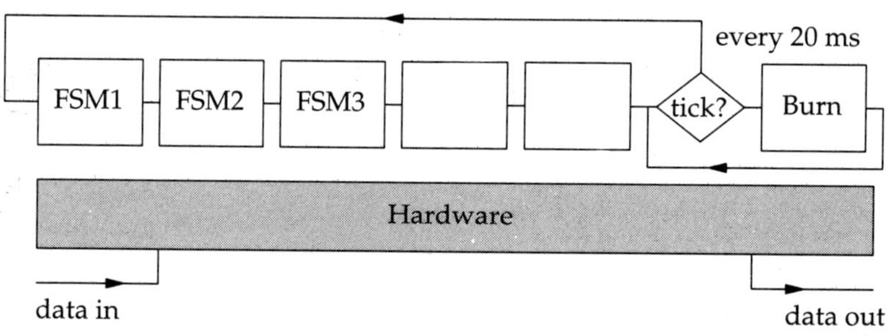

Cyclic executive hosting multiple FSMs

A cyclic executive offers enough scheduling facilities to host several FSMs running concurrently. But the application code still has to deal with all the hardware initialization and input and output activity.

An operating system, or real-time executive, takes all the responsibility for task scheduling, which makes the job of the application programmer a lot simpler. And it also provides a set of device driver routines for the local hardware so I/O programming can be carried out at a more abstract level of coding. The overall sophistication of the application may warrant the use of a multi-tasking operating system. If so, many extra facilities, such as signals,

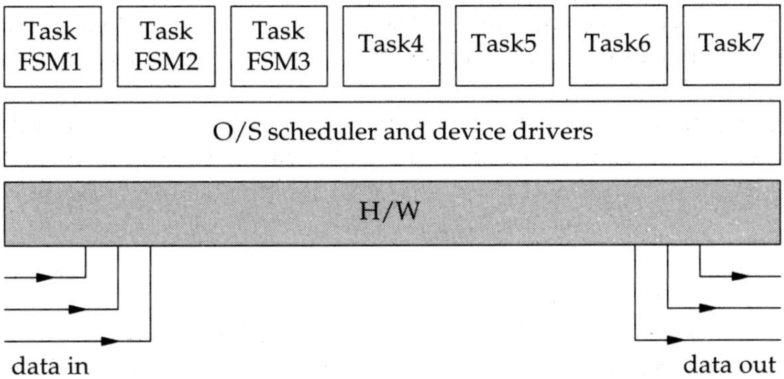

Full multi-tasking on an O/S

semaphores, a file system, timing, dynamic prioritization and memory access protection, are normally provided.

6.11 Chapter summary

There are five alternative transformation techniques for obtaining runnable code from an FSD: sequential coding, switch-case, goto-label, finite state table, OOP. The need to pre-process incoming data and interrupt signals into a single FSM event number is discussed. This activity has been described as the 'laundry'. Several FSMs may readily be run concurrently to fully implement a parallel real-time system. Using C++ or Java to implement an FSM using object-oriented techniques can offer difficulties and new opportunities for dynamic expression.

6.12 Problems and issues for discussion

1. What different methods of directly implementing a finite state machine are available? Discuss the advantages and disadvantages of each of them.
2. Draw up a finite state table, in C, for the dual loop vehicle detector presented on p. 100.
3. Convert the dual loop vehicle detector FSD into an ASM diagram, and then into sequential C code (or VHDL if you are able to).
4. How would you go about selecting suitable loop scan and state dispatch rates for the vehicle detector system? How would you implement an amber flashing, speed warning facility through software?
5. Transform the burglar alarm FSD, in Question 8 in the preceding chapter, into an FST for use with a C program. Some programmers prefer

to use two or three tables in place of the single one presented earlier in this chapter. This would avoid the need to use structs. What do you think of this?

6. Consider the following three FSDs, try to express each of them directly in sequential C code. Now draw up FSTs to describe each system. Which method was easier? Note that the transition activities have not yet been written in.

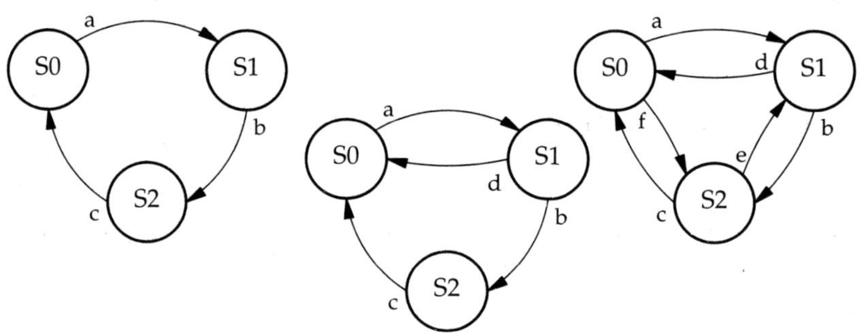

FSD 1 FSD 2 FSD 3

7. Include a 'defroster' state in the FSD for the toaster application (p. 111) to deal with items taken directly from the deep freeze.
8. Implement the Teas-made example, presented on pages 102–103 using the GOTO/LABEL method and then the FST method. Now investigate the ease with which either implementation can absorb the following changes:
   (i) Include a tea now button
   (ii) Select buzz in place of radio when the tea has been brewed
   (iii) Offer a selectable snooze option for silencing the radio for 10 mins
   (iv) Include a personalized message record and playback facility
   (v) Include facilities to control the timing for an electric blanket.
9. Examine how each of the FSM implementation methods deals with events which occur during the 'wrong' state. This can be a tricky issue, especially as frequently occurring events may effectively block out less salient events from being serviced.

6.13 Suggestions for reading

Allworth, S. & Zobel, R. (1990). *Introduction to Real-time Software Design.* Macmillan.

Cureington, J. (2001). Finite State Kernel Creator (FSKC). From: http://fskc.source forge.net

Harel, D. (1987). Statecharts: a visual formalism for complex systems. *Sci. Comp. Prog*, 8, 231–274.

Lawrence, P. & Mauch, K. (1988). *Real-time Microcomputer Systems Design.* McGraw-Hill.

van Gurp, J. & Bosh, J. (1999). On the Implementation of Finite State Machines. Proc. 3rd IASTED Conf SWEng & Applications. Oct 1999, Scottsdale, Arizona.

Chapter 7

Why multi-task?

7.1 Chapter overview

Dividing a program into several component tasks increases the complexity of the implementation. But a full multi-tasking application does offer several advantages to the systems developer which are described in this chapter. Most real-time, multi-tasking applications employ pre-emptive scheduling, and thus the need to protect critical data arises. The different multi-tasking environments are described.

7.2 Recognizing a real-time application

The most likely situation that demands a multi-tasking solution is where there are several rather unpredictable input/output activities which need to be handled at the same time as some core processing. If the equipment includes a user front panel keyboard and display, special device interaction, intermittent LAN comms and critical control activity, then perhaps a programmer's mind turns to a multi-tasking solution. In part, this is to defer

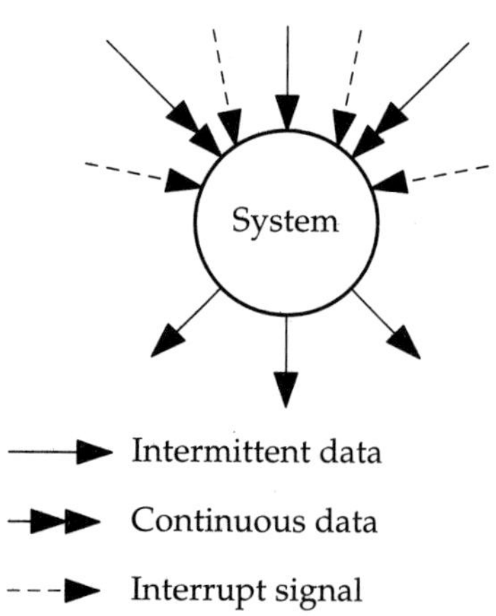

Complex I/O may suggest a multi-tasking solution

until run-time some important decisions about code sequencing, and then delegate responsibility for it down to the RTE! Although the programmer *could* serialize all these activities by using test-and-skip operations in a single loop, such a crude scheme suffers from increasing disadvantages as the systems grows in size and the relative demands of each of the component activities varies. Perhaps even more significant than the provision of convenient demand-driven code sequencing is the influence that multi-tasking can exert on system design. Design methods that support the decomposition of problems into multiple, semi-independent tasks for concurrent processing offer a straightforward method for dealing with complexity. In this way, big systems can be handled by partitioning them into many smaller, separately running tasks. Suitable design methods also clearly specify the steps to follow from analysis, through design and into code implementation.

7.3 Multi-tasking and multi-threading

The use of multi-tasking to improve the throughput and efficiency of large mainframe computers was introduced during the late 1950s to make the expensive, centralized resources more available. Those affected were usually university researchers or government scientists. In that situation, the tasks were generally owned by different users who were simply sharing access to the CPU, memory and peripheral devices. The main aim was to separate the

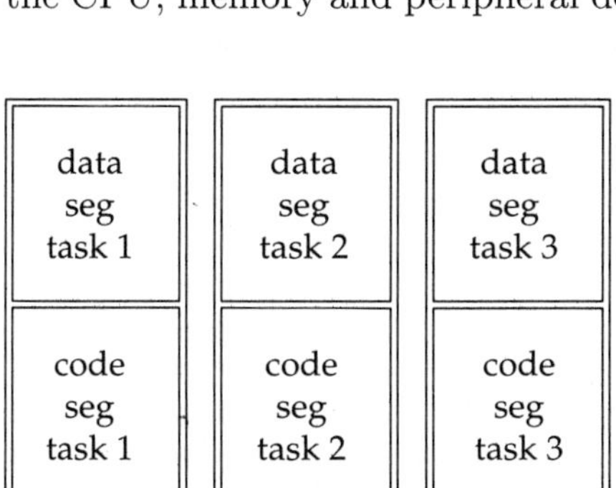

Three separate tasks

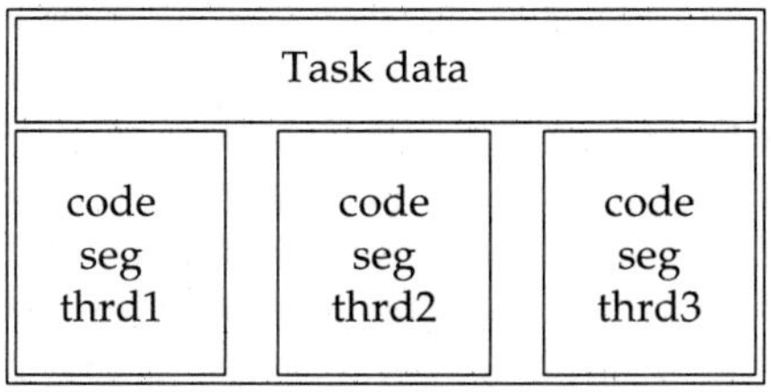

Three threads in a single task

Threads and tasks

tasks, making sure that when one crashed it did not pull down the others! We now refer to this arrangement as 'multi-user'. Clearly you cannot offer multi-user facilities without at least basic multi-tasking support. The slightly different concept of running several tasks to work cooperatively together to accomplish something is a more recent idea. In this case, the tasks would all be owned by the same user, and be organized to communicate between each other. A further development which is becoming very popular with programmers is 'multi-threading'. The principal disadvantage of using separate tasks is the effort that the system has to expend in swapping between them. This *context switching* activity can take up to a couple of milliseconds, partly due to the need to carefully save the current task's volatile processing environment and partly due to the security constraints in place to protect tasks from damaging each other. In the case of threads this is not so burdensome because several processing threads can share the same volatile environment, all being owned by the same user. All threads created by a task can access the same address space, global data variables, file descriptors, pending timer alarms, signals, signal handlers and operating system accounting information. A thread can be realized as either a *periodic* (clock-driven) or an *aperiodic* (event-driven) process. In order to reduce blocking time, threads typically communicate using an asynchronous model, via shared data areas. The use of concurrency raises a number of other design issues: mutual exclusion, deadlock, livelock, starvation and race conditions.

But each thread does get allocated its own CPU register set values and state information. Threads are also sometimes known as 'lightweight processes', indicating the much reduced activity that has to be carried out to swap between threads.

7.4 Run-time support environment

The problem with discussing real-time systems is the wide variation that exists between different types of real-time applications. This is especially apparent when the run-time support environment is being considered. Broadly speaking there are four major styles of implementing a real-time system as shown below. To further complicate the comparison, the chosen programming language may also offer specific run-time support for real-time systems. This could include tasking facilities, critical resource management, synchronization and memory allocation routines. Thus a program implemented in ADA, loaded onto a bare board, benefits as much from run-time support as one coded in assembler, running on an RTE. The IEEE, in 1998, offered a new API standard, POSIX 1003.1/b, in an attempt to rationalize the diversity of programming interfaces to operating system facilities. Embedded systems in particular were the focus of attention, and some commercial RTEs have now adopted some of the POSIX recommendations, providing them in parallel with their own proprietary facilities. To

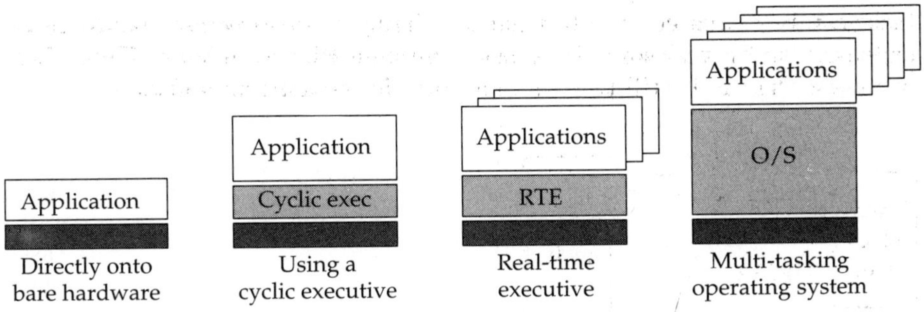

Different implementation environments

be expected, the bigger operating systems – Windows, Solaris, Linux – now offer developers a fuller range of POSIX compliant API facilities.

For simple systems not requiring much run-time support, application code can be developed to load directly into bare RAM or Flash memory. All the hardware initialization, software setup and hardware device handling would then have to be included with the application code. Some real-time programmers prefer this approach because although it requires more software to be produced, it reveals all aspects of the system, hiding nothing behind the opaque complexities of an operating system. Managers, who care more about budgets, become suspicious of this approach when it dawns on them that each new product is being redeveloped from scratch. They also worry that the organization is too dependent on key staff who hold the 'secrets' of their software rather too close to their chests. This may be the moment when they decide to move on, to cyclic executives or RTEs.

Both cyclic executives and RTEs strip the scheduling activity away from the application code. This means that new products can inherit large chunks from previous projects, saving a lot of development and testing. Also, should a product survive long enough to be enhanced or redeveloped, the work is much easier to carry out.

But bespoke development still results in much smaller code, tailored to the exact needs of the application. If the tasking involves periodic scanning, it is convenient to use a cyclic executive to host the application code. Such a primitive scheduling facility offers little except regular, periodic execution. If further run-time facilities such as memory management and semaphore handling are required it is common to acquire a special RTE such as VXWorks or CExec. A full operating system such as Linux or Windows can offer all the previous facilities as well as a sophisticated file manager and resident development tools.

A task or process comprises some code, its associated data and a control block data structure which the operating system uses to define and manipulate the task. These are commonly held in a dynamic link-list (p. 154) to assist with rapid access and manipulation. Tasks can mostly be developed and tested as independent programs, if the intercommunications to other tasks can be emulated by a test harness. Truly *multi-processor* solutions are expensive and reveal some intertask communication problems. Thus, single processor sharing is still the common form for concurrent software.

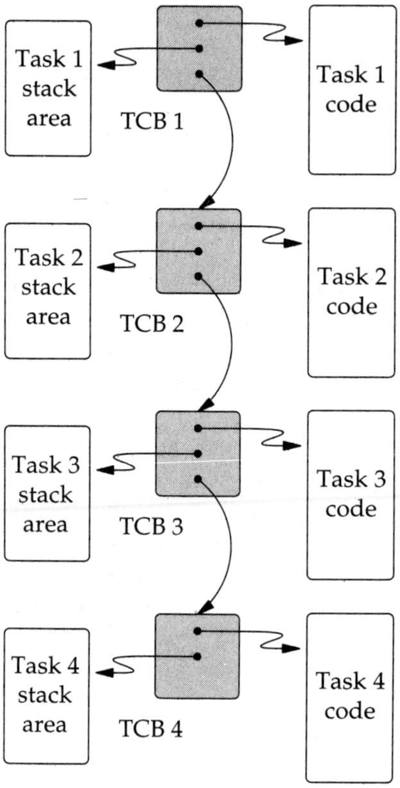

Task control block queue

7.5 Run-time scheduling

Systems implemented in software have become so large and complex that they have to be broken into components in order to design, build and maintain them. Traditionally this was achieved using functions and modules. More recently, object-oriented encapsulation has been promoted to deal with this problem. Whatever structuring method adopted, the software components were seen as running in a pre-planned sequence, each completing a subordinate part of the total job. With real-time systems it is not always possible to know the run-time sequence in advance, often the only way to partition the work is to have several subprograms ready to run, depending on the prevailing conditions. Thus the code is partitioned into schedulable units, tasks, which are linked by strictly defined communication channels and synchronization facilities. Only at run-time, through the mediation of the scheduler, will a particular task be selected for execution. This scheme of functional decomposition readily allows design, implementation, testing and maintenance activities to be carried out on selected tasks, greatly assisting with resource planning and allocation.

The cyclic executive, described in Chapter 4, offers interrupt, clock and base levels of task priority. The interrupt task is scheduled pre-emptively by the CPU hardware, and so is capable of immediately breaking into main tasks to achieve its goal. The latency can be very low, 20 μsec from device request to software response. For such activity, as long as the required processing is not too heavy, it is likely that the Interrupt Service Routine (ISR) will carry out all of the processing itself. But if this would take too long, the ISR is split and the majority portion will be deferred to a main task, to be completed later. Clock-level tasks are cooperatively scheduled on a round-robin basis. This can appear somewhat inflexible, as the relative task priorities can only be varied by the programmer by running higher priority clock tasks more frequently than lower priority neighbours. This leaves little opportunity for run-time adjustment, such as 'aging' which is used by some RTEs and also Linux. The base tasks can be operated on a round-robin or 'first come first served' scheme. Neither offer much opportunity for dynamic priority adjustments in response to changing circumstances.

Task	Scheduling	Priority
Interrupt	Pre-emptive	High
Clock	Cooperative	Middle
Base	FCFS Low	

Broad task priorities

Dispatching is the action of restoring a task to the CPU so that it can continue executing. Before that can occur, the current task status, known as the volatile environment, has to be saved away for the future. This could involve all the CPU register values being pushed onto the stack and the task stack pointer saved in the PCB. With more sophisticated hardware, consideration has to be given to the cache, memory management unit and other intelligent peripherals. For example, if a data transfer has been started, what will the action be when it completes should the initiating task no longer be running?

7.6 Justifying the use of multi-tasking

Using a multi-tasking approach to solving a real-time problem can end up being more complex, needing more programming skills, and can take more resources than the simple looping solution. So why would anyone choose to go down that route? In summary, a task-based solution can be formally justified by at least six good arguments as listed below. Also, the extra difficulty of implementing a dependable multi-tasking application has been somewhat reduced by the range of facilities offered by modern HLLs. Java in particular provides the programmer with convenient multi-threading capability which will be described in more detail in Chapter 14.

- Dependable system responsiveness
- Intellectual simplicity during design
- Rigour of implementation
- Easy of unit testing
- System integrity
- Exploiting multi-processor hardware

Advantages of multi-tasking

7.7 Responsiveness

Despite our concentration on other features, the principal role of a real-time system is to respond to asynchronous, unpredictable events in an orderly and timely fashion. Often the requirements will specify explicitly the maximum response latency times which are acceptable. Even then there may be further implied timing constraints which the system has to satisfy in order to successfully interact with connected equipment. To achieve

Instant response?

this, real-time systems frequently rely on hardware interrupt signals to evoke the necessary service routines. The executive software will convert interrupt signals into software flags or software signals so that processing can be more effectively scheduled, in an appropriate sequence, with the mainline application code. Thus, although some small amount of processing may take place within the ISRs, this must be reduced to a minimum because the ISRs are usually beyond the control of the scheduler, their relative priorities being permanently fixed by the hardware. Some increase in latency, or loss of responsiveness, is unavoidably incurred in order to retain control of the overall scheduling. How the interrupt service routines communicate with the main tasks is another of the features that distinguishes cyclic executives from the more developed real-time executives.

7.8 Intellectual simplicity of design

The specification and design of multi-tasking systems can appear initially to suffer from unnecessarily increased complexity, and thus offer greater scope for errors than a monolithic solution. However, the clean separation and allocation of functionality into discrete tasks can directly express the way designers analyse and specify their plans. Partitioning the functionality of the whole system into separate, cooperating activities may offer a good opportunity to rationalise analysis, design and implementation. With explicitly defined interfaces between the tasks, the need to understand fully the internal workings of all the tasks is reduced. It offers an alternative means of implementing *data hiding*, which supporters of the object-oriented design approach

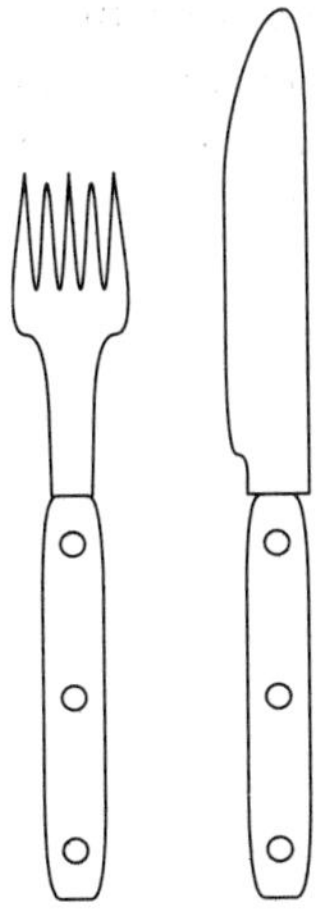

Design simplicity

strongly advocate. Indeed, on a more philosophical level, a model which includes concurrent operations more closely reflects the real, parallel world that we live in.

7.9 Rigour of implementation

The disciplined structure imposed by an RTE or cyclic executive, through the necessary use of prescribed system calls, successfully constrains application programmers and largely eliminates the worst 'creative' excesses from their code. True, this does limit the freedom that some programmers cherish, but the long-term payback comes from well-structured, predictable code that readily supports the occasional maintenance activity and easily accommodates reworking with new features. By accepting the need to conform to a standardized software environment provided by an RTE or cyclic executive, the programmer becomes a member of a larger community, with all the supportive benefits that come with that position.

7.10 Unit testing

An extra advantage gained from using a well-partitioned multi-tasking solution is the ease with which individual tasks can be separately tested. This does involve the production of some extra testbench software to provide a substitute stream of input data and events, but experience tells us over and over again that money is saved the earlier a bug is detected in the development cycle. Such simulation testing can initially be done on a convenient host computer, supplied with full debugging and profiling tools, rather than the much less convenient target board. A well-recognized problem, however, with software testing is the exponential explosion of different execution pathways through the code due to the use of conditional instructions such as IF-ELSE and SWITCH-CASE. For a completely exhaustive test, every

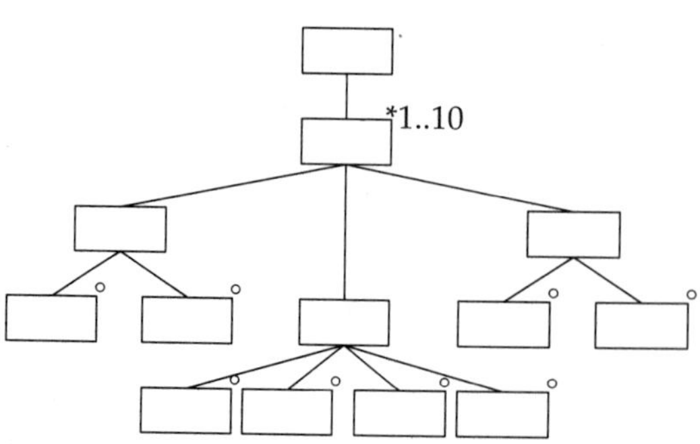

Testing complexity: 10^6 pathways

legal pathway should be tried out, which is totally unfeasible with most normal programs. The straightforward example presented on p. 158, a four-way SWITCH-CASE bracketed by two IF-ELSE statements, still results in about one million alternative pathways. Should this structure be evoked ten times, say within a function, the test combination count shoots up to 10^{60}. Interleaved threads, arising from a multi-tasking system, further increase the large number of pathways which require checking.

Because of the impossibility of completing full coverage tests within a reasonable time, software testing is usually carried out by a reduced sampling technique. This is either 'blind', also termed black box, with randomly constructed data sets, or 'informed', also termed white box, with carefully chosen data values which are of particular sensitivity or significance to the key algorithms.

7.11 System integrity

A significant advantage to the multi-tasking approach when implementating an application is the independence and isolation that it gives to component tasks. This means that one task can fail and not bring the whole application crashing down. Mutual checking of one task by another can also be carried out with ease. Extra facilities can be inserted, or modifications carried out

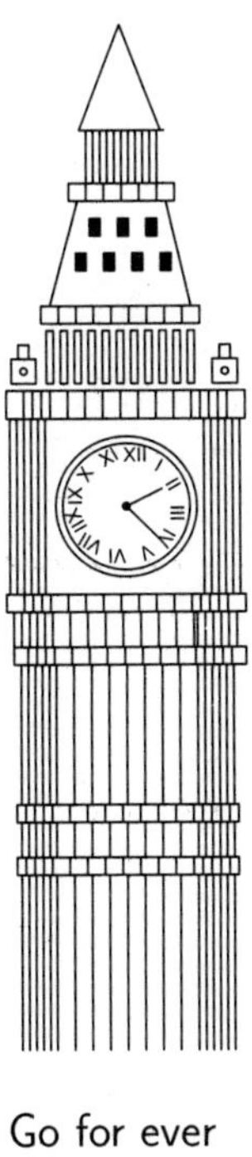

Go for ever

on existing tasks, with minimum impact on the other tasks. Indeed, dynamic updating of tasks can be achieved, enabling the system to have the previous code releases available in standby mode, should the newest version of the code fail. This leads to the concept of a *high integrity* system assembled from imperfect components. When newly installed components fail, they can be immediately withdrawn or replaced without interfering with the overall availability of the system. Perhaps this is more like a biological organism than an electrical machine.

7.12 System integration testing

The bringing together of all the software and hardware components for the first time often highlights surprising incompatibilities which have somehow slipped through earlier checks and reviews. Because the full integration test is more complex than previous unit tests, it is essential to make careful action schemas and contingency plans. This may involve the use of performance monitoring and code profiling to watch the system components interacting in real-time.

7.13 Exploitation of multi-processor hardware

It is now common for suppliers of even standard, commodity PCs to have multi-processor systems in their catalogues. For the most part, they are acquired to act as powerful networked file servers, or database engines, providing many users with a centralized service. The dual benefits of faster performance and failure resilience can justify the extra hardware complexity and cost. But to write software which can benefit from multi-processor capability requires a specific approach to program design and implementation. Cutting an application program into cooperating tasks is one way to assist the operating system when it tries to spread the processing load between the available CPUs.

Symmetric multi-processor hardware

A multi-processor can be configured in many ways. The Symmetric Multi-processor (SMP) arrangement is one of the most common schemes, with several identical CPUs sharing access to main memory and I/O devices through the system bus. As normal, the operating system has to decide where to load program pages in physical memory, but then it also has to allocate processors to the individual execution threads. This introduces an extra possibility for corrupting shared data which can result from a CPU having a bus request granted by the bus arbitrator, potentially giving it access to shared data areas in the same way that interrupt routines can burst

31	0	
I/O map base address	T	64H
	LDT segment selector	
	GS	
	FS	
	DS	
	SS	
	CS	
	ES	
EDI		
ESI		
EBP		
ESP		
EBX		
EDX		
ECX		
EAX		
EFLAGS		
EIP		
CR3 (PDBR)		
	SS2	
ESP2		
	SS1	
ESP1		
	SS0	
ESP0		
	Prev task link	00

Pentium Task-state Segment (TSS), hardware Task Control Block (TCB)

into a vulnerable activity. Because of this, bus lock instructions have been introduced and are used in the same way that the Disable Interrupts (DI) instruction has to be applied to prevent pre-emeption at critical moments. Now it is important that mutual exclusion semaphores are accessible to all the CPUs which are executing threads from the same program. A particularly nasty problem comes from the use of cache memory within each CPU. Thus, if several CPUs are reading and writing to a single variable, as they might with a semaphore, they will all have different local copies of the variable in cache, unless something is done to prevent it. This issue of *cache consistency* gets worse. Consider the situation where CPU-1 is modifying variable A, and CPU-2 is modifying variable B. Each will write back the changed value to main memory for others to read. So far so good. But what if variables A and B share the same cache line? Then CPU-1 will have a local, stale copy of variable B to hand, and CPU-2 will have a local, stale copy of variable A. This problem is resolved by building cache controllers with bus *snooping* capability. With this, cache controllers can monitor all bus cycles and so detect the occurrence of write activity to main memory which might invalidate local copies of cache data. The same problem could happen when DMA is enabled for input data channels. The normal solution in this case is to disable CPU caching of the relevant page of memory.

7.14 Processor support for task swapping

At the bottom of most real-time applications is a timer-counter which ticks away at a fixed rate, maintaining periodic polling activity and time-slice scheduling. So the need for interrupt handling facilities is practically too obvious to mention to real-time programmers! At one time there was a considerable difference between the various interrupt facilities offered by microprocessors from different producers. This has diminished, with most microprocessors now offering a similar pattern of prioritized multi-level, nested, vectored-response interrupts. With some devices, such as the ARM processor, targeted more at the smaller embedded systems market, multiple sets of CPU registers are provided to allow extremely rapid context switching when servicing interrupts. But this is not helpful when swapping dozens of tasks in and out.

Because computers usually run multi-tasking operating systems, there is also great advantage to be gained by choosing a CPU which incorporates hardware support for task management. So the relevant features of the Pentium processor will be described as an example of what is possible in the way of hardware support for multi-tasking. The Pentium defines a standard data structure which acts as a task control block (p. 61). When a task is declared and initialized, a new task control block data structure is linked into the task chain so that the scheduler can quickly locate the associated code, data and stack segments for each task, through their segment pointers (CS, DS, SS). The TCB images in the Pentium are known as Task-state Segments (TSS), and are standardized in format in order to allow for hardware acceleration of load and store operations. The TSSs are located using pointers (TSS Segment Descriptors) held in the Global Descriptor Table (GDT), along with the Segment Descriptors (SD) and Local Table Descriptors (LTD). Any task must be identified by a segment selector pointing into the GDT, and accessing a task descriptor which holds the location and size of the TSS block. The location of the GDT is confirmed by the address held in the Global Descriptor Table Register (GDTR). All the active TSS descriptors, holding the start and end addresses of TSS task control blocks, have to be stored in the Global Descriptor Table (GDT).

TSS base addr 31..24	G	0	0	AVL	Limit 19..16	P	DPL	0	Type 10B1	TSS base addr 23..16

TSS base addr 15..0	TSS segment limit 15..0

31 0

Eight byte TSS descriptor, GDT entry

When a task is swapped out, the volatile environment is rapidly copied back into the TSS block and the data held in the next task's TSS is copied into the CPU registers to restart that task.

The task register holds a 16 bit segment selector to index into the Global Descriptor Table (GDT) and access the relevant TSS descriptor. This contains base and limit address values for the intended TSS block. To speed further access, a copy of the TSS descriptor is cached in another part of the task register (10 bytes wide) for faster access to the TSS block. All the addresses so far referred to are logical, not physical. The translation from virtual to physical is not only used to extend limited RAM space onto a disk swap volume, but it also administers strong access permissions and is the base of effective run-time security. So even with fairly 'static' real-time systems, there is a great advantage to running a system with the virtual memory management facilities turned on, even if the address mapping is simply one to one. Not only can each task be allocated separate logical segments (CSEG, DSEG, SSEG), but also they can each use a different page mapping table. The TSS blocks hold copies of the usual CPU registers, the CR3/PDBR (Page Directory Base Register), and the three segment base and limit addresses (CSDCR, DSDCR, SSDCR). They will all be saved and restored on task swapping. The full address mapping and checking may involve segment offset addition, followed by a page-to-frame lookup, determining the final physical address. On the Pentium, both segment descriptors and page attributes offer access permission and security protection. In this way, a task has no idea where the other tasks reside in RAM. In fact, this could be freshly determined when

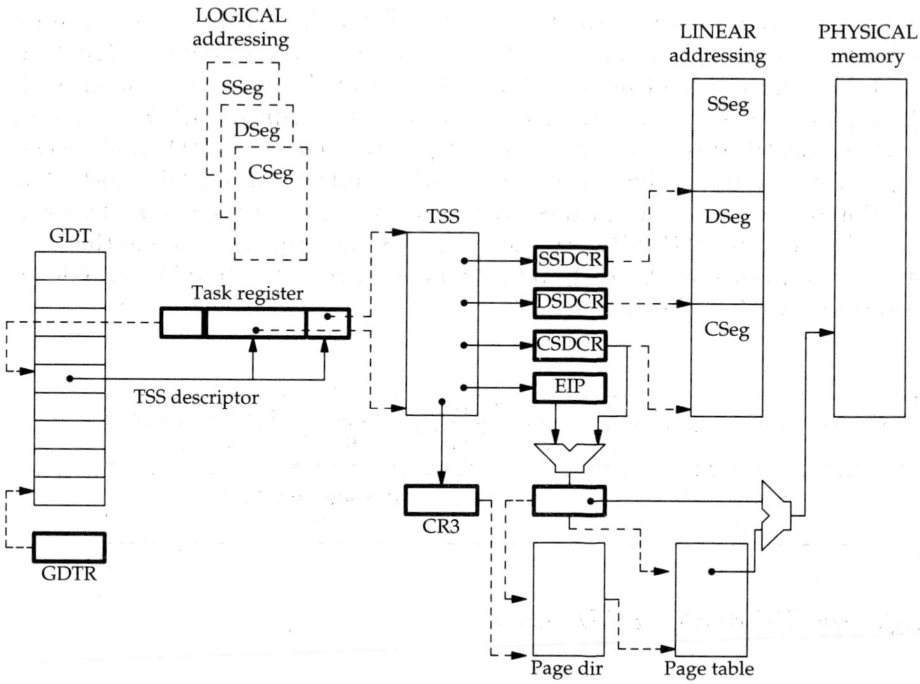

Task address translation on the Pentium

tasks are dynamically forked, making determined mutal interference even more unlikely.

One interesting feature of Pentium task handling is the provision for task *nesting*. This looks as if it has been provided for pre-emptive interrupt and exception processing, but reveals the problem of non-re-entrant task code. Unlike in the case of subroutine nesting, where the stack offers a fresh data frame for each evocation of a function, should a task try and call itself, or be evoked a second time before the first version has completed, there is no provision for holding the state of the earlier task. Because of this problem, tasks on the Pentium are functionally non-re-entrant. The CPU EFLAGS register provides the Nested Task (NT) flag to record when a task has been entered through an interrupt event or a `CALL` instruction, rather than a non-returning, straightforward `JMP` instruction. This enables the dispatcher to either restore the pre-empted task, or put up the next scheduled task in a correct manner. To protect against an erroneous attempt to call an active task, there is a *BUSY* flag provided in the TSS descriptor to protect against such an error. Normally only supervisor privilege software can dispatch a task. This can be assured by the Descriptor Privilege Level (DPL) which holds a 2 bit value from 0 to 3, indicating the privilege level required to activate the associated task. Any task with a Current Privilege Level (CPL) equal to or less (higher privilege) than the TSS DPL value may dispatch the new task.

The situation with interrupt service routines is slightly different, even though the ISRs are classified as tasks and not functions. Instead of directly accessing a TSS descriptor stored in the GDT, the interrupt vector will first index into the Interrupt Descriptor Table (IDT) and obtain a Task-gate Descriptor (TGD), which then points to an entry in the GDT or the Local Descriptor Table (LDT), and so on to an interrupt handler. Where the CPU goes after the interrupt has completed depends on whether the entry was achieved by a `CALL` or a `JMP` instruction.

7.15 Starting new tasks in Linux

The normal way to start up new tasks in Unix is to use the `fork()` system call. This duplicates the existing *parent* task, creating all the data structures needed to launch a new, *child* task. Both continue executing the same code from the fork point, but they can distinguish themselves as parent or child by the PID value returned by the call to `fork()`. The parent gets the child's PID, while the child gets a zero. The following code fragment illustrates the basics of using `fork()`. To reduce the delay introduced by forking, under Linux the fork uses 'copy-on-write'. This means that memory pages are not duplicated until a *write* occurs, at which point the affected page is duplicated to give completely separate versions for each task. So the only penalty incurred by evoking a `fork()` is the time and memory space required to initialize new task page tables, and a new TCB for the child task.

```
#include <sys/types.h>
#include <unistd.h>

pid_t fork(void);
pid_t pid;

main() {
 • • • • •
   switch (pid = fork()) {
      case -1:
          /* The fork failed */
          /* Some possible because no more process slots, or
             virtual memory */
          perror("Sorry, fork failed\n");
      break;
      case 0:
          /* child code continues here */

            _exit(0);
       break;
       default:
          /* parent code continue here */
```

```
        printf("Child's pid is %d\n",pid);
    }
  • • • • •
}
```

In place of the switch/case, it is common to use an if/else clause, but there are three possible outcomes, making the use of switch/case a more suitable choice. Of great interest to the programmer is what values the child inherits from the original parent task. This does depend somewhat on the version of Unix being used, but mostly they comply to a common list. Note that the child gets copies of these things, not access to the original.

The lists presented below summarize the inheritance position for new tasks. Perhaps the most confusing situation concerns the sharing of file

- Process credentials
  (real/effective/saved UIDs and GIDs)
- Process environment
- Stack contents
- Data and code
- Open file descriptors
  (position index are shared with parent)
- Close-on-exec flags
- Signal handling settings
- Nice value
- Scheduler class
- Process group ID
- Session ID
- Current working directory
- Root directory
- File mode creation mask (umask)
- Resource limits
- Controlling terminal

Attributes inherited by child from parent task

- New process ID for child
- Different parent process ID
- Private copies of file descriptors
- Process, text, data and memory locks
- Process times
- Resource utilizations
- Pending signals
- Timer_create() timer values
- Asynchronous input or output operations

Attributes *not* inherited by child task

position indexes. So either child or parent can read forward into an open file, and affect the next item read by the other task. Should a completely different task be required, the `exec()` system call has the power to bring in an new executable file from disk, and overlay the code on top of an existing task's code segment.

7.16 Chapter summary

The design-side advantages of partitioning a system into discrete tasks are explained. Multi-tasking code can also provide a more flexible response to changing environmental conditions because the scheduling decisions are modified according to ongoing processing demands. Task scheduling strategies vary from host system to host system: pre-emptive, cooperative, first come first served, time sliced. But dividing a program into several interacting component tasks does increase the overall complexity of the implementation. Some modern CPUs offer hardware support for tasking, this requires the TCBs to conform to a predefined structure.

7.17 Problems and issues for discussion

1. What are the main reasons for implementing real-time applications in a multi-tasking format? Do real-time applications necessarily benefit from a pre-emptive multi-tasking scheduling regime?
2. Why are external interrupts so important for real-time programmers? As interrupts are mainly 'wired in' during board design, how can a programmer retain some control over the relative priorities assigned to interrupt service processing activity?
3. Will multi-tasking *always* provide a better response-time performance (reduced latency)? If not, why do programmers prefer multi-tasking solutions?
4. What is the principal difference between multi-tasking and multi-threading? In what circumstances would a programmer choose to use either?
5. The computer bus is a shared resource. How does hardware deal with the problem of resource contention?
6. Testing interrupt-rich code has always been recognized as difficult. This is due in large part to the unpredictability, and unreproducibility, of real-world events. In my personal experience, however, the most unpredictable element in the equation is always the *human being*. Comment on the wisdom or otherwise of this opinion. Are human users more dangerous than interrupts? How can this risk be reduced?
7. Investigate how the Windows and Linux operating systems provide run-time support and scheduling on multiprocessor hardware, dual Pentium motherboards.

7.18 Suggestions for reading

Bach, M. (1986). *The Design of the Unix Operating System.* Prentice Hall.

Heuring, V. & Jordan, H. (2004). *Computer Systems Design and Architecture.* Addison Wesley.

Intel (1999). *Intel Architecture Software Developer's Manual*, Vols 1–3.

Tanenbaum, A. (2002). *Structured Computer Organisation.* Prentice Hall.

Chapter 8

Task communication and synchronization

8.1 Chapter overview

Multi-tasking software relies on system functions to provide intertask communications and synchronization facilities. Semaphores, lock files, signals, pipes and sockets are all described with code examples. Commercial RTEs and most operating systems offer these functions.

8.2 Data sharing

Multi-tasking implementations can suffer from difficulties when using shared resources. In particular, reader tasks have to be sure that the data is stable and valid, and writer tasks must guard against simultaneous operations which would leave data structures in an inconsistent condition. When several concurrent tasks are able to access a shared data area, and pre-emptive rescheduling can take place, it is essential to look out for the possibility of task rescheduling right in the middle of an update. In such circumstances, the data will be abandonded for a period in an inconsistent condition until the writer task is restored. Several well-established techniques are available to programmers to deal with this problem and these are listed below and will be further described in the next sections.

- Serialize the critical accesses with cooperative scheduling
- Disable interrupts to inhibit the scheduler during access to shared data
- Bit flags, set and tested by application tasks, tasks spin poll
- Semaphores, flags and task wait queues supplied by the kernel
- Monitors, exclusive access procedures associated with data
- Control queues, MASCOT solution
- Synchronous rendezvous, ADA solution
- Synchronized methods (Java)

Techniques for critical data protection

Previously in Section 3.15 the need to protect shared resources from possible corruption, arising from simultaneous access, has been highlighted. The time-of-day display example revealed the problem, and employed the serialized access method to solve it. Any of the intertask synchronization techniques can be used by a programmer to protect vulnerable, shared resources from corruption. But another difficulty then emerges which involves the fair and timely scheduling of tasks which are running with different priorities. The problem is termed priority *inversion* and refers to a situation when a high priority task is delayed by lower priority tasks because they have control over a critical resource which the high priority task requires in order to run. The scheduler would normally dispatch the low priority task. It would run to completion, relinquish the resource and allow the high priority task to come in. The higher priority task cannot pre-empt the lower priority task because it is not fully ready to run without the resource requested. However, if there is a third task of *medium* priority ready to run, it will intervene, and run ahead of the low priority task, preventing the freeing of the resource. In this way the high priority task gets locked out by two lower priority tasks which are effectively 'hogging' a shared resource. Scheduling decisions depend not only on relative priority, but also the availability of resources.

Perhaps the 1997 Mars Pathfinder probe offers the most famous priority inversion incident. After the successful, if bouncy, landing, and the deployment of the rover vehicle, the onboard equipment began taking meteorological readings and relaying them back to earth. All seemed to be perfect, until the computer system began to experience sudden, unaccountable shutdown events, which rebooted the system with inevitable loss of data. The problem was tracked down to a shared data area, protected by a semaphore, and accessed by several tasks of differing priority. An infrequent low priority task gathered meteorological data for storing in the shared area.

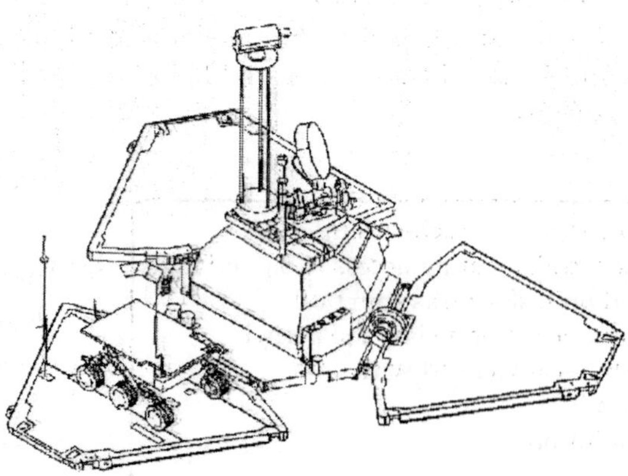

NASA Mars Pathfinder

A medium priority task was responsible for craft communications, while a high priority task, scheduled by incoming interrupts, also required access to the shared area. Most of the time this scheme worked reliably; however, occasionally there was an opportunity for the medium priority task to be scheduled just at the moment when the low priority task was running with the semaphore, and so blocking off the eligible high priority task. In such a case, the medium priority task could pre-empt the low priority task, thus holding up the release of the mutex, necessary for the high priority task to run. The unexpected delay that occurred enabled a watchdog timer to kick in and reset the whole system.

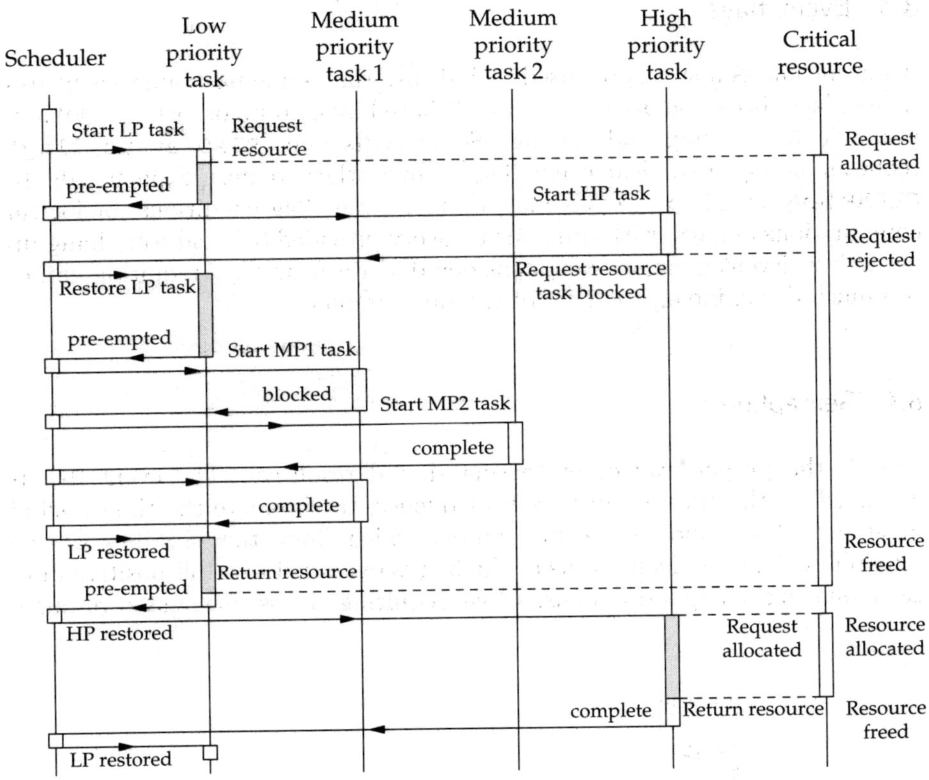

Priority inversion with critical resources

In commercial RTEs (VxWorks, PSOS, MTOS and VRTX) a variety of facilities are provided (see p. 172) to help deal with intertask communication, synchronization and critical resource protection.

- Event flags
- Semaphores
- Lock files
- Mailboxes, channels, pipes and queues
- Signals
- Sockets
- Rendezvous
- Synchronized

Communication and synchronization facilities

8.3 Event flags

An event flag is a status bit used to indicate that some particular event has taken place. It can be private to a task, shared by a group of tasks or globally available for reading and setting. Some APIs offer `READ(event_flag)` requests arranged to clear event flags, while others require explicit calls to `CLEAR(event_flag)`. Tasks may wait on event flag conditions, or logical combinations of flags, with time-out recovery provided to avoid total hang-up occurring. Event flags are now considered quite primitive, requiring rather too much discipline on the part of the programmer.

8.4 Semaphores

This is the proper way of protecting shared resources! The event flag is extended by the addition of task wait queues, to eliminate the time wasted in spin polling, and access procedures which limit the visibility of the semaphore. The Boolean status of the flag is extended to a full positive integer (counting semaphore). Thus, a task requiring access to a shared resource

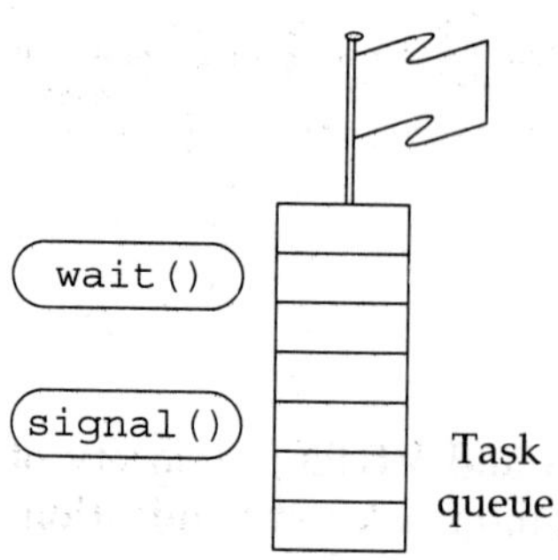

Semaphore schematic

will request exclusive control, which may be deferred by the kernel blocking and queuing the task until the semaphore indicates free entry. This method avoids the tasks spin polling on event flags, and wasting the CPU even if the period is limited by time-slicing.

However, the operation of semaphores does involve quite considerable overhead in kernel activity. Priority reassessment and task rescheduling can take place after every `wait(semaphore)` and `signal(semaphore)` system call.

Because semaphores are system variables, they require a set of control functions for user-level access: `init()`, `wait()`, `signal()`. The application programmer has to arrange for each critical, exclusive resource to have a dedicated semaphore protecting it. This is done by calling the operating system and requesting the allocation of a new semaphore using: `init(sem_1)`. So now, before accessing the critical data protected by sem_1, all tasks are required to query the relevant semaphore: `wait(sem_1)`. Note that this system call will probably generate task rescheduling, so even if the resource is available, it is not certain that the running task will be allowed to jump straight in and access the data. Should the semaphore indicate that its associated resource is not currently free, the requesting task will be swapped out, inserted into the semaphore waiting queue, and an alternative ready task restored to running.

The binary flag semaphore has been extended to include a *counting* capability so that it can serve a wider range of needs. With counting semaphores, the `signal()` call can be set to *increment* the semaphore value, while its `wait()` partner function carries out a *decrement*. This enables the semaphore to maintain a count of items held in a critical buffer, or the current number of resource users.

When a task has finished with the critical activity, it is essential that it calls the exit routine: `signal(sem_1)`, otherwise the critical resource will be permanently reserved, and denied to other tasks. This can quickly lead to run-time problems, which are not uncommon. Some operating systems offer the alternative of a 'mutex' (mutual exclusion) or a 'semaphore'. The distinction rests on who is allowed to release a locked resource. In the case of the mutex only the *original* task that acquired the resource, by requesting the mutex, is permitted to release it. Other tasks will be blocked if they attempt to carry out a `mutex_unlock()`. While, with a semaphore, any task is capable of executing a `signal()` operation to release the resource. The subject of semaphores will be encountered again in Chapter 9 when dealing with the facilities offered by the POSIX API.

8.5 Lock files

Because the initialization of a file has to be an uninterruptible action, it has formed the basis of a mutual exclusion technique. Although rather 'clunky'

Lock files

it is still used to detect whether an application is already loaded and running. Check your home directory using `ls -al` for the `.netscape` directory. List the contents and see if there is a `.lock` file present. If not, fire up Netscape and look again. Then fire up a second Netscape and read the warning message. Two versions of the same executable may result in corrupt initialization files. By ensuring that the 'file exists' test is also uninterruptible, the system can safely use temporary, invisible dot files for retaining status information.

8.6 Intercept signals

These are a kind of software interrupt which a device or task may fire at another task. A single data word will be transferred through a signal call which is often named rather disturbingly, as in Unix: `kill()`. This does not mean that a task will necessarily die when a signal arrives. It is up to the programmer to specify what action will follow reception of signals. The two essential parameters for the `kill(pid, signal)` function call are destination process identity and signal code number. The target, receiving process

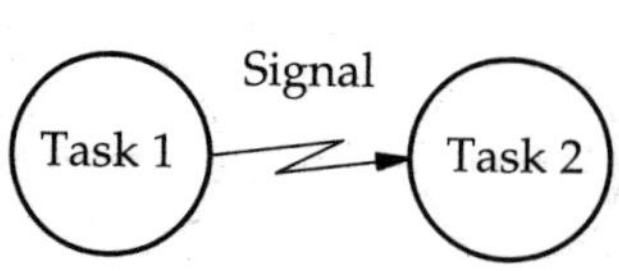

Intertask signals

may be sleeping, in anticipation of the incoming signal, using `pause()` or `wait()`.

Signals are a useful way of handling intermittent data arrival, or rare error conditions. The RTE might offer the facility of directly tying a device interrupt to a particular signal, which acts as if to route the interrupt to a mainline task. If this is not available, it can always be coded explicitly in the associated ISR.

Try the following signal demonstration program which instals a Unix signal handler to count and display the number of signal hits received by a process.

```
#include <stdio.h>
#include <signal.h>
#define MYSIG 44


/* Signal handler function, evoked by sig 44
   reinstalls after each sig hit, prints number of hits
*/
void getsig(int s)
{
   static int count = 0;
   printf("signal %d again, %dth time \n", s, ++count);
   signal(MYSIG, getsig);
}


/* Process to demonstrate signals, sets up a sig handler to
   count the number of sig hits received. Loops forever.
   Start using "kbdcnt &" and make note of pid value returned
   Recommend to use "kill -44 pid" to send signals
   Remove using "kill -9 pid"
*/
int main(void)
{
     signal(MYSIG, getsig);
     printf("start counting kbd kills\n");
     while(1) { };
     return 0;
}
```

Example signal code for Unix

Signals are directed software interrupts which are serviced by a designated signal handler routine within the target task. The main functions include error recovery, intertask signalling and synchronization but the simple flexibility of the method lends itself to many other uses. Note that cyclic executives and VRTX, as the smallest of the RTEs, do not support signals. In summary, software signals are similar to hardware interrupts, transferring control to special routines when a signal arrives at a task. So the target task code must include a function set aside and initialized for this purpose.

Timed signals, known as *alarms*, are also provided. The kernel handles the identification and delivery of the signal to the correct process. Typically, a 32 bit code is available with the signal to identify it, so a process may deal differently with signal intercepts from different sources by checking this value. The lowest range of signal numbers are generally reserved for use by the operating system, the rest are freely available for application use. A process receiving a signal without a properly initialized intercept routine will normally take it as a kill instruction and abort itself.

As you can see, the installation of a function to catch the signal as it comes into the process is achieved by using the `signal()` system call. Note

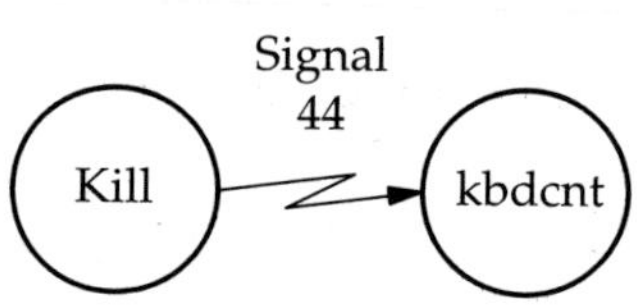


```
rob [262]
rob [263] gcc kbdcnt.c -o kbdcnt
rob [264] kbdcnt &
[1] 9539
rob [265] start counting kbd kills
kill -44 9539
rob [266] signal 44 again, 1th time
kill -44 9539
rob [267] signal 44 again, 2th time
kill -44 9539
rob [268] signal 44 again, 3th time
kill -44 9539
rob [269] signal 44 again, 4th time
rob [270] kill -9 9539
```

Compile the code
Run kbdcnt process
Send signal to kbdcnt

Running the example signal code from p. 175

that it has to be repeated after every signal event because the system resets to the default handler. The signal handler itself receives the incoming signal number as a parameter which may be used within the function to take decisions on what to do. In this way it is possible to have a single function catching all the incoming signals. To send a signal from the console keyboard to a process the shell-level `kill` command can be borrowed. Normally this is used to remove errant processes from the machine, but it can also send less final notifications! Signal number 9 is known for its lethal effectiveness, but here we are using signal number 44 which has not been otherwise allocated.

Notice that the Unix process is detached from the keyboard and made to run in the background by including an ampersand (&) after the command (`a.out &`). In this example it is not so important, we could always use another window to fire `kill -44`, but elsewhere it is an essential facility. You may find the Unix `script` tool useful to record the console I/O during debugging sessions. Type `script /tmp/log.file` before the command you are testing, and all the console dialogue will be copied into /tmp/log.file. Logout or ^D will terminate the recording activity. Remember to do this, or you will end up with a very large log file!

The actual signal handling routines should be kept as short as possible because queuing and nesting intercept signals are not possible. As with interrupt routines, the best plan is to set a global flag to indicate subsequently to the mainline code that the relevant processing is now required. Avoid direct input or output instructions within an intercept routine. Commonly the mainflow process code will `pause()` awaiting the arrival of a signal. This effectively unblocks the waiting process which then continues after the `pause()`.

Unix and other operating systems use *signals* to 'nudge' processes to execute one of their specially designated functions, in a similar fashion to interrupts evoking an ISR. Signals, like interrupts, do not carry parameter data, and usually only offer a minimum self-identification in the form of an integer number. Unix has some publically defined values, which are listed on the following page.

The command line `kill` command sometimes fails if a task is set to ignore or intercept the signal for some other action. To ensure a 100 per cent success, use the `kill -9` command, known as 'kill with severe prejudice', but it is too immediate in some circumstances, not allowing the target task to carry out the normal clean-up operations before closing down. The routine use of the keyboard ^C to kill a foreground process works by the current shell sending a number 2, 'interrupt' signal to the target task which evokes a default action to close down the task. Should a parent task die before its children, the child tasks enter a 'zombie' state when they die. This means that they do not properly relinquish their allocated resources for reuse. In Unix, the base `init` task will then adopt the zombies and recover their resources.

```
#define   SIGHUP      1         /* hangup */
#define   SIGINT      2         /* interrupt (^C) */
#define   SIGQUIT     3         /* quit (ASCII FS) */
#define   SIGILL      4         /* illegal instruction (not reset when caught) */
#define   SIGTRAP     5         /* trace trap (not reset when caught) */
#define   SIGIOT      6         /* IOT instruction */
#define   SIGABRT     6         /* used by abort, replace SIGIOT in the future */
#define   SIGEMT      7         /* EMT instruction */
#define   SIGFPE      8         /* floating point exception */
#define   SIGKILL     9         /* kill (cannot be caught or ignored) */
#define   SIGBUS      10        /* bus error */
#define   SIGSEGV     11        /* segmentation violation */
#define   SIGSYS      12        /* bad argument to system call */
#define   SIGPIPE     13        /* write on a pipe with no one to read it */
#define   SIGALRM     14        /* alarm clock */
#define   SIGTERM     15        /* software termination signal from kill */
#define   SIGUSR1     16        /* user defined signal 1 */
#define   SIGUSR2     17        /* user defined signal 2 */
#define   SIGCLD      18        /* child status change */
#define   SIGCHLD     18        /* child status change alias (POSIX) */
#define   SIGPWR      19        /* power-fail restart */
#define   SIGWINCH    20        /* window size change */
#define   SIGURG      21        /* urgent socket condition */
#define   SIGPOLL     22        /* pollable event occured */
#define   SIGIO       SIGPOLL   /* socket I/O possible (SIGPOLL alias) */
#define   SIGSTOP     23        /* stop (cannot be caught or ignored) */
#define   SIGTSTP     24        /* user stop requested from tty */
#define   SIGCONT     25        /* stopped process has been continued */
#define   SIGTTIN     26        /* background tty read attempted */
#define   SIGTTOU     27        /* background tty write attempted */
#define   SIGVTALRM   28        /* virtual timer expired */
#define   SIGPROF     29        /* profiling timer expired */
#define   SIGXCPU     30        /* exceeded cpu limit */
#define   SIGXFSZ     31        /* exceeded file size limit */
#define   SIGWAITING  32        /* process's lwps are blocked */
#define   SIGLWP      33        /* special signal used by thread library */
#define   SIGFREEZE   34        /* special signal used by CPR */
#define   SIGTHAW     35        /* special signal used by CPR */
#define   SIGCANCEL   36        /* thread cancellation signal used by libthread */
#define   SIGLOST     37        /* resource lost (eg, record-lock lost) */

/* insert new signals here, and move _SIGRTM* appropriately */

#define   _SIGRTMIN  38         /* first (highest-priority) realtime signal */
#define   _SIGRTMAX  45         /* last (lowest-priority) realtime signal */
```

Unix standard intercept signals

```
/* pingpong.c
 * Demonstrating the use of Signals by Unix Processes
 */

#include <stdio.h>
#include <signal.h>
#include <errno.h>

#define PSIG 43     /* check the value of NSIG in          */
```

```
                    /*      /usr/include/sys/signal.h          */
#define CSIG 42     /* before choosing the signal values */

int ccount = 0;
int pcount = 0;
char str[] = "error message";

void psigfunc(int s)
{
      pcount++;
      signal(CSIG, psigfunc);
}

void csigfunc(int s)
{
      ccount++;
      signal(PSIG, csigfunc);
}

main() {
int ke, tpid, ppid, cpid;

      ppid = getpid();
      cpid = fork();    /* spawn child process */
      if (cpid == -1) {
            printf("failed to fork\n");
            exit(1);
      }
      if (cpid == 0)  {
      /* Child process executes here */
            signal(PSIG, csigfunc);
            printf("Child started\n");
            while (1) {
              pause();
              printf("Child hit! count = %d\n",ccount);
              sleep(rand()%10);
              if((kill(ppid, CSIG))) perror(str);
            }
      } else {
      /* Parent process continues execution from here */
            signal(CSIG, psigfunc);
            printf("Parent started\n");
            while (1) {
              sleep(rand()%10);
              if((kill(cpid, PSIG))) perror(str);
              pause();
              printf("Parent hit! count = %d\n", pcount);
            }
      }
}
```

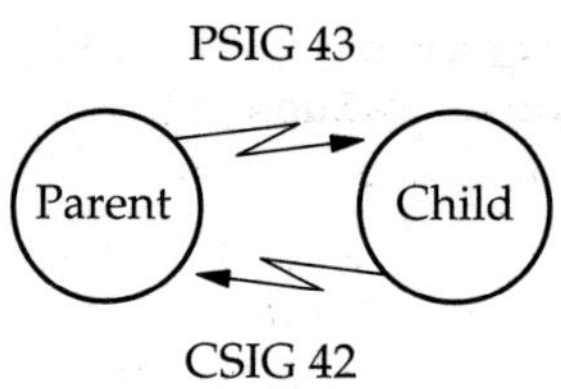

When you actually run the previous example code the results will appear as below:

```
rob [52] pingpong
Child started
Parent started
Child hit! count = 1
Parent hit! count = 1
Child hit! count = 2
Parent hit! count = 2
Child hit! count = 3
Parent hit! count = 3
Child hit! count = 4
Parent hit! count = 4
Child hit! count = 5
^C
rob [53]
```

Demonstrating the use of intercept signals using pingpong.c

A useful Unix utility to investigate running processes is `strace`. This can be evoked to monitor the pingpong program:

```
strace -v -o /tmp/strace.log ./pingpong
```

The log file can then be inspected to reveal all the user-to-kernel system calls and also any signal activity:

```
execve("./pingpong", ["./pingpong"], [/* 58 vars */]) = 0
uname({sysname="Linux", nodename="linux47", release="2.6.2-3mdk",
   version="#1 Fri Feb 13 19:29:11 CET 2004", machine="i686"}) = 0
brk(0)                                  = 0x804a000
old_mmap(NULL, 4096, PROT_READ|PROT_WRITE, MAP_PRIVATE|
     MAP_ANONYMOUS, -1, 0) = 0x40017000
open("/etc/ld.so.preload", O_RDONLY)    = -1 ENOENT (No such file
                                          or directory)
```

```
open("/etc/ld.so.cache", O_RDONLY)          = 3
fstat64(3, {st_dev=makedev(3, 5), st_ino=1927360, st_mode=S_IFREG|
     0644, st_nlink=1, st_uid=0, ...
old_mmap(NULL, 51800, PROT_READ, MAP_PRIVATE, 3, 0) = 0x40018000
close(3)                                    = 0
open("/lib/tls/libc.so.6", O_RDONLY)        = 3
read(3, "...ELF..."..., 512) = 512
fstat64(3, {st_dev=makedev(3, 5), st_ino=718135, st_mode=S_IFREG|
     0755, st_nlink=1, st_uid=0, ...
old_mmap(NULL, 1343148, PROT_READ|PROT_EXEC, MAP_PRIVATE, 3, 0)
      = 0x40025000
old_mmap(0x40167000, 16384, PROT_READ|PROT_WRITE, MAP_PRIVATE|
     MAP_FIXED, 3, 0x141000) = 0x40167000
old_mmap(0x4016b000, 7852, PROT_READ|PROT_WRITE, MAP_PRIVATE|
     MAP_FIXED|MAP_ANONYMOUS, -1, 0) = 0x4016b000
close(3)                                    = 0
old_mmap(NULL, 4096, PROT_READ|PROT_WRITE, MAP_PRIVATE|
     MAP_ANONYMOUS, -1, 0) = 0x4016d000
set_thread_area({entry_number:-1 -> 6, base_addr:0x4016d080,
     limit:1048575, seg_32bit:1, ...
munmap(0x40018000, 51800)                   = 0
getpid()                                    = 5211
clone(child_stack=0, flags=CLONE_CHILD_CLEARTID|CLONE_CHILD_SETTID|
     SIGCHLD, child_tidptr=0x4016d0c8) = 5212
rt_sigaction(SIGRT_10, {0x804852c, [RT_10], SA_RESTORER|SA_RESTART,
     0x4004d718}, {SIG_DFL}, 8) = 0
fstat64(1, ({st_dev=makedev(0, 9), st_ino=3, st_mode=S_IFCHR|0620,
     st_nlink=1, st_uid=501, ...
mmap2(NULL, 4096, PROT_READ|PROT_WRITE, MAP_PRIVATE|MAP_ANONYMOUS,
     -1, 0) = 0x40018000
write(1, "Parent started\n", 15)            = 15
rt_sigprocmask(SIG_BLOCK, [CHLD], [], 8)    = 0
rt_sigaction(SIGCHLD, NULL, ({SIG_DFL({, 8) = 0
rt_sigprocmask(SIG_SETMASK, [], NULL, 8)    = 0
nanosleep({3, 0}, {3, 0})                   = 0
kill(5212, SIGRT_11)                        = 0
pause()                                     = ? ERESTARTNOHAND
                                              (To be restarted)
--- SIGRT_10 (Real-time signal 9) @ 0 (0) ---
rt_sigaction(SIGRT_10, {0x804852c, [RT_10], SA_RESTORER|
   SA_RESTART, 0x4004d718}, {0x804852c, ...
sigreturn()                                 = ? (mask now [])
write(1, "Parent hit! count = 1\n", 22)     = 22
rt_sigprocmask(SIG_BLOCK, [CHLD], [], 8)    = 0
rt_sigaction(SIGCHLD, NULL, {SIG_DFL}, 8)   = 0
rt_sigprocmask(SIG_SETMASK, [], NULL, 8)    = 0
nanosleep({6, 0}, {6, 0})                   = 0
kill(5212, SIGRT_11)                        = 0
pause()                                     = ? ERESTARTNOHAND
                                              (To be restarted)
--- SIGRT_10 (Real-time signal 9) @ 0 (0) ---
rt_sigaction(SIGRT_10, ({0x804852c, [RT_10], SA_RESTORER
   |SA_RESTART, 0x4004d718}, {0x804852c, ...
sigreturn()                                 = ? (mask now [])
write(1, "Parent hit! count = 2\n", 22)     = 22
```

```
rt_sigprocmask(SIG_BLOCK, [CHLD], [], 8)    = 0
rt_sigaction(SIGCHLD, NULL, {SIG_DFL}, 8)   = 0
rt_sigprocmask(SIG_SETMASK, [], NULL, 8)    = 0
nanosleep({7, 0}, 0xbffff4c4)               = ? ERESTART_RESTARTBLOCK
                                                (To be restarted)
--- SIGINT (Interrupt) @ 0 (0) ---
+++ killed by SIGINT +++
```

When a program seems to be getting lost in a maze of system calls, the printout from `strace` can be an invaluable means to disentangling the mystery. Although the log file looks rather awesome at first sight, it can be printed out, marked up with coloured pens and discussed at leisure with colleagues.

8.7 Shared data buffers

The use of global data is regarded suspiciously by many programmers, especially where system-wide visibility may be necessary. But many situations exist where it is the only effective solution to a communication problem because of the amount of data involved or the need to maintain records throughout the application's run-time. There is an obvious danger of data corruption should a pre-emptive task swap occur during a write operation, leaving the data half updated. This can be resolved by using a semaphore in the classical producer-consumer alternation pattern. In this example, the pool is a fixed size buffer which holds the current value of some data which may be read repeatedly, but is overwritten (erased) by subsequent writes. Note that for this example, the reader can depend on data being available, and a writer will always leave a value successfully.

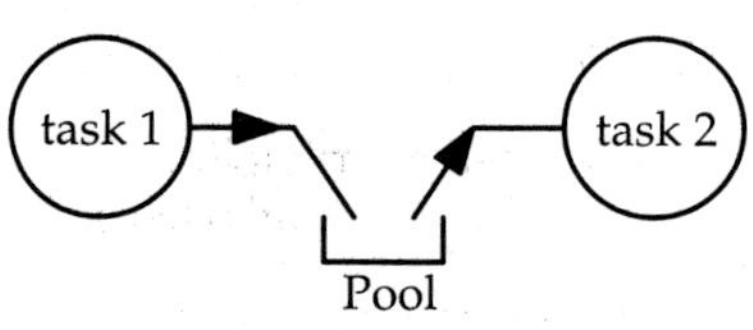

Shared data

```
WRITER task1                          READER task2
 produce new item for READERs           WAIT(sem_avail)
  WAIT(sem_avail)                         read copy from buffer
   overwrite item in buffer             SIGNAL(sem_avail)
  SIGNAL(sem_avail)                   process the item
END_WRITER                            END_READER
```

A more complex problem, involving a variable size data buffer and employing three semaphores, is dealt with in the next section.

8.8 Pipes

Pipes are FIFO channels set up between tasks. They are usually handled in a similar manner to traditional files. Both named and unnamed pipes are supported by Unix, but named pipes are much easier to set up and debug. The messages are usually of unlimited length because they are mediated by pointers. On some RTEs, either *synchronous* (blocking) or *asynchronous* (non-blocking) operation can be specified, allowing the programmer to pause the receiving task while it awaits a message, or carry on doing something else. Named pipes use space in the file system, possibly in /tmp, and can be accessed, as for any files, by pathname. Unnamed or anonymous pipes are associated with the fork command issued by the parent task and are only shared with the immediate child task, which makes their use much more problematic and subtle. The use of centralized message exchanges to pass data, asynchronously or synchronously, between cooperating tasks is a common feature of most RTEs. The maximum size for messages varies, the scheme may be FIFO or prioritized, time-out facilities for suspended readers may be optional. Pipes may be allocated in a similar manner to files, and so appear as entries within the file structure.

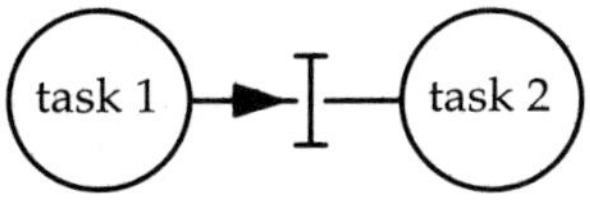

Piping data between tasks

The data flows between the different processes are mediated by pipes which are technically similar to the storage-buffers or FIFOs used to hold data coming and going to disk. Each process in the pipeline is running as independently as is possible when relying on other processes for the essential input data. When no data is available the process will block. When more data arrives it can proceed as fast as it can until an EOF (end of file) marker is received. Pipelines can also include a program written by you in C, or some other language. Such a program may be saved and used later in other pipelines, thus becoming a tool!

The previous pipeline example employed 'anonymous' pipes in that they did not have explicit names. There is an alternative form, 'named' pipes, which you can demonstrate using the Unix 'mknod p' or 'mkfifo' command. This will create a pipe buffer in the nominated directory.

Setting up a pipe or FIFO for one task privately to pass a stream of data to another is a very useful facility. A more complex net of pipes running between several tasks can be also be established. Providing this kind of facility is essential when implementing a multi-tasking application. Here is a simple two process example to run under Linux.

```
rob@kenny [80] mkfifo /tmp/pipe1 -m 660
rob@kenny [81] mkfifo /tmp/pipe2 -m 660
rob@kenny [82] mkfifo pipe3 -m 660
rob@kennyy [83] ls -al /tmp/pipe*

prw-rw-r--   1 rob csstaff 0 Oct 14 18:39 pipe1
prw-rw-r--   1 rob csstaff 0 Oct 14 18:39 pipe2
prw-rw-r--   1 rob csstaff 0 Oct 14 18:39 pipe3

rob@kenny [84] cat letter.tmp > pipe1 &
rob@kenny [85] cat pipe1 > pipe2 &
rob@kenny [86] cat pipe2 > pipe3 &
rob@kenny [86] cat pipe3
  UWE
  Frenchay
  Bristol
  BS16 1QY
```

Creating, and passing data through, named pipes

```
/* speaker.c
   to create a named pipe and write into it
*/
#include <stdio.h>
#include <fcntl.h>

main() {
      int npipe1;
      int i;

      if (mkfifo("/tmp/pipe1", 0666)) {
             fprintf(stderr, "Error in initializing pipe\n");
             exit(0);
      }

      if ((npipe1 = open("/tmp/pipe1", O_WRONLY)) == 0) {
             fprintf(stderr, "Error in pipe opening\n");
             exit(0);
      }

      for(i=0;i<5;i++) write(npipe1, "hello, hello\n", 13);

      close(npipe1);
      unlink("/tmp/pipe1");
      exit(0);
}
```

```
/*-----------------------------------------------------------*/
/* listener.c
   to open a named pipe and read single lines of text from it
*/
#include <stdio.h>
#include <fcntl.h>

int errno;

main() {
      int npipe1;
      int nl=0, i, letter;
      char message[100];

      if ((npipe1 = open("/tmp/pipe1", O_RDONLY)) == 0) {
            fprintf(stderr, "Error attaching to pipe %d \n",
            errno); exit(0);
            }
      while (read(npipe1, &letter, 1) > 0) message[nl++]
         = letter;

      message[nl] = 0;
      printf("%d\n%s\n", nl, message);

      close(npipe1);
      exit(0);
}

/* speaker2.c
   to create a named pipe with a command line name, and write a
      message into it
*/
#include <stdio.h>
#include <modes.h>
#define CBUFF_SIZE 100

char pdev[] = "/pipe/";

main(int argc, char * argv[]) {
      int pid, nchar, i;
      char cbuff[CBUFF_SIZE];
      char * argname;
      char pipename[20];
      char * here;
      char * there;

      if(argc < 2){
            fprintf(stderr,"%s usage:\n %s %s \n",
                  *argv,
                  *argv,
```

```
                 "Pipe_Name\n  Type in message, terminate with
                    esc\n");
                 exit(1);
        }
        here = pipename; /* build full pipe name from command
          line parameter */
        i = 0;
        while (*here++ = pdev[i++]);
        here--;
        there = argv[1];
        while (*here++ = *there++);
        printf("final Pipe name: %s\n", pipename);

        if (mkfifo(pipename, 0666)) { /* open the new pipe */
              fprintf(stderr, "Error creating pipe\n");
              exit(1);
        }
        pid = open(pipename, S_IWRITE);     /* open the new pipe */
        if(pid < 0){
              printf("Error opening pipe\n");
              exit(1);
        }

        nchar = readln(0, cbuff, CBUFF_SIZE);

        while(nchar > 0) {
              writeln(pid, cbuff, nchar);  /* send data down the
                pipe */
              nchar = readln(0, cbuff, CBUFF_SIZE);
        }

} /* end */
/* listener2.c
   to open a named pipe using a command line name, and read a
     message from it
*/

#include <stdio.h>
#include <modes.h>
#define CBUFF_SIZE 100

char pdev[] = "/pipe/";

main(int argc, char* argv[]) {
      int pid, nchar, i;
      char cbuff[CBUFF_SIZE];
      char * argname;
      char pipename[20];
      char * here;
      char * there;
```

```
    if(argc < 2){
          fprintf(stderr,"%s usage:\n %s %s \n",
                *argv,
                *argv,
                "Pipe_Name\n");
          exit(1);
    }
    here = pipename;
    i = 0;
    while (*here++ = pdev[i++]);
    here--;
    there = argv[1];
    while (*here++ = *there++);
    printf("final Pipe name: %s\n", pipename);

    pid = open(pipename, S_IREAD); /* open an existing pipe */
    if(pid < 0){
          printf("Error opening pipe\n");
          exit(1);
    }

    nchar = readln(pid, cbuff, CBUFF_SIZE);

    while(nchar>0){
          writeln(1, cbuff, nchar);
          nchar = readln(pid, cbuff, CBUFF_SIZE);
    }
} /* end */
```

When a task is forked in Unix, producing 'child' tasks, there is a facility to link the resulting tasks through anonymous pipes. Thus a parent can set up pipes through to children, and children can also be interlinked to the parent task, and to each other.

Every task has a file descriptor table which maintains pointers into the system's main file table for open files, pipes and active devices. From here the appropriate inode number can be obtained for any open file, locating the stored data or the device driver for the device in question. Accessing a pipe will look much like a truncated access to a file: a data buffer is held in memory, but no interrupt routine or DMA chip shifts the data to and from the hardware! To open a file requires the kernel to search through the file system for the file name, and build a new entry in the system file table. From then on, all accesses to that file or device will use a file descriptor index and not the file name.

Programmers write Unix tasks with the universal agreement that position 0 in the file descriptor table will deal with *stdin*, position 1 with *stdout* and position 2 with *stderr*. But this is only a long standing, and very useful convention which may be occasionally broken when necessary. Note that the

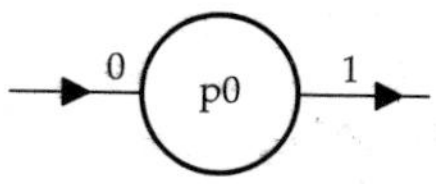

Initial, parent process with path descriptors 0, 1 and 2 already allocated to stdin, stdout and stderr.

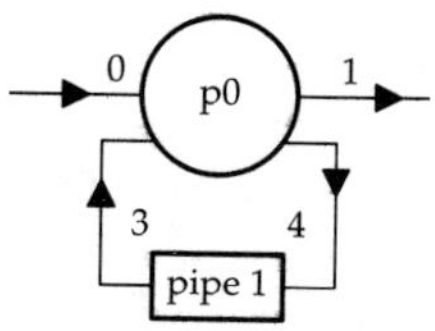

Create a new pipe connected to the original process through descriptors 3 and 4.

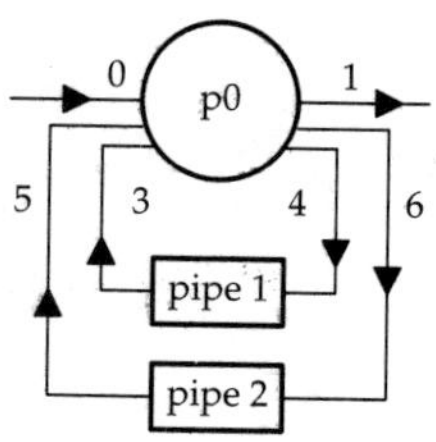

Add a second pipe taking descriptors 5 and 6.

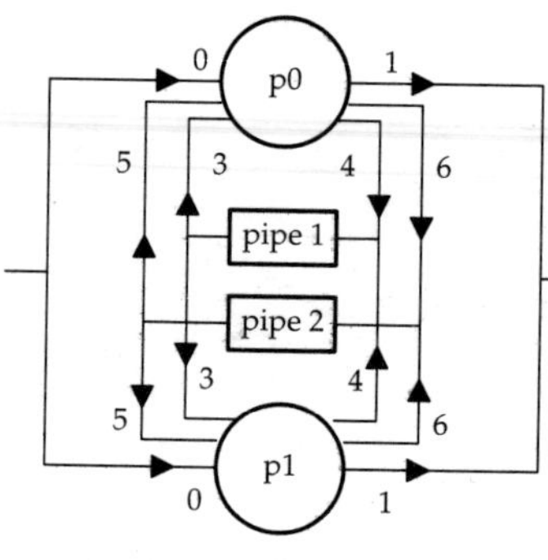

Fork the parent process and create a child process which executes a copy of the same code, shares the same open files and accesses them through a copy of the parent's descriptor table. This means that information about devices, files and pipes are all copied into the child process space by the fork operation. The diagram shows how muddled the duplication is!

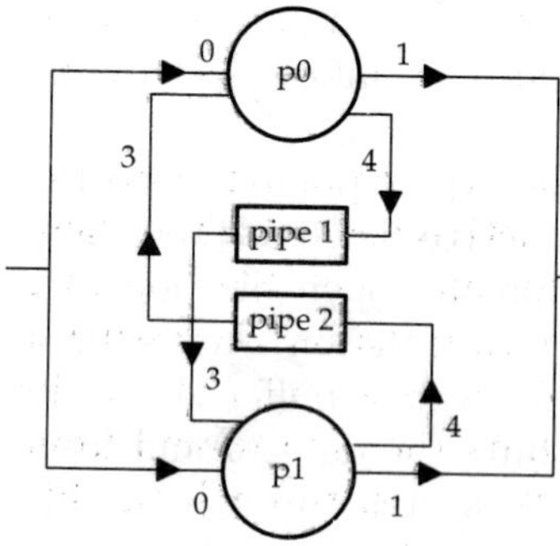

By child and parent closing down the correct set of pathways, a clearer communication network appears. The path descriptor numbers are finally rearranged for clearer operation.

Arranging anonymous pipe communication pathways

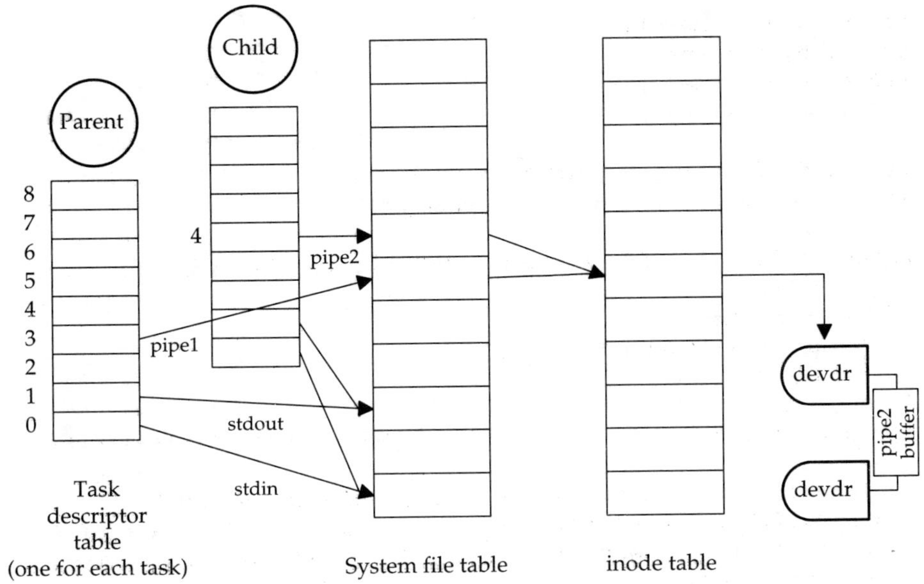

How a task accesses files, devices and pipes

Unix command line piping facility exploits this when it redirects input and output data to build a process pipeline.

```
/* Demonstration code for Linux, showing forking and anonymous
      piping
*/
#include <stdio.h>
#include <time.h>
#include <sys/types.h>
#include <unistd.h>

int main() {

 struct timespec ts1, ts2;
 pid_t newpid;
 int fd1[2], fd2[2];
char m0[] = "\nabout to fork....\n";
 char m1[] = "message from parent to child\n";
 char m2[] = "message from child to parent\n";
char m3[] = "\ndone....\n";
 char rbuf1[256];
 char rbuf2[256];
 int cn1, cn2;
```

```
  ts1.tv_sec=(time_t)1;
  ts1.tv_nsec=(long)1;
  ts2.tv_sec=(time_t)1;
  ts2.tv_nsec=(long)1;

  if ((pipe(fd1)==-1)) printf("error\n");
  if ((pipe(fd2)==-1)) printf("error\n");

  printf("fd1 %d %d fd2 %d %d\n", fd1[0], fd1[1], fd2[0],
     fd2[1]);
  if ((newpid=fork()) ==-1) {
     printf("failed to fork\n\n");
     return 0;
  }
  if (newpid > 0) {                          // parent ***************

    close(fd1[1]); close(fd2[0]);            // closing 4 and 5
    dup(fd2[1]); close(fd2[1]);              // taking 4 in place of 6
     write(4, m1, sizeof(m1));               // parent_to_child messg
     usleep(10000);
     cn1=read(3, rbuf1, 256);
     write(1, rbuf1, cn1);
   } else {                                  // child ***************

     close(fd1[0]); close(fd2[1]);           // closing 3 and 6
     dup(fd2[0]); close(fd2[0]);             // taking 3 in place of 5
     write(4, m2, sizeof(m2));               // child_to_parent messg
     usleep(10000);
     cn2=read(3, rbuf2, 256);
     write(1, rbuf2, cn2);
    }

     write(2, m3, sizeof(m3));
 return 0;
}
```

As probably expected, once again there is a critical resource problem when accessing such shared data areas. In this case, because the pipe can be full or empty, there are extra difficulties for writers and readers respectively. Because there is a risk of a writer gaining access to the buffer and then discovering that it is full, at which point it blocks, hogging the resource. To avoid this situation, another semaphore is employed to give advanced warning of the full condition. Equivalently, a reader could gain access and discover the buffer was empty, and then block. So it is important only to grant exclusive access to tasks which are guaranteed to complete and release.

```
WRITER task1                        READER task2
produce new item for READER          WAIT(sem_data)
WAIT(sem_space)                       WAIT(sem_free)
WAIT(sem_free)                         remove item from buffer queue
add item to buffer queue              SIGNAL(sem_free)
SIGNAL(sem_free)                     SIGNAL(sem_space)
SIGNAL(sem_data)                    process the item
END_WRITER                          END_READER
```

8.9 Control queues

The old real-time design and implementation method known as MASCOT (Modular Approach to Software Construction Operation and Test) used passive access procedures to protect the critical data held in pools and channels. These procedures use two pairs of kernel primitives: `JOIN() & LEAVE()`, and `STIM() & WAIT()`. They provide mutual exclusion facilities similar to the `wait()` and `signal()` operations with semaphores. MASCOT divided the critical data access problem, encountered when using interconnecting data channels to connect tasks, into two distinct areas. Protecting resources from simultaneous, interleaved writing activity and the prevention of simultaneous reading and writing. Separate task queues were installed for readers and writers. The sharing of IDA (pool or channel) procedures by all the contending tasks gives an efficient implementation by not requiring further monitor tasks.

8.10 Sockets

The TCP/IP communications protocol includes a useful construct known as a socket. For programmers in any language, this has become the de facto standard for communicating between processes running on different machines connected by a LAN or even a WAN. Thus processes may exchange data across the Internet using socket calls. In fact, it is now also common to employ sockets to communicate between tasks running on a single machine,

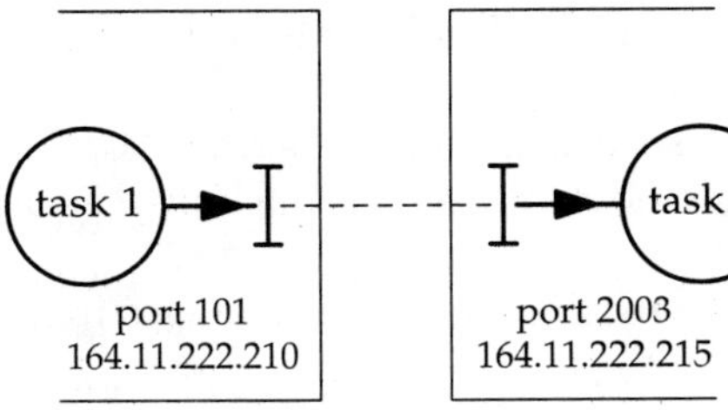

Remote socket communications

even though more efficient alternatives are available. Such flexibility allows software to be quickly distributed across several interconnected hosts after it has been tested on a single platform.

Sockets are addressed by specifying the IP number of the host machine and the port number associated with the targeted application or service. All operating systems now offer socket libraries to assist with building programs which communicate over the network. Client–server pairs, running on different operating systems, can transparently communicate with little trouble.

The system calls that you will be using are listed here, but for the full details, you need to use the on-line help/man facilities.

`socket()` – creates the data structures describing a socket end-point, returning an integer 'socket descriptor', like the file descriptor which gets returned by `fopen()`. Used by both client and server to carry out the communication. The type of communication, datagram (UDP) or virtual circuit (TCP) is also specified by this call. Sockets usually have to be 'bound' or 'connected' before they are useful.

`bind()` – used by server to bind a publically visible address (IP and port number) to the local socket. This will be the address used by remote clients to make contact by using the `connect()` call. Thus some method has to be used to inform clients of the address. This is where the widely published Well-Known-Ports (WKP) come in.

`connect()` – used by client to contact a server socket in preparation for a SOCK_STREAM (TCP) session. After connecting, the `send()` function may be used, which does not require the server address as a parameter, which is mildly convenient.

`listen()` – places a server socket in 'passive' mode, awaiting incoming requests. And it sets the maximum length for the incoming data queue which is provided to avoid simultaneous requests being lost.

`accept()` – this blocks, waiting for incoming requests. It is used with TCP server sockets. When a client request arrives, `accept()` will allocate a new socket for the client to use, thus freeing the original socket for subsequent requests. The port number of the new socket is returned to the client in the acknowledgement packet.

`recv()` – acquire incoming data from the named socket.

`send()` – send data via a TCP socket, after the bind/connect has been achieved.

`sendto()` – used by clients and servers to send complete datagram (UDP) messages to a remote socket. The remote address is included as a parameter to this call.

`recvfrom()` – used by clients and servers to receive complete messages from remote socket.

close() - close down INET domain socket connection.

`unlink()` – deletes Unix domain socket structures.

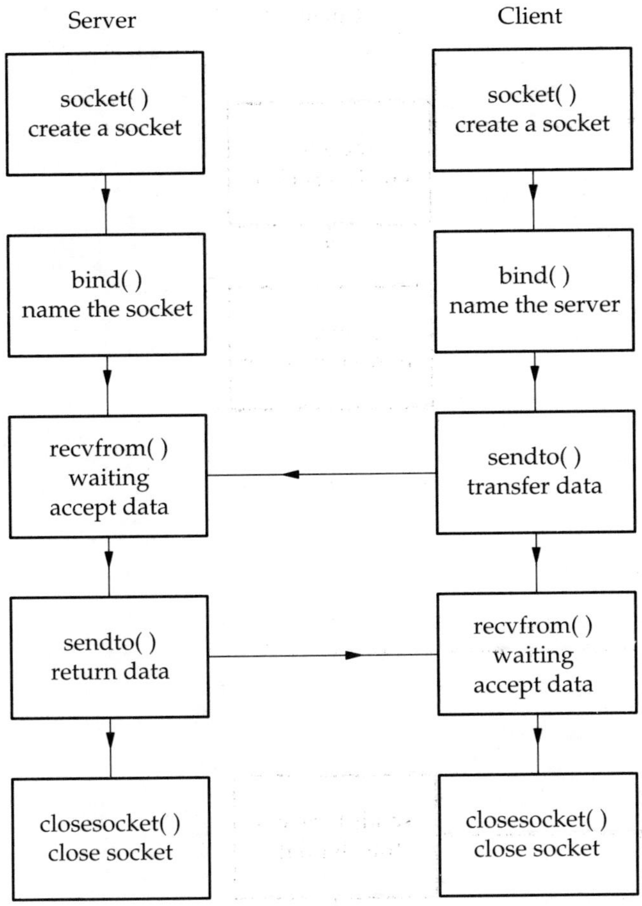

Communication with client–server connection-less (DGRAM) sockets

The next example programs will communicate using UDP datagrams which could be sent between different computers connected to the same LAN.

```
/* Unix Internet DOMAIN (AF_INET), UDP (SOCK_DGRAM) */
*
/*  Server side */

#include <stdio.h>
#include <sys/types.h>
#include <sys/socket.h>
#include <netinet/in.h>
#define SERVER_PORT 4097  // replace port # to suit local
                             situation
                          // look in /etc/services
```

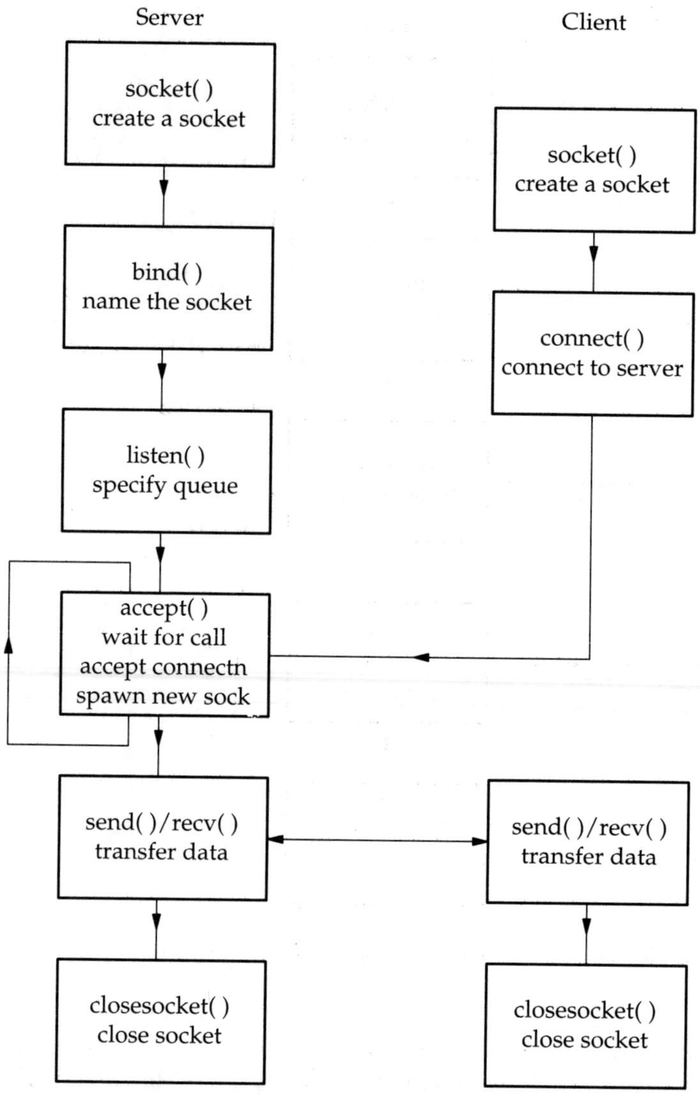

Communication with client–server connection-based (STREAM) sockets

```
int main(void) {

struct sockaddr_in myaddr, youraddr;
int mysock, yoursock, ns, k;
char ibuf[50];
int errno;

      mysock = socket( AF_INET, SOCK_DGRAM, 0);
```

```
      if (mysock < 0) {
           printf("sock err: %s\n", strerror(errno));
           exit(1);
      }

      myaddr.sin_family = AF_INET;
      myaddr.sin_port = htons(SERVER_PORT);
      myaddr.sin_addr.s_addr = INADDR_ANY;

      errno = bind(mysock, (struct sockaddr*)&myaddr, sizeof
        (myaddr));
      if (errno < 0) {
           printf("socket binding error- %s\n", strerror(errno));
           exit(1);
      }
    while (1)  {
      printf("waiting for incoming messg ...\n");
      ns = recv(mysock, ibuf, sizeof(ibuf), 0);
      if (ns < 0) {
           printf("server: recv error\n");
           close(mysock);
           exit(1);
      }
      ibuf[ns] = 0;
      printf("Messg received by Server: %s\n",ibuf);
    }

    close(mysock);

return 0;
}
```

htons: an endian byte swap function

On the i80x86/Pentium the byte ordering within a multi-byte data type, such as `int`, follows the little-endian convention (least significant byte first). Whereas the network byte order, as used throughout the Internet, follows Sun and Motorola with big-endian (most significant byte first). To assist with converting the byte ordering between the host and network formats, there are several transformation functions available: `htons()`, `htonl()`, `ntohs()`, `ntohl()`. These mnemonics refer to *host*, *network*, *short* (16 bits) and *long* (32 bits). So converting a 16 bit word from host (small-endian) to network (big-endian) format requires `htons()`.

```
/* Unix Internet DOMAIN (AF_INET), UDP (SOCK_DGRAM) */
 *
/*  Client side */

#include <stdio.h>
#include <sys/types.h>
```

```
#include <sys/socket.h>
#include <netinet/in.h>
#define SERVER_PORT 4097

int main(void) {

int mysock, n, errno;
char obuf[] = "Hello from client \n";
char ibuf[50];

struct sockaddr_in myaddr, youraddr;

      mysock = socket(AF_INET, SOCK_DGRAM, 0);
      if (mysock < 0) {
        printf("socket error: %s\n", strerror(errno));
        exit(1);
      }

      youraddr.sin_family = AF_INET;
      youraddr.sin_port = htons(SERVER_PORT);
      youraddr.sin_addr.s_addr = inet_addr("164.11.253.36");
                                               //Use your own server addr
      sendto(mysock,
            "Hello from a client!",
            20,
            0,
            (struct sockaddr*)&youraddr,
            sizeof(youraddr));
      printf("sent message to server\n");

close(mysock);
return 0;
}
```

8.11 Remote Procedure Calls (RPC)

The RPC facility was introduced by Sun Microsystems in the 1980s and was used to develop their widely successful Network File System (NFS). It allows an application to run a procedure on a remote host, and receive the results back. Note that the remote procedure must be properly registered on the remote server for this to work! Whereas socket programming passes data back and forth between client and server, RPC programmers deal in function calls and parameters. RPC still uses TCP/UDP ports, which it allocates to requesting applications. So, applications are not tied to particular port numbers, as with the 'well known port number' (WKP) scheme. RPC offers a port mapping service whereby port numbers above 1024 get temporarily assigned to applications which need them. The lookup and routing service is referred to as portmapper and rpcbind. The portmapper works by providing a WKP at 111, either UDP or TCP, to which a remote application can request a connection. This lookup service demon is normally started at boot time and runs continuously.

RPC UDP header

transn ID	SDI	RPC ver	Type	Prog #	Prog ver	Proc #	Authn	Host name	len	UID	GID	grps	verif	len

RPC TCP header

transn ID	SDI	RPC major ver	RPC minor ver	Type	Prog #	Prog ver	Proc #	Authn	Host name	len	UID	GID	grps	verif	len

RPC frame structure

Whereas a local function call would perhaps use stack or CPU registers to pass parameters across, the RPC operates by forming packets, and dispatching them through ports across the network. The operation starts with the client process dispatching a call message to the server process and then blocking while it waits for the reply. The server process carries out its action and returns a reply message containing the results. At which point the client can restart and continue executing. The internal structure of the two RPC message types, call and a reply, are presented in the above figure.

RPC works on a call/reply basis where the calling program is allocated a port and then blocks waiting for a reply. Meanwhile other programs will be able to make new requests to the WKP 111 and the portmapper.

RPC data is encoded using an external data representation (XDR) as defined in RFC 1832, which defines how integers, floating point numbers and strings are represented. This presentation layer protocol enables different computers with different operating systems to interact smoothly. There is no formal message header or protocol system for XDR. XDR uses an 8 bit byte, with the lower bytes being the most significant. The RFC defines that all integer data types are converted to 4 byte integers. While floating point numbers use IEEE 754 32 bit format. If the user data is smaller than 4 bytes, it gets padded out.

RPC is a presentation-level protocol, and provides techniques for authenticating calls from one machine to another, so NFS can be used safely between registered machines and users.

8.12 ADA rendezvous

The real-time language ADA had synchronous rendezvous facilities built in. It operates in a similar mode to the RPC (Remote Procedure Call). The calling task will be suspended until it receives a result back, and the called task may block at an entry point (`accept()`) awaiting a request. In this way two tasks may synchronize their threads of execution, or just pass data across as a message. The code may also be set up to guard critical data from simultaneous accesses.

8.13 Java synchronization

As Java facilities encourage programs to employ multiple threads, there is a basic need to protect shared resources from corruption due to simultaneous access. Java achieves this by offering the `synchronized` statement:

```
synchronized (object)
      statement;
```

In this way, a method which offers access to a shared data resource can be declared as `synchronized` which then ensures that only a single thread can be active on the resource at any time, guarding against corruption. The `synchronized` method can be seen as an *exclusive* gate, controlling access to the resource. Normally, however, a shared data buffer requires both `put()` and `get()` methods, and so to use this access control facility both methods are covered by the `synchronized` command. This is achieved by categorizing the containing *object* as a *monitor*, thus enabling all the different synchronizing methods to be coordinated. When a thread finishes executing a `synchronized` method the object will be unlocked, allowing the next queued thread to gain access. Alternatively, a thread can execute the `wait()` method to relinquish the protected resource and return to the queue. If the thread has finished with the resource it calls `notify()` to signal to the other waiting threads, the highest priority one is then given access to the resource.

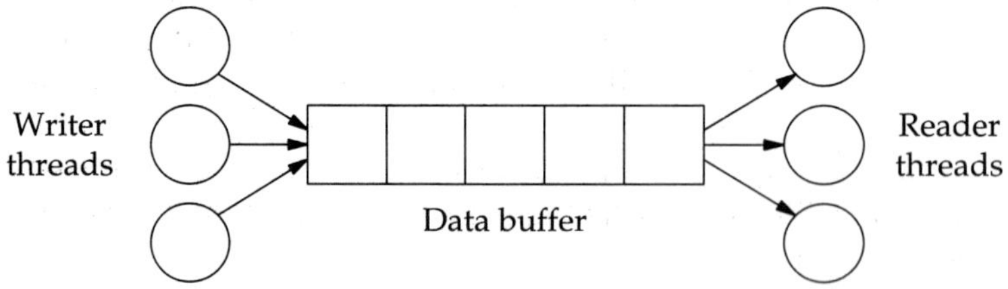

Reader and writer threads accessing a critical data buffer

```
import java.util.*;
public class Queue extends Vector {
```

```
    public synchronized void putIt(Object obj) {
        addElement(obj);
        notify();
    }

    public synchronized Object getIt() {
        while (isEmpty())
            try {
            wait();
        }
        catch (InterruptedException e) {
            return null;
        }
        Object obj = elementAt(0);
        removeElementAt(0);
        return obj;;
    }
}
```

8.14 Chapter summary

An introduction to the syntax and use of several multi-tasking communication/synchronization functions has been presented, so that the variety of facilities available to programmers can be appreciated and compared. Different programmers adopt different styles of implementation, requiring different underlying support. This is often highlighted by a preference for or against the use of intercept signals. For multi-tasking implementations, it is common to use pipes or sockets to provide communication channels between tasks. The use of remote procedure calls by application programmers has fallen into disfavour, perhaps because of security issues.

8.15 Problems and issues for discussion

1. Use the Unix `lockfile` facility to control access to a shared data area which is acting as cyclic buffer between supplier and consumer tasks. Repeat the experiment using the `semaphore` facilities. Carry out some comparative timing experiments. Is there a great difference in the performance of the two methods?
2. Set up a socket connection between a pair of PCs running Linux and Windows. Use TCP and arrange for the Linux server program to respond to a request for a spell check from a client. This should be carried out on a variable length string. The corrected string will then be returned to the client.

3. Investigate the Unix named `pipe` facility for passing data between two tasks. Use `mknod -p` to create the pipe buffers in the /tmp directory. Make sure the access permissions are correct.
4. Using anonymous pipes, launch two processes, spawned from a single parent, which communicate with each other through stdin and stdout.
5. Implement signal passing between two separate tasks, which have been launched independently from the command line. How can they discover the agreed signal numbers and each other's PID?

8.16 Suggestions for reading

Quinn, B. & Shute, D. (1998). *Windows Sockets, Network Programming.* Addison Wesley.

Stevens, W. R. (1994). *TCP/IP Illustrated*, volume 1. Addison Wesley.

Stevens, W. R. (1998). *Unix Network Programming.* Addison Wesley.

Williams, R. (2001). *Computer Systems Architecture – A Networking Approach.* Addison Wesley.

http://www.rfc.net, An RFC (Request For Comment) is one of a series of documents describing the protocols and standards that the Internet is built on. An RFC starts life as an Internet draft. Then the draft is proposed to the IETF, whereupon voting and modification occurs until it either becomes obsolete due to lack of interest or is accepted by the IESG and formally assigned an RFC number for publication. The decision processes are described in more detail in RFC 2026. Further information on RFC documents and the IETF can be had at http://www.rfc-editor.org, the home of the RFC Editor. While the RFC Editor was once a single individual, the legendary Jon Postel, it is now operated by a group funded by the Internet Society.

Chapter 9

Real-time executives

9.1 Chapter overview

Tasks require a system to service their basic needs for scheduling, memory allocation, mutual exclusion and communication. All these can of course be offered by full operating systems, such as Linux, but a more streamline option is provided by Real-time Executives (RTE). This chapter describes the normal range of facilities offered by RTEs, and compares them with those provided by Linux. RTEs can offer more flexible tuning of the task scheduling to fit in with the precise needs of the application, and easier installation of device drivers to handle new hardware. The POSIX standard for system calls is introduced, which many RTEs and operating systems fully or partly adhere to.

9.2 Real-time systems implementations

It is common for real-time programs to be divided into many semi-independent concurrent tasks which are scheduled by an RTE or operating system. Each task deals with one aspect or function of the total system activity. Alternatively, simple real-time systems can be implemented in a single program using procedural loops or incorporating a cyclic executive. This results in several problems occurring, such as inflexible timing for device polling, fixed task priorities and limited intertask communication. Also the performance of such systems rapidly deteriorate if the user requirements become more elaborate as extra facilities are demanded or timing constraints vary from those originally specified. It is under similar circumstances that programmers start looking around for a suitable RTE to release them from

- VxWorks – Wind River
- VRTX – Microtec
- OS 9000 – Microware
- QNX – QNX SS Ltd
- pSOS – Integrated Sys
- MicroC/OS – Microsis
- LynxOS – LynuxWorks

Available RTEs

the deepening quagmire. Programmers usually recognize that while they can realistically build their own cyclic executives, where RTEs are concerned, it is preferable to acquire an existing example. Their time is better spent on dealing with the application itself.

9.3 RTE vs O/S

Fully featured operating systems and a real-time executive

Most programmers want to know what exactly are the differences between a normal operating system, such as Windows or Linux, and a dedicated RTE. This is important when your time and money are on the line! Well, it is rather like comparing a motorized caravan or recreational vehicle (RV) with a racing car. One is built for easy weekend tripping, the other for fast cornering. The RV has everything you could need in most circumstances, and you rarely bother to sort out and unpack the less used items before driving off somewhere. The racing car, however, is fully stripped down for each race. Equipped with the most suitable tyres, suspension tuned to the circuit conditions, and filled with just the right amount of fuel. I wouldn't go on holiday in a single seater racing car, nor tackle a Grand Prix race in an RV. Mind you, RV racing may be occurring somewhere at this very moment, there is no accounting for the human ingenuity. Some of the more familiar facilities which are offered by general operating systems, but not often by RTEs, are listed in the figure below.

- Demand paged virtual mem mngt
- Disk filing system
- Windowing user interface
- Intertask security
- Full networking facilities
- Multi-user support

Extra facilities, beyond most RTEs

There are many RTEs available, commercial, shareware and open source. Each offers a range of facilities which go beyond anything possible with a cyclic executive. However, the variation in the facilities and the Application Programmer Interface (API) offered by current RTEs makes for a serious problem when attempting to reuse or port code. It also means that real-time programmers rather resent changing RTE, because they suspect that they will be required to learn a completely new set of system calls. Partly to address these issues, the IEEE POSIX standard (1003.1/b) for a generic API suitable for RTEs has been launched. And this has been incorporated into operating systems (Linux, Solaris) and RTEs (VxWorks) for programmers to use if they so choose.

9.4 Porting application code for RTEs

Frequently, application code used on real-time systems has not been freshly created, but ported from existing, well-tested sources. Of the four possible sources of code highlighted below, three require porting. Unfortunately, this entails other significant problems which are frequently encountered when changing any of the principal factors affecting implementation: hardware platform, operating environment (API) or compiler suite. When changing them all together, a good deal of time should be allowed for debugging and testing the newly ported code.

- Code from an existing RTE system
- Unix workstation legacy code
- Proprietary cyclic executive code
- Freshly minted code

Provenance of real-time code

9.5 Hardware support for an RTE

Selecting the hardware for a real-time system is often an exercise in cost minimization. If the target system is intended for consumer goods, or embedded within some mass produced equipment, the unit hardware cost is of major concern. Other applications may be unique products; consider a robotic controller to be installed within a \$250 m manufacturing plant. In this case, the possibility of an identical repeat order is very slim, and the major issue would be controlling the spiralling cost of the development work. In the former scenario, a small reduction in chip count would be enthusiastically welcomed, whereas in the latter, such an achievement would be an irrelevance.

Choosing a target platform often starts with comparing the performance of suitable CPUs. To carry out such an assessment requires a fairly accurate estimate of the maximum processing requirements of the new application.

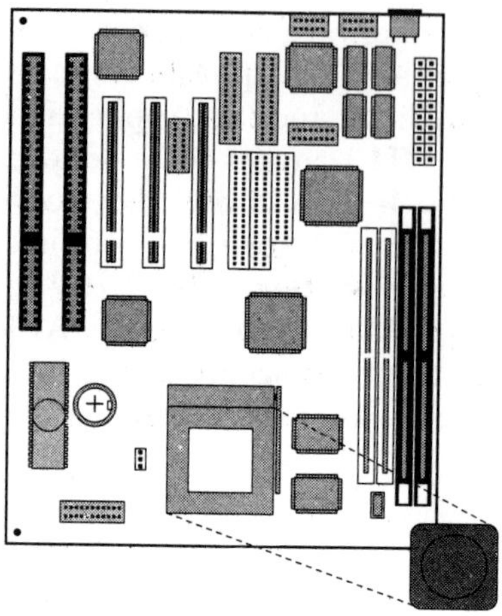

A single board computer

- CPU processing speed
- Arithmetic power
- Addressing range
- Interrupt capability
- Co-processor requirements
- Boot ROM/Flash
- RTC tick source
- MMU availability
- LAN port for loading
- File system hosting
- RS232 as a debugging port
- JTAG loading and debugging

Supporting the RTE

This can involve simulation studies, theoretical calculations, relying on practical experience or simply inspired guesswork. After this stage, the peripheral devices which come as part of the microcontroller, or as discrete components installed on the SBC (Single Board Computer), are considered. To provide support for an RTE will certainly need a source of real-time ticks and a suitable interrupt handling capability. Some of the more sophisticated RTEs require an MMU to translate virtual to physical addresses and to implement the intertask protection controls. The amount of memory, and the balance between RAM and ROM/Flash, needs to be carefully assessed, taking into account immediate debugging needs and possible future system expansion. Some RTE debuggers use up extra target memory to hold their symbol tables, and all of them need some manner of host–target interconnection: LAN, RS232 or JTAG. It is common for the RTE and application code to be held in PROM or Flash, eliminating the need for a boot disk. The majority of the RTE is generic for the CPU type, any board-specific hardware differences are dealt with through the Board Support Package (BSP) which is provided separately or is the responsibility of the development programmer. These issues will be further discussed in Chapter 18.

9.6 RTE facilities

The distinction between fully featured operating systems and RTEs can be blurred. Linux is being adapted to supply the needs of some real-time applications by changing the scheduling system and allowing programmers to recompile the kernel to include only the bare essentials. At the opposite pole, Microware's OS/9000 grew from its original form as a small 8 bit executive for the Motorola 6809 CPU, and now supports most of the facilities associated with larger operating systems such as Unix. The principal facilities offered by RTEs are listed below.

- Hardware device initialization
- Use of memory management H/W for intertask security
- Loading task code into memory, RAM or Flash
- Task initialization and ongoing management
- Task scheduling
- Real-time clock maintenance
- Critical resource protection
- Intertask communication
- Intertask synchronization
- I/O management
- Multiple interrupt servicing
- Free memory allocation and recovery
- Assistance with debugging live systems

Principal RTE facilities

The choice of an RTE can be considered as the straightforward comparison of technical parameters. In practice the situation is more complex. Licence agreements and prices differ widely. Standards of documentation and technical support cannot always be relied upon. Target processor, language interface, satisfactory development tools or the cost of host environments may turn out to be the crucial factors.

An RTE kernel has eight major groups of system functions, listed below, which serve the application tasks through calls to a standardized API.

In this chapter we will discuss the facilities supporting concurrency, or multi-tasking, although separating task scheduling from communication and

- Providing support for system calls (TRAPs)
- Managing memory allocation and recovery
- Carrying out system initialization actions
- Implementing multi-tasking: scheduling and task swapping
- Handling intertask communication
- Dealing with task synchronization
- Managing all I/O processing
- Taking responsibility for exception (interrupt) servicing

RTE system function groups

synchronization is rather artificial because they are all closely related. So intertask communication and synchronization will be the subject of the next chapter, followed by I/O handling.

Task and thread creation are handled by a range of system calls which can initially appear confusing. But code for at least one task has to be available in main memory to run through the action of either a boot loader, a startup script or by being blown permanently in ROM or Flash RAM. From then on the initial task can spawn and load the other tasks that are required for the application to fully run. Remember, threads are the basic execution unit, and a task may contain several threads which are scheduled independently, having separate stacks but sharing common global and heap data.

9.7 Linux

Unix was nurtured into life by Ken Thompson and Dennis Ritchie at Bell Labs around 1970. Because it was freely distributed to universities, ran well on standard DEC hardware, and provided economical access to a multi-user programming environment, it won a strong following in the educational arena. Unix came to dominate the server and technical workstation markets where ease of use was not a major issue, and support for large file systems was essential. In 1991, Linus Torvalds, then a student at the University of Helsinki, started to develop Linux as a free, open source, Unix-like operating system. It has now shrugged off its origins as something only fit for geeky computer science students to play with. In recent year, it has become a major alternative for commercial systems, particularly after its adoption by IBM within their server business. There is also a mass of documentation available, usually on-line through the web, for Linux developers (Linux Documentation Project 2004). As is quite apparent, this provenance sets Linux quite far from the traditional approach to applications in the real-time field. In fact, the comparison of interrupt latencies, or response times, shown below, clearly distinguishes Linux from the RTEs. More seriously, a similarly adverse comparison can be made with regard to *variation* in response timings, known as 'jitter'.

	Response delay
Standard o/s	1–100 ms
Desktop Linux	1–10 ms
RTE	1–10 μs
RTLinux	1–10 μs

Response times

In addition to the slow response timings, standard Linux needs a 32 bit CPU with virtual memory support, more to maintain separation between tasks than to support collaborative dynamics. The I/O timing is rather unpredictable, calls which start access to devices are routed through the filesystem which leads to a more complicated minimum configuration. The kernel code before the 2.5 release was non-pre-emptible which resulted in an occasionally longer response latency, contributing to the poor jitter figures. The scheduling algorithm is more concerned with 'fairness' than deadline priorities. Many development managers will still not countenance its use within their products because it is a commercial orphan; there is no supplier to take the blame.

For those still interested in using Linux for a real-time application there are several strategies used to make it smaller and more responsive when handling external events. So far there have been two principal approaches taken to make Linux behave better:

- a micro-kernel HAL, as used by RTLinux and RTAI
- a modified kernel, as offered by TimeSys.

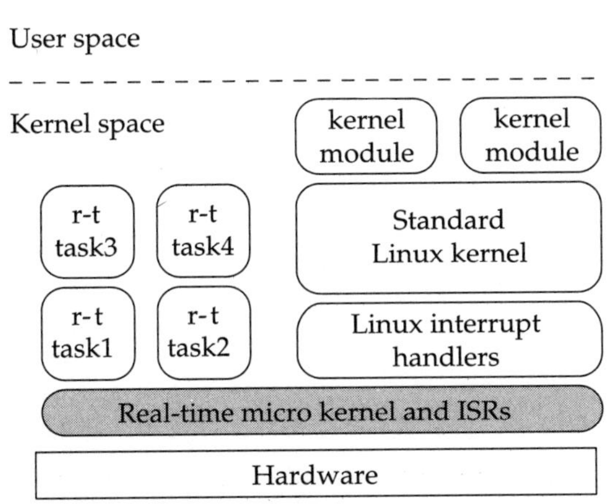

RTAI Linux architecture

The first micro-kernel was created by Victor Yodaiken (RTLinux) but unfortunately a lot of this code is now protected by patent, and no longer available under the GPL licence agreement. An alternative project was completed by Paolo Mantegazza (RTAI), who also left the Linux kernel largely unmodified, developing a new emulator layer, or micro kernel, between the standard kernel and hardware. The layer is referred to as the Real-time Hardware Abstraction Layer (RTHAL). This effectively treated the kernel as a low priority, real-time task, along with any other real-time tasks. The RTAI HAL schedules the tasks and handles all incoming interrupts, passing them on to the Linux kernel if necessary.

The TimeSys Linux real-time upgrade is offered as a GPL distribution as well as commercial, support products. Their modifications to the standard Linux kernel include the addition of more sophisticated mutex pre-emption facilities in place of the existing spinlock arrangements. Also, schedulable interrupt service routines reduce the length and variability of response time latency. There is also an improvement in the system timer resolution.

9.8 POSIX facilities

In order to provide a more detailed, but generally applicable, description of common RTE services, we will use the POSIX definitions as a basis for discussion. In practice, this is still relevant because RTEs such as VxWorks and QNX include most of these system calls, in addition to their own proprietary versions. The POSIX (Portable Operating System Interface Standard) 1003.1 API came about in 1988 in an attempt to rationalize the growing diversity of programmer interfaces being offered by proprietary systems. In 1998 a real-time extension was issued, which has developed into the standard followed by this text.

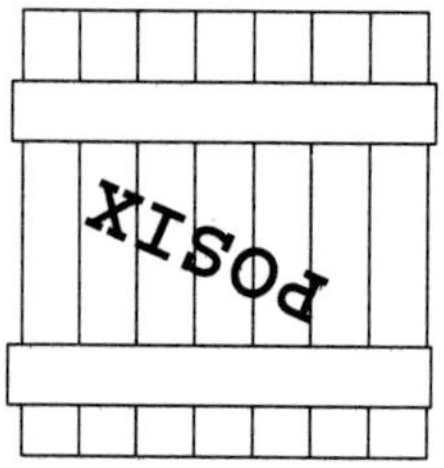

Box of tricks

- *Tasks* In Linux the `fork( )` system call creates a child task, or task, with the same code as the original parent task. It differs from the parent task only in having a different process id (PID) and parent process id

(PPID), and in the fact that resource utilizations are set to 0. Any already existing file locks or pending signals are also not inherited.

In fact, under virtual memory Linux, the child task runs initially with the parent's pages. Separate, new pages are created for the child only when a memory write occurs. This policy is termed 'copy-on-write', and reduces the immediate startup penalty for new tasks when forking. It is then common to use the system call `execv( )` to load in from disk a new executable on top of the child task code! In fact, with Unix, all tasks are spawned in this manner from the single `init` startup task. The two stage fork/execv operation does appear somewhat cumbersome for those more familiar with the RTE style of directly starting up new tasks.

```
#include <sys/types.h>
#include <unistd.h>

pid_t cpid;
cpid = fork();                  // duplicates current task,
                                // TCB & data stack


execv("/home/rob/a.out",        // loads an executable over
      NULL, NULL);              // current task,
                                // starting a new task
```

- *Threads* Threads have become a key facility in the development of complex applications for Linux. Both client and server programs benefit from the use of multi-threaded software architectures. Multi-function programs, like web browsers, rely on threading to provide responsiveness in several contexts simultaneously. Threads can provide a natural programming model for application with basic concurrency requirements.

```
#include <pthread.h>           // use gcc -lpthreads
int rv;
pthread_t tid;
pthread_attr_t attr;
int status;
void * startarg;

main() {
// runs the function startfunc() as a independent,
// schedulable thread
      rv = pthread_create(&tid, &attr, startfunc, startarg);

// waits for tid_1 thread to join it
      rv = pthread_join(tid_1, &rv);

// detach a thread so it doesn't need to be joined
```

```
            rv = pthread_detach(pthread_t);

            rv = pthread_attr_init( );
            rv = pthread_attr_destroy( );
   // terminates the calling thread, returning to the parent
   // pthread_exit(&status);
            rv = pthread_cancel(tid);
   }
```

- *Signals* A signal is like an interrupt, which allows one task, using the operating system, to notify another task. Signals are considered to be *asynchronous* because they can be sent and responded to at any time. There are several special terms associated with POSIX signals.

  A signal is said to be *delivered* when it has been sent to a task. Signals can be *blocked*, being held up and not immediately delivered to the target task. When the block is removed, any blocked signal is then delivered to its target task. To complicate matters for the programmer, signals are not queued, so if a signal is blocked, another signal arriving will overwrite the first. Only one signal will be delivered when the block is removed. Signals may be blocked in two ways. Either a signal mask can be set or the task can be already busy executing a signal handler. A signal is *caught* using either `sigaction()` or `signal()` which register a task function to act as the signal handler. So, when the signal is delivered to your task, it is caught and your signal handler, which will be a function with the signature `void handler(int signo)`, is executed. If the signal handler is set to SIG_DFL, the default handler is used. Alternatively, it may be set to SIG_IGN, in which case incoming signals will be ignored.
- *Semaphores* POSIX 1003.1b semaphores can offer an efficient vehicle for intertask synchronization or communication. Cooperating tasks can use semaphores to arbitrate access to centralized resources, which most frequently means: shared or global memory. Semaphores can also protect from uncontrolled access those resources available to multiple threads. In some circumstances there may be a need to control access to hardware such as printers, disks or ADC/DAC equipment.

Function call	Operation
sem_init	Initializes an unnamed semaphore
sem_close	Deallocates the specified named semaphore
sem_destroy	Destroys an unnamed semaphore
sem_t *sem_open	Opens/creates a named semaphore
sem_getvalue	Gets the value of a specified semaphore
sem_post	Unlocks a locked semaphore
sem_trywait	Performs a semaphore lock on a free semaphore
sem_wait	Performs a semaphore lock
sem_unlink	Removes a specified named semaphore

POSIX semaphore function calls

```
#include <sys/types.h>
#include <stdio.h>
#include <errno.h>
#include <unistd.h>
#include <semaphore.h>

main()  {
sem_t   mysem;
int     pshared = TRUE;
unsigned int value = 5;
int     sts;
   sts = sem_init(&mysem, pshared, value);
   if (sts) {
     perror("sem_init() failed");
   }
}
------------------------------------------------------------
#include <sys/types.h>
#include <stdio.h>
#include <errno.h>
#include <fcntl.h>
#include <unistd.h>
#include <sys/mman.h>
#include <semaphore.h>
#include <sys/stat.h>

main()  {
sem_t   *mysem;
int     oflag = O_CREAT;
mode_t  mode = 0644;
const char semname[] = "/tmp/mysemaphore";
unsigned int value = 3;
int     sts;
   mysemp = sem_open(semname, oflag, mode, value);
   if (mysemp == (void *)-1) {
      perror(sem_open() failed ");
   }
}

/*
** These examples use POSIX semaphores to ensure that
** writer and reader processes have exclusive, alternating
** access to the shared-memory region.
*/

/* Shared memory WRITER task, contends with reader task for
 * access. Access resolution by single semaphore
*/

#include <unistd.h>
#include <semaphore.h>
#include <errno.h>
#include <sys/types.h>
#include <sys/mman.h>
```

```
#include <sys/stat.h>
#include <sys/fcntl.h>

char shm_fn[] = "my_shared_mem";
char sem_fn[] = "my_sem";

main() {
  caddr_t shmptr;
  unsigned int mode;
  int shmdes, index;
  sem_t *semdes;
  int SHM_SIZE;

  mode = S_IRWXU|S_IRWXG;

  if ( (shmdes = shm_open(shm_fn,O_CREAT|O_RDWR|O_TRUNC,
     mode)) == -1)  {
     perror("shm_open failure");            // open shared memory

     exit();
    }

  SHM_SIZE = sysconf(_SC_PAGE_SIZE);        // preallocate shared
                                            // memory

  if(ftruncate(shmdes, SHM_SIZE) == -1){
    perror("ftruncate failure");
    exit();
  }

  if((shmptr = mmap(0, SHM_SIZE, PROT_WRITE|PROT_READ, MAP
    _SHARED,b  shmdes,0)) == (caddr_t) -1){
    perror("mmap failure");
    exit();
  }

semdes = sem_open(sem_fn, O_CREAT, 0644, 0); // create semaphore
                                             // in locked state
if(semdes == (void*) -1){
  perror("sem_open failure");
  exit();
}

 if(!sem_wait(semdes)){  // lock the semaphore
      for(index = 0; index < 100; index++){
        shmptr[index] = index*2;             // write to the
                                             // shared memory
        printf("write %d into the shared memory
            shmptr[%d]\n", index*2, index);
      }
    sem_post(semdes);                        // release the
                                             // semaphore
 }
```

```
    munmap(shmptr, SHM_SIZE);                // release the
                                             // shared memory


    close(shmdes);
    shm_unlink(shm_fn);

    sem_close(semdes);                       // return thes emaphore
   }

   /*********************************************************/

   /* Shared memory READER task, contends with writer task for
    * access. Access resolution by single semaphore
   */
   #include <sys/types.h>
   #include <sys/mman.h>
   #include <semaphore.h>
   #include <errno.h>
   #include <sys/stat.h>
   #include <sys/fcntl.h>

   char shm_fn[] = "my_shared_mem";
   char sem_fn[] = "my_sem";

   main(){
     caddr_t shmptr;
     int shmdes, index;
     sem_t *semdes;
     int SHM_SIZE;

     SHM_SIZE = sysconf(_SC_PAGE_SIZE);

     if ( (shmdes = shm_open(shm_fn, O_RDWR, 0)) == -1 ){
        perror("shm_open failure");          // open the shared
                                             // memory area
        exit();
      }

     if((shmptr = mmap(0, SHM_SIZE, PROT_WRITE|PROT_READ,
       MAP_SHARED, shmdes,0)) == (caddr_t) -1) {
       perror("mmap failure");
       exit();
     }

     semdes = sem_open(sem_fn, 0, 0644, 0); // create the semaphore
     if(semdes == (void*) -1){
       perror("sem_open failure");
       exit();
     }

     if(!sem_wait(semdes)) {                 // lock the semaphore
         for(index = 0; index                // access shared memory
            < 100; index++)                  // area for reading
            printf("The shared memory shmptr[%d] holds %d\n",
                index, shmptr[index]);
```

```
        sem_post(semdes);                       // release the semaphore
    }

    munmap(shmptr, SHM_SIZE);

    close(shmdes);                              // close shared memory
                                                // area

    sem_close(semdes);                          // cancel semaphore
    sem_unlink(sem_fn);
}
```

POSIX offers both named and unnamed semaphores. The former would be used between multiple processes, while the latter is suited for multi-threading, or within a single process. Care needs to be taken because some semaphore functions are intended to perform operations only on named or unnamed semaphores. An unnamed semaphore can be created using the `sem_init()` call. This initializes a counting semaphore with a specific value and can then be accessed. To create a named semaphore, call `sem_open()` with the O_CREAT flag specified. This establishes a connection between the named semaphore and the task.

Semaphore locking and unlocking operations can be done with `sem_wait()`, `sem_trywait()`, and `sem_post()` functions. These apply to named and unnamed semaphores. A call to `sem_getvalue()` returns the semaphore's value.

When the application finishes with using an unnamed semaphore, it can be destroyed with a call to `sem_destroy()`. To deallocate a named semaphore, the `sem_close()` function must be called. The `sem_unlink()` function is then called to remove the named semaphore when all other user processes have deallocated it.

9.9 Scheduling

Multi-tasking using uniprocessor equipment involves the multiplexing of distinct tasks onto an exclusive central processor. Only the main program instruction fetch-execute sequence is limited to a single active task. Autonomous input/output, arithmetic and similar subsidiary activities may be carried on simultaneously if co-processors are installed and used. The strategy used by schedulers to determine which task runs next can vary considerably.

The provision of pre-emptive scheduling within an RTE depends on the availability of interrupts and a range of system calls which enable the RTE scheduler to regularly regain control of the CPU and reschedule the tasks when the situation demands. This is particularly useful when

- Round-robin – simple task queue, used by cyclic executives at clock and base level
- First come first served – simple task queue, but no time slice pre-emption
- Prioritized queuing – static or dynamic allocation of relative priorities
- Deadline – task priority increases as the deadline approaches
- Shortest job first – popular priority scheme with typists

Task scheduling strategies

the effective relative priorities of ready tasks have been altered by external events.

Real-time executives tend to employ pre-emptive, fixed priority schemes with time-slicing available for tasks set at the same priority level. Unix has a task 'aging' facility which increases the priority of tasks as they sit on the ready queue. The longer they wait the more chance they have of selection. Allowing the relative task priorities to vary during system execution provides for more flexibility and better responsiveness. However, the extra problems and difficulties incurred in tuning such systems must be acknowledged.

The moment of rescheduling may be determined on a regular time-sliced pattern (RTC interrupt) or on an irregular, pre-emptive basis using external event interrupts. The problem of swapping tasks, often called *context switching*, transparently without too much loss of processing time is of principal concern to CPU architects. New CPUs often have extra features in hardware or microcode to assist with this crucial activity.

The task's status is saved, partly on the task stack and partly in the TCB itself and another task is allocated time on the CPU. Eventually the dispatcher will restore the original task which will resume execution, hopefully without hiccough. The choice of which task to move forward to the running state is left to the main scheduler.

Real-time executives support pre-emptive task scheduling in addition to the more normal time-slicing. An age-based scheme provides fair access to all tasks. When a task is entered into the active queue its age is initialized by setting it equal to the priority value. Whenever a new task enters the queue all the age values are incremented. The age is also incremented every time task switching occurs. On Linux, the priority of tasks may be altered from the keyboard using the `nice` command. The range of priorities runs from 1 (lowest) to 65 535 (highest).

Tasks can also influence the scheduling by setting the initial priority parameter in the `fork()` call.

9.10 Unix Filesystem Hierarchy Standard (FHS)

The number of files on a standard Linux system amounts to several tens of thousands, and these require a standardized hierarchical directory structure to maintain some reasonable sense of order for the user. The intention is for the file systems of all Unix installations to be similar and so recognizable to new users. Files can be classified as *static* when they hold code or constant data, or *variable* when they can accept write requests from running programs. Files can also be *private* or *public* depending on their ownership and access permissions.

9.11 Configuring and building the Linux kernel

Recompiling the kernel before breakfast is a badge of honour or rite-of-passage for many embedded systems developers. Such activity is possible because all the source code for Linux is readily available via the Internet. This freedom does not mean that everyone is recoding kernel modules or testing out freshly created scheduling algorithms everyday. Rather, it offers the realistic opportunity to selectively configure the operating system, using existing modules, to more exactly suit the requirements of your application. In particular, the need to adjust Linux to include real-time support is important for developers of embedded systems. This involves downloading fresh source files from http://www.kernel.org, obtaining the particular architecture patch files, then the special real-time patch files, applying the patches to the kernel sources, configuring the make script and finally compiling and linking the kernel module. Beginners need to understand that Linux releases are numbered in a three field format: 2.6.4. The left digit is the major version number, which has been 2 for some seven years. The middle digit gives the current 'patch level', identifying subversions, where an *even* value indicates reasonable stability, but an *odd* value warns of an experimental release. The right-hand digit is known as the 'sublevel', referring to the current state of bug fixes. The latest Linux kernel is numbered 2.6, but 2.4 is still more popular with embedded systems developers. The whole operation is complex and not easy to describe exactly for all hosts and all target CPUs. Some more details are given later in Chapter 19, but the seriously interested reader is referred to the Redhat website for more information and the few specialist texts, such as Beekmans (2003), which describe how to build new Linux kernels in much

- Select system components
- Download and unpack tgz files
- Apply architecture patch code to kernel
- Configure and build target kernel
- Build root file system for target
- Select and set up booting arrangements
- Download and boot

Creating an embedded Linux

more detail. There is also a full and useful description of the porting process for Linux 2.4 onto an XScale target provided by Kumar *et al.* (2004).

9.12 Linux for embedded applications

There are two main options for developers who want to use a version of Linux for real-time applications RTLinux and RTAI. Both require a working memory management unit, which limits the choice of CPU to the larger microcontrollers, such as ARM or 386 -based. A smaller Linux derivative, μCLinux, has removed the MMU dependencies, and is viable for smaller targets. The memory requirements are also reduced to less than 1 MB. But the latest 2.6 version of the Linux kernel includes several features of interest to real-time developers. The kernel code is now pre-emptible, removing some of the latency variability encountered with the 2.4 predecessor. Also, use of the Native POSIX Threading Library (NPTL) greatly improves multi-threading performance, which is of direct relevance to many embedded systems. A new scheduling algorithm (O(1)) should have superior performance, especially under higher loading and with multi-processor platforms. Of particular interest is the possibility that the 2.6 kernel may be configured to run with physical addressing, obviating the need for MMU support, an ability offered, until now, only by the μCLinux kernel.

9.13 Booting embedded Linux

The normal way to boot Linux is to load the kernel image onto a hard disk partition, mark it as 'bootable' and use a boot manager, such as the Linux Loader (LILO), to direct control to that partition when the system boots. Such an arrangement does allow the user to boot different operating systems, or revert to an earlier version of Linux if the new one fails. For some larger real-time systems this might be appropriate description, but for smaller, embedded systems, which do not have access to hard drives, a different procedure has to be employed.

9.14 Language support

Real-time systems can be coded using special HLLs such as ADA or Modula-2 which include the necessary facilities to support tasking. Standard HLLs such as Pascal or C can be linked to an RTE which provides task scheduling and a lot of other support not encompassed by the HLL libraries. Special purpose executives, written in C or ASM, may also fulfil basic task scheduling requirements. Application programs then run with the assistance of this executive or operating system. The run-time support offered by the RTE may be 'included', linked or available at runtime through TRAP windows.

In addition, multi-tasking programs need subroutine linkage support, I/O handling and error management. The HLL run-time support routines can be selected from the associated library, to a limited extent, during the linking phase. Many RTEs allow tasks to share code modules in memory, even auto-loading from disk if necessary.

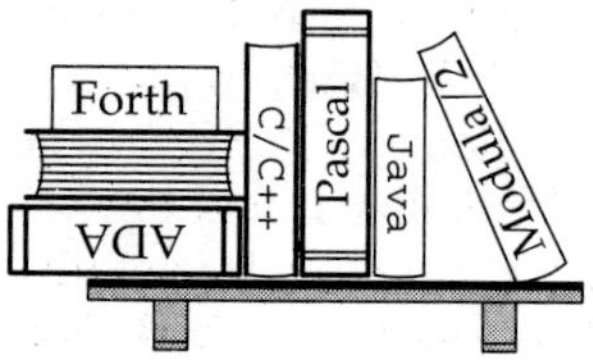

Language diversity

RTEs provide system calls/TRAPs for application programs which support tasking, memory management, I/O handling, interrupt servicing, intertask communication, critical resource protection and error recovery. Specialist libraries are now available for graphics and numeric routines. These can be linked into the application module before loading takes place, or provided as memory resident PROM code at run-time.

An advantage of HLL compilers is that the Operating System interface is handled through the run-time support code: changing the host Operating System doesn't (shouldn't) require any alterations in a C/C++ application program. Only the compiler library package would be changed. If a development is intended to be installed onto a 'bare board' the run-time support package will need to be specially prepared and linked into the main code in place of the normally used package.

There are a number of particular problems involved in dealing with multi-tasking systems which require special facilities for their resolution. Data integrity must be ensured when multiple tasks have access to the same data pool. The tasks may need to communicate information or mutually synchronize to ensure effective job completion. The danger of tasks becoming permanently deadlocked must be removed as far as possible and the fair allocation of CPU time must be ensured to avoid task starvation. Provision for debugging and testing should be planned from the start of the design.

Before programmers start worrying about intertask communication they need to know how to launch a task, and then how to launch several related tasks. The simplest scheme simply involves developing and compiling *discrete programs* which are started from the command line, or a batch file. They all have the same owner permissions, and can communicate through preagreed, named pipes or files, known sockets or common data modules. Such schemes work, but suffer from too much 'independence', making development more difficult. For example, signals are nearly impossible to use because of the difficulty of separate tasks assertaining each other's task number. Similarly, the compiler does not have the advantage of knowing all the names and types used in all the different programs. The imposition of order and consistency is left to the humans.

An alternative technique launches a single parent program which then spawns from itself all the concurrent tasks required by the application. This allows the resulting child tasks to know some of each other's PIDs, enabling signals to be employed to a limited extent between tasks. Pipes, named and anonymous, can be set up between all the tasks.

9.15 Licensing issues

Although this text is clearly prepared for students mainly interested in technical issues, the financial and legal side needs to be contemplated when considering the acquisition of software from an outside supplier. This is of particular significance in the embedded field where an executive or operating system may need to be modified in some way. There are several alternative legal structures which software developers can adopt when deciding to acquire and reuse software from outside sources.

- Outright source code purchase
- OEM licence agreement
- Open source
- BSD-style open licence
- GNU GPL

Legal/financial structures for software development

Richard Stallman states in his introduction to the GNU GPL (General Public License) that: 'The licenses for most software are designed to take away your freedom to share and change it. By contrast, the GNU General Public License is intended to guarantee your freedom to share and change free software – to make sure the software is free for all its users.' GNU/Linux is distributed under the terms of the GPL licence, making it a strict requirement that any new additions or amendments to the original code should be made available in source format.

The conditions of GPL have been adopted by many other free software and open source developers, and these conditions need to be clearly understood by those seeking to sell products which include some GPL code.

Although initially some commercial suppliers were worried about the impact of GPL software on their business, there are now many examples of GPL-covered commercial programs which have established themselves in the marketplace. The availability of proprietary software, such as compilers and databases, does not appear to have suffered. This may be due to the nervous reluctance of professional managers to move away from traditional 'support' agreements, or, perhaps, the unchallengeable excellence and value for money of commercial software.

Richard Stallman guru of GNU

Interestingly, the Indian and Chinese governments have now openly committed to using Linux for desktop and server computer facilities within civil service departments as official policy. This may be because of their suspicions about Microsoft's motives, or simply for financial advantage. But still, the general uncertainty over the legal position of open source software means that developers often find it hard to convince managers to rely on GPL code at the core of a new project.

Software is also distributed under similar conditions: Artistic License, GNU Lesser General Public License, IBM Public License, Mozilla Public License, Open Software License, Academic Free License, Sun Industry Standards Source License, W3C Software Notice and License, and the BSD Public Licenses.

The BSD licence comes after GNU GPL in popularity as free software licence. The significant difference between the two being that BSD does not require any altered sections of source code to be made available to purchasers. For example, Apple has used parts of Mach, FreeBSD, and NetBSD to create Mac OSX. So large parts of the latest, proprietary Mac operating system are derived from source software.

The use of GPL software in the embedded marketplace is more difficult than with desktops or servers. In the latter cases, it is fine to install proprietary applications alongside GPL programmes. There is no infringement of the GPL conditions if this is done. However, in the embedded situation, where kernel modules or device drivers are commonly amended when porting the operating system to a new platform, the requirement is to hand over full source listings to all customers. With the genuine risk of competing organizations obtaining a free view of precious code, it is not surprising that managers are cautious to accept the GPL conditions. To get around this dilemma, some firms take advantage of the Linux facility to dynamically load device driver modules, thus hopefully avoiding the GPL strictures. Whether such an arrangement using loadable, proprietary modules rigorously complies with the letter of GPL is debatable! The worry for managers is that GPL itself has not yet been tested through a court case, so the report that Linus Torvalds accepts the validity of loadable proprietary modules within the Linux community is the best reassurance available.

Unfortunately, for real-time developers there is a particular legal issue relating to the use of RTLinux from FSMlabs due to the US patents which have been filed covering aspects of the RTLinux/PRO, but not the other product. RTLinux/GPL (RTLinux Patent 1999). To confuse the issue, the patent licence is not totally clear, introducing some doubt which deters GPL users. FSMLabs have tried to balance the requirements to generate revenue to fund further development work, with the expectations of the open source community.

Worrying doubts have also been raised about the use of GPL libraries by proprietary software. Distributing non-free, copyrighted software that uses GPL-covered software is forbidden. This is particularly sensitive in the case of dynamic shared libraries (DLLS), whose GPL status may be unknown, and even unknownable, to the original developer. The fact that a GPL-covered program takes the form of a library makes no difference to the conditions of the GPL licence. An alternative licence, the Lesser General/GNU Public Licence (LGPL), has been published to deal with this situation. So when permission is required for non-free software to access a GPL library, the LGPL can be used.

Serious problems could rapidly arise for GPL users if a legal challenge to the status of their software were launched by a malign organization, more interested in disrupting the smooth running of their competitors than winning the case.

In the end, 'cost is always king'. But this should be understood as the *complete* product cost, maybe over a 10 year development and maintenance cycle.

9.16 Chapter summary

The many advantages of using an RTE to support multi-tasking systems is explained. Tasks require: scheduling, memory allocation, mutual exclusion and communication. Linux can of course offer all these, but it is also much larger because of all the other unnecessary facilities that it provides. The normal range of facilities offered by RTEs is described and compared with those provided by Linux. RTEs do offer more options for tuning task scheduling, which helps to keep the application running smoothly. Also, access to hardware is considered easier from an RTE. The availability of a POSIX standard for system calls makes programming for a new RTE and porting code much easier. More details about task communication and synchronization facilities are provided in the next chapter. Legal issues surrounding the many different licensing agreements are introduced as significant for many commercial OEMs.

9.17 Problems and issues for discussion

1. Using Google, search out a couple of downloadable RTEs which provide enough documentation for you to get an idea of the facilities they offer

to programmers. Are they POSIX compliant? Does this really matter for an embedded systems development?
2. What are the main facilities required of an RTE for an embedded application?
3. Check out the improvements to the threading capabilities offered by the Linux 2.6 kernel, beyond those offered by the 2.4 release.
4. What disadvantage might become evident if you were to employ a non-pre-emptive scheduling strategy for implementing a multi-channel data router? Would traffic composed of fixed size packets make any difference?
5. Check out the differences between standard and real-time enhanced Linux. How significant is the introduction of kernel pre-emption?
6. Report on the different versions of r-t Linux that are available: RTAI, LynuxWorks/BlueCat, KURT, Monta Vista, TimeSys, FSM-Labs/RTLinux, and any others you can discover.

9.18 Suggestions for reading

Abbott, D. (2003). *Linux for Embedded and Real-time Applications.* Newnes.
Beekmans, G. (2003). Linux from scratch, version 5. GNU LDP. From: http://www.tldp.org/LDP/lfs/lfs.pdf
DEC (1996). Guide to realtime programming.
From: http://h30097.www3.hp.com/docs/base_doc/DOCUMENTATION/V40F_PDF/APS33DTE.PDF
Describes the use of the POSIX library under Unix.
Well worth reading, even though rather dated.
Gallmeister, B. (1995). *POSIX.4.* O'Reilly Books.
Kumar, K., Bhat, A. & Hongal, S. (2004). Porting of Linux 2.4.21 onto the XScale Mainstone board.
From: http://www.linuxgazette.com/node.9786
Labrosse, J. (2002). *MicroC/OSs-II: The Real-time Kernel.* CMP Books.
Labrosse, J. (2002). *Embedded Systems Building Blocks.* CMP Books.
Michaelson, J. (2003). Open Source Licensing: What every OEM should know.
Michaelson, J. & Brownlee, D. (2003). BSD or Linux: Which Unix is best for embedded applications?
From: www.wasabisystems.com/data_sheets
POSIX 1003.13, Standards document, real-time & embedded application support.
From: http://www.unix-systems.org/version3
Proctor, F. (2002). Introduction to Linux for real-time control. Aeolean Inc.
From: http://www.isd.mel.nist.gov/projects/rtlinux/
Ready, J. & Weinberg, B. (?2001). *Leveraging Linux for Embedded Applications.* MontaVista Software.
RTLinux Patent (1999). http://www.patents.ibm.com/details?pn=US05995745
Russell, R. & Qinlan, D. (2000). Filesystem Hierarachy Standard – version 2.2.
From: http://www.pathname.com/fhs
Simon, D. (1999). *An Embedded Software Primer.* Addison Wesley.
VxWorks Programmer's Guide 5.5 (2002). WindRiver.

Yaghmour, K. (2003). *Building Embedded Linux Systems.* O'Reilly.
Yaghmour, K. (2003). Embedded systems, Linux, and the future.
From: http://www.linuxdevcenter.com/pub/a/linux/2003/06/09/embedlinux.html
http://www.fsf.org, for information on the Free Software Foundation.
http://www.stallman.org, Richard Stallman's home page.
http://www.realtimelinuxfoundation.org, source of much up-to-date information.
http://www.uclinux.org, source of information about μCLinux for MMU-free hardware.
http://tldp.org. The Linux Documentation Project. A gold mine of information.
http://www.armoid.com/literature.html, a very useful compilation of documents in pdf form.

Chapter 10

Using input/output interfaces

10.1 Chapter overview

A common characteristic of embedded, real-time systems is often the significance of input/output data transfers. Much equipment in the field of communications does little else. Where an operating system will provide the run-time support, it is important to investigate its API before making a firm decision to purchase. To assist with sizing and scoping the application, either simulation or queuing theoretic studies can be carried out before finalizing the design.

10.2 Input and output operations

To many desktop programmers, the extent to which real-time systems explicitly pass data to and from the external world is their most defining characteristic. This only reflects the success with which contemporary operating systems mask the details of I/O activity from application programmers. However, accessing I/O hardware from *within* an operating system environment can involve more software complexity than the direct hardware methods described earlier in Chapter 3. So, partly to avoid hidden software complexity, and partly to improve run-time performance, many real-time programmers

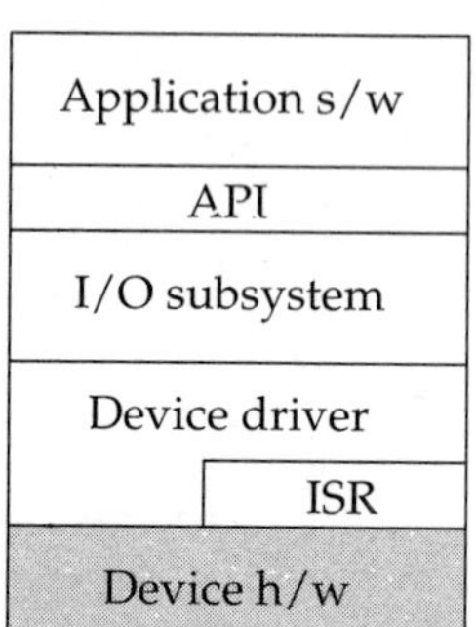

Device handling

prefer to access ports directly, even though such activity effectively cancels much of the run-time protection provided by the operating system.

From the perspective of the systems programmer, the provision of device drivers, which interface to the external devices and carry out the various service requests arising from the application tasks, is an essential part of the operating system. By identifying families of similar devices which can share at least part of the device driver code, an initial level of abstraction is introduced, insulating the application code from the peculiarities of a particular device. In the same vein, data transfer operations are generally categorized as either *serial* or *block*, depending on the characteristics of the attached device. A magnetic disk is a block device, while the COM port is serial. With Unix, most block devices are supplied with both block and serial device drivers, the latter to allow for 'raw' access. To confuse the matter, the Ethernet LAN interface behaves more like a block device, because there is a minimum packet size.

10.3 Categories

I/O activity is often identified as dealing with either blocks of binary data or a serial streams of ASCII characters. This categorization appears to distinguish data transfers according to the *amount* of data handled, but really it is more concerned with how the data is *erased*. Block-oriented data channels can usually be addressed and repeatedly read a block at a time. The data is held on *random access* devices, but these constrain the accesses to deal with a minimum amount of a block, which then requires buffering for later processing. Only when a *write* occurs will a block of data be erased. It is unusual for a serial, character-oriented channel to behave in this way. More commonly, the bytes of data are erased when *read*, denying any second chance to read the item.

Such a simplistic classification of I/O operations into only two categories is based on historic differences, but does still enable the programmer to more readily reuse existing software. However, when a new form of data transfer

Database access	Pro*C library
Indexed-sequential files	ISAM library, e.g. ObjecTrieve
Standard C I/O (buffered)	FILE * fopen(), fseek(), fput()/fget(), fwrite()
File I/O	int open(), lseek(), read(), write()
Kernel level access	device driver routines
Direct h/w access	h/w init: *pUARTwrite = letter, or outb()

Levels of software access to devices

appears, such as happened when networking facilities became available, it may not fit easily into either camp.

The various types of access available to the Unix programmer when handling devices are listed above. Programmed reading and writing to I/O ports can be accomplished directly, if the access permissions are favourable, either in C or assembler, but the more common technique is to employ only operating system device driver routines. These can be simple, byte-oriented port access functions, or more complex, offering sophisticated system facilities, which have built-in 'understanding' of the devices involved. So disks are normally managed to support a logical file system, with directories and dynamically sized sequential file structures. Even more complex function libraries can be obtained to assist with handling record-oriented indexed-sequential files to deliver faster access. While at the maximum level of sophistication are the libraries, such as Pro*C, which allow programs to exchange data with full databases using SQL statements. Pro*C is implemented as a preprocessor for the C compiler. It allows programmers to embed SQL statements within their programs. Thus Pro*C tries to combine the advantages of the C procedural language with the ability to directly access an Oracle database using standard SQL.

10.4 Operating system support

Though system calls regarding task scheduling and synchronization are dealt with directly by the kernel, those relating to I/O are often passed onto other modules with special responsibility for data transfers. This also offers the possibility of the dynamic installation of new device driver modules while the system is up and running. Repeatedly having to reboot the PC, when installing new devices, was one of the most annoying aspects of the earlier versions of Windows. While for critical 'non-stop' applications, the requirement to reboot after every upgrade or trial installation would certainly not be acceptable. As with Unix, accessing device driver read and write facilities provided by an RTE may appear to the programmer much the same as accessing a disk file. The device driver has to be acquired, and its use registered by the task, before any data transfer can take place. This treats the device driver and device ports as a critical resource which only a single task can access at any time.

Unix treats all data I/O through its file handling facilities and structures. The internal representation of a file or device is an *inode*, which holds a description of where file data is actually located on disk and which device driver to use for data I/O. Every file has a single inode, but this may be linked to more than one directory entry, resulting in multiple aliases to a single file. A call to `open("file_name",1)` will effect a search through the directory to locate an entry for the name, and retrieve the associated inode. If all goes well, a new entry to the file descriptor table will be constructed for that task, and that will then be used subsequently to access the data. To assist with accessing files and devices, an expanded inode table is constructed in memory from the principal, disk-based inode data after the system boots, and the file system is mounted. The in-memory inode table adds extra fields containing the associated device major number, inode numbers, which are needed because the information is arranged in hash queues, not ordered arrays as on disk, using additional pointers to other inodes. The boot block is physically positioned in the first block of the storage device, so that it can be located on power-up by the BIOS ROM loader. It can contain a system loader program, so, although every file system on each partition will have a boot block, normally only one will contain initial bootstrap code. The master boot block will then mark this partition as a bootable partition. When using boot managers, such as LILO or GRUB, it is possible to give the user a choice of several bootable partitions. The super block holds information about the size of the file system and where to find free space for new files. Immediately adjacent to the super block lies the inode list, the first of which is the *root* inode for that file system. So for Unix the 64 byte inode structure is the key to accessing both file data and I/O devices.

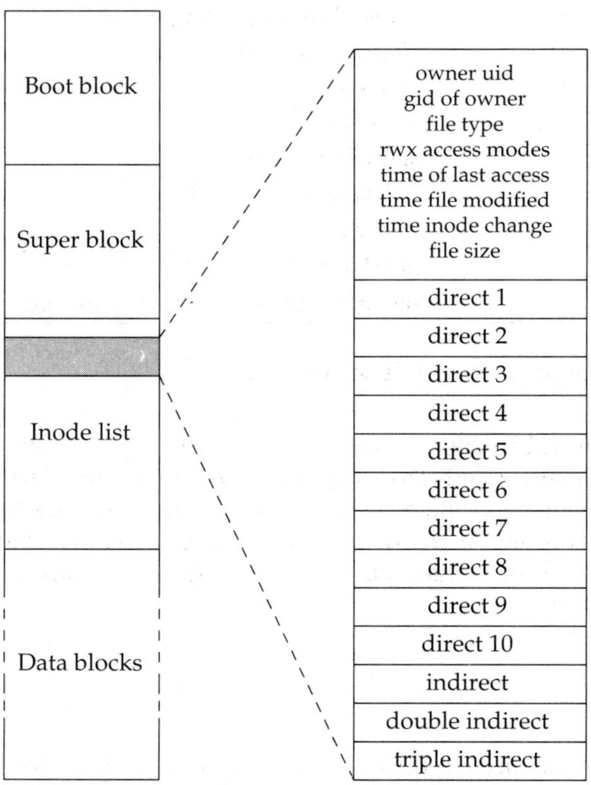

Disk-based Unix file system records

With different types of file system residing on separate partitions, scattered over several disk packs, Unix maintains control over the potentially chaotic situation by placing a super block in each partition. The position of each partition is available from the master boot record written into the very first sector of the disk. Then the super blocks can be read into the `super_block` structure when the file systems are `mounted`. Each super block table entry holds the major number and minor number identifiers of the device driver and physical device holding the designated file system, as well as the location of the root inode. To cater for secondary, mounted file systems, there is also space for the inode of the mount point on the hosting file system.

For each task, the user file descriptor table identifies all active files and devices. Each entry in this table is indexed by the application code using so-called *file descriptor* integers. Positions 0, 1 and 2 are dedicated to `stdin`, `stdout` and `stderr`, which are often responsible for handling the console keyboard and screen.

System call	Activity
`fd=creat("filename", mode);`	allocate an inode and data buffer
`fd=open("filename", mode);`	access through existing inode
`close(fd);`	close an active file
`read(fd, pbuffer, count);`	read data
`write(fd, pbuffer, count);`	write data
`fcntl(fd, cmd...);`	special file controls
`ioctl(fd, cmd...);`	special device controls
`unlink(fd);`	delete a file
`stat(fd);`	get status information
`lseek(fd, offset, w);`	move pointer in a random access file

Principal Unix system calls for data file and device accesses

Connection to the real-world frequently requires data buffering and interrupt service routines. Flow control and error trapping must also be provided. At higher levels, the problems of dealing with time-out failures should be thought through at an early stage in the design. It too often happens that distinct error codes are ignored or merged just because higher-level software cannot manage the information.

10.5 Raw I/O

Programmers involved with writing interface handlers or device drivers have to become proficient at reading and interpreting the technical sheets produced by chip suppliers such as Intel and Motorola. The problem with these documents comes from their hardware-oriented style. From the software point of view there may only be three paragraphs, and a couple of diagrams, of vital importance: the rest is only of relevance to an electronic engineer or circuit designer. The essential information from a programmer's point of view is highlighted below.

- The overall functionality of the chip
- The number of internal registers and their physical addresses
- Which registers are READ and which WRITE
- General register function and the specific action of each bit
- Available interrupt functions and which are used in this circuit
- What handshaking is used to regulate data flow rates
- Initialization requirements for the functions used
- Error handling capabilities.

Data sheet information for programmers

10.6 I/O with Linux

With Linux, as with many other Unix-based operating systems, accessing attached devices is done using the same system facilities as provided for the main file system. So the serial port could be referred to as '/mnt/com1', the parallel port as '/mnt/parport'. The actual title given to a device is arbitrary, as are file names. The command `mknod` is used to create file system nodes for new devices. The information held in the so-called *inode* indicates which device driver is to be used with which specific piece of hardware. As with files, devices need to be *opened* before any read or write activity can be started. Opening a device means registering the current ownership of the device with the operating system, setting up administrative data structures and transfer buffers, and returning to the task a reference handle to be used for all future accesses. In addition to reading and writing, there are often special actions which are only relevant to a particular device. In this situation, the required functions are installed as identified calls to the `ioctl()` system function.

- Obtain an access number (handle)
- Identify correct device driver
- Request access to the port
- Register task ownership of resource
- Request buffer space
- Initialize the hardware

Opening a device

The following example demonstrates the use of an `ioctl()` system call to the keyboard console device handler. It exploits a special function to toggle the keyboard LEDS: NumLock, CapsLock and ScrollLock.

```
/*
 * kbdleds.c
 * has to run with root privilege
 */
#include <stdio.h>
#include <errno.h>
#include <fcntl.h>
#include <sys/ioctl.h>
#include <linux/kd.h>                       // LED_SCR (scroll lock),
                                            // LED_NUM (num lock),
                                            // LED_CAP (caps lock)
int main() {
   int led = 0;
   int consolefd = open("/dev/tty0", O_RDONLY);

   while (TRUE) {
            led ^ = LED_SCR;                // flash LED
        if (ioctl(consolefd, KDSETLED, led )) {
            fprintf(stderr, "%s: ioctl(): %s\n", "kbdleds",
              strerror(errno));
            exit(2);
        }
        usleep(500000);
     }
     close(consolefd);
     exit(0);                               // never happens
}
```

The next example shows how to direct a signal from a device into a process. Using Linux, the PC serial port COM1 emits a SIGIO signal when data arrives. To get this to work, the process opens the port, registers a signal handler function, claims the signals, and sits back, awaiting the arrival of a signal. There is also code to set up the serial port tx/rx parameters.

```
#include <termios.h>
#include <stdio.h>
#include <unistd.h>
#include <fcntl.h>
#include <sys/signal.h>

#define BAUDRATE 9600
#define MODEMDEVICE "/dev/ttyS0"
#define _POSIX_SOURCE 1 /* POSIX compliant source */
#define FALSE 0
#define TRUE 1
```

```
int wait_flag=TRUE;                   /* TRUE while no signal received */

/*********************************************************************
* signal handler. sets wait_flag to FALSE, to indicate above loop     *
* that characters have been received.                                 *
*********************************************************************/

void signal_handler_IO (int status) {
     puts("SIGIO received");
     wait_flag = FALSE;
 }

/*********************************************************************
*/
main() {
    int fd, nc, quitf;
    struct termios oldtio, newtio;
    struct sigaction saio;           // definition of signal action
    char buf[80];

// open the device to be non-blocking (read will return immediatly)

    fd = open(MODEMDEVICE, O_RDWR | O_NOCTTY | O_NONBLOCK);
    if (fd <0) {perror(MODEMDEVICE); exit(-1); }

// install the signal handler before making the device asynchronous

    saio.sa_handler = signal_handler_IO;
    saio.sa_mask.__val[0] = 0;
    saio.sa_mask.__val[1] = 0;
    saio.sa_mask.__val[2] = 0;
    saio.sa_mask.__val[3] = 0;
    saio.sa_flags = 0;
    saio.sa_restorer = NULL;

    sigaction(SIGIO,&saio,NULL);

// allow the process to receive SIGIO

   fcntl(fd, F_SETOWN, getpid());

/* Make the file descriptor asynchronous (the manual page says only
   O_APPEND and O_NONBLOCK, will work with F_SETFL...) */

   fcntl(fd, F_SETFL, FASYNC);

   tcgetattr(fd, &oldtio); // save current port settings

// set new port settings for canonical input processing

   newtio.c_cflag = B9600 | CRTSCTS | CS8 | CLOCAL | CREAD;
   newtio.c_iflag = IGNPAR | ICRNL;
   newtio.c_oflag = 0;
   newtio.c_lflag = ICANON;
   newtio.c_cc[VMIN] = 1;
```

```
   newtio.c_cc[VTIME] = 0;
   tcflush(fd, TCIFLUSH);

   tcsetattr(fd, TCSANOW, &newtio);

// loop while waiting for input. normally we would do something here
   quitf = FALSE;
   while (!quitf) {
      usleep(1000000);
      putchar('*');
      fflush(stdout);
// after receiving SIGIO, wait_flag = FALSE,
// input is available and can be read
        if (wait_flag == FALSE) {
        nc = read(fd, buf, 80);
        buf[--nc] = 0;
        printf("%s : %d\n", buf, nc);
        if (nc == 0) quitf = TRUE;  // stop loop if only a CR was input
        wait_flag = TRUE;           // wait for new input
      }
   }
// restore old port settings
    tcsetattr(fd,TCSANOW,&oldtio);
}
```

10.7 Direct device driver

With Linux it is possible to use the `/dev/port` device to access all the I/O ports on the PC. This is somewhat dangerous because it potentially gives unregulated access to all hardware, such as the hard disk controller and video card. Generally this is only used for educational demonstrations with the parallel printer port, so do be careful running the example on your system. Access to the `/dev/port` device file must first be enabled for all users, so that the call to `fopen()` will be allowed.

```
#include <unistd.h>
#include <time.h>
#include <sys/types.h>
#include <sys/stat.h>
#include <fcntl.h>
#include <errno.h>

int errno;

main() {

   int fd;
   unsigned int i;
   struct timespec rem, attends = { 0, 500000000 };
```

```
    if((fd = open("/dev/port", O_WRONLY)) <=0 ) {
       printf("not opened, %d %d\n", fd, errno);
       exit(0);

    }
    printf("fd = %d\n", fd);

    for (i=0; i<=0x0FF; i++) {
      putchar('\n');
      printf("  %d  \r", i);
      lseek(fd, 0x378, SEEK_SET);
      write(fd, &i, 1);
      nanosleep( &attends, &rem);
    }
    close (fd);
}
```

Note that you will have to re-seek before every write operation because the file position pointer is auto-incremented. 0x378 is the standard I/O address for this output register. You will need to relax access permissions on the `/dev/port` device special file if you want to run the program with non-root permissions. This is *not* a safe technique to be generally recommended. It is preferable to employ standard device driver routines to access hardware registers. These will be dealt with more fully in Chapter 19.

10.8 Device drivers under interrupt

The outline structure and action of interrupt device drivers is presented on p. 234. You can see that the device driver code is split into two parts: the front-end and the interrupt service routine. Between them is the data buffer where data is temporarily stored before moving onward. Consider a data output operation. The application program calls an output function with the data item as a parameter (`putc()`). Control then passes to a library routine which in turn calls an operating system routine. This checks to see if there is space in the transmit buffer associated with the specified device. If there is space, the item is entered at the back of the queue, the queue pointers are updated and control returns to the original program. If there happens to be no space in the buffer, perhaps due to a failure of the link, an error status code is returned to the program. The data will hang about in the transmit buffer for a moment before it gets transferred to the output port by the transmit ISR. This is triggered by the port hardware when it is ready to receive more data. So an application program may appear to have satisfactorily written some data out to a device, when the data actually got no further than the transmit buffer.

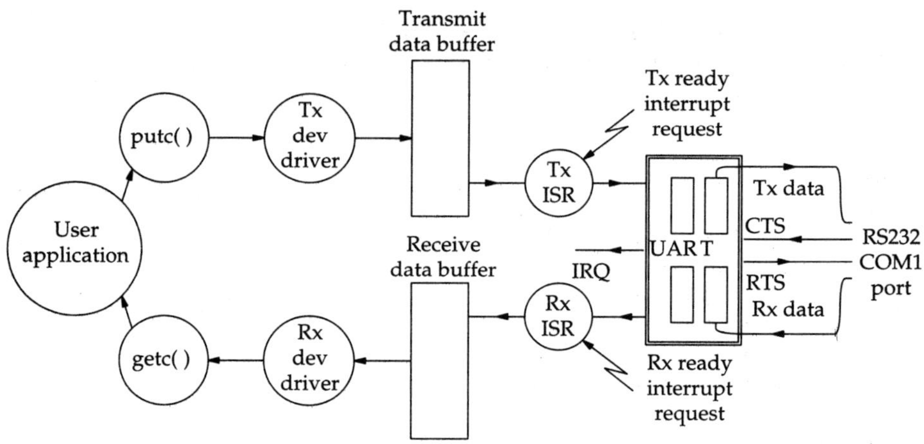

A bi-directional buffered, interrupt-driven serial channel

The sequence of operations is similar for the receive channel. Data arrives at the receive port and triggers an interrupt which evokes the receive ISR. This moves the data into the receive buffer, from where it may be read by an application program.

When such a communication channel is used in a master/slave situation, with the master computer emitting a query and the slave computer responding, it is important to have the capability to flush stale data from the input buffers. Consider the master system switching over to reading the input buffer after successfully transmitting a request. The data read from the receive buffer might have been left over from earlier, aborted transactions. Such 'synchronicity' errors are sometimes difficult to detect and recover from. This problem can be expected to occur if line switching takes place which can generate bursts of spurious signals when a changeover occurs. The receive buffers will store this in the form of random data, ready to confuse the next reader.

Another difficult situation can occur when transferring data across an RS 232 link. Because the link was originally intended for use with terminals or teletypes, several functions were included in the device drivers to assist with interactive sessions. An example of this would be code editing, where a line of data is held in the keyboard buffer to facilitate second thought corrections. So various ASCII codes, such as BS, XOFF and EOF are recognized as link commands and not transferred directly through as data. This can completely disrupt further attempts at raw data transfers or simple text communications applications until the unwanted code filtering activities are disabled.

A further difficulty may occur when automatic echoing is enabled. The transmitter will send a stream of characters along the link to the receiver. These may get auto-echoed back to the original transmitter. There they could accumulate in the transmitter's receive buffer until it is full. At which point the flow control mechanism kicks in to stop more echoed characters being transmitted back by the receiver. In which case, if the receiver is not allowed to transmit echo characters, it will trigger a flow control order in the other direction, halting the primary stream of incoming data. The clear indication of this problem is a transmission which always stops after 255 characters: a buffer load. Thus, perversely, the transmission fails because the transmitter is not reading enough!

10.9 Queuing theory

Many real-time systems are now incorporated into large networked infrastructures. This means that data transmission bandwidths, processing rates and throughput performance can be critical to the success of the project. When planning to handle an incoming data stream, it is necessary to obtain some estimate of the likely resource implications such as required size of memory buffers, mean interrupt rate, the number of hardware channels required to deal with the peak demand, the worst case CPU loading and even the file space to be reserved. Such estimates can be calculated using statistical queuing theory, or measured from empirical simulation studies. The starting point is often a set of traffic figures presented in terms of likely events per second or likely inter-event interval periods. The assumption is then made that arrival patterns are random, equally probable in any period of time. This leads to the Poisson probability distribution for event occurrence, as shown below, where the average number of arrival events is 5 per second.

If the system is stable, and the arrival rate can be described by a Poisson curve, with a mean value of $\bar{n}$, the period between arrivals will follow an exponential pattern, with an average value of $1/\bar{n}$.

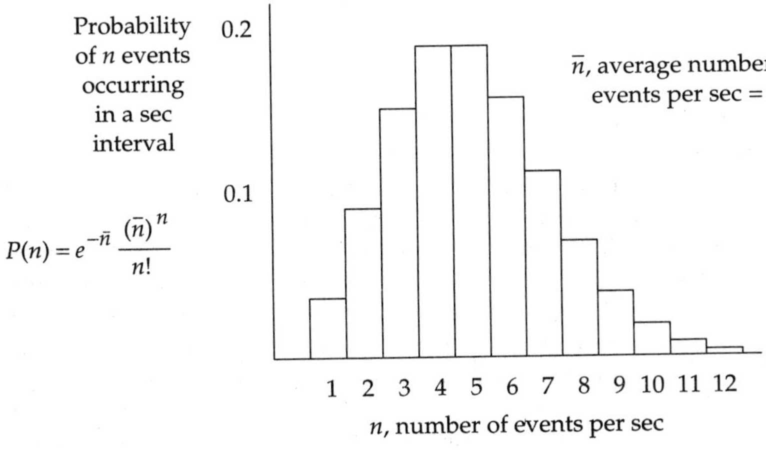

Poisson distribution of probability

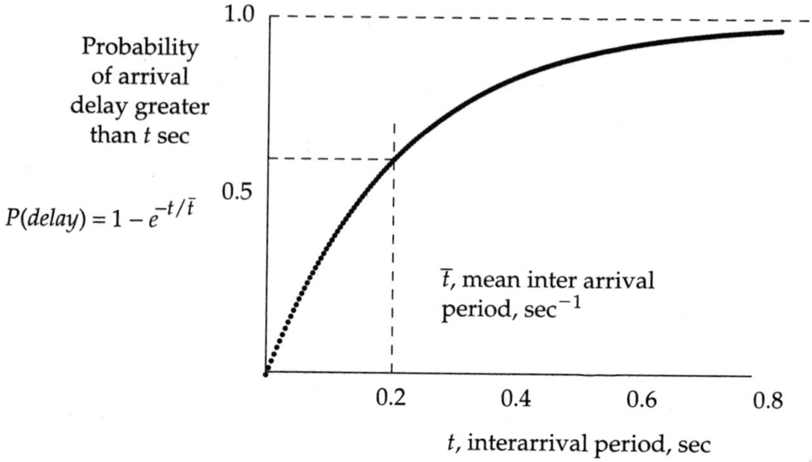

Exponential distribution of interarrival intervals

Consider the situation where a server can deal with 6 transactions a second. If the average arrival rate is 5 per second, what is the probability of a fluctuation in the random arrival pattern which exceeds the server's capacity? The probability of transactions arriving *within* the server's performance capability can be calculated by adding up the probabilities for 1, 2, 3, 4, 5 and 6 arrivals per second.

$$P(\leq 6) = \sum_{n=1}^{n=6} \frac{e^{-5}5^n}{n!}$$

$$P(\leq 6) = e^{-5}\left(\frac{5}{1} + \frac{25}{2} + \frac{125}{6} + \frac{625}{24} + \frac{3125}{120} + \frac{15\,625}{720}\right)$$

$$P(\leq 6) = 0.75$$

So for the probability of *not* enjoying less than 6 transactions per second, we only need to subtract 0.75 from 1, giving a final result of 0.25 – a 25 per cent risk of overloading the server, resulting in a queue developing, and clients having to wait for a response. The value could also be computed by adding up the heights of the 6 columns from the Poisson bar graph. Designers work in the reverse order. First find out what loading, mean arrival rate, the system has to deal with. Then decide what risk of overloading is acceptable (0.01 per cent or 25 per cent?). With these the Poisson tables can be consulted to find what the minimum steady state server throughout has to be to achieve these targets.

To estimate the average queue length and queuing time requires some extra assumptions regarding the service time and its variation. But if only steady state situations are dealt with, and the service time distribution is

- Utilization factor (% busy)
- Probability of 100% utilization
- Mean number in queue awaiting service
- Mean number in the system
- Mean queuing time
- Mean delay time (queuing and service)
- Probability of queuing delay
- Probability of n requests in the system

Useful parameters obtainable from queuing theory analysis

taken to be exponential, the following equations can be taken as valid if the service time is constant:

$n_a = n_q + n_s$ — n_q – *number in queue*, n_s – *number being served*

$t_a = t_q + t_s$ — t_q – *queuing time*, t_s – *service time*

$\rho - \bar{n} \cdot \overline{t_s}$ — n – *incoming request rate, events secs*$^{-1}$

$\overline{n_a}$ – *average number in system*

$\overline{n_a} = \rho + \frac{\rho^2}{2(1-\rho)}$ — ρ – *the fractional utilization*

$\overline{t_a} = \overline{t_s}\left[1 + \frac{\rho}{2(1-\rho)}\right]$ — $\overline{t_a}$ – *average time in system*

On a newly proposed system, if there are anticipated to be 100 transactions per second demanded at peak time, and each transaction takes 7.5 msec to process,

$$\rho = \frac{100 \times 7.5}{1000} = 0.75 \quad \overline{n_a} = 0.75 + \frac{0.5625}{2(1-0.75)} = 1.85$$

So the system is normally only 75 per cent busy, and with a single server, there is an expected mean queue length of less than a single transaction waiting in the buffer. The expected queuing time would be calculated:

$$\overline{t_q} = 7.5\left[1 + \frac{0.75}{2(1-0.75)}\right] - 7.5 = 11.25\,\text{ms}$$

When the service time is not constant but is randomly distributed, following an exponential curve, the predicted queuing numbers and mean delay times are slightly simpler:

$$\overline{n_a} = \frac{\rho}{(1-\rho)} \qquad \overline{t_a} = \frac{\overline{t_s}}{(1-\rho)}$$

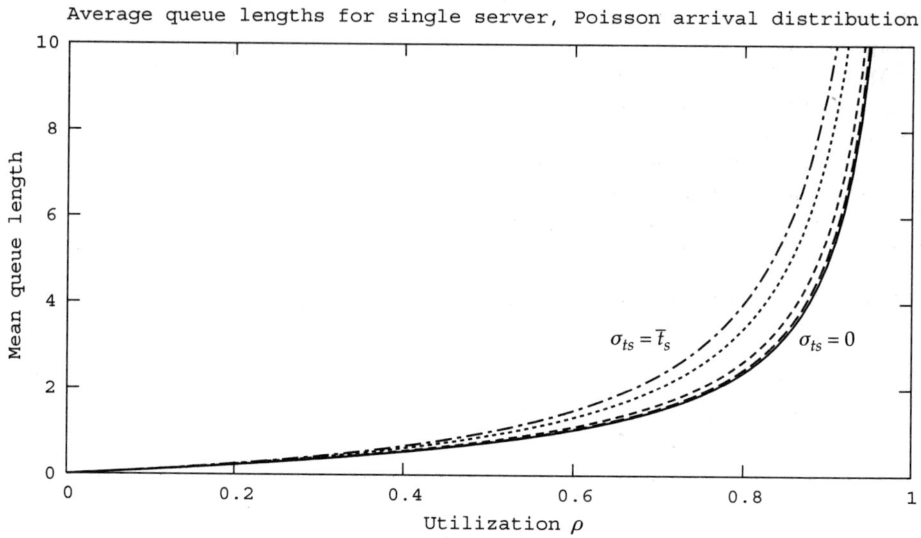

Mean queue length for a single server, providing exponential service times, and dealing with a Poisson arrival pattern

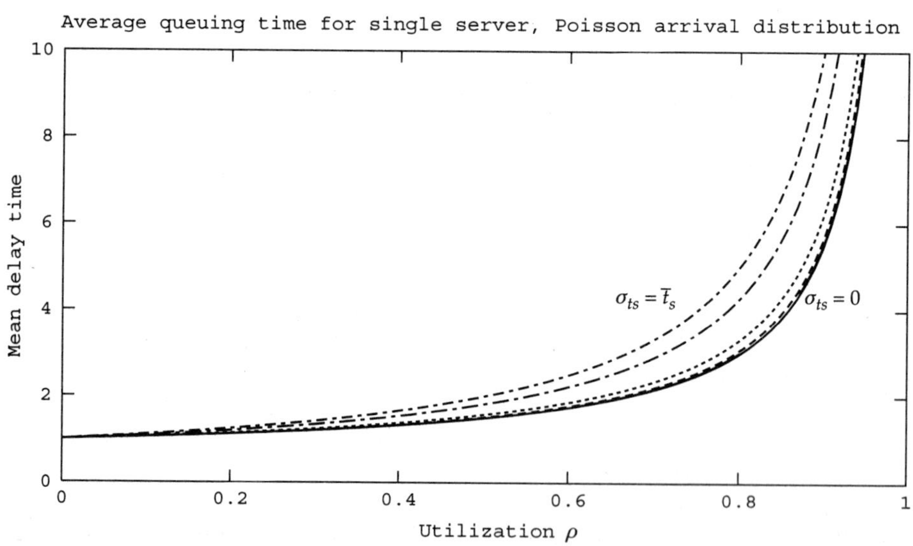

Mean queuing times for a single server, providing exponential service times, dealing with a Poisson arrival pattern

The most common way to deal with traffic analysis and load prediction, with queuing theory, is to use a set of lookup tables or graphs, as printed opposite.

Referring to the curves, the multiple traces are drawn to represent several different situations, when service timing is fixed ($\sigma = 0$) through to when it varies maximally for an exponential distribution. Now place a ruler across the x axis at the 0.75 value. Where it intersects the $\sigma = 0$ curves should give the same y values as we calculated earlier in this paragraph, $\overline{n_a} = 1.85$, and $\overline{t_q} = 11.25$ ms. The former is easy to confirm, but the latter requires some interpretation. The graph delivers a value of 2.5, how does this reconcile with the computed value of 11.25 ms? Well, the 2.5 is not in ms but in units of *service time*, which in this case is 7.5 ms. So we have to multiply 2.5 by 7.5 ms to get the mean *total* delay time (queuing and being serviced) which gives 18.75 ms. As computed earlier. This has only been a short introduction to the powerful mathematical techniques offered by queuing theory, and the reader is referred to more specialist texts in this area.

10.10 Chapter summary

Embedded, real-time systems often involve a significant amount of input/output data transfers. Indeed, some equipment in the large field of data communications does little else. The Unix operating system handles devices using device drivers accessed through its standard file system. Interrupts play an important part in the transfer of data into and out from computer systems. Simulation and queuing theoretic studies are available to assist with finalizing a design.

10.11 Problems and issues for discussion

1. Does the Linux USB device driver think it is a block or char device? Can more than one device driver service the same physical device? What are the potential dangers of this arrangement should it occur?
2. What advantages and disadvantages are there to the application programmer accessing hardware directly, rather than relying on operating system device drivers?
3. What does the system call `open()` achieve? When would you need to use the `ioctl()` system call?
4. When installing new port hardware to interface to a special device, what information does a programmer require to write a device driver to install into either a Linux or RTE-based system?

5. A website can cope with 5 queries per second. On Monday morning there is an average arrival rate of 3 events per second. What is the probability of exceeding the system's capacity?
6. Investigate the unit of data traffic known as the Erlang.

10.12 Suggestions for reading

Bennett, S. (1995). *Real-time Computer Control.* Prentice Hall.
Buchanan, W. (1999). *PC Interfacing, Communications and Windows Programming.* Addison Wesley.
Martin, J. (1998). *Systems Analysis for Data Transmission.* Prentice Hall.
Stevens, W. R. (1998). *Advanced Unix Programming.* Addison Wesley.

Chapter 11

Structured design for real-time systems

11.1 Chapter overview

Structured Analysis and Design (SA/SD), although increasingly abandoned in favour of Object-oriented Design (OOD) methods, retains popularity in the field of real-time systems to gain improved performance. This chapter explains that the original Yourdon SA/SD method was extended for use with real-time systems design. Finite State Machines (FSM), Data-flow Diagrams (DFD) and entity relationship diagrams (ERD) are unified within real-time Yourdon. The routes through to implementing code are also described.

11.2 Design methods

It is now widely recognized that appropriate design methods are essential for the successful production of good software. The preliminary activities for any software development usually involve research, analysis and self-education, before real design can start, so development methodologies have to support many different activities within the software lifecycle. In short, design must assist in finding the best way to implement the functional requirements. In particular, real-time systems have several special areas which demand strong support through the design phase and into implementation.

- Guidance for code structuring
- Data definitions
- Identification of tasks
- Task sequence model with initial priority settings
- Intertask dependencies and communication needs
- Highlight critical sections
- Reveal potential deadlock situations
- Guide the production of test data
- Offer flexible/adaptable implementations
- Assistance during debugging

Requirements for a real-time design method

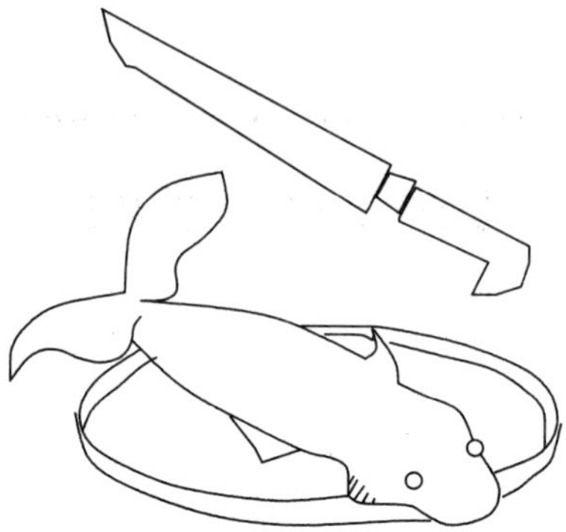

Designer's dilemma: where to make the first cut

When choosing a design method, an important aspect concerns the moment when decisions are taken. If important decisions have to be taken early in the project lifecycle the risk incurred with using that method might be unacceptable because reversing these decisions becomes increasingly expensive, even impossible – I call this the fish bones problem. On visiting a restaurant for a significant dinner party with someone you really want to impress, you unwisely follow her advice and choose fish for the main course. Now this turns out to be a very odd decision because you have never actually tackled a *whole* fish before. At home you only eat microwaved fish fingers or pre-prepared cod cakes. This is the first time you have realized the vital need for anatomical information shedding light on the internal construction of fish. The penalty is severe: an evening spent picking handfuls of fish bones from your mouth while trying to pay attention to the conversation, and appear relaxed and appreciative. The first knife cut most probably determines the success or otherwise of the evening. It is impossible to reverse the activity, short of cooking another fish and rerunning the dinner party. A thick, creamy, opaque sauce doesn't help, either. The initial activities will require support in several areas, listed below.

- Unambiguous nomenclature for expressing ideas and relationships
- Disciplined sets of questions
- Clear timetable of activities
- Language for communicating with colleagues and clients
- Support for the identification of core data structures
- Guidelines for problem decomposition

Initial project needs

Later on during the project, eyes turn to other imperatives but truly effective designers never lose sight of their ultimate goal: well-structured code.

All design decisions should be clearly related to the target implementation, otherwise unnecessary, new difficulties can be picked up en route which create chaos later in the lifecycle. A theoretically ideal decomposition may fail to map onto available platforms. An efficient, 'clever' algorithm can exclude subsequent product expansion. Specially devised protocols will cut off your equipment from interworking with others. The required size of ROM and RAM turns out to be way beyond commercial constraints. Such situations may arise when design is carried out in isolation from practical considerations.

- Clear route for implementation
- Code documentation for reference during debugging sessions
- Trial data for acceptance tests
- Documentation for customer's records
- Support for continuing maintenance activity

Subsequent project needs

11.3 Incremental functional decomposition

When dealing with complex problems it is common to break them down into more manageable sized parts. This method is often characterized as 'top down design by incremental decomposition'. So there appears to be a steady progression from the *what?* question towards an answer to the *how?* question. Structured analysis and design follows this prescription but unfortunately, although the method is still popular, there are several serious risks entailed in its use.

- Decisions too early
- Problem segmentation
- Semantic gap
- Code repetition
- Critical problems

Design issues

- *Critical design decisions* These occur too early in the project lifecycle, well before the full scope of the application has been determined. These initial choices, if *wrong*, may completely flaw the project, leading inevitably to delays, reworking and even complete abandonment: those fish bones again!

- *Problem segmentation* The method offers little guidance when the designer is making important decisions about problem partitioning. Despite its significance, it is really left to the individual's experience and judgement.
- *Semantic gap* The target level is too far below the initial specification level. The language used to describe the requirements is abstract and relevant to the customer's daily activities, while the final solution is expressed in programs containing machine instruction codes. Translating from the first to the last is the difficult job of the analyst–programmer.
- *Top-down divergence* Working down from top to bottom, and splitting into a multiplicity of functional units, leads to duplication of effort. Often nearly identical code is rewritten again and again within the same project. It is difficult to identify the base functional units from the start.
- *Late crises* Sometimes the real killer problem is only tackled towards the end of the project. A seriously challenging algorithm or the need for a novel implementation will only emerge on the critical path when it is nearly too late to rectify a serious situation.

11.4 Use of diagrams in design

It has now become standard practice to undertake coding only after preparatory design activity and long hours spent drawing up schematic diagrams. The exact formulation of the diagrams may change: flowchart, structure chart, data flow diagram, object collaboration diagram, state transition diagram, all being turned out by the barrowload using diagram editors and laser printers. Nevertheless, diagrams still appear to hold a special position within the design process. Put simply, these two dimensional, graphical models greatly assist with the successful development of text-based programs.

- Communication with others
- Abstraction of relevant aspects
- Intellectual discipline
- Temporal → spatial mapping
- Record of decisions
- Unambiguous representation

Reasons for using diagrams

So after the design diagrams have been completed it is still necessary to transform them into a programming language. Some progress has been made to provide translators which can automatically generate standard code from graphical descriptor languages, but these are still limited in quality and scope. Good communications between all those involved with a project has to be facilitated. There is no better method of presenting complex ideas and subtle, abstract relationships than through pictures. Having some reliable means of communication with others is an invaluable asset during all phases of a developmental project. The activity of design is a modelling process. Relevant objects have to be identified, and irrelevant objects excluded. Using diagrams, such important decisions can be documented for inspection and debate. Of particular relevance to real-time programmers is the mapping from the time dimension onto the space dimension, a technique well known in physics and maths. So if a temporal sequence of events needs to be recorded or reviewed, it is produced as a spatial graph, with time on one axis.

11.5 Data Flow Diagrams (DFD)

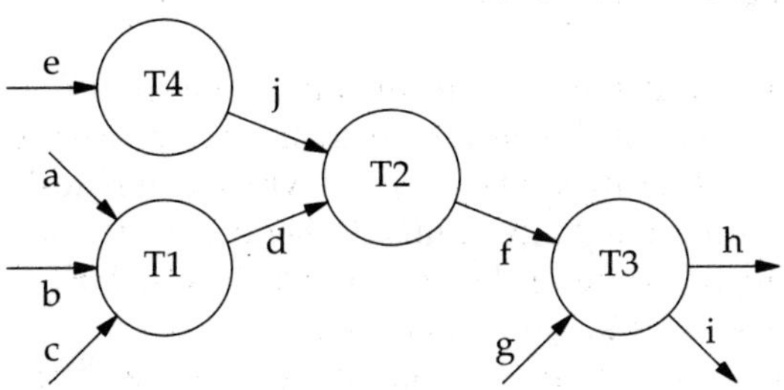

Data flow diagram (DFD)

During the era of COBOL and mainframe computers, data flow modelling for large data processing systems was well established, but there remained a number of problems when attempting to adapt this method for real-time systems. The first step is for designers to draw up a context diagram, introduced in Section 5.2. As shown below, the attached data sources and sinks, known as *terminators*, are conventionally drawn in square boxes. Next, a top-level DFD can be derived by partitioning the functionality into separate processes, or transformations, which are then interlinked by data flows. The DFD represents a sequence of actions, rather like a factory production line or a data flow pipeline. Each transformation process reads in data from designated input streams, carries out its transformation, and then outputs the results. The basic scheduling scheme for data transformations is fully synchronous, with each process triggered by the arrival of data items on input streams.

A serious deficiency of the DFD schematic is its failure to fully specify the *timing* and *functionality* of each component data transformation. For this reason, it is strongly recommended to retain a textual description with each data transformation. These paragraphs are known as process specifications

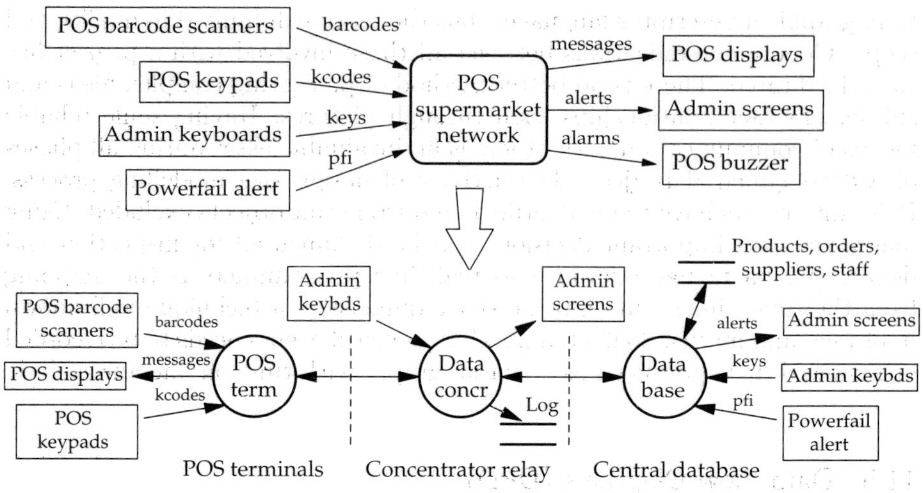

Further partitioning of a context diagram into level-1 DFD

(PSpecs) or mini-specs. In this way a fuller specification can be referred to at all times. The progressive decomposition of the data transformation processes is carried on, layer after layer, until a description is achieved which can readily be expressed directly in a programming language. Thus, the context diagram is expanded into a level-1 DFD, which is then broken down into level-2 DFDs, which in turn decompose into level-3 and so on as necessary.

Maintaining complete consistency between the context diagram and the derived data flow diagrams is obviously essential. Initially this is limited to checking that all the terminators are included at all levels, but subsequently also involves reconciling all the internal data streams. When to stop design activity and move on to code implementation varies with each situation. If a relatively familiar application is being reworked, the need for detailed analysis and extensive design structuring is less evident. An important outcome of the analysis and design phases of software development is self-education, learning about the application, its purpose and desired behaviour. So when dealing with a familiar scenario, these activities can safely be abbreviated.

When decomposing context diagrams into lower-level DFDs, it is often useful to consider the likely hardware architecture or execution environment. Thus, if the intended environment comprises several networked platforms, it is sensible to split the DFDs and their PSpecs to comply with this situation. The data flows between the subsystems then get represented by physical channels or IP sockets.

11.6 Implementing a DFD

The implementation of a straightforward DFD, using a high-level programming language, can be carried out directly by walking through the chain of processes, explicitly translating each in the order in which they appear on the diagram. The data flows are implemented as either local variables, getting passed as parameters into and out of the transformation functions, or as uniformly accessible global variables. This linear strategy, however, is not well suited to modern block structured languages and quickly runs out of control with increased DFD complexity. If there are many arms merging on the DFD, the order of coding is not clear, but may be significant at run-time, especially where several input reads are involved, with operational sensitivity to the input sequencing.

```
while (1) {
  a = read();
  b = read();
  c = read();
  d = doT1(a, b, c);

  e = read();
  j = doT4(e);

  f = doT2(j, d)

  g = read();
  doT3(f, g, &h, &i);
  write(h);
  write(i);
}
```

Straightforward coding of DFDs on p. 245

Perhaps a better approach, illustrated below, is first to transform the whole DFD into a structure chart in readiness for coding. This is sometimes likened to seizing the middle link of a chain and lifting it straight up and shaking it. The two sides of the DFD diagram, to the left and to the right, termed the input/afferent and output/efferent arms, hang down towards the ground. In this way a hierarchical tree of functions is established to guide the programmer. It is also similar to the transformation known as *program inversion* which plays a central role during the implementation phase of Jackson Structured Programming (JSP) methodology, and is redeployed as *process inversion* in the more general Jackson Structured Design (JSD) methodology. A pipeline of processes is converted to a hierarchy of functions, with data passing as parameters between the levels. Although overall the structured code can be longer, it is more rationally organized and can be amended with much less difficulty.

It should be understood that *timing* information is excluded from DFDs, only *ordering* is represented by the sequence of transformation processes. DFDs do not contain any information about timing, synchronization or events. Only the arrival of items of data can activate the otherwise blocked processes. Signals and interrupts cannot easily be represented. Because discrete data and continuously available data are treated similarly, the use of discrete data for control information appears even more confusing. This results in a very limited data-driven view of scheduling.

With more complex systems, it is not desirable, or even possible, to transform the complete DFD into a structure chart for implementation. Considerable decomposition of the level-1 DFD has to be carried out first. When this has been completed, and the bottom-level data transformations are all judged to be suitable for coding, there remains the issue of how to present the bottom-level design to the programmer. The DFDs themselves lack sufficient detail to pin down the code structure, so this is where the textual PSpecs (Section 11.5) can be exploited. A common tactic is to expand the PSpecs into pseudocode, but perhaps a better, more expressive option is to draw up a structure chart for each data transformation, based on the PSpec and the bottom-level DFD. This will follow the conventional diagrammatic structure chart conventions, with the addition of an extra indication of where process input and output occurs which may entail the likelihood of blocking. This enables the reader to gain more insight into the possible dynamics of the code, beyond the fundamental: seq/it/sel, and see how the individual components interact. The example illustrated below is based on the 'monitor' data transformation from the top diagram on p. 257.

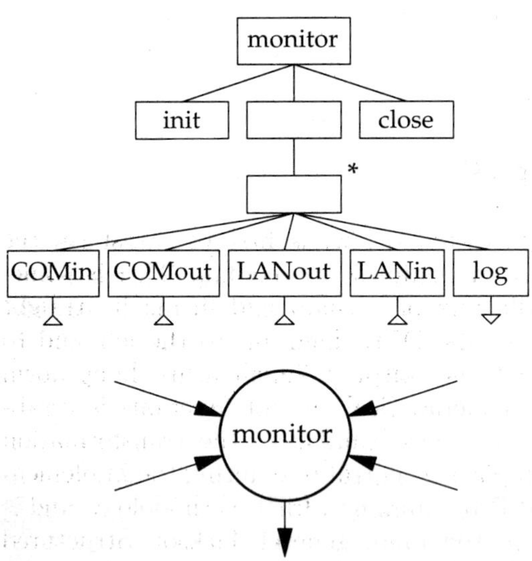

Structure chart for the monitor process on p. 257

By separating the implementation of each data transformation, the possibility emerges of dealing with them as independently scheduled *tasks* within a multi-tasking system. This outcome is dealt with more fully in Chapter 12, but such a mapping is not essential, as the implementation of the data transformations can be dealt with as multiple functions within a single task, and simply called in correct order. A real advantage in the multi-tasking approach, however, is the way that the implementation closely follows the structure of the design, assisting with debugging and future extensions. It is interesting to observe that the difference in coding hinges on the placement of the *forever* iteration loop. For multi-tasking, all the transformation tasks loop independently, blocking on their I/O data channels. By contrast in a uni-task solution, there is a single iteration loop within which all the transformation functions take their turn to be evoked.

		Rules								
Conditions		1	2	3	4	5	6	7	8	9
Destn	to me	1		1		1	1	1		
	to other		1		1				1	1
Source	from me	1		1		1			1	1
	from other		1		1		1	1		
Type	login	1	1							
	logout			1	1					
	data					1	1		1	
	ACK							1		1
	NAK									
Actions										
	pass on		1		1					
	delete	1		1		1		1		
	display					1	1			
	send ACK		1				1			
	send NAK									
	logon	1								
	logoff			1						
	update		1	1	1	1				
	re-tx									
	1	1								

Decision table for decoding a store-and-forward ring LAN packet

A useful alternative to the structure chart is the decision table. In the situation where many interacting conditions lead to many overlapping outcomes, there is a pressing need for a method which delivers clear analysis and documentation. This can be provided by the decision table which offers diagrammatic openness, with a direct route to code. The 'rules' express the combinations of the inputs, or conditions, which have to hold in order to generate any particular output. The example given above corresponds to a packet store-and-forward ring LAN, where incoming packets may be addressed to someone else, and so need to be immediately forwarded. A data packet contains a short text message for the addressee, who should then acknowledge its receipt. If no ACK packet is received within a fixed period, a series of retries will be attempted by the sender, until the transmission is abandoned. Decision tables list the actions which are required by the various combinations of conditions and circumstances. So, when a packet arrives addressed *to* some other station, *from* some other station, it will simply be forwarded. There are five legal types of packet which are distinguished by the type field. When

To	From	Type	Comment	
me	me	login	successful login request, init directory	00000
		logout	successful logout request, clear directory	00001
		data	test messg, display, return ACK	00010
		ACK	for earlier test messg sent, del from pending tbl	00011
		NAK	for earlier test messg sent, resend from pending tbl	00100
	other	login	error	01000
		logout	error	01001
		data	messg arrives, display, return ACK	01010
		ACK	for earlier messg sent, del from pending tbl	01011
		NAK	for earlier messg sent, resend from pending tbl	01100
other	me	login	error	10000
		logout	error	10001
		data	returned packet, destination problem, resend	10010
		ACK	returned packet, destination problem, del, display	10011
		NAK	returned packet, destination problem, del, display	10100
	other	login	pass packet onward, ACK, update directory	11000
		logout	pass packet onward, update directory	11001
		data	pass packet onward	11010
		ACK	pass packet onward, update directory	11011
		NAK	pass packet onward	11100

Alternate format for decision table from the previous figure

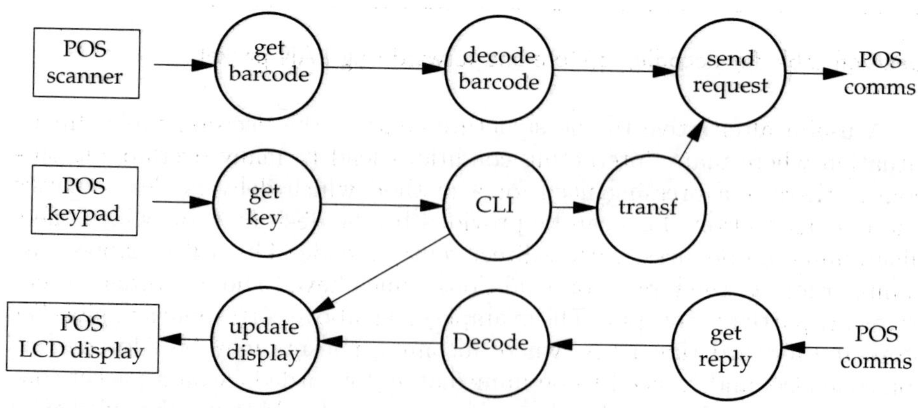

DFD for one of the POS terminals

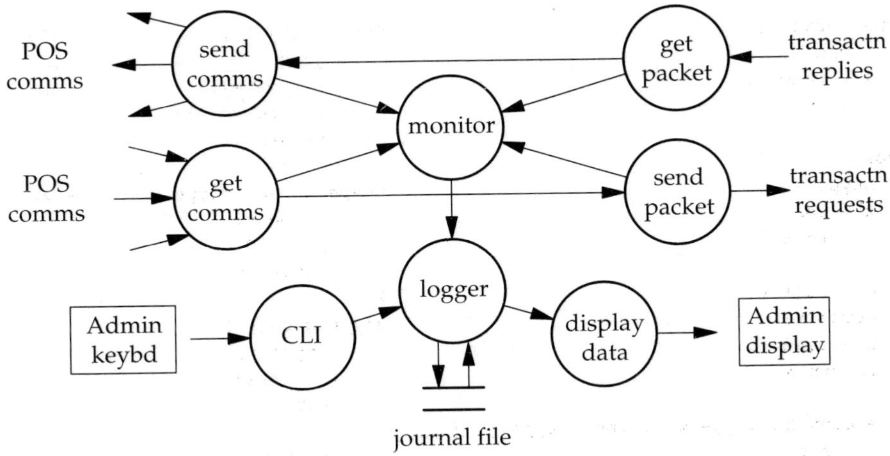

DFD for the data concentrator

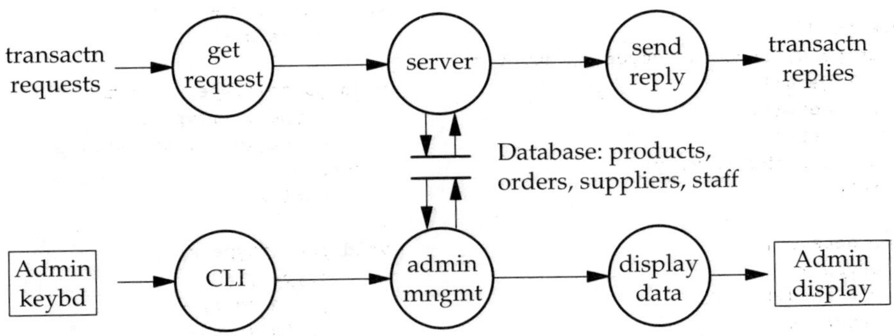

DFD for the database server

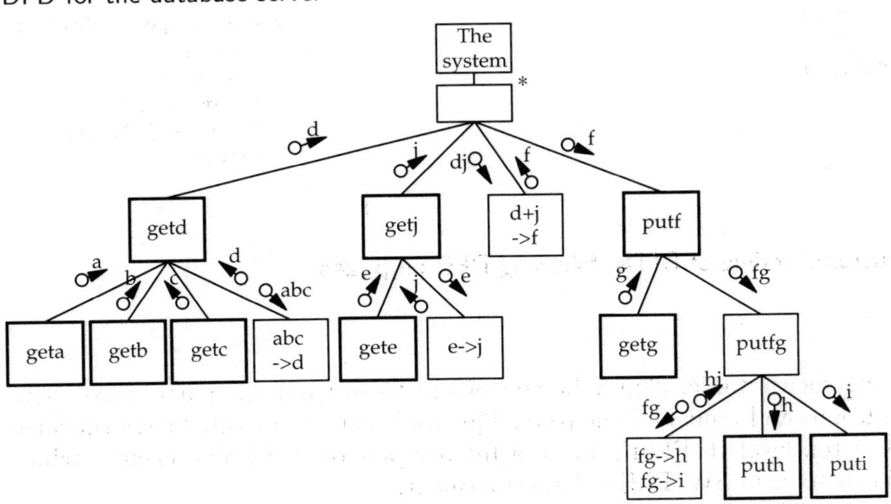

Structure chart derived from the DFD on p. 247

```
atype geta() {
    atype x;
    x = read();
    return x;
}
btype getb() {
    btype x;
    x = read();
    return x;
}
ctype getc() {
    ctype x;
    x = read();
    return x;
}
dtype convabc(atype w, btype, ctype y) {  }
    dtype z;
    z = f(w, x, y);
return z;
}
dtype getd() {
    atype w; btype x; ctype y; dtype z;
    w = geta();
    x = getb();
    y = getc();
    z = convabc(w, x, y);
    return z;
}
etype gete() {
    etype x;
    x = read();
    return x;
}
jtype conve(etype x) {
     jtype y;
     y = f(x);
 return y;
}
jtype getj() {
     jtype y;
     e = gete();
     y = conve(e);
     return y;
}
ftype convdj(dtype x, jtype y) {
     ftype z;
     z = f(d, j);
     return z;
}
gtype getg() {
     gtype x;
     x = read();
     return x;

void puth(htype x) {
     write(x);
}
void puti(itype x) {
     write(x);
}
void putfg(ftype w, gtype x) {
     htype y; itype z;
     convfg(w, x, &y, &z);
  puth(y);
     puti(z);
}
void putf(ftype x) {
     gtype y;
     y = getg();
     putfg(x, y);
}
main() {
     dtype d; jtype j; ftype f;
     while (1) {
         d = getd();
         j = getj();
         f = convdj(d, j);
         putf(f);
     }
}
```

Structured coding of DFDs, following DFD on p. 245

coding such a table, it may be convenient to sort out the pairs of exclusive conditions and render all the rows. This table can then easily be transformed into a top-level IF-ELSE, above a further pair of IF-ELSEs, each of which holds a six arm SWITCH-CASE statement.

Although this hierarchical style of implementation fits well with HLLs such as C and C++, it does not appear to be as efficient or maintainable as expected. When faced with the challenge of implementing a large decision table, the possibility of using a computed jump table comes to mind. To achieve this, the 'conditions' have to be reformatted to give a number which can be used as an index into a table of function pointers, which dispatch the necessary action functions. Looking back to p. 250, a possible 5 bit selector code can be seen on the right. The status of the 'TO', 'FROM' and 'TYPE' conditions can be used to generate a 5 bit code. This indexes into an array of pointers to functions, delivering the correct response for any set of input conditions. You may agree that this is the more elegant solution.

11.7 Reading structure charts

If you are already familiar with structure charts, and need no guidance in their interpretation and translation into code, please feel confident to skip this section.

When first confronted with structure charts, especially if your prior experience has been with flowcharts, there is an urgent need to adapt to a different way of reading the diagrams, and converting them into program code. Unlike the flowchart, the horizontal as well as the vertical position of items on the page are very significant. The diagrams are read from top to bottom, with passes from left to right being made as necessary to give the order of execution

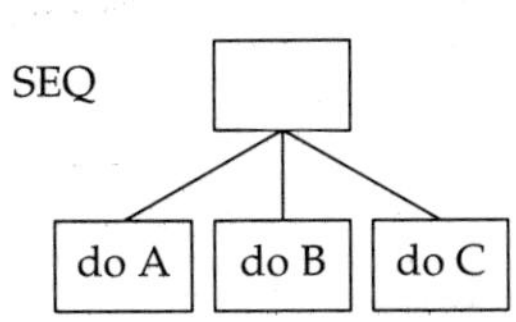


```
void doitall(void) {
    doA( );
    doB( );
    doC( );
}
```

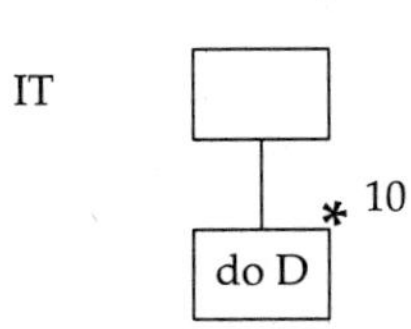


```
for(i=0; i<10; i++) {
    doD( );
}
```

or

```
x = 0;
while (x < 10) {
    doD( );
    x++;
}
```

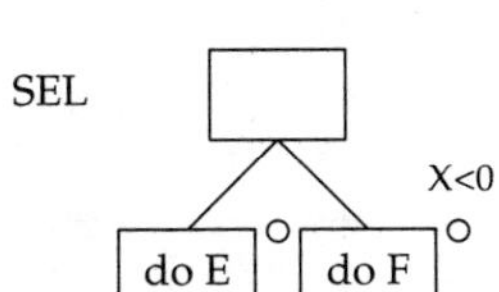


```
if (x >= 0) {
    doE( );
} else {
    doF( );
}
```

Structure chart representation of SEQ, IT and SEL

of the activities. A structure chart represents the three basic programming structures: SEQ, IT and SEL (sequence, iteration and selection) and maps directly onto program code if a modern structured language, such as C/C++ or Java, is being employed.

In a structure chart, the top activity boxes represent top-level functions in the program which call the lower level functions, passing parameters downwards and receiving results back. If a more tangible method of visualizing the mapping from structure chart to program code is required, the manipulation demonstrated below may help. This suggests that a sheet of thin paper holding a structure chart is pinned by the top right-hand corner, and seized by the bottom left-hand corner. The paper should then be folded upwards, diagonally, revealing only the back of the sheet.

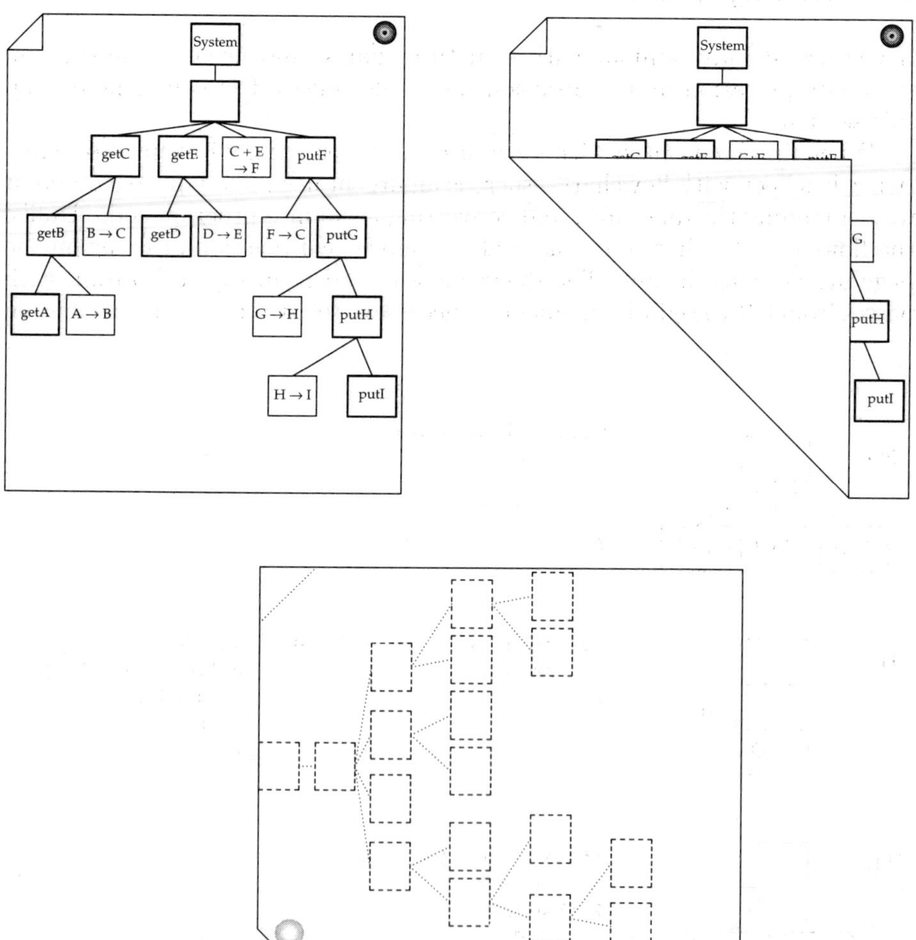

Reading a structure chart for program code ordering

By reading the diagram through the back of the paper, from top to bottom, the correct ordering of the actions can be seen. Starting at the top of the reversed page and running downwards, take the right-most modules in sequence. This might convince you that a structure chart is a very close representation of the final code, even though it is graphical and two dimensional.

11.8 Yourdon structured analysis and design for real-time systems

The Yourdon structured approach to systems specification, design and implementation was initially established for DP applications, but it has been extended to fit the specific needs of real-time systems development. Here we will follow the expanded methodology proposed by Paul Ward and Stephen Mellor: Yourdon SA/SD with Ward–Mellor Extensions. The resultant method is suitable for building large multi-tasking systems, and has gained popularity due to the availability of automated tools and ease of use. The initial step, conventionally, involves the context diagram as described in Section 5.2. The initial context diagram sets out the perimeter of the system to be developed, with all the external data sources and sinks. This gives the designer an opportunity to start to think about data structures and estimate flow rates, which will give some value for the likely processing load to be encountered. At the same time, especially

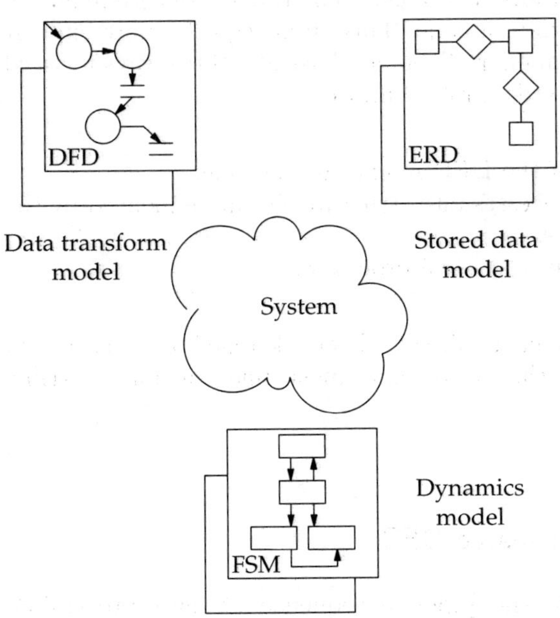

The three Yourdon modelling perspectives

when confronted with an unknown application field, a structured 'viewpoint analysis' can help in establishing more accurately the system's functional requirements.

The Yourdon method, with real-time extensions, successfully unifies three design approaches with distinct diagrammatic methodologies.

After drawing up a system context diagram, the top-level DFD can be derived, partitioning the system into its principal functional units, or subsystems. This separation may actually be driven by the practical need to distribute the software over several discrete platforms, or separate the processing load among available hosts. Alternatively, you can start with: 'Input', 'Process', 'Output' if no other useful guidance comes to mind! A further fragmentation can then be undertaken to generate the more detailed second-level DFDs based on the previous data transformations.

The Entity Relation Diagram (ERD) often plays Cinderella to its two sister diagrams because dynamic processing rather than large, complex data sets are seen as the key issue for real-time systems. So the ERD is often neglected, unless an actual database is required. The data modelling approach can, however, offer an alternative to the context diagram as a first step in the design process. A high-level description is initially developed involving real-world entities and their relationships. This ERD is far removed from the practicalities of implementation, and serves to sort out confusions and uncertainties in the early stages of a project. It is, in fact, rather similar to the more abstract Class Diagram (CD) which we will encounter later in Chapter 14.

By the time that the second-level DFD has been drafted, concern may usefully turn towards the production of code. This often requires more explicit guidance than the raw DFD can offer. There are basically three ways forward from the final DFD phase towards implementation:

1. Direct implementation of the DFD in executable code.
2. Expansion of the data processes into structure charts, sequenced by the input and output streams.
3. Introduction of event-driven control processes.

The first two approaches have already been sketched out earlier in this chapter. There remains the third, and most relevant for real-time programmers.

11.9 Implementing an event-based DFD

The DFD bubble chains give the pipeline sequence of data processing, and are generally interpreted as indicating that each process is started by the arrival of the necessary data at its input. Such a limited specification of scheduling is not really sufficient for concurrent systems. In fact, all the data transformation processes could be active simultaneously if multi-processor hardware were available. More likely, they would all be implemented as separate tasks running concurrently on a single CPU.

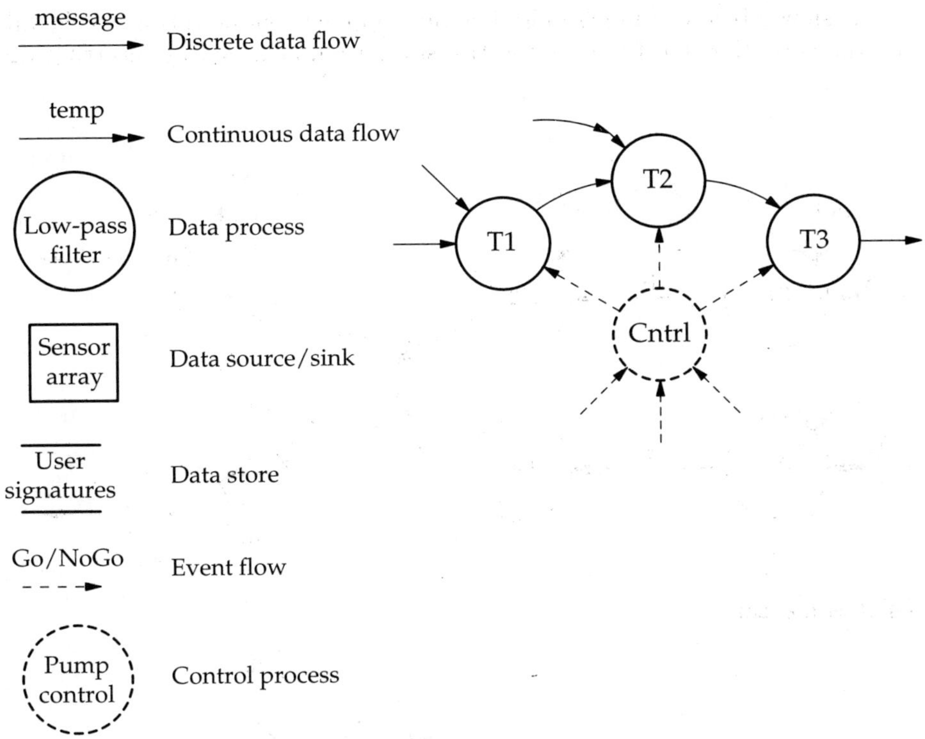

DFD with control process

Paul Ward and Stephen Mellor (1985) (and independently by D. Hatley and I. Pirbhai) proposed modifications and additions to make the Yourdon SA/SD method more suitable for use with real-time systems. The principal change saw the inclusion of 'control processes' which acted on the data processes as schedulers. In this way the scheduling activity could be explicitly separated from activity on the incoming data stream.

In order to deal with incoming events and use them to schedule processes, the DFD has to be restructured for the mutation into FSM form. Principally, control processes are inserted at the centre of local clusters of data transformation processes. How to group data processes around a control process may be an issue, but generally the close sequencing of activities, and the data involved, guides the selection so as to satisfy the requirements of FSM activities. Incoming events are then reattached from the original data processes to the new control processes, and internal trigger events are introduced to link control processes to activities. Once this has been completed, the full choice of FSM coding method, as presented earlier in Chapter 6, can be made.

It should be noted that the data flows between data processes can be implemented in many different ways: parameter passing within a function call, FIFO queues between autonomous tasks, or global data areas.

As shown below, a much more flexible approach can be taken to scheduling the activities, P1–P9 after the transformation achieved by inserting the

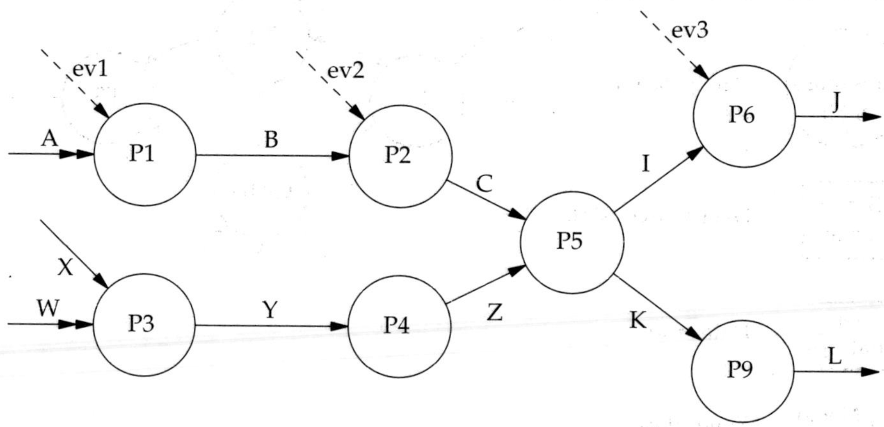

DFD with events

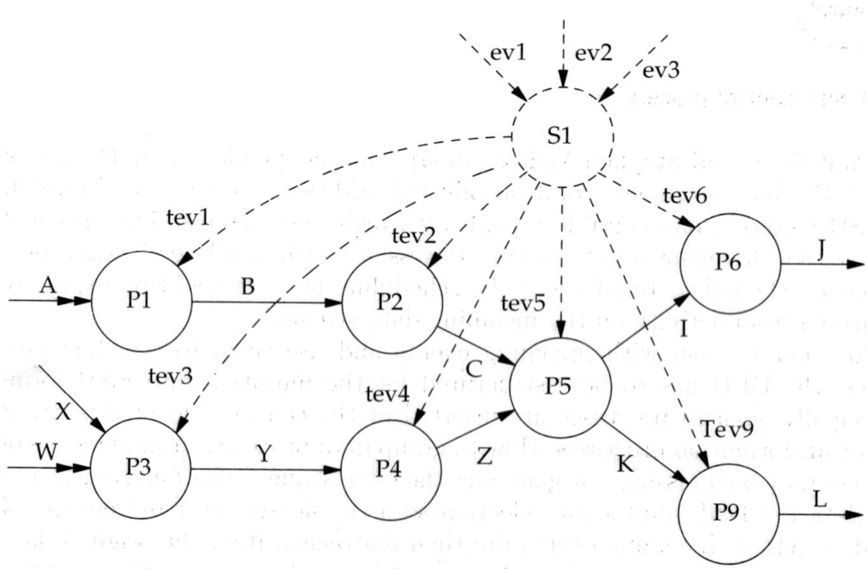

DFD with control process inserted

control process S1. In fact, the reliance on data arrival events to trigger processing is removed, and the new possibility emerges of dealing with processes that don't actually *receive* discrete data! Looking again at the DFD from the POS example, it might be considered appropriate to carry out the FSM

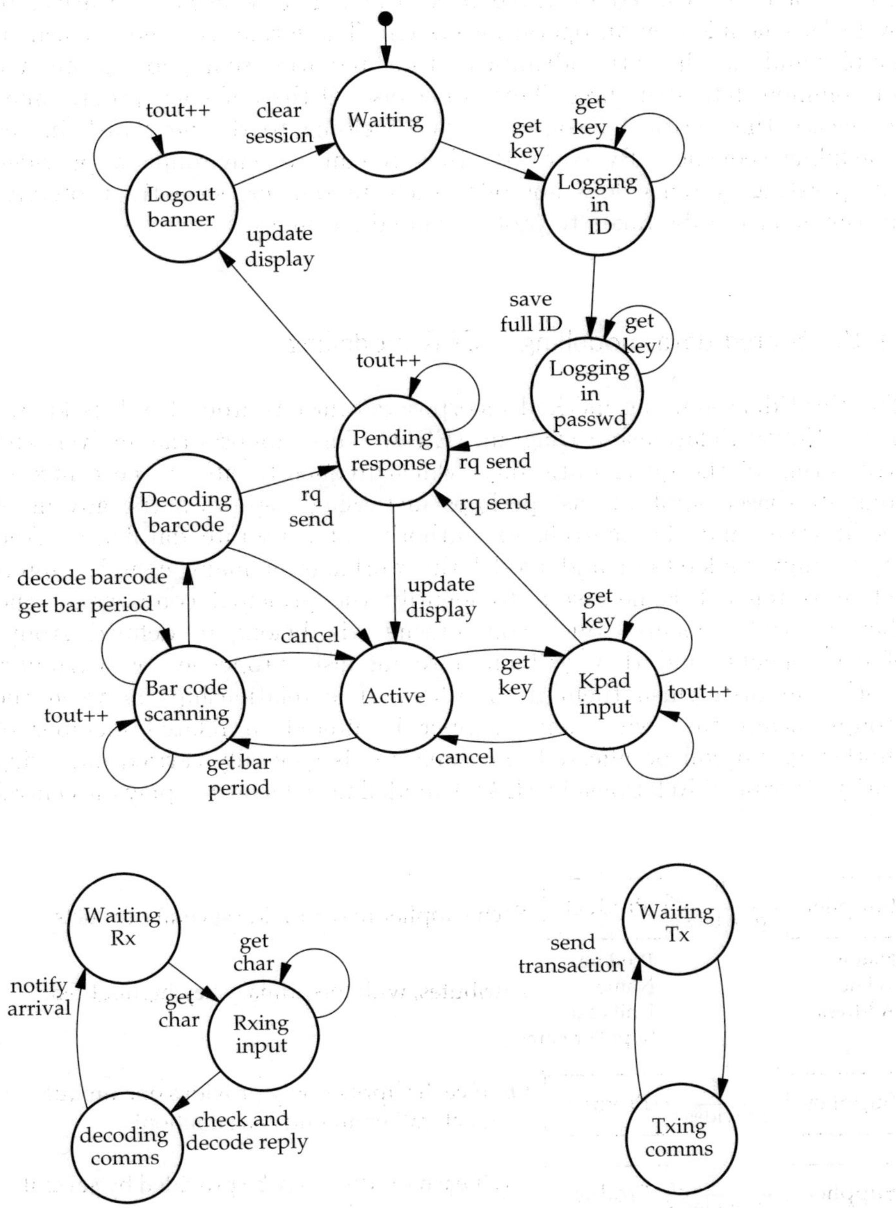

Three concurrent FSMs for the POS terminal, derived from p. 250 – keypad and scanner, serial receiver and serial transmitter

transformation, as above. The POS terminal takes responsibility for monitoring the barcode scanner, the keypad, and the incoming serial link, while transmitting transaction requests to the data concentrator and updating the local display panel. Such a situation, where simultaneous activities demand a multi-tasking implementation, can be handled by three concurrent FSMs. These could be realized by three tasks running on a cyclic executive, or by tasks scheduled by an operating system. The former scheme is cheaper, simpler and has the extra advantage of not requiring semaphore protection for common data structures. This is because all the tasks are programmed to release their critical resources before yielding to the next task in the scheduling sequence. By contrast, the pre-emptive environment provided by operating systems does not offer such guarantees, so extra protective measures have to be taken to protect shared resources.

11.10 Stored data modelling – EAR modelling

The third diagramming method incorporated into Yourdon SA/S is known as the Entity Relationship Diagram (ERD). This supports the analysis and structuring of the quasi-static data which frequently sits at the centre of computer-based applications, perhaps increasingly so, with the advent of the Internet and the centralizing authority of corporate databases. And so, to fully understand and model the workings of many complex interactive systems it is necessary to identify the principal components and their interrelationships. Such components will belong to defined groups of components, and they will all have intrinsic properties or attributes which will distinguish them from others. The relationships between the groups means that when one member is altered, a related member of another group will be affected. The analysis is generally carried out using Entity Attribute Relationship (EAR) modelling which also plays a central

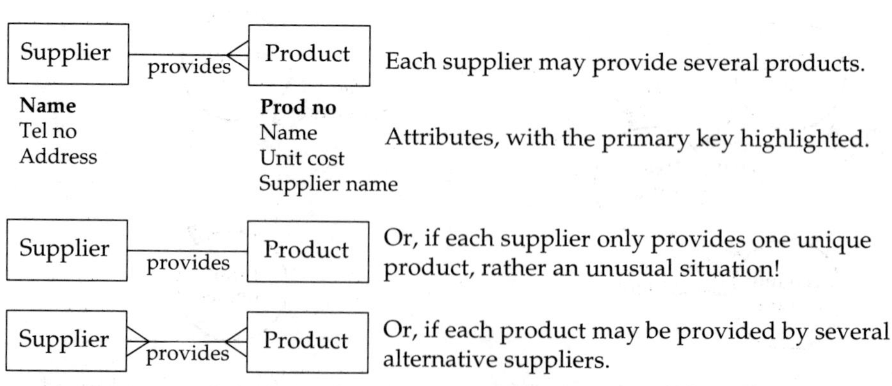

Entity relationship diagrams

role in database systems development. EAR modelling employs a topdown approach, developing a high-level description of the system's objects, their properties, and the relationships between them. Using an example from retailing illustrates three alternative relationships between supplier and product data. Only one of the three will be correct for a particular system's operation.

Important entities are identified and grouped into entity sets. The figure above shows that there are two entity sets represented: supplier and product. But entities can be conceptual (sales transaction) as well as physical (customer). They can usefully be viewed as clusters of particular properties, such as: {CustomerID, Name, Address, CreditCardNo}, which uniquely distinguish them from each other. The legal range of values of a property, or attribute, is termed the domain, and will be limited in the same way a language TYPE constrains the values which a variable can assume. So an instance of an entity is really a set of attribute values which are unique within the entity set. Each entity instance is represented as a row of attribute values in the relation table. The attribute names are seen at the top of the columns. The attributes can also be listed near the entity box on the ERD. The minimum group of attributes, which ensure the uniqueness of an entity instance, is termed the *primary* key. The supplier relation table has the **Name** attribute as its primary key, whereas the product table uses **Prod No**. Keys may concatenate several attributes to discriminate between entity instances, in which case they are termed *complex keys*.

Alternative nomenclature for the ERD

Attributes which are not part of the primary key are known as *non-primary attributes* and should be fully dependent on the whole primary key; that is, all the non-primary attributes of an entity instance should be predictable given the entity's primary attribute values. This must hold true for currently stored entities, as well as future entities. Thus, the primary key, and the possibility of deriving non-primary attribute values from it, are due to the nature of the data itself, and not the actual instances which happen to be recorded.

An entity may have a relationship with another entity. This does not refer to any particular *instance* of an entity, rather, all the possible entity instances that could occur within that entity set. So, the entity *supplier* is linked to the entity *product*, through the relationship *delivers*.

The use of lookup tables to implement functional relationships between data items is not the only way. It is perfectly possible to employ mathematical

Supplier Name	Tel no	Address
Smiths	123 4567	The Brewery, AX1 2XA
CojaCola	321 7654	Drinks Factory, MS1 2SM
Mcvista	789 0123	Biscuit Corner, RN1 2NR
Tartan	678 9876	The Bakery, SA1 2AS

Product Number	Name	Price	Supplier
01296891	Keg Ale	540	Smiths
01298650	Brown Stuff	125	CojaCola
01273214	Crackers	75	Mcvista
01274521	Oats	45	Tartan
01293245	Lager	225	Smiths
01291552	Cider	185	Smiths
01273221	Digestives	85	Mcvista

Product Number	Name	Price	Supplier
01296891	Keg Ale	540	Smiths
01298650	Brown Stuff	125	CojaCola
01273214	Crackers	75	Mcvista
01274521	Oats	45	Tartan

Product Number	Name	Price	Supplier
01296891	Keg Ale	540	Smiths
01298650	Brown Stuff	125	CojaCola
01273214	Crackers	75	Mcvista
01274521	Oats	45	Tartan
01274521	Oats	45	Mcvista
01293245	Lager	225	Smiths
01291552	Cider	185	Smiths
01273221	Digestives	85	Mcvista
01296891	Keg Ale	540	Smiths
01273214	Crackers	75	Tartan
01274521	Lager	225	Smiths

Example supplier and product relation tables representing the three alternative relationships from p. 260

functions or algebraic expressions to map from one entity instance to another. The database technique simply serves the role of an arbitrary, modifiable function, in which parameters are set and a unique return value is supplied, with the extra facility of easy, ongoing modifiability. Being able to tweak the `sin()` function in order to improve data fit is a luxury not widely available!

So the value of the ERD within the Yourdon SA/SD methodology principally concerns data stores, where the 'product database' requires analysis and normalization in order to eliminate redundant items and streamline the update activities. As central databases play an increasingly important role in on-line, interactive systems, it is clear that real-time programmers should not neglect the ERD!

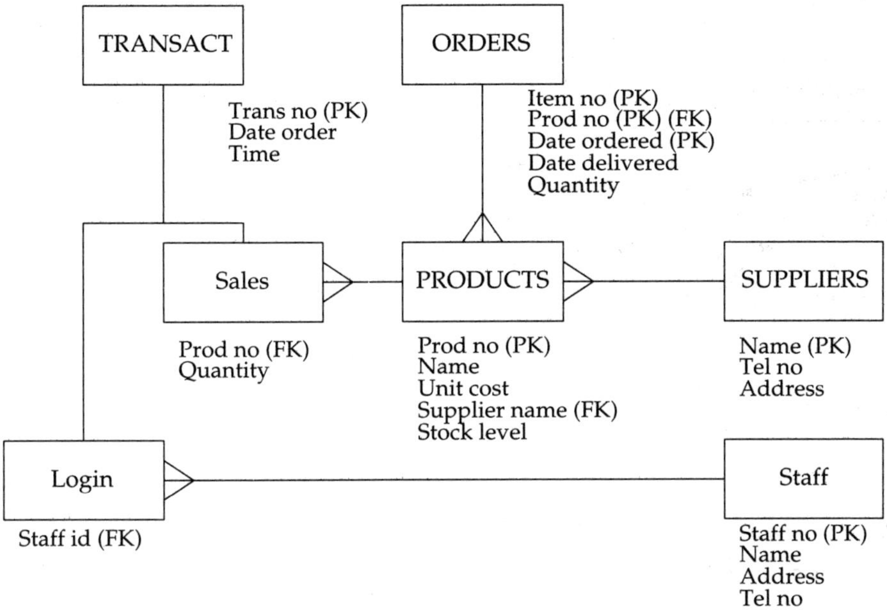

ERD for POS system

11.11 Transforming ERD to DFD

An ERD description may be used in either of two circumstances. The most common is to analyse and describe a component database which holds enduring data for the system. In this case the ERD will require translating into SQL script to handle the creation, updating and queries involving the database. The other situation requires the transformation of an initial ERD model, covering the complete or part system, into a form of expression closer to implementation. For this, there are no universally accepted rules. If discrete files are used in place of a centralized database, or if individual relation tables may be represented separately without confusion, The figure below illustrates an ERD fragment and the related DFD for generating a replenishment order to a supplier. Entities within an ERD can thus represent data stores, or terminator devices, where quasi-stable data is maintained for the system. If the relationship between two entities is complex, even involving the introduction of more attributes, the DFD data transformation can be realized by the use of another lookup table, which supplies the necessary mappings. The relation between two entities becomes an active function serving a request. Exactly *when* this happens is not specified by the ERD model, only that it is available, the assumption being that any change to data will trigger a ripple of actions across the model to reconcile all the tables.

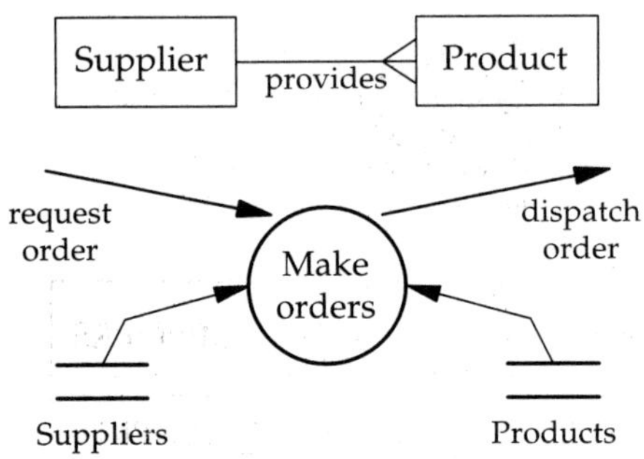

Transforming ERD into DFD

11.12 Normalizing stored data

Data sets often contain functional dependencies, which constrain the values which are allowed. Thus, the variables do not change their values independently, they are not *orthogonal.* In fact, the values of the *primary* variables can be used to determine the values of *non-primary* items. Whenever sets of data are stored for processing and inspection it is important to minimize the quantity and rationalize their interrelationships. In the field of database systems, it has long been recognized that storing redundant or repeated data is inefficient and will probably lead to continuing maintenance problems when inconsistences creep into the data. This situation has been effectively addressed through the work of Codd (1971) and Chen (1976). Data relations can now be normalized to comply with specific conditions, and so reduce, or even eliminate, redundancy. So data can be presented in a number of conditions which have been designated as:

- 1NF First Normal Form, item instances listed in simple attribute relation table may contain redundant data.
- 2NF Second Normal Form, same as 1NF but with non-prime attributes fully dependent on whole primary key attribute(s).
- 3NF Third Normal Form, same as 2NF but with no functional dependencies between non-prime attributes.
- BCNF Boyce–Codd Normal Form, same as 3NF but with multiple primary key relation tables, the keys are interdependent.
- 4NF Fourth Normal Form, same as BCNF but no multi-valued dependencies.

- 5NF Fifth Normal Form, same as 4NF but with no non-prime dependencies.

The transformation to higher-level normal forms to eliminate redundant data involves splitting relation tables into smaller subrelations.

11.13 Chapter summary

The method of structured analysis and design, which consistently includes FSD, DFD and EAD, can assist effectively with real-time systems development. Both static and dynamic viewpoints are catered for. Functional decomposition and system partitioning, from context diagram, through multi-level DFDs, down into structure charts and FSDs, can deliver well-structured real-time programs. Some methods are explained for transforming all three schematic diagrams into code. Good designers keep one eye on implementation at all times.

11.14 Problems and issues for discussion

1. Draw up a context diagram, followed by a top-level DFD for digital telephone answering software which operates on a PC using a PCI telephone line interface card.
2. Draw up a context diagram, followed by subsequent DFDs for the text messaging facility provided by your mobile phone. See how far you get.
3. Further partition the DFD presented in Section 11.6. Perhaps a multi-threading approach would be attractive for such an application: comms-receive, comms-reply, command-line-interpreter.
4. Derive a structure chart from the DFD presented on p. 250 as an alternative implementation route.
5. Derive a decision table to describe how a Sony Mini-disc unit, with microphone recording, downloading and playback facilities, operates.
6. Using the SA/SD methods of DFD and FSM, analyse the user-side operation of your mobile handset.

11.15 Suggestions for reading

Cooling, J. (1997). *Real-time Software Systems.* Thomson Computer Press.
Edwards, K. (1998). *Real-time Structured Methods.* Wiley.
Goldsmith, S. (1995). *Real-time Systems Development.* Prentice Hall.
Gomaa, H. (1993). *Software Design Methods for Concurrent and Real-time Systems.* Addison Wesley.

Hawryszkiewycz, I. (1990). *Relational Database Design.* Prentice Hall.
Jackson, M. A. (1975). *Principles of Program Design.* Academic Press.
Jackson, M. A. (1985). *System Development.* Prentice Hall.
Parnas, D. L. (1972). On the criteria to be used in decomposing systems into modules. *Comm. ACM*, 15(2), 1053–1058.
Pressman, R. P. (2003). *Software Engineering: A Practitioner's Approach.* McGraw-Hill, chs 7, 11.
Stevens, W., Myers, G. & Constantine, L. (1974). Structured design. *IBM Systems Journal*, vol. 13/2, 115–139.
Ward, P. & Mellor, S. (1985). *Structured Development for Real-time Systems*, Vols 1, 2 and 3. Prentice Hall.

Chapter 12

Designing for multi-tasking

12.1 Chapter overview

Traditional SA/SD methods need extending to deal with real-time systems and multi-tasking implementations. Splitting a project into concurrent tasks during the preliminary phase of systems design can be difficult. A few guidelines can be offered to assist with this activity. Task diagrams can provide a good system overview by expressing task functions and communication channels. When dealing with multi-tasking software, there are some special requirements to be kept in mind when selecting languages and compilers.

12.2 SA/SD for multi-tasking

All software designers need guidelines, derived from the functional specification, which will shape the emerging software structure. In this vein, the

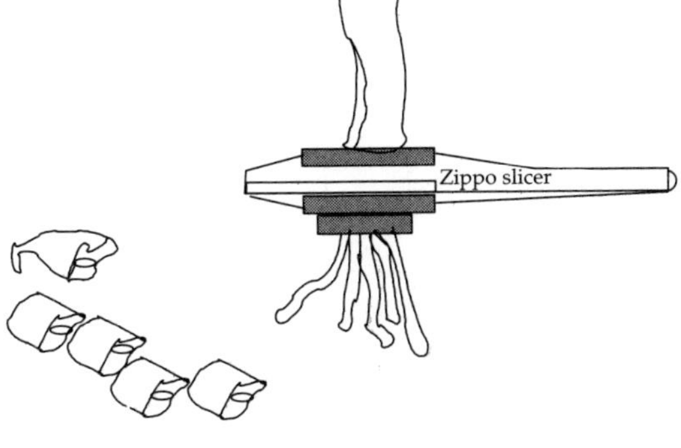

Chopping or slicing the beans?

Jackson Structured Programming (JSP) method proposes that the *static* patterns of input and output data files should be matched to identify *correspondences* which effectively give the fundamental code structure. In a similar way, SA/SD starts with the context diagram which ties down the terminal ends of the DFD pipelines with the external data sources and sinks. These are primary constraints on the subsequent code structure. The SA/SD methodology as described in Chapter 11 involves drawing up a top-level DFD, and then expanding and partitioning it into lower-level DFDs in preparation for implementation. In general, we could look at the choices involved in the decomposition process from the same point of view as a cook preparing green beans. This poses the lifestyle dilemma of whether to cross-chop or length-slice the bean pods. The cross-chopping method is how SA/SD advises programmers to partition a process pipeline, so you end up with a sequential series of activities to be run one after the other. However, length-slicing beans mimics the division of an activity into several semi-independent, long-running concurrent tasks.

Another part of the system's foundation which can be identified early in the design phase is the requirement for internal data stores which endure for the lifetime of the application. These can be in the form of database, disk files or even linked lists and arrays. They may hold transaction records, error logs, customer accounts, flight paths, anything that is essential to the operation of the system. Once the primary data structures are recognized, the update and read rates can be estimated, with the likely number of sources and destination which could be involved, and, most important of all, whether concurrent accesses are to be catered for.

12.3 Partitioning into tasks

Students often ask what rules should be followed when dividing a job into tasks or threads. This is not an easy question to answer because every

- Platform constraints
- Concurrent functionality sequential and parallel
- Simultaneous I/O activity
- Response priorities
- Heavy algorithms
- Periodic activities
- Overlapping for efficiency
- Data transfer streams
- Possibility of blocking
- Exception trapping
- Testing purposes

Guidelines for partitioning into tasks

application is different and will require a different group of answers. Advisory guidelines are not 100 per cent reliable because of this wide variation between applications, but they may still serve as a useful starting point. The previous figure, with the associated notes, lists 11 significant characteristics which can be helpful when attempting to identify candidate tasks. The initial step of identifying all the various functions to be carried out by the system has already been completed through the context diagram and subsequent DFDs. But the technique of isolating *tasks* to run concurrently has still to be described.

- *Platform constraints* A single top-level DFD can be chopped vertically into separate tasks, which then map onto different CPUs. This approach is clearly necessary in a distributed system where several CPUs are available, perhaps on discrete platforms linked by communications channels, or where specialist processors, such as DSP or graphic accelerators, are being exploited.
- *Functional concurrency* At the centre of all multi-tasking systems will be tasks carrying out recognizably distinct activities, often in the form of service loops, usually with different periodic or sporadic scheduling patterns. Once the list of system functions has been drawn up, the problem of sifting through them for candidate tasks can begin. As suggested above in Section 12.2, existing DFD process pipelines may be separable into concurrent subactivities. More simply, key DFD transformation processes may become discrete tasks in their own right. Others may be broken down further into lower-level DFDs before the identification of tasks can be completed.
- *Simultaneous I/O activity* Inspecting the system input and output requirements is normally very fruitful when attempting to identify potential tasks. Some systems clearly require multiple I/O events to be occurring simultaneously. A serial communications or LAN port could be receiving incoming messages, while other servicing has to continue undisrupted. In this case, encapsulating the different activities within separate tasks would offer a good solution.
- *Response priorities* The preliminary analysis phase may reveal some idea of the relative priority levels which all the various activities will require to supply an effective service. So the response to an alarm button being pressed should not be held up by a routine adjustment to the room temperature. Activities with dissimilar priorities will require separate tasks. In the extreme, an interrupt could be dedicated to the event, achieving maximum priority.
- *Heavy algorithms* Heavy, CPU-bound processing can take too much time to run through to completion. Unacceptably, the job would block out all the other system activities. The simplest way to deal with such a situation is to place the algorithm within a low priority task, which may readily be pre-empted by more urgent requests.

- *Periodic activities* When some processing has to happen at regular intervals in time, such as input polling, it is convenient to place the code within a task which can sleep until an event alarm wakes it up for immediate execution. After the task has completed, it reinitializes the event alarm, returns to the sleeping state, and waits for the next event alarm.
- *Overlapping for efficiency* Some activity appears initially to be multi-phase, serial in nature, each phase completing before the next phase can start. But with more analysis it may be possible to reconfigure so that it can be carried out by several overlapping activities. In this way, a greater throughput can be achieved, with a more flexible response to partial failures and unexpected conditions. Data pre-fetching and command line editing are examples of this approach. Another familiar example is that of Unix, splitting up data flow pipelines into separate concurrent processes for efficient execution, as can be seen by inspecting the process list while data is being processed.
- *Data transfer streams* Once you have gained some idea of how the system could be partitioned into discrete tasks, it is then possible to take a look at the emerging intertask communication requirements. Where large quantities of data are being copied from task to task, there may be efficiency issues to be taken into account. One solution is to merge neighbouring tasks, and so eliminate the need to transfer so much data.
- *Possibility of blocking* One strategy for handling intermittent processing requests is to block a task on each data source. When data items arrive, the associated task will be woken and be able to complete the necessary processing. This will require that the blocked task does not hold up other processing activities, quite easily satisfied within a multi-tasking environment.
- *Exception trapping* With the possibility of run-time errors occurring, the propagation of their influence can readily be limited to the task which generated them. So an extra level of security is gained from splitting the processing into semi-autonomous tasks.
- *Testing purposes* Unit testing can be greatly facilitated by partitioning the program into semi-autonomous tasks for design, coding and test. This requires that the interfaces between tasks be clearly defined at an early stage within the development: this is no bad thing.

12.4 Cohesion and coupling

Another way to approach the issue of how to partition into multiple tasks is to revisit the set of criteria used for assessing module cohesiveness and coupling. This was published by Constantine (1979) with a more general intention of improving the quality of all software, rather than assisting the realtime programmer. It had been noted that various types of interaction, or coupling, between modules made maintenance much more difficult. Thus, if this could be reduced, it was hoped that the large cost of bug fixing and future maintenance could be reduced.

Applying these criteria during design may be challenged because they work retrospectively! First do the segmentation, then carry out the assessment.

a. Platform, CPU sharing by several modules	WEAK
b. Coincidental, e.g. compile/edit convenience	↓
c. Logical, design-driven problem segmentation	
d. Temporal, e.g. run-time initialization	
e. Procedural, library code sharing	
f. Communicational, common data sharing	
g. Sequential, run-time scheduling	
h. Functional (cooperating on a single task)	STRONG

Within module cohesiveness (intramodule cohesiveness)

a. No direct referencing (fully independent tasks)	WEAK
b. Value parameters passed (function or task)	↓
c. Reference parameters passed (pointers)	
d. Control variables used (switch flags)	
e. `EXTRN/PUBLIC` data declarations exchanged	
f. `COMMON` or `GLOBAL` data used	
g. Internal data referenced by physical address	STRONG

Between module coupling (intermodule coupling)

The partitioning of an application into a process network requires important extra decisions about the data passing methods to be used which affect the overall scheduling pattern of the system. If a DFD, bubble diagram is directly mapped onto a network of tasks, too many tasks may result, leading to a somewhat inefficient implementation.

12.5 Designing for intertask communication

The nomenclature and approach presented in this section is loosely based on MASCOT (Modular Approach to System Construction Operation and Test), a method which was developed in the early 1970s by Hugo Simpson and Ken Jackson (1979) at the Royal Signals and Radar Establishment (RSRE), Malvern. It was mainly intended for use by UK defence contractors implementing real-time embedded systems. It is very close in conception and style to the Concurrent Design Approach for Real-time Systems (CODARTS) which was proposed in the US for a similar range of applications (Gomaa 1993).

Although tasks are intended to run independently of each other, as far as the application functionality permits, they still need to communicate and influence each other's execution patterns. To enable these interactions to take place safely and efficiently, most operating systems and RTEs provide several primitive facilities through APIs and code libraries. They are illustrated below: channels, pools, flags and signals. These have been described in more detail already in Chapter 9, so only the diagrammatic icons and their correct use for systems design will be dealt with in this section.

The channel, already introduced in Section 8.7, represents a means of passing items of data between tasks asynchronously. So if the receiver is not ready to receive the item, the sender leaves the item 'on the doorstep' for later. The role of the asynchronous channel is to reduce blocking to a minimum by providing enough temporary FIFO storage to decouple the execution threads of the communicating tasks. Note that the data items are *destroyed on read*, they do not endure in the channel. Should a channel become full, the writer will block, and similarly if the channel is empty the reader will block. The associated functions are: `open(&chan, size, type)`, `write(chan, item)`, `read(chan, &item)`. Channels, also called *pipes*, would normally be RAM based for speed of access. If no specific run-time support is available, channels can be coded as circular buffers, with all the read/write accesses regulated by semaphores.

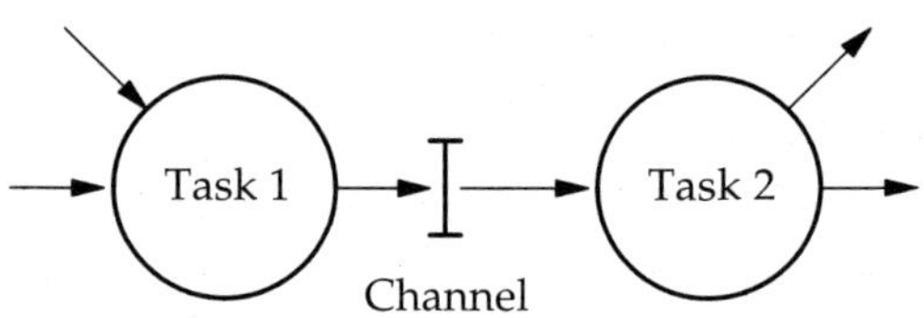

FIFO communication channel between tasks

The signal represents a convenient means of providing intertask control. One task may voluntarily sleep, and a companion task then directs a signal at the right moment to wake it up. Alternatively, asynchronous error conditions can be quickly transferred around the system using the signal facility to evoke a special function within the receiving task. Operating systems manage signal delivery and task sleep/wake-up operations with little indication of the complexity of the underlying structures. But if no run-time support for

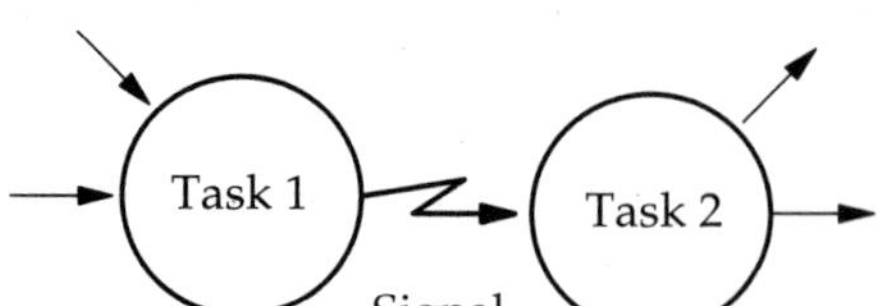

Signalling between tasks

signal handling is available, a similar facility can be hand coded using dual semaphores.

The pool is simply a defined global data area in RAM which has access functions provided to protect against critical data corruption. Items get overwritten by the writer, but otherwise endure. So multiple readers are possible. Should the run-time support environment not contain such a facility, it can be hand coded using two semaphores as illustrated in Section 8.6. It is useful to recognize the curved symbols as *active*, while the straight edges represent passive objects. Only items of *dissimilar* character may be linked. The code within the passive item is run as part of the execution thread of the active caller. This is much the same as DLL modules sitting in memory waiting to be used. So channels and pools are passive, while tasks are active. Tasks are connected to channels or pools, and vice versa. Tasks cannot be directly connected to other tasks.

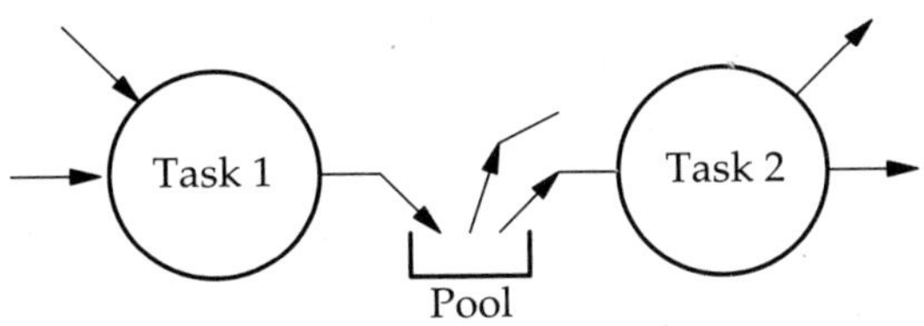

Pool storage buffer

As might be expected, in a pre-emptive, multi-tasking environment, the data within channels and pools represents a 'critical resource' which could easily be corrupted by uncontrolled simultaneous access, as described in Section 3.15. Thus, the access procedures associated with channels and pools must take this problem into account, by queuing requesting tasks until safe access is possible. The circle now represents an autonomous task containing an independent, looping thread of execution. In practice, with a single CPU, only one task will be executing at any time, but the real-time system designer works as far as possible without thinking about the scheduling issues, concentrating on successfully representing the application requirements. In some ways, a task bubble could be seen as a kind of mini-context diagram in its own right.

12.6 Device interfacing

When dealing with device drivers the interconnectivity picture is slightly confused because they can be active (interrupt driven) or passive (polled). So the connection pathways to tasks have to reflect this difference. In the next figure, Task 1 is receiving data from an external device which fires an interrupt to wake up the driver with each new delivery. Task 1 may be blocked on the channel until data arrives, or only intermittently checking

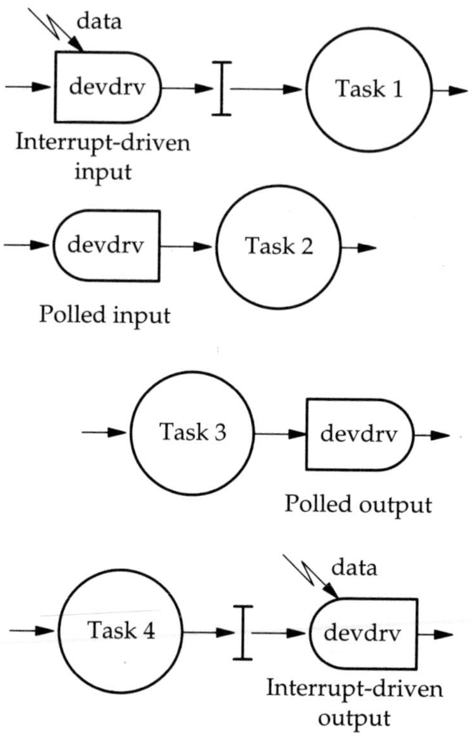

Device drivers

it, or even waiting for a signal which informs it of the incoming data. The lightning flash symbol represents an external interrupt when directed at an *active* device driver, and a software signal when directed at a task. Task 2 illustrates a straightforward polling operation, which could suffer badly from data overrun if the source of data is faster, on the average, than Task 2 itself!

Another confusion which arises when coding multiple, communicating tasks, is the order of initialization, and where the responsibility lies for creating the shared communication facilities. Unlike with IP sockets, where the master and client roles are clearly defined, with channels and pools it can be slightly ambiguous as to who should instantiate the shared resource. It is possible to centralize all the initialization code into a single setup task, which may kill itself off having done its work. But more often, one task out of the group using a pool or channel will set up the shared resource, to which the others can connect.

12.7 Task diagrams

Before presenting the task diagram for a PnD machine, it is worth defining the context diagram and bandwidth estimates which have to be drawn up first.

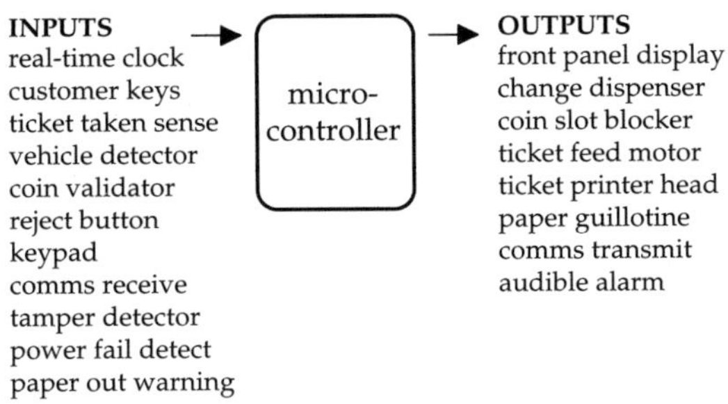

	Type	Rate Hz
Input		
real-time clock	bit	0.2
customer keys	bit	0.01
ticket taken sense	bit	0.01
vehicle detector	byte	0.3
coin validator	byte	1
reject button	bit	1
keypad	byte	0.3
comms receive	byte	10 K
tamper detector	bit	1
power fail detect	bit	100
paper out warning	bit	1
Output		
front panel display	bit	0.01
change dispenser	bit	10
coin slot blocker	bit	0.2
ticket feed motor	bit	0.2
ticket printer head	byte	200
paper guillotine	bit	1
comms transmit	byte	10 K
audible alarm	bit	1

Context diagram for a pay and display ticket vending machine

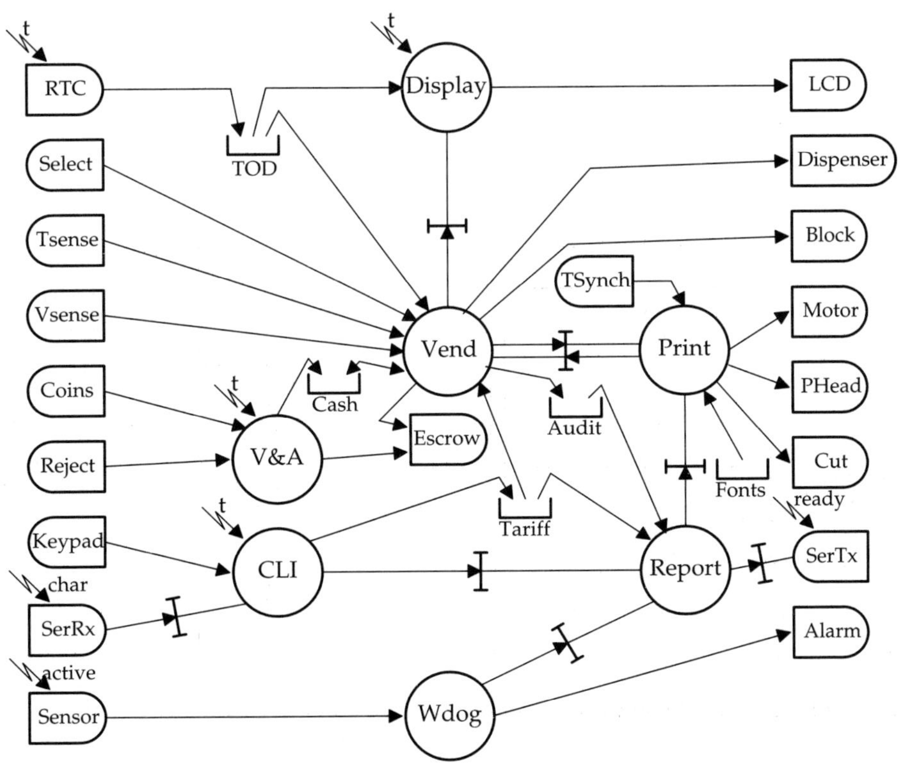

Task diagram for a pay and display ticket vending machine

Task diagrams, constructed from the components described in the previous section, can be very helpful in providing a schematic overview. They can, however, be easily confused with DFDs, or even FSMs, so care must always be taken when presented with a 'bubblearrow' diagram for the first time to establish its real meaning. There is also an important

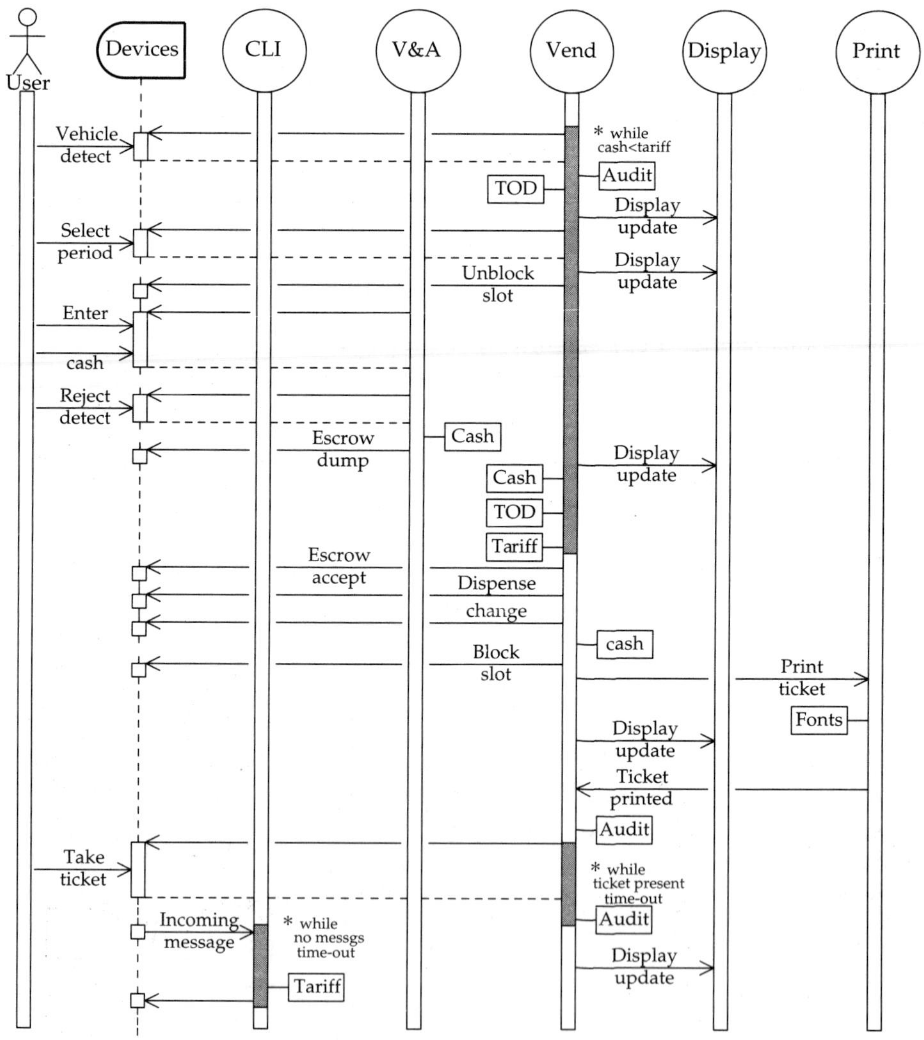

Execution sequence diagram for a pay and display ticket vending machine

part of the system which often gets omitted, namely, the support services which provide the execution environment for the individual tasks. The most salient contribution is undoubtedly the real-time *tick*, usually derived from a hardware crystal oscillator.

In the pay and display, ticket vending example, shown above, several of the tasks operate in periodic polling mode, handling an input or output device. This requires a cyclic wake-up tick event, which may be represented by a signal/interrupt flash. The next useful step is to undertake a preliminary analysis of the dynamic execution pattern likely to occur with an average level of I/O activity. Obviously, guessing every possible execution route is not needed, at this stage anyway. Employing an approximate UML sequence diagram is probably a good choice when trying to reveal a particular execution scenario, rather than an FSD which better suits the prescription of a complete range of legal activities. Although this is somewhat anachronistic, UML not arriving until several years after SA/SD was well established, it appears perfectly justifiable in the circumstances. Designers and programmers should be free to select processes and techniques to suit their needs, rather than being forced to conform to a single, unified paradigm. If you wish to review the use of UML sequence diagrams, it is introduced in the following chapter, but I think it is fairly self-explanatory in this context. It allows the designer to express a single, typical scenario, with messages and task activities displayed in time ordered sequence. The input and output reads and writes are drawn in because of their importance when trying to gain some idea of the likely run-time pattern of scheduling.

The vertical execution lines are drawn as *active* boxes, rather than inactive dashed lines, which emphasizes the existence of multiple independent threads. This could be modified if a synchronous wait, or blocking read, is anticipated as a normal part of the scheduling pattern. The open headed arrow signifies an asynchronous message, as would be sent via a channel. Pool accesses have been inserted as named boxes, on the left of the execution line for a read, on the right for a write. Where a task regularly loops, waiting for a status change, the execution line is greyed in, and the iteration guard conditions annotated. Should a blocking read, or synchronized channel access, be intended (an ADArendezvous), the arrow head can be fully blacked to emphasize the important effect on task scheduling which will then occur.

The next step following production of the task diagram and a preliminary analysis of patterns of dynamic activity is to take each task individually and produce either an FSD or structure chart to guide the code realization. Constraints to be satisfied now include: input and output channels, access to pools, and response to signals, including time-driven scheduling.

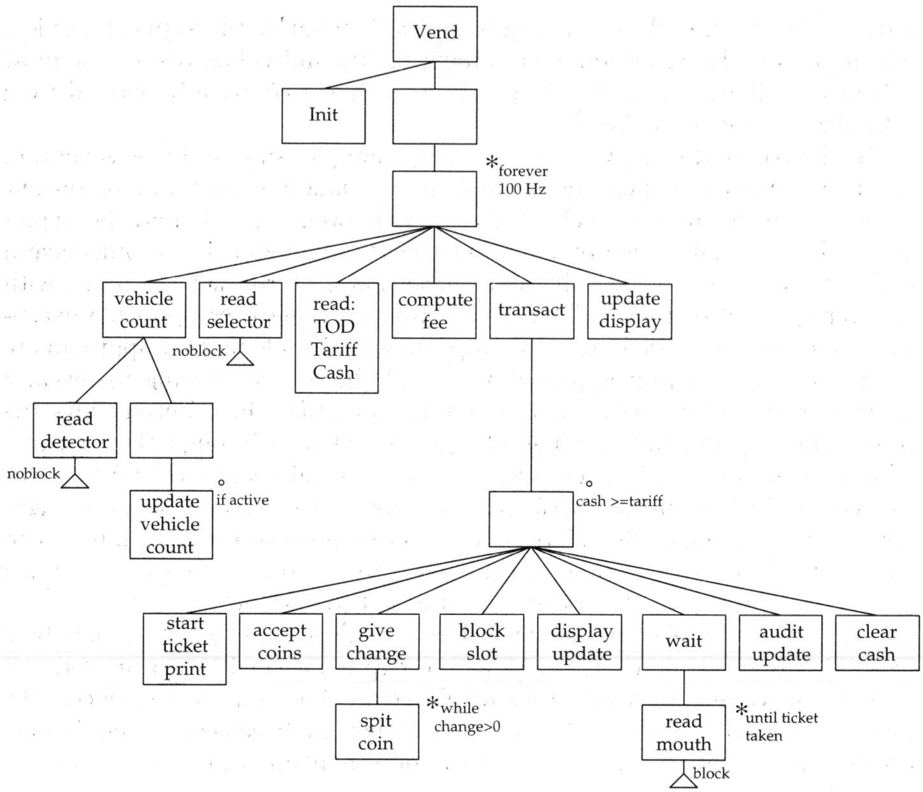

Structure chart for the Vend task from the figures on pp. 275 and 276

12.8 The CODARTS method

The Concurrent Design Approach for Real-time Systems was developed in the early 1980s to assist with the design and development of multi-tasking systems. It is based on the earlier DARTS (Design Approach for Real-time Systems) (Gomaa 1993), which itself emerged from the SA/SD methodology. In DARTS, the task identification activity takes a DFD, and groups neighbouring data transformations together to form tasks. The tasks can then communicate *asynchronously*, unlike the earlier chains of synchronous data transformation processes. The main cohesion criteria would then be temporal sequence, which is not the strongest alternative, as listed on p. 271. The steps needed to carry out the DARTS/CODARTS development are listed below, but are very similar to those already described earlier in this chapter for the extension of SA/SD into a tasking architecture. The final products are task diagrams, defining the tasks and their interactions, and structure diagrams for each task giving a static description of the code.

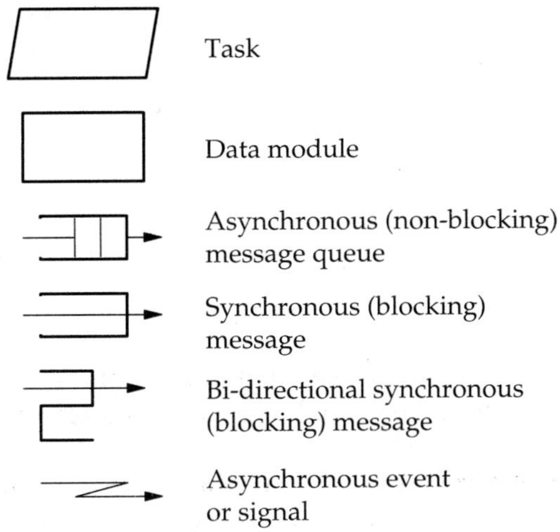

Elements for DARTS task diagrams

- Draw a system context diagram and hierarchically decompose into subsystems of DFDs for allocation to platforms. Define the behavioural characteristics of each component, similar to SA/SD methods.
- Identify and form the principal tasks, based on standard criteria as listed in Section 12.3.
- Identify the message channels and where the need for synchronization primitives may occur between the schedulable tasks.
- Establish the significant, enduring application data which has to be stored in datahiding modules, establish their initialization and access functions.
- Task and data module interrelationships are defined.
- Fully define all component interfaces, including data and control flows.
- Incremental software development within the separate tasks using structure diagrams.

12.9 Re-entrant code

An important aspect of implementing multi-threaded and multi-tasking programs is the need for pure, re-entrant code. While most modern compilers and support libraries recognize this requirement, there is always the possibility that some rogue subroutine is imported without a thorough assessment as to its suitability. The real problem relates to task pre-emption. Consider the situation when a task calls a function which uses a set of variables. Then it gets interrupted or time-sliced off the CPU, with the variables still active. What happens if the next task to run calls the same subroutine? It is essential that each evocation of the subroutine uses a different set of variables. This is easily achieved by ensuring that all functions only use local variables

Re-fientrant code problems

positioned on the evoker's stack, or semaphore protected global variables. So, many tasks can concurrently execute the same code, but each uses a private set of data variables.

Some algorithms are most efficiently coded as recursive functions, which, while executing, incestuously call themselves. Although these can be tricky to understand and worse to debug, they do offer a memory efficient solution to specific problems. Although they employ a kind of cooperative scheduling, they are clearly re-entrant and require the same separation of code and data segments, as with pre-emptive multi-tasking.

A related but less common version of the re-entrancy problem occurs if some code indulges in self-modification; a horrific practice, long deprecated by all sane programmers. If a function is different every time it gets called, you clearly have a real challenge! However, I must confess that I did do it once, and it was great fun. My justification came from a very limited CPU instruction set which did not support register-indirect I/O, all port numbers had to be compiled in as immediate values. Unfortunately the equipment included a large array of display units, amounting to nearly 128 discrete digits. Each had to be periodically addressed at its own port, and updated. It transpired that using 1 Kbyte of precious PROM for front panel digit addressing was not a popular suggestion with my colleagues. So using a small, self-modifying routine to loop around, incrementing the port number byte and refreshing the digits in sequence, turned out to be the best solution. As the program code was stored in PROM, the whole routine needed to be copied across to RAM to permit execution. But honestly, this is not to be recommended.

12.10 Setting task priorities

With multi-tasking systems, the priority given to a task sets the amount of time it has on the CPU, relative to the other tasks, and how long it waits for access to the CPU when becoming ready. It is intended that lower priority tasks will give way to high priority tasks, either by pre-emption or at least at the end of the current time-slice. Operating systems differ in the way this is handled, but most allow an initial value to be set by the programmer, which then evolves throughout the lifetime of the task. For periodic tasks, the 'Rate Monotonic' (RM) method is often used to compute a static priority value. The RM method assigns priorities inversely proportional to the likely run period of each task. This effectively sets the priority in direct proportion to the desired scheduling frequency: the shorter the run period, the more frequently the task is likely to be evoked. Dynamic priority schemes change task priorities in response to the task's success in getting access to the CPU, and the approaching deadlines. An example is the aging algorithm, where the task priority is incremented at each time-slice that passes until it eventually has to be dispatched. To avoid insignificant tasks gaining an inappropriately high priority, tasks are generally consigned to fixed bands which stop them moving too far away from their starting point.

12.11 Execution timing

Once the design work for a multi-tasking application has been completed and some outline code structures for the tasks are available, the need for estimates of likely execution times become more urgent. This is partly to ensure that the intended hardware is sufficiently powerful to carry out the processing and deliver the required response timings, and partly to generate a better understanding of the likely scheduling patterns which may occur at run-time. A major goal is to determine the worst case execution time for each task, so that the values can be inserted into the sequence diagrams and permit some arithmetic to be carried out on different scenarios. There are several approaches to determining values for run-times, as listed below. If there is already prior experience with similar algorithms, a reasonable estimate may be gained in discussions with a colleague. With larger, better funded projects, simulation trials may have been undertaken which may deliver quite reliable run length values. Having to write simulation code specifically to generate early estimates of timing parameters is not often justified, but other aspects of the proposed system could also be prototyped at the same time, such as communication handlers and screen GUIs. Sitting down quietly and counting sequences of machine instructions is never a popular or reliable activity, but there are now software tools to assist with this approach. Inserting a couple of temporary 'software probes' into the prototype code can give timing printouts on screen, as the system runs. But adding a system call, data formatting

- Algorithm estimation
- Simulation run
- Instruction audit
- Software probes
- Physical measurement

Predicting execution times

and screen output instructions, can disturb the fundamental timing. If extra equipment can be brought into play, the In-circuit Emulator (ICE) will offer timing facilities with no change to the target software. But finally, the easiest and most ubiquitous technique is to measure the timing performance of prototype code using a logic analyser or oscilloscope. This approach does require external equipment, although not as expensive as a full ICE probe, and a couple of temporary 'debug' output instructions to be added to each task, so that short pulses can be seen on the screen. In addition, a new generation of low priced, logic analyser and digital oscilloscopes are now available, which are really 'virtual instruments', implemented through software running on PCs. They simply employ special hardware probes which plug into standard USB sockets (USB-INSTRUMENTS 2004). If you are as yet unfamiliar with this use of oscilloscopes, Appendix A presents more details.

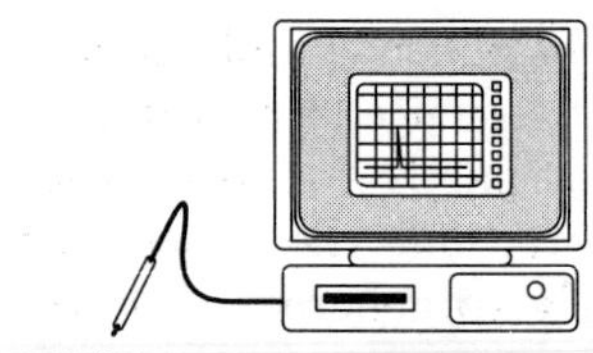

Measuring execution times

12.12 Run-time support

When developing a system based on a cyclic executive, the programmer expects little in the way of support code to be available at run-time. The basic C compiler library and perhaps a couple of standard libraries for socket or maths functions might be used. The majority of the executable code has been directly written by the application programmer. With multi-tasking implementations this is less likely to be the case because they normally employ an RTX or full operating system to manage the tasks, handle communications and deal with exceptions. Much of the code that carries out these functions is supplied in binary format, and is not available for inspection or modification. A fuller listing and description of the common list of support functions is provided in Section 9.6.

12.13 Chapter summary

The original SA/SD methods needed supplementing in order to deal with real-time systems and multi-tasking implementations. The Yourdon method was extended by Ward and Mellor to include dynamic modelling, but not task partitioning. Knowing the best way to split a project into concurrent tasks during the preliminary phase of systems design can be difficult. Some guidelines have been presented and discussed to assist with this activity. Task diagrams can provide a good system overview by expressing task functions and communication channels. The CODARTS method extends SA/SD in a way which brings forward the task as the principal design component. When dealing with multi-tasking software, there are some special requirements to be kept in mind when selecting languages and compilers. Intertask synchronization and communication becomes an important part of any multi-tasking implementation.

12.14 Problems and issues for discussion

1. What standard facilities offered by Linux would be suitable to implement channels, pools, flags and signals as described in this chapter?
2. To reduce the 'prowling' time spent by motorists searching for an available space within pay and display car parks, vehicle sensors and publicly visible redirection (SPACE/FULL) signs are to be installed. Modify the context and task diagrams in Section 12.7 to include the extra facility. Note that traffic signs and vehicle sensors must be interfaced to the nearest ticket unit, but all the units will be informed of the current occupancy through the serial communications link.
3. Draw up structure charts or pseudocode PSpecs for the remaining tasks in the PnD system on p. 275.
4. Estimate the run-time length of a short program you have written. Then measure it using both software timing probes and external equipment, such as oscilloscope, logic analyser or ICE. Is the program running alone on bare hardware, or as one task on a multitasking system? How will this affect the recorded values?
5. Check out the accessible system timers provided by Windows and Linux. What API calls are available, and what is the minimum quanta (granule) of time supported?
6. Draw up a context diagram and then a task diagram for a supermarket POS terminal. This should interface to the following devices: laser barcode scanner, sales assistant's keyboard and screen, credit card validator, customer price display, product weighing scales, receipt printer, cash drawer release, network connection, and two conveyor belts with product sensor beams.

12.15 Suggestions for reading

Allworth, S. & Zobel, R. (1989). *Introduction to Real-time Software Design.* Macmillan.

Bate, G. (1986). Mascot 3: an informal introductory tutorial. *SWEng. J.*, May.

Cooling, J. (1997). *Real-time Software Systems.* Thomson Computer Press.

Gomaa, H. (1987). Using the DARTS software design method for real-time systems. *Proc. 12th Structured Methods Conf (Chicago)*, August.

Gomaa, H. (1993). *Software Design Methods for Concurrent and Real-time Systems.* Addison Wesley.

Jackson, K. & Simpson, H. (1975). MASCOT – a modular approach to software construction, operation and test. RRE Technical Note no. 778.

JIMCOM (1983). *Official Handbook of MASCOT.* RSRE, Malvern.

Shaw, A. (2001). *Real-time Systems and Software.* Wiley.

Simpson, H. & Jackson, K. (1979). Process synchronisation in MASCOT. *BCS J.*, 22(4), 332–345.

http://www.usb-instruments.com/hardware.html, a range of USB oscilloscopes and logic analysers.

Chapter 13

UML for real-time systems

13.1 Chapter overview

UML is a graphical language available to describe systems by expressing their constructs and relationships. This includes both static and dynamic relationships. For real-time systems, the availability of statecharts and sequence diagrams fulfils the requirement to describe run-time dynamics which are an important part of real-time systems development. Object-oriented Design (OOD) is the normal methodology that UML supports.

13.2 A Unified Modelling Language

Any design method must support the move from the often slim set of functional requirements provided by a customer, to the burgeoning complexity of a computer-based system. As a graphical language, UML can help to record information and relationships which emerge during the analysis and design stages of the software lifecycle. It is a visual language, *not* a design method, and so supports the activities of analyst–programmers, over a spectrum of methods, but especially in the area of Object-oriented Design (OOD). The supporters of UML advocate its accepted uniformity and flexibility to adopt new extensions covering other design methods should they emerge in the future.

[TM]The UML cube icon is a worldwide trademark of the Object Management Group, Inc.

- Use-case diagram
- Object collaboration diagram
- Class diagram
- Sequence diagram
- Statechart (FSM)
- Implementation diagram
- Activity diagram

UML diagrams

Listed above are the seven principal, interrelated diagrams offered by UML.

13.3 Use-cases

Use-case diagrams are drawn up during the preliminary analysis phase of a project to record the interactions of the proposed system with people and other external systems. They also explicitly lay out the functional expectations of those users for the new system. Although it is not intended as a replacement for the context diagram, it does fulfil some of its functions in displaying potential I/O channels with the associated functions. The terminal points are often users, engineers and administrators, but the stickman symbol, termed *actor*, can also represent equipment or connected systems. In effect, usecase diagrams provide a high-level view of what the system does and how it is used. The users, their functional requirements and the assocations between all the major parts, can be clearly exposed. The use-case diagram does not carry detailed information about the sequencing of actions; this behavioural information can only be noted in associated text which can be very useful when subsequently drawing up sequence diagrams.

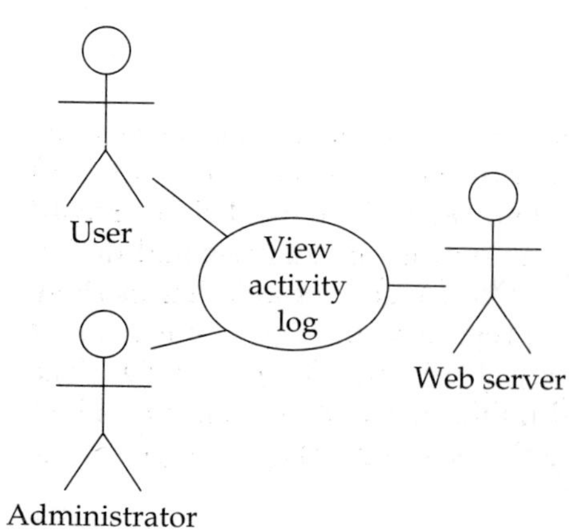

Example use-case diagram

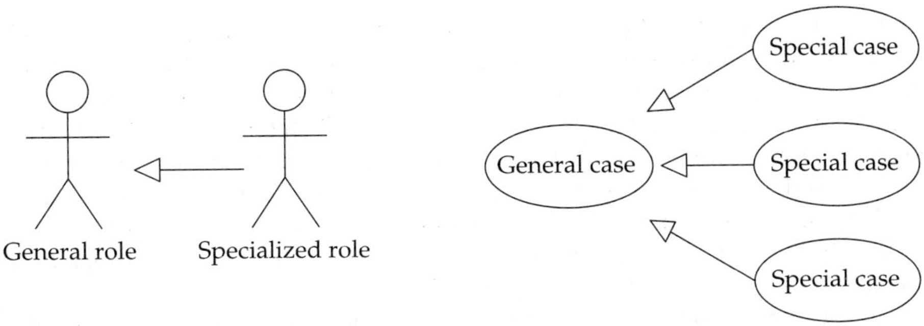

Use-case generalizations

Another part of analysis which can be documented with use-case diagrams is the identification of *generalizations*. Two or more actors may appear to be representatives of a more general category of 'super' actor. Where an existing use-case contains some functionality which can be separated out for use elsewhere, the '≪include≫' notation provides the power to express this decomposition. Similarly, where some elaboration of functionality is identified as applicable, there is the '≪extend≫' option as shown below. Both these notations encourage a top-down, incremental approach to use-case analysis.

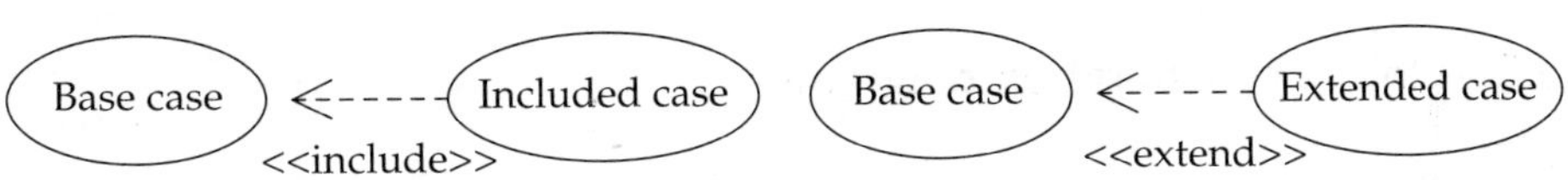

Use-case extension and inclusion

Note that the use-case is not based on a flow of information; it does not require consideration of data types or transfer rates like the context diagram. The concern is at a higher level of abstraction with no immediate view to implementation. However, the successful identification of actors, in the use-case diagram, may assist later on with the specification and implementation of system interfaces.

13.4 Objects and classes

Structured analysis and design separates data from function, and decomposes systems into sequences of actions, which then get further decomposed into primitive functions prior to implementation. Data streams link the functions, and central data stores hold enduring system variables. This separation of data from function has been rejected by the object-oriented camp of developers. They saw the big advantage to expanding Abstract Data Types (ADT) and tying all functions to the data they act on. This arrangement is termed a *class*, although it is little more than a `struct` which includes several pointers to functions. Then, complex data items can be declared of a particular class type, and then be referred to as objects. So objects represent things that encapsulate attributes and behaviour. The real-world things they represent can be concrete or abstract. Thus, when several objects have a lot of variables and actions in common, it can be useful to group them all together as belonging to the same *class*. So a class can be seen as the *type* of a set of similar objects. Objects instantiated from the same class share actions and all contain the same number and types of data.

The object, incorporating together data and operations, may initially appear only as a minor extension of the C `struct` or the Pascal record in terms of implementation, but it has led to a major revolution in the way designers do their work and the way we all view computer systems.

An important distinction needs to be drawn between *passive* and *active* objects. The former are little more than ADTs, offering their methods for other objects to use, like library units. The latter can, however, start and sustain their own threads of execution, holding state information and acting as independent tasks. The sequence diagram is the most helpful in identifying active objects, as the start point of execution sequences which endure throughout an extended time period, evoking other actions and controlling outcomes.

13.5 Object collaboration diagrams

The collaboration diagram provides a schematic overview of the possible interactions between objects within an active system. In some ways this is a simpler alternative to the sequence diagram, but without the graphic representation of message ordering.

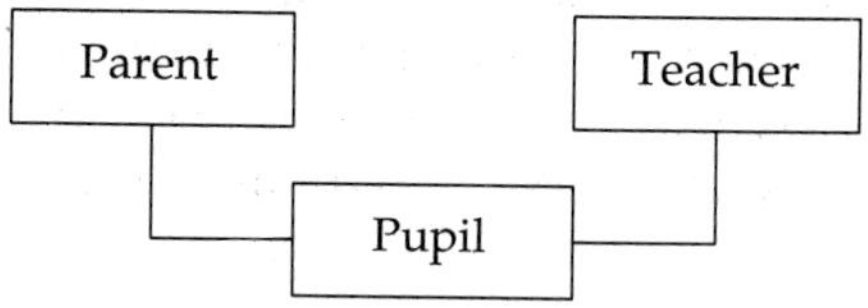

Object collaboration diagram

Many texts introduce the abstract idea of a class type before dealing with the objects which they govern. As programmers and engineers approach new problems by looking out for individual objects, rather than *similarities* between objects, it seems more reasonable to talk about objects before classes. In support of this view, the methodology is described as OOD, not COD. In object-oriented software, the functionality is provided by the close interaction of objects, not classes. The UML collaboration diagram is helpful in recording possible interactions between objects which may occur while the system is running. In many ways it is like an FSD; it indicates legal routes, but does not say which are taken, when and how often.

13.6 Class diagrams

Classes are basic design component of Object-oriented (OO) systems. Class instances, termed objects, are the building blocks. The various relationships between classes are shown on class diagrams. These present a static, relational view of the model system. Classes are frequently derived from an existing *base* class. This facilitates software reuse by the *inheritance* of properties, parent class to child class. Derived classes can then be extended by the addition of new attributes and operations. Attributes and operations can be designated as *private*, *public* or *protected* to show the visibility and access allowed for other objects.

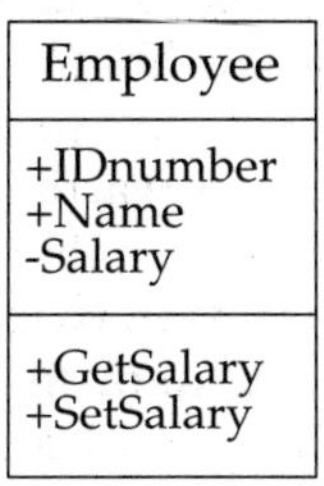

Class component

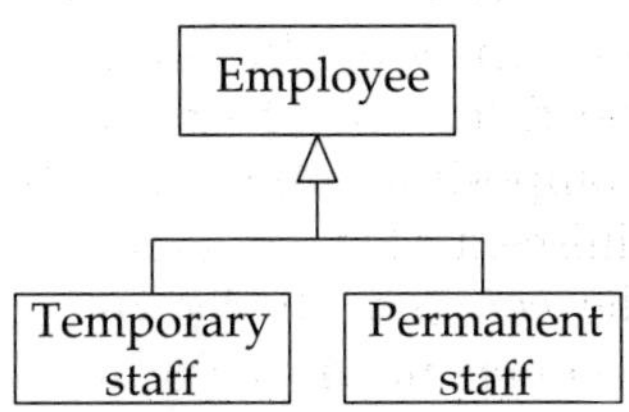

Derived class generalization

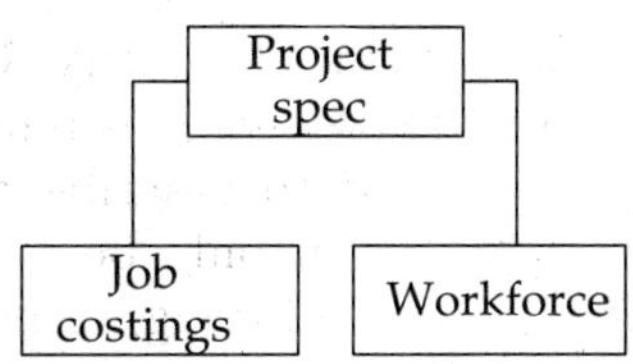

Association

When devising OO models and producing UML diagrams from the original specification, it can still be useful to employ *functional delegation* to partition the system. Thus, data and its associated methods should reside in the most appropriate class. The identification and allocation of data and operations are at the centre of the OO method of class creation.

Generalization, or derivation, is a way of reusing attribute type definitions and method interfaces and bodies. It is one technique of providing OOP *inheritance* capability. If code works with the base class (superclass) it should work with the derived classes (subclasses), too. A subclass may include a new version of an existing, inherited method, effectively using the same interface with different code. Derivation, or specialization, occurs when a new subclass is defined from an existing base class. The subclass then inherits attributes and methods from the superclass, but it may also add new ones of its own, or even substitute for the inherited versions. Of special interest are *abstract* superclasses and interfaces which constrain offered facilities in conformance with established standards.

Association represents a loose form of coupling between objects, usually implemented in code by method calls. The association lines marked between classes represent relationships which will be evoked by the objects at run-time. They are the pathways for run-time messages. Associations can be given *role* names to distinguish each of them. A role may also offer multiplicity, which means that more than one object of a class may participate in the association. An OO system is based on class types that interact with each other by passing messages and receiving responses. Message passing may be implemented using functional parameters, remote procedure calls or any other technique. When the system runs, it declares class instances, or objects. When objects evoke a method from another object, an *association* is confirmed between the defining classes.

There are two other interclass relations, besides derivation and association, which can be displayed in class diagrams: aggregation and composition. Composition expresses a situation where a primary object, such as an 'oil field' can be usefully broken down into component 'oil wells'. Any dealings with individual wells then have to be undertaken through the oil field. If the oil field is closed, all the wells are abandoned, too. The whole is made up of its parts. In fact, this is exactly the decompositional relationship that a traditional structure chart expresses. In essence the wells could be seen as multiple attributes of the field, but of sufficient complexity to warrant some individual identity. Composition allows an object to be disassembled diagrammatically. It is reminiscent of the manner in which a structure chart can be used to describe the component records and fields of a data file. An object can only be a component of one other object. But aggregation is different, allowing an object to be associated with more than one other object. So because a composite object can be linked to more than a single parent, it needs to survive when one parent or more dies.

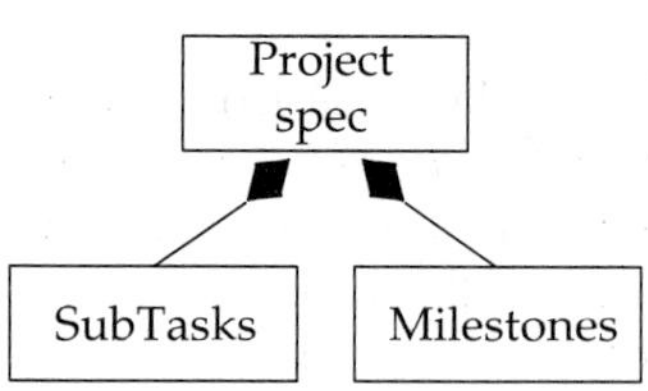

Composition

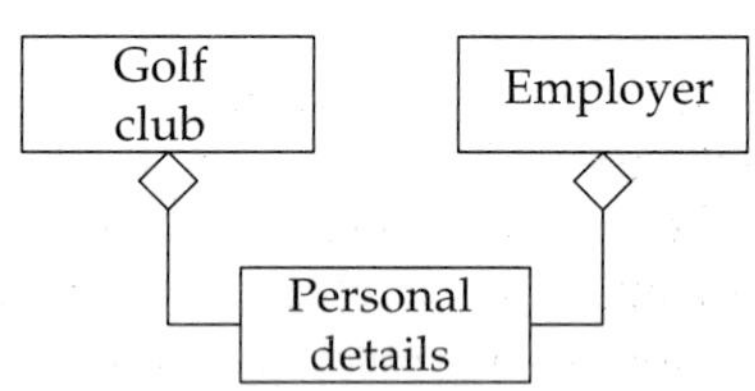

Shared aggregation

The use of base classes to provide a standard interface for several derived subclasses can be very useful. In such circumstances, it is not even necessary to equip the base class with method code. This can be supplied later by the derived classes. Such an empty base class is called an *abstract* class or an *interface.* Abstract classes may be supplied with a partially complete set of implementation code, while an interface has none at all. This is a necessary facility for Java, where multiple inheritance is not provided, which can be an inconvenience when attempting to create a class which then needs attributes and methods only found in different superclasses. This difficulty can be resolved by *extending* one superclass and *implementing* the others as interfaces.

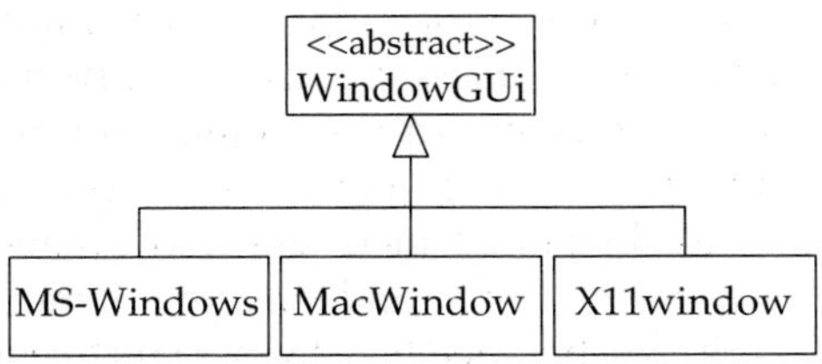

Abstract base class

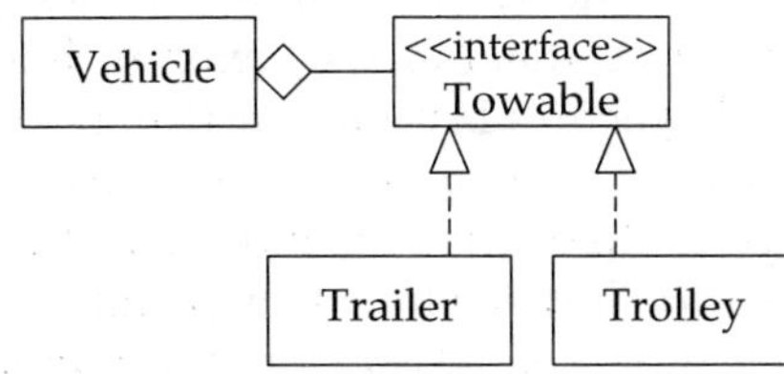

Implementing an interface

13.7 Interobject messaging

UML represents the various different types of communication that can take place between objects with a single *message* generalization. So an abstract UML message could be implemented by a straightforward call to a method, a remote procedure call (rpc), a piped message queue, sockets, or other techniques. The type of message used depends on the situation. If the recipient is a 'passive' object without an intrinsic thread of execution, it is appropriate to use conventional procedure calls with parameters and return values. If, however, the message is passing between two 'active' objects, executing semi-independently, the situation is very different, and signals or data pipes might be the selected means of communication. UML designates messages

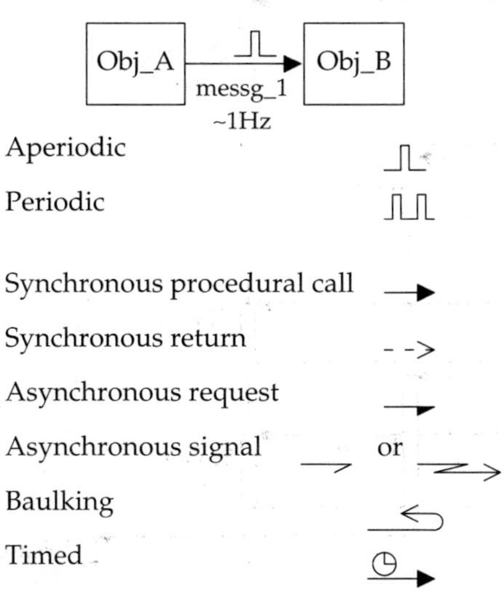

UML message types

as asynchronous or synchronous, which could be referred to as *blocking* or *non-blocking*. The former could be implemented by a system signal in addition to the mechanisms listed above. Although messages usually involve only two objects, the originator and recipient, they can also be *multicast*, single to many. The symbols allow the designer to annotate object collaboration and sequence diagrams to express information about message arrival patterns and synchronization constraints. Parameters relating to the timing requirements can be captured and inserted onto the message paths. The average arrival frequency, or interarrival interval for incoming messages and events, is very important when planning processing capacity and memory buffering provision. Also response requirements can be specified by a *worst case* or average performance. These are especially significant for hard real-time systems, where a single late result could be catastrophic.

13.8 Interaction diagrams

UML offers three diagram formats to express the dynamic interactive characteristics of a system: the Finite State Diagram (FSD), the Object

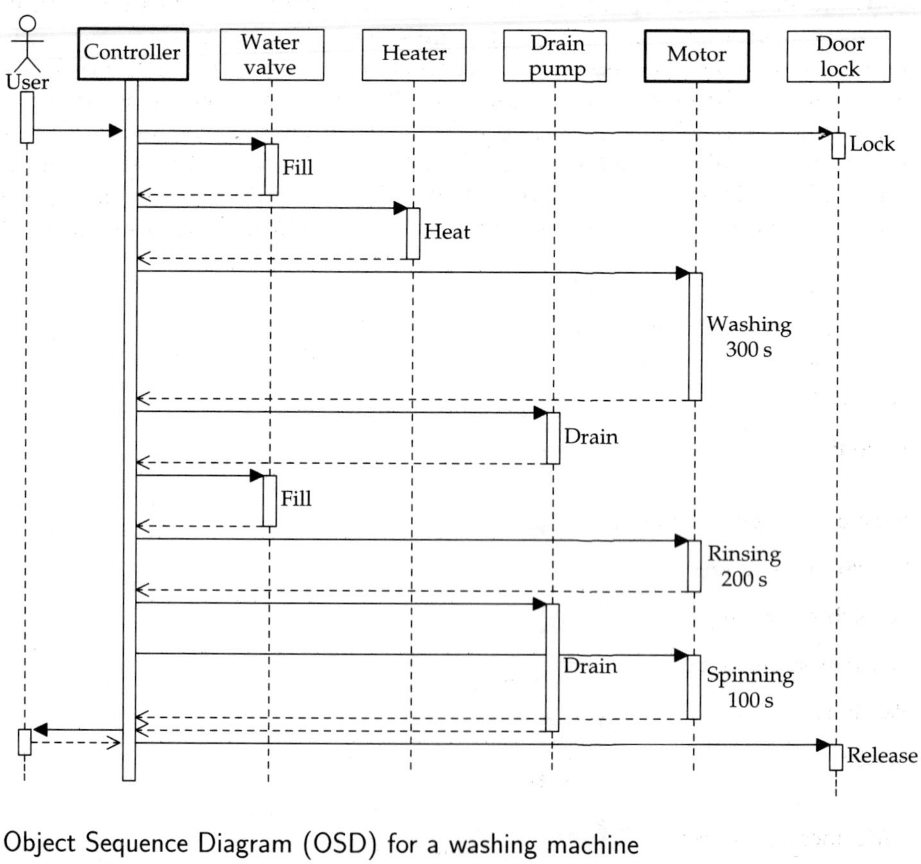

Object Sequence Diagram (OSD) for a washing machine

Collaboration Diagram (OCD) and the Object Sequence Diagram (OSD). FSDs are very useful when detailing the lifecycle of an individual object, but do not deal so effectively with systems comprising many closely interacting objects. This is where the OCD or OSD can be deployed. I have already presented in Chapters 5 and 6 sufficient description of how the FSM can be used and so will not repeat the details here. OCDs and OSDs are used to describe the interlocked lifecycle of several objects and show the exchange of messages, including their relative orderings. The advantage of the OSD is the linear, spatial mapping of the message streams, which permits the inclusion of more timing information than with an OCD. In an OSD, the normal way to represent the lifecycle is to follow a particular sequence of events associated with the chosen scenario. The objects involved are arrayed across the page, with individual 'lifelines' running down from them. Messages are then time ordered down the page, with arguments and control conditions appended.

The washing machine OSD expresses the autonomy of the objects responsible for the water valve, heater, drain pump and motor. They all take independent decisions regarding the terminating conditions: water level, temperature, timing. In such a situation, it might be desirable to implement these objects as active objects, threads or processes. In this case, due to the lack of any other activity for the controller object to get preoccupied with, the expansion into a full multi-tasking implementation could not really be justified. However, the motor object has to control the speed of rotation by frequent (100 Hz) adjustment of the driving pulse widths. With this in mind, it has been decided that the motor object could take on an autonomous role, and assume the responsibility of an active object.

Unlike implementations derived by SA/SD methods, object-oriented code tends to be more dispersed, with the thread of execution skipping between

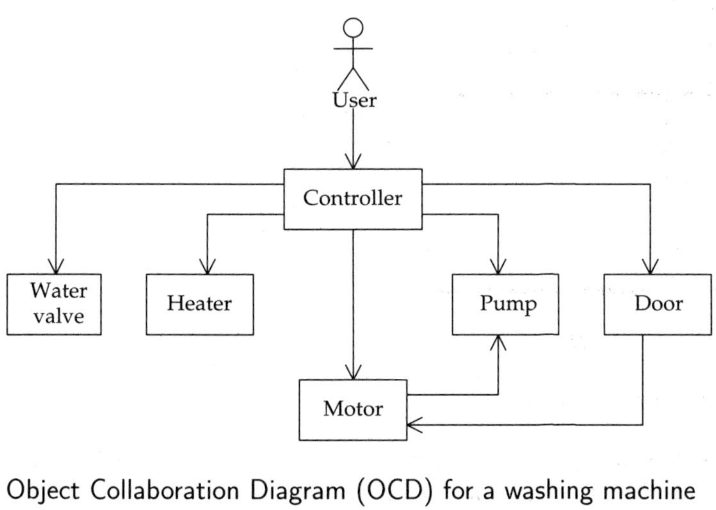

Object Collaboration Diagram (OCD) for a washing machine

many objects, making the actual sequence of execution more difficult to trace out when debugging systems. The sequence diagram can be very helpful in this regard, tracing out the overall flow of control through the collaborating objects which make up the system.

13.9 Activity diagrams

The activity diagram is closely related to the Petri Net Diagram (PND), dealing with the synchronization of objects as they execute in parallel. The desire to avoid deadlocks and investigate the sequencing of interlocked threads of execution is at the base of this type of analysis.

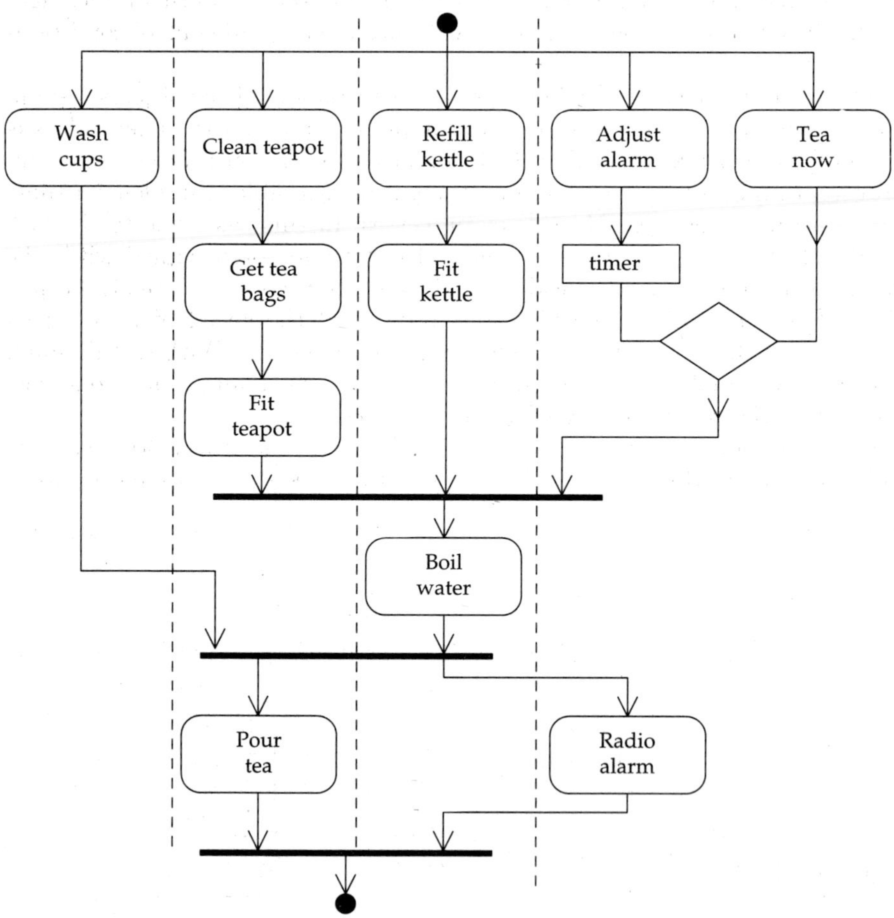

Activity diagram displaying swim lanes

But the activity diagram can also be used to structure the objects into collaborating groups which can then usefully be drafted into semi-independent tasks during the implementation phase. This is where the separation into discrete, vertical *swim lanes* can be helpful to visualize the parallel activities and identify the intertask synchronization points. These are represented by the thick bars, as in the Petri net diagrams. The synchronization bars also can be used to express occurrence of the Unix tasking primitives `fork()` and `wait()`.

Activity diagrams are sometimes disregarded as a odd mixture of Petri nets and flowcharts, but for real-time programmers they can be used to express many important system characteristics of great relevance when developing a multi-tasking implementation.

13.10 Chapter summary

The group of iconic conventions and diagrams (use-case, object sequence diagram, statechart, object collaboration diagram, class diagram, activity diagram) which UML offers comprises a graphical modelling language which can be used to describe systems by expressing their components and relationships. UML can express both static and dynamic relationships, and especially for real-time systems, the availability of statecharts and sequence diagrams can be used to describe run-time dynamics which are so significant for modern real-time systems development. Object-oriented Design is particularly popular when OOD and OOP are being used for GUI-based applications.

13.11 Problems and issues for discussion

1. Carry out a use-case analysis of the operations performed by a parking ticket vending machine. Consider end user (motorist), maintenance technician, auditor, coin collector and traffic warden.
2. What characteristics would you use to designate an object as *active* or *passive*? Which of the UML diagrams allow such a decision to be recorded?
3. Draw up a sequence diagram based on the washing machine FSM represented on p. 99. Which diagram do you consider most useful to the programmer? Does the simplicity of this application promote a fair comparison?
4. Does the use of a single central controller object, which takes responsibility for all the sequencing (scheduling) activity, in any way undermine any of the OOD principles?
5. The use of OOD and OOP made great progress when they were applied to the development of graphical interfaces (GEM, X-windows, MS-Windows). Do real-time, multi-tasking applications exhibit any similar hierarchically ordered characteristics which lend themselves to OO analysis and modelling?

13.12 Suggestions for reading

Barclay, K. & Savage, J. (2004). *Object-oriented Design with UML and Java.* Elsevier.

Bennett, S., Skelton, J. & Lunn, K. (2002). *UML. Shaum Outline Series.* McGraw-Hill.

Booch, G., Jacobson, I. & Rumbaugh, J. (1997). *UML Distilled.* Addison Wesley.

Douglass, B. (2004). *Real-time UML 2nd ed.* Addison Wesley.

Harel, D. (1987). Statecharts: a visual formalism for complex systems. *Science of Computer Programming*, Vol. 8, 231–274.

http://www.omg.org, source for the UML specification documents.

Chapter 14

Object-oriented approach for real-time systems

14.1 Chapter overview

Object-oriented Design and Programming (OOD/P) extends the principles of information hiding, as already offered by abstract data types. There is a close association between the functions and the data on which they operate. The separation of data from code was an essential part of structured methods, but with OOD/P, the methods are grouped with their data to form objects. Also, similar objects are identified as sharing the same type or class. The concept of a *task* is not commonly employed by OO developers, who often work at a more abstract level, ignoring the implementation constraints which will rear up when the time for implementation arrives. Design patterns are a valuable tool for software developers because they offer proven solutions to common problems.

14.2 Real-time object-oriented design and development

This chapter is not intended as a comprehensive introduction to object-oriented design and programming methods, as there are many excellent texts to which the reader can turn for guidance. Here we are limiting the discussion to the application of such ideas to the design and implementation of real-time systems.

Object-oriented Design (OOD) and Object-oriented Programming (OOP) are now well-established techniques. Their commercial popularity stems partly from the success with which they can be applied to GUI development for Windows applications, although the theoretical heritage goes back further to Smalltalk, Simula and before. Perhaps unsurprisingly, language development always seems to precede the development of appropriate design tools. Currently C++, Java and C# are the major languages of choice for OO programmers, but others will certainly appear at regular intervals. The OOD method is organized about the production of abstract models of the intended system. In the preliminary analysis stages, a conceptual model is

Activity	Process	Deliverables	
Analysis	Requirements analysis	Use-case models with scenarios	Use-case diagrams with descriptive text Message lists
	Systems analysis	High-level initial architectural model Refined control algorithms	Class diagrams at the subsystem level Component diagrams Activity diagrams
	Object structural analysis	Structural object model	Class diagrams Object diagrams
	Object behavioural analysis	Behavioural object model	Object sequence diagrams Statecharts
Design	Architectural design	Concurrency model Deployment model Component model	Identify active objects Deployment diagrams O/S tasking model
	Mechanistic design	Collaboration model Message sequence diagrams	Class diagrams Patterns State execution model
	Detailed design	Class details	Methods, attributes, user-defined types, package members
Translation		Executable application	Fully executable code generated from structural and behavioural models
Testing	Unit testing Systems integration and validation	Code corrections Design defects list	Design-level debugging Test reports

Object-oriented software lifecycle

drawn up as a vehicle to express the overall structure and functionality, but with a low level of detail. Next, the specification model incorporates more information about the user requirements and is taken as the end product of systems analysis. Transforming this representation of what the client requires to how it is to be provided is the principal design activity. Finally, the coding takes place after an implementation model has been created. It can be seen as a welcome simplification, or a confusing disadvantage, that all three phases are annotated with the same set of UML diagrams. Only the level of detail distinguishes them.

14.3 Designing for real-time

The recent development of large distributed systems, which have to deal with high transaction rates while acting as internationally available web servers, has thrown up major issues for real-time software developers. Although faster processors now offer the flexibility to handle high rates of asynchronous events, it is the possibility of exploiting *multi-threading* which has had the biggest influence on server development. This technique is widely used to formulate software solutions for large servers.

The need to rapidly port applications onto new 'state-of-the-art' hardware has frequently been a challenge for real-time developers. But the wider acceptance of HLLs and more abstract design techniques, which allow platform-independent specification and initial design work to be carried out, has gone a long way to remove this as a significant problem. Perhaps, also, the frantic pace of the silicon industry has slowed down, resulting in fewer new processors to choose from.

The OOD/P approach offers both static and dynamic viewpoints, conceptual frameworks and diagrammatic support. While the FSM paradigm remains the best way to prescribe all the potential execution routes, the sequence diagram, which describes a particular scenario followed by the application, may be a better way to expose system dynamics to clients and less technical colleagues.

The initial design steps, employing use-case diagrams, must be supplemented by parallel work for the development of class and sequence diagrams, or the whole process can 'deteriorate' into functional decomposition, which would be inappropriate for OOD!

Sequence diagrams show when messages are exchanged between objects, and this superficially defines the problem's flow of control, on a broader view, outside the methods themselves. These messages are viewed as requests for service directed at passive recipients which then join the active caller's thread of execution. Thus the programmed activity sequence is held in the caller object and it has to know where to send the request message, the implementation must already know that the other object exists and that it can satisfy the service request. These latter two requirements in some measure contravene the pure aims of module isolation and data encapsulation, unfortunately increasing the degree of intermodule coupling.

14.4 Objects, objects

Objects are seen as containers for data and the associated routines which are allowed to process that data. This important characteristic is generally referred to as *encapsulation*. Objects communicate with each other by messages which, on arrival, evoke a method in the receiver to carry out the requested processing. So the interaction between objects follows the client–server (active–passive) model. Data belonging to an object is generally private to that object, but conforms to the typing specification set out in the relevant class definition. So objects created from the same class will all have the same set of variables, but with distinct private values. Their methods are provided only once by the class definition, much like a shared library, and are accessed through pointer tables.

14.5 Finding the objects

With all design methods, there can be hurdles for newcomers. Particularly for an unfamiliar application area, there may be preliminary activities or judgements which stall the whole process if not carried out effectively. Earlier, in Section 11.2, we remarked that SA/SD demanded critical partitioning very early in the design process. For object-oriented analysis and design, a similar issue arises with the identification of objects and then the definition of appropriate classes. A class is a type or descriptor for a set of objects with similar structure, behaviour and relationships. There are a number of well-accepted 'can opener' tactics which can help the less confident designer through the early stages of class identification. Based on the suggestions in Douglass (1999), a list of eight techniques, some of which may suit the project in hand, can be offered.

Identify →	
key nouns	This suits when a written specification is available
causal sources	Sources of events, actions, messages
services	Targets for events or messages, providing actions for others
real-world items	The system will be a real-world model
devices	Terminal equipment such as sensors and actuators
concepts	Such as bank account, subscription, signal spectrum
transactions	Objects are bound together by transactions
data	Persistent data, becoming an object's attribute

Methods to help identify useful objects

Identifying component objects, and specifying their attributes and behaviour, goes only part way to understanding how a system will behave. Perhaps it is like announcing the rules of football and claiming that is sufficient to express all the variety and subtlety of every possible game. In addition, having determined the likely objects, and perhaps identified potential classes and relationships, for a real-time programmer, an allied issue is to distinguish the *active* objects from the *passive* ones. As an OO application can benefit from a multi-tasking implementation in the same way that a program realized by SA/SD, the identification of tasks, or active objects will be an important goal. In order to execute any of their methods, the *passive* objects will rely on *active* objects for calls to their methods. This suggests a congruence between an active object and an SA/SD task, while passive objects offer their methods and attributes for others to use, rather as a dynamic library facility. A system with multiple active objects can be implemented as a multi-threaded application. Unfortunately, when differentiating between active and passive objects, inspection of an object collaboration diagram will not be of much assistance. All objects contain attribute data and method code, but only the active objects start execution, and schedule the code sequences by maintaining threads. Operating systems environments commonly support tasking as well as threading. The latter is seen as a more efficient way to implement a program containing several active objects because switching between different tasks is much more demanding than a thread switch. The volatile environment for a thread is mostly shared with other sister threads in the program.

An approach to requirements analysis, centred around the UML use-case diagram, is currently popular, partly due to the availability of graphics tools, and partly because it does lead easily into the identification of the principal system *actors* and the range of messages which get exchanged between them. These messages are intended to elicit information or an action, the latter then transforms into an object's method. So a set of use-cases describe the system capabilities and allocate the actions among a preliminary group of objects, with origination from the *active* participants. So in this way, the active objects may be identified as the source of message sequences. If several message sequences emerge and run in parallel, there is probably a bit of multi-tasking taking place!

14.6 Analysis class stereotypes

When attempting to identify useful objects, and classes within which they can be grouped, there are three particular kinds of class that are encountered over and over again. Such a framework can be related to the original model–view–controller architecture proposed as part of the Smalltalk-80 programme (Krasner & Pape 1988). This demarcation can also be helpful when dealing with real-time systems because the Boundary class represents 'interfacing' and the Control class represents 'scheduling'.

- *Boundary classes* These represent the software interfaces to external devices, human users or even external software resources. They can arise from use-case analysis, where interfaces to the real world are revealed and need to be modelled. The advantage of clearly expressed system boundaries, carried by specified components in the final implementation, makes porting much easier because the majority of the revisions will occur within the boundary class objects. Boundary class objects could end up being implemented with interrupt-driven or polled routines, depending on the circumstances.

- *Entity classes* These are classical abstract data types, modelling important information and associated behaviour, which could relate to an abstract concept, concrete thing or service, directly paralleling a real-world entity beyond the system perimeter. In general, an entity class will be passive, offering access methods to other objects.
- *Control classes* Perhaps the central role in any application is taken by control class objects. These provide the coordinating activity, the thread of control, which binds all the objects together in the correct order, to build the dynamic application. They hold the 'game plan', without which the other modules would sit passively waiting for something to happen. So the control class objects are responsible for the core sequencing and coordination of the application.

A class definition describes the common characteristics of all the objects (instances) declared *of that class*, and these may include attributes and methods inherited from the original parent class. It is important to realize that this inheritance is accumulative; more attributes and methods may be added, even if they override existing definitions, but they cannot be removed.

14.7 Tasking

Although every identified object could be implemented as an individual thread, this is not always practicable. So objects need to be clustered around the principal active objects to form threads. Each active object can become an aggregate composite which helps to simplify the system architecture. Perhaps the best starting point to achieve this grouping is the sequence diagram, where the basic active objects are easily associated with passive co-objects.

First, you should choose a well-understood scenario which exercises as wide a range of capabilities as possible, then draw up the sequence diagram. When objects require to evoke a service provided by passive objects, a local or remote procedure call will be sufficient to carry out the operation, so these are marked as *synchronous* interactions, with the caller blocked waiting for the return value. However, with active objects, maintaining concurrent threads of control, the more convenient communication techniques would be data pipes, signals or sockets. In this case, the *asynchronous* decoupling of the tasks should be maintained throughout the exchange of information by using *asynchronous* message passing, where the sender is not blocked, waiting for a value to be returned. It continues directly along its execution path without regard to the immediate outcome of the transmission. If, as is most likely, the receiver does not find it convenient to deal with the message immediately, it has to be stored in some way for later processing. When the initial selection of objects has been completed, and their

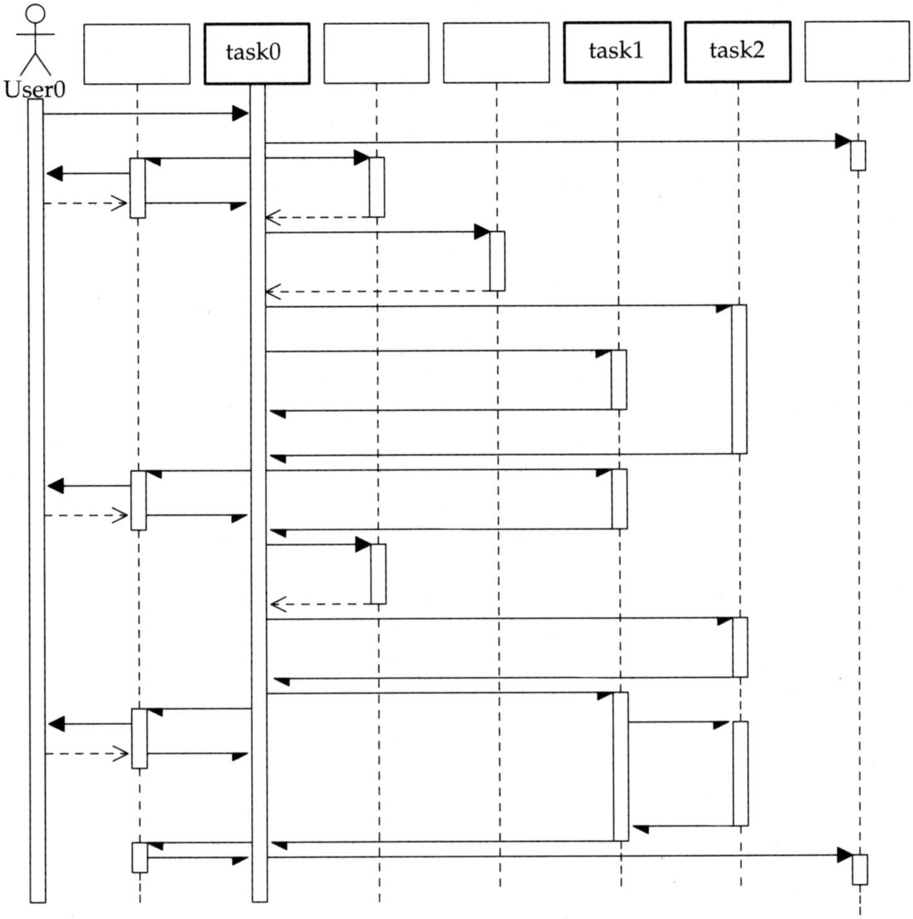

Sequence diagram with asynchronous messages between concurrent tasks

communication sequences plotted out, they can be clustered around the control objects to form implementation components. The partitioned sequence diagram can then be transcribed into a modified style of collaboration diagram, known as a task diagram, or into an activity diagram showing task swim lanes.

14.8 Multi-threading with Java

As has been discussed in Chapters 7 and 12 the advantages of implementing a real-time application using a multi-tasking approach is quite convincing.

For some time, operating systems and HLLs have offered support for a lightweight version of multi-tasking which is referred to as *multi-threading.* At the moment, it cannot be denied that Java is having a very great influence on the design style and manner of implementation of a wide spectrum of applications, not simply those destined for the web. Other languages could have been used in its place without much difference, but perhaps with less panache.

The `java.lang.Thread` class holds all facilities necessary to initiate a concurrent thread on the JVM, or as an applet running in a browser. To create a thread, reference to a `Runnable` object must be passed to the constructor, `Thread()`. So, to implement a thread in Java requires access to the `Thread` base class. This class provides the useful methods: `start()`, `run()`, `sleep()` and `yield()`. To gain access to these, it is convenient to declare one derived class within your program as `extends Thread` with a method called `run()` containing the thread code, probably as a loop. Then, from `main()`, all that is required, after the derived Thread object has been instantiated, is for `object.start()` to be called, and a thread is initialized which is immediately exercised through the `run()` method. When `start()` is called it also informs the Java Virtual Machine (JVM) of the existence of the thread, and this ensures that the system scheduling is adjusted to take into account the new arrangements. A similar arrangement can be instituted as a Java applet to run from an HTML page within a web browser. In this case, the `main()` function is dropped in favour of an `init` method.

Java also offers convenient facilities for safe thread synchronization and the protection of shared resources with the `synchronized` method qualifier. This stops more than one object using the method code at any time, in much the same way that a semaphore could be deployed. In addition, the `notify()` and `wait()` signalling primitives allow threads to *rendezvous* with each other and so synchronize their execution paths.

Threads are assigned a priority number between 1 and 10 the default value being 5. This may be adjusted using the `setPriority()` call. But limits are placed on the range of modification that will be accepted.

There is some confusion over the policy adopted for scheduling multiple threads on different platforms. The original Sun JVM implementation for Solaris did not support time-slice pre-emption, whereas that for Windows did. Without time-slicing, threads of equal priority could suffer starvation if the running thread never blocked or yielded to its sisters. This was of no real consequence in the normal mode of use, where a thread would be given responsibility for a single asynchronous data channel. It would block until data arrived, then it would be restored to the runnable state, and be entered onto the runnable queue. This event would pre-empt the current thread and rescheduling would take place. So effectively, a cooperative scheduling scheme would take place, reliant on regular and dependable thread blocking.

14.9 Design patterns

Design patterns represent another attempt to organize the sharing of programmers' experiences. It is a continuation of the search for *reusability* of effort, and the dissemination of good practice. A design pattern describes how to assemble a small set of classes and methods to solve a problem. Frequently encountered design problems, with their solutions, are offered as a kind of library of accepted recipes which then become available to other systems designers. This facilitates the more rapid production of high quality software products by offering a set of proven solutions to common problems. It also assists with easier communication between designers by publishing an open vocabulary of solutions, aiding the development of new system architectures. For the most part, C++ and Java are the languages of choice for designers working in this area. Design patterns are now classified into four categories: Factory, Delegation, Control and Algorithm. There are now a wide range of accepted design patterns, and only a small selection of examples will be described here. For further details the reader is referred to Reiss (1999), Barclay & Savage (2004) or any other acceptable OOD text.

- *Interface pattern* (Delegation) The interface pattern is one of the most useful, even though it initially appears very straightforward. The cleanest way to create such an interface is through class inheritance. All the methods are delegated by the interface to derived subclasses. By using an abstract base class, which provides no method code, only interface definitions, all the actual method code is provided by the subclasses. The interface appears to offer all the services of an input device. While in fact it delegates the requests. In order to conform to an interface, a class must implement all of its services by providing method bodies for all of the declared services in addition to any augmented services. The use of interface classes is common in Java because this language does not offer multiple inheritance. So when a new subclass could benefit from deriving behaviour from more than a single superclass, the common solution is to `extend` one superclass and `implement` the other as an interface for the new subclass.

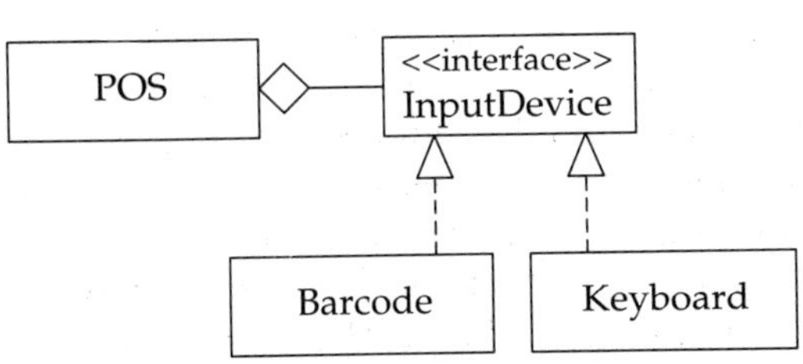

Implementing an interface

- *The Facade pattern* (Delegation) This is also referred to as the Adapter pattern and is a very useful technique, often required in a wide range of systems. It attempts to further encapsulate a group of already interconnected classes in a 'container' which hides the underlying complexity, and presents a single, simple interface to the user. It thus provides a black-box component which can then interact with the main system. Facades can be new classes created for the purpose, or they might already exist as system components. Sometimes a class may present the wrong set of methods to a client. By using a class within the Facade pattern it is possible to remedy the situation with a minimum of wider disruption. The top *adapter* object passes on the request for services to the lower *delegate* object. It maps the requests onto the delegate's methods. In this way new services can be added with only minor amendments to existing code.

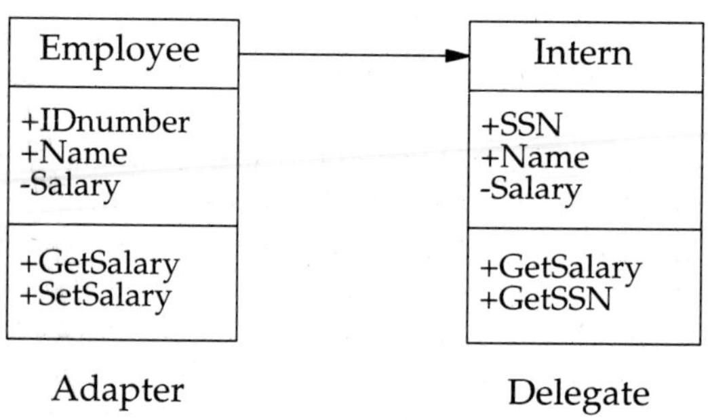

Facade pattern

- *Singleton pattern* (Factory) This ensures that only a single object of the class exists at any time. Without this restriction, any number of objects of any class could be instantiated while the system runs, which may not always be acceptable. This is achieved by hiding the constructor method from further access.
- *Model-View-Controller (MVC) pattern* Most effective user-interface designs try to separate the code arranging the visual interface elements from that carrying out the core functionality. This distinguishes the separate concerns for the two parts into logically separate components, which delivers great benefit if the application needs to be ported to a new platform, demanding serious modifications to the interface. Consider the changes resulting from a move from MS-Windows to X-windows. It could also be necessary to improve the user interface without changing the underlying system functionality, should the product be successful and require a fresh look. Such a separation is achieved, in OOP, by creating different classes, one for the underlying computation, the Model, and one for the visual interface, the View.

The two classes could simply be *associated*, then all that would be required would be a reference to the View object, as an attribute of the Model object, and for the identity of the View to be passed to the Model at creation time, or at some later moment. So, when the Model undergoes a change of state, it immediately sends a message to the View informing of the changes and enabling the View to implement the necessary updates to the display screen.

Such a scheme initially appears to work fine, but it suffers from a number of problems. The reference to the View object has to be explicitly coded in the Model class. This means that if other views are included or a different View object employed, the Model, too, has to be revised. The call to the View's change method passes the information needed by the View to update itself. So if the View is modified or a new view is used requiring different information, the Model must again be changed. Indeed, if the View is completely removed, the Model will have to be modified. As a result, the degree of isolation achieved between Model and View is not actually successful. To deal with this overcoupling situation, the Observer pattern has been proposed.

- *Observer pattern* (Algorithm) The problems with the MVC pattern can be overcome by the use of the Observer pattern which is also supported directly by Java through its Observable class and Observer interface. This also solves the problem of informing a number of observer objects when the state of another object changes. In essence, many Views are made available, and the Model interacts with them to pass over the necessary information at an update point. This approach is often called a *publish–subscribe* methodology where the item under observation informs the *registered* observers of the change. To be an observer, a class must implement the observer interface. The intention is that the subject can then inform all the observers of any change in its own state by sending out notify messages to all the registered observers. This pattern assists with implementing code to coordinate the actions

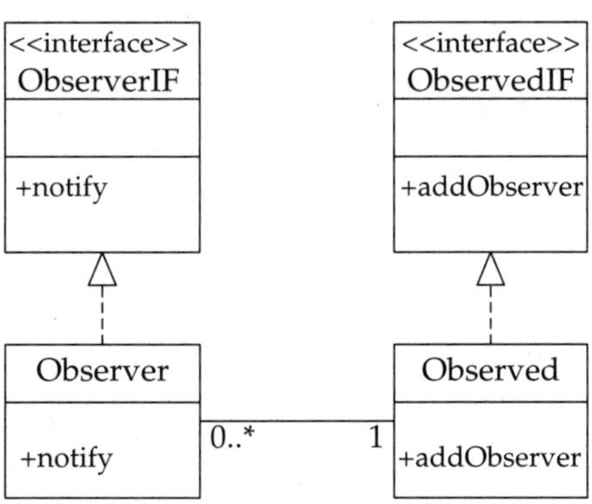

Implementing an observer pattern

of a diverse set of objects, even when they do not know of each other's existence.

- *The Visitor pattern* (Control) The idea behind a Visitor pattern is to allow additional functionality to be added to an existing system at a later date without the need to modify the system in any way. An abstract class, Visitor, is defined to implement virtual operations. The main system is then created with the visitor pattern in place so that all components of the system are prepared to accept a new visitor object via an `accept(Visitor v)` method.

Factory patterns	
Builder	a simple factory class to generate instances of *concrete* classes
Abstract factory	multiple factory classes for a common set of objects
Flyweight	constructing shared objects
Singleton	limits object instantiation by hiding the constructor
Factory method	putting the factory inside another class
Prototype	cloning new objects
Delegation patterns	
Interface	Abstract interface to all methods
Adaptor	delegating functionality to another object
Bridge	treating a class as a pointer to another
Decorator	using delegation to include new behaviour
Facade	creating subsystems of objects, encapsulated together
Proxy	placeholders for remote objects
Control patterns	
Composite	using objects to achieve groupings
Interpreter	interpreting a command language
Command	reorganizing commands
Iterator	stepping though a composite structure
Visitor	providing indirect methods in a class hierarchy
Mediator	controlling the interaction of other objects
Observer	publish–subscribe messaging framework
Algorithmic patterns	
Strategy	using an object to contain an algorithm
Template	subdividing an algorithm into fixed and variable parts
Momento	saving and restoring the internal state of an object

Categorization of design patterns, based on Reiss (1999)

14.10 Chapter summary

Object-oriented design and programming is based on the principles of information hiding, derived from abstract data types, and the close association of functions with data, not their separation as promoted by structured methods. Functions, or methods, are clustered together with their data to form objects. Similar objects are identified as sharing the same type or class. Classes are defined by inheritance from an existing parent or base class and additional augmentation. The concept of the *task* is not commonly employed by OO developers, who often work at a more abstract level, ignoring the implementation constraints which will rear up when the time for implementation arrives. To assist developers, there is a growing library of design patterns available which offer proven solutions to common software design problems.

14.11 Problems and issues for discussion

1. Explain how the concept of *tasks* fits into the OOP methodology.
2. Using Java threads to gain the necessary multi-tasking capability, develop a small joke server, which clients can connect to through a published port and request a new joke.
3. Focusing on the POS terminal example from Chapter 11, carry out a software design and implementation exercise following the OO methodology.
4. Provide the definition of a 'document' class, where you need to include all kinds of data-containing objects, such as audio files, video clips, text files, images and any combination and sequence of them. You may like to check out the DICOM (Digital Imaging and Communications in Medicine) standard to gain some idea of the relevance of this kind of analysis.
5. Carry out the preliminary analysis and design work for a vehicle charging scheme which is to be implemented for the your local town centre. All participating vehicles will be equipped with transponder units which, when passing, link with roadside radio beacons which check the user's registration and transmit the appropriate debit request to the driver's account. The user accounts need to be recharged on a monthly basis. If an unknown vehicle is detected passing into a restricted traffic area, a digital image is taken by an associated camera, and saved for future investigations. Prepare use-case and sequence diagrams to describe the action of the system, including vehicle transponders, roadside beacons, penalty cameras, and central monitoring unit with user database.

14.12 Suggestions for reading

Barclay, K. & Savage, J. (2004). *Object-oriented Design with UML and Java.* Elsevier.

Cooling, J. (1997). *Real-time Software Systems: An Introduction to Structured and Object-oriented Design.* Thomson Computer Press.

Deacon, J. (2005). *Object-oriented Analysis and Design.* Addison Wesley.

Kelly, J. (1987). *A Comparison of Four Design Methods for Real-time Systems.* ACM.

Krasner, G. & Pope, S. (1988). A cookbook for using the model view controller user interface paradigm in Smalltalk-80. *J. OOP.*, Aug. 26–49.

Reiss, S. (1999). *Software Design with C++*. Wiley.

Selic, B., Gulleksen, G. & Ward, P. (1994). *Real-time Object-oriented Modelling.* Wiley.

Zeigler, B. (1997). *Objects and Systems.* Springer.

Chapter 15

System integrity

15.1 Chapter overview

The often discussed 'software crisis' has its roots most often in deficient requirements specification. The reasonable expectation of clients that their computer systems will provide a dependable service is too frequently disappointed. With embedded systems, in particular, developers should be aware of a range of techniques and tools that will assist with the design and realization of more reliable software. The concept of system *integrity* rather than *reliability* is useful when self-recovery, following component failure, is an achievable feature of modern computer systems. The reuse of well-tested software components is often recommended as a fast route to reliable systems, but porting software incurs its own problems. Run-time bugs are often traced back to failures of understanding during the determination of system requirements.

15.2 Software crisis

There always seems to be a crisis simmering away somewhere within the software industry. Productivity levels are not improving, project budgets overrun, delivered systems fail to work reliably and efficiently. The software maintenance mountain is not showing any signs of diminishing. Unsurprisingly, customers become disillusioned with their suppliers as these issues roll on and on. Only the fashionable panaceas change from month to month.

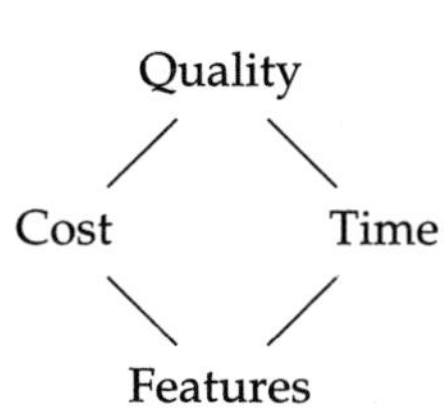

Conflicting commercial pressures

Quality assurance activity within the software industry is still relatively new and it largely involves implementing well-established project management techniques, adapted from traditional engineering practice. These include a tight control on timescales, regular review sessions, clear product requirements from the start, agreed test schedules, and well-managed team work. Projects often commence with an 'Outline Requirements Document' or a similarly sketchy work called the 'Statement of Needs'. There is a genuine example, to illustrate the problem, reproduced below. Shamefully, this document was the only written record of a high-level preliminary product

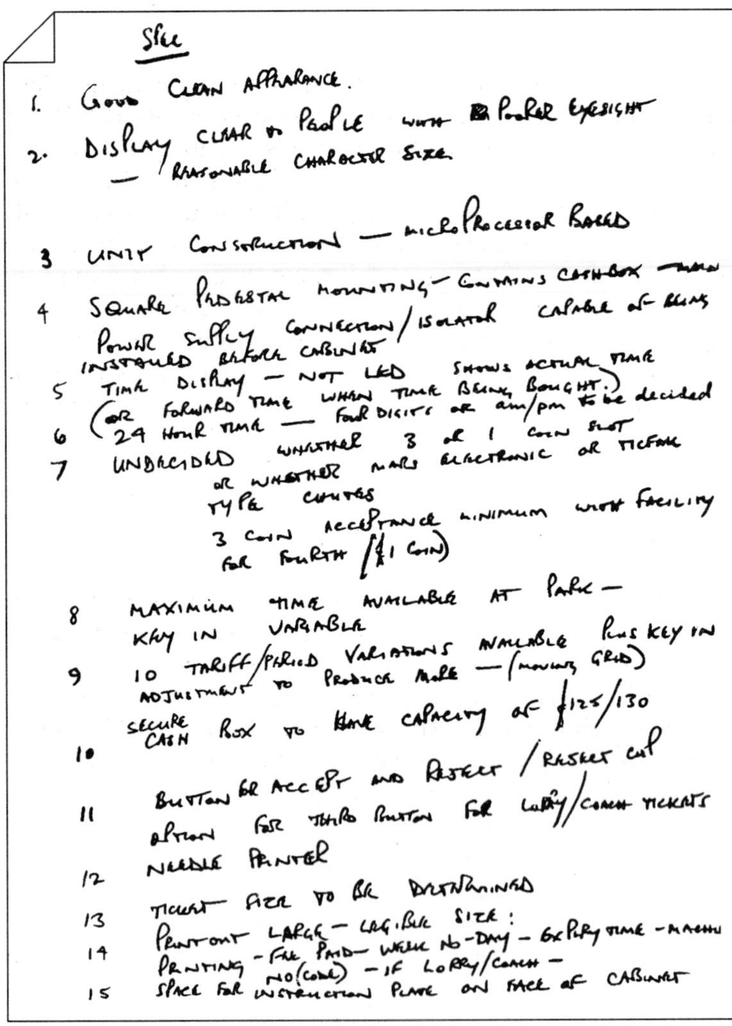

SPEC

1. GOOD CLEAN APPEARANCE.
2. DISPLAY CLEAR TO PEOPLE WITH POORER EYESIGHT — REASONABLE CHARACTER SIZE
3 UNIT CONSTRUCTION — MICROPROCESSOR BASED
4 SQUARE PEDESTAL MOUNTING — CONTAINS CASHBOX — MAIN POWER SUPPLY CONNECTION/ISOLATOR CAPABLE OF BEING INSTALLED BEFORE CABINET
5 TIME DISPLAY — NOT LED SHOWS ACTUAL TIME (OR FORWARD TIME WHEN TIME BEING BOUGHT.)
6 24 HOUR TIME — FOUR DIGITS OR am/pm to be decided
7 UNDECIDED WHETHER 3 OR 1 COIN SLOT OR WHETHER MARS ELECTRONIC OR TICFAK TYPE COINTES 3 COIN ACCEPTANCE MINIMUM WITH FACILITY FOR FOURTH (£1 COIN)
8 MAXIMUM TIME AVAILABLE AT PARK — KEY IN VARIABLE
9 10 TARIFF/PERIOD VARIATIONS AVAILABLE PLUS KEY IN ADJUSTMENT TO PRODUCE MORE — (MOVING GRID)
10 SECURE CASH BOX TO HAVE CAPACITY OF £125/130
11 BUTTON OR ACCEPT AND REJECT / BASKET CUP OPTION FOR THIRD BUTTON FOR LORRY/COACH TICKETS
12 NEEDLE PRINTER
13 TICKET SIZE TO BE DETERMINED
14 PRINT OUT LARGE — LEGIBLE SIZE: PRINTING — FEE PAID — WEEK NO-DAY — EXPIRY TIME — MACHINE NO (CODE) — IF LORRY/COACH —
15 SPACE FOR INSTRUCTION PLATE ON FACE OF CABINET

A *real* requirements document

development meeting, lasting all day, involving managing director, marketing director, technical director, sales manager, development manager and the author. Anyone can see that to start a software development based only on such flimsy and irrelevant information is likely to end in a disaster. Designing on the back of the proverbial cigarette packet can still be witnessed in practice! This is where most of the really difficult problems begin. The initial investigations, involving research, interviews and detailed negotiations are notoriously underresourced. Sometimes inexperienced staff, with little background knowledge of previous products, are expected to reconcile conflicting demands placed by senior colleagues. The requirements are sometimes subtle and often complex.

15.3 Fault tolerance

The ability to continue responding to events, processing data, even after components have failed, is not an unusual requirement for real-time systems. Such robustness of performance does not come without a cost, the hardware may have to be carefully selected for proven reliability, and even duplicated to provide immediate failover, hot standby capability. In the case of software, the cost is driven up by the extra complexity of an operating environment which protects data from corruption, even when alternative modules are being reinstalled or reconfigured on a live system.

A small server problem

In fact it is possible, by careful configuration, to design and build a computer system which works more reliably than its hardware and software components. This is achievable through the deployment of redundant resources, backup facilities which can be swapped-in when a failure occurs. So a real-time system must be able to detect exceptions, record them, and undertake a recovery procedure which does not jeopardize the smooth operation of the whole system. Designing for failure is a true challenge for programmers, requiring imagination, detailed analysis and costing. There are various ways to build strong software systems, and the choice depends on the type of error or exception anticipated, and the facilities provided by the target language. Large database systems use the method of *check-pointing* and *roll-back* to recover when a transaction, for some reason, fails to be confirmed. With real-time systems, errors can occur due to invalid input data, application bugs, or even incompatibilities in a shared library. Dynamically recovering may be as simple as reading the next item of data, but could demand switching over to an earlier release of a software module or library code. Both may involve other code units which could be executing correctly at the time of failure. So isolating and swapping the faulty software may affect several tasks, directly or indirectly. We will return to this topic in Chapter 16.

15.4 System requirements

A requirements document is meant to clearly and unambiguously specify what the final system should be able to do without saying how this should be achieved. The precise, consistent, unambiguous description of essential, functional aspects should also be separated from the auxiliary constraints or desirable features. However, during the normal run of a project, the often strained negotiations with clients might be shortened by adopting a reverse approach: use the requirements document also to declare what the system will *not* provide. In this way the client will not be expecting some undeclared, implied functionality which they see as 'obviously' necessary for that class of product.

Mistakes or misunderstandings which slip through to later stages are like timebombs which are well hidden until revealed as much more serious problems by programmers or users. Many systems subject to expensive catastrophic failures have had the cause traced back to early mistakes made

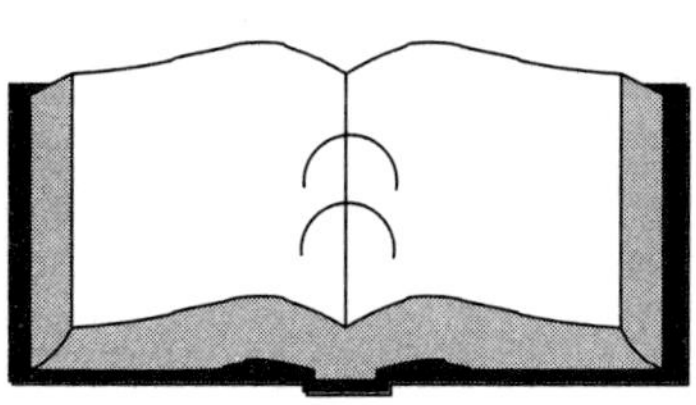

- Underresourced activity carried out by inexperienced staff
- Complications due to attempting to reuse previous documents
- Customers unprepared with only vague ideas
- Irreconcilable viewpoints from different departments
- 'Hi-tech' enthusiasm from senior managers: feature creep
- Design decisions put in too soon
- Ambiguous customer descriptions
- Customer continually changing ideas
- No commitment to agreeing test data
- Hidden agendas or constraints
- Clients' requirements too ambitious

Common problems for the requirements team

during the requirements phase. With this in mind, some of the common problems associated with the requirements analysis phase of the software lifecycle are listed above.

15.5 Requirements analysis techniques

The Controlled Requirements Expression method (CORE) was introduced as a requirements analysis front end to the MASCOT (Modular Approach to Software Construction Operation and Test) development method for real-time software. It provided a disciplined, structured framework for the capture, analysis and expression of project requirements: the *what* of the design not the *how*. All too often, small errors incorporated into the project at this early stage can result in expensive revisions occurring late in the testing phase. Because of this, requirements analysis and specification is recognized as a crucial activity: would you try to construct Concorde using a fuzzy photograph as your only working plan? CORE was intended to help formulate a consistent model of the new system by documenting and synthesizing the views of all the individuals concerned with the project. By using a clearly defined method, communication within large teams can be improved, as can client–analyst discussions.

Unfortunately, the terms 'viewpoint analysis' and 'activity diagrams' are practically the only remaining contribution of this nearly abandoned but

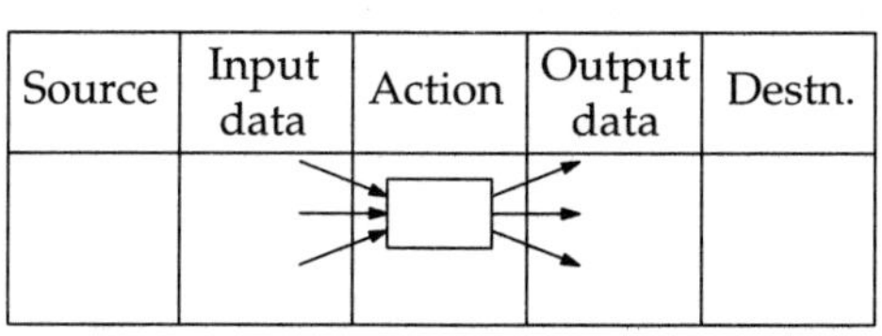

CORE viewpoint diagram

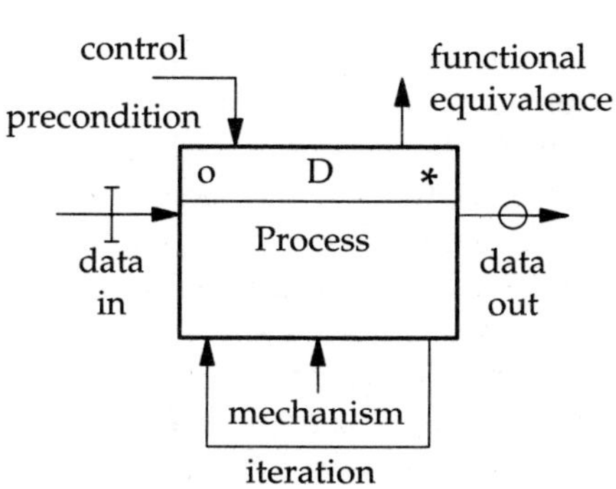

CORE activity diagram

valuable technique. Practising engineers often scorned the method as too abstract, making problems out of thin air, or top-heavy. Certainly the management of the large amount of paperwork was a central issue, but that can be contained by the use of automated diagramming tools. CORE was a practical and effective method for requirements analysis and specification which attracted some measure of support in the real-time community. Recently the UML use-case diagram has replaced the CORE viewpoint analysis technique, as described in Chapter 13.

15.6 Verification and validation

The establishment of a set of requirements is a good start, but from then on, there is an obvious need to *verify* that the developing product complies with the list of established requirements. In addition to this ongoing comparison and assessment activity, the quality of the design and implementation work has to be scrutinized under the banner of *validation*. So 'VnV' is widely regarded as an essential activity within any substantial development project.

Verification and validation (VnV)

15.7 Good design

The fact that all successful systems are founded on a good design is often only really apparent some years after the project has been completed and the product is undergoing routine maintenance. Good design leads to code that offers open, well-organized structures. It must be said that some design techniques are easier to relate to the eventually generated code than others. Some methodologies, such as JSD, seem to advocate the exclusive use of automatic code generation, something that would make debugging activity very difficult because it becomes nearly impossible to relate code to design. Finite state diagrams, however, can be implemented directly into easily understood code through several different methods. Object-oriented techniques successfully encapsulate functionality and encourage system partitioning with clearly defined coupling between components. The choice of an appropriate method for the job in hand is a primary skill of the experienced developer. As we have observed before, the main purpose of carrying out any design activity is to structure code. Design without implementation is like planning a summer holiday; and then not actually going.

Clifton suspension bridge, a good, enduring design by Isambard Brunel (1864)

15.8 Simulation studies

Preliminary simulation studies can greatly assist with understanding the more complex aspects of system functionality before committing to the full design. By using simulation trials, extra information can be provided for the systems analyst, this can be especially useful where variable processing loads are anticipated, or optimum task scheduling could be a critical

Life, the Universe and Everything? (Adams 1979)

factor. Simulation can also provide an intermediate step between design and full implementation. It is frequently possible to carry out a prototype implementation before completely committing the code to a rather inconvenient embedded target processor. If the majority of software testing can be carried out in the relative convenience and security of a desktop PC, why not benefit from the better debugging facilities on offer? Although introducing this new intermediate step within the implementation phase will increase the workload, partly because of the extra software harness required, it can easily pay back manyfold through fast bug fixing. This technique of running code within a harness on a host machine should be termed 'emulation' rather than 'simulation', but it has a common aim: to improve the final product.

A final simulation stage may also be carried out to stress test the release software. In this case the simulation refers to the replacement of the system context, the surrounding environment, by a software harness. This harness code can be divided into *stubs* and *drivers*. Drivers are active routines which pass data down the hierarchy onto others. They expect to receive back appropriate values. Stubs operate by receiving function calls from above, perhaps intended for input and output interfaces, and satisfy them with test data values. This allows the tester to artificially introduce changes in data rates and flow-control signals. Such an arrangement can provide preliminary performance statistics, and reveal some tricky aspects of system activity, only apparent under full CPU or I/O loading.

15.9 Petri nets

It is estimated that in production-grade software, as much as 60 per cent of the delivered code is concerned with intercepting error conditions and dealing with them. In some circumstances, this does appear to be more like online testing than handling rare exceptions. If preliminary simulation studies were employed more widely, many of the early batch of problems which get delivered to customers with their new software might be avoided. An interesting way of carrying out preliminary system testing through simulation is offered by Petri nets (Peterson 1981).

This technique was devised in 1962, specifically to model and investigate concurrent systems with mutual sequential dependencies. Petri net modelling can be used throughout the design phase of development. There are some automated tools to speed up investigations, but not too many. The principal focus concerns the causal interaction of events due to the intercommunication or synchronization of independent processes. Deadlock susceptibility and load sensitivities can be identified. The technique is still the subject of primary research work which, unfortunately, leads to continual changes in the symbolism and some basic assumptions. There is a tendancy for novices to muddle Petri Net Graphs (PNG) with the FSM diagrams, which look superficially

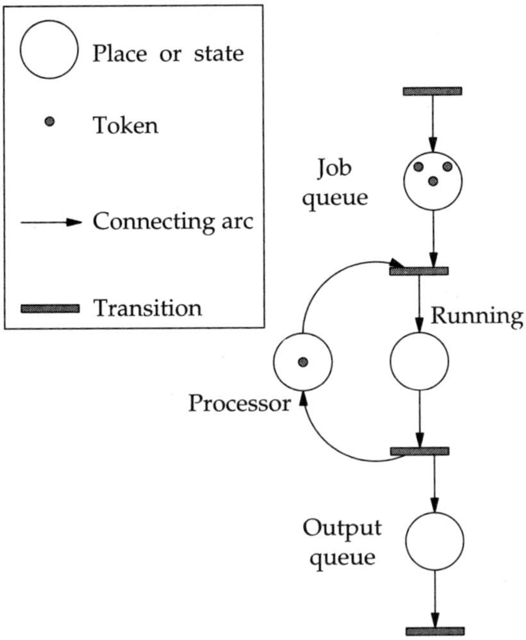

Petri net diagram for a process queue

somewhat similar. But PNGs are more similar to the UML activity diagram, which we discussed in Chapter 13. The PNG can be identically represented by an algebraic statement which enables the automatic manipulation of Petri net representations.

Places – possible states of the system
Transitions – allowed system events, state $\rightarrow$ state
Inputs – preconditions for a transition
Outputs – postconditions for a transition
Tokens – shows current system resource status

Petri net graph components

The execution of a Petri net is controlled by the position of the tokens. Tokens sit in places and move like Ludo counters around the graph. Graphs with tokens are said to be 'marked'. The 'firing' of a transition is determined by the number of preconditions and the position of the tokens. A transition may only fire if all the inputs are marked. Then the tokens are repositioned on the outputs.

Petri net techniques are used to investigate various properties of parallel systems: boundedness, conservation, coverability, equivalence, liveness,

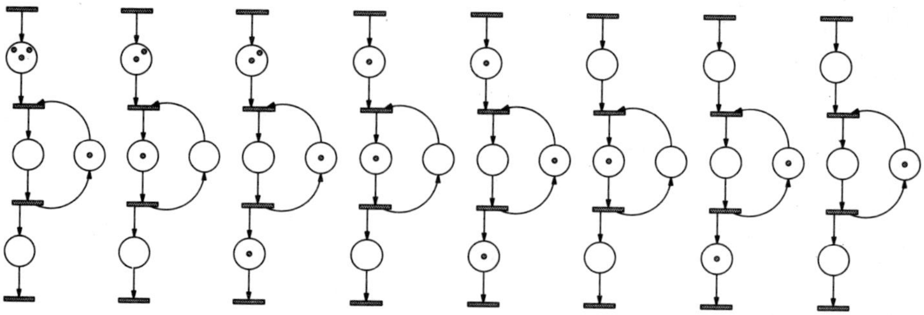

A sequence of Petri net activity with three simultaneous requests for an single exclusive resource

reachability, safeness. This is achieved by drafting a textual description of the dynamic sequence of activity within the Petri net by using a reachability tree. In the semaphore example (below) there are five places, represented by a five component vector. The token count at each place is written into the vector, thus indicating the dynamic changes which the net reveals. From the initial state, with only three tokens present, in this case of the two contending processes, the semaphore can deliver either of two sequences, depending on which of the processes gains control. Either path ends up with the semaphore open, and no requests to enter a critical region. Drawing in reachability trees can be tedious. You stop when all tokens are exhausted, or a transition is permanently blocked, indicating a deadlock situation. It is also possible to enter a never ending repetitive loop, which may be detected by recognizing a repeating pattern of tokens.

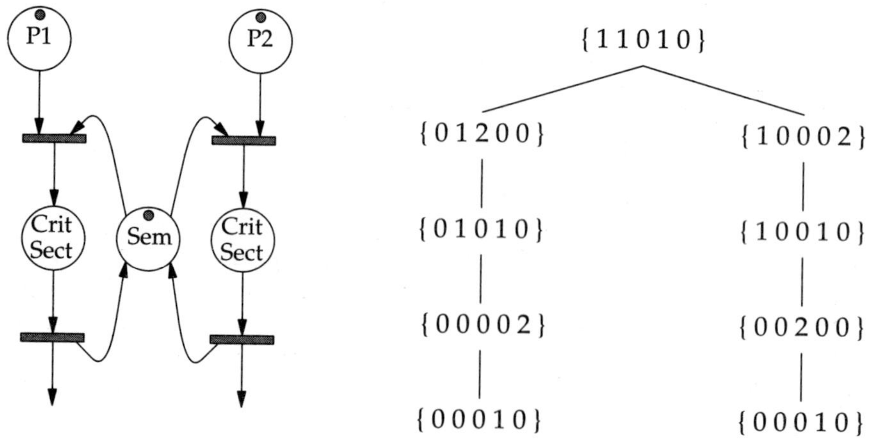

Modelling semaphore action using reachability tree

15.10 Design for security – source code checking: lint

Before compilers became acceptably reliable and helpful in the production of error messages, it was common practice to run code through a static program verifier, such as `lint`. This utility detects syntax errors and anomalies which may give rise to run-time errors or problems later on. Lint actually offers a severity of checking not found in most commercial compilers. It will detect many 'dodgy' code situations including: unreachable statements, all type mismatches, the possibility of an unintentioned NULL pointer, functions returning pointers to automatic (local) variables, incorrectly entered loops, unused local variables, constant logical expressions. In addition, it checks functions to make sure they have the correct number of arguments and always return a value, and that the returned value is used. For multiple file compilations, the mutual compatibilities are also checked.

A touch of lint

The use of auxiliary code checkers has now become much less common, perhaps due to the improvement in the quality of compiler error and warning messages. But the severity of the checking standards implemented by lint still goes far beyond most C compilers. So in the field of high reliability software production, the use of lint has re-emerged to provide a warning to programmers about potentially risky features and unsafe usages. Nowadays, with much better compiler technology, the application of `lint` has fallen into disuse, and it is no longer routinely bundled with Unix, and obtaining a version is not the easiest thing (SPLINT 2003). If you cannot get hold of a copy of lint, the GNU gcc/g++ compilers can be put into an extra 'fussy' mode using the `-Wall` and `-pedantic` flags. So it is important at the outset of a new contract to ensure that the necessary software tools are available. Where extreme C code correctness is demanded, the use of `lint` would be advisable.

15.11 Code reuse

The confident recommendation that by recycling old code from well-used, existing applications, better systems will be delivered, needs to be evaluated cautiously. In particular, projects involving embedded systems may be different, because porting old code to new hardware is a more complex process than upgrading a PC package from Windows 98 to Win2k. There are many pitfalls which are not readily appreciated by inexperienced programmers.

At the start, when trying to resurrect five year old source code, it is not uncommon for archive tapes to be unreadable, for makefiles to have vanished, and for no test data to be available. Translating from legacy languages, such as Fortran or Z80 assembler, into Java or C may reveal teeth grinding inconsistencies. In such circumstances, it is hardly surprising when nobody else volunteers to help with a project that threatens to become a modern day archeological investigation!

Even if the programming language has not been changed, it is probable that the new compiler will distinguish itself by sporting many incompatible 'improvements' over the original version, revealing many syntactic discrepencies. Although it is likely that the new CPU is more powerful, it could alternatively have been selected for its cost advantage. In which case, floating-point instructions may no longer be welcome. Some major system difficulties can emerge when the true differences in memory management and protection become more apparent.

Sometimes the hardware is not the principal source of problems. It is the change in O/S API that generates the programmer's headaches. When specialized I/O devices are involved, the need to port the device drivers can demand a lot of time and skill. Any I/O mismatches have to be quickly resolved, especially those arising from hardware limitations, such as number of interrupt lines, priority assignments, buffer sizes and device bandwidths. Confusion and delay, due to badly commented code, can outstrip practically any other source of frustration. Code reuse, which involves interplatform porting, may not save you time or money. The likelihood that comments and code will drift apart, during the years of contract maintenance, is very high. When you are unfamiliar with the application, and the code does not look consistent with the comments, which do you trust?

15.12 Compile-time checking

If you do not have a copy of lint, the GNU gcc/g++ compilers can be put into an extra 'fussy' mode using the `-Wall` and `-pedantic` flags which enables a whole set of extra messages, warning the programmer about anomalies and irregularities in the code which may be the cause of problems at some time in the future. Try `man gcc` and scroll forward to the flags section containing details of the `-w` options.

15.13 Code testing

An extra advantage gained from using a well-partitioned, multitasking solution is the ease with which individual tasks can be separately tested. This does, however, involve the production of testbench software or harness, to provide a substitute stream of input data and events. Such simulation testing can initially be done on a convenient host computer, supplied with full debugging and profiling tools, rather than the much less convenient target board. A well-recognized problem, however, with software testing is the exponential explosion of different execution pathways through the code due to the use of conditional instructions such as IF-ELSE and SWITCH-CASE. For a totally exhaustive test, every legal executable pathway should be tried out, which is totally unfeasible with most normal programs. In the straightforward example presented below, a fourway SWITCH-CASE is bracketed by two IF-ELSE statements, and delivers about one million alternative pathways to be tested. But should this structure be evoked ten times, say within a function, the test combination count shoots up to 10^{60}. Interleaved threads, arising from a multi-tasking system, further increase the large number of pathways which require checking.

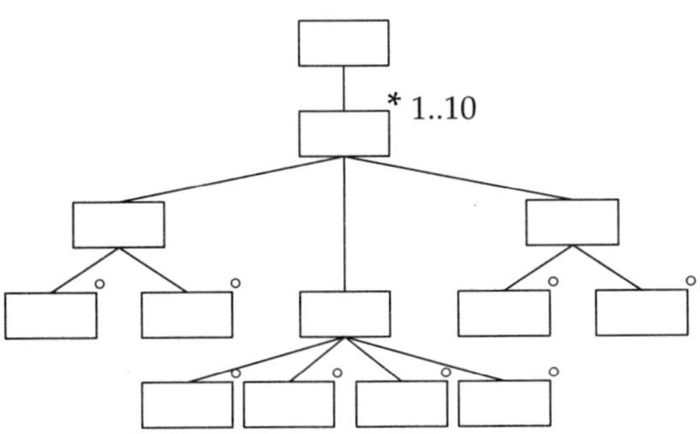

Testing complexity: 10^6 pathways

Because of the impossibility of completing full coverage tests within a reasonable time, software testing is usually carried out by a reduced sampling technique. This is either *blind*, also termed black box, with randomly constructed data sets, or *informed*, also termed white box, with carefully chosen data values which are of particular sensitivity or significance to the key algorithms.

15.14 System integration testing

The bringing together for the first time of all the software and hardware components often highlights surprising incompatibilities which have somehow slipped through earlier checks and reviews. Because the full integration test is much more complex than previous unit tests, it is essential to make careful action schemas and contingency plans.

15.15 Run-time error trapping

The sequence of system run-time checks, illustrated below would include aspects such as: power-fail, bus error and memory access violation, division by zero and watchdog time-out. The next level of checking intercepts software traps, variable range checks, stack overruns and module checksum inconsistencies. Task checking focuses on scheduling problems and uses inter-task checking. If some system-wide consistency checking is being carried out on global data, such as integrity, capacity or timing limits, it takes place at the fourth level. Finally, system supervisory checks may be required on distributed or parallel systems to ensure an equal allocation of process loading.

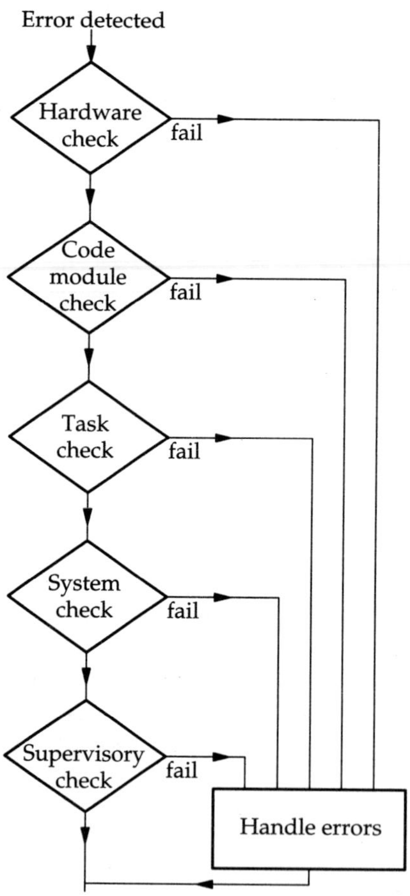

System run-time checks

The availability of a well-tried RTE may initially appear to be an attractive prospect when considering software from the reliability point of view. However, for high integrity systems the cooperative, cyclic executive model can still be justified in order to retain a deterministic view of dynamic system operation. RTEs modify their task scheduling behaviour in response to environmental changes which makes it difficult to exactly predict their performance under all combinations of external conditions.

15.16 Run-time checking: assert

A noteworthy advantage of some programming languages is the provision of exception handling. When an error occurs inside a block of code, or subroutine, the programmer can insert explicit instructions to deal with the situation immediately. This prevents what starts as a minor inconvenience escalating into a major catastrophy. ADA and Java both offer such interception facilities. But it should be remembered that if Ariane 5 had been programmed in simple C and not 'failsafe' ADA, the integer overflow exception from the gyroscope might not have led to the disastrous loss.

Beyond the preliminary lint and compile-time checks, further precautionary measures can be inserted into the code to act at run-time. Some languages have been provided with special facilities to support such run-time checking and error trapping. Of course any additional, redundant code carries the unnecessary risk that it will itself introduce more bugs into the program! The C language `assert()` macro helps with debugging by checking for an anticipated value, reporting immediately if that value is not correct and passing control to the `abort()` function. Popular uses are to check for incorrect NULL pointers and valid parameter values. On Linux, the `assert` macro is defined within the assert.h header file, and its compile-time inclusion is controlled by the NDEBUG macro flag. If the macro NDEBUG is defined TRUE before the `#include <assert.h>` statement occurs, the macro will *not* be active, generating no code, and doing nothing. However, for a debugging session, the code needs to be recompiled with NDEBUG defined as FALSE. The macro `assert(trial)` will then print an error message to standard output and terminates the whole program by calling `abort()` when the expression `trial` is valued at zero (FALSE). The Linux header file definitions are as follows:

```
# define assert(expr) (__ASSERT_VOID_CAST((expr) ? 0 :\
  (__assert_fail(__STRING(expr),__FILE__,__LINE__,__ASSERT_
# FUNCTION),0)))

# ifdef         __USE_GNU
# define assert_perror(errnum) (__ASSERT_VOID_CAST(!(errnum) ? 0 :\
  (__assert_perror_fail((errnum),__FILE__,__LINE__,__ASSERT_
#  FUNCTION),0)))
# endif
```

The purpose of this macro is to help development programmers to identify bugs in their code. It is not intended to provide messages to end users.

But if you prefer not to halt the whole program when an assertion fails, you may install a custom handler in place of the default `assert_fail()` and `assert_perror_fail()` functions. In case of an assertion failure, an LED could be toggled, an ouput bit pulsed, or a value dumped to a prearranged location for later inspection. There would be little disruption to normal system performance and timing with these actions.

Once the debugging session has been completed, all that is necessary is to set the NDEBUG flag and recompile the code. All the `assert` macros will then be ignored by the preprocessor and take up no space in the executable program.

```
assert(pdata != NULL);
```

15.17 Run-time checking: exceptions and hardware watchdog

This is very powerful technique often used with multi-tasking applications, but it does require access to some dedicated hardware in the form of a programmable counter/timer (such as the i8254) or an analogue retriggerable monostable (such as the LM555). The scheme works by the watchdog timer having access to the system reset line. Every 50 ms or so the timer can emit a pulse which resets the whole system. This drastic action is normally cancelled before it happens by resetting the timer back to the beginning of its 50 ms interval. So software, running periodically faster than 20 Hz, has the responsibility of holding off the watchdog timer reset pulse by continually restarting the timer. In this way, hardware can check on the health of periodic tasks. The watchdog can reset all the hardware and fully reboot the software should the system crash, or the watchdog task fail. So to avoid system reinitialization, the programmer must insert output instructions to be evoked at regular intervals by the scheduler. These output signals will restart the counter

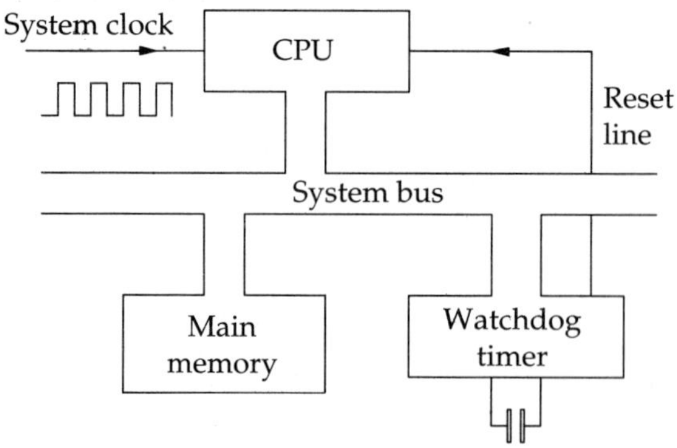

Watchdog timer

or retrigger the monostable, maintaining a constant output, incapable of resetting the system.

15.18 Run-time checking: stack length checking

Another useful run-time ploy is to routinely check the system stack length. As users of some PC packages know, it is not uncommon for complex software to suffer from 'memory leakage'. One way that this can occur is for the stack to slowly increase in size, possibly due to an inbalance in the use of PUSH and POP instructions, or a failure to scrub parameters after a function call. A suitable technique involves clearing the stack area during initialization, filling it with a particular, recognizable data pattern (such as 0X55AA55AA). In this way it is easy for the code to check intermittently and see how far down the stack it has extended, even if it has retreated upwards in the meanwhile, leaving stale data values behind in memory.

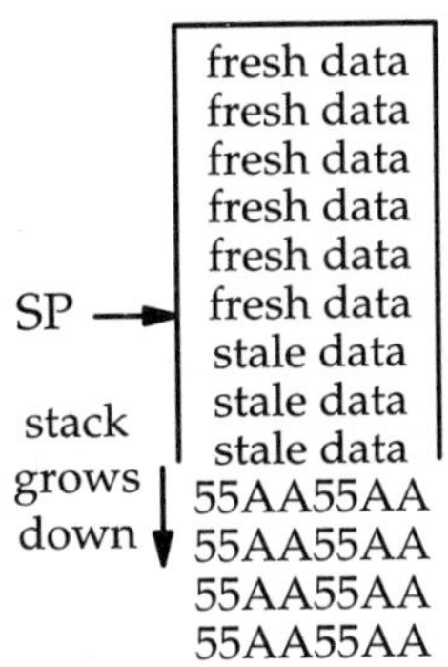

Stack length checking

15.19 Visual assistance

When you first start working on real-time systems, it is often time itself that is the source of the greatest confusion. The best way round this is to provide a visual display of the ongoing events. Now these may be occurring millions of times a second, although it is much more common for realtime systems to work at the millisecond level, i.e. thousands of events a second. The most suitable tool for this job, as already promoted in the first chapter, is an oscilloscope. Unfortunately most programmers do not welcome sight of this kit, perhaps it brings back horrific memories of long Wednesday afternoons in a dusty physics lab. This is a pity, because all that is needed is a couple of output instructions to be judiciously inserted into the critical piece of code, blipping an output port for a fraction of a microsecond, for the display to spring into life and present a crystal clear image of the previously invisible code timings. A short introduction to using an oscilloscope, to assist non-physicists when debugging software, can be found in Appendix A.

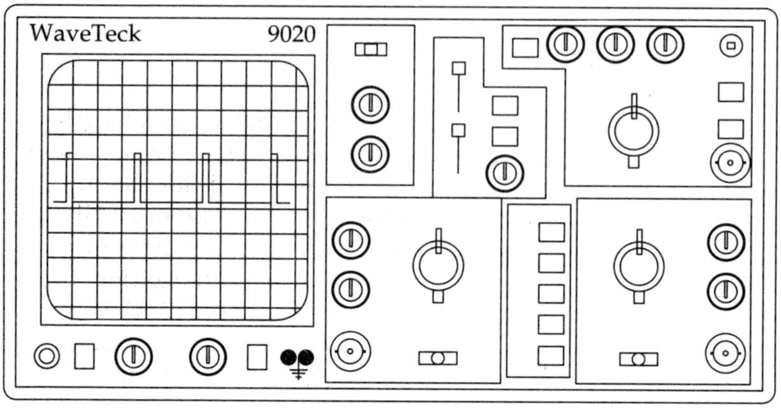

Visual debugging aid

15.20 A wet Monday morning

Students often find the discipline of software engineering a tedious and unexciting subject. But when *working* rather than *studying*, every now and then a stunning incident occurs which screams out to teach us something about the importance of routine, administrative processes in the struggle to maintain quality products. So, here is a half-imagined scenario:

> It is a normal, ordinary Monday morning. You arrive in the office and start to engage in a routine software maintenance task. Perhaps a couple of minor but annoying problems have been identified by the client, and finally they are to be fixed. Alternatively, the system required an unscheduled reboot and you are detailed to track down its cause. Sometimes maintenance is triggered by the need for enhanced functionality: the problems of having a successful product! And finally, older systems can require porting to newer, cheaper platforms. Whatever the exact scenario, you are pottering around in the source archive playing with project directories and `make` files. At this moment you may find yourself unexpectedly in a rapidly accelerating downward spiral.

- On close inspection, the client's run-time binaries do not seem to match the archived source code. And the official site files, which record software releases, have not been kept up to date. Perhaps the only way to resolve the uncertainty is to visit a customer's site and carry out some clandestine code copying in order to ascertain exactly which version of your software

they are running. This is unprofessional, embarrassing and possibly illegal.
- Maybe the system configuration and build completely fails and so you are unable to regenerate the most recently released binaries. Is it even clear which of the multiple source files are the current versions? Then, if the build does complete successfully and you end up with a running system, no authorized acceptance tests are available. And, of course, nobody in the office can, or wants to, remember what the software actually does.
- The worst situation, sending a shudder down your spine, is the sudden realization that you are confronted not by a simple two hour update, but by a complete system overhaul because your trivial amendment to a single module has produced completely inexplicable side-effects within a distant segment of code.

All these events have happened to me, and they will probably happen to you, unless your office procedures are a lot better than the average development unit chaos! Maintaining or debugging unfamiliar, ill-structured code drives home the need for good design, documentation and project archiving more securely than any classroom talk. So, code release management and site tracking are an essential, if tedious associate of the more exciting activity of software creation and marketing.

15.21 Concurrent version control system (CVS)

The CVS source code management system helps with the management of large, multi-file, multi-programmer projects. A constant issue when working on such developments is keeping track of the latest versions of each module. With parts of the system being developed and continually modified, sometimes by remote unknown colleagues, it becomes increasingly difficult to ensure that the latest releases are being used.

During multi-person developments, there is an ever-present risk of *simultaneous* code updates being attempted on the same module. Two or more programmers might initiate independent editing sessions on the same file, and then, eventually, attempt to write their individual, amended copies back onto disk. This circumstance can be handled by imposing a file locking scheme, as offered by SCCS and RCS, an earlier source code control system. In this case, extra facilities have to be provided beyond the simple owner–group–everyone, read–write–execute file permissions provided by Unix. RCS only allowed a single programmer to access a file with *write* permissions at any moment. The file is dealt with as an exclusive resource. But RCS did allow multiple simultaneous *read* accesses.

CVS operates by maintaining a single copy of all the master source files. These copies are termed the source repository, which also contains all the information permitting programmers to extract previous software releases using either a symbolic revision tag, or the repository registration date. Most usefully, CVS servers are happy to operate over LANs or even the internet.

CVS has a more sophisticated capability which tolerates simultaneous, independent repository checkouts on a single file, only issuing a warning to the parties involved, and then merging the amended files when they are restored to the repository, resulting in a single, updated version. This conflict resolution is impressive, but remains problematic from the users' point of view. The reliance on files as a unit of protection does not accord with the current object-oriented paradigm where classes, methods and data attributes are seen as the essential units. Thus it would be more useful to issue class code for modification, irrespective of the file containing it. In addition, CVS does not keep track of component interdependencies, as offered by the `make` utility. Any amendment will only be revealed to co-workers when their compiles fail or test suites are run. Programmers would also welcome a convenient 'roll-back' facility to reverse unsuccessful amendments which have already been registered by CVS.

A list of the principal CVS user commands are available on-line with `cvs * -H`, and more information on any of these commands can be obtained with `cvs -H <command>`:

add	Add a new file/directory to the repository
admin	Administration front end for RCS
annotate	Show last revision where each line was modified
checkout	Checkout sources for editing
commit	Check files into the repository
diff	Show differences between revisions
edit	Get ready to edit a watched file
editors	See who is editing a watched file
export	Export sources from CVS, similar to checkout
history	Show repository access history
import	Import source files into CVS repository
init	Create a CVS repository if it doesn't exist
log	Print out history information for files
login	Prompt for password for authenticating server
logout	Removes entry in .cvspass for remote repository
pserver	Password server mode
rannotate	Show last revision where each line of module was modified
rdiff	Create 'patch' format diffs between releases
release	Indicate that a module is no longer in use
remove	Remove an entry from the repository
rlog	Print out history information for a module
rtag	Add a symbolic tag to a module

server	Server mode
status	Display status information on checked-out files
tag	Add a symbolic tag to checked out version of files
unedit	Undo an edit command
update	Bring work tree in sync with repository
version	Show current CVS version(s)
watch	Set watches
watchers	See who is watching a file

15.22 Setting up a CVS repository

To set up a CVS repository requires the designation of a root directory (CVSROOT) from which a directory tree can grow. The repository contains the master source code files, RCS history files ('file,v', yes it is a comma) and necessary administrative information. CVSROOT can be declared using:

```
cvs -d ~/cvsroot/projectA
```

or initializing an environment variable:

```
export CVSROOT=~/cvsroot/projectA.
```

The system also needs to know the position of the local, working directory, often termed the 'sandbox':

```
export CVSAREA=/tmp/projectA.
```

Both these can be added to the .bashrc shell initialization file. After declaring the position of the repository and the local working area, cvs creates the repository with:

```
cvs init
```

Actually, the repository declaration and creation can be rolled into one with: `cvs -d ~/cvsroot init`. The root directory will now contain several administration files ready to receive some source code files.

When the project source code is archived, so that in the future the application can be rebuilt correctly, thought should also be given to preserving a working system and tool set. There is little point in storing source code for 20 years, only to find that the correct cross-compiler with its libraries and hosting system have themselves all been thrown away. Will a DOS-based compiler always be compatible with the latest version of Windows? In fact, the problem of compatibility may be more worrying in the Linux arena, where releases and revisions are frequent occurrences.

15.23 Conducting design and code reviews

The detection and correction of errors can be a time consuming and frustrating activity. Often the most resilient bugs relate to a misunderstanding in the initial statement of requirements or an implied expectation on the part of the client, not appreciated by the analyst or programmer. The sooner such hiccoughs are identified and corrected, the better. The extra cost of sorting out code which has been delivered to the client can be phenomenal: travel, hotel bills, disruption to ongoing schedules, replacement equipment, loss of market position. So, any ideas that might help to identify bugs as early as possible would be worth their weight in gold. One such idea, now well established, is the 'Code Review'.

Review meetings

An early paper from IBM (Fagan 1970) highlighted the advantages of development staff participating in regular review meetings, and offered some guidelines as to the best way to conduct these reviews. A major source of misgivings for those planning to hold a regular sequence of design and code reviews is the fear that the activity may become competitive, even vindictive. If some members of staff use the meetings to assert their technical superiority, very little would be gained, perhaps even the reverse would occur with staff becoming defensive, resentful and demotivated. Such a sensitive issue must be handled carefully. Here, some straightforward guidelines are offered which can be used when starting to hold design/code reviews for the first time. Eventually you can devise your own rules, tailored to your own particular situation.

Regular design and code reviews can trap errors early in the development lifecycle. The sooner a bug is spotted, the cheaper it is to correct. Even quite insignificant errors, in this litigious age can have expensive consequences. A coding mistake which substituted a time value of 18:00 in place of the intended 20:00 cost a local hospital much lost revenue, but the site management contractor ended up forfeiting a lucrative contract and suffering legal proceedings. But Fagan does warn developers that where review meetings are adopted as a method for detecting project flaws, the likely cost may amount to 15 per cent extra on project budgets. A very useful remedial activity to be

- Review the product not the producer – take the pressure off the individual whose work is under scrutiny.
- Stick to the prepared agenda – don't allow the meeting to be hijacked for other purposes.
- Guillotine debate strictly – senior staff are busy, if they fear that the meeting will overrun, they may withdraw their vital support.
- Summarize problems, don't try to solve them – discussion on solutions can take place later, around the coffee machine.
- Make public notes on a flipchart – remove the suspicion that line managers may take away incriminating notes, to be brought out at annual appraisals.
- Establish a follow-up procedure – reduce the administrative variation, make it a routine activity.
- Be warned and prepare for sessions – most of us need to read through the material ahead of the meeting to make our contribution worthwhile.
- Train staff for review work, establish mutual trust.
- Use impersonal tick sheets as far as possible – routine recording.
- Schedule reviews as part of normal product development – budget for them.
- Review the reviews – learn from experience and get better at reviewing.
- All participants sign the formal acceptance – corporate responsibility.

Rules governing a successful review meeting

undertaken at the conclusion of projects would be to backtrack through the error logs and records from review meetings, during which, it now appears, serious bugs remained undetected: how was this possible? What was done wrong? What measures could be introduced to prevent such expensive slip-ups reoccurring? Learning from experience is an important lesson to learn!

15.24 Extreme Programming

An interesting development in recent years has been the adaptation of the rapid prototyping development method into something called Extreme Programming (XP) (Beck 1999). This is suitable to small/medium sized software development teams and addresses some of the main difficulties encountered by programmers. The best known principle which practitioners need to observe is the *pair* programming. This means that all design and programming activity is carried out by teams of two. This enforces a constant regime of peer reviewing, reducing, if not eliminating, the need to carry out formal code review meetings. But of equal significance is the rule governing the production of test suites for all code units. By having agreed test harnesses, before the components are created, it allows for frequent testing to prevent bugs propagating into the main source store. Because the development will be embarked on by several pairs of programmers in parallel, there is a vital need for a source code release control which can handle simultaneous updating. The CVS tool is sufficiently powerful to handle this central role. An advantage of working in pairs, and encouraging an impersonal approach to code production, is skill sharing and a collegiate attitude to error correction and maintenance activities. In line with the aim of good, informal communications between all the team members, there should be total access to the customer, or an informed representative, throughout the project. Perhaps a worrying point for those considering adopting the XP technique, is the frequency with which the word 'courage' occurs in the descriptions used by those already committed!

- Test harnesses produced first
- Pair programming: constant peer review
- Rapid prototyping
- Frequent unit testing
- Code release control (CVS)
- Simple code is best
- No personal code ownership
- Small teams: good communications
- Customer representation

Principles of **XP**

15.25 Software standards

There are a wide range of published standards which are used by software developers and their clients. Unsurprisingly these are more often intended for

Level		Description
1	Initial	Utter chaos when things go wrong, no agreed s/w standards, poor project management. Product quality unpredictable. Organization sustained by outstanding staff effort and commitment.
2	Repeatable	Standard processes established and repeatable. Management does carry out retrospective reviews to improve future performance.
3	Defined	The whole organization has adopted a standardized software development and maintenance process which can be repeated for all s/w projects. Because the procedures are well understood, management has good insight into the day-to-day progress on all projects.
4	Managed	The organization has adopted quantifiable measures of quality which are applied to both process and product. The process can be adapted in an effective way to suit the needs of each individual project.
5	Optimized	Mature disciplined process which is being continuously refined. Improvement occurs both by incremental advancements in the existing process and by innovations using new technologies and methods.

Level definitions for the capability maturity model

military or aerospace contracts. The Capability Maturity Model (CMM) is used in the USA to provide a scaled assessment of organizations involved in software project management. It was started in 1980 by the US airforce who were dissatisfied with their supplier vetting procedures. Its aim is to offer guidelines for improving software development. The CMM framework can also be used by software managers, in government and industry, to select, adopt, and apply sound organizational and technical practices as applied to large software projects. The principal levels of compliance are summarized above. Assessments are carried out by teams of appraisers under the auspices of the Software Engineering Institute (SEI) at Carnegie-Mellon University.

ISO9001 is a similar organizational accreditation scheme which focuses on the process, its improvement and the maintenance of customer satisfaction.

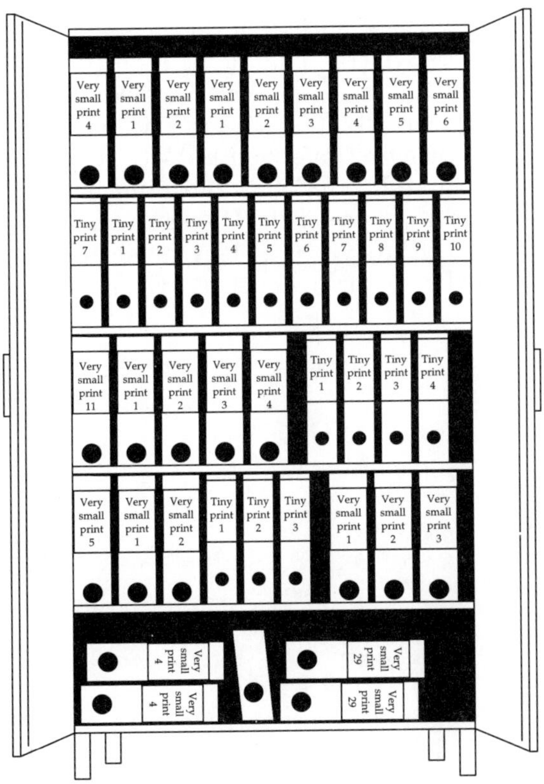

MIL-STD-498 documentary trail for a 50 page program

For aerospace and military contracts it is common to have to follow the MIL-STD-498. The purpose of this standard is to establish a uniform approach to software development and documentation. It specifies processes and documents that may be demanded at each stage in the contract lifecycle by the client. There are now 22 document types, described in the Data Item

Descriptions (DIDs). Although MIL-STD-498 is intended to be applicable to any type of software project, and independent of any particular methodology, the extra burden of work involved in following it means that only large, life critical developments can justify the cost. To gain an idea of the scale of the extra documentation generated by following MIL-STD-498, a five shelf 7 ft cabinet filled with specified documents, was needed to support a 3000 line program written mainly in C. The source code itself contributes a meagre 100 pages.

15.26 MISRA

Different commercial sectors have established their own software standards and practices to which group members adhere. The Motor Industry Software Reliability Association (MISRA) is a group of vehicle manufacturers, component suppliers and engineering consultants who are concerned with promoting best practice in the development of safety-critical electronic systems for road vehicles. Of particular interest to real-time programmers are a set of recommendations they publish for the use of the C programming language for safety-critical applications (MISRA 1998). Many developers, far removed from the motor industry, refer to these guidelines when safety is paramount.

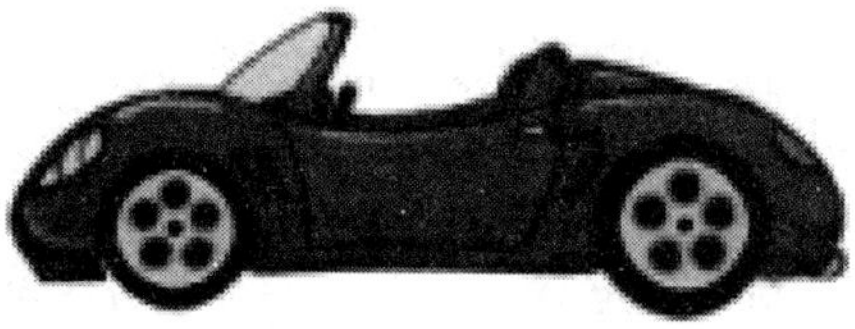

Motor vehicle control software

Developers concerned with high integrity or life-critical applications often expose some of the well-recognized deficiencies within the C language: free access to pointers, relaxed TYPING constraints, algebraic expression complexity, arcane operator precedence rules, widely available language extensions, risky dynamic memory allocation procedures, but for some the worst of all is the availability of a `goto` instruction! Serious technical problems can emerge when porting well-trusted C source code from one platform to another. The commercial compilers provided by different chip manufacturers are sometimes exasperatingly incompatible. The use of a single, well-tested compiler suite, such as GNU gcc, would resolve this problem.

15.27 Final advice

As the use of embedded microprocessors within life-critical systems becomes more and more widespread, so the concern for their correct deployment grows. Subtle, hidden bugs in engine management code, hospital equipment or avionics computers, could have extremely serious repercussions. On a less morbid scale, even bugs in desktop code can bring companies to the point of bankruptcy when clients react vindictively. Although this chapter focuses on tools, methods and processes, the single most significant factor by far in achieving a high quality, reliable product is the motivation and commitment of the development team. Whatever design process adopted, however secure in its checking procedures, if the users are only half interested in their work, it is unlikely that the final product will be a winner. So the first priority of management should be to assemble and retain an excellent development team. Maintaining the commitment and enthusiasm of all the members of this team can be quite a challenge. Often programmers expect to be treated somewhat differently to 'normal' office staff. They may demand to be given more freedom, arriving late, and then working on into the night to complete a project. The disruption and inconvenience of such behaviour has to be offset against the value of their contribution to a project's success. Smaller companies often cope better in this area than

Yesterday,
All those backups seemed a waste of pay.
Now my database has gone away.
Oh I believe in yesterday.

Suddenly,
There's not half the files the reused to be,
And there's a milestone hanging over me,
The system crashed so suddenly.

I pushed something wrong
What it was I could not say.

Now all my data's gone
and I long for yesterday-ay-ay-ay.

Yesterday,
The need for backups seemed so far away.
I knew my data was all here to stay,
Now I believe in yesterday.

Yesterday, by Colin and the Beatles. A useful reminder to take regular backups larger enterprises, perhaps because the managers cannot risk losing important staff. A team of prima-donna programmers can be worse than a bag of cats!

15.28 Chapter summary

This chapter has presented a very diverse set of ideas and advice relevant to the production of good quality software. Flaws in the initial phase, which lays down the system specification, can undermine the whole project. A good designer should always maintain a view of the intended target platform to ensure a successful implementation. Preliminary simulation studies can assist with determining likely performance parameters before any executable code becomes available. Source code should be thoroughly checked through peer review, public review, using compilers with full warnings enabled, and the application of syntax checkers such as lint. Run-time checking enables failed modules to be trapped and recovered. Most commercial projects employ some form of software management tools, such as make and CVS, to avoid the wasted time and embarrassment which results from confused software administration. But the most important factor which influences product quality is the motivation of the development team.

15.29 Problems and issues for discussion

1. Explain in your own words the following Petri net schema.

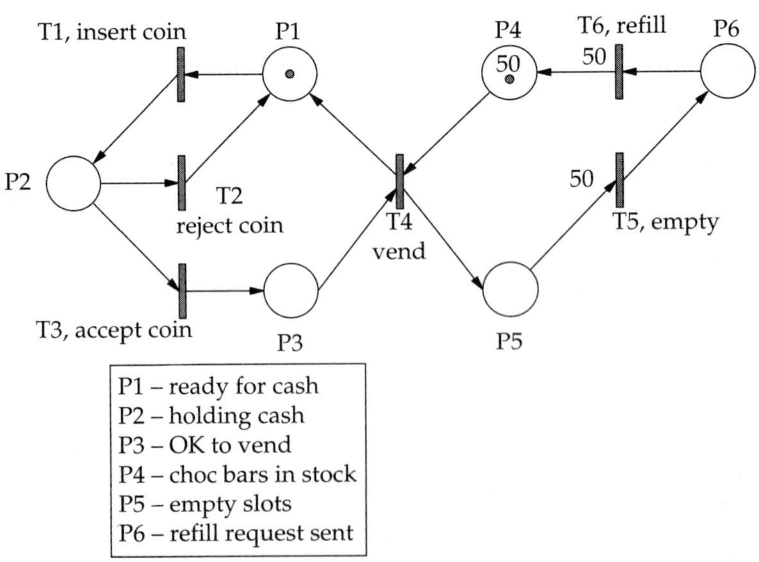

Provide a Petri net schema for a coffee vending machine which offers tea *or* coffee. Request refill servicing after 100 cups of tea or 200 cups of coffee. Do not vend if a selection has not been made on the front panel keypad.

2. Take your largest C program and recompile it with the compiler set to 'pedantic' mode, in order to get maximum checking and warning. Then seek out a usable version of Lint and see if it reveals anything more of interest about your code. You may like to pass the code for a large open source program through lint, and see how it performs!
3. Take one of your programs and scan through it by hand, from beginning to end, checking all the calls to library functions. Be sure to use the on-line help facilities to confirm your understanding of all the system function return values. This is especially important when opening files and reading an uncertain number of items from a channel. Will the code recover gracefully should any of these calls fail?
4. For a common exercise, swap code with a friend and individually devise a small change to the original specification which requires revision to the design. Discuss how well the two original design structures manage to incorporate the changes.
5. If, during a work placement or industrial internship, you have been involved in a project review meeting, compare its conduct with the advisory guidelines offered here on p. 333.
6. Inspect the criteria listed on p. 334. Have you ever worked for an organization which behaves better than Level 1?

15.30 Suggestions for Reading

Adams, D. (1979). *Hitchhiker's Guide to the Galaxy.* Tor Books.

Beck, K. (1999). *Extreme Programming Explained: Embracing Change.* Addison Wesley.

Dittrich, G. & Fehling, R. (1991). PetriLab: A Tool for Hierarchically Representing Nets.

Evans, D. (2003). *SPLINT Manual.* SPG, Dept CS, Univ. of Virginia.

Fagan, M. (1970). Design and code inspections to reduce errors in program development. *IBM Systems Journal*, 15(3), 181–211.

Hatton, L. (1994). *Developing Software for High-integrity and Safety-critical Systems.* McGraw-Hill.

IEE. Process maturity model of software. *IEEE Software*, 10(4), July 1993.

MISRA (1998). The MISRA guidelines for the use of the C language in vehicle based software.

Peterson, J. L. (1981). *Petri Net Theory and the Modelling of Systems.* Prentice Hall.

http://www.extremeprogramming.org, a gentle introduction to the method.
http://www.sei.cmu.edu, details about the Capability Maturity Model (CMM) assessment.
http://www.iso.org
http://archive.adaic.com/standards/mil-std-498
http://.cse.dcu.ie/essiscope/sm3/process/mil498.html
http://www.misra.org.uk

Chapter 16

Languages for RTS development – C, Ada and Java

16.1 Chapter overview

Over the years, there have been many programming languages developed for real-time applications. A set of criteria has emerged to compare their facilities and suitability for the role. With the central importance of compilers in the production of code, their performance must also be carefully assessed. There has been a change in the field of real-time systems from 'hard' embedded applications coded in Ada or C, to distributed, Internet-enabled products where Java may be more suitable.

16.2 The choice

Choosing a language suitable for real-time applications is complex and time consuming. In most circumstances, the implementation language adopted for your project is never really in question: you use what is available. Taking time to browse the shelves for a new language, or even a new compiler, is a rare luxury which few project teams can afford. Perhaps a less satisfactory recent development has been the growing domination of commercial suppliers, such as Microsoft and Sun, who effectively make decisions on our behalf by determining what compilers will be provided with their operating systems. The heroic activities of Richard Stallman and the GNU contributors can only go some way to mitigating this undesirable situation which increasingly reduces programmers' choice.

While designing and implementing a language suitable for real-time is not a project to be undertaken lightly, as can be confirmed by reading the historic articles concerning the birth of Ada, over the years several have appeared: RTL/2, CORAL66, CHILL, Modula/2, OCCAM, Esterel, realtime Euclid, Erlang and of course Ada. A variety of specialist requirements is demanded in addition to the normal HLL features which have evolved from the continuing general experience with assembler code, C/C++, C# and Java. The current favourite for embedded systems is undoubtedly C, which actually fails to

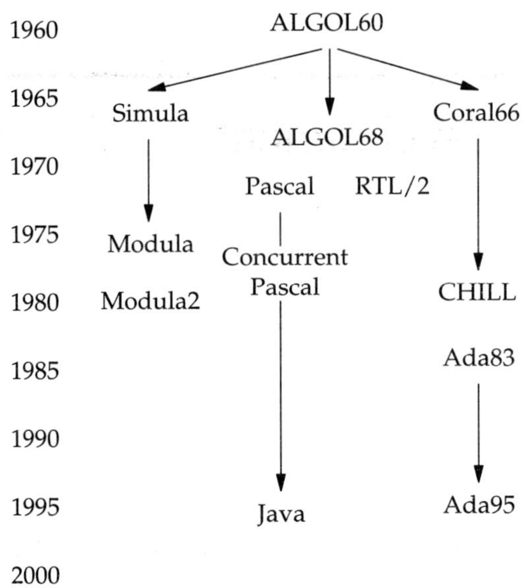

R-t languages

satisfy nearly all of the real-time wish list presented below. In its day, C was seen as a welcome step forward from hand polished assembler, where each instruction was carefully crafted to save a few bytes in program length. Its great success was making the dissemination and rapid porting of Unix a possibility. Later, the US Department of Defense (DOD) was influential in nudging the whole real-time industry with its sponsorship of Ada. But even now, there is widespread reluctance in some parts of industry to invest hard cash in new compilers and software tools.

In addition to the syntax verification and language translation that compilers offer, they also contribute the run-time support code and many extensive libraries stuffed with useful functions. So, when choosing a compiler all these aspects should be reviewed.

16.3 General criteria for programming languages

The primary determinant which influences language selection is, unsurprisingly, cost. This entails not only the initial purchase price and annual maintenance fee, but also the necessary investment in staff training, the

- **All the 'bilities**

General needs

upgrading of host computers, and subsequent enhanced salaries required to retain the newly skill-rich staff. Common to all commercially viable programming languages, there is a group of technical requirements which are expected whatever the application area. These may nonchalantly be referred to as the 'bilities, and are described next in further detail.

- *Readability* Software is a public asset not a private puzzle, and must be as easy to read and understand as possible. Poor documentation and opaque code multiplies debugging problems as well as maintenance costs. The high development cost of large software systems leads to an extended lifetime which will involve large numbers of secondary programmers who have no first-hand knowledge of the original design and implementation.
- *Flexibility* Perhaps surprisingly, software has emerged as a *conservative* influence on industry, due to the large development costs. So many products will get repeatedly modified to extend their useful life. Software designers and programmers must build-in flexibility to their systems to more easily support this maintenance phase. It is often only during the later phases of the product lifecycle that genuine *quality* can be assessed. On the other hand, programmers immediately want to express themselves in a manner that the language facilities rigorously deny. So some flexibility on the part of the programmer will also be required!
- *Portability* Compilers must be available on a wide range of operating systems and host machines to allow easy porting of application code. Accepted standards and APIs, such as POSIX and WIN32, help with this.
- *Understandability* Difficult language syntax will never achieve wide acceptance in spite of powerful abstract expressiveness. A lack of relevant skills within the project team can be the final deciding factor when selecting languages and tools. Complex languages can generate their own crop of errors beyond those contributed by careless programmers. Easy modularization of code provides an aid to both readability and design simplicity.
- *Reliability* Compilers clearly carry out code checks at compile-time using syntax and TYPE consistency rules, but they also may insert extra code to perform intermittant runtime checks as the program executes. Examples of this facility would be stack length inspection and maintaining array bounds constraints. However, such run-time checking and error trapping do incur speed and code size penalties which may be unacceptable for some applications. Slow compilers are more tolerable than slow target systems. The earlier the error is flagged in the development process the better. The distinction between the terms *reliability* and *integrity* may be usefully drawn when dealing with software systems which can be set to reconfigure themselves and recover when failures occur.

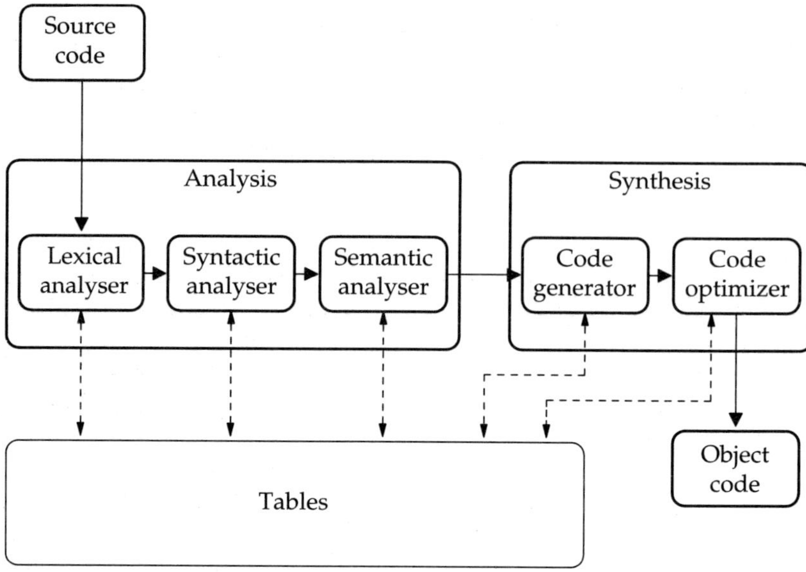

Components of a HLL compiler

- *Supportability* Most programmers hit a brick wall at some time, when a problem with the compiler seriously jeopardizes their progress. Then the benefit of having accessible telephone support or a friendly email guru really strikes home. When comparing different commercial compilers, it might be wise to try out the support facilities before making a final decision. A helpful support service can stop projects from stalling. More often now, with open source GNU compilers, web-based user discussion groups and FAQ sites provide the mutual help and support that programmers require.
- *Maturity* Well-used code is well-tested code. This is equally true for compilers as for application programs. If a new compiler has been acquired, there are likely to be undiscovered bugs waiting to be activated. Operating as a beta test site for your compiler supplier might not be convenient when you are hurtling towards your own deadlines.
- *Efficiency* With cheaper, faster processors the paramount importance of tight, fast code has diminished. Nevertheless, the generation of efficient code is still a significant criterion when choosing a HLL compiler. The maths library may not yet be using a group of faster machine instructions which are available on a newer version of the target CPU.

16.4 Special criteria for real-time compilers

Surprisingly, not all languages which claim a real-time pedigree offer real-time facilities. Neither Coral66 nor RTL/2 included ready-to-use tasking facilities.

Pascal, in its heyday, was also inexplicably promoted in the commercial press as a panacea for real-time systems development. Programmers would then have to use the tasking facilities from a host operating system or write all the task swapping routines themselves. The principal set of special real-time requirements for a HLL compiler are now outlined below and then discussed in further detail.

- Multi-tasking facilities
- Re-entrant code generated
- Initialization source code
- Run-time efficiency
- Interrupt handling
- Error recovery
- Predictable performance
- Hardware access
- Linker facilities
- Excellent debugger
- Specialist libraries

R-t compilers

- *Multi-tasking facilities* Processes need to be registered with the scheduler, started, stopped and deregistered. These facilities are normally supported by an underlying operating system but they may also be incorporated into the language run-time support code. This latter arrangement has the real advantage of giving the compiler the chance to expand its checking capability to encompass the tasking activities. The more compile-time checking, the better.

  Once a system undertakes multi-tasking, the need immediately arises for intertask communication and synchronization facilities, such as semaphores, pipes and signals. When tasks share data, it must be protected from inadvertent corruption.
- *Re-entrant code generated* Functions written with re-entrant code can be shared by many tasks because each task sets up its own set of variables within private stack and data segments. So all tasks possess data separate from the other tasks. Although the requirement for re-entrant code is now seen as essential for any decent compiler, there may still exist compilers and languages which do support this. In particular, when you are selecting a C compiler for a small microcontroller it is worth determining if the generated code is safely re-entrant. For pre-emptive multi-tasking environments, it would be impossible to run tasks using a shared library if the compiler generated non-re-entrant code.
- *Initialization* It is often very helpful for the programmer to have access to the source of run-time support code, as employed by the compiler for hardware and software initialization. This is especially significant when

multi-language developments are being undertaken, with the possibility of differing standards in parameter passing and stack frame structuring.

- *Run-time efficiency* The speed and efficiency of target code generated by the compiler is always of great interest to real-time programmers who frequently do not have the luxury of using the very latest multi-GHz microprocessor. For the recent generation of programmers, desktop PCs have offered so much spare processing capacity that the need to consider size and efficiency has somewhat dropped out of mind.
- *Interrupt handling facilities* Although there is still some support for the idea that all interrupt service routines should be tightly coded in assembler, many real-time HLL compilers can also generate code to handle external interrupts. The loss of run-time efficiency needs to be balanced against the likely gain in code maintainability.
- *Error recovery* Low-level errors can be dealt with through exception handling provided by the compiler and language library. It is very important to be able to recover gracefully from system failures.
- *Predictable run-times* A language which includes automatic garbage collection may help the novice programmer and eliminate memory leakage bugs, but it wipes out any attempt to estimate accurately run-time performance. The possibility of a bedside patient monitor occasionally taking a break to reclaim deallocated memory fragments is ludicrous. But other less obvious applications may also put vulnerable people at risk indirectly through unexpected interludes in their throughput.
- *Hardware access* Frequently, embedded real-time systems require direct access to hardware ports. However, general purpose operating systems, such as Linux or Windows, are built, for security reasons, to deny this kind of activity to application processes. So a Linux process needs to run with root permission to access a port directly. Real-time executives recognize this problem and, taking into account that normally all processes running on an embedded system are owned by the same user, relax the security constraints. Otherwise programmers would have to develop and install a standardized device driver for every new hardware port, demanding more effort and resulting in poorer run-time performance.
- *Linker facilities* Retaining the atmosphere of a software backwater, the development and consideration of linker tools has only ever come a poor second to compilers and assemblers. But this neglect can be very misleading. The most tricky error messages often come from a confused linker. With embedded real-time systems, linkers need the ability to cross link for a non-host environment, combining object modules, libraries, and assembler-coded modules. When considering the provision of library code, real-time systems often use static linking rather than the dynamic alternative. This removes the need to hold the complete dynamic library on backing store just in case some function is called. The smaller penalty of having to load multiple copies of some library functions with each task may not be unacceptable.

- *Debuggers* Most valued by a desperate programmer is the source-level debugger. This can quickly reveal logical errors by tracking the executing code and offering convenient facilities to detect and diagnose run-time bugs. Break points may be temporarily inserted to halt the program at a critical point, or variables can be scanned for target values. If a trace facility is available, the program can be run full speed into a crash, and the immediately preceding events revealed from the contents of the trace memory, much like an in-flight, black-box recorder. On Linux, gdb only offers a command-line interface for the debugger, but this can be supplemented by a GUI such as gvd, DDD or kdbg running on KDE.
- *Specialist libraries available* Often special requirements in numeric processing or graphic displays are required to support some aspect of the system.

16.5 Compiler optimization

HLL compilers use a variety of techniques to improve the performance of the generated code. Sometimes these techniques do not suit real-time applications. With invisible interrupt routines accessing variables concurrently, seemingly redundant instructions can be 'optimized' out. This painful situation has been dealt with through the introduction of the `volatile` qualifier into the newer ANSI C language, but real-time programmers have to remain vigilant for subtle compiler tricks which may disrupt the intended workings of their code. It is important to realize that during the debugging phase a compiler may generate significantly different code from the final, release version. This can be due to the inclusion of extra TRAP instructions, the disabling of the code cache, the cancellation of compiler optimizations, or the use by the linker of special libraries for operation with the debugger. All these can seriously alter run-time performance.

Speed and dependability

Most compilers offer a straightforward command-line option to minimize code size or to maximize the speed of execution, seemingly contradictory alternatives. But this choice has to be treated with some caution. Now that CPUs are equipped with large on-chip code caches, the performance is often closely related to the number of cache miss penalties that occur, rather than the number of instructions executed. So *small* code, which fits nicely into cache, is also *fast* code. Longer code, which has had its functions rolled out as in-line macros, in an attempt to speed up execution, may deliver more time wasting cache misses and so execute more slowly. Does the compiler take into account whether the functions being called are widely referenced from other modules, too?

Some of the more common compiler optimization techniques are as follows:

- *Elimination of ineffectual code* The recognition that multiplication by 1, addition of 0, or redundant, repeated assignments are not contributing to the calculation, and so can usually be safely deleted.
- *Reduction in arithmetic strength* In an attempt to speed up the code, alternative machine instructions may be substituted, such as left shift instead of integer multiplication and right shift in place of integer division. This only works directly for powers of two, but may be topped up with a couple of subtractions or additions to complete the required arithmetic operation. So a $\times 10$ could be achieved by three left shifts and a couple of additions. When inspecting code such changes can lead to some confusion.
- *Identification of common subexpressions* Repeated groups of operations may be identified as suitable for a discrete expression and reused subsequently. This may introduce new variables.
- *Substitution of in-line macros for functions* In-line code could run faster because all the `call/ret` and stack frame instructions are eliminated. But refer above to the cautionary discussion concerning the role of the CPU code cache in this argument.
- *Compile time arithmetic* When the arithmetic takes place on constant values, it may be conducted at compile-time rather than at run-time, reducing the execution load.
- *Removal of loop invariants* If an operation is being carried out within a loop, every opportunity is made to reduce the number of repeated instructions to a minimum. This can be done by identifying constant subexpressions and pre-evaluating them. Also, if there is more than one loop terminating condition, there may be a possibility of eliminating the extra conditions. A common example is the insertion of a false target item as a *terminating sentinal* at the end of an array which is to be searched. Now the search loop only has to check for the item, rather than the final index value as well, on each iteration.
- *Use of loop index variable* More use may be made of the loop index variable (i) when coding loop algorithms. This can be illustrated by the

addition of the loop index to an array base pointer to more efficiently access elements within the array.

- *Registers and caches* Repeatedly accessed variables should be stored in CPU registers for fast referencing. Similarly, algorithms can be written so that variables may be pre-loaded and retained in data cache to reduce access times. Probably, all local variables in scope on the stack will automatically be copied into data cache and require no special arrangements.
- *Unused instructions* Compilers are quick to detect and remove unused code such as abandoned debug statements.
- *Optimization of flow-of-control* Rationalization of complex IF-ELSE spaghetti, or the concatenation of jmp strings can be achieved by some compilers.
- *Constant propagation* Initialization code can be rationalized, with the precalculation of constant expressions.
- *Redundant store elimination* Interim, temporary variables, which were included in a data manipulation, may be removed by a rearrangement of code.
- *Dead-variable elimination* Identification of unaccessable variables which can safely be deleted from the program.
- *Boolean expressions* Simplification of complex Boolean formula to speed up evaluation.
- *Loop unrolling* Short loops may be converted to in-line sequential code with the consequent elimination of terminating tests and conditional branch instructions.
- *Loop amalgamation* Two or more loops can be combined into a single longer loop.
- *Reduction of conditional switches* In SWITCH statements, it is occasionally possible to combine several CASE arms and eliminate some conditional checks.

The gcc command-line options for alternative optimizations are:

```
-falign-functions=n -falign-jumps=n -falign-labels=n
-falign-loops=n -fbranch-probabilities -fcaller-saves
-fcprop-registers -fcse-follow-jumps -fcse-skip-blocks
-fdata-sections -fdelayed-branch -fdelete-null-pointer-checks
-fexpensive-optimizations -ffast-math -ffloat-store -fforce-addr
-fforce-mem -ffunction-sections -fgcse -fgcse-lm -fgcse-sm
-floop-optimize -fcrossjumping -fif-conversion -fif-conversion2
-finline-functions -finline-limit=n -fkeep-inline-functions
-fkeep-static-consts -fmerge-constants -fmerge-all-constants
-fmove-all-movables -fnew-ra -fno-branch-count-reg
-fno-default-inline -fno-defer-pop -fno-function-cse
-fno-guess-branch-probability -fno-inline -fno-math-errno
-fno-peephole -fno-peephole2 -funsafe-math-optimizations
-ffinite-math-only -fno-trapping-math -fno-zero-initialized-in-bss
-fomit-frame-pointer -foptimize-register-move -foptimize-sibling-calls
```

```
-fprefetch-loop-arrays -freduce-all-givs -fregmove
-frename-registers -freorder-blocks -freorder-functions
-frerun-cse-after-loop -frerun-loop-opt -fschedule-insns
-fschedule-insns2 -fno-sched-interblock -fno-sched-spec
-fsched-spec-load -fsched-spec-load-dangerous -fsignaling-nans
-fsingle-precision-constant -fssa -fssa-ccp -fssa-dce
-fstrength-reduce -fstrict-aliasing -ftracer -fthread-jumps
-funroll-all-loops -funroll-loops --param name=value
-O -O0 -O1 -O2 -O3 -Os
```

And that does not include the group of linker options!

16.6 C for real-time

Comparisons between anything as complex and flexible as programming languages is fraught with difficulties. In 1978 Brian Kernighan and Dennis Ritchie introduced the C language in the preface to their definitive text in this way:

> C is a general-purpose programming language which features economy of expression, modern control flow and data structures, and a rich set of operators. C is not a *very high level* language, nor a *big* one, and is not specialized to any particular area of application. But its absence of restrictions and its generality make it more convenient and effective for many tasks than supposedly more powerful languages.
>
> Kernighan & Ritchie 2002

While some developers still judge C as an ideal, elegant language, others view it with suspicion, considering that it should have been abandoned long ago. It lacks object-oriented features, strong typing, tasking support, exception handling, pointer protection, array bounds checking and dynamic string types. It offers a syntax which is algebraic in its cryptic minimalism, allowing programmers readily to write correct code that nobody else can fathom. But despite its limitations, or because of them, it offers programmers the freedom to code what they want, in the way they want to. When evaluating C for a project, it is reassuring that Unix and many other operating systems are implemented in C. Also, when a new microprocessor is launched, the first compiler to be provided is always for C. It can monitor input port bits,

The C language from Kernighan & Ritchie

and talk to corporate Oracle databases. Dennis Ritchie has given us an adult language that expects the programmer to use it correctly. The popular gcc compiler suite is available for Linux and Windows, with output code configurable for a wide range of CPUs, making it ideal for embedded system cross-development.

16.7 Ada

During the 1970s, the US Department of Defense ran an extended international competition to select a new HLL language which would satisfy their burgeoning requirements in the real-time embedded systems field. The rate of failure of large software projects had been a source of alarm within the DOD, and a reduction in the diversity of programming languages was the hoped for panacea. In the event, the winning team was led by Jean Ichbiah from Honeywell/Bull in France, and the final outcome was Ada. Ada is a large, strictly typed language with the ability to express object-oriented designs (Barnes 1989). Superficially it looks like Pascal, but has many extra facilities: exception and interrupt handling, packages, intrinsic tasking and rendezvous primitives. Ada compilers are required to be officially validated against an extended test suite before they can be sold under the name. Although Ada programs tend to be large, and normally execute with full operating system support, it is fairly easy to link in a board support package, or HAL, and run the code directly on bare hardware. Ada certainly attracts enthusiastic followers who admire its vision of structure and order. Unfortunately, partly due to the cost of compilers, it has not been adopted by the non-military sector, and has even been somewhat abandoned by its initial sponsors. Its original tasking model was the target of much criticism, and was modified for the release of the enhanced Ada85. Ada offers good exception handling capabilities and an extensive package of timing facilities.

Countess Ada Lovelace (1815–1852)

16.8 Java

The Java programming language was developed, during the early 1990s, by a team led by James Gosling at Sun Microsystems. Initially the intention was for a new language, then called Oak, to be suitable for downloading into embedded systems, such as domestic and consumer equipment. There were a number of significant problems involved with this application area which made C/C++ unsuitable, and Basic was considered not reliable enough. What emerged was Java, which uses partial compilation into an intermediate byte code language, which then needs a run-time interpreter for execution. Like Ada, it offers intrinsic support for concurrency, unlike C and C++ which have to make direct calls in the underlying operating system to achieve the same thing. Clearly, the Java interpreter (JVM) has to use operating system facilities, it is not running on bare hardware, but the issues of *localizing* the software to fit into the hosting hardware and operating system have been delegated to the JVM, reducing the application programmers' workload. Java has now become a major object-oriented programming language in education and commerce. There was great enthusiasm for its features, such as: object orientation, dynamic loading, platform independence and a secure execution environment. Although the application target of the proposal has been altered by commercial circumstances, the language itself remains true to the original vision, with web page animation and interactive websites becoming the main focus for Java developers. When version 2.0 of the Netscape browser was released with an integral Java interpreter, the value of the technical vision and its future popularity for Internet programming was assured.

Fresh brewed Java

Despite its original role for the development of small embedded systems, the language confronts real-time programmers with some negative as well as positive characteristics. It is definitely object oriented, supports multi-threading, handles exceptions, but runs on an interpreter, carries out automatic, uncontrollable memory retrieval operations (garbage collection) in the background, and originally tried to deny all access to the local hardware. The latter group of features would seem to be clear evidence for dismissing it from all consideration as a real-time language. On the other hand, it has tightened up on C laxities with type checking, imposing tougher compile-time checking, and eliminating explicit pointer operations, which have always been acknowledged as the primary source of many run-time errors in C and C++. Perhaps inconsistently, it provides strong exception trapping and handling, but does not offer asynchronous signals.

Nevertheless, over recent years, there have been changes to the Java programming environment to better suit real-time applications by improving the multi-threading capability and the ability to access local hardware. To initiate multiple threads, the fundamental `Thread` class can be subclassed with the `extends` directive, with each such class providing a `run` method. The Java thread capability is well suited for the implementation of active objects.

```
public class MyThread extends Thread {
   public

 run()  {
            while (true) {
                                  // insert my thread code loop here
            }
   }
}

public class YourThread extends Thread {
   public void run() {
            while (true) {
                                 // insert your thread code loop here
            }
   }
}

public class TestThreads {
   public static void main( String args[]) {

      MyThread thread_1 = new MyThread();    // create a new
                                             // thread object
      MyThread thread_2 = new YourThread(); // create a different
                                             // thread object
      thread_1.start();                      // and run by calling
                                             // start
      thread_2.start();
   }
}
```

Note that although the thread code is contained in the `run()` method, to actually get it running, the `start()` method has to be evoked. Threads, like tasks, will introduce the scheduling problems of deadlock and starvation, as well as the danger of critical data corruption. This is dealt with using the facilities offered by Java `synchronized()` methods.

Thread priority assignments are fixed, but with pre-emptive capability whose behaviour unfortunately depends on the execution platform. Priority inversion is prevented by the use of priority inheritance, whereby the priority of the lower-level thread is promoted to that of the blocked higher-level task, to speed up the release of the critical resource. The real-time thread classes offer a large number of new methods that can be used to tune the threads and control their scheduling pattern. So there is a choice of periodic or aperiodic thread activation.

As already stated, Java programs are pre-compiled into intermediate byte code, and then offered to the Java Virtual Machine (JVM) interpreter for execution. This does lead to some loss of performance when compared to a fully compiled language but with newer, more efficient compilers and faster processors, this problem has diminished in significance. In addition, so called Just-In-Time (JIT) compilers are available which take the intermediate Java byte code and, during the first execution, build machine code executable segments which can then be used subsequently to speed things up. Java continues to benefit from very active development resulting in growing class libraries which are often made available free on the Internet for downloading. The newer Embedded Java has been installed onto cellular telephone handsets and games consoles, indicating its success in a variety of distinct application areas.

A major concern with the Java language has always been security. As we are all too well aware, downloading executable code, even something as modest as a Word macro, can have devastating effects worldwide. So a primary requirement was to ringfence all untrusted 'foreign' code, and protect the local host from malicious or accidental interference. In particular the physical resources are hidden as far as possible from direct access by Java applets.

The intention was always to present the JVM as a universal 'virtual machine', identical to all, regardless of the actual hosting computer and operating system. This is possible because the source code for JVM is written in C, and so readily ported to new architectures when they emerge onto the market. The compiler itself is held as a Java program, so can immediately follow the JVM as it starts up on a new machine.

Perhaps the most notorious issue for real-time programmers is the autonomous garbage collector that has the responsibility for finding and reclaiming dynamically allocated space on the heap after it has been finished with. This activity can pre-empt applications at any moment and run for unpredictable periods. But the recent real-time extensions to the Java

	C	*Ada*	*Java*
Cost	free/commodity price	expensive	free/commodity
Readability	programmer dependent notoriously cryptic	good, Pascal-like OOP style possible	C-like OOP style normal
Flexibility	free style	constrained	constrained
Portability	generally very easy, compilers available, bare-board or hosted	few compilers, few BSPs available, usually hosted	first needs JVM ported, then easy, needs native classes to access local h/w
Understandability	limited syntax expression	modular structure OOP possible	modular structure OOP normal
Reliability	questionable, programmer dependent	exception handling, certified compilers	exception handling
Supportability	good	good	good
Maturity	well established ANSI/ISO	well established ANSI/MIL-STD/ISO	still evolving
Efficiency	fast compiled code	fast compiled code	slower interpeted
Multi-tasking scheduling	programmed with o/s or cyclic executive	built-in tasking facilities	multi-threading
Multi-tasking protection	none	compile-time checking	none
Hardware access	normally	possible	deprecated
Interrupt handling	possible with direct h/w access	built-in facilities	none
Safety critical use	doubtful	yes	no
Linker facility for foreign modules	yes	yes	by DLL provision
Init source code available	usually	sometimes	never
asm inserts	yes	yes	no

language include two new subclasses to `Thread`: `RealtimeThread` and `NoHeap RealtimeThread`. Thread instances of the `NoHeapRealtime Thread` subclass have higher priority than the garbage collector, allowing for more accurate and reliable scheduling schemes.

Access to time values in the millisec range are obtainable through the `Date` class, and `wait()`, `sleep()` and `join()` are also supported within Java, but with some uncertainty surrounding the exact periods of time which actually result.

16.9 Cross-compilers

When working with embedded systems, if the target is incapable of supporting its own software development, because it has no storage devices attached or the processor is really too feeble to cope with X-windows, emacs and gcc, the need arises to prepare a suitable host to handle cross-compilation. This often means configuring a second version of gcc to run on the host computer, but which produces native code for the *target* CPU, not the (Pentium) host. A cross-assembler and cross-linker will also be required. So, if the target system sports a StrongArm microcontroller, the cross-compiler needs to generate machine code for the ARM CPU. In addition to gcc-ARM, in place of gcc-386, a matching version of the support library glibc-ARM, or an equivalent such as μClibc, must be created to work on the target board.

There are several important differences between the principal support libraries, μClibc and glibc, which need to be recognized when choosing which one to employ. Because μClibc is smaller, it does not offer all the facilities of the glibc, but for embedded applications this may not be a problem. The subject of cross-compilation will be returned to in Chapter 17. When building cross-compilers it is useful to distinguish three platforms: the *build* machine on which the cross-compiler suite is being developed; the *host* machine on which the cross-compiler will be used; and the *target* machine which will execute the code generated by the cross-compiler. Often the first two, build and host, are the same machine, but they do not have to be.

16.10 Chapter summary

The many different programming languages which have been developed for real-time applications all have particular advantages and disadvantages. But a clear set of criteria has emerged to allow the comparison of their facilities and performance. Modern compilers are mostly offer high quality in the production of code, but overall their suitability must still be carefully appraised. In the field of real-time systems, there has been a shift from small, embedded applications often coded in C, towards large, distributed, network-connected products, often accessing large central databases. After a torrid flirtation with Ada, the attention of fashion-conscious developers has now switched to Java, especially where soft real-time systems are concerned.

16.11 Problems and issues for discussion

1. As C is so deficient in all the characteristics expected of a real-time language, why has it remained so popular for so long?
2. Compare the work required to port a JVM onto a new microprocessor board, with that of preparing a C cross-compiler for the same target. How would you recompile the JVM?

3. Check out the optimization controls offered by your current compiler.
4. List and explain the advantages and disadvantages of using an interpreted language, such as Basic or Java, for a real-time monitoring and control application.
5. Seek out information on the programming language called Forth, which was strongly supported, at one time, for real-time applications. Assess its current suitability for small embedded systems developments.

16.12 Suggestions for reading

Barnes, J. (1989). *Programming in ADA.* Addison Wesley.

Hill, A. (1991). The choice of programming language for highly reliable software, a comparison of C and ADA. *ADA User*, 12, 11–31.

Hoare, C. (1988). *The OCCAM2 Reference Manual.* Prentice Hall.

Kernighan, B. & Ritchie, D. (2002). *The C Programming Language.* Prentice Hall.

Shaw, A. (2001). *Real-time Systems and Software.* Wiley.

Smedema, C., Medema, P. & Boasson, M. (1983). *The Programming Languages: Pascal, Modula, CHILL, Ada.* Prentice Hall.

Stallman, R. (2000). *Using and Porting GNU CC.* Free Software Foundation.

Young, S. (1982). *Real Time Languages: Design and Development.* Ellis Horwood.

http://www.rtj.org, the real-time specification for Java.

http://cpan.cybercomm.nl/pub/linux/libs/uclibc/Glibc_vs_uClibc_Differences.text

http://www.forth.org, and forth.com, central sites for information about the Forth language.

Chapter 17

Cross-development techniques

17.1 Chapter overview

Cross-development means that the software development activity is largely carried out on a separate host system, before installing the code onto the target system for delivery. Such an arrangement requires a separate 'cross-compiler' to be used, with different header files and libraries to suit the target processor and run-time support environment. Carrying out debugging with the limited facilities offered by most Single Board Computers (SBCs), which are often used for embedded applications, can be difficult. The JTAG boundary scan test facility is now being used to download code into memories, configure FPGAs and debug running code.

17.2 Host–target development

Many real-time systems employ microprocessors or microcontrollers intimately bound into dedicated equipment. Such systems are now termed *embedded* and require a special approach to software development. This is mainly because the target platform is not often capable of supporting the

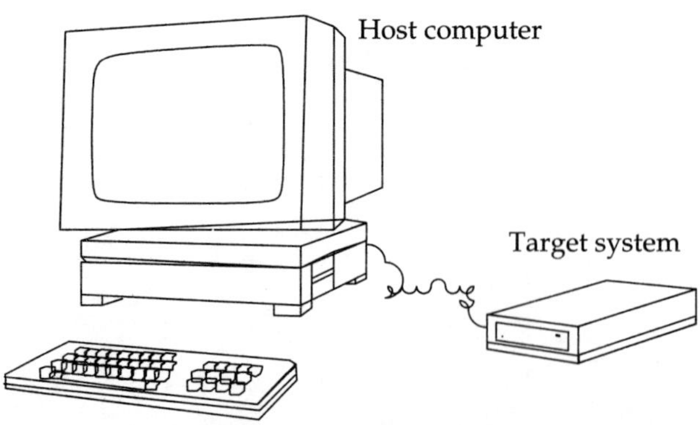

Host–target development

editors, compilers, linkers and code control tools essential for the development task. So a second, larger computer is used for the actual code production. This is the *host* platform and is commonly a desktop PC running Windows or a version of Unix. In this way all the hardware and software facilities of a larger computer system can be utilized during the development cycle. Only the production code actually executes on the small target processor. If the selected target system has a different CPU to that in the host computer, a very likely circumstance, it can be somewhat confusing to produce and store executable files on the host computer that cannot be executed by the host CPU. Additional problems occur with the need for *cross-compilers* and associated target libraries. The host file system has to be carefully organized so as to keep the native and cross-compilers and libraries well apart.

The necessary interconnection between the two systems, for downloading executable files and controlling the target system during debugging, can be a slow serial cable, a fast Ethernet channel, or a specialized JTAG or BDM link. These latter two are described in more detail later in this chapter under the section on debugging.

17.3 Cross-compilers and linkers

Often newcomers to real-time systems are surprised when confronted with their first embedded project to discover the complexity of the routine operations: compiling, linking, locating and loading. Desktop PCs have been around for so long, their sophisticated Integrated Development Environments (IDE) now successfully hide the actual operations of the compiler suite behind pre-initialized GUI screens. Which libraries are linked to the produced object modules, and what format is used by them, can be completely unknown, until something falls over, and questions have to be answered.

The main sources for cross-compilers and linkers are Kiel, IAR and GNU. The first two are well-respected commercial suppliers, and the latter is Richard Stallman's organization for the development of open source software. There is a clear advantage to using the GNU gcc/g++ compiler suite because of the availability of all the source code, and the worldwide community of expert users. Many gcc cross-compilers have already been built for the more common host–target combinations, and made available on the web for general usage.

For the gcc compiler suite, the quite impressive list of recognized CPU names are:

> 1750a, a29k, alpha, arm, avr, cn, clipper, dsp16xx, elxsi, fr30, h8300, hppa1.0, hppa1.1, i370, i386, i486, i586, i686, i786, i860, i960, m32r, m68000, m68k, m6811, m6812, m88k, mcore, mips, mipsel, mips64, mips64el, mn10200, mn10300, ns32k, pdp11, powerpc, powerpcle, romp, rs6000, sh, sparc, sparclite, sparc64, v850, vax, we32k.

While the recognized target operating systems are:

> 386bsd, aix, acis, amigados, aos, aux, bosx, bsd, clix, ctix, cxux, dgux, dynix, ebmon, esix, freebsd, hms, genix, gnu, linux, linux-gnu, hiux, hpux, iris, irix, isc, luna, lynxos, mach, minix, msdos, mvs, netbsd, newsos, nindy, ns, osf, osfrose, ptx, qnx, riscos, rtu, sco, sim, solaris, sunos, sym, sysv, udi, ultrix, unicos, uniplus, unos, vms, vsta, vxworks, winnt, xenix.

These lists were obtained from the document 'Using and porting the GNU Compiler Collection (GCC)'. If, however, a completely new target CPU has been selected, the gcc compiler can be configured for use by setting up the machine architecture definition files: target.h, target.c and target.md. But this has generally been carried out by the hardware supplier. How else could they reasonably claim to have tested their product?

In general, there are two major aspects to be organized: the configuration of a GNU gcc compiler with an associated binutils package, and the provision of header and library files tailored to the needs of the target system. If the target is a bare board, several basic initialization and device driver routines will also have to be prepared before the compiled code can finally be linked and downloaded to run. Indeed, if the new hardware is truely *bare*, the practical problem of how to load boot code onto the system will have to be solved. If the target is to run Linux, there will be a couple of target libraries to choose from, the main ones being: glibc, μClib and newlib. The latter, newlib, originated with Cygnus, and was intended specifically for use on embedded systems.

17.4 The gcc compilation process

Gcc by itself only compiles the C or C++ code into assembler. Normally gcc assumes responsibility for invoking all the passes required for a complete build. These are: cpp, cc1, gas, and ld. Where cpp is the C preprocessor, which merges all the required include files, expands all macro definitions, and processes all the #ifdef conditional sections. To see the output of ccp, invoke gcc with the -E option, and the preprocessed file will be displayed. The actual compiler is cc1, which produces assembler code from the preprocessed source file. In fact, gcc is really only a driver program to evoke all the compiler passes. Although it is seen as a compiler command line, gcc will deal with command-line options intended for any of the other passes. The

gcc
GNU

The GNU compiler suite

usual gcc command line will ask ld to link in the necessary startup code and additional libraries by default.

GNU `gas` started its life as a single phase within the compiling operation, but now it can also be used as a stand-alone, source-level assembler. When used as a source-level assembler, it has a companion assembler preprocessor called gasp. This has a syntax similar to most other assembler macro packages. Gas generates a relocatable object file from the assembler source.

The linker, `ld`, is responsible for resolving the values of logical symbols and addresses, swapping numbers for the symbols, by using the symbol table. Some RTEs use relocatable object file formats like a.out, but more commonly the final image for small embedded systems will only be provided with absolute physical addresses. This enables the code to be burned directly into PROM or Flash. To produce an executable image, `ld` inserts a startup object file called crt0.o. This startup code usually defines a special symbol like _start that is the default entry address for the application, and the first symbol in the executable image. For target systems which run without operating system or RTE, before the application can use functions from the standard C library, the library code needs to be ported to the particular hardware involved.

There are several important differences between the alternative libraries: newlib, μClibc and glibc, which need to be recognized when choosing which one to employ. Because μClibc is smaller, it does not offer all the facilities of the glibc, but for embedded applications this may not be a problem. Newlib is more readily ported to new hardware, because it has been planned with a clearly defined interface comprising 17 stub functions, below which there is needed a HAL. By coding a new HAL, newlib can then be used in a 'bare-board' situation, but it can also be used in a Linux environment if the correct system function calls are used.

Option	Description
-nostartfiles	no default startup files
-nostdlib	no default libraries
-Xlinker option -Xlinker param	pass the option and parameter directly to the linker
-Wl, option param	pass the option and parameter directly to the linker
-v	verbose display
-fpic	generate position-independent code

Useful gcc options for embedded systems developers

Most of the gcc options of interest for embedded systems developers can be offered to the gcc compiler driver for passing onto the gas assembler and the ld linker.

17.5 Startup code

A program written in C and compiled with gcc will need a startup routine to run first. This preliminary code is called crt0 (C Run-time) and may require some modification according to the target environment that is to be used. Startup code is usually written in assembler, and it has to be linked to run first and thus set up the basic facilities for the rest of the application. A template source file crt0.S is usually provided to assist with the development of bespoke versions for particular target systems. So, returning to the gcc cross-compilation example, the newlib library comes with a whole group of architecture-dependent crt0.S files in the ${PREFIX}/newlib-1.12.0/newlib/libc/sys/directory. Here is one of the few opportunities that a programmer has to indulge in assembler-level coding, albeit only a dozen lines of code! The startup code needs to do the following things:

- Initialize anything that still needs to be initialized. This varies from system to system. If the application gets downloaded using a ROM monitor, then there is usually no need for any hardware initialization. The ROM monitor probably handles it for you. If the plan is to burn the code into a ROM, then the crt0 typically has to do all the hardware initialization required to run the application. This can include initializing the stack and heap, as well as serial port hardware and the memory management unit.
- The .bss section for uninitialized data can be cleared to zero. In this case, all the pointer variables in this section will also be set to zero, so that programs that forget to check variables' initial values may get unpredictable results.
- Initial values have to be copied into the .data variables from the .text section where they have been parked for downloading and storage.
- If the ROM monitor supports it, the `argc` and `argv[]` command-line arguments will be picked up along with an environment pointer. For embedded systems, this code can often be deleted as unnecessary.
- At the end of crt0, it must transfer control onto the `main()` function. This is basically what starts the application running. For C++, the main routine gets a branch to __main inserted by the code generator at the very beginning because __main() is used by g++ to initialize its internal tables. `__main()` then return to the original `main()`.

Startup arrangements

- After main() has completed, there needs to be a clean-up operation, and relinquishment of control of any allocated hardware resources. Sometimes the best thing to do in this case is to force a hardware reset, or branch back to the start address all over again. When a ROM monitor is present, a user trap can be called and then the ROM monitor retrieves control.

The options set for a gcc compiler can be inspected by using the -v flag option, as presented below. Note the startup and shutdown files inserted by the linker, highlighted in bold.

```
rts-rob@kenny> gcc -v world.c
Reading specs from /usr/lib/gcc-lib/i386-linux/3.3/specs
Configured with: ../src/configure -v --enable-languages=c,c++,
     java,f77,pascal,objc,ada,treelang
--prefix=/usr
--mandir=/usr/share/man
--infodir=/usr/share/info
--with-gxx-include-dir=/usr/include/c++/3.3
--enable-shared
--with-system-zlib
--enable-nls
--without-included-gettext
--enable-__cxa_atexit
--enable-clocale=gnu
--enable-debug
--enable-java-gc=boehm
--enable-java-awt=xlib
--enable-objc-gc i386-linux
Thread model: posix
gcc version 3.3 (Debian)
 /usr/lib/gcc-lib/i386-linux/3.3/cc1 -quiet -v -D__GNUC__=3
  -D__GNUC_MINOR__=3-D__GNUC_PATCHLEVEL__=0 world.c -quiet
  -dumpbase world.c -auxbase world -version -o /tmp/cclRrmoi.s
GNU C version 3.3 (Debian) (i386-linux)
         compiled by GNU C version 3.3 (Debian).
GGC heuristics: --param ggc-min-expand=100 --param ggc-min
     -heapsize=131072
ignoring nonexistent directory "/usr/i386-linux/include"
#include "..." search starts here:
#include <...> search starts here:
 /usr/local/include
 /usr/lib/gcc-lib/i386-linux/3.3/include
 /usr/include
End of search list.
 as -V -Qy -o /tmp/ccv94vCj.o /tmp/cclRrmoi.s
GNU assembler version 2.13.90.0.18 (i386-linux)
using BFD version 2.13.90.0.18 20030121 Debian GNU/Linux
/usr/lib/gcc-lib/i386-linux/3.3/collect2 --eh-frame-hdr
     -m elf_i386 -dynamic-linker
```

```
/lib/ld-linux.so.2
/usr/lib/gcc-lib/i386-linux/3.3/../../../crt1.o
/usr/lib/gcc-lib/i386-linux/3.3/../../../crti.o
/usr/lib/gcc-lib/i386-linux/3.3/crtbegin.o
-L/usr/lib/gcc-lib/i386-linux/3.3
-L/usr/lib/gcc-lib/i386-linux/3.3/../../..
/tmp/ccv94vCj.o
-lgcc -lgcc_eh -lc -lgcc -lgcc_eh
/usr/lib/gcc-lib/i386-linux/3.3/crtend.o
/usr/lib/gcc-lib/i386-linux/3.3/../../../crtn.o
rts-rob@kenny>
```

Notice that the position where you might expect the linker ld to be evoked is occupied by **collect2**. This is used on nearly all systems to call various initialization functions at run-time. Collect2 operates by first linking the program and checking the output file for symbols with certain names indicating they are C++ constructor/destructor functions. If collect2 finds any, it creates a temporary file containing a table which it then compiles and links by carrying out a second linker pass.

The actual calls to the constructors are carried out by a subroutine called __main, which is called (automatically) at the beginning of the body of main (provided main was compiled with gcc). Calling __main is necessary, even when compiling C code, to allow linking C and C++ object code together. Collect2 has to call ld itself to carry out the linking activity.

17.6 GNU linker, ld and linker script file

GNU's linker, `ld`, offers a very wide range of options and facilities, `man ld` reveals nearly 25 pages of Unix style cryptic flag option summaries to whet your appetite. An important role for the linker is to resolve any external references which remain outstanding, or unsatisfied, from the application code. The linker uses the `-L/-l` command-line flags to locate library files. For static linking, this means searching through designated library files for the outstanding labels, and extracting the associated function code. If dynamic, shared libraries are to be used, the linker extracts only short stub code which will then be used to make the run-time requests to the operating system to gain access to the DLL module. Effectively this introduces a secondary linking activity, when the operating system has to discover where the called-for shared library modules are stored on disk. This is done through the LD_LIBRARY_PATH environment variable, or paths stored in the `/etc/ld.so.conf` file. But if this file is changed, the `/etc/ld.so.cache` file needs to be updated by running the `/sbin/ldconfig` program. For embedded systems, it may be preferable to force the use of static library code, which can be done using the gcc `-static` flag.

The ld user can become very confused by the wide range of command-line options, and Gatliff (2001a) helpfully recommends some basic selections.

Although generally used only to produce executable programs for desktop PCs, ld can also act as a *cross-linker* in the production of embedded systems software for a range of different CPUs. It is evoked by default when the command `gcc` has finished compiling all the source files entered on the command line. So the well-known C language initiation command, `gcc hello.c`, after bringing in header source files, such as `stdio.h`, and compiling the C source code, evokes the `ld` linker to insert the `crt0.o` initialization code, and link in stub functions to access dynamic, shared libraries, such as `libc.so`, before finally generating the default executable `a.out`. It is possible to take over explicit command for separate compile and link phases:

```
> gcc -c hello.c
> ld /lib/crt0.o hello.o -lc -o hello
>
```

To direct the way the linker does its job, a *linker command file* is produced with instructions as to the placement of the final module in main memory, the execution entry point, the type of memory required for each segment and the anticipated usage demands. It is customary to use `.lds` as a file name extension for linker scripts, but this is not enforced. The ld linker accepts the name of a linker command file using the `-T script-file` command-line option. However, if ld is being invoked indirectly by gcc, the command-line option has to be written: `gcc hello.c -Wl,-T script-file -o hello`. The alternative gcc `-Xlinker` flag, which also passes commands straight through to the linker, would require the longer configuration: `-Xlinker -T -Xlinker script-file`, to handle the two parts of the linker instruction.

Understanding linker scripts remains one of the extra activities which embedded developers have to undertake. For desktop programmers, the linker remains hidden because its parameters rarely have to be changed from the default setup. This is not the case for real-time, embedded applications, where memory type and size is routinely changed in mid-project, several times.

Here is a linker script that can be used to produce code for a target board.

```
STARTUP(crt0.o)                    /* file for first position in
                                      link list */
OUTPUT_ARCH(arm)
INPUT(libc.a libg.a testprog.o)  /* input file list for
                                      linking */
OUTPUT_FORMAT("arm-elf")
OUTPUT_FILENAME("testprog")        /* can be overriden by command
                                      line */
SEARCH_DIR(.)
ENTRY(_start)                      /* ignored by reset vector */
__DYNAMIC = 0;
```

```
MEMORY {                              /* target memory map */
  vect (RX)  : ORIGIN = 0x000000, LENGTH = 0.25K
  rom (RX)   : ORIGIN = 0x000000, LENGTH = 16M
  ram (WX)   : ORIGIN = 0x1000000, LENGTH = 32M
}

SECTION {                         /* setup RAM map */
  .vect :  {
              __vect_start = .;
              *(.vect);
              __vect_end = .;
       }       > vect

  .text :  {                      /* .text, CODE SECTION */
              CREATE_OBJECT_SYMBOLS
              __text_start = .;
              *(.text)          /* insert code sections for files
                                   named on the ld command line
                                     */
              *(.strings)       /* char strings from all files on
                                   ld command line */
              __text_end = .;
       }      > rom

  .bss :   {                      /* .bss, UNINITIALIZED DATA
                                   SECTION */
              __bss_start = ALIGN(0x8);
              *(.bss)           /* bss sections from all command
                                   line files */
              *(COMMON)
              __bss_end = .;
       }      > ram

  .data : AT(__text_end {         /* .data, PREINITIALIZED DATA
                                   SECTION */
              __data_start = .;
              *(.data)          /* data sections from all command
                                   line files */
              __data_end = .;
       }      > ram

  .stack : {
              __stack_start = .;
              *(.stack)         /* stack sections from all command
                                   line files */
              _stack_end = .;
       }      > ram
```

```
  .stab.(NOLOAD): {            /* .stab, SYMBOL TABLE SECTION */
  *( .stab )
  }
  .strtab.(NOLOAD) : {           /* .strtab, STRINGs TABLE */
  *( .strtab )
  }
}
```

17.7 Entry point

The entry address for an executable file can be set in a number of different ways, as listed below, which can be confusing to the programmer. A similar situation exists when deciding how to locate the initial stack in an embedded system. The linker can build a stack segment, but this is of little value, because it does not actually initialize the stack pointer, it simply reserves space in the memory map.

- ld command-line `-e entrypoint` option
- Use of `ENTRY(entrypoint)` within the linker script
- Relying on the `start` symbol
- Default to the beginning of the .text section
- Use the hardware reset to force entry at address 00000000

Ways to set the main entry point

17.8 Building a gcc cross-compiler

If there is no suitable ready-configured compiler available, you will have to 'roll your own' from the gcc sources. Before building a new gcc cross-compiler, the latest compatible versions of the gcc, newlib (or glibc) and binutils source code packages have to be obtained, either on CD or by downloading directly

Impression of a gnu

from gcc.gnu.org or an equivalent mirror site. The packages are available in tgz or bz2 compressed tar format and will be labelled something like: gcc-3.2.3.tar.gz and binutils-2.13.90.tar.gz. You will need about 500 MB of free disk space to carry on with this operation. In the end, this reduces to about 100 MB after the removal of all the interim, temporary files. The availability of the particular CPU instruction set has to be investigated before too long. But it is probable that the gcc tool-chain has already been configured for any well-known processor, as evidenced by the list provided in Section 17.3.

A tool-chain refers to the series of processing steps required to generate a binary file that will execute on the target system. For C, the translation requires several passes: cpp, gcc, gas, ld. The preprocessor, cpp, handles all the source header files and macros. The compiler, gcc, takes the source file and produces assembler code for gas, the GNU assembler. This then produces object files containing machine code for the target CPU. Finally the linker, ld, combines several object files and libraries, by binding symbolic labels to address values in order to produce a final executable image that will run on the target system. Since the gcc cross-compiler itself generates assembler mnemonic code, a cross-assembler will also be required to generate relocatable object files. In addition, the cross-linker will expect object libraries containing routines suitable for the target CPU. These will have to be generated and installed on the host machine along with the associated header files. Also, the linker will search for the initial startup file (crt0.o) which, when any task starts, has to be executed first to set up stack and global data areas.

After a source file has successfully passed through the preprocessor, compiler and assembler phases, gcc calls up the linker and hands on the remaining command-line flags and options. So, once linker support is provided, gcc should be able to produce a fully linked executable image. However, the linker will need access to appropriate target libraries and target initialization code usually held in an object file called crt0.o. The linker also has to be told where the code is to be loaded in target memory, how big the stack might grow, and where the data heap should be initialized. If the target is running an operating system or RTE, the code will make system calls to the available API, but if no such facilities exist, low-level device handling routines will have to be written and linked into the application code before it can be installed on the target.

Compiling compilers is a lengthy and processor intensive operation. It is considered rather a good check on the health of your system! Be prepared to remove competing jobs to speed up the process, and check before you start that all necessary software is installed and available. In particular the unusual language development tools: `bison`, `yacc`, `lex and` `flex` will be required at some stage. If you are working on a network, try telneting across to the fastest processor available and use local /tmp file space, if it is big enough, to reduce network transfer delays. Plan the compiler building operation from the beginning to avoid corrupting the host's existing compiler and libraries. A cautious approach is to set the location of the install directory to /tmp/install rather than to /usr/local. Eventually, when you are satisfied with the results, change PREFIX to /usr/local, and repeat the build. New directories are created to house all the interim files. Assuming the target processor will be an ARM and the chosen library to be used will be newlib, this is now available on the Redhat site. It is advisable not to assume root privileges while you are testing out the sequence. After everything has been built and tested, *then* the time will have arrived to review the location of all the files and the state of their access privileges. Using `make install` can be a convenient option for installing the binary, header and library files in the correct locations.

A listing of the process of building a cross-compiler is now presented in full. This is to reassure first-timers that it is possible, even sometimes easy, to produce new versions of the gcc compiler. However, things do go wrong, and so some determination, personal initiative and an experienced friend are all highly recommended.

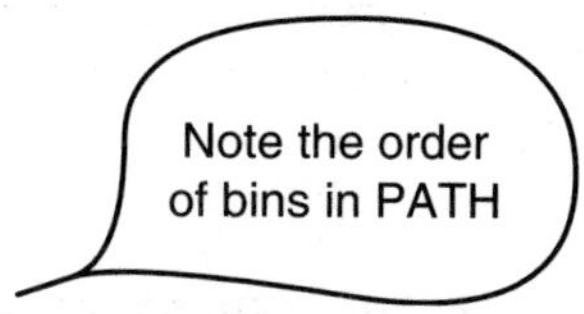


```
rob: > export TARGET=arm-elf
rob: > export PREFIX=/tmp/install
rob: > export PATH=${PREFIX}/bin:${PATH}
rob: > cd /tmp
rob:/tmp> mkdir build-gcc build-binutils build-newlib build-glibc install

rob:/tmp> ftp gcc.gnu.org
Connected to gcc.gnu.org.
220 FTP server ready.
Name (gcc.gnu.org:rwilliam): anonymous
331 Guest login ok, send your complete e-mail address as password.
Password:*******
230 Guest login ok, access restrictions apply.
ftp> binary
200 Type set to I.
ftp> dir
200 PORT command successful.
150 Opening ASCII mode data connection for directory listing.
total 3200
dr-xr-xr-x   2 root     root       4096  Feb 14  2004  bin
dr-xr-xr-x   2 root     root       4096  Feb 14  2004  etc
drwxr-xr-x   2 root     root       4096  Feb 14  2004  lib
-rw-r--r--   1 root     root    1449788  Oct 28 06:00  ls-lR
-rw-r--r--   1 root     root     154770  Oct 28 06:00  ls-lR.gz
drwxrwxr-x  45 root     root       4096  Oct 28 12:07  pub
drwxr-xr-x   3 root     root       4096  Nov  8   1999 usr
drwxr-xr-x   3 root     root       4096  Dec  7   2001 www
226 Transfer complete.
499 bytes received in 0.27 seconds (1.79 Kbytes/s)

ftp> cd /pub/binutils/releases
250 CSD command successful
```

```
ftp> get binutils-2.15.tar.gz
200 PORT command successful.
150 Opening ASCII mode data connection for binutils-2.150.tar.
     gz (15134701 bytes).

ftp> cd /pub/gcc/releases
250 CSD command successful
ftp> Bget gcc-3.4.2.tar.bz2
200 PORT command successful.
150 Opening ASCII mode data connection for gcc-3.4.2.tar.bz2
     (27246826 bytes).

ftp> cd /pub/glibc/releases
250 CSD command successful
ftp> get glibc-2.3.3.tar.gz
200 PORT command successful.
150 Opening ASCII mode data connection for glibc-2.3.3.tar.gz
     (17489958 bytes).
ftp> quit


rob:/tmp> ftp sources.redhat.com
Connected to redhat.com
220 FTP server ready.
Name (redhat.com:rwilliam): anonymous
331 Guest login ok, send your complete e-mail address as
     password.
Password:******
230 Guest login ok, access restrictions apply.
ftp> binary
200 Type set to I.

ftp> dir
200 PORT command successful.
150 Opening ASCII mode data connection for directory listing.
total 3200
dr-xr-xr-x    2  root    root      4096  Feb  14  2004  bin
dr-xr-xr-x    2  root    root      4096  Feb  14  2004  etc
drwxr-xr-x    2  root    root      4096  Feb  14  2004  lib
-rw-r--r--    1  root    root   1449788  Oct  28 06:00  ls-lR
-rw-r--r--    1  root    root    154770  Oct  28 06:00  ls-lR.gz
drwxrwxr-x   45  root    root      4096  Oct  28 12:07  pub
drwxr-xr-x    3  root    root      4096  Nov   8  1999  usr
drwxr-xr-x    3  root    root      4096  Dec   7  2001  www
226 Transfer complete.
499 bytes received in 0.27 seconds (1.79 Kbytes/s)

ftp> cd /pub/newlib/
250 CSD command successful
```

```
ftp> get newlib-1.12.0.tar.gz
200 PORT command successful.
150 Opening ASCII mode data connection for newlib-1.12.0.tar.gz
     (6684150 bytes).
ftp> quit
```

Now to unpack the compressed tar files. This will create four new directories: /tmp/gcc-3.4.2, /tmp/binutils-2.15, /tmp/newlib-1.12.0 and /tmp/glibc-2.3.3.

```
rob:/tmp> tar -jvxf gcc-3.4.2.tar.bz2
rob:/tmp> tar -zvxf binutils-2.15.tar.gz
rob:/tmp> tar -zvxf newlib-1.12.0.tar.gz
rob:/tmp> tar -zvxf glibc-2.3.3.tar.gz
```

The source trees are all initialized by tar within separate directories. Then the `configure` utility is run to build the necessary makefiles. This operation requires some key parameters to be given to configure, so that it knows which host and target systems it will be preparing for. Configure runs a script which checks for the availability of resources on the host platform and creates many makefiles which will then be capable of building the required tools. It is possible to run configure from a remote directory, but it is simpler to attach to the empty build directory before running it, and refer from there to the source tree directories.

```
rob:/tmp> cd build-binutils
rob:/tmp/build-binutils> ../binutils-2.15/configure \
? --target=$TARGET --prefix=$PREFIX
rob:/tmp/build-binutils> make all install
     2>&1|tee binutils_make.logfile
rob:/tmp/build-binutils> cd ..
rob:/tmp>
```

Remember the space before the \

When only the –target option is used, and not –host, the configuration assumes that a cross-compiler is required. The `2>&1| tee` construction enables the bash shell to blend stdout and stderr for the same output, and duplicates this data stream to screen and logfile. For csh or tcsh shell the same is achieved using: `>&|tee`. Depending on the speed of your machine, after about five minutes of processing of the makefile, the assembler (arm-elf-as) and linker (arm-elf-ld) have been built and are ready for use in the directory ${PREFIX}/bin. There will also be a couple of utility programs, arm-elf-objcopy which translates formats, and arm-elf-objdump which displays the contents of elf object files. Copies of some of the binutil tools are also placed in $PREFIX/$TARGET/bin for later use. The next step is to build an interim, *bootstrap* version of the gcc compiler with which to build newlib run-time libraries for the ARM target. If you type the options for make exactly in this order, it will be easier to run the same command line again, after some painless editing. But remember, a space character is need before the \ line extender.

```
rob:/tmp> cd build-gcc
rob:/tmp/build-gcc> ../gcc-3.4.2/configure --target=$TARGET --prefix=$PREFIX \
? --with-gnu-ld --with-gnu-as --enable-languages=c \
? --with-newlib --without-headers --disable-shared
rob:/tmp/build-gcc> make all-gcc install-gcc 2>&1|tee gcc_make.logfile
rob:/tmp/build-gcc> cd ..
rob:/tmp>
```

At this point there will be a preliminary 'bootstrap' compiler, arm-elf-gcc, in ${PREFIX}/bin which can be used to build a target versions of newlib and associated header files.

```
rob:/tmp> cd build-newlib
rob:/tmp/build-newlib> ../newlib-1.12.0/configure
     --target=$TARGET --prefix=$PREFIX
rob:/tmp/build-newlib> make all install 2>&1|tee newlib_make.logfile
rob:/tmp/build-newlib> cd ..R
rob:/tmp>
```

In ${PREFIX} will be the static libraries: libc.a, libg.a and libm.a. At last the full cross-compiler can be built as follows:

```
rob:/tmp> cd build-gcc
rob:/tmp/build-gcc> rm -rf *
rob:/tmp/build-gcc> ../gcc-3.4.2/configure --target=$TARGET --prefix=$PREFIX \
?        --with-gnu-as --with-gnu-ld --enable-languages=c,c++
rob:/tmp/build-gcc> make all install 2$>$&1|tee make.logfile
rob:/tmp/build-gcc> cd ..
rob:/tmp>
```

At this point there will be a cross-compiler, arm-elf-gcc, available in the temporary /tmp/install/bin directory. This, along with the newlib library and include files, will all need to be installed in the correct location in the file system, perhaps /usr/local/bin, /usr/local/lib and /usr/local/include. This could be done by copying the directory contents, or repeating the whole process with PREFIX set to /usr/local.

17.9 Tips!

Should any of the makefiles fail to complete (which is quite likely in my experience!) the build-xxxx directories need to be cleaned, either by running `make distclean` or `rm -rf *`, or both, before repeating the configure/make sequence. Check the environment variables to make sure they have not been lost, and ensure you do not run as root. Read carefully the *first* error message dumped to the screen and log file. Identify any offending source file where possible, and have a good look at the error line. An advantage of running through the whole procedure under /tmp is that there is less opportunity for confusing native-CPU and target-CPU files. Also cleaning out directories becomes quick and thoughtless. Which versions of gcc, newlib and binutils to work with may be significant, and little advice beyond personal experience is available. So, although it may be attractive to choose the most recent releases, that may not be advisable. The popular combination is: gcc-2.95.3, binutils-2.11.3 and newlib-1.9.0. But the more recent binutils-2.15 appears to work with the two other versions as well.

17.10 Executable and Linking Format (ELF)

The object file format produced by the gcc compiler will conform to either 'COFF' (Common Object File Format) or more currently 'ELF' (Executable and Linking Format). Most recent compilers have switched to ELF as default because of its increased flexibility. ELF was originally developed by Unix System Laboratories and has become the standard compiler output because it supports more facilities than the previous a.out and COFF formats, notably in the area of dynamic, shared libraries. So it now appears as the default binary format on Linux and Solaris because it offers dynamic loading, dynamic linking, run-time control, and improved support for shared libraries (DLLs). The ELF file format is platform independent and permits object files to be identified, parsed, and interpreted uniformly, making the object files 'portable' across platforms of similar architectures.

ELF defines three principal formats for executable, relocatable and shared object files. These hold the code, data, and information which the operating system and linker need to access in order to take appropriate action. An *executable* file has to contain machine code but also all the information needed for the operating system to create and run a task. A *relocatable* file describes how it can be linked with other object files to create an executable file, or a shared library. A shared object file contains information needed for both static and dynamic linking. An ELF object file will be divided into several sections: status header, code, data, symbol table, relocation table and information to assist with debugging. Using an industry standard file format such as this allows users to acquire compatible tools from several different suppliers. There are really two views for each of the three ELF file types (relocatable, executable, library) which support the linking and execution phase of a program. The two views are summarized below where the link view is on the left, and the execution view is on the right. The object file link format is partitioned by sections and the execution view by segments.

Linking view	Execution view
ELF header	ELF header
Program header table (optional)	Program header table
Section 1	Segment 1
Section 2	
Section N	Segment N
Section header table	Section header table (optional)

ELF file format views

Thus, if the programmer is concerned with aspects of program production such as symbol tables, relocation, executable code or dynamic linking, the link view would be more useful. But if the concern is with loading segments into memory, requiring information about the location of the text and data segments, the execution view would be more appropriate. The ELF access library, libelf, provides a programmer with tools to extract and manipulate ELF object file contents for either view. The ELF header describes the layout of the rest of the object file. It provides information on where and how to access the other sections. The section header table gives the location and description of the sections and is mostly used in linking. The program header table provides the location and description of segments and is mostly used in creating a program's process image. Both sections and segments hold the majority of data in an object file including: instructions, data, symbol table, relocation information, and dynamic linking information.

ELF object files are recognized by the gcc linker and the loader. The former is concerned with resolving external references, translating symbolic names into their correct numeric values, and uniting independently compiled modules with library routines and then creating a larger relocatable object file or even the final, executable module. While the latter is used to load the executable binary into main memory and registering it with Linux so that it can be dispatched by the scheduler at the earliest opportunity.

Assembly source code programs contain several sections as shown below which are then transformed into object module sections by the assembler. Compilers also produce output object modules divided into sections. The linker will merge the text sections from all the object modules that are presented on the command line and produce a single text section for the output module.

Each ELF module contains a single main program header and headers for each of the contained sections. These data structures may be

Section	Content
.text	program code and constant data
.data	initialized data items
.bss	uninitialized data area
.symtab	module symbol table
.strtab	program strings table
.shstrtab	section names
.rela***	relocation info for module***

ELF object module sections

inspected on Linux using the `readelf` utility, and the definitions are held in /usr/include/linux/elf.h.

The ELF file and section header structures are given next, with the fields commented with summary descriptions. The `readelf` tool decodes the fields and presents the information in a more convenient format.

```
typedef struct {
  unsigned char e_ident[EI_NIDENT]; /* 16 char identifier */
  Elf32_Half     e_type;         /* file type 1-rel, 2-exe, 3-so, 4-core */
  Elf32_Half     e_machine;      /* CPU ident */
  Elf32_Word     e_version;      /* ELF file version, 0-inval, 1-current */
  Elf32_Addr     e_entry;        /* virtual address entry point */
  Elf32_Off      e_phoff;        /* program header offset */
  Elf32_Off      e_shoff;        /* section header offset */
  Elf32_Word     e_flags;        /* processor-specific flags */
  Elf32_Half     e_ehsize;       /* ELF header size, in bytes */
  Elf32_Half     e_phentsize;    /* prog header's field size in bytes */
  Elf32_Half     e_phnum;        /* prog header number of fields */
  Elf32_Half     e_shentsize;    /* section header size in bytes */
  Elf32_Half     e_shnum;        /* section header number of entries */
  Elf32_Half     e_shstrndx;     /* section name string index */
} Elf32_Ehdr;

typedef struct {
  Elf32_Word     sh_name;        /* indexes into sectn header string table */
  Elf32_Word     sh_type;        /* 1-progbits, 2-symtab, 3-strngtab, 4-rel */
  Elf32_Word     sh_flags;       /* section attributes */
  Elf32_Addr     sh_addr;        /* if loadable, virtual address of sectn */
  Elf32_Off      sh_offset;      /* sctn offset within loadable image */
  Elf32_Word     sh_size;        /* sctn size in bytes */
  Elf32_Word     sh_link;        /* link to index table */
  Elf32_Word     sh_info;
  Elf32_Word     sh_addralign;   /* 0, 2, 4, 8 word alignment */
  Elf32_Word     sh_entsize;     /* entry size in bytes */
} Elf32_Shdr;
```

Definitions of ELF main and section headers

The following listing is the output from `readelf` for the a.out (ELF format) generated by gcc from a trivial hello.c program.

```
ELF Header:
  Magic: 7f 45 4c 46 01 01 01 00 00 00 00 00 00 00 00 00
  Class:                             ELF32
  Data:                              2's complement, little endian
  Version:                           1 (current)
  OS/ABI:                            UNIX - System V
  ABI Version:                       0
  Type:                              EXEC (Executable file)
  Machine:                           Intel 80386
  Version:                           0x1
  Entry point address:               0x80482a0
  Start of program headers:          52 (bytes into file)
  Start of section headers:          7452 (bytes into file)
  Flags:                             0x0
  Size of this header:               52 (bytes)
  Size of program headers:           32 (bytes)
  Number of program headers:         7
  Size of section headers:           40 (bytes)
  Number of section headers:         33
  Section header string table index: 30

Section Headers:
  [Nr] Name              Type     Addr     Off    Size   ES Flg Lk Inf Al
  [ 0]                   NULL     00000000 000000 000000 00      0   0  0
  [ 1] .interp           PROGBITS 08048114 000114 000013 00   A  0   0  1
  [ 2] .note.ABI-tag     NOTE     08048128 000128 000020 00   A  0   0  4
  [ 3] .hash             HASH     08048148 000148 000028 04   A  4   0  4
  [ 4] .dynsym           DYNSYM   08048170 000170 000050 10   A  5   1  4
  [ 5] .dynstr           STRTAB   080481c0 0001c0 00004c 00   A  0   0  1
  [ 6] .gnu.version      VERSYM   0804820c 00020c 00000a 02   A  4   0  2
  [ 7] .gnu.version_r    VERNEED  08048218 000218 000020 00   A  5   1  4
  [ 8] .rel.dyn          REL      08048238 000238 000008 08   A  4   0  4
  [ 9] .rel.plt          REL      08048240 000240 000010 08   A  4   b  4
  [10] .init             PROGBITS 08048250 000250 000017 00  AX  0   0  4
  [11] .plt              PROGBITS 08048268 000268 000030 04  AX  0   0  4
  [12] .text             PROGBITS 080482a0 0002a0 0001b4 00  AX  0   0 16
  [13] .fini             PROGBITS 08048454 000454 00001a 00  AX  0   0  4
  [14] .rodata           PROGBITS 08048470 000470 000015 00   A  0   0  4
  [15] .eh_frame         PROGBITS 08048488 000488 000004 00   A  0   0  4
  [16] .data             PROGBITS 0804948c 00048c 00000c 00  WA  0   0  4
  [17] .dynamic          DYNAMIC  08049498 000498 0000c8 08  WA  5   0  4
  [18] .ctors            PROGBITS 08049560 000560 000008 00  WA  0   0  4
  [19] .dtors            PROGBITS 08049568 000568 000008 00  WA  0   0  4
  [20] .jcr              PROGBITS 08049570 000570 000004 00  WA  0   0  4
  [21] .got              PROGBITS 08049574 000574 000018 04  WA  0   0  4
  [22] .bss              NOBITS   0804958c 00058c 000004 00  WA  0   0  4
  [23] .comment          PROGBITS 00000000 00058c 00012c 00      0   0  1
  [24] .debug_aranges    PROGBITS 00000000 0006b8 000078 00      0   0  8
  [25] .debug_pubnames   PROGBITS 00000000 000730 000025 00      0   0  1
  [26] .debug_info       PROGBITS 00000000 000755 000a4f 00      0   0  1
```

```
  [27] .debug_abbrev   PROGBITS 00000000 0011a4 000138 00       0  0   1
  [28] .debug_line     PROGBITS 00000000 0012dc 000272 00       0  0   1
  [29] .debug_str      PROGBITS 00000000 00154e 0006af 01   MS  0  0   1
  [30] .shstrtab       STRTAB   00000000 001bfd 00011e 00       0  0   1
  [31] .symtab         SYMTAB   00000000 002244 0006a0 10      32 52   4
  [32] .strtab         STRTAB   00000000 0028e4 0003ad 00       0  0   1
Key to Flags:
  W (write), A (alloc), X (execute), M (merge), S (strings)
  I (info), L (link order), G (group), x (unknown)
  O (extra OS processing required) o (OS specific), p (processor
          specific)
Program Headers:
  Type     Offset    VirtAddr    PhysAddr    FileSiz  MemSiz   Flg  Align
  PHDR     0x000034  0x08048034  0x08048034  0x000e0  0x000e0  R E  0x4
  INTERP   0x000114  0x08048114  0x08048114  0x00013  0x00013  R    0x1
      [Requesting program interpreter: /lib/ld-linux.so.2]
  LOAD     0x000000  0x08048000  0x08048000  0x0048c  0x0048c  R E  0x1000
  LOAD     0x00048c  0x0804948c  0x0804948c  0x00100  0x00104  RW   0x1000
  DYNAMIC  0x000498  0x08049498  0x08049498  0x000c8  0x000c8  RW   0x4
  NOTE     0x000128  0x08048128  0x08048128  0x00020  0x00020  R    0x4
  STACK    0x000000  0x00000000  0x00000000  0x00000  0x00000  RW   0x4

Section to Segment mapping:
  Segment Sections...
   00
   01     .interp
   02     .interp .note.ABI-tag .hash .dynsym .dynstr .gnu.version
          .gnu.version_r
          .rel.dyn .rel.plt .init .plt .text .fini .rodata .eh_frame
   03     .data .dynamic .ctors .dtors .jcr .got .bss
   04     .dynamic
   05     .note.ABI-tag
   06
```

17.11 C++ global constructors and destructors in ELF

The C++ global constructors and destructors are handled conveniently within the ELF format. Constructors all have to be called before entering the `main()` function, and destructors evoked after exiting from `main()`. The GNU g++ compiler inserts two auxiliary startup files (crti.o and crtbegin.o) in front of main, and two after it (crtend.o and crtn.o). Crtbegin.o contains a list of pointers to the constructor functions, arranged in the correct order.

17.12 Debugging techniques

Debugging using ICE, BDM, JTAG, Logic analyser and CPU simulators will now be described.

- *ICE* An early technique used to debug embedded real-time systems relied on In Circuit Emulator (ICE) equipment. This required the target

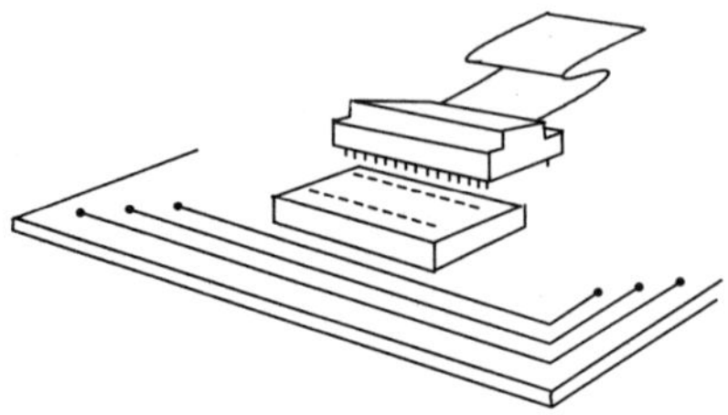

ICE probe and socket

microprocessor to be removed and replaced by a multi-way plug and umbilical cable leading back to an emulator card set within the host ICE workstation. The emulator card would use a very similar microprocessor to run the execution cycles in place of the target processor. With some equipment, the emulation processor card can be swapped for other 'personality' cards holding alternative microprocessors. In this way, a general ICE station can be obtained, dealing with several target CPUs. Prototype development cards for use with ICE probes were generally equipped with Zero Insertion Force (ZIF) sockets to make swapping out the microprocessor easier and less risky. The alternative of locating an extra socket on the circuit board, with all the bus signals mapped onto its pins, allows an ICE probe to be connected without removing the microprocessor. This scheme does require the target microprocessor to be held in *reset* throughout the debugging sessions so that its tristate output pins are all in the OFF state. In this way all the functions of the target microprocessor can be observed and controlled by a programmer sitting at the host workstation. The aim is to achieve complete transparency, so that the target system performs identically whether running with microprocessor or ICE probe. Unfortunately this is not really achievable, signal timing differences may require the target under ICE to run at a slower clock speed, one of the interrupts may be taken by ICE, or areas of the main memory map may have to be dedicated to the operation of the probe. But despite these drawbacks both hardware and software engineers frequently rely on ICE to get new systems up and running for the first time. Most ICE equipment provides advanced debugging facilities at basic logic, machine instruction and HLL instruction level. Hardware comparators, watching data and address buses, can be set to break execution on 'interesting' values. Most usefully, a high speed trace memory maintains a push-through history queue of several hundred instructions with their results, which allows system crashes to be retrospectively analysed and diagnosed. Sometimes extra emulation or overlay RAM can be temporarily mapped into the target memory map to substitute for unavailable RAM chips, inconvenient PROM, or to cope with the greater size of debug code. Also, unused output ports can be set to trigger external hardware on reaching a debug breakpoint

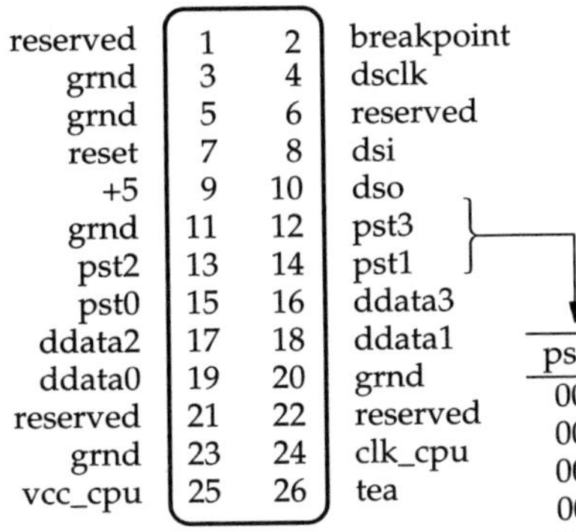

pst3-0	Signal definition
0000	continue execution
0001	begin instruction execution
0010	reserved
0011	enter user mode
0100	begin execution of PULSE or WDDATA
0101	begin execution of taken branch
0110	reserved
0111	begin execution of rte instr
1000	begin 1 byte transfer on DData
1001	begin 2 byte transfer on DData
1010	begin 3 byte transfer on DData
1011	begin 4 byte transfer on DData
1100	exception processing
1101	emulator-mode entry exception
1110	processor stopped, waiting interrupt
1111	processor halted

BDM interface

in the code. This is a useful trick when trying to capture oscilloscope traces of elusive data transmission patterns.

- *BDM* As more sophisticated on-chip integration became possible, new microcontrollers were produced which didn't offer enough signal visibility, on their external pins, to fully synchronize to an ICE probe. Vital system signals were retained internally, inaccessible to the probe. As a response, the Background Debugging Mode (BDM) facility was introduced by Motorola with their 32 bit 68300 microcontroller range, offering a viable alternative to ICE. Irrespective of systems integration, the provision of ICE equipment was becoming more and more technically problematic due to the higher levels of performance offered by the faster, parallel pipelined CPUs.

  BDM supports processor control and also real-time status tracing through the PST0-3 and DData0-3 signal lines. There are 14 PST codes available indicating CPU status. The Motorola Coldfire CPUs also offer the PULSE instruction to signal across the BDM link to assist with time auditing. The necessary interface pins are led to a 26-way connector on the motherboard which accepts the cable and interface pod which plugs into the host PC.
- *JTAG test access port* With the constraints imposed by miniature Surface Mount Packaging (SMP), and the physical limitations on the

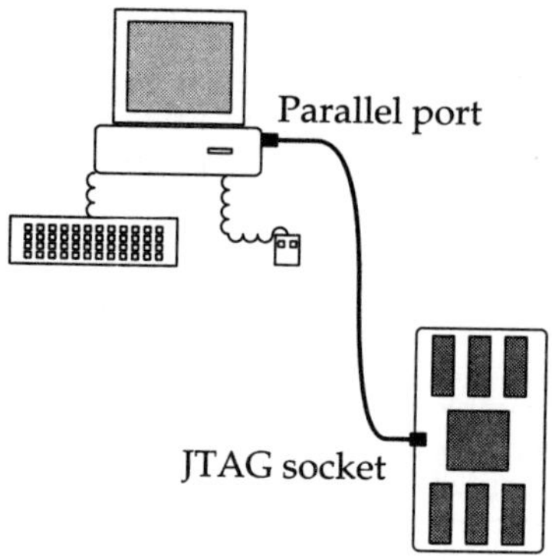

JTAG connection between host and target

number of easily accessible pins, it became essential to develop alternative approaches to debugging. So chip suppliers started to include special debugging facilities, for software as well as hardware, fully integrated into the primary functionality. Initially, this came about as an extension of existing JTAG hardware test facilities. The Joint Test Action Group (IEEE 1149.1, JTAG) had already specified a technique and protocol to support boundary scan testing, for Printed Circuit Boards (PCB) through a four/five line serial interface. This replaced the traditional ATE (Automatic Test Equipment) 'bed of nails' with internal shift registers directly built into the chips. Each I/O pin, and all the register bits of interest during a debugging session, are twinned with a bit in the JTAG shift register loop. This can result in JTAG loops being hundreds of bits long, and even longer, when several chips are connected in series. For the Intel StrongARM SA1110, the BSR has 292 cells, while for the Altera APEX20K 1500E, it winds its way around 2190 cells! The Boundary Scan Register (BSR) is made up of a string of logic cells around the periphery of a device, at the interface between the core logic and the solder pins. The BSR cell logic can be used to disconnect pins from the core, allowing either the pin or the associated core track to be driven or monitored. Target boards are provided with an 8 pin JTAG header to connect with a host computer, often through a standard parallel port. The connecting, umbilical cable usually provides voltage shifting drivers, to change the signal voltage from the lower working voltage of the target CPU to the 5 V used by the PC parallel port. Because there are now a number of 'standard' CPU voltages, the interface cable must be carefully selected to fit with the intended target hardware. The BSR receives a serial stream of bits through the Test Data Input (TDI) pin. These are clocked on the rising edge of the test clock signal (TCK). So, to obtain the logic value on one particular pin, the full BSR loop has to be clocked out serially through TDO and unpacked by the host computer. Similarly, pins can have their values set for testing, by clocking in the correct chain of bits through TDI. As alluded to above, if several chips on a circuit board have JTAG ports, their TDO and TDI pins can be wired together in series, chip to chip. This also requires all the TCK, TMS and TRST pins to be connected together for synchronous operation. If only one of the chips is being investigated by JTAG, all the others may be placed in 'bypass' mode to reduce the length of the joint BSR. But remember, bypass does still introduce a single bit delay in the extended BSR chain!

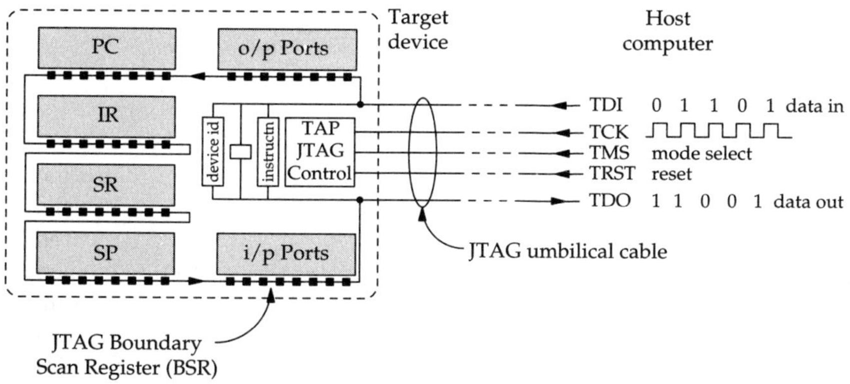

JTAG loop accessing CPU registers

The IEEE JTAG protocol has now been extended by commercial chip suppliers to assist with software debugging, hardware configuration, and in-circuit programming. These extra functions are often available in addition to boundary scan, hardware testing. In any case, the IEEE 1149.1 specification only encompassed the *communications* format and not the *control* of devices. The circuit details of a cell within the JTAG boundary scan register are not really important to a programmer about to use a JTAG umbilical for code debugging, but they do define the range of possible actions that a JTAG scan mode can complete. So notice that the circuit shown below represents one of the little dark square cells in the figure above. Each of these cells may control the interconnection between pin and core, core and pin or register bit and internal device bus. In the figure below the BSR chain runs across the page, with the monitored data pathway running from top to bottom. The `updateDR` control line to the second multiplexor enables direct, normal connection for the data, or isolate the data-in from data-out, interposing a value stored in the shadow, assert flip-flop. This can be changed with the value from the capture flip-flop, which sits within the actual BSR loop. When a string of data is being clocked through the BSR loop, it steps from one capture flip-flop to the next. There are three routes that the serial data may take when entering the JTAG TDI port. It may be set to bypass everything, and

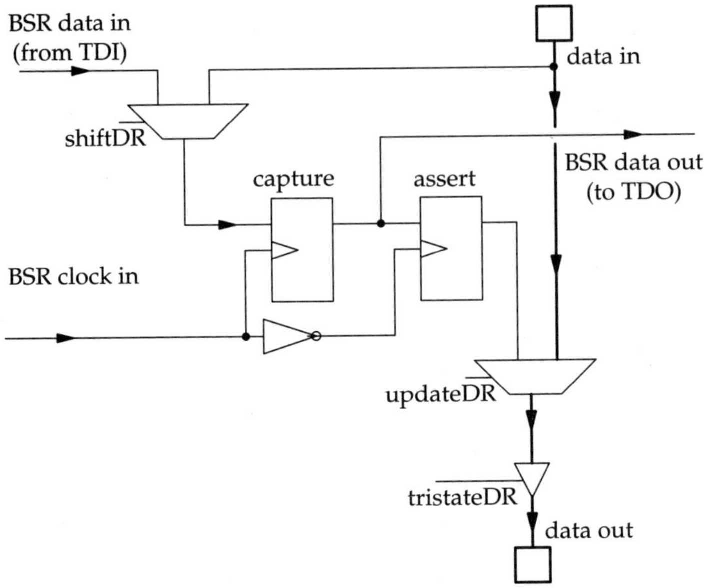

A boundary scan register data cell

come straight out of the TD0 pin; only useful if several devices are connected end to end on a single JTAG loop. Alternatively, it can step data into the TAP instruction register, where it will be decoded and control subsequent JTAG events. Or, it may pass through the full BSR loop from TDI to TDO, taking many TCK clock cycles to complete.

JTAG interfaces are provided for the ARM range of microcontrollers and the StrongARM and XScale chips. A serial interface, known as ICSD, which works in a very similar manner to JTAG, is offered by Microchip for its PIC microcontrollers. This supports program loading into on-chip Flash and run-time debugging. How the JTAG loop interacts with elements of the device, such as CPU registers, is determined by the manufacturer, and may not be publically available. An attempt to standardize the full set of JTAG-related facilities has been launched by a group of motor manufacturers: the Global Embedded Processor Debug Interface Standard Consortium (GEPDISC), rebadged in 2001 as the Nexus 5001 Forum.

In the TAP FSM, shown below, note that all the states only have two exit transitions which makes it possible to steer a route through the FSD using only the single bit TMS signal. The clock TCK is used to sample TMS and so activate the transitions. Which data register is selected to receive the serial data stream from the BSR loop, when the Data arm is being stepped through, has to be previously set by the instruction register. Data bits are shifted into the selected register when a capture state is entered, and output to the BSR on exit from the shift-into state.

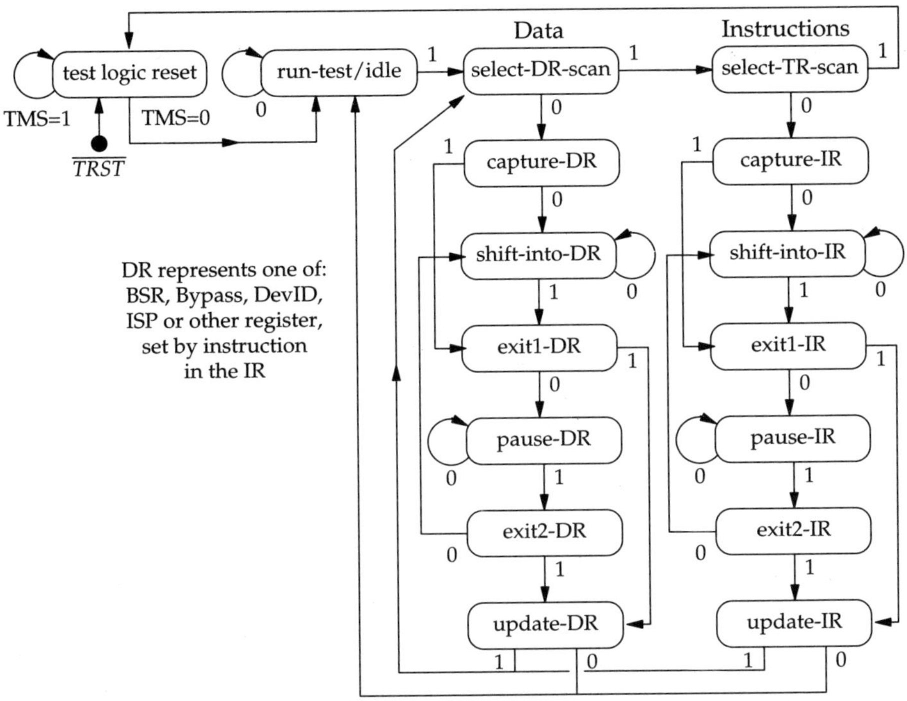

FSD for a TAP JTAG controller

Considering the FSD above, which describes the functionality of the JTAG TAP controller, all transitions between states are driven by the clock rising edge (TCK) with the single mode line (TMS) selecting which transition will be taken. The asynchronous reset line, TRST, restores the FSM back to the initial state. A reset can also be achieved by clocking TCK five times with TMS set at 1. By stepping one of the JTAG instruction codes into instruction register, a variety of interconnections and actions may be selected. So, if a control sequence as presented below is toggled into the StrongARM chip, a 32 bit identifier code will emerge, lsb first. At the start, either zeroing TRST,

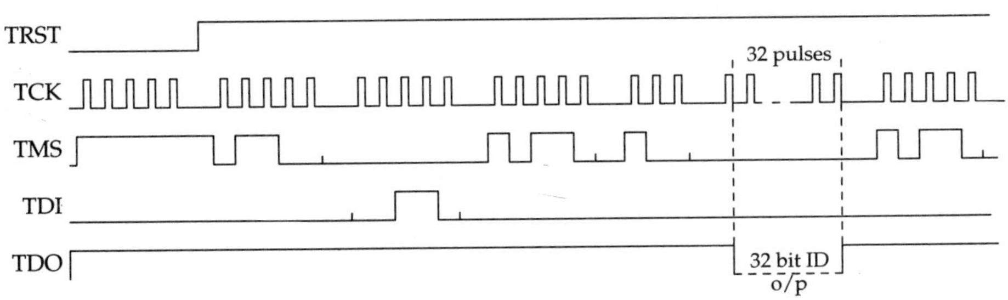

JTAG logic sequence to read a chip ID

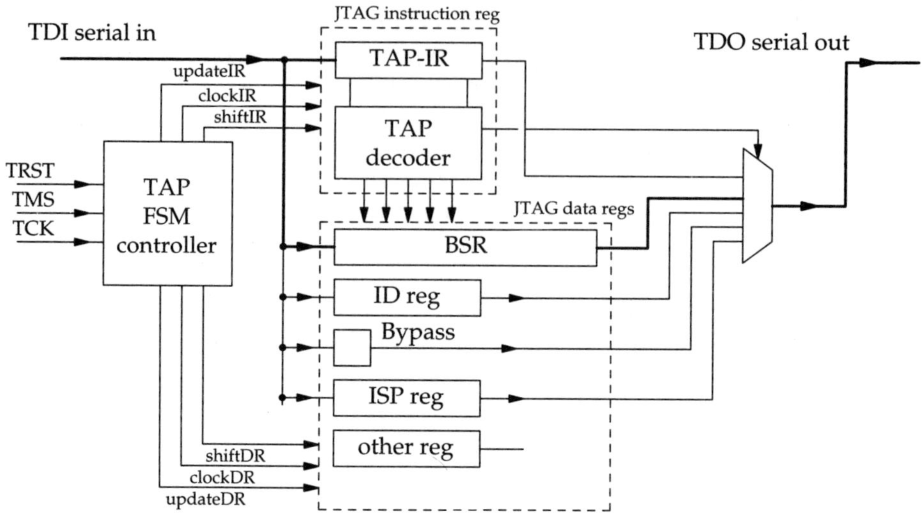

Data paths through the JTAG circuitry

or pulsing a high into TMS for five clock periods, will reset the TAP FSM back to origin. If TRST is not being used, it is essential to hold it at logic 1 with a 10 K pull-up resistor.

Debugging activity has to be carried out through the JTAG serial loop by directly modifying a CPU register, single stepping through some machine instructions, and inspecting the result. Reading and writing to external memory is an even more protracted exercise using JTAG protocols because each bus cycle has to be set up and then executed explicitly. Nevertheless, this does offer one way to initialize a Flash boot ROM when it has already been soldered onto a board. Issue an EXTEST instruction to isolate the CPU core from peripheral pins, and then force the address, data and control bus lines to execute a sequence of bus write cycles into the Flash memory.

Instruction	Code	
EXTEST	0000	BSR is connected between TDI and TDO, cells latch incoming pin data on entering CAPTURE_DR state, and it gets passed on when exiting from SHIFT_DR state. New contents of BSR are applied to output pins during UPDATE_DR state. Used to test the pack's solder connections.
INTEST	0001	BSR is connected between TDI and TDO, cells latch outgoing core data on entering CAPTURE_DR state, and it gets passed on when exiting from SHIFT_DR state. New contents of BSR areapplied to the core logic during UPDATE_DR state. Used to exercise the core without affecting the board connections.
IDCODE	00110	A device id code can be sifted out of the id register.
BYPASS	11111	Select the single cell bypass, TDI to TDO.

Basic set of JTAG instruction codes

- *Logic analyser* A useful piece of equipment, which functionally sits between ICE and a digital oscilloscope, is the logic analyser. Some managers prefer to invest in this type of debugging tool, rather than a microprocessor ICE probe, because it offers a more general functionality, applicable to a wider range of problems and hardware situations. In a similar arrangement to that described for ICE, the target system is monitored by a host unit. But rather than removing the microprocessor, each of the principal pins is hooked up to a multiway umbilical, and the digital signals detected and recorded. However, with the increasing miniaturization of packaging, moving from a pin pitch of 0.1 inch down to 0.05 inch, the safe attachment of pin clips has become a significant problem. The front end of a logic analyser is similar to that of a multichannel, digital oscilloscope, but behind the signal capture hardware are often sophisticated translation facilities which can interpret the raw signal data and display it in a more meaningful format. So when monitoring signals from a CPU bus, disassembly software can be run on the logic analyser to display instruction mnemonics on the screen alongside the signal traces. Or, when dealing with communications protocols, the packets can be captured, unpacked and the component fields conveniently decoded. There are now ranges of reasonably priced logic analyser equipment based on standard PCs, some using the USB port for umbilical interfacing, available to assist with debugging.

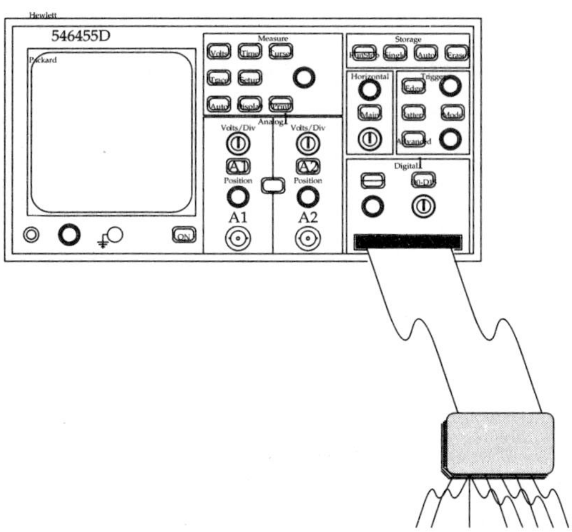

Multichannel logic analyser with umbilical connectors

- *CPU simulator* The original technique offered to developers by microprocessor vendors was the simulator, running on a large host computer. Such a simulator is a completely host-based program that runs as an interpreter for the target CPU's instruction set. With this, it is possible to start testing out new executables in a safe environment, with many extra debugging aids on hand. Checks on execution timing and device access has to be deferred until the genuine target is ready, but some useful testing can still be carried out in this way. Nowadays, if the real hardware is actually available, very few developers choose to try out their software on a simulator, which may be a mistake when dealing with complex software bugs obscured by unfamiliar hardware.

17.13 Program memory options

Usually, system code needs to be stored on a media which is unaffected by power loss so that, on rebooting, it can be reactivated without human intervention. For PCs this means holding the major part of the operating system on hard disk, with a small initial loader available in Flash or EEPROM. The situation is different for embedded microprocessors, where commonly all the executable code, system and application, is held in non-volatile Flash memory. This offers the real advantage of providing *in-circuit* programmability, unlike some earlier field programmable devices. Flash memories are divided into segments, and when deleting or writing data, a full segment has to be involved, rather like data sectors on a disk. Most Flash devices offer different size segments to deal efficiently with different application needs. So the first and last segments are seen as dedicated to boot code or lists of initialization parameters. Having the option of 'locking' a segment against inadvertent corruption is incredibly useful, when the risk of losing the initial loader code, or even the routine which reprogrammes the Flash memory itself, is recognized.

17.14 Flash memory

With the change from employing EPROM and EEPROM, for storing bootloader and application code, to Flash devices, programmers have had to learn how to deal with much more complex hardware. An initial concern is that Flash devices have finite lifetimes, which can eliminate them from certain very active applications. Although Flash carries out *read* operations in a very similar manner to SRAM, the approach to *writing* is very different and requires much longer time periods to be allocated. Because of this asymmetry between the read/write operations, there are several points to take into account when understanding Flash write cycles. First, Flash memory has to be explicitly erased before it can be rewritten, otherwise a logical AND, or OR, mix will be the result. But individual locations cannot be erased, only complete segments, or blocks. Their size depends on the manufacturer's policy, and varies according to the intended application. There may even be several block sizes provided within a single memory device. Finally, the timing sequence of write attempts and test reads is not a simple unitary action, and is best encapsulated within special Flash driver functions. These can be obtained from the websites of the manufacturers but usually include a couple of initial writes to 'special' addresses to unlock the device for subsequent erase and write operations. Also, post-write checking is carried out on each location before progressing to the next one.

Flash devices

To assist programmers in the minefield of changing Flash devices, manufacturers have adopted a standardized format for an information block to be read out from Flash memory chips so that systems can discover the correct values of working parameters. This standard is called the Common Flash Interface (CFI) and is accompanied by the Basic Command Set (BCS) and the Scaleable Command Set (SCS). Using the CFI, it is easier for systems designers to allow users to select from a wider range of devices with slightly different characteristics. This is especially important when providing a Flash card socket which might receive ... anything! CFI allows the system to interrogate a Flash chip, while BCS and SCS are used to command the chip to carry out the desired functions. As Flash devices do not accept standard WRITE requests, the CFI is able to define writing 98H to address 55H as a query. Some CFI-enabled devices simply ignore the address bus signals on WRITE cycles, anyway. If the queried device is CFI-compliant, it will return the ASCII letters 'Q', 'R' and 'Y' when three consecutive READs are executed starting from 10H. These must be normal full bus width READs. To cancel the query sequence, 0FFH can be written to any location. Older Flash devices do not offer a response to the CFI query, but do provide the JEDEC-compliant facility of holding manufacturer and device identifier numbers at locations 00H and 01H respectively. To get access to these, the value 90H has first to be written to location 00H, then the two reads from 00H and 01H are executed, followed by an FFH write to any location to reset the Flash to normal running.

A major disadvantage of Flash technology is its slow write speed. Flash devices are only suitable for program memory which is to be used in a read-frequently, write-rarely mode. If data is to be stored, a RAM caching scheme will be needed to hide the write delays. This does introduce another risk, however; when the power fails, there may not be enough time to fully write all the data from volatile RAM into Flash. So some level of battery backup may be required for this operation to be secure. On the positive side, with remote equipment, if a modem or Internet link is available, Flash memory makes possible the convenient distribution of upgrades and code patches, without the need to make a site visit.

Using Flash does reintroduce a previously abandoned responsibility for the programmer: the need to keep track of the *physical* addresses of data loaded into Flash when rewriting occurs. These rather inconvenient characteristics of Flash actually make it a suitable candidate for secondary storage, holding a file system rather than program variables, and handled as a block device, through the file management subsystem.

17.15 Installing target code

Application code is commonly loaded into memory using the normal operating system facilities available to the user. If, however, the target hardware is completely bare of code, devoid of any bootable firmware in PROM, the likely recourse is to obtain an EEPROM, preloaded with suitable initialization code, and physically insert it into the first memory socket on the target board. If the memory decoding logic on the target board is correctly set up (see Section 3.2 for more details of the memory decoding logic), when the reset button is released, the fetch–execute sequence should be directed to the boot PROM. Alternatively, as introduced in Section 17.12, a BDM or JTAG link can be used to insert a short boot routine into target memory, either RAM or Flash. This can be achieved by using any JTAG device connected to the common bus as a host, or Trojan horse. A processor, memory or peripheral chip supporting JTAG can be used. Only connectivity to all the relevant bus lines is needed so that they can be forced high or low by the JTAG BSR to effect a data write cycle for any valid address on the bus. The length of time required to carry out a sequence of bus write cycles, using only the JTAG access port on a neighbouring chip, can be easily estimated. First, you need to determine the length of the BSR for the host chip. If the board has several chips linked serially into the JTAG loop, all the other chips can be reset to *bypass* mode, leaving only one bit delay in the overall JTAG loop as evidence of their existence. In this case, it is important to set all those chips to a safe, tristate condition before asserting the bus lines via the JTAG port.

$$totaltime = \frac{(no\_of\_words * bus\_cycles/write * (lenBSR + updateCycles))}{clockHz}$$

For a 16 Kbyte segment in FLASH, accessed by 16 bit word; using a host chip with a BSR of 224 cells; and a TCK capable of 100 kHz through the parallel port:

$$totaltime = \frac{(8192 * 4 * (224 + 5))}{100\,000} = 75\,\text{secs}$$

If this is too painfully slow, a faster USB umbilical can be obtained. A JTAG port will typically work up to half the operational clock speed for the chip. Alternatively, with the benefit of an ICE probe, the target

• Operating system	disk file USB dongle, local file LAN/NFS, disk file native development
• RTE	floppy disk, module file serial port, module file LAN/FTP,module file
• Monitor	serial line, hex file hex code from keypad
• JTAG connector	serialized binary
• PROM socket	executable program

Methods of loading code

hardware can be controlled by software running out of overlay RAM in the host workstation. In this way, a monitor program can be written directly into the onboard Flash memory, by a loader routine running in ICE overlay RAM, after any necessary address adjustments for the relocation had been carried out.

Commercial prototype boards are usually supplied with an extended loader, or monitor program in PROM. Immediately after a system reset, control is handed to this program which offers the options of reading in other modules from serial or LAN ports, assisting with debugging or just jumping into any other executable which is ready and loaded. Such monitor programs can differ greatly in their sophistication, but generally they are at the hex end of the facility spectrum, with rather primitive file loaders. There are several accepted file formats for code downloading onto target systems: Intel Hex format, Motorola S-Record, ELF binary. These must be serviced by a monitor loader program already installed in memory on the target board. This can be accomplished using a removable EPROM or an in-circuit programmable EEPROM or Flash ROM. When the executable code module has been compiled, the linker can be set to produce a special format output file for downloading onto the target board. For serial link transfers, the Intel Hex or Motorola S-Record formats have been popular. But these double the size of the download file by splitting each byte into two nibbles and converting them to ASCII. This relates way back to the use of 7 bit paper tape and the need to restart failed transfers. With the reliability of TCP/IP, there is no longer any real need for these conversions, and it is now common to download executable binary files via the LAN.

2 bytes	2 bytes	6 bytes	<256 bytes	2 bytes
Type	Length	Address	Data	Checksum

Motorola S-record format with trailing checksum bytes

The data in Motorola S-Records and Intel Hex files is all in ASCII format. Before transmission, each byte is split into two nibbles which are then converted to ASCII representation of hex digits (0–F). This explains why a single byte checksum suddenly appears as two bytes at the end of the record.

```
S0 03 0000 FC
S2 24 010400 46FC26002E7C000808006100005E61000082610003 3C46FC270023FC00010678 6B
S2 24 010420 000C011023FC00010678000C011423FC00010678000C011823FC00010678000C 6D
S2 24 010440 011C610003A4303C271053406600FFFC46FC21006100057A4E4B000000004E75 3B
.......
S2 24 012200 0968584F4878004C4EB900010928584F206EFFFC524810BC0004602248790001 7D
S2 24 012220 21CA4EB900010968584F487800484EB900010928584F206EFFFC524842104E5E 84
S2 08 012240 4E750000  D1
S8 04 000000 FB
```

Example fragment of a Motorola S-Record format file

Above is an example fragment of a Motorola S-Record file which has been artificially spaced out to help you identify the fields. You should now confirm the checksum arithmetic. Choose one of the shorter data records (S2 Type), the penultimate is convenient, and add up, in hex, the length, address and data fields. Some calculators have hex mode, so try and borrow one:

08 + 01 + 22 + 40 + 4E + 75 + 00 + 00 = 12E
forget the 1 as overflow, leaving 2E (0010 1110)
invert the bits 1101 0001 (**D1**)   THE CHECKSUM!

Objcopy can convert a binary executable image into an S-Record format file for downloading:

```
rts-rob@kenny> objcopy -O srec file.bin file.sr
```

When producing and installing Linux, or another version of Unix, onto a target board during an embedded systems development, in addition to the kernel module, an extra problem arises because Unix needs at least the root file system, containing a minimum set of files and tools, to be available at boot time. This has to be built on the host and downloaded with, or after, the kernel to enable the full system boot to be achieved. From then on, any extra file systems can be dynamically loaded and linked into the root file system using the `mount` command.

17.16 Chapter summary

Developing code to run on embedded systems involves the use of host development stations and a suite of cross-compilers, linkers and debuggers. The development system frequently uses a different CPU to that installed on the target which gives rise to more problems with libraries and header files.

Installing code onto the target system may not be as straightforward as expected. The compiler, linker, target monitor and hardware communications facilities must be carefully considered before deciding how to deal with this phase of the development. Cross-debugging can also provide serious problems for the programmer. Extra equipment may be needed to assist with system testing and debugging. The JTAG boundary scan test facility is now being used to download code into memories, configure FPGAs and debug running code. Some SBC loaders still require ASCII format files for downloading, but this practice is going out of fashion with the move to using the much faster LAN interface.

17.17 Problems and issues for discussion

1. Trace out the sequence of states on the JTAG TAP controller on p. 383 followed by the ID request instruction.
2. Take one of your well-tested real-time programs, identify an output port with a spare line. It could be a parallel port bit or an RS232/RTS pin. Then insert two output instructions into one of the cyclical tasks to 'blip' the line. Use an oscilloscope to observe the trace. Is the timing exactly as you had imagined it?
3. Check out the linker options available on your normal compiler suite. Can it handle both native and cross compilations? What target hardware (CPU) and operating environment can it cope with?
4. Obtain/download the hardware and software manuals for a microprocessor that you are already familiar with and investigate the debugging facilities offered to developers.
5. Investigate the format of Intel Hex and Motorola S-Record files, as often used to download executable code to target systems. What error checking is provided? Are there any retransmission arrangements? Do you think the doubling of loading time which results from adopting ASCII Hex file formats is still justified?
6. Obtain the Flash user manuals from the Intel website, and read them through with a 'programmer's eye', paying particular attention to the write protocols.

17.18 Suggestions for reading

Free Software Foundation (2003). Installing GCC.
From: http://www.gcc.gnu.org

Gatliff, W. (2001a). An introduction to the GNU compiler and linker.
From: http://www.billgatliff.com

Gatliff, W. (2001b). Porting and using newlib in embedded systems.
From: http://www.billgatliff.com

Intel (2000). Common Flash Interface (CFI) and Command Sets, AN 646.

Lu, Hongjiu (1995). ELF: The Programmer's Perspective,
Nilsson, H-P. (2000). Porting gcc for dunces.
From: ftp.axis.se/pub/axistools/
Yaghmour, K. (2003). Building Embedded Linux Systems. *O'Reilly Books.*
http://crossgcc.billgatliff.com, a cross-compiler FAQ.
http://www.gnu.org, the source of information about GNU products.
http://www.intel.com/design, source of the common Flash interface documents.
http://sources.redhat.com/newlib, the main site for Cygnus' newlib.
http://sources.redhat.com/ml/crossgcc, gcc cross-compiler mailing list.

Chapter 18

Microcontroller embedded systems

18.1 Chapter overview

Programmable, or stored program controlled, devices were made possible with the invention of the microprocessor. There now exists a range of devices targeted at applications demanding anywhere from from 4 to 64 bit processing capability. Microcontroller devices have progressed beyond microprocessors to incorporate processor, memory and I/O units onto a single chip. Two commercial applications are described for the i8051 and StrongARM processors.

18.2 Microprocessors and microcontrollers

With the introduction of small integrated CPUs, in the form of microprocessors, came the possibility of many new computer-based applications. But

Type	Size	Speed	Examples	Roles
Low cost microcontroller high volume	4/8 bits	12 MHz	Intel 8051 Microchip 16F84	domestic white goods, toys, games
General purpose microcontroller	8/16 bits	25 MHz 80 MHz	80186 Infineon c166S	technical equipment, automotive applications
High performance graphics support	32 bits	3 GHz	Intel Pentium IBM Power PC	desktop PC
High performance graphics support power save mode	32 bits	2.4 GHz	Intel Pentium Transmeta crusoe	laptop/portable PC
Good performance low power	32 bits	400 MHz 200 MHz	Intel XScale StrongARM	handheld equipment, PDA, pocket PCs, real-time power computing
Top performance wide address range	32/64 bits	800 MHz	Alpha Itanium	network server, database server

Categories of microprocessor/controller

the early microprocessor chips still had to be supported on the PCB by up to a dozen peripheral chips: crystal oscillator, bus drivers, memory controller, UARTs (serial comms), PIOs (parallel I/O), interrupt controller, SRAMs, DRAMs and PROMs. Although the single chip *processor* had arrived, the single chip *computer* remained some way off. However, when circuit masks could be shrunk sufficiently, and cost effectively, it became feasible to integrate CPU, memory and I/O all on the same chip. These new highly integrated microcomputers were referred to as *microcontrollers* and reduced the cost of implementing embedded systems by a further substantial factor. Currently there is a fairly clear distinction between different categories of microprocessor, as summarized above.

18.3 Intel 8051 8 bit family

One of the most successful and enduring processor families was started by Intel in the mid-1970s. It was introduced in the form of the 8 bit, i8048 microcontroller. One of its principal features was the 27 I/O lines that it offered to system designers. These came as three byte-wide ports (P0, P1 and P2), but many of these potential port lines are dual function, and thus get reserved for more important roles. The family included several variants, including the 8748, an innovative prototyping model with 1 Kbyte of resident EPROM program memory. Intel expanded the 8048 facilities to give the 8049, and then created the 8051, which remains commercially important both as a device and in the form of IP files, for installation in customers' ASICs and FPGAs. Interestingly, the basic CPU architecture is Harvard, offering split memory for code and data, to more readily cope with the requirement for embedded systems to store program code in some form of PROM, separate from read/write data. The Program Counter (PC), also termed the instruction pointer, is 12 bits wide, limiting program memory pages to 4 Kbytes. It should also be noted that the external address and data buses are multiplexed to reduce the number of solder pins required. So if an external program memory is to be used, a bus demultiplexer latch will be needed. The internal stack pointer requires only 3 bits to handle the resident eight-level, 16 byte, stack. This occupies data RAM from locations 8 to 24. Should subroutine nesting inadvertently exceed eight in depth, not unlikely if nested interrupts have been enabled, a rollover stack error occurs, resulting in a quick system crash!

The CPU is provided with only a single byte-wide accumulator (A) and further 8 byte-wide general purpose data registers (R0–R7). The bottom 32 bytes of the internal, resident data RAM can be divided into four alternate banks of data registers. Which of these banks is selected and active is indicated by a pair of bits (RB0, RB1) in the Program Status Word (PSW). The bank switching capability is offered for convenient context saving when servicing an interrupt request. Importantly, the first two registers of a bank, R0 and R1, can act as pointers for indirect access to data RAM, but for the

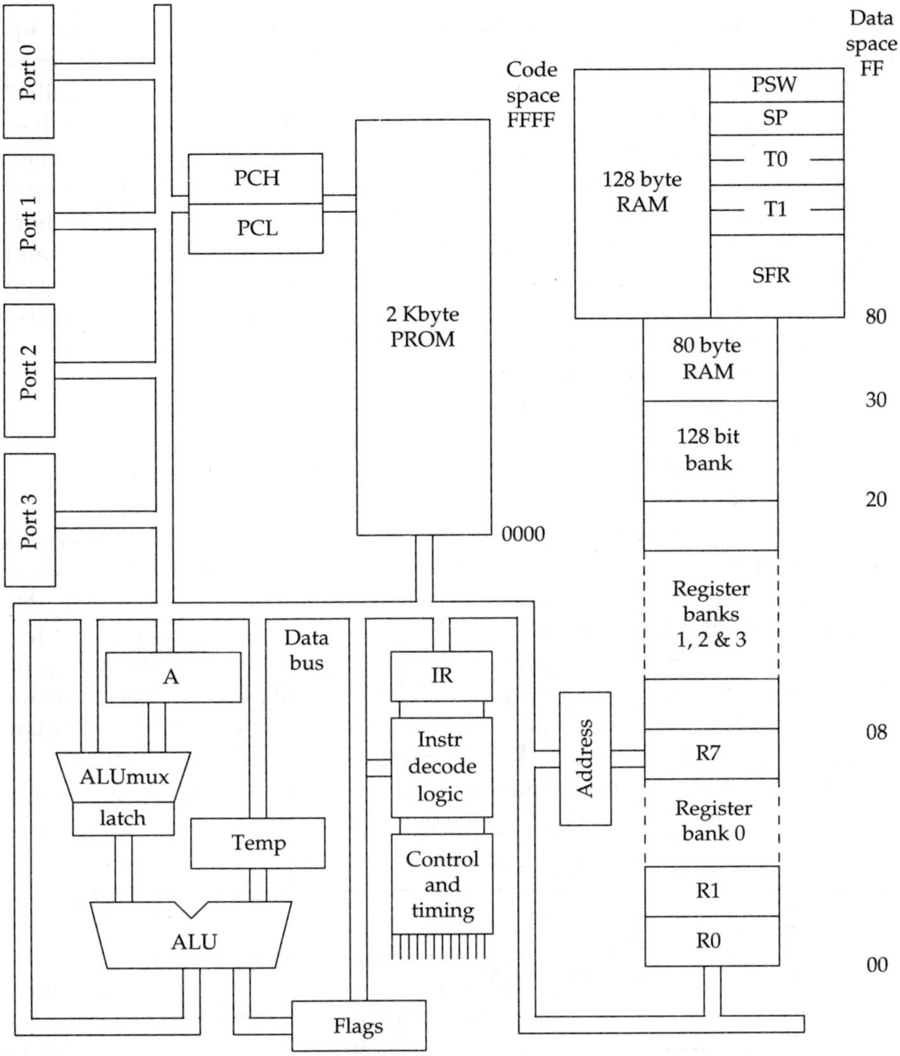

Intel 8051 internal block schematic

lower 128 bytes, memory direct addressing is also available. An interesting facility designates the next 16 bytes of resident RAM as 128 individual bit flags for status and control purposes. Above the bit flags sits a further 80 bytes of general purpose data RAM. For chips which contain 256 bytes of RAM, there are another 128 bytes which can be accessed indirectly using R0 or R1 as pointers. In parallel, overlaying the same upper 128 bytes of data space, are the Special Function Registers (SFR). These use the same address *values*, but a different addressing *mode*. Whereas the SFRs are accessed *directly*, the upper 128 bytes of data RAM can only be accessed with R0 or R1 as pointers, using the *register indirect* addressing mode. If an extended external RAM is required, possibly up to 64 Kbytes, it also has to be addressed through register indirect means, using a special `MOVX` instruction. An extra 16 bit register (DPTR) is provided in the SFR block to access the full 64 Kbyte range. SFR also holds the 8 bit extended Stack Pointer (SP) limiting the maximum stack length to 256 bytes. There are the usual `PUSH/POP` and `CALL/RET` instructions to make efficient use of the stack. Because these instructions use the register *indirect* addressing mode, the extended stack can conveniently be located in the upper 128 bytes of data memory.

The `CALL` and `JMP` instructions use either short range relative (+128/−128 byte) or long range absolute (64 Kbyte) addressing. This may result in the need to recompile and relink all executables when a minor code change occurs. The 8051 instruction set does not really support Position Independent Code (PIC).

Although the 8051 has external data and program memory spaces extending to 64 Kbytes without paging, this may still appear to be too small for many modern, GUI-based applications. But with such cheap microcontrollers, a genuinely multi-processor implementation is cost-effective. So a VCR could contain four 8051 microcontrollers, each dedicated to a particular function, communicating over an I^2C bus.

In practice, when the program is stored on-chip, in Flash memory, the 64K maximum is constrained to the availability of 4K, 8K, or 16K capacity devices. This varies depending on the speed, cost and power constraints that the project has to work within. Each version offers specific capabilities but certainly one of the distinguishing factors from chip to chip is how much ROM/EPROM/EEPROM/Flash space the chip has.

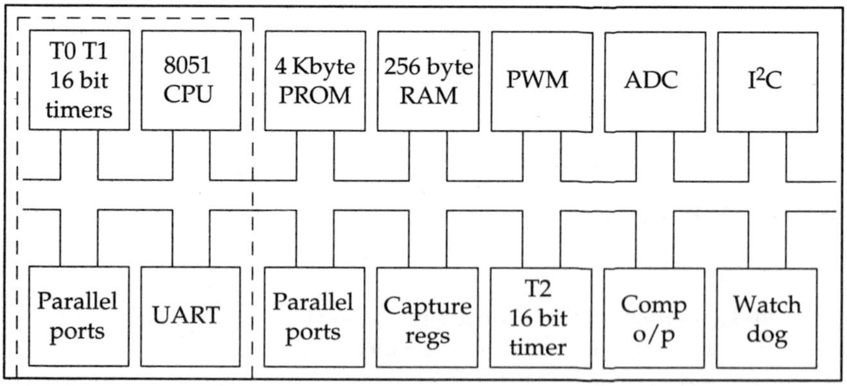

Schematic for Philips PCB83C552 microcontroller, based on the 8051 core

The continuing survival of this rather odd architecture has been due to the energetic revisions and extensions to the associated peripheral interface circuits that have been undertaken by Intel and other suppliers. Philips, for example, have included: ADCs for analogue monitoring, PWMs for motor control, counter timer circuits, I^2C for communication, onto their PCB83C552. An alternative approach can now be taken by OEM system designers. Instead of seeking out the most suitable microcontroller for their application, they can get access to a CPU design, in the form of an IP licence, and lay down their own microcontroller using an FPGA chip. To programmers used to processors offering more rational, orthogonal instruction sets, the 8051 does appear quirky, even ad hoc. But it has stood the test of time, benefited from the change to HLL programming, and now rides the IP wave into ASICs and FPGAs. Who knows how much longer it can survive?

18.4 Automatic vending technology

A major application area for microcontrollers is the vending machine market. Chocolate bars, hot drinks, pizza, and tickets of all kinds get dispensed for cash or credit by the million, at all times of day and night. This requires a pretty reliable performance, else the resentful revenge, which too often follows a failed transaction, may cost the operator a lot more than a cup of coffee in damaged equipment. Car parking is an interesting example of automatic vending because the value of an individual transaction varies from 50p for 30

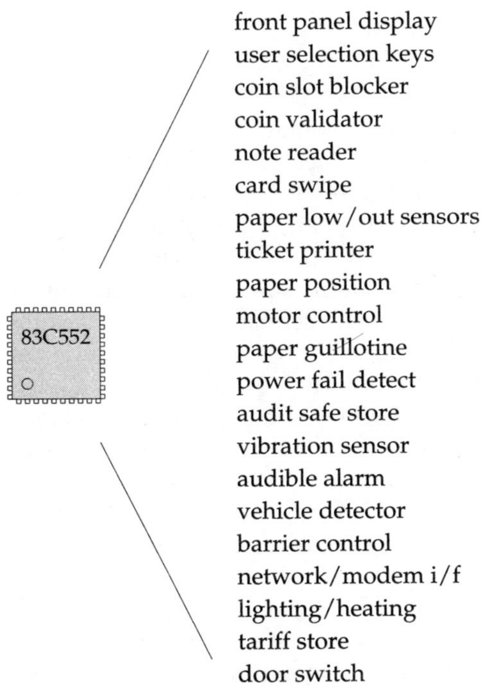

Ticket machine: I/O diversity

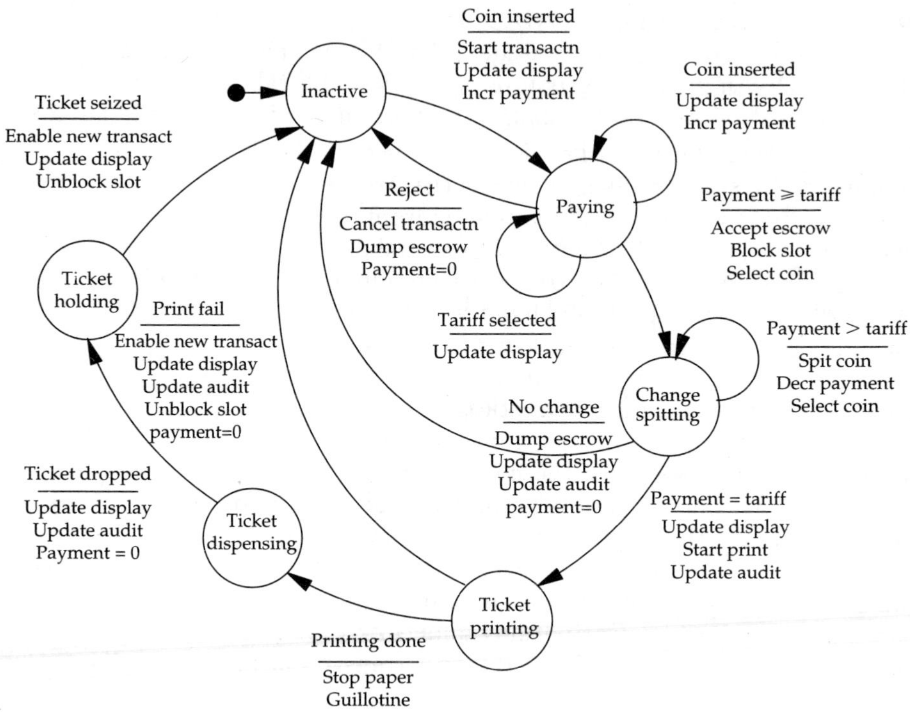

FSD for a simple Pay and Display machine

minutes in a local car park, to many hundreds of pounds for a fortnight's stay at Heathrow airport. The same equipment has to deal with a broad spectrum of client and end-user expectations. The range of typical peripheral devices is surprisingly diverse, which makes the systems design problem more interesting. And although this application is rarely seen as life threatening, a sales accountant responsible for the monthly audit can become dangerously unpredictable when confronted with a financial discrepancy in the machine records after a busy bank holiday. So be warned, get the audits right! The large number of attached devices, with a wide range of interfacing requirements, provides the developer with a good number of hardware and software problems. This project will also undoubtedly be subjected to intense cost cutting pressures due to the number of units that could be manufactured, and the international competition that already exists in this market sector. Analysing the functional requirements of a ticket issuing machine reveals a straightforward linear sequence of interactions with the user. Little justification emerges to warrant a multi-tasking implementation until a more flexible approach to the user interface, and on-line communications are included in the requirements. Should the operator want to connect all their vending machines to a network, or install dial-up modems, the software then has to deal with multi-tasking.

18.5 ARM 32 bit family

The first ARM 32 bit RISC CPU, running at 8 MHz, was designed in 1985 by Acorn as a replacement for the 8 bit 6502. The intention was to use the faster RISC processor in a new version of the very successful BBC Micro educational computer. The new machine, known as the Archimedes, gained some market share in schools and colleges, but suffered from the unanswerable criticism of being *different* from the IBM PC. The original design evolved through several versions, but when a static, low power circuit was developed, the demand for a CPU to work in portable, handheld devices was recognized. The figrst portable device which adopted low power ARM technology was the Apple Newton. But the arrival of cellular telephony, with the exploding marketplace for handsets running sophisticated voice compression/decompression and error correction algorithms, rapidly accelerated global demand for low power, high performance CPUs. The original Acorn company then evolved from a manufacturer into a supplier of circuit designs, or Intellectual Property (IP) as it had become known. This means that the VHDL code specifying a full CPU can be licensed for use by other OEM suppliers, for use within their own devices. In this way, Digital Equipment Corporation (DEC) purchased a licence for the ARM design, and the rights to extend it further. This led on to the SA-1100 StrongARM which was transferred to Intel with the unfortunate demise of DEC in 1998.

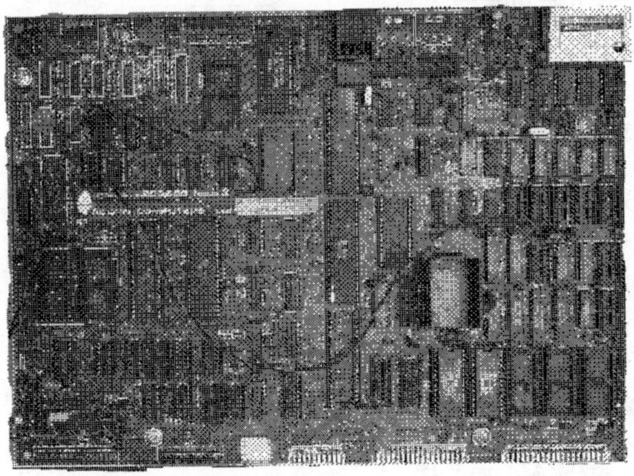

The 1980 BBC Micro motherboard with 6502 processor

18.6 StrongARM processor

The high performance 32 bit StrongARM microcontroller was developed by Digital Equipment Corporation using the original ARM-4 CPU design. Then Intel continued the development introducing the SA-1110 and recently the

XScale range of processors. The StrongARM is supplied in a 256 pin mini ball grid array (BGA) package. The integrated peripheral facilities include: 6 channel DMA, PCMCIA interface, 28 parallel I/O lines, SDRAM interface, JTAG testing and five, high speed serial channels serving RS232, I^2C, and USB.

DEC used the same technology as developed for their advanced Alpha processors, implemented the first 200 MHz StrongARMs using a 0.35 μm CMOS process, which employed triple layer metal masking to interconnect around 2.5 million transistors on a 50 mm^2 die, clocking at 200 MHz but dissipating less than a watt of heat. This compares with the familiar 15–50 watt Pentium! The DEC StrongARM worked with a five stage decode pipeline, supported by data forwarding to reduce the impact of data dependency, and had separate 16 Kbyte code and data caches.

The 26 address lines which are available *outside* the package only span a 64 Mbyte memory range, so with a 5 bit bank selector, leaving 27 bits for *within bank* addressing, only half of each of the 32 memory banks is accessible. But demonstrating its versatility, the 32 bit virtual memory management unit (MMU), with translation look-aside address caching (TLB), handles the 4 Gbyte virtual to 64 Mbyte physical page mapping. The SA1110 also has a full memory address decoding and segment selection circuitry.

Bank	Sel line	Mbytes		Physical address
		384	Reserved	FFFF_FFFFH
3		128	Zeros	
3	RAS/CAS3	128	DRAM bank 3	
3	RAS/CAS2	128	DRAM bank 2	
3	RAS/CAS1	128	DRAM bank 1	
3	RAS/CAS0	128	DRAM bank 0	
2		256	LCD & DMA registers	internal to SA1110 StrongARM
2		256	Expansion & memory	internal to SA1110 StrongARM
2		256	SCM registers	internal to SA1110 StrongARM
		256	PM registers	internal to SA1110 StrongARM
		768	Reserved	
1	CS5	128	Flash/SRAM bank 5	
1	CS4	128	Flash/SRAM bank 4	
0	PSTSEL	256	PCMIA socket 1	
0	!PSTSEL	256	PCMIA socket 0	
0	CS3	128	Flash/SRAM bank 3	
0	CS2	128	Flash/SRAM bank 2	
0	CS1	128	Flash/SRAM bank 1	
0	CS0	128	Flash bank 0	0000_0000H

SA1110 StrongARM 4 Gbyte memory map

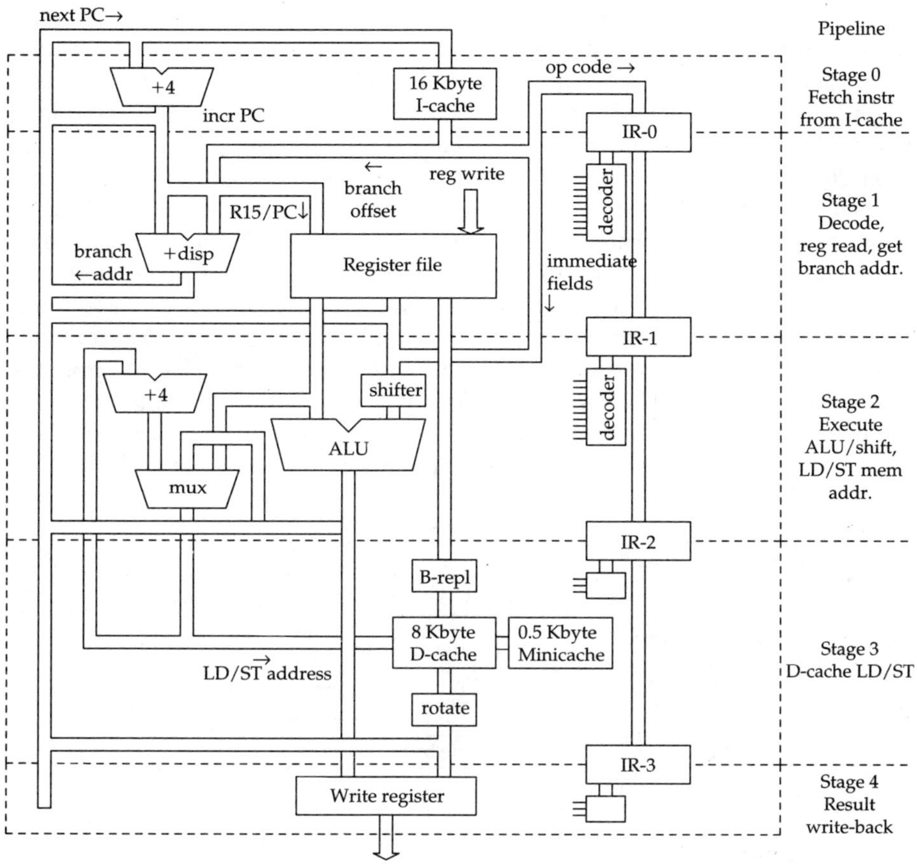

Block diagram for the StrongARM core

After a system reset the CPU starts to fetch instructions from location 0000_0000H, which is the base entry of the system's eight element interrupt vector table. To deal with this situation, it is essential to install valid branch instructions into the vector table to handle exception events.

In the StrongARM, the instruction and data caches are upstream of the MMU, meaning that they operate with *virtual* addresses. This is unlike the Pentium which pre-maps the addresses, and so passes *physical* addresses to the LI and LII caches. A problem arises with D-cache operating in virtual space. Should the same physical main memory location be mapped into more than one virtual address, in the same way that a Unix file can be 'linked' to be accessible through different directory entries, more than one cache entry will be involved with writing to the same main memory location, so it will not easily be possible to be sure that all cache items are up to date. This may be a significant issue for shared variables, and the recommended solution, to avoid cache inconsistencies with doubly mapped virtual addresses, is to block caching or to build in *bus snooping* circuitry.

A significant issue with all pipelined CPUs is the resolution of data dependencies which would otherwise stall the progress of instructions through the pipeline. Such a situation could occur if two instructions in immediate proximity share a register as operand. The first one calculates a result and stores it in register Rn, while the next instruction requires the value in Rn for its operation. This is termed a 'read-after-write' hazard because the result is not written back to the Rn register until the final pipeline step, causing the next instruction to already pass its execution step. One solution is to separate the two interlinked instructions by a NOP, or allow the compiler to carry out a spot of judicious code reordering. The StrongARM takes a different approach by providing a special backstreets short cut for the required value, before it is finally written into its register. This is known as 'data forwarding', even though it often involves sending the value backwards from the ALU!

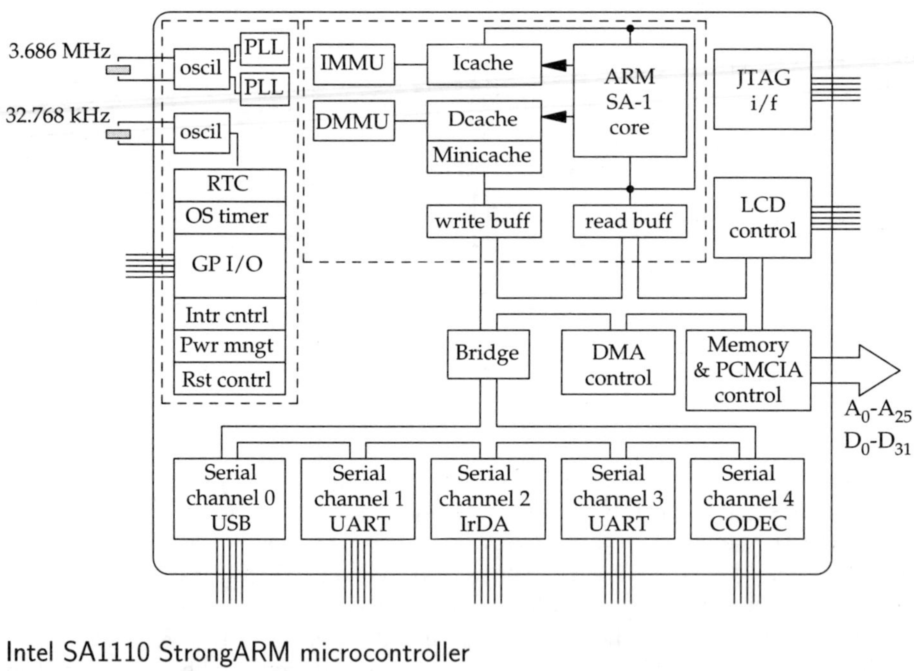

Intel SA1110 StrongARM microcontroller

18.7 Puppeteer StrongARM microcomputer

As shown in the next figure, the Puppeteer SBC has a double-sided, 150 × 100 mm PCB supporting a StrongARM CPU, one large FPGA, two CPLDs, the Ethernet chip, SRAM, Flash, four high density expansion connectors, power regulator, lithium battery for real-time clock chip, and all the other

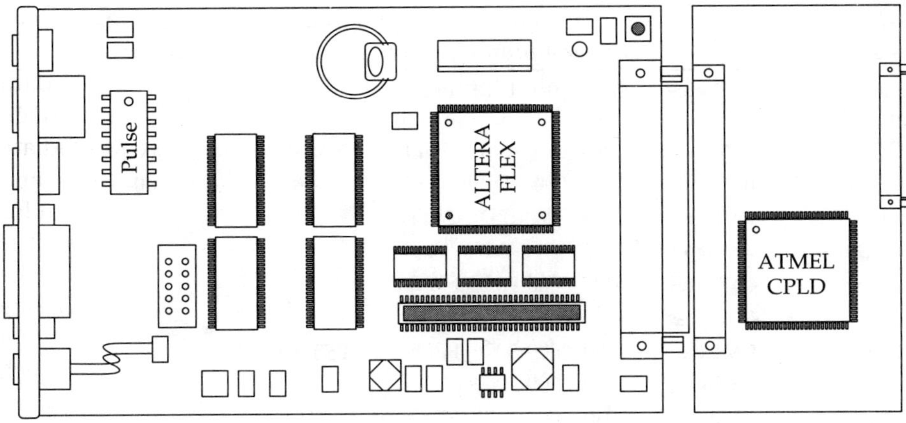

Front side of Puppeteer SBC and a plug-in I/O expansion card

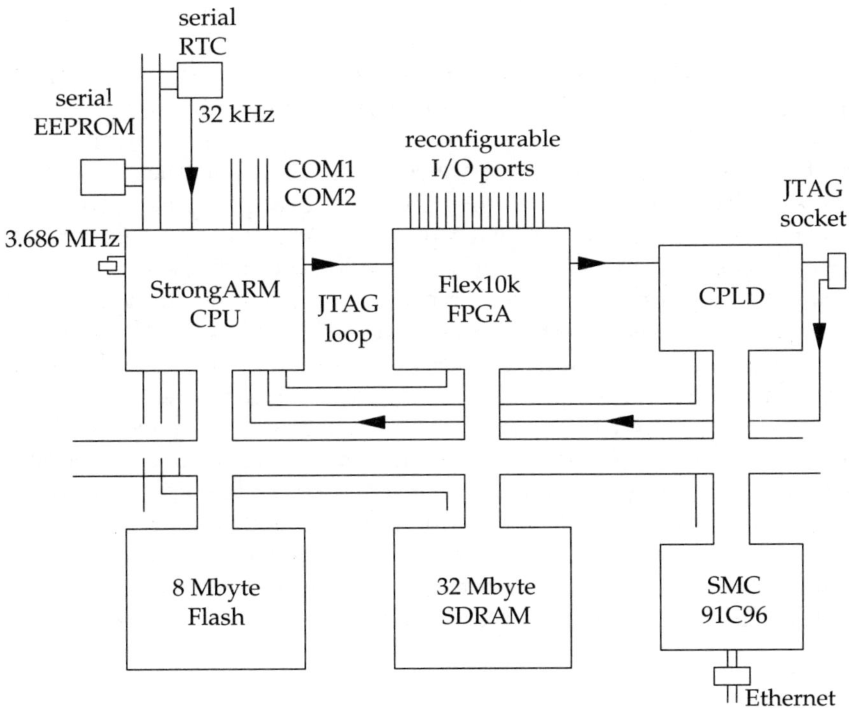

System layout for the StrongARM Puppeteer board

essential electronics to keep the system functioning. There is also an extension socket at the right-hand side to allow a variety of specialist I/O cards to be plugged into the main CPU board. The one illustrated is a flexible reconfigurable CPLD card, providing 24 bits of programmable parallel I/O

Device range	Size	Physical address	Select line	Virtual address with caching
Zero Bank cache flush	4 Mbytes	E000_0000-E03F_FFFF		
SDRAM1	16 Mbytes	C800_0000-C8FF_FFFF	RAS1	8100_0000-81FF_FFFF
SDRAM0	16 Mbytes	C000_0000-C0FF_FFFF	RAS0	8000_0000-80FF_FFFF
ASB	4 Mbytes	B000_0000-B03F_FFFF		
MMU	4 Mbytes	A000_0000-A03F_FFFF		
	4 Mbytes	9000_0000-903F_FFFF		
Sys Cntrl	4 Mbytes	8900_0000-893F_FFFF		
PCMIA1	1 Mbyte	3000_0000-300F_FFFF	PSTsel	
Ethernet	4 Mbytes	2000_0300-2000_03FF		
FPGA	4 Mbytes	1040_0000-107F_FFFF		
Flash	8 Mbytes	0000_0000-007F_FFFF	CS0	9140_0000-91BF_FFFF

Memory map for StrongARM Puppeteer

which can emulate the legacy facilities of an i8255! The I/O card has a JTAG port through which the CPLD can be reconfigured when necessary.

The Puppeteer boots up through several different memory configurations, initially to make loading and hardware setup simpler, and then to benefit from the security offered by the StrongARM MMU access control facilities. The first phase, immediately following powerup, and reset, disables virtual memory mapping, effectively using the 32 bit logical addresses in the code directly as 32 bit physical addresses: a one-to-one mapping. In addition all CPU caching is disabled. In the second phase of boot-up, CPU caching is enabled through a virtual address range for user-level processes. Thus the MMU page mapping tables are used to control access and caching for processes running on the CPU, rather than providing a swap space extension for the available 4 Gbyte space. In addition, a gap between the blocks of installed SDRAM in physical space is removed in the virtual space by appropriate mapping. This simplifies the production of software. Perhaps it is worth thinking about this alternative use of virtual memory mapping. There is no longer any need to spill main memory over into disk swap files. So the MMU plays the different role of access controller.

18.8 Application

The Puppeteer was selected for a high profile application within a public exhibition. This involved driving a game aimed principally at children who were challenged to participate without any explanation of the game's rules (my thanks to Jeff Graham for these application details and producing the awesome, artistic impression). Not only were the players required

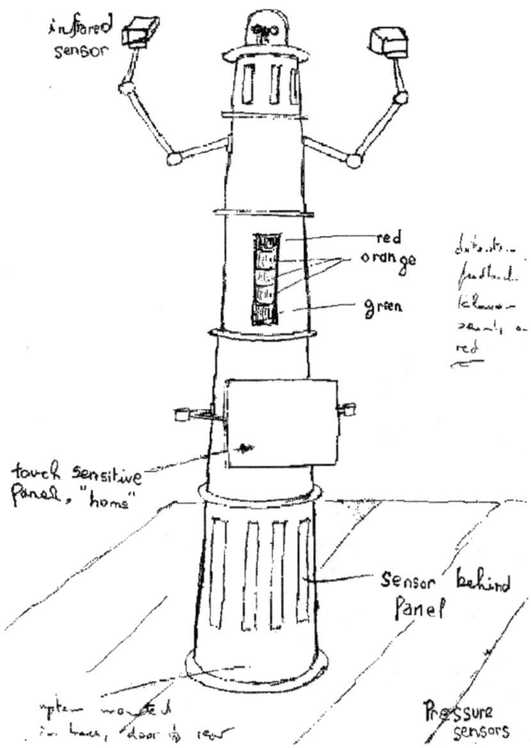

The intelligent goal post

to deduce the rules and develop winning strategies, but also the software monitored the success rate of the game and the algorithm tightened the rules if the players succeeded too often. Worse still for the players, if they were judged as winning too easily and regularly, the rules were changed, meaning that in effect a completely different game was being played. This was ruthlessly done without explanation or warning. The children had to work out what the rules were and pass on tips to other players. As their level of expertise rises, the rules can again change to confound the increasingly confident participants. Each new set of rules has to be guessed and countered.

The game is based on a set of sensors that monitor movement, pressure, heat, and light. Players are required to pass through a series of traps to reach 'home'. A stack of green, amber and red lights is used to indicate what the system has succeeded in detecting. As more detections are made, more and more lights are lit, until the last red lamp indicates that the player has lost. Sounds are also used to give more exciting feedback and build a sense of drama. The volume level is controlled automatically by monitoring ambient noise levels and adjusting accordingly.

The staff at the centre where the game is installed wanted easy control over all the critical parameters, such as audio volume and average brightness. They also wanted to be able to monitor game usage statistics in order to implement later modifications. The ability to select different sound files, perhaps to use seasonal sounds, and to alter the base game rules were both seen as essential facilities. To make this possible, the Puppeteer runs a web server which provides a number of interactive pages allowing all these settings to be altered. The staff can access the web server from their offices, over the LAN.

All of this is managed by a single Puppeteer, programmed in Java, using multiple threads. The web server runs in one major thread, spawning further threads for each client that connects. The sensors are monitored through individual threads. The game has been a great success and has revealed a lot about the way children play and deal with non-explicit rule sets.

18.9 FPGA usage

A modern SBC, such as the Puppeteer board, offers the system designer the potential for hardware as well as software development through the configuration of large FPGAs. This facility might be used to implement significant peripheral devices, such as an Ethernet or USB interface, or contribute to accelerating an important algorithm by installing a special DSP co-processor. An SVG video controller could be implemented if the need for a locally attached monitor arose. The risky opportunity even exists to dynamically change the FPGA configuration during normal operational system usage if the required JEDEC files can be stored in Flash. Further details concerning the language VHDL and mapping logic designs onto the internal architecture of commercial FPGAs are beyond the scope of this text, but the reader is encouraged to continue investigating this subject by reading a suitable text (e.g. Zwolinski 2000).

18.10 Serial access memory

With very tight space constraints, the need to shrink embedded hardware beyond that possible simply by using single chip microcontrollers has led to

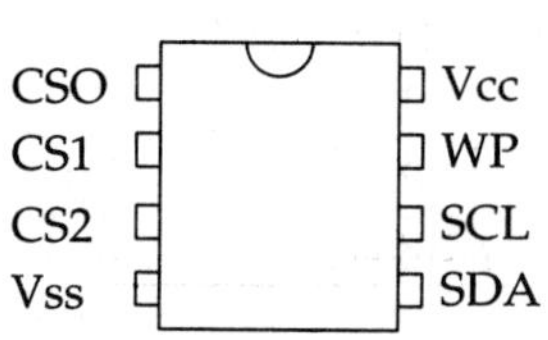

ATMEL serial EEPROM

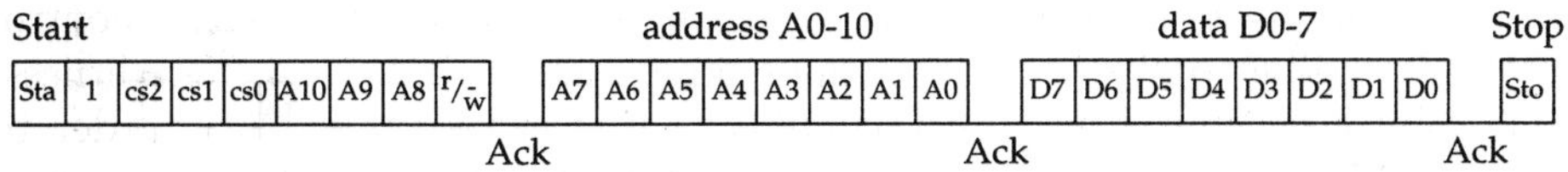

Command sequence for a 1 Kbyte serial EEPROM

the development of serial buses, such as I^2C and SPI. There are now quite a range of I^2C devices offered to system designers. In the Puppeteer example system described earlier, the FPGA has to be loaded with a configuration file during the power-on sequence. If this does not happen the FLEX 10k FPGA will have no useful role to play. The SDA/SCL serial bus follows a master/slave operational protocol very similar to that defined by I^2C. The CS0-2 pins designate a 3 bit address for the device, allowing up to eight similar devices to coexist on the same serial bus. To write data into a serial EEPROM, a data bit value is set up on SDA and the clock line, SCL, dropped from high to low. The EEPROM acknowledges reception of a byte by pulling SDA low. The master supplies the clock, and requests data from one slave at a time.

The maximum clock speed for a serial EEPROM is typically only 100 kHz, giving a rather slow single byte write time of 300 μsec. Because it then takes at least 77 msec to write out the full 256 bytes, careful consideration has to be given before using serial EEPROMS to save critical data in the event of a power failure. To avoid unintentioned corruption of data, perhaps during the power-up interlude, a write protect pin (WP) can be used to hold off any write activity until the system is fully operational.

18.11 Chapter summary

Stored program controlled devices emerged as a dominant influence in the 1970s when microprocessors were commercially introduced by Intel. The range of such devices has expanded to include specially developed versions for many particular applications, using anywhere from 25 MHz, 4 bit to 500 MHz, 64 bit CPUs. The processing capability can be selected to match the need. Microcontroller devices have progressed beyond microprocessors to incorporate processor, memory and I/O units onto a single chip. The use of large FPGAs to host complete systems, including two or more processors, is a new development in the embedded field.

18.12 Problems and issues for discussion

1. Take the example of a microcontroller you are familiar with and consider the problems of writing a new application for it using a PC as host. Take into account the commitment you have made to the client

to demonstrate a simulation of the functionality on your laptop before continuing toward the target implementation.

2. Why cannot you use a microcontroller I/O pin to supply the C/S signal to RAM or ROM? Why are there only three address lines on the typical UART chip? Explain why a certain 256 Mbit DRAM chip has only 13 address lines.
3. Consider a car park traffic monitoring scheme which uses induction loop detectors as illustrated in Section 5.4. Draft out a rough proposal for a microcontroller-based system which would be intended for installation at a major airport. This would have to deal with a range of large parking areas, some multi-storey, others open field. Network communications would clearly be a central part of the facilities offered, as would several central monitoring stations positioned in offices.
4. Given the pressing need for remote feline care and management equipment, which microcontroller would you recommend to a friend who is trying to write a business plan to convince a bank to fund the venture? Local and remote interfaces to the domestic LAN, GSM text messaging, and a variety of Internet modems are desirable. Supply a top-level system architecture plan, including both the principal hardware and software components.
5. As any new parent knows, babies are easily pleased by novelty, but fickle in their attention span. Until now, toy manufacturers have been content with offering large, static arrays of dangling plastic items which often survive critical appraisal, and physical damage, for as long as 10 minutes. What if a computer-driven, interactive panel could be used, with a reasonably powerful audio output unit? The display would be driven by suitably complex algorithms, generating regular sensory changes, to hold the attention of the most challenging client. A cunning blend of coin-slot, arcade know-how and developmental, cognitive psychology should quickly achieve worldwide market domination. Sketch out the software architecture for such a device, taking into account your desire to sell a regular string of 'educational' updates from your firm's on-line server.

18.13 Suggestions for reading

Berger, A. (2002). *Embedded Systems Design.* CMPBooks.

Furber, S. (2000). *ARM System-on-Chip Architecture.* Addison Wesley.

Intel (2001). *i8251 Microcontroller, Developer's Manual.*

Intel (2001). *StrongARM SA-1110 Microprocessor, Developer 's Manual.*

Kreidl, H. (2000). Using C++ in embedded applications on Motorola's 8 and 16 bit microcontrollers. *Embedded System Engineering*, 8(5), 42–60.

Li, Q. with Yao, C. (2003). *Real-time Concepts for Embedded Systems.* CMPBooks.

Shaw, A. C. (2001). *Real-time Systems and Software.* Wiley.

van Someren, A. & Atack, C. (1995). *The ARM RISC Chip.* Addison Wesley.

Wilmshurst, T. (2001). *An Introduction to the Design of Small-scale Embedded Systems*. Palgrave.
Yeralan, S. & Ahluwalia, A. (1998). *Programming and Interfacing the 8251 Family of Microcontrollers*. Addison Wesley.
Zwolinski, M. (2000). *Digital Design with VHDL*. Prentice Hall.
http://www.vhdl.org, source of information concerning the VHDL language standards.
http://www.iPuppeteer.com, information about the StrongARM Puppeteer board.

Chapter 19

Linux device drivers

19.1 Chapter overview

The availability of several real-time variants, and its increasing popularity for desktop and server usage, has meant that Linux is now being seriously evaluated for embedded applications. Device drivers are collections of subroutines which together offer a software interface to an I/O device. They may be bound into the kernel, or dynamically loaded into a running system. All device drivers have to comply with a standardized interface (API) by having their code organized into a small set of functions which fit in with the published system calls. To further 'virtualize' the device interface, in Unix they are accessed through the file system directories.

19.2 Embedded Linux

Recently there has been increasing interest in the use of the Linux kernel for real-time embedded systems, as described in Chapter 9. This is curious because Linux is far from being suitable for real-time applications. It was created for a multi-user, mini-computer with large file system, a 'fair-shares' scheduler, and virtual memory support. This discrepancy reminds me of the time when Pascal was enthusiastically greeted as the final solution for real-time programming, despite all its immediately obvious shortcomings. But for whatever reasons, Linux is being used for an increasing number of high-profile products and services. Of particular note, when writing this chapter, is the TomTom GPS in-car navigation system which provides a 3D model of the road ahead with text and voice synthesized driving advice. In addition, a variety of PDAs and high functionality mobile phones have been announced with Linux as their first choice cperating system.

19.3 Porting Linux

Since its early days, one of the principal advantages that Unix offered to computer system builders was its readiness to be ported to new architectures. This was partly because it was mainly coded in C, but also because the source code was freely available for inspection and modification. With the advent of Linux, the situation has further improved, with widespread support for porting activities. However, as indicated in Section 9.11, the configuring and recompilation of Linux kernels is still not something to be undertaken while perfecting your skills as a pastry chef. It can be unpredictable and time consuming, and rarely goes according to the recipe. So what follows is only an optimistic scheme which can be used as a guide. Refer to Abbott (2003) and Duffy (2004) for more detailed advice and guidance. An essential tool in porting Linux is gcc, configured as a cross-compiler for the target architecture, as described in Chapter 17. First, it might be a good idea to check out the version of cross-gcc you intend to use for the target kernel production. This can be done by running the cross-compiler with the -v flag: `arm-elf-gcc -v`. Working with the 2.4 series kernel will require a compiler version later than 2.95.3, but too recent a version may also be incompatible. It is not unknown for Linux releases to come with 'incompatible' gcc compilers, because they have been updated subsequent to production of the kernel. Anyway, here we go.

1. Change your current directory to /tmp, or similar development directory, to avoid the possible corruption of your host PC system files.
2. The source package for the chosen version of Linux, such as linux-2.4.18.tgz, should be downloaded from a convenient server site (http://www.kernel.org or ftp.kernel.org).

```
rob:/tmp> ftp ftp.linux.org
Connected to ftp.linux.org.
220 FTP server ready.
Name (ftp.linux.org:rwilliam): anonymous
331 Guest login ok, send your complete e-mail address as password.
Password: *******
230 Guest login ok, access restrictions apply.
ftp> binary
200 Type set to I.
ftp> dir
200 PORT command successful.
```

```
150 Opening ASCII mode data connection for directory
    listing.
total 3200
dr-xr-xr-x    2 root     root       4096 Feb 14  2004 bin
dr-xr-xr-x    2 root     root       4096 Feb 14  2004 etc
drwxr-xr-x    2 root     root       4096 Feb 14  2004 lib
-rw-r--r--    1 root     root    1449788 Oct 28 06:00 ls-lR
-rw-r--r--    1 root     root     154770 Oct 28 06:00 ls-lR.gz
drwxrwxr-x   45 root     root       4096 Oct 28 12:07 pub
drwxr-xr-x    3 root     root       4096 Nov  8  1999 usr
drwxr-xr-x    3 root     root       4096 Dec  7  2001 www
226 Transfer complete.
499 bytes received in 0.27 seconds (1.79 Kbytes/s)
ftp> cd /pub/linux/releases/2.4
250 CSD command successful
ftp> get linux-2.4.18.tar.gz
200 PORT command successful.
150 Opening ASCII mode data connection for linux.2.14.tar.gz
ftp> quit
```

3. Next, the compressed Linux tar file sitting in /tmp has to be decompressed and unpacked:

```
> tar -vzxf linux-2.4.18.tar.gz
```

4. This builds the Linux source file directory tree, with multiple configure and makefiles, based on a new directory /tmp/linux. To adjust the kernel to deal with the target CPU architecture a special patch file has to be obtained and inserted into the source tree. In this case, the ARM patch produced by Russell King is being downloaded, using ftp as before, but from a different ftp server:

```
rob:/tmp> ftp ftp.arm.linux.org.uk
ftp> cd /pub/linux/arm/source/kernel-patches/v2.4
ftp> binary
   . . . .
ftp> get patch-2.4.18-rmk7.gz
ftp> quit
```

5. Before applying the architecture patch, it may be necessary to clean up the distribution, perhaps to remove the results of failed earlier attempts.

```
> make distclean
```

6. To apply the architecture amendment patch to the main kernel source:

```
> gzip -cd patch-2.4.18-rmk7.gz | patch -p0
```

This takes the diff format changes held in the patch file, and applies them to the list of files which it also contains. In this case, there are too many files all to be cited on the command line! It is probably worth scanning through `man patch` to understand what effect it is having on the original files, but the -p flag indicates whether to truncate the path names by deleting leading /s.

7. Now the top-level kernel makefile, contained in the /tmp/linux directory, needs to be edited appropriately for your setup:

   ARCH:= ARM
   CROSS-COMPILE = arm-linux-

8. At this moment, even though the source tree has been adjusted for the target CPU (ARM), the kernel code still needs further adjustment for compilation to work for the target board's memory and I/O devices. One strategy to speed things up is to look out for an existing configuration which is similar to your new target. Each of the available config files could be inspected in /tmp/linux/arch/arm/ and the best option chosen. In this case, as an example, we will take the Pangolin board as closest.

```
>make pangolin
```

   This produces a .config file to be used as a starting point for the next make operation, and needs to be placed in /tmp/linux.

9. Stay in the /tmp/linux directory and run the principal, top-level makefile to configure the kernel. The choice of make targets usually includes: config, xconfig or menuconfig, they all run interactively to allow the correct target system options to be selected. The xconfig version is not quite as fully featured as the other two, but perhaps, more convenient.

```
>make menuconfig
```

   The response choices offered to each of the config options are Y, N, and ? for more help. The configuration process is driven by the config.in text file. While all the information captured is entered into the .config file. The config.in file is located in /tmp/linux/arch/arm, if the target architecture is ARM. If you look inside, the structure and sequence of the menuconfig questions can be recognized. More information about the configuration scripting language can be found in the file: /tmp/linux/Documentation/kbuild/config-language.txt. The main result of passing through the *make menuconfig* configuration process is to set the values for variables, or macros, used by the many makefiles held in the Linux source tree. The makefiles will read out these values to determine which components to include in the new kernel, and also to pass #define values into various source code files.

10. The next step configures the memory assignments for loading, decompressing and running the kernel. This requires the address values in the /tmp/linux/arch/arm/boot file to be edited, as well as a few other memory value revisions to convert to the specific target configuration. Check the address values in the linker script file, vmlinux.lds, ensure they are in accord with the target board memory layout for TEXT segment, BSS segment and start addresses.
11. If necessary change back to /tmp/linux-2.4.18 and then run the makefiles. This make operation is complex and recursive. There are many makefiles scattered over the Linux source tree, so it can be 30 minutes before completion, depending on the speed of your processor.

```
> make dep
 > make clean
 > make zImage
```

12. Now there should be `vmlinux` in /tmp/linux/arch/arm/boot/ compressed, this is the compressed kernel with its decompressor code waiting to be downloaded. It can be checked using a bintools utility, `objdump`:

```
> arm-linux-objdump -D vmlinux
```

13. There is also `zImage` in /tmp/linux/arch/arm/boot, and `vmlinux` in /tmp/linux. But before the compressed kernel boot module can run, a root file system has to be provided for the target system, where it will reside in an 8 MB RAMdisk. The mkfs variant command formats the RAMdisk volume for an ext2 file system with 2 KB inode size.

```
> dd if=/dev/zero of=imagefile bs=1k count=8192
> /sbin/mke2fs -F -m0 -I 2000 imagefile
> mount -t ext2 -o loop imagefile /loopfs
> cd /loopfs
> mkdir /dev /etc /bin /sbin /lib /usr /proc /tmp /etc
    /init.d /usr/bin
```

14. Several scripts and files can now be copied into the /etc directory from the host file system: /etc/fstab, /etc/init.d/rcs, /etc/inittab, /etc/passwd.
15. Also all the necessary special device files with major and minor numbers have to be setup in /dev using mknod, but this requires root permissions. All the major and minor number values are conventionally standardized and so may be copied from an existing desktop version of Linux.

```
> su
$ mknod -m 0888 tty c 5 0
```

Repeated for: tty0, S0, S1, SA0, SA1, SA2, cusa0, cusa1, cusa2, ram, null, pt0, pt1, pt2, pt3, ptmx, ptyp0, ptyp1, ptyp2, ptyp3, ttyp0, ttyp1, ttyp2, ttyp3.

16. The basic set of Unix tools, grep, sed, ls, etc., can conveniently all be obtained with `busybox`, which can be downloaded from http://www.busybox.net.
17. The most suitable library to use with embedded systems might be μ`clibc`, which is obtainable from http://www.uclibc.org and rebuilt from source.
18. In place of the normal login utility, the smaller `tinylogin` is often preferred for small embedded systems.
19. There remains to figure out how to download the compressed kernel module and compressed root file system module into target memory. The best way requires an onboard monitor which can handle Ethernet transfers, probably using TFTP. But there are several other alternatives as discussed in Section 17.15.

19.4 The role of device drivers

Linux, in common with most operating systems, prefers to hide from programmers the specific operational details of peripheral hardware behind a screen of software. This promotes programmability, strengthens system security and raises run-time resilience. The principal component in this 'defensive' wall is the device driver, which represents the associated hardware by offering a limited software interface of several function calls. These in their turn are mapped onto the standard programmer interface which offers a small set of generic facilities for every device: `open()`, `read()`, `write()` and `close()`. The kernel maintains *device switch tables* to map access requests to the versions of these open/read/write functions appropriate for the device in question. The device major number operates as an index into this table. In this way, Linux ensures that all devices are accessed by programmers in a standardized manner. Not all the functions are provided for every device, but a formal error will be returned to avoid crashing should an unimplemented function be called. It is possible for user processes to have device registers mapped into their virtual address space, but this is rarely done, because of the problems it would generate, especially if interrupts were involved. The special, privileged role of device drivers means they are classified as *system* rather than *application* software.

Interestingly, one peripheral device may enjoy the attentions of more than one device driver, each presenting a different set of hardware characteristics to the user, while one device driver often deals with a whole family of similar devices. In Unix, a device 'major number' selects the device driver, while a 'minor number' may be used to specify the device itself. This is further explained in the next section. Device driver code can be bound within the booting kernel, or installed later, as a *loadable module*, into an already operational system. Linux conveniently now offers both alternatives.

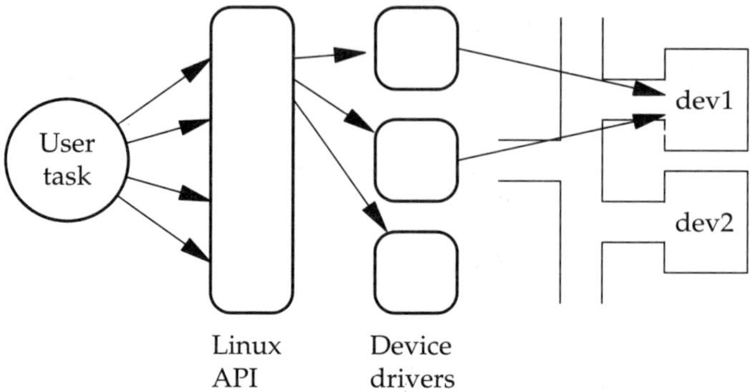

User task access route to devices

19.5 Major and minor numbers

In Unix, all device drivers are allocated a 'major number'. This is used by the operating system to identify the device driver, index into the device table, and from there to access the correct set of read/write functions. The major numbers can be inspected by listing /proc/devices. Complete device numbers

```
[rob@local] cat /proc/devices
Character device  Block device
    1 mem             1 ramdisk
    2 pty/m%d         2 fd
    3 pty/s%d         3 ide0
    4 tts/%d          9 md
    5 cua/%d         11 sr
    6 lp             22 ide1
    7 vcs
   10 misc
   14 sound
   29 fb
  116 alsa
  128 ptm
  129 ptm
  130 ptm
  131 ptm
  136 pts/%d
  137 pts/%d
  138 pts/%d
  139 pts/%d
  162 raw
  180 usb
[rob@local]
```

Major device numbers

are constructed by concatenating the 8 bit device driver 'major number', with the 8 bit device 'minor number'. As stated, the former is used by the kernel to identify the device *driver*, while the latter is only relevant to the device driver itself, distinguishing the actual *device* which will be accessed. So the minor number is in effect an abstraction of the device's port addresses and interrupt number. Using `ls -al`, the major and minor numbers can be inspected. For IDE disk devices, the minor number can often be further split down, with the top two bits holding the disk number, and the bottom six bits referring to the partition. The 10 partitions, on the first IDE (main master) drive, have minor numbers in the range 1–11 (00_000001–00_001011). The second IDE (main slave) drive is described by minor numbers 65–75 (01_000001–01_001011). While, the secondary master and secondary slave have allocations: 129–139 (10_000001–10_001011) and 193–203 (11_000001–11_001011).

The device driver's major number can be assigned statically by the programmer and edited into the driver code, or allocated dynamically at device installation time by request to the kernel. But, of course, the major and minor numbers all have to be unique within the system. To access a raw device, in principle all that is needed is its major number, identifying the correct driver routines, and the minor number which translates into the device port addresses. However, this is never done. All access to peripheral devices is carried out by first looking up their logical *names* through the file system. Then using the returned pointer, or index, to evoke the access functions through the inode which holds the major and minor numbers.

```
[rob@local] ls -ls ide/host0/bus0/target*/lun0/part*
 0 brw------- 1 root root 3,  1 Jan 1 1970 ide/host0/bus0/target0/lun0/part1
 0 brw------- 1 root root 3, 10 Jan 1 1970 ide/host0/bus0/target0/lun0/part10
 0 brw------- 1 root root 3, 11 Jan 1 1970 ide/host0/bus0/target0/lun0/part11
 0 brw------- 1 root root 3,  2 Jan 1 1970 ide/host0/bus0/target0/lun0/part2
 0 brw------- 1 root root 3,  5 Jan 1 1970 ide/host0/bus0/target0/lun0/part5
 0 brw------- 1 root root 3,  6 Jan 1 1970 ide/host0/bus0/target0/lun0/part6
 0 brw------- 1 root root 3,  7 Jan 1 1970 ide/host0/bus0/target0/lun0/part7
 0 brw------- 1 root root 3,  8 Jan 1 1970 ide/host0/bus0/target0/lun0/part8
 0 brw------- 1 root root 3,  9 Jan 1 1970 ide/host0/bus0/target0/lun0/part9
 0 brw------- 1 root root 3, 65 Jan 1 1970 ide/host0/bus0/target1/lun0/part1
 0 brw------- 1 root root 3, 74 Jan 1 1970 ide/host0/bus0/target1/lun0/part10
 0 brw------- 1 root root 3, 75 Jan 1 1970 ide/host0/bus0/target1/lun0/part11
 0 brw------- 1 root root 3, 66 Jan 1 1970 ide/host0/bus0/target1/lun0/part2
 0 brw------- 1 root root 3, 69 Jan 1 1970 ide/host0/bus0/target1/lun0/part5
 0 brw------- 1 root root 3, 70 Jan 1 1970 ide/host0/bus0/target1/lun0/part6
 0 brw------- 1 root root 3, 71 Jan 1 1970 ide/host0/bus0/target1/lun0/part7
 0 brw------- 1 root root 3, 72 Jan 1 1970 ide/host0/bus0/target1/lun0/part8
 0 brw------- 1 root root 3, 73 Jan 1 1970 ide/host0/bus0/target1/lun0/part9
[rob@local]
```

Major and minor device numbers

19.6 Index blocks, the Unix inode

Devices under Linux are categorized as character, block or network. Each needs servicing in a different fashion and this is reflected in the actions of the device driver. A *character* device supplies, or consumes, a stream of bytes, with no defined structuring. The associated inode, or pseudo-file, such as /dev/ttyS0 holds the major and minor numbers to provide an access route to the correct device driver when a process calls the `open()` function with that device name. Block devices, such as disks, deal in blocks of data, and require some internal structuring, usually an intrinsic file system, to facilitate data access. If the device concerned holds the root file system, then access to data blocks, through the root directory and inode pointers, is already established during the booting process. However, if the required data exists on a secondary device, an inode has to be created, such as '/dev/hdb0', on the root device to give access to the device driver for the secondary disk. Then normal file accessing can be achieved by *mounting* the new device onto a suitable position within the root file system. This relies on the new mount point inode holding major, minor and superblock details, so that file references can be passed on to the secondary device driver.

Unlike in other operating systems, Unix users access peripheral devices and data files as a unified hierarchical file system, hanging down from the single root directory. Compare this with Windows offering up to 26 file device identifiers, A:–Z: and many device identifiers: COM2, LPT1, CON. Unix has always dealt with devices simply as another aspect of file handling. The file system administrative structure starts with a boot device containing a master boot block. This holds the initial system loader, information about the disk's partitioning, and, in particular, which partition holds the bootable kernel image. Next on the disk, the superblock contains information about where the root file system is to be found by holding the location of the root inode and directory.

As we have already seen, Unix file systems depend heavily on a data structure known as an *inode* (index node). The structure of an inode block can be seen in the header file: /usr/include/linux/fs.h. The *mode* field indicates what type of file this inode represents, regular, directory, or device. You can see the fields used for accessing the data blocks. Every file, device and directory has a unique, identifying inode block which holds pointers to further data blocks. The data blocks may then actually contain file data, a subdirectory or device information. From the next figure a disk inode block can be seen to hold access control information as well as 12 direct pointers to data blocks which contain the data for that file. With a 4 KB storage block size, the 12 direct pointers (0..11) handle files up to 48 KB in size. Should the file require more storage capacity, pointer 12 leads to a slave index block pointing to a further 1 K data blocks. When this is exhausted, pointer 13 acts as a doubly indirect pointer, linking into 1 M (1 K $\times$ 1 K) further data blocks. Finally, to cater for massive files, pointer 14 is triply indirect, giving

```
/*
 * Constants relative to the data blocks
 */
#define  EXT2_NDIR_BLOCKS     12
#define  EXT2_IND_BLOCK       EXT2_NDIR_BLOCKS
#define  EXT2_DIND_BLOCK      (EXT2_IND_BLOCK + 1)
#define  EXT2_TIND_BLOCK      (EXT2_DIND_BLOCK + 1)
#define  EXT2_N_BLOCKS        (EXT2_TIND_BLOCK + 1)

/*
 * Structure of an inode on the disk taken from /usr/include/
     linux/ext2_fs.h
 */
      struct ext2_inode {
            __u16     i_mode;       /* File mode */
            __u16     i_uid;        /* Low 16 bits of Owner Uid */
            __u32     i_size;       /* Size in bytes */
            __u32     i_atime;      /* Access time */
            __u32     i_ctime;      /* Creation time */
            __u32     i_mtime;      /* Modification time */
            __u32     i_dtime;      /* Deletion time */
            __u16     i_gid;        /* Low 16 bits of Group Id */
            __u16     i_links_count;/* Links count */
            __u32     i_blocks;     /* Blocks count */
            __u32     i_flags;      /* File flags */
            union { . . . } osd1; /* OS dependent 1 */
            __u32     i_block[EXT2_N_BLOCKS];   /* Pointers to blocks */
            __u32     i_generation;/* File version for NFS */

            /* ACL stuff here */

            union { . . . } osd2; /* OS dependent 2 */
};
```

Unix inode structure on disk

access to 1 G ($1\,\text{K} \times 1\,\text{K} \times 1\,\text{K}$) more data blocks. Thus, the largest file size would be: $(12 + 1\,\text{K} + 1\,\text{M} + 1\,\text{G}) \times 4\,\text{KB}$, over 4 terabytes.

There is some confusion when referring to an inode structure, because there are two slightly different forms, that stored on disk and that held in memory for faster run-time access. The latter is extended with extra fields of status information as summarized below. The C structure used by programmers to access the information is also presented.

The fields 'st_ino' and 'st_dev' are the most important because they hold the inode number and device major and minor identifiers. Only through these numbers it is possible to find the file data on disk, or the device driver routines to carry out the I/O operations required. The inode number needs to be addded to the in-memory inode structure because they are no longer sorted in order, as on disk. Rather they are reorganized in a hash list for faster

- Inode status – locked/free
  – task waiting
  – memory inode changed
  – file data changed
  – inode is a mount point
- Device number (major and minor)
- Inode number
- Pointers to other inodes in list
- Count of active references

Extra data held by in-memory inodes

```
struct stat {
      dev_t        st_dev;     /* major-minor device number */
      long         st_pad1[3];/* reserve for dev expansion, */
      ino_t        st_ino;     /* inode number */
      mode_t       st_mode;
      nlink_t      st_nlink;   /* number of active links to the file */
      uid_t        st_uid;     /* file owner's ID */
      gid_t        st_gid;     /* designated group id */
      dev_t        st_rdev;
      long         st_pad2[2];
      off_t        st_size;    /* file size in bytes */
      long         st_pad3;    /* reserve for future off_t expansion*/
      timestruc_t              st_atime;/*last access time*/
      timestruc_t              st_mtime;/*last write time (modification)*/
      timestruc_t              st_ctime;/*last status change time*/
      long         st_blksize;
      long         st_blocks;
      char         st_fstype[_ST_FSTYPSZ];
      long         st_pad4[8];/* expansion area */
};
```

Structure used to access in-memory inode information

access. Programmers obtain the inode information for a file by using the system function `int stat(const char *path, struct stat *buf)`.

There is a bit of a chicken-and-egg problem when trying to discover the identity of a device driver from its associated inode. How can we originally access the root file system device, when the device inode information is on disk and we cannot read the major and minor numbers? So at boot time, the root disk's device driver is specially declared, and the root file system inodes are read into memory from disk. Here, a dynamic linked list inode data structure is constructed to support much faster file accessing.

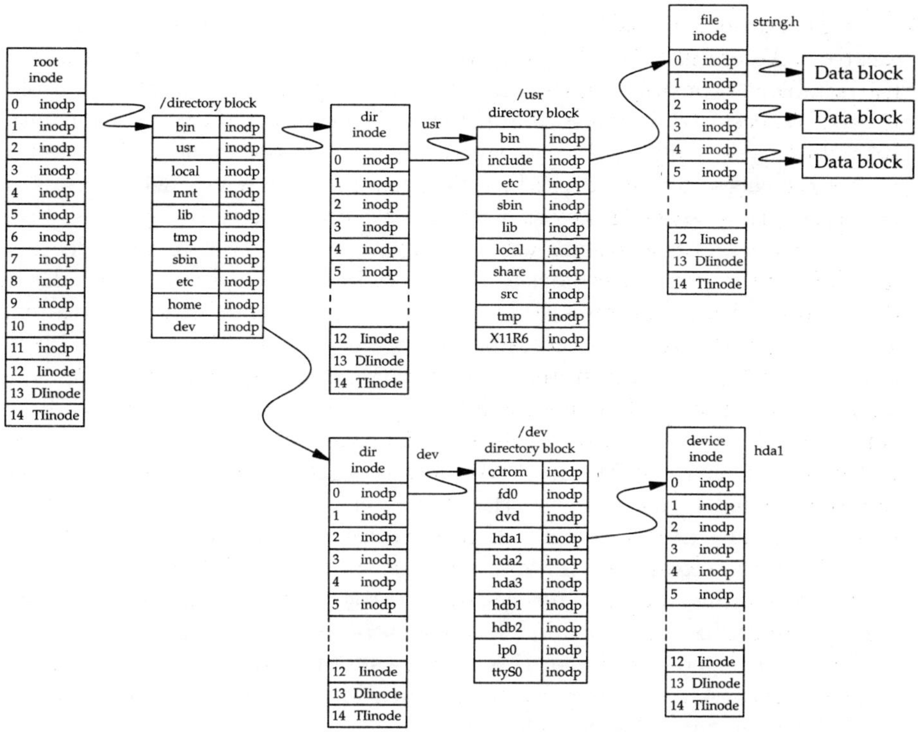

Relating Unix directories, inodes and devices as used for opening

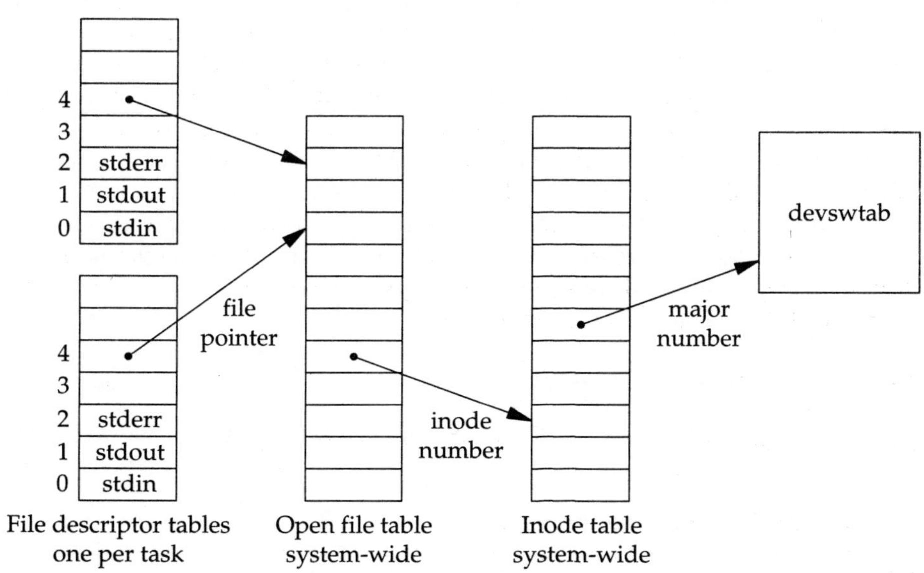

Kernel data structures for open files/devices

A file name is translated into the associated inode number through the directory. Accessing the file inode will then give the location on disk of all the data blocks comprising the file. Similarly, a device name (ttyS0, console) is used to access the device special file which contains the device major number which indexes into the system's device descriptor table. From here a pointer connects to the correct file structure for that device which leads to the appropriate access functions within the device driver code. Thus, both device drivers and file systems are accessed through entries in the directory. The Unix file system uses blocks of inode pointers to locate on disk all the data blocks which comprise a file. While companion directory entries can point at device drivers for accessing hardware devices. Both device drivers and file systems are 'registered' with the operating system using the same `mount()` command. This command links the device and driver to a directory identifier, which looks much like a normal file name, and can be used in the normal shell pipeline and redirection constructions. Where the device nodes are actually positioned on the file system hierarchy is largely down to convention, the /dev and /mnt directories are popular for this. Using the `mount` and `df` commands, you can see how your own system is set up.

Starting at the top of the file system, the root directory inode will have its pointers indicating directory blocks, each representing a subdirectory, such as /etc, /bin or /home. The entries in these subdirectory blocks will point to further directory inodes, which in their turn locate directory blocks, and so on, building up the file system hierarchy.

The management of hierarchical directories, and also the facility to use file names in place of inode numbers to access file data is realized through directory data blocks. These hold a list of file_name/inode_pointer pairs for a particular directory, to allow the symbolic to numeric translation to be carried out when accessing files. It is important to remember that there are several types of inode blocks, dealing with: data files, directories, devices and pipes. Thus a data file inode has pointers indicating the location of data blocks, while a directory inode has pointers which indicate the location of blocks containing file_name/inode_number pairs.

For data files, inodes are reserved when a file is created or expanded, but for devices, inodes are reserved with the `mknod` command which then links up the device name with its type (character or block) and the device driver routines (major and minor numbers):

```
rob@local> mknod /dev/ttyS0 c 4 64
```

All devices have major and minor numbers, which can be viewed using `ls -l`:

```
rob@local> ls -al /dev/ttyS0
lr-xr-xr-x    1 root    root 5 May 28 19:32 /dev/ttyS0 -> tts/0
rob@local> ls -al /dev/tts/0
crw-rw----    1 rob     tty 4, 64   Jan  1  1970 /dev/tts/0
rob@local>
```

This shows that the inode for /dev/ttyS0 refers to a character-oriented device, with a major number of 4, which designates the correct set of device driver routines, and a minor number of 66, which designates the actual hardware device to be opened and accessed. On the other side, the device driver must have been associated, at installation, with this major number using the `register_chrdev()` system call. This would have set up an entry in the system tables `chdevs[]` along with all the other character devices.

Directories appear as a special type of data file containing file names and corresponding inode numbers. The utility fsck (file system check) will run a thorough check on the file system integrity, and attempt to mend any errors.

Unix treats files as linear sequences of bytes. Any internal structuring is the responsibility of the application programmer. I/O devices are included as a file type to provide a more unified approach to handling data input/output. Disks, terminals and printers are assigned inodes within the file system directory at **/dev**. This can be seen as a software map of all the attached devices. In this way they can be treated the same as files; for example, devices can have data directed to them using the same commands as for a file:

```
cat device.h test.c > /dev/tty.

[rob@localhost rob] mount
/dev/hda1 on / type ext3 (rw)
none on /proc type proc (rw)
none on /dev type devfs (rw)
none on /dev/pts type devpts (rw,mode=0620)
none on /dev/shm type tmpfs (rw)
/dev/hda8 on /home type ext3 (rw)
/dev/hda5 on /local type ext3 (rw)
/mnt/cdrom on /mnt/cdrom type supermount
       (ro,dev=/dev/hdc,fs=iso9660,--,iocharset=iso8859-15)
/mnt/cdrom2 on /mnt/cdrom2 type supermount
       (rw,dev=/dev/scd0,fs=iso9660,--,iocharset=iso8859-15)
/mnt/floppy on /mnt/floppy type supermount
       (rw,sync,dev=/dev/fd0,fs=vfat,--,iocharset=iso8859-15,
           umask=0,codepage=850)
/dev/hda10 on /tmp type ext3 (rw)
/dev/hda9 on /usr type ext3 (rw)
/dev/hda6 on /var type ext3 (rw)
none on /proc/bus/usb type usbdevfs (rw,devmode=0664, devgid=43)
/dev/hdb1 on /DOS type vfat (rw)
[rob@localhost rob]

[rob@localhost rob] df
Filesystem                 Size  Used  Avail Use% Mounted on
/dev/hda1                  5.8G   73M   5.3G   2% /
none                       125M     0   124M   0% /dev/shm
```

```
/dev/hda8              3.9G  283M   3.6G    8% /home
/dev/hda5              478M  8.1M   445M    2% /local
/dev/hda10             5.1G   34M   4.8G    1% /tmp
/dev/hda9              2.0G  969M   929M   52% /usr
/dev/hda6              1.0G  109M   887M   11% /var
/dev/hdb1              503M  297M   206M   59% /DOS
[rob@localhost rob]
```

19.7 Types of Linux device drivers

In Linux, device drivers are generally classified into one of three categories as listed below.

- Discrete char devices handling byte streams, sometimes termed *raw* devices, such as:

/dev/console	c 5, 1
/dev/ttyS0 c 4, 64	serial port
/dev/tty1 c 4, 1	terminal

- Block data devices, handling 1, 2 or 4 Kbyte blocks of data in single operations.

/dev/fd0 b 2, 0	floppy disk
/dev/hda1 b 3, 1	IDE hard drive
/dev/sda1	SCSI hard drive
/dev/cd0 b 22,0	CDROM drive

- Network interface.

With regard to Unix network devices, here is 'the exception which proves the rule'. They are managed completely differently. The device eth0 is not found in the /dev directory.

Device drivers and other special modules can be included with the kernel for loading at boot time, or, with Linux, inserted later while the system is running. The tools `lsmod`, `insmod`, `rmmod` and `modprobe` are available to list, dynamically insert and remove kernel modules. The kernel maintains a symbol table to allow dynamic linking of new modules. My current system holds 18328 symbols, as shown below.

```
[rob@localhost rob] cat /procs/kallsyms | wc -l
 18328

[rob@localhost rob] cat /procs/kallsyms
c0105000 t rest_init
c0105020 t do_pre_smp_initcalls
```

```
c0105030 t run_init_process
c0105060 t init
  . . . .

e0c197e0 t journal_write_revoke_records    [jbd]
96d91461 a __crc_journal_dirty_data        [jbd]
c0129650 U __mod_timer   [jbd]
c0141e30 U __kmalloc     [jbd]
c01415c0 U kmem_cache_destroy    [jbd]
c0154d60 U bh_waitq_
head          [jbd]
[rob@localhost rob]
```

Kernel modules do not use normal library code, such as found in `libc`, only functions already exported by other kernel modules. So, `printf()` is off limits, the kernel equivalent `printk()` should be used instead. All modules need to contain the functions: `init_module()` and `cleanup_module()` to register and deregister the module with the kernel. The traditional introductory 'Hello World' application can be produced as follows, but of course this has no particular hardware device associated with it. Use one of the text consoles ([CNTRL][ALT][F1]) to test out kello.c rather than an xterm, otherwise the output from printk will end up appended to the /var/log/messages file.

```
/* kello.c kernel module,
   - gcc -c -DMODULE kello.c
   - switch to root, using su
   - insert module using /sbin/insmod -f ./kello.o
   - remove using /sbin/rmmod
   - exit from root
*/
#define MODULE
#define __KERNEL__
#include <linux/module.h>
#include <linux/init.h>

module_init(testit_init);
module_exit(testit_exit);

int testit_init(void) {
     printk("<1>Hello from kworld!!\n");
     return 0;
}
void testit_exit(void) {
      printk("<1>Goodbye kworld??\n");
}
```

To compile and run the kernel module use the following instructions:

```
[rob@localhost] su
password ******
[root@localhost] gcc -c -O2 -Wall -DMODULE hello.c
[root@localhost] insmod -f ./hello.o
    Hello from kworld!!
[root@localhost] rmmod hello
    Goodbye kworld??
[root@localhost]
```

An important part of most device driver activity involves reading or writing to registers inside an I/O chip, such as a UART, PIO or network interface. Before this can be done safely, the port addresses have to be checked and reserved with the kernel, to ensure that the device driver has exclusive access. Surprisingly, this is more a helpful convention than a technical necessity. If two device drivers access the same ports, there will be no crashing disaster, only a confused piece of equipment. There is no enforcement on port registration in the same way that the MMU assigns regions of memory to tasks.

```
struct resource {
      const char *name;
      unsigned long start, end;
      unsigned long flags;
      struct resource *parent, *sibling, *child;
};

struct resource *request_region(unsigned long base_port,
                                unsigned long port_range,
                                char *name);
void release_region(unsigned long base_port,
                    unsigned long port_range);
```

The call to `request_region()` returns a NULL pointer if it fails to succeed. Before the 2.4 kernel was issued, there was an additional need to call `check_region()` before requesting its allocation.

Adding a new device driver to the kernel requires an exclusive major number to be assigned, and then communicated to the file system so that it can be stored in the special device file inode for later reference when the device is being opened by an application program. New major numbers can be allocated manually by the programmer, or dynamically by the system. The current allocation list can be seen in `/proc/devices`, making the manual choice possible.

Device drivers supply function bodies to fulfil the operations listed in the kernel's `file_operations` structure. In this way, all device drivers should respond correctly, even if only with a valid error message, to any of these formal requests. Most programmers will instantly recognize open, read, write, ioctl, lseek and flush. Because the kernel maintains a *global* symbol table, it is very important to choose the function names so as not to clash with existing modules. The `struct file_operations` structure mostly houses pointers to the actual functions needed for that particular major number device.

```
struct file_operations {
  struct module  *owner;
  loff_t     (*llseek) (struct file*, loff_t, int);
  ssize_t    (*read) (struct file*, char __user*, size_t,
              loff_t*);
  ssize_t    (*aio_read) (struct kiocb*, char __user*, size_t,
              loff_t);
  ssize_t    (*write) (struct file*, const char __user*, size_t,
              loff_t*);
  ssize_t    (*aio_write) (struct kiocb*, const char __user*,
              size_t, loff_t);
  int        (*readdir) (struct file*, void*, filldir_t);
  unsigned int  (*poll) (struct file*, struct poll_table_struct*);
  int        (*ioctl) (struct inode*, struct file*, unsigned
              int, unsigned long);
  int        (*mmap) (struct file*, struct vm_area_struct*);
  int        (*open) (struct inode*, struct file*);
  int        (*flush) (struct file*);
  int        (*release) (struct inode*, struct file*);
  int        (*fsync) (struct file*, struct dentry*, int
              datasync);
  int        (*aio_fsync) (struct kiocb *, int datasync);
  int        (*fasync) (int, struct file*, int);
  int        (*lock) (struct file*, int, struct file_lock*);
  ssize_t    (*readv) (struct file, const struct iovec*,
              unsigned long, loff_t*);
  ssize_t    (*writev) (struct file*, const struct iovec*,
              unsigned long, loff_t*);
  ssize_t    (*sendfile) (struct file*, loff_t*, size_t,
              read_actor_t, void __user*);
  ssize_t    (*sendpage) (struct file*, struct page*, int,
              size_t, loff_t*, int);
  unsigned long (*get_unmapped_area)(struct file*, unsigned long,
             unsigned long, unsigned long, unsigned long);
};
```

A new set of unique function names can be registered for use with the device functions as follows, demonstrating the order-free, tagged structure initialization syntax.

```
struct file_operations my_fops = {
   llseek:my_llseek,
```

```
    read:  my_read,
    write: my_write,
    ioctl: my_ioctl,
    open:  my_open,
    release:   my_release,
};

  . . .
if (nret = register_chrdev(MY_MAJOR_NUM, "mydev", &my_fops)) < 0)
  printk(KERN_ERR "register_chrdev: %d\n", nret);
```

When a file is opened, it is assigned a file structure in kernel space, supplying all the generic function calls with enough information to be routed to the correct versions of their code for the device in question. The major number has been used to locate the correct device driver, but the minor number then often comes into play to select a particular hardware unit belonging to that device family. The device driver has access to the kernel-level `struct file`. This is distinct and *different* from the user space `FILE`, as offered by the C library for opening and accessing files from application code.

```
struct file {
   struct list_head f_list;
   struct dentry    *f_dentry;     //directory entry, gives
                                   //access to inode
   struct vfsmount  *f_vfsmnt;
   struct file_operations *f_op;   //pointer to device
                                   //specific operations
   atomic_t         f_count;
   unsigned int     f_flags;        //file flags from open()
   mode_t           f_mode;         //read or write access
   loff_t           f_pos;          //offset of pointer into
                                    //data
   struct fown_struct  f_owner;
   unsigned int     f_uid, f_gid;
   int              f_error;
   struct file_ra_state  f_ra;
   unsigned long    f_version;
   void             *f_security;
   void             *private_data; //needed for tty driver
   struct list_head f_ep_links;
   spinlock_t       f_ep_lock;
   void             *f_supermount; //used by supermount
};
```

The kernel will call the `init_module()` function when the module is loaded by `insmod`, but often the initialization and clean-up functions are renamed by using `module_init(my_init)` and `module_exit (my_cleanup)`. Giving unique names to all the module initialization and clean-up functions will assist greatly with debugging. Note that a vital responsibility of the `init_module()` function is to claim a major number from the kernel as an identifier which will be the link with the device special file inode on the file system. So when the device is opened by an application program, using the /dev/device_name entry within the file system, the associated inode will contain the correct major number to select the required device driver code. In addition, `module_init()` is likely to check up on the presence of hardware and all the necessary data structures. To obtain a new value for a major number requires the use of `register_chrdev()` which can either be told what number to use or to find a valid number and return it. The latter option is probably the best.

```
new_maj_num = register_chrdev(0,        //request a new major
                                        //number
                                   const char *dev_name,
                                   struct file_operations * my_fops);
```

To summarize, the `mknod` command initializes a special device file with the chosen major number, while on the other side, the `register_chrdev()` operation tells the kernel which device driver, with particular open/read/write/close functions, to associate with that value of a major number. Herein lies a problem for dynamically loaded modules. How can we be sure that the major numbers arising from these two separate activities successfully match up? Rubini & Corbet (2001) offer an interesting solution. When loading modules, run an installation script which first evokes `/sbin/insmod` to insert the module, relying on dynamic allocation for its major number. This will then appear in the `/proc/devices` file, where the script can scan for its entry and record the new major number. At which point it is safe to evoke `mknod`, with this value for the major number, to create the special device file inode. Dealing with major numbers in this manner is reminiscent of auto-detecting port numbers or receiving IP numbers dynamically from a DHCP server.

```
#!/bin/sh
# based on chpt 3 example, Rubini & Corbet

module="my_module"
device="my_device"
mode="644"
group="staff"

# insert module and accept a major number

/sbin/insmod -f ./$module.o || exit 1

rm -f /dev/${device}[0-3]            #delete stale drivers
```

```
# find and record the new major number
major_num = 'gawk '/'$ module'/ {print $1}' /proc/devices'

# create special device file inodes
mknod /dev/${device}0 c $major 0
mknod /dev/${device}1 c $major 1
mknod /dev/${device}2 c $major 2
mknod /dev/${device}3 c $major 3

# set file permissions
chgrp $group /dev/${device}[0-3]
chmod $mode /dev/${device}[0-3]
```

Device drivers eventually have to earn their keep by transferring data between a data buffer in user space and the device buffer in kernel space. Because of operating system security controls, implemented using CPU and MMU facilities, such operations cannot simply be done with `memcpy()`. The macros and function definitions to carry out these transfers are listed in /usr/include/asm/uaccess.h. Copying 'across the fence' introduces a number of tricky problems which do not occur when using `memcpy()` in user space. The relevant user data pages may be swappped out onto disk, incurring a delay which results in a task swap. In such circumstances, it is important to prepare the code for re-entrancy, in case it gets re-evoked by another task. In addition, the mapping from logical to physical addresses use different page tables for user and kernel spaces which requires some consideration. The main functions available to the programmer are `copy_to_user()` and `copy_from_user()`, but as can be seen from the excerpt taken from uaccess.h, they are both resolved down to kernel primitives after some base checking has been completed.

```
unsigned long __copy_to_user_ll(void __user *to,
                                const void *from,
                                nsigned long n);

static inline unsigned long __copy_to_user(void __user *to,
                                           const void *from,
                                           unsigned long n) {
    if (__builtin_constant_p(n)) {
   unsigned long ret;
   switch (n) {
   case 1:
       __put_user_size(*(u8 *)from, (u8 *)to, 1, ret, 1);
       return ret;
   case 2:
       __put_user_size(*(u16 *)from, (u16 *)to, 2, ret, 2);
       return ret;
   case 4:
       __put_user_size(*(u32 *)from, (u32 *)to, 4, ret, 4);
```

```
        return ret;
    }
      }
      return __copy_to_user_ll(to, from, n);
}

static inline unsigned long copy_to_user(void __user *to,
                                          const void *from,
                                          unsigned long n) {
    might_sleep();
    if (access_ok(VERIFY_WRITE, to, n))
        n = __copy_to_user(to, from, n);
    return n;
}

unsigned long __copy_from_user_ll(void *to,
                                  const void __user *from,
                                  unsigned long n);


static inline unsigned long
  __copy_from_user(void *to, const void __user *from,
     unsigned long n) {
  if (__builtin_constant_p(n)) {
  unsigned long ret;


  switch (n) {
  case 1:
      __get_user_size(*(u8 *)to, from, 1, ret, 1);
      return ret;
  case 2:
      __get_user_size(*(u16 *)to, from, 2, ret, 2);
      return ret;
  case 4:
      __get_user_size(*(u32 *)to, from, 4, ret, 4);
      return ret;
    }
  }
  return __copy_from_user_ll(to, from, n);
}
static inline unsigned long
  copy_from_user(void *to, const void __user *from, unsigned
     long n) {
   might_sleep();
   if (access_ok(VERIFY_READ, from, n))
                      n = __copy_from_user(to, from, n);
   else
                      memset(to, 0, n);
   return n;
}
```

19.8 The new devfs

A new approach to handling devices within the Unix file system has been adopted by many. The Device File System (devfs) groups devices in subdirectories in a more orderly fashion:

cdroms	console	discs	dsp	floppy	full
ide	initctl	input	kmem	kmsg	log
mem	misc	mouse	null	port	psaux
printers	ptmx	pts	pty	random	rd
root	rtc	scsi	sequencer	shm	snd
sound	random	usb	vc	vcc	vcs

If you inspect the directory entry for `/dev/hda1`, you may see that it is linked to another entry: `/dev/ide/host0/bus0/target0/lun0/part1` which represents the devfs way of organizing the special device files. These entries are built dynamically at boot time from the specifications held in the `/etc/devfsd.conf` file. When a new device driver module is loaded with `insmod`, devfsd will automatically create a new file system entry.

The principal reason for changing the way of dealing with devices under Unix was the increasing problems with the allocation of major and minor numbers. For suppliers this had become a significant headache, similar to the IRQ situation. Looking into the traditional `/dev`, an enormous range of device references, sometimes 1200, can be seen, many of which will never be used. They have been inserted into the directory, just in case. Under devfs, the use of major and minor numbers has been abandoned in favour of a naming scheme.

There is an important difference between the way the device driver routines are located when using the new devfs. With the old system, the 8 bit major and minor numbers were obtained from the device inode and used to identify the device drivers and the associated service routines by indexing into a 128 entry table. The ceiling that this imposed on the maximum number of active devices which could be handled was also a serious problem for larger systems.

With device driver modules destined for installation onto a system running devfs, the system calls `devfs_register()` and `devfs_unregister()` have to be employed in the init and clean-up functions. The major number registration function also needs to be updated to a new version: `devfs_register_chrdev()`. For the moment, device driver code needs to work well in both environments.

19.9 Chapter summary

R-t variants of Linux, such as RTAI and RTLinux, have introduced Linux as a possibility for real-time applications. So Linux is now being seriously evaluated for jard, embedded applications. In these circumstances, the need to introduce bespoke device drivers for special equipment is often essential. Linux device drivers are collections of subroutines (`open()`, `read()`, `write()` and `close()`) which together offer a software interface to the associated equipment. With Linux, they may be bound into the kernel, or dynamically loaded into a running system. To further 'virtualize' the device interface, in Unix they are accessed through the name translation scheme operated by file system directories. A new arrangement, devfs, is being introduced to rationalize the management of devices under Unix.

19.10 Problems and issues for discussion

1. Use the `open()` system call on the parallel printer device `/dev/port` to access the parallel port on your PC. Check out the mini-howto (Saikkonen). This technique does not require root access, but you do have to have permissions to read/write to /dev/port. Why is this a serious security risk?
2. Investigate the μCLinux kernel which is set up without any virtual memory support and no separation between kernel and user spaces. All tasks run at privilege level 0. It is intended for use on smaller microprocessors and microcontrollers.
3. Investigate the kernel module commands: `lsmod`, `modprobe`, `insmod`, `rmmod`. How does Linux keep track of all the loaded modules and their function names?
4. Use the /dev/port device on your computer to access the parallel printer port. You should be able to use: `fd=open("/dev/port",O_WRONLY);` and then apply the following code to write to the byte-wide output port: `lseek(fd, 0x378, SEEK_SET); write(fd, &idata, 1);`. Note that you will have to re-seek before every write operation because the file position pointer is auto-incremented. 0x378 is the standard I/O address for this output register. You will need to set access permissions on /dev/port if you want to run as non-root.
5. Investigate the use of `ioctl()` calls. Review man ioctl, man ioctl_list, /usr/include/sys/ioctl.h and /usr/include/linux/asm/ioctl.h.

19.11 Suggestions for reading

Abbott, D. (2003). *Linux for Embedded and Real-time Applications.* Newnes.

Duffy, C. (2004). eRTSD course worksheets. From http://www.cems.uwe.ac.uk/~cduffy/rtem_sys.html, worksheets 1–6.

Rubini, A. & Corbet, J. (2001). *Linux Device Drivers.* O'Reilly.

Saikkonen, R. An alternative method for I/O port programming on Linux. From: file:/share/doc/HOWTO/HTML/en/mini/IO-Port-Programming

Selvakumar, D. & Rebeiro, C. (2004). RTLinux on memory constrained systems. From http://www.linuxdevices.com/files/rtlws-2004/ChesterRebeiro.pdf

Yaghmour, K. (2003). *Building Embedded Linux Systems.* O'Reilly.

http://www.tldp.org, the Linux documentation project, come here for manuals, FAQs, HOW-TOs, manual pages, etc.

http://www.tldp.org/LDP/khg/HyperNews/get/devices/devices.html, Linux Kernel Hackers Guide, section on building device drivers.

http://www.realtimelinuxfoundation.org, a SIG site.

http://www.kernel.org, main server for Linux source code, download tar balls.

http://www.rtai.org, real-time application interface.

http://www.fsmlabs.com, owner and supplier of RTLinux.

http://www.bluecat.com, a limited version of RTLinux supplied by LynuxWorks.

Chapter 20

Hardware/software co-design

20.1 Chapter overview

Reconfigurable hardware is becoming available with large enough capacity and performance to support complete systems. Opportunities for taking an integrated software/hardware approach to systems development will increase, and need to be assessed for many applications. FPGAs and PLDs can be configured using software techniques not unfamiliar to software engineers working in the field of real-time systems. This chapter does not attempt to introduce the VHDL or Verilog languages, but rather the context for their use, in the development of modern real-time systems.

20.2 Systems-on-chip

Many electronic engineers and programmers think that we are on the threshold of another major technical paradigm shift which will again adjust the functional dividing line between hardware and software. This could be compared with the emergence of microprocessors in the 1970s, and the subsequent change in everyone's expectation of commodity electronic components which could, for the first time, be used to build 'stored program

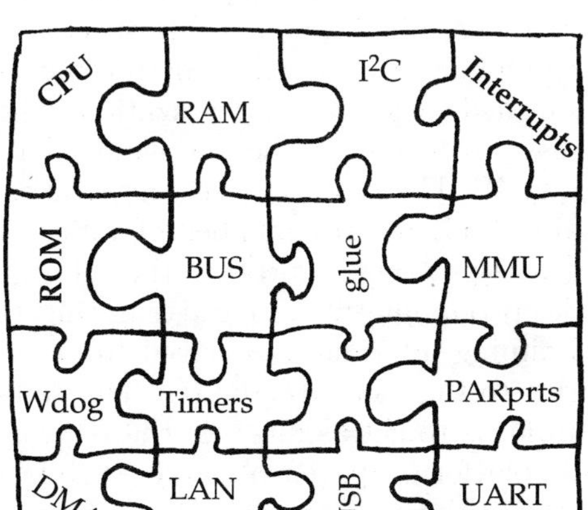

Solving the IP jigsaw puzzle

control' equipment. The current discussion concerns Field Programmable Gate Arrays (FPGAs) which are reconfigurable circuits, large enough to carry out all the systems functions for many common applications. Thus, in many circumstances, it is actually possible to shrink a complete motherboard with electronic components to a single monolithic chip of silicon. Such an opportunity is of major interest to real-time systems designers. The possibility of implementing dynamically self-reconfiguring hardware may also excite attention.

The capability of such 'systems-on-a-chip' has rapidly improved over the last decade as production competence within the chip fabrication industry moved ahead. Five years ago people referred to a very similar vision as systems-on-silicon, with various microcontrollers in mind as successful examples. This description covered devices from the 8 bit Philips 8XC552, through the 16 bit Mc68C11, up to the 32 bit DEC StrongArm, as described in Chapter 18. But then, even earlier, the remarkable achievement of placing several transistors together on a monolithic chip, to act as a basic logic gate, was lauded as a 'silicon system'. Now the Pentium processor and top-of-the-range FPGAs, benefiting from submicron manufacturing techiques, deploy millions of gates routinely to achieve a complexity which requires teams of engineers and programmers to exploit effectively for commercial products. In the coming years, the real-time application platform is likely to become a single FPGA, carrying several CPUs, peripheral interfaces, network ports, special bespoke circuitry and cache memories. The configurable devices which can support such sophisticated application circuits are certainly capable of supporting small to medium sized projects which previously required multiple VLSI chips and substantial PCB surface area.

20.3 Intellectual property

The expected commodity market in 'IP', intellectual property hardware designs, has for the most part not yet taken off. A few notable successes, such as ARM, have shown that it can be made to work when the product is good enough, but mostly it is only established within large organizations who are running their own internal marketplace to encourage the reuse and distribution of virtual components, proprietary IP. The problems with integrating designs, supplied as 'soft', synthesizable RTL from a number of different sources, have not been fully solved. These problems centre on the internal dependencies and interactions which keep popping up when attempting to carry out a joint synthesis. Typically, timing information derived from the separate unit tests are no longer relevant to the merged circuitry. The common approach to overcoming these hurdles is to get as much of the IP from a single source, now termed taking a 'platform approach', and establishing a good working relationship with that principal supplier. Basically, the interface between IP modules, as currently specified, is inadequate to ensure compatibility under all circumstances. Perhaps it could be compared to

Si.ware

a naive architect attempting to build up a new city using neighbourhood plans borrowed from a dozen existing cities around the world. The width of the roads may be the same, but the traffic could be travelling on different sides of the road. What happens when a US-style urban motorway enters an Italian piazza? Then there are the incompatibilities in the subterranean services: water, sewage, telephone, gas and electricity. At the moment similar issues in the IP world lead to a nearly overwhelmingly large amount of verification and validation work to check out the new builds at every stage.

Despite these problems, the advent of OEM configurable target hardware may mean that very soon the specialized microcontroller, built around an industry standard CPU, will be abandoned in favour of an off-the-shelf FPGA, onto which the chosen CPU design has been configured. This could be a bought-in design, or an in-house development, perhaps extending an open source design. The current teaching to university undergraduates of VHDL and Verilog skills will result in a generation of engineers and programmers open to such ideas, and capable of exploiting the opportunities for integrated hardware/software developments.

Unfortunately there seems to be a growing productivity gap between design and production capabilities, rather reminiscent of the situation that existed with software before the widespread acceptance of HLL compilers. Currently, the time and resources needed to bring new designs to the point of manufacture are often underestimated, and new design tools have not yet caught up with the improvements in fabrication technology. The engineering of new circuit designs is in great need of better tools and methods if it is to fully exploit the enormous potential of modern FPGAs. The accepted solution for this problem is generally stated to be increased 'IP design reuse'. But this, as yet, has failed to deliver the predicted benefits.

20.4 Reconfigurable hardware

The basis of reconfigurable logic is either the hardware Lookup Table (LUT) or a PLA switch matrix 'fuse map'. The former can be implemented as a block of memory cells which uses the input word as an address to access the desired output pattern. For LUT-based devices, configuration will involve loading the

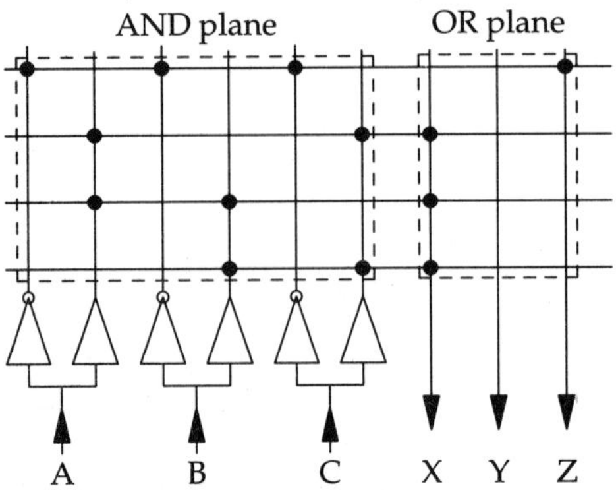

$X = B.C \quad A.B \quad A.C$

$Z = \bar{A}.\bar{B}.\bar{C}.$

Y – *unused*

Three term AND-OR product term matrix

correct bit patterns into the LUT memory cells as well as setting all the circuit interconnections across the chip. Alternatively, with the AND-OR, product term matrix, it is the cross point switches which need to be controlled by memory bits. In the figure above, the rows in the AND plane represent four 6-input AND gates, while the columns in the OR plane represent three 4-input OR gates.

Reconfigurable hardware devices can be obtained in non-volatile and volatile technologies. The latter, commonly referred to as Programmable Logic Devices (PLDs), employ integrated Flash/EEPROM memory to hold their configuration data. This ensures that they retain their interconnections during a power-down. The alternative method is only to hold configuration data in RAM, which is then lost when power is withdrawn. These devices are referred to as FPGAs and are generally larger, with more complex facilities. The two most popular families of large FPGA devices are currently the Altera APEX and the Xilinx Virtex ranges. They are both offered with an optional preconfigured 'hard' 32 bit RISC CPU, or the capability to accept whatever configuration, including 'soft' CPUs, the user wishes to install. Using these devices for prototype testing, followed by a production commitment to ASIC,

- 10^9 transistors
- 4×10^7 logic gates
- Packages with 2000 pins
- 1.5 Gbps I/O data rates
- Up to 1 GHz CPU clock
- 1.0 V core voltage
- 24 MB internal RAM
- 16×10^7 configuration bits

Next generation FPGA capacity and performance

may have been the original intention, but more often than not, they are now being delivered as a significant part of final products.

Some possible applications which could usefully exploit such devices could be:

- Bespoke microcontrollers, using a standard CPU core, but customized with specialized peripheral interfaces.
- SMP, symmetric multi-processor compute engines for dedicated algorithmic solutions.
- Multi-tasking platforms, offering one CPU per task: true parallel processing.
- High performance synchronous logic, migrating an existing application from sequential software executed on a processor, to dedicated hardware.
- Secure application requirements, where conventional ROM software would be too vulnerable to theft. The FPGA configuration file is encrypted and stored in ROM for loading into the FPGA at power-on, using an OTP decryption microcontroller.
- Dynamically self-reconfigurable application hardware, such as switching between encryption and decryption, or compression and decompression, functionality.
- Application specific instruction set extensions, adding extra functionality to an existing 'soft' CPU. In the same manner that CISC microcode could be upgraded to include new instructions.

The likely capacity and performance parameters for advanced FPGAs in development at the moment are given above. But the pressure to improve VLSI fabrication technology to deliver even smaller feature sizes, by working with masks and wavelengths well below the optical spectrum range, is still increasing.

20.5 Software support

The issues involved with successful design and implementation using large FPGA and PLD devices are becoming the focus of much research and development work. The languages VHDL and Verilog have been coerced into use from their original context as ASIC specification languages, but there is still a long way to go in the evolution of more suitable tool chains which can simultaneously cope with hard and soft virtual components (IP imports), as well as supporting behavioural and structural designs. VHDL was commissioned for the US DOD Very High Speed Integrated Circuits (VHSIC) program to provide a single VLSI specification and simulation facility. The IEEE now supervise its maintenance and evolution under the 1076 standard. VHDL offers the capability to describe functional (behavioural) as well as relational (structural) information. VHDL compilers generate output files for simulation testing or circuit synthesis. Frequently this results in the specification of how base components are interconnected: a wiring schema, or netlist. The input–output operational details of all the components are described by behavioural elements, an arrangement which enables simulation testing to take place. For a hardware implementation to be achieved, all the basic components have to be substituted by hardware cells configured for identical functionality, and the wiring schema must be implemented using the interconnection highways available on the FPGA. This final transformation is carried out by the *Fitter* program normally obtainable from the FPGA supplier.

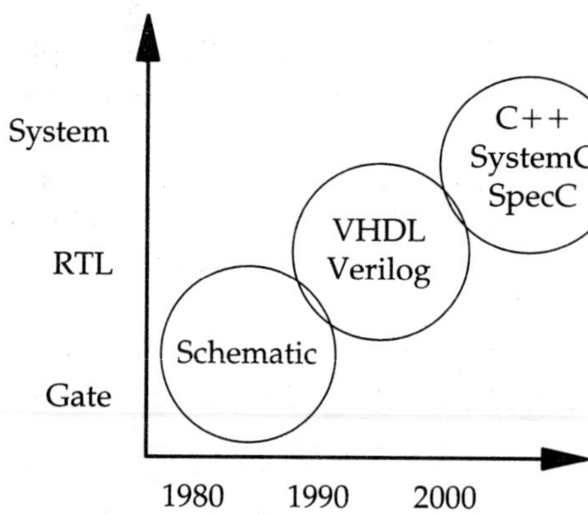

Trends in chip modelling

There has recently been the emergence of devices capable of offering both analogue and digital circuitry, which cannot be handled by standard VHDL and Verilog. This technical development is especially important for the production of mobile handsets, digital radio, and a range of other consumer equipment to be operated without keypads.

20.6 Altera APEX/Excalibur device

As mentioned above, there is an increasing trend to use a single source architecture as the platform for complex System on Programmable Chips (SOPC) developments. This benefits from all the previous compatibility tests and checks carried out by the supplier and earlier OEM engineers. As an example platform we are describing the Altera APEX cPLD family, which offers considerable logic capacity and decent clock speeds. The basic functional unit within the Altera APEX reconfigurable device is the Logic Element (LE), see below for a schematic diagram. At the moment, 51 840 of these are available to be configured and interlinked when developing an application circuit with the largest member of the APEX family. LEs have been designed to operate in three modes: arithmetic, counter or normal, and are blocked together in groups of 10, referred to as Logic Array Blocks (LABs). At the next level, 24 LABs are grouped together into MegaLab cells. Associated with each MegaLAB is a configurable memory block containing 2 Kbits, which is called the Embedded System Block (ESB). The memory can be arranged as dual-port RAM, ROM, FIFO, or CAM, with a variety of word width/memory length combinations: 2048×1, 1024×2, 512×4, 256×8 or 128×16. Alternatively, each ESB can be configured into 16 macrocell logic blocks, offering

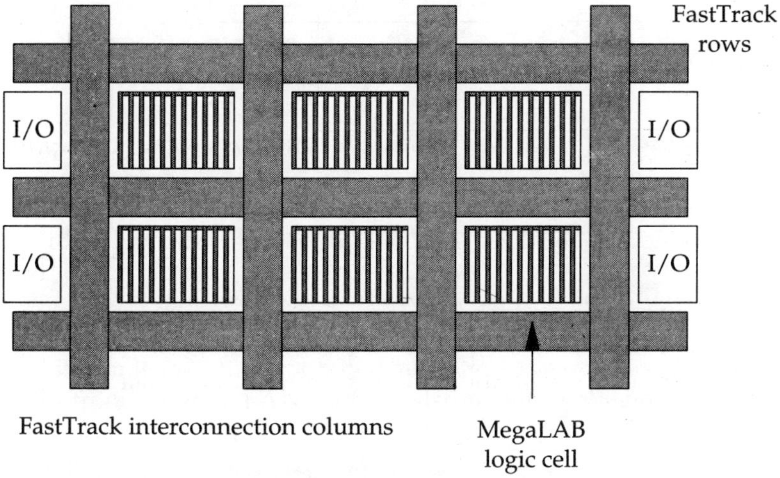

Block layout of an Altera APEX20K cPLD

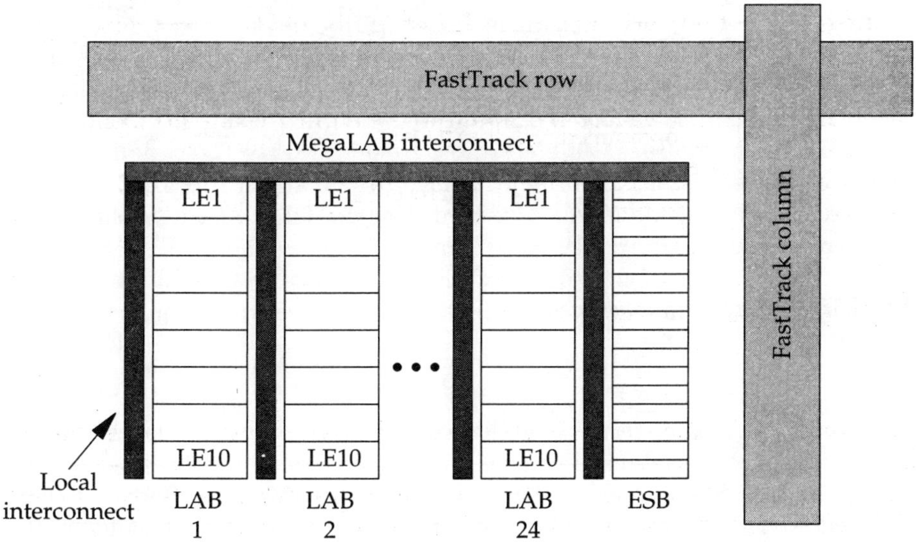

A single MegaLAB logic cell from an Altera APEX20K cPLD

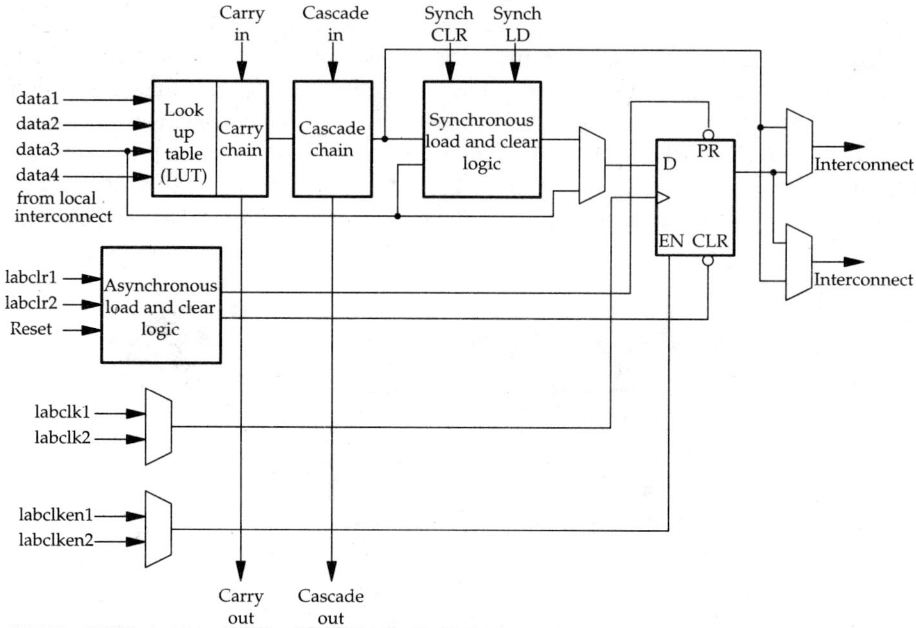

APEX20k Logic Element (LE)

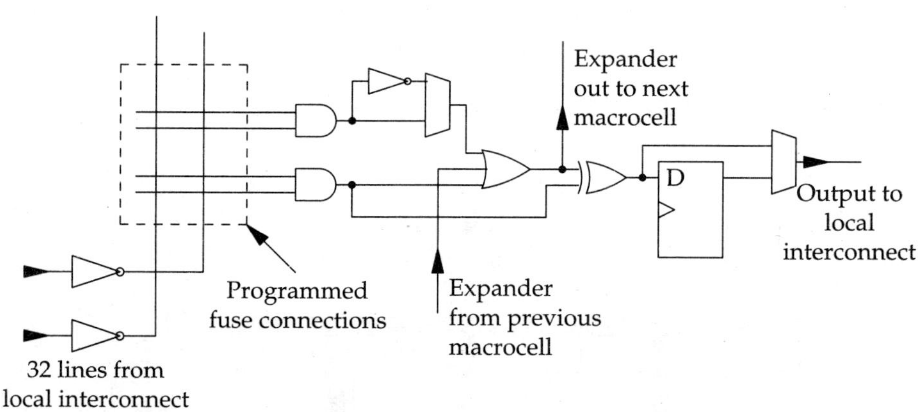

APEX20k product-term macrocell

combinatorial, product-term capability, see the above figure. The AND-OR product terms can be stacked to give a 32 product-term width, if all macrocells in a single ESB are used. In this way Altera are offering a choice between LUT and AND-OR product-term implementation on a single reconfigurable chip. These approaches would traditionally be separated onto FPGA or PLD chips. Whether it is better to use a combinatorial logic net or a RAM lookup to generate a solution depends very much on the problem in hand. Somewhat surprisingly, Altera state that the silicon area used for a 16-way LUT is only 70 per cent that of a two input product-term circuit as used in the ESB macrocell.

To provide effective reconfigurable links, there is a hierarchy of interconnection highways available throughout the device. The 10 LEs within a LAB have direct access to a 65 line local interconnect highway. Each LE can access two local interconnect highways, giving fast links to 29 other LEs. So an application circuit based on *30 bit* words might be a better choice with this device. The LABs can be linked by the next level, MegaLAB interconnect. While FastTrack interconnects, aligned horizontally and vertically, are provided for high speed links between components across the chip.

20.7 Processor cores

Altera offer two processor cores for implementation in the APEX 20KE cPLD. A hard coded ARM922T 32 bit RISC CPU can be preinstalled and purchased as the Excalibur device, or the NIOS, a soft HDL coded RISC CPU, can be installed by the application engineer or programmer after it has been configured to fit the end-user needs.

20.8 Chapter summary

Systems-on-chip, using reconfigurable hardware in the form of FPGAs or CPLDs, are becoming a popular form for embedded systems, often because of their reduced power requirements. This approach demands an integrated approach to hardware and software development if it is to be successful. Opportunities for all kinds of new applications will emerge using this cost-effective technology. FPGAs and PLDs can be configured using software techniques not unfamiliar to software engineers working in the field of real-time systems. The two most common hardware specification languages are currently VHDL in Europe and Verilog in the US.

20.9 Problems and issues for discussion

1. Investigate the gate count for common proprietary microcontrollers and compare them with the capacity of a range of commercial FPGAs offered by suppliers such as Altera, Xilinx and Atmel.
2. Take a microcontroller, and an idea for a suitable application, then assess what percentage of the hardware facilities provided you would actually use. Do you think that the flexibility to 'roll-your-own' circuitry and avoid purchasing redundant circuits will win over still sceptical development managers?

3. Check out the principal differences between Verilog and VHDL for FPGA configuration.
4. Start by looking at www.opencores.org, then draw up a list of CPU cores which are available in the form of IP files for downloading.
5. Consider the design and development of a voice-operated washing machine. Carry out a study of the h/w-s/w tradeoff with regard to the provision of the expected functionality.

20.10 Suggestions for reading

Altera Corp. (2002). *Nios Embedded Processor Peripherals Reference Manual.*

Altera Corp. (2002). Custom instructions for the Nios embedded processor. Application Note 188.

Altera Corp. (2004). *APEX20K Programmable Logic Device Family Data Sheet.*

Carpinelli, J. (2002). *Computer Systems Organization and Architecture.* Addison Wesley.

Jerraya, A. & Wolf, W. (2005). Hardware/software interface codesign for embedded systems. *IEEE Computer*, vol. 38, no. 2, 63–69.

Martin, G. & Chang, H. (2000). *Surviving the SoC Revolution.* KAP.

Martin, G. & Chang, H. (2003). *Winning the SoC Revolution.* KAP.

Smith, J. (1998). *Application-specific Integrated Circuits.* Addison Wesley.

http://www.opencores.org, source for open source IP files.

Appendix A

Appendix A: Using an oscilloscope for software debugging

A1.1 Overview

A few simple procedures involving an oscilloscope can help the real-time programmer gain an immediate insight into the dynamics of a running program. This can save a lot of time and pain while debugging. When computers actually break down or the hardware misperforms, an oscilloscope remains the most universal diagnostic tool.

A1.2 Using an oscilloscope

It is important to gain confidence with all new tools in a situation where you don't have too much pressure on you. All too often, the need to use an oscilloscope happens in the middle of a fraught, last-minute debugging session, when little time is available to learn the niceties of trigger-level adjustment. Also it is probably advisable to start with a basic 20 MHz model, which could be an analogue oscilloscope or a small, hand-held LCD model. The normal professional lab kit has become a 500 MHz digital scope, based on fast microprocessors, which can serve as oscilloscope, hardware logic analyser, signal storage scope, and software debugger. Such versatile instruments should not be neglected in the struggle to catch elusive real-time bugs.

A1.3 Turning on an analogue CRT scope

An oscilloscope front panel, even for a basic model, can appear very complex at first sight. However, the confusion will soon disappear if you view the parts of the panel separately, and practise using the controls, one by one. Also, if you progress to using a digital storage scope, you will look back at the basic model as a very simple affair.

There is often the same problem when starting a session with an unfamiliar oscilloscope, rather like setting time-record on an unfamiliar video recorder. In this case the trace just vanishes, and no matter how much you

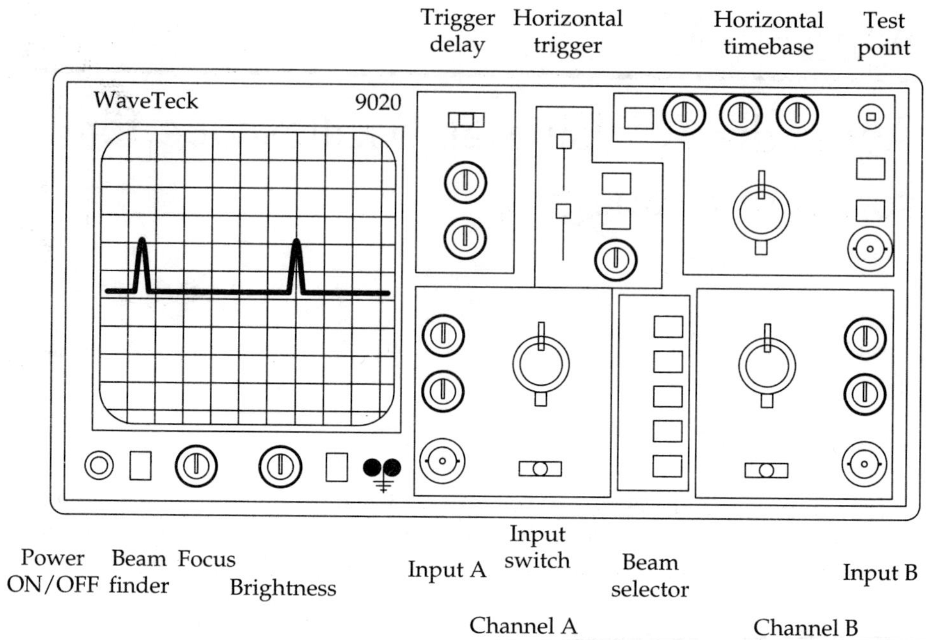

A budget-level, dual channel, 20 MHz analogue oscilloscope

twiddle the knobs and flick the switches, it does not reappear. However, if you cling on to the basic principles of operation, it will definitely help the trace to return to its rightful position at the centre of the screen.

I hope these simple guidelines will get you going, with a good strong trace running across the screen. But first, you really must understand what all the buttons and knobs do, so turn the power on and follow the instructions:

1. Select both channels A and B for display, and centre both channel A and B vertical position knobs (pushbuttons bottom middle).
2. All timebase and signal amplification should be set to mid range (big rotary knobs).
3. Trigger selection set to AUTO on channel A. No trigger filtering or TV synch pulse handling (vertical sliders top middle).
4. Both channel A and B i/p switches should be set to GND. Check the probe switches, too, which can offer ×10, ×1 or OFF (next to i/p sockets).
5. Trigger delay, in the OFF or normal position (slider top left).
6. Is the trace visible? Try pressing the trace finder button.
7. When a trace is visible, plug a probe into channel A, and hook it onto the test point. Change the i/p switch for that channel to DC. Then try adjusting channel A vertical position and gain, and the horizontal timebase speed. See how the display changes. Adjust the controls so that the regular test pattern is conveniently viewable.

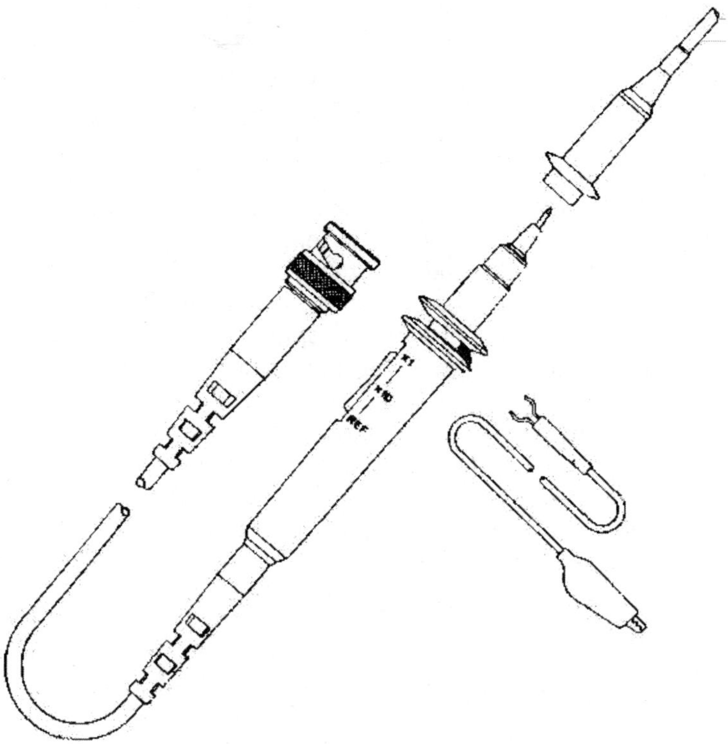

Traditional high impedance, passive scope probe with earthing fly lead

A1.4 Introduction to the oscilloscope

The traditional Cathode Ray Tube (CRT) oscilloscope is really only a faster and more flexible version of the black and white television. Inside the box is an evacuated glass tube, which is shaped like a square bottle. This lies on its side with the flat base towards the viewer. The whole operation depends on coating the inside of the tube with a special paint which glows (gives out light) when pelted with electron particles. A fine beam of electrons is accelerated from the 'electron gun' in the neck of the tube straight towards the viewer and bangs into the front screen, making the phosphor glow.

If all that is required is to draw light patterns on a screen, a laser beam might have been a better choice. However, particles of light (photons) are not easily deflected; while electrons, because they are negatively charged, are simple to move about in space using electric or magnetic fields. In fact, televisions use magnetic coils to steer the electron beam, while oscilloscopes use electrostatic plates.

In the case of a CRT analogue scope, if you can obtain a small (SMALL!) magnet it is quite fun to hold it up to the screen and watch the effect on the startled electrons. Doing this with a modern flat screen LCD model will be unremarkable.

In the CRT oscilloscope, the electrons in the beam can be pulled sideways, or up and down, as they zoom from the gun towards the screen, by applying voltages to the X and Y plates. If the voltage applied to the plates is not constant it will result in the electron beam executing sympathetic wiggles. These will get drawn in light on the phosphor, resulting in a diagram representing the original voltage oscillations.

Before the probe tip is connected to a pin, to pick up a signal, the earth lead must be attached to a convenient earthing point. This can be anywhere on the circuit board, or power supply output connector. It might require an extra wire to be soldered onto the board just to provide an accessible earthing point.

For the purposes of software debugging, it is possible that an existing I/O port may have a spare output line. This can then be driven high and low again by a couple of instructions inserted judiciously into the doubtful code. The RS232 port offers the RTS output line which can be toggled by using the `ioctl()` system call.

A1.5 Digital storage scopes

Digital scopes work differently to the analogue equipment. After the high impedance input amplifiers, the signals are routed through fast ADCs to convert the analogue voltages into streams of binary numbers. These are directed to a fast memory for storage, ready to be displayed on the LCD panel.

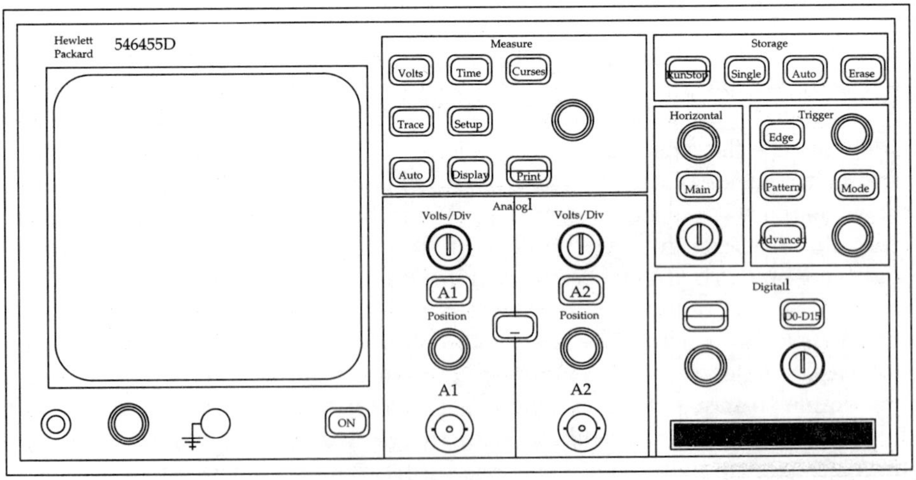

A typical digital storage scope with analogue and digital input channels

Digital storage scopes are much more like *computers* than televisions. The signals being monitored are immediately digitized through fast ADC units, operating at 200+ MHz. The resulting stream of binary sample values is then stored in fast memory for later display, dispatch to a printer, or transfer to a PC for further post-processing In this way a single event can be captured and viewed at leisure afterwards. The sampling rate needs to be set correctly using the Time knob. If you set the rate too fast the memory will quickly fill up, and the window of viewing will be too narrow to be of interest. If you set the sample rate too slow, quick events might happen between sample points, and be lost to view. Once the data is held in memory it can be viewed at differing resolutions, fine or coarse, giving the user a lot of flexibility.

The HP 54845D not only offers the traditional twin analogue inputs, but also 24 digital input channels. These only accept 5 V TTL logic signals, they are not provided with ADC units. In many circumstances when dealing with computer signals, it might be better using the digital inputs instead of analogue.

Index